JavaServer Faces in Action

JavaServer Faces in Action

KITO D. MANN

Greenwich
(74° w. long.)

For online information and ordering of this and other Manning books, please go to www.manning.com. The publisher offers discounts on this book when ordered in quantity. For more information, please contact:

Special Sales Department
Manning Publications Co.
209 Bruce Park Avenue
Greenwich, CT 06830

Fax: (203) 661-9018
email: orders@manning.com

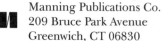

Manning Publications Co.
209 Bruce Park Avenue
Greenwich, CT 06830

Copyeditor: Liz Welch
Typesetter: Denis Dalinnik
Cover designer: Leslie Haimes

ISBN 1-932394-12-5

Printed in the United States of America
2 3 4 5 6 7 8 9 10 – VHG – 08 07 06 05

To my beautiful wife and best friend, Tracey.

This book would not exist without you, and I'm eternally grateful
for the positive influence you've had on my life,
always pushing me to be the best I can be.

brief contents

ONLINE EXTENSION

The five chapters in part 5 (plus four additional appendixes) are not included in the print edition. They are available for download in PDF format from the book's web page to owners of this book. For free access to the online extension please go to www.manning.com/mann.

contents

online extension

The online extension consists of five chapters in part 5 as well as four appendixes that are not included in the print edition. They are available for free download from the book's web site at www.manning.com/mann. This is the table of contents for the online extension.

foreword

As I write this foreword, I am collaborating with four leading user interface (UI) component vendors on a presentation for the 2004 JavaOne℠ conference. In our presentation, the vendors will show how they leverage JavaServer™ Faces technology in their products. While developing the presentation, I am learning some things about the work we've been doing on JavaServer Faces for the past three years. The vendors have their own set of concerns unique to adapting their product for JavaServer Faces, but they all voice one opinion loud and clear: they are very relieved to finally have a *standard* for web-based user interfaces.

The absence of a standard for web-based UIs forced these component vendors to write special case code for every integrated development environment (IDE) into which they wanted to plug. Now that we have the JavaServer Faces standard, any IDE can declare compliance to that standard, and any vendor that also complies with the standard can plug components into the IDE with much less work. Of course, this means that any components you develop will also be able to plug into tools without too much additional work.

The JavaServer Faces specification was developed by a community of leading minds in the field of web UI development. We took the best ideas from many different approaches to UI frameworks and assembled them into one coherent whole. The trouble with standards is that they get rather complex in order to solve the problems they are addressing. For JavaServer Faces, that problem is providing an easy-to-use UI framework built on top of a collection of technologies not well suited to UIs at all. This has led to a particularly complex specification to implement. Thankfully, the number of people actually implementing the spec is relatively small compared to those using those implementations, but as it turns out, knowing the specification in detail is still helpful in order to use it.

As a member of the expert group developing the next version of JavaServer Pages, Kito is no stranger to technology standards. Kito grasps the key value-adds of JavaServer Faces and has explained them in a book that is accessible and in-depth. You will see what sets JavaServer Faces apart from other web UI frameworks, including its first-class component model, its well-defined state management system, and its conceptual similarity to JavaBeans. Kito is familiar with the abstractions being used by the specification, and, more important, he *understands* why we used those abstractions. Understanding the *why* of the specification leads to a superior explanation for you, the reader. For example, look at the "relationship of concepts" diagram in chapter 2. This is a great way to understand the rationale for the design of JavaServer Faces.

Kito also understands the marketplace into which this technology fits. This means you get the most important information first, so you can get your job done quickly and completely. He spends just enough time building a firm foundation of the technology underlying JavaServer Faces, making the book ideal for getting started from scratch.

Finally, the book has all the things you've come to expect from a top-quality software technology book: a descriptive table of contents that can serve as a framework for understanding, chapter goals and summaries to save you time, and lots of working examples that you can use in your own projects. One thing I've seen in this book that I haven't seen in others is an in-depth look at the currently shipping IDEs that support JavaServer Faces. This is especially valuable because such tools can save you time, once you understand the underlying technology they support.

In addition to the unique insight this book offers on shipping IDEs, Kito brings to bear his experience as the principal of JSFCentral.com to inform the entire book. This site is a high-quality aggregation of articles, interviews, and, most important, an up-to-the-minute picture of the state of industry and community offerings related to JavaServer Faces. Kito has separate sections that cover components, render kits, implementations, and more. I think you'll find this site—and this book—extremely valuable as you explore JavaServer Faces programming.

ED BURNS
JavaServer Faces Specification Lead

preface

I've always enjoyed writing. I was one of those computer geeks who found humanities classes easier, in some ways, than computer science courses—that is, if I could manage to convince my professors that I had actually read the dozens of books they gave me. In the late 1990s, I finally fused my affection for writing with my obsession for software development by writing magazine articles and performing technical book reviews. Then, in 2000, after years of financial consulting with Fortune 500 companies, I took the start-up plunge.

Okay, so it was a little late. But I was jealous of my friends who had joined start-ups and intrigued by all of those wonderful stories in magazine articles. The start-up I chose was an educational application service provider (recently acquired by McGraw-Hill) that, surprisingly, had a real business plan. A key part of our product was a web-based application, and one of my tasks, as chief architect, was to build it (with, of course, the help of other poor souls). Instead of using my own homegrown web application framework, I chose Struts, which at the time was a good decision. As I directed development through a couple of release cycles, I gained an understanding of the good and bad parts of Struts, as well as the issues involved with developing a mission-critical web application with team members who all had different backgrounds.

After two years of burning myself out and neglecting my girlfriend Tracey, I resigned and spent some time getting to know the stranger called Sleep. After we had been sufficiently reacquainted, I inhaled as much information as possible about new technologies, and stumbled across the Java Specification Request (JSR) 127—JavaServer Faces (JSF). JSF seemed like an answer to the growing problem of framework mania. Moreover, since JSF abstracts so many tedious details of web application development, it seemed superior to Struts in many ways. It was clear to me that JSF was the Next Big Thing in Java web development.

Because I was anxious to get back into writing something other than architecture specifications and memos, writing a book on JSF seemed like a good idea. I had reviewed several books for Manning, so I contacted the publisher to discuss writing one about JSF. After some lobbying, Manning agreed, and the *JavaServer Faces in Action* project was born. Little did we know that the specification would go through radical changes before its final (late) release in March 2004. (If I had a crystal ball, I would certainly not have written so much of it in early 2003; rewriting is just not fun.)

Throughout the last year and half, a lot has happened. In May 2003, I married Tracey (I suppose leaving the start-up was a good thing after all). Later that year, I launched JSF Central, a web site dedicated to the JSF community, chock-full of resources and a handy FAQ. And finally, on March 3, 2004, JSF 1.0 was released (with the 1.1 maintenance release appearing in May). The result is a solid technology that I believe will add fire to the world of Java web development, not only by making life easier for day-to-day development but also by igniting a third-party user interface (UI) component industry, à la Microsoft's ASP.NET Web Forms.

To that end, I've worked hard to ensure that this book will serve as a catalyst on both fronts, not only helping you understand what JSF is, how it works, and how to use it, but also teaching you how to write your own UI components. I've also worked with representatives from Oracle, IBM, and Sun to paint a picture of how JSF is integrated into different IDEs. In addition, this text was influenced by my role as editor-in-chief of JSF Central, where I have gained a unique vantage point of the growing JSF ecosystem.

So, there you have it. I hope *JavaServer Faces in Action* will inspire in you the enthusiasm that I have for this technology and serve as a useful tool in your own projects. In the meantime, I intend to reacquaint myself with that old friend, Sleep. Feel free to send your comments about this book to kmann@virtua.com or post them in the Author Online forum for this book at www.manning.com/mann; once awake, I'll be happy to read them.

acknowledgments

Most projects are not one-person endeavors, even if they start out that way. Technical books require the talents of an enormous range of people, many of whom donate their free time. (I will, however, take the prize for that particular sacrifice.) Let's start at the beginning with Clay Anders, the person at Manning who believed that this book was a good idea, well before anyone else was talking about JavaServer Faces. Then, there's Marjan Bace, Manning's publisher, who authorized the project, then promptly ripped the first draft of my introduction to shreds. Without Marjan, this book would have already put you to sleep. (If you're holding open your eyelids with your fingertips right now, blame him.)

Next, there's Jackie Carter—I couldn't dream of a better developmental editor. Jackie didn't just critique and guide my work; she was a true partner throughout the process. I'd also like to thank the legions of technical reviewers who let my words consume their evenings without compensation: Roland Barcia, Todd Cunningham, Jeff Duska, Carl Hume, Will Forster, Aleksandar Kolundzija, Jason LeCount, Josh Oberwetter, Michael Nash, Russ Pearlman, Mark Pippins, Matthew Schmidt, Keyur Shah, Sang Shin, and Henri Yandell. Ted Kennedy (rest in peace) and Dave Roberson deserve mention for doing a commendable job coordinating the review process.

Several members of the JSF Expert Group (Eric Lazarus, Brian Murray, Adam Winer, and especially Michael Nash) helped ensure the technical accuracy of this book, and Ed Burns (the co-spec lead) wrote an excellent foreword.

Along the same lines, several vendors gave me insight into their products well before they had public releases available. Beverly Dewitt provided general information about IBM WebSphere Studio, and Roland Barcia wrote the portion of online extension appendix B about that product (in addition to providing an extremely thorough technical review). Jim Inscore from Sun Microsystems made sure I had access to early releases of Java Studio Creator.

Jonas Jacobi and his team at Oracle (Brian Albers, John Fowler, and Adam Winer) went above and beyond the call of duty by not only providing details about JDeveloper but also conducting informal reviews and serving as a general JSF resource. Jonas also wrote about JDeveloper's JSF support and Oracle's ADF Faces Components in online extension appendix B.

In addition, I enlisted the assistance of my good friend Ed LaCalle for Spanish translations, as well as my world-traveling brother, John A. Mann II, for Russian translations. My wife Tracey Burroughs provided general technical guidance and support. She also wrote most of appendix E—she has an uncanny knack for detail, and she's way too brilliant for her own good.

There's also the production team, who worked to create the early-access version of this book (available in PDF) as well as the print version. Henri Yandell is an extremely meticulous technical editor who made sure that everything I wrote made sense. Liz Welch, the copyeditor, corrected all of my bad grammar and made sure I followed Manning's guidelines. Susan Forsyth proofread every word, Denis Dalinnik typeset every single page, and Susan Edwards tackled the extremely tedious job of indexing. Finally, Mary Piergies coordinated the production process.

If you have seen this book mentioned on a web site or received a free copy or excerpt, you have Helen Trimes to thank—she's done an outstanding marketing job. I'd also like to thank a few others at Manning: Lianna J. Wlasiuk, Susan Capparelle, Syd Brown, and Iain Shigeoka.

And then there are my parents—the strongest and kindest people I know. Whenever I look at where I am in life, I can see a profound imprint of their love and encouragement.

All of these people worked hard to make *JavaServer Faces in Action* a quality product. Lastly, I'd like to thank you, the reader, for buying this book. (Okay, maybe you're just flipping through it, but that counts for something too.)

about this book

This book is written for people who currently develop Java web applications—architects, application developers, and front-end developers. From my perspective, architects worry about the application's design, which technologies are used, and how the development process will work. Application developers build model objects, application logic, and so on, while front-end developers concentrate on building the GUI, usually with a display technology like JavaServer Pages (JSP) or Velocity. In many shops, these roles are performed by the same people, or those in different roles have overlapping skill sets. JSF is a web application framework like Struts, WebWork, or Tapestry, but this book is accessible even if you haven't used a web framework before.

JavaServer Faces in Action is divided into five parts. The first part covers JSF basics. Chapter 1 explains the motivation behind JSF, examines how it fits into the current landscape, and has the requisite Hello, world! example. This chapter also provides a brief overview of the foundation technologies JSF uses: HTTP, servlets, portlets, and display technologies like JSP. Chapter 2 delves further into JSF by examining its core concepts and explaining in detail how JSF performs its magic. Chapter 3 covers everyday topics like configuration, JSP integration, JavaBean initialization, and navigation. Chapters 4 and 5 cover the standard UI components, and chapter 6 examines internationalization, validation, and type conversion. All of these chapters explain JSF as a technology, but also reveal how it is used within tools.

Part 2 is focused on building a UI using all of the concepts outlined in part 1. It begins with chapter 7, which introduces the case study that is used throughout parts 2 and 3. Chapters 8, 9, and 10 build a working prototype of the case study using UI components and JSP without any Java code.

Part 3 focuses on the application code required to turn the prototype into a real application. Chapter 11 outlines JSF's Java API from an application developer's perspective, while chapters 12 and 13 walk through design and development of the application. Chapter 14 examines integration with existing frameworks like Struts.

Part 4 looks at the other side of the coin: extending JSF with UI components, renders, validators, and converters. Chapter 15 examines the JSF API from a component developer's perspective. The print edition ends with appendix A, which looks at using JSF without JSP.

Following appendix A is an online extension (part 5) which is downloadable at no charge from http://www.manning.com/mann. The online extension is chockfull of examples that build upon the foundation laid in part 4. Chapter 16 shows how to develop a basic UI component, and chapter 17 examines renderers. Chapters 18 and 19 show how to build more sophisticated UI components, and chapter 20 walks through developing a validator and a converter. All of these chapters use examples that are applicable to everyday web development.

The online extension ends with four appendices that cover a range of additional topics. Appendix B provides thorough coverage of JSF support in Oracle JDeveloper, IBM WebSphere Studio, and Sun Java Studio Creator. Appendix C looks more closely at JSF's architecture and shows how to extend it with pluggable classes. The last two appendices are references: appendix D covers every configuration element, and appendix E lists time zone, language, and country codes.

How to use this book

This book is part tutorial, part case study, and part reference. It's written so that it can be read sequentially, but I have tried to ensure that individual sections make some sense in isolation. That being said, if you have the time, just start from the beginning and skip the sections that don't seem relevant. Be careful skipping entire chapters, because each chapter may have a nugget of information that you find useful.

Of course, few people believe that they have *any* time (let alone *the* time), so here are a few guidelines. If you're an architect, you should peruse most of this book, but pay close attention to chapters 1, 2, 3, 6, 8, 12, 13, and 15. You may also want to peruse appendix A, and online extension appendices B and C.

Application developers should read most of parts 1–3, but you can skim chapters 4 and 5. You only need to read chapter 14 if you're working with an existing web application, or if you're currently using Struts. Advanced developers should certainly read parts 4 and 5 (online), as well as appendix A, and online extension appendices B and C.

Front-end developers should read all of parts 1 and 2, with the possible exception of parts of chapter 2. In general, this book becomes more complicated as you get closer to the end.

References

References to web sites, books, and articles are denoted in brackets ([]) and can be found in the References section at the end of this book. For example, the author's community site, JSF Central [JSF Central] is a great place to find out more information about JSF news, products, and resources. In the References section, the bracketed text maps to the actual URL:

[JSF Central] JSF Central community web site, http://www.jsfcentral.com.

The bracketed name looks the same regardless of whether it's a web site, a product, a book, or an article.

Conventions

Like in any good book, this text is mostly self-explanatory. I do, however, use a few conventions, which are explained in the following sections.

Boldface type

I use boldface type to emphasize portions of code segments (which could be in Java, XML, or JSP). Usually I'm trying to point out the meat of the code or draw attention to text that was added to a previous listing.

Italicized type

Italics are used when I'm defining a word. I also use them to emphasize particular words, in the usual way.

Courier type

Courier type (`like this`) is used for code (Java, XML, or JSP). I use it in code listings, but also for Java class names, XML tags, and anything else you might type into a development tool.

Component tables

In chapters 4 and 5, I use specialized tables to describe JSF UI components. The first is a Component Summary table; here's an example:

`HtmlOutputText` summary

Component	`HtmlOutputText`
Family	`javax.faces.Output`
Possible IDE Display Names	Output Text
Display Behavior	Converts the value to a string and displays it with optional support CSS styles. (If the `id` or `style` property is set, encloses the text in a `<span>` element.)
Tag Tibrary	HTML
JSP Tag	`<h:outputText>`
Pass-Through Properties	`style, title`
Common Properties	`id, value, rendered, converter, styleClass, binding` (see table 4.2)

Property	Type	Default Value	Required?	Description
`escape`	`boolean`	`true`	No	Controls whether or not HTML or XML characters are escaped (displayed literally in a browser).

Don't worry about what this means quite yet—the point is that all of the standard JSF UI components are described this way. The idea is to give you all of the basic details about the component in one single table.

UI component examples are handled in tables as follows:

`HtmlOutputText` example: Text is escaped by default.

HTML	`What are <i>you</i> looking at?`
Component Tag	`<h:outputText value="What are <i>you</i> looking at?"/>`
Browser Display	What are <i>you</i> looking at?

Here, I show the HTML output, the JSP component tag, and the browser display, all in one table. This way, you can easily see how the three different pieces are related. The HTML is displayed first for those who think in terms of HTML.

Code annotations

I use code annotations because they look much cooler than comments. Here's an example:

```
public String myAction()      <-- (1) This is an action method
{
   // Do something
}
```

Sometimes I'll expand upon annotations in paragraphs after the code listing, using numbered cueballs like this: (1).

Callouts

I use the typical callouts like NOTE, WARNING, DEFINITION, and so on throughout the text to emphasize specific points that may otherwise get buried in ordinary text. Here's an example:

DEFINITION A *UI component*, or *control*, is a component that provides specific functionality for interacting with an end user. Classic examples include toolbars, buttons, panels, and calendars.

In addition, I use a couple of unique ones:

BY THE WAY Makes a point that isn't essential to the current text, but may be useful anyway. Usually, I'm attempting to address related questions you may have.

SOAPBOX My own personal opinion. Take these with a grain of salt.

Source code and the online extension

All of the source code for this book can be downloaded from the book's web site: http://www.manning.com/mann. The downloadable files contain instructions for installation and compilation. From the same site, book owners can also download an additional 300 pages of this book, called the online extension, in PDF format.

Author Online

Manning maintains a forum for us authors to spew our biased views at our beloved readers. The one for *JavaServer Faces in Action* is available at http://www.manning.com/mann. If you have any questions about JSF or comments about this book, feel free to drop by. I will personally be checking this forum from time to time, as I'm keenly interested in what you have to say.

About the author

Kito D. Mann is a consultant specializing in enterprise architecture, mentoring, and development. A programmer since the tender age of 12, he has written several articles on Java-related technologies, and also speaks at user groups and conferences. He has consulted with several Fortune 500 companies, and has been the chief architect of an educational application service provider. Kito is also the founder of the JSF Central community web site, and a member of JSF 1.2 and JSP 2.1 expert groups. He holds a B.A. in Computer Science from Johns Hopkins University, and lives in Stamford, Connecticut, with his wife, four cats, and two parrots. In his spare time, he enjoys making incomplete compositions with electronic music equipment.

about the title and cover

About the title

By combining introductions, overviews, and how-to examples, the *In Action* books are designed to help learning and remembering. According to research in cognitive science, the things people remember are things they discover during self-motivated exploration.

Although no-one at Manning is a cognitive scientist, we are convinced that for learning to become permanent it must pass through stages of exploration, play, and, interestingly, re-telling of what is being learned. People understand and remember new things, which is to say they master them, only after actively exploring them. Humans learn in action. An essential part of an *In Action* book is that it is example-driven. It encourages the reader to try things out, to play with new code, and explore new ideas.

There is another, more mundane, reason for the title of this book: our readers are busy. They use books to do a job or solve a problem. They need books that allow them to jump in and jump out easily and learn just what they want just when they want it. They need books that aid them in action. The books in this series are designed for such readers.

About the cover illustration

The figure on the cover of *JavaServer Faces in Action* is a "Saka," or a Turkish water carrier. The illustration is taken from a collection of costumes of the Ottoman Empire published on January 1, 1802, by William Miller of Old Bond Street, London. The title page is missing from the collection and we have been unable to track it down to date. The book's table of contents identifies the figures in both English and French, and each illustration bears the names of two artists who worked on it, both of whom would no doubt be surprised to find their art gracing the front cover of a computer programming book...two hundred years later.

The collection was purchased by a Manning editor at an antiquarian flea market in the "Garage" on West 26th Street in Manhattan. The seller was an American based in Ankara, Turkey, and the transaction took place just as he was packing up his stand for the day. The Manning editor did not have on his person the substantial amount of cash that was required for the purchase and a credit card and check were both politely turned down.

With the seller flying back to Ankara that evening the situation was getting hopeless. What was the solution? It turned out to be nothing more than an old-fashioned verbal agreement sealed with a handshake. The seller simply proposed that the money be transferred to him by wire and the editor walked out with the bank information on a piece of paper and the portfolio of images under his arm. Needless to say, we transferred the funds the next day, and we remain grateful and impressed by this unknown person's trust in one of us. It recalls something that might have happened a long time ago.

The pictures from the Ottoman collection, like the other illustrations that appear on our covers, bring to life the richness and variety of dress customs of two centuries ago. They recall the sense of isolation and distance of that period‹and of every other historic period except our own hyperkinetic present.

Dress codes have changed since then and the diversity by region, so rich at the time, has faded away. It is now often hard to tell the inhabitant of one continent from another. Perhaps, trying to view it optimistically, we have traded a cultural and visual diversity for a more varied personal life. Or a more varied and interesting intellectual and technical life.

We at Manning celebrate the inventiveness, the initiative, and, yes, the fun of the computer business with book covers based on the rich diversity of regional life of two centuries ago brought back to life by the pictures from this collection.

Part 1

Exploring JavaServer Faces

Part 1 introduces and explores the world of JavaServer Faces programming. We provide an overview of the technology and explain how JSF fits into the current web development landscape. Next, we discuss a sample application, explore how JSF works, and examine its fundamental concepts. This part of the book concludes with chapters that cover all of the standard JSF components, as well as features like internationalization and validation.

1 Introducing JavaServer Faces

This chapter covers

- What JavaServer Faces is, and what it's not
- Foundation technologies (HTTP, servlets, portlets, JavaBeans, and JSP)
- How JavaServer Faces relates to existing web development frameworks
- Building a simple application

Welcome to *JavaServer Faces in Action*. JavaServer Faces (JSF, or simply "Faces") makes it easy to develop web applications by bringing support for rich, powerful user interface components (such as text boxes, list boxes, tabbed panes, and data grids) to the web development world. A child of the Java Community Process,[1] JSF is destined to become a part of Java 2 Enterprise Edition (J2EE). This book will help you understand exactly what JSF is, how it works, and how you can use it in your projects today.

1.1 It's a RAD-ical world

A popular term in the pre-Web days was *Rapid Application Development* (RAD). The main goal of RAD was to enable you to build powerful applications with a set of reusable components. If you've ever used tools like Visual Basic, PowerBuilder, or Delphi, you know that they were a major leap forward in application development productivity. For the first time, it was easy to develop complex user interfaces (UIs) and integrate them with data sources.

You could drag application widgets—UI controls and other components—from a palette and drop them into your application. Each of these components had properties that affected their behavior. (For example, `font` is a common property for any control that displays text; a data grid might have a `dataSource` property to represent a data store.) These components generated a set of events, and event handlers defined the interaction between the UI and the rest of the application. You had access to all of this good stuff directly from within the integrated development environment (IDE), and you could easily switch between design and code-centric views of the world.

RAD tools were great for developing full-fledged applications, but they were also quite useful for rapid prototyping because they could quickly create a UI with little or no code. In addition, the low barrier to entry allowed both experienced programmers and newbies to get immediate results.

These tools typically had four layers:

- An underlying component architecture
- A set of standard widgets
- An application infrastructure
- The tool itself

[1] The *Java Community Process* (JCP) is the public process used to extend Java with new application programming interfaces (APIs) and other platform enhancements. New proposals are called *Java Specification Requests* (JSRs).

The underlying component architectures were extensible enough to spawn an industry of third-party component developers like Infragistics and Developer Express.

Of course, the RAD philosophy never went away—it just got replaced by other hip buzzwords. It's alive and well in some Java IDEs and other development environments like Borland Delphi and C++Builder. Those environments, however, stop short of using RAD concepts for web projects. The adoption of RAD in the web development world has been remarkably slow.

This sluggishness is due in part to the complexity of creating such a simple, cohesive view of application development in a world that isn't simple or cohesive. Web applications are complex if you compare them to standard desktop applications. You've got a ton of different resources to manage—pages, configuration files, graphics, and code. Your users may be using different types of browsers running on different operating systems. And you have to deal with HTTP, a protocol that is ill suited for building complex applications.

The software industry has become good at masking complexity, so it's no surprise that many RAD web solutions have popped up over the last few years. These solutions bring the power of visual, component-oriented development to the complex world of web development. The granddaddy is Apple's WebObjects,[2] and Microsoft has brought the concept to the mainstream with Visual Studio.NET and ASP.NET Web Forms. In the Java world, many frameworks have emerged, several of them open source. Some have tool support, and some don't.

However, the lack of a *standard* Java RAD web framework is a missing piece of the Java solution puzzle—one that Microsoft's. NET Framework has covered from day one. JavaServer Faces was developed specifically to fill in that hole.

1.1.1 So, what is JavaServer Faces?

In terms of the four layers of a RAD tool, JavaServer Faces defines three of them: a component architecture, a standard set of UI widgets, and an application infrastructure. JSF's component architecture defines a common way to build UI widgets. This architecture enables standard JSF UI widgets (buttons, hyperlinks, checkboxes, text fields, and so on), but also sets the stage for third-party components. Components are event oriented, so JSF allows you to process client-generated events (for instance, changing the value of a text box or clicking on a button).

Because web-based applications, unlike their desktop cousins, must often appease multiple clients (such as desktop browsers, cell phones, and PDAs), JSF

---

[2] WebObjects has a full-fledged environment that includes a J2EE server, web services support, and object persistence, among other things.

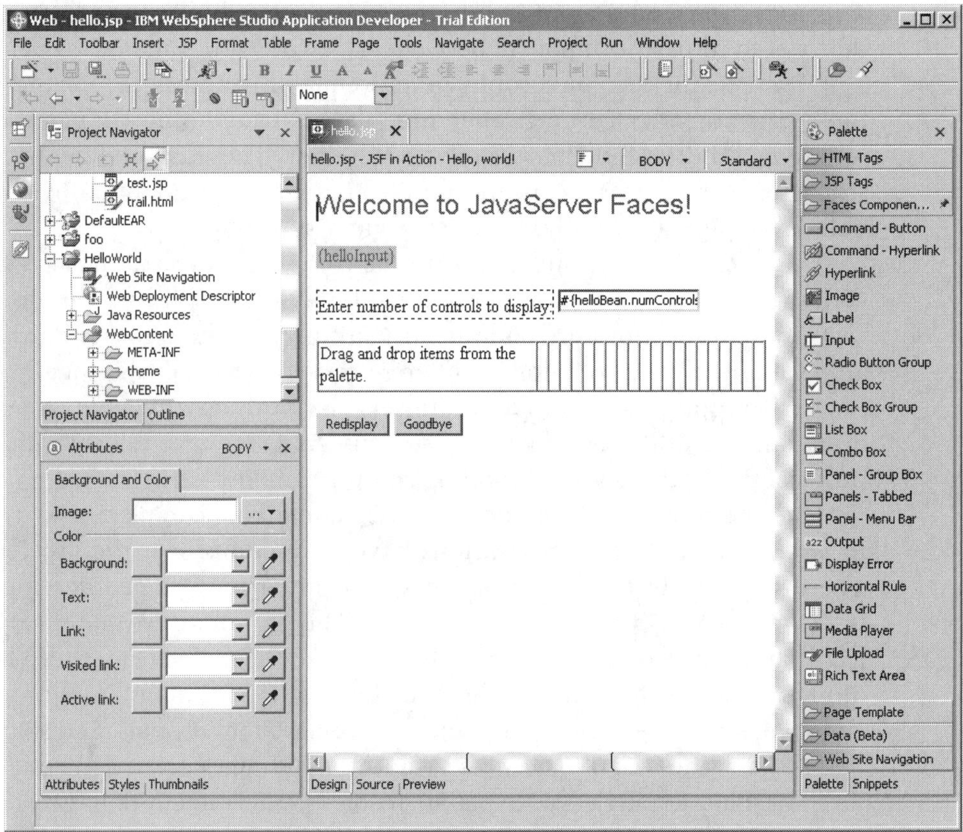

Figure 1.1 IBM's WebSphere Application Developer (WSAD) has been expanded to support JSF applications in addition to the seemingly endless amount of other technologies it supports. You can visually build JSF applications, and mix-and-match other JSP tag libraries using WSAD's familiar Eclipse-based environment.

has a powerful architecture for displaying components in different ways. It also has extensible facilities for validating input (the length of a field, for example) and converting objects to and from strings for display.

Faces can also automatically keep your UI components in synch with Java objects that collect user input values and respond to events, which are called *backing beans*. In addition, it has a powerful navigation system and full support for multiple languages. These features make up JSF's application infrastructure—basic building blocks necessary for any new system.

JavaServer Faces defines the underpinnings for tool support, but the implementation of specific tools is left to vendors, as is the custom with Java. You have

Figure 1.2 Oracle's JDeveloper [Oracle, JDeveloper] will have full-fledged support for JSF, complete with an extensive array of UIX components, which will integrate with standard JSF applications. It will also support using JSF components with its Application Development Framework (ADF) [Oracle, ADF]. (This screen shot was taken with UIX components available with JDeveloper 10g, which are the basis of JSF support in the next version of JDeveloper.)

a choice of tools from industry leaders that allow you to visually lay out a web UI in a way that's quite familiar to users of RAD development tools such as Visual Studio. NET. (Figures 1.1, 1.2, and 1.3 show what Faces development looks like in IDEs from IBM, Oracle, and Sun, respectively.) Or, if you prefer, you can develop Faces applications without design tools.

Just in case all of this sounds like magic, we should point out a key difference between JavaServer Faces and desktop UI frameworks like Swing or the Standard Widget Toolkit (SWT): JSF runs on the *server*. As such, a Faces application will run

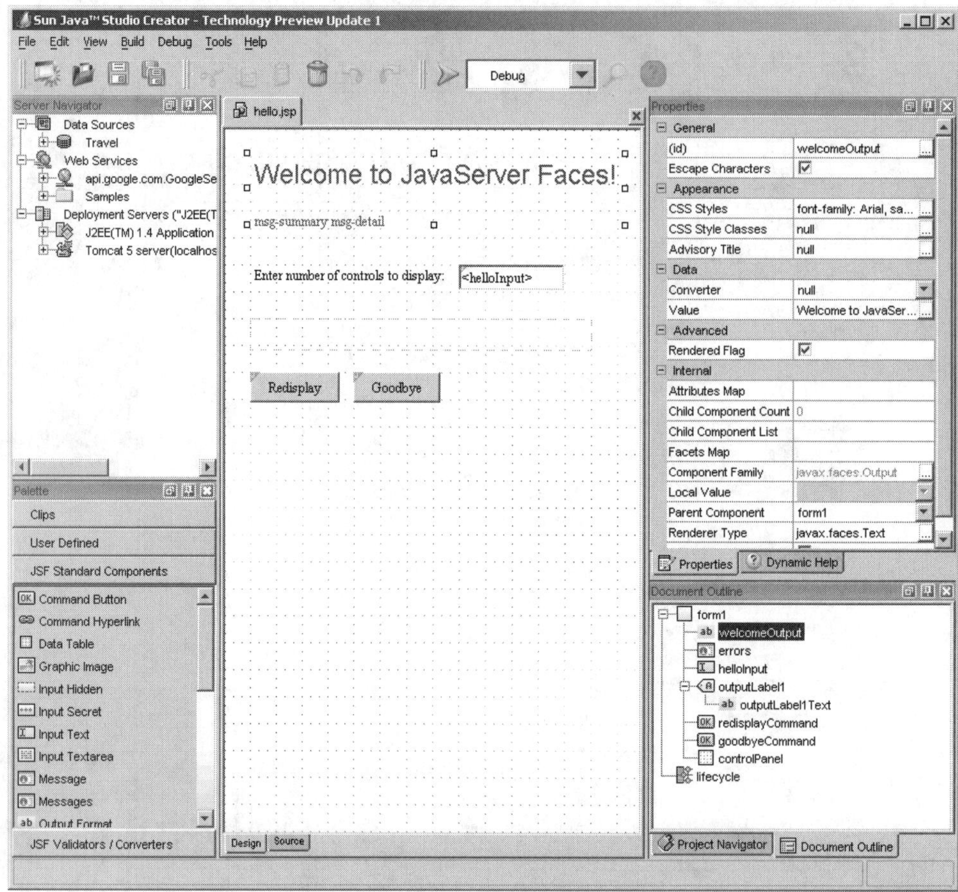

Figure 1.3 Sun's Java Studio Creator [Sun, Creator] is an easy-to-use, visually based environment for building JavaServer Faces applications. You can easily switch between designing JSF pages visually, editing the JSP source, and writing associated Java code in an environment that should seem familiar to users of Visual Studio.NET, Visual Basic, or Delphi.

Widget Toolkit (SWT): JSF runs on the *server.* As such, a Faces application will run in a standard Java web container like Apache Tomcat [ASF, Tomcat], Oracle Application Server [Oracle, AS], or IBM WebSphere Application Server [IBM, WAS], and display HTML or some other markup to the client.

If you click a button in a Swing application, it will fire an event that you can handle directly in the code that resides on the desktop. In contrast, web browsers don't know anything about JSF components or events; they just know how to

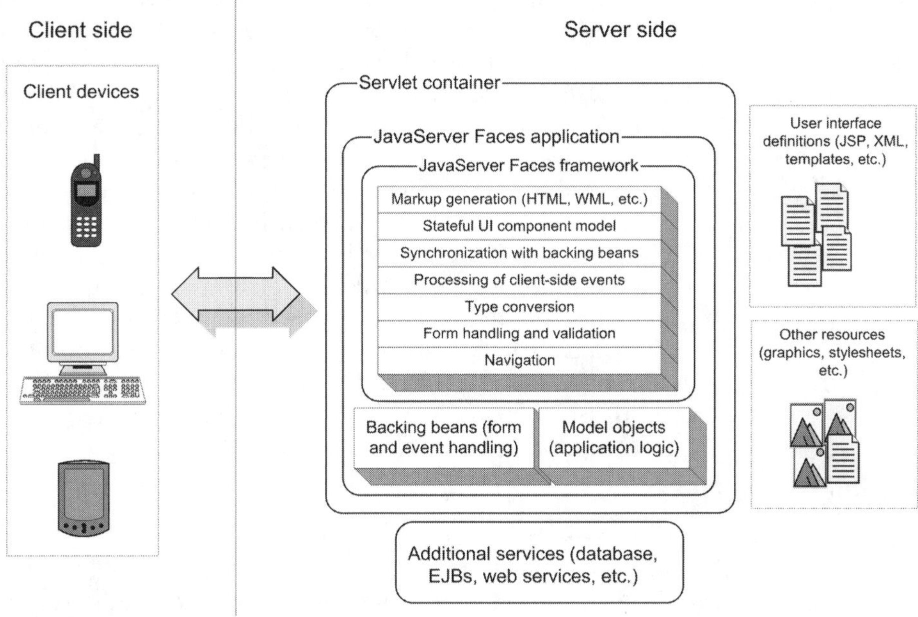

Figure 1.4 A high-level view of a JavaServer Faces application. JSF makes web development easy by providing support for UI components and handling a lot of common web development tasks.

display HTML.[3] So when you click on a button in a Faces application, it causes a request to be sent from your web browser to the server. Faces is responsible for translating that request into an event that can be processed by your application logic on the server. It's also responsible for making sure that every UI widget you've defined on the server is properly displayed to the browser.

Figure 1.4 shows a high-level view of a Faces application. You can see that the application runs on the server and can integrate with other subsystems, such as Enterprise JavaBeans (EJB) services or databases. However, JSF provides many additional services that can help you build powerful web applications with less effort.

JavaServer Faces has a specific goal: to make web development faster and easier. It allows developers to think in terms of components, events, backing beans, and their interactions, instead of requests, responses, and markup. In other words, it masks a lot of the complexities of web development so that developers can focus on what they do best—build applications.

[3] Technically, they do a lot of other things, like execute JavaScript or VBScript, display XML and XHTML, and so on.

NOTE JSF is a technology, and this book covers it as thoroughly as possible in several hundred pages. Tools sugarcoat a lot of pieces of the development puzzle with graphical user interface (GUI) designers that generate JSP, screens that edit configuration files, and so forth. Throughout this book, we'll show you the real Java, JSP, and XML code and configuration that JSF uses, while giving you a sense of where the tools can make your life easier. With this approach, you'll have a full understanding of what an IDE does behind the scenes, which is extremely useful for maintenance of your application after it's built, and also for situations where you need to move from one IDE vendor to another. And, of course, if you don't like IDEs at all, knowing how things actually work is essential. (If you are a big IDE fan, don't worry—we show screen shots of different tools throughout the book, and online extension appendix B covers three of them in detail).

1.1.2 Industry support

One of the best things about the Java Community Process (JCP), Sun Microsystems's way of extending Java, is that a lot of great companies, organizations, and individuals are involved. Producing a spec through the JCP isn't exactly speedy, but the work can be quite good. JavaServer Faces was introduced as Java Specification Request (JSR) 127 by Sun in May 2001; the final version of the specification, JSF 1.0, was released on March 3, 2004, and JSF 1.1 (a maintenance release) arrived on May 27th, 2004. The companies and organizations (other than Sun) involved in developing Faces include the Apache Software Foundation, BEA Systems, Borland Software, IBM, Oracle, Macromedia, and many others.

The products developed by these companies can be put into three categories (many fit in more than one): J2EE containers, development tools, and UI frameworks. Because JavaServer Faces is a UI component framework that works with tools and runs inside J2EE containers, this makes good sense. What's significant is the fact that the group includes many industry heavyweights. This means that you can expect JSF to have a lot of industry support. And if your vendor doesn't support JSF, you can download Sun's reference implementation for free [Sun, JSF RI].

To keep up with the latest JSF news, articles, products and vendors, check out JSF Central [JSF Central], a community site run by the author.

1.2 The technology under the hood

All JSF applications are standard Java web applications. Java web applications speak the Hypertext Transfer Protocol (HTTP) via the Servlet API and typically use some sort of display technology, such as JavaServer Pages (JSP), as shown in figure 1.4. The display technology is used to define UIs that are composed of components that interact with Java code. Faces applications can also work inside of portlets, which are similar to servlets. JSF's component architecture uses JavaBeans for exposing properties and event handling.

In this section, we briefly describe these technologies and explain how they relate to JSF. If you're already familiar with Java web development basics and understand how they relate to JSF, you may want to skip this section.

1.2.1 Hypertext Transfer Protocol (HTTP)

Diplomats and heads of state come from many different cultures and speak many different languages. In order to communicate, they follow specific rules of ceremony and etiquette, called *protocols*. Following protocols helps to ensure that they can correspond effectively, even though they come from completely different backgrounds.

Computers use protocols to communicate as well. Following an established set of rules allows programs to communicate regardless of the specific software, hardware, or operating system.

The World Wide Web (WWW) started as a mechanism for sharing documents. These documents were represented via the Hypertext Markup Language (HTML) and allowed people viewing the documents to easily move between them by simply clicking on a link. To serve up documents and support this hyperlinking capability, the Hypertext Transfer Protocol (HTTP) was developed. It allowed any web browser to grab documents from a server in a standard way.

DEFINITION The Web was originally designed for *static* content such as academic documents, which do not change often. In contrast, *dynamic* content, such as stock information or product orders, changes often. Dynamic content is what applications usually generate.

HTTP is a simple protocol—it's based on text headers. A client sends a request to a server, and the server sends a response back to the browser with the requested document attached. The server is dumb[4]—it doesn't remember anything about the client if another document is requested. This lack of memory means that HTTP is a "stateless" protocol; it maintains no information about the client between requests.

[4] Web servers have grown to be quite sophisticated beasts, but initially they were pretty simple.

The stateless nature of HTTP means that it's able to scale well (it is, after all, *the* protocol of the Internet, and the Internet is a huge place). This property isn't a problem for the static documents that HTTP was originally developed to serve.

But imagine what it'd be like if a valet parked your car but didn't give you a ticket and didn't remember your face. When you came back, he'd have a hard time figuring out which car to retrieve. That's what it's like to develop an application in a stateless environment. To combat this problem, there are two possibilities: cookies and URL rewriting. They're both roughly the same as the valet giving you a ticket and keeping one himself.

No matter what language you use, if you're writing a web application, it will use HTTP. Servlets and JSP were developed to make it easier to build applications on top of the protocol. JavaServer Faces was introduced so that developers can forget that they're using the protocol at all.

1.2.2 Servlets

HTTP is great for serving up static content, and web servers excel at that function out of the box. But creating dynamic content requires writing code. Even though HTTP is simple, it still takes some work to write programs that work with it. You have to parse the headers, understand what they mean, and then create new headers in the proper format. That's what the Java Servlet application programming interface (API) is all about: providing an object-oriented view of the world that makes it easier to develop web applications.[5] HTTP requests and responses are encapsulated as objects, and you get access to input and output streams so that you can read a user's response and write dynamic content. Requests are handled by *servlets*—objects that handle a particular set of HTTP requests.

A standard J2EE web application is, by definition, based on the Servlet API. Servlets run inside a *container*, which is essentially a Java application that performs all of the grunt work associated with running multiple servlets, associating the resources grouped together as a web application, and managing all sorts of other services. The most popular servlet container is Tomcat [ASF, Tomcat], but J2EE application servers such as IBM WebSphere [IBM, WAS] and the Sun Java System Application Server [Sun, JSAS] provide servlet containers as well.

As we mentioned in the previous section, one of the big problems with HTTP is that it's stateless. Web applications get around this problem through the use of

---

[5] Technically, the Servlet API can be used to provide server functionality in any request/response environment—it doesn't necessarily have to be used with HTTP. In this section, we're referring to the `java.servlet.http` package, which was designed specifically for processing HTTP requests.

sessions—they make it seem as if the users are always there, even if they're not. Sessions are one of the biggest benefits that the Servlet API provides. Even though behind the scenes they make use of cookies or URL rewriting, the programmer is shielded from those complexities.

The Servlet API also provides lots of other goodies, like security, logging, lifecycle events, filters, packaging and deployment, and so on. These features all form the base of JavaServer Faces. As a matter of fact, JSF is implemented as a servlet, and all JSF applications are standard J2EE web applications.

JSF takes things a bit further than the Servlet API, though. Servlets cover the basic infrastructure necessary for building web applications. But at the end of the day, you still have to deal with requests and responses, which are properties of the underlying protocol, HTTP. JSF applications have UI components, which are associated with backing beans and can generate events that are consumed by application logic. Faces uses the Servlet API for all of its plumbing, but the developer gets the benefit of working at a higher level of abstraction: You can develop web applications without worrying about HTTP or the specifics of the Servlet API itself.

1.2.3 Portlets

Most web applications serve dynamic content from a data store—usually a database. (Even if the business logic is running on another type of server, like an EJB or Common Object Request Broker Architecture [CORBA] server, eventually some code talks to a database.) Since the early days of the Web, however, there has been a need for software that aggregates information from different data sources into an easy-to-use interface. These types of applications, called *portals*, were originally the domain of companies like Netscape and Yahoo! However, more and more companies now realize that the same concept works well for aggregating information from different internal data sources for employee use.

So a variety of vendors, including heavyweights like IBM, BEA, and Oracle, offer portal products to simplify this task. Each data source is normally displayed in a region within a web page that behaves similarly to a window—you can close the region, customize its behavior, or interact with it independent of the rest of the page. Each one of these regions is called a *portlet.*

Each of these vendors developed a completely different API for writing portlets that work with their portal products. In order to make it easier to develop portlets that work in multiple portals, the JCP developed the Portlet specification [Sun, Portlet], which was released in late 2003. All of the major portal vendors (including Sun, BEA, IBM, and Oracle) and open source organizations like the Apache Software Foundation have announced support for this specification in their portal products.

The Portlet specification defines the Portlet API, which, like the Servlet API, defines a lot of low-level details but doesn't simplify UI development or mask HTTP. That's where JSF comes into the picture; it was developed so that it can work with the Portlet API (which is similar in many ways to the Servlet API). You can use ordinary JSF components, event handling, and other features inside portlets, just as you can inside servlets.

NOTE Throughout this book, we mostly talk about JSF in relation to servlets. However, most of our discussions apply to portlets as well.

1.2.4 JavaBeans

Quite a few Java web developers think that JavaBeans are simply classes with some properties exposed via getter and setter methods (accessors and mutators). For example, a Java class with the methods `getName` and `setName` exposes a read-write property called `name`. However, properties are just the tip of the iceberg; JavaBeans is a full-fledged component architecture designed with tool support in mind.

This is significant, because it means there's a lot more to it than just properties. JavaBeans conform to a set of patterns that allow other Java classes to dynamically discover events and other metadata in addition to properties. As a matter of fact, JavaBeans is the technology that enables Swing and makes it possible for IDEs to provide GUI builders for desktop applications and applets. Using JavaBeans, you can develop a component that not only cooperates nicely with a visual GUI builder but also provides a specialized wizard (or *customizer*) to walk the user through the configuration process. JavaBeans also includes a powerful event model (the same one used with Swing and JSF components), persistence services, and other neat features.

Understanding the power of JavaBeans will help you comprehend the full power of JSF. Like Swing components, every JSF component is a full-fledged JavaBean. In addition, Faces components are designed to work with backing beans—objects that are implemented as JavaBeans and also handle events.

If you're just planning to write application code or build UIs, then a basic knowledge of JavaBeans (mutators and accessors) is sufficient. If you're going to be developing custom components, a deep understanding of JavaBeans will make your life much easier.

1.2.5 JSP and other display technologies

Servlets are great low-level building blocks for web development, but they don't adequately simplify the task of displaying dynamic content. You have to manually write out the response to every request.

Let's say that every line of HTML you were sending was written as a separate line of Java code. You have about 30 pages in your application, and each page has about 80 lines of HTML. All of the sudden, you have 2400 lines of code that looks a lot like this:

```
out.println("This is a <b>really</b> repetitive task, and \"escaping\"" +
        " text is a pain. ");
```

This is really tedious work, especially because you have to escape a lot of characters, and it's hard to quickly make changes. Clearly there has to be a better way.

To solve this problem, Sun introduced JavaServer Pages (JSP) as a standard template mechanism. JavaServer Pages look like an HTML page, but they have special tags that do custom processing or display JavaBean values, and can also have Java code embedded in them.[6] Ultimately, they behave like a servlet that looks a lot like the previous code snippet. The JSP translator does the boring work so that you don't have to.

You can create your own custom tags[7] to perform additional processing (such as accessing a database), and there's a useful set of standard tags called the JavaServer Pages Standard Tag Library (JSTL) [Sun, JSTL]. The idea is that you can define the UI with HTML-like tags, not Java code.

Even though JSP is the industry standard display technology, you can choose among many alternatives. You could use a full Extensible Markup Language/Extensible Style Sheet Language Transformations (XML/XSLT) approach with something like Cocoon [ASF, Cocoon], or a stricter template-based approach like Velocity [ASF, Velocity] or WebMacro [WebMacro]. Many other options are available as well.

One of the key design goals of JSF was to avoid relying on a particular display technology. So JSF provides pluggable interfaces that allow developers to integrate

---

6 The ability to have Java code embedded in JSPs is considered bad design (and a bad practice) by many and is the topic of one of those huge religious wars. The main argument is that it doesn't enforce separation between display and business logic. That "feature" is one of the main reasons there are different choices for display technologies. In JSP 2.0, you can turn off this feature.

7 Custom tags are technically called "custom actions," but we use the more common term "custom tags" throughout this book.

it with various display technologies. However, because JSF is a standard Java technology, and so is JSP, it's no surprise that Faces comes with a JSP implementation (via custom tags) right out of the box. And because JSP is the only display technology that *must* be integrated with JavaServer Faces, most of the examples in this book use JSP as well.

1.3 Frameworks, frameworks, frameworks

Earlier, we said that JavaServer Faces is a "framework" for developing web-based UIs in Java. Frameworks are extremely common these days, and for a good reason: they help make web development easier. Like most Java web frameworks, JSF enforces a clean separation of presentation and business logic. However, it focuses more on the UI side of things and can be integrated with other frameworks, like Struts.

1.3.1 Why do we need frameworks?

As people build more and more web applications, it becomes increasingly obvious that although servlets and JSPs are extremely useful, they can't handle many common tasks without tedious coding. Frameworks help simplify these tasks.

The most basic of these tasks is form processing. HTML pages have forms, which are collection of user input controls like text boxes, lookup lists, and checkboxes. When a user submits a form, all of the data from the input fields is sent to the server. A text field in HTML might look like this:

```
<input maxLength=256 size=55 name="userName" value="">
```

In a standard servlet application, the developer must retrieve those values directly from the HTTP request like this:

```
String userName = (String)request.getParameter("userName");
```

This can be tedious for large forms, and because you're dealing directly with the value sent from the browser, the Java code must also make sure all of the request parameters are valid. In addition, each one of these parameters must be manually associated with the application's objects.

Forms are just one example of tasks that servlets and JSP don't completely solve. Web applications have to manage a lot of pages and images, and referencing all of those elements within larger applications can become a nightmare if you don't have a central way of managing it.

Management of the page structure is another issue. Although JSP provides a simple mechanism for creating a dynamic page, it doesn't provide extensive support for *composing* a page out of smaller, reusable parts. Other fun things that servlets don't handle include internationalization, type conversion, and error handling.

To handle all of these tasks in a simplified manner, several frameworks have emerged. Some of the more popular ones are Struts [ASF, Struts] and WebWork [OpenSymphony, WebWork]. The goal of any framework is to facilitate development by handling many common tasks.

1.3.2 She's a Model 2

Basic organization and management services are a necessity for larger web applications, but they need structure as well. Most web frameworks, including JSF, enforce some variation of the Model-View-Controller (MVC) design pattern. To understand exactly what MVC is, let's look at a driving analogy.

When you're driving down the highway in one direction, there's usually a median between you and the traffic heading in the opposite direction. The median is there for a good reason—fast traffic moving in opposite directions doesn't mix too well. Without the median, a rash of accidents would inevitably result.

Applications have similar issues: Code for business logic doesn't mix too well with UI code. When the two are mixed, applications are much harder to maintain, less scalable, and generally more brittle. Moreover, you can't have one team working on presentation code while another works on business logic.

The MVC pattern is the standard solution to this problem. When you watch a story on the news, you view a version of reality. An empirical event exists, and the news channel is responsible for interpreting the event and broadcasting that interpretation. Even though you see the program on your TV, a distinct difference lies between what actually took place, how people doing the reporting understand it, and what you're seeing on your TV. The news channel is *controlling* the interaction between the TV program—the *view*—and the actual event—the model. Even though you may be watching the news on TV, the same channel might be broadcasting via the Internet or producing print publications. These are alternate views. If the pieces of the production weren't separate, this wouldn't be possible.

In software, the view is the presentation layer, which is responsible for interacting with the user. The model is the business logic and data, and the controller is the application code that responds to user events and integrates the model and view. This architecture ensures that the application is loosely coupled, which reduces dependencies between different layers.

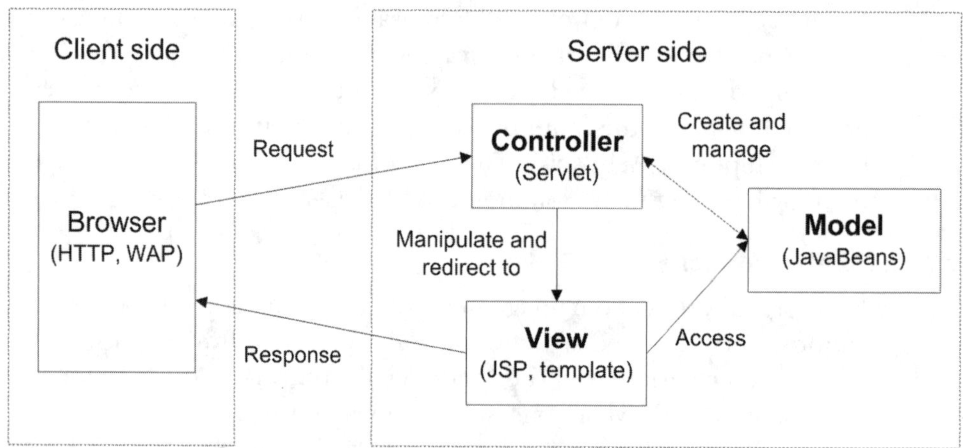

Figure 1.5 Most web frameworks use some variation of the Model 2 design pattern.

Model 2 (shown in figure 1.5) is a variation of MVC that's specific to web applications. The basic point is that:

- The model can consist of plain old Java objects (POJOs), EJBs, or something else.
- The view can be JSPs or some other display technology.
- The controller is always implemented as a servlet.

So if the JSP page contains an error, it doesn't affect the application code or the model. If there's an error in the model, it doesn't affect the application code or the JSP page. This separation allows for unit testing at each layer, and also lets different parties work with the layers independently. For instance, a front-end developer can build a JSP before the business objects and the application code are complete. Portions of some layers can even be integrated before all three have been completed.

These benefits are exactly why most frameworks, including JSF, support some variation of the MVC design pattern.

1.3.3 JSF, Struts, and other frameworks

Let's face it: there are a lot of Java web frameworks available. Some of them, like Struts [ASF, Struts] and WebWork [OpenSymphony, WebWork], help with form processing and other issues such as enforcing Model 2, integrating with data sources, and controlling references to all of the application's resources centrally via

XML configuration files. These *foundation frameworks* provide extensive underpinnings but don't mask the fundamental request/response nature of HTTP.

Other frameworks, like Tapestry [ASF, Tapestry], Oracle's Application Development Framework (ADF) UIX [Oracle, ADF UIX], and SOFIA [Salmon, SOFIA], provide a UI component model and some sort of event processing. The purpose of these *UI frameworks*, which include JSF, is to simplify the entire programming model. Often, foundation and UI frameworks have overlapping functionality.

To understand this overlap, you can think of web application infrastructure as a stack of services. The services close to the bottom of the stack don't abstract too many details of the underlying protocol; they're more like plumbing. The services toward the top of the stack hide more of the gory details; they provide higher levels of abstraction. The lowest services are handled by web servers, the Servlet API, and JSP. Most frameworks provide some subsection of the additional services. Figure 1.6 shows this stack in relation to JSF, Struts, servlets, JSP, and a traditional web server.

You can see from the figure that JSF supports enough services to make it quite powerful by itself, and in many cases, it's all you'll need. Subsequent releases of Faces will most likely cover additional services as well.

However, even though Faces overlaps with frameworks like Struts, it doesn't necessarily replace them. (As a matter of fact, the lead developer of Struts, Craig McClanahan, was instrumental in the development of JavaServer Faces.) If you integrate the two, you get access to all the services of the stack (chapter 14 covers Struts integration). You can also use JSF with other frameworks like Spring [Spring-Faces].

For UI-oriented frameworks, JSF may overlap with a large set of their functionality. Some of those projects have pledged support for JSF in future versions. Faces has the distinction of being developed by a consortium of industry heavyweights through the JCP and will be part of J2EE. As a result, it enjoys heavy tool support and will ship standard with many J2EE servers.

1.4 Components everywhere

Sadly, overuse of the term "component" is rampant in the industry today. An operating system is a component, an application is a component, EJBs are components, a library is a component, and so is the kitchen sink. Numerous books about components are available, and the good ones point out that many definitions exist.

The excessive use of this word isn't that strange if you know what it really means. If you look up "component" in the dictionary, you'll see that it's a

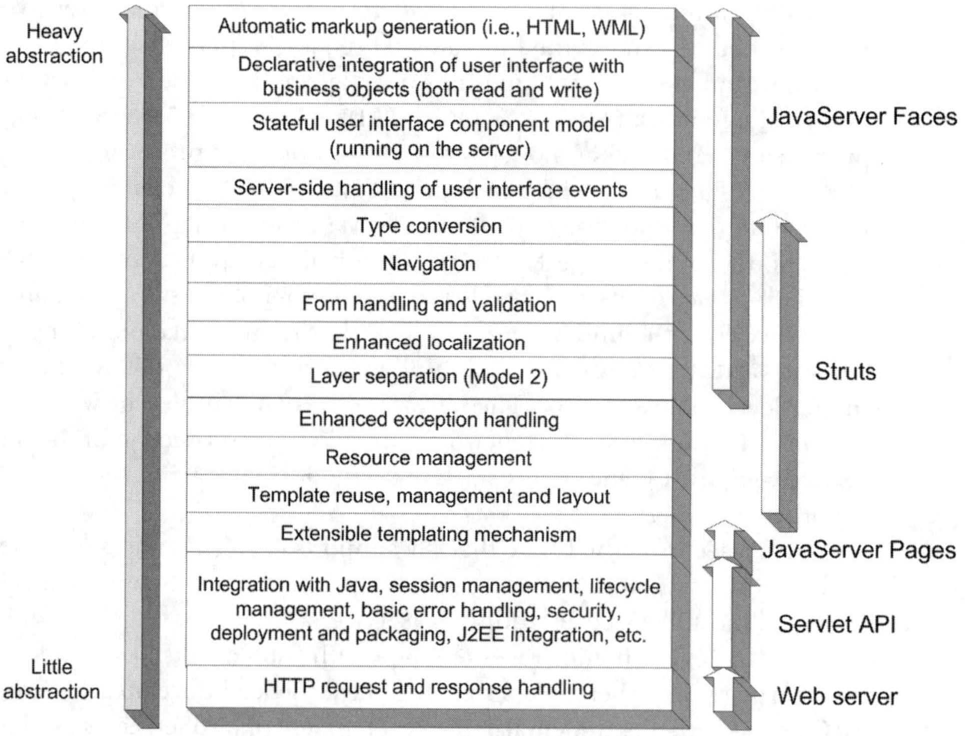

Figure 1.6 Web application infrastructure can be viewed as a stack of services. The services on the bottom provide basic plumbing but little abstraction. The services at the top of the stack provide more abstraction. Having all of the services together is extremely powerful.

synonym for *constituent*—a part of a whole. So, if you use the literal meaning of the word, an operating system really is a component in the context of a distributed application.

What's funny is that conceptually, a kitchen sink has more in common with Faces components than an operating system does. If you remodel your kitchen, you get to pick out a kitchen sink. You don't have to *build* it from scratch—you just have to pick a sink that fulfills your requirements: size, color, material, number of bowls, and so on. The same thing goes for other kitchen items, like cabinets and countertops. All of these components have specific interfaces that allow them to integrate with one another, but they depend on specific environmental services (plumbing, for instance). The end result may be unique, but the whole is made up of independent, reusable parts.

If we take the concepts of kitchen components and apply them to software, we end up with this definition:

DEFINITION A *software component* is a unit of composition with contractually specified interfaces and explicit context dependencies only. A software component can be deployed independently and is subject to composition by third parties [Szyperski].

The "context dependencies" in a kitchen are things like the room itself, plumbing, and electrical circuits. In essence, the context is the container for all of the components. A *container* is a system that hosts components and provides a set of services that allow those components to be manipulated. Sometimes that manipulation is within an IDE (during *design time*); sometimes it's in a deployment environment, like a J2EE server (during *runtime*).

The phrase "deployed independently" means that a component is a self-contained unit and can be installed into a container. Kitchen sinks are individual, self-contained items made to fit into a countertop.

When you remodel your kitchen, you hire a contractor, who assembles the components you've selected (cabinets, drawers, sink, and so on) into a full-fledged kitchen. When we build software using component architectures, we assemble various components to create a working software system.

JSF components, Swing components, servlets, EJBs, JavaBeans, ActiveX controls, and Delphi Visual Component Library (VCL) components all fit this definition. But these components concentrate on different things. JSF and Swing components are aimed solely at UI development, while ActiveX and VCL controls may or may not affect the UI. Servlets and EJBs are much more *coarse-grained*—they provide a lot of functionality that's more in the realm of application logic and business logic.

Because JSF is focused on UI components, let's narrow our component definition appropriately:

DEFINITION A *UI component*, or *control*, is a component that provides specific functionality for interacting with an end user. Classic examples include toolbars, buttons, panels, and calendars.

If you've done traditional GUI development, then the concept of a UI component should be quite familiar to you. What's great about JavaServer Faces is that it brings a standard UI component model to the web world. It sets the stage for things desktop developers take for granted: a wide selection of packaged UI functionality with extensive tools support. It also opens the door for creating custom components that handle tasks specific to a particular business domain—like a report viewer or an interest calculator.

1.5 Hello, world!

Now that you have a basic understanding of the problems JavaServer Faces is meant to solve, let's begin with a simple Faces application. This section assumes you're familiar with Java web applications and JSP. (For more about these technologies, see section 1.2 for an overview.) We'll dissect a simple HTML-based web application that has two pages: hello.jsp and goodbye.jsp.

The hello.jsp page does the following:

- Displays the text "Welcome to JavaServer Faces!"
- Has a single form with a text box that requires an integer between 1 and 500
- Stores the last text box value submitted in a JavaBean property called `numControls`
- Has a grid underneath the text box
- Has a button labeled "Redisplay" that when clicked adds `numControls` output UI components to the grid (clearing it of any previous UI components first)
- Has a button labeled "Goodbye" that displays goodbye.jsp if clicked

The goodbye.jsp page does the following:

- Displays the text "Goodbye!"
- Displays the value of the JavaBean property `numControls`

JSF performs most of the work of our Hello, world! application, but in addition to the JSP pages, there are a few other requirements:

- The `HelloBean` backing bean class
- A Faces configuration file
- A properly configured deployment descriptor

Some tools will simplify creation of some or all of these requirements, but in this section, we'll examine the raw files in detail.

Before we get into those details, let's see what Hello, world! looks like in a web browser. The application starts with hello.jsp, as shown in figure 1.7. The text box on this page is associated with a JavaBean property of the `HelloBean` class;

Figure 1.7 The Hello, world! application before any data has been submitted.

when someone enters a value into this box, the property will be updated automatically (if the value is valid).

If you enter the number "64" into the text box and click the Redisplay button, the page redisplays as shown in figure 1.8—a total of 64 UI components are displayed in the grid. If you clear the text box and click the Redisplay button, you'll get a validation error, as shown in figure 1.9. You'll also get a validation error if

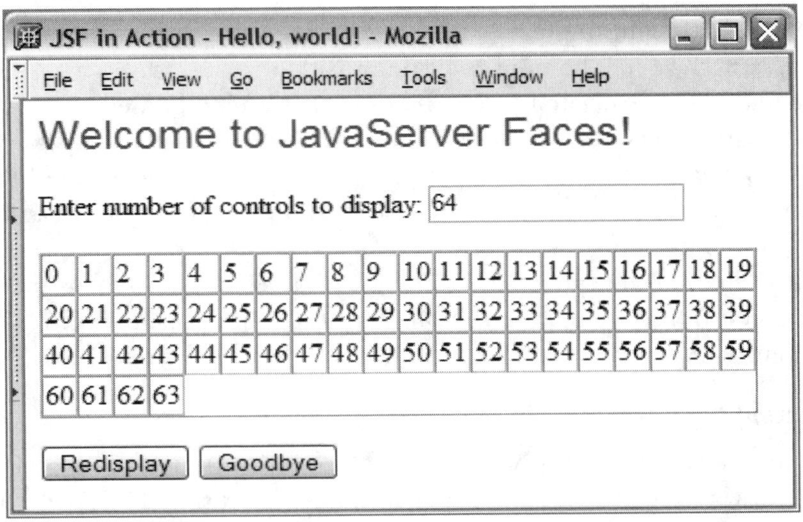

Figure 1.8 The Hello, world! application after you enter "64" and click the Redisplay button. The grid is populated with 64 UI components.

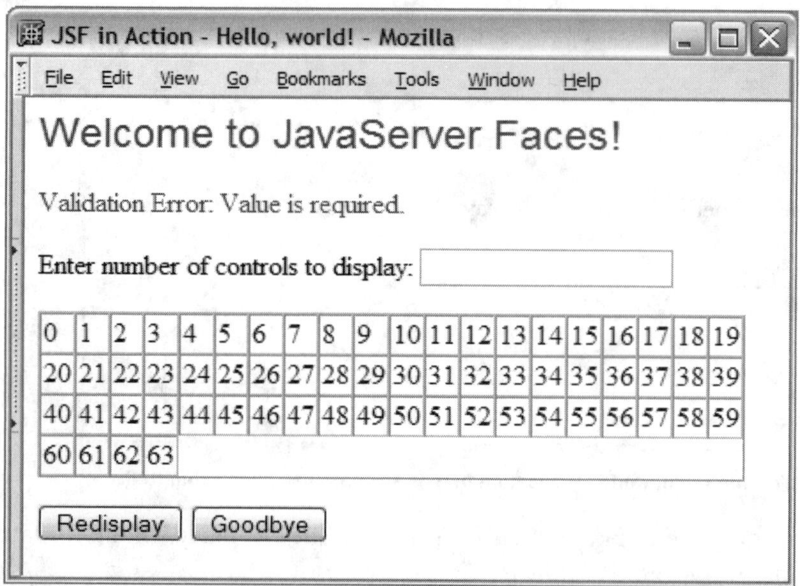

Figure 1.9 The Hello, world! application after you submit a blank value for the required text box field and click the Redisplay button. Because a validation error occurred, the value of the associated JavaBean property didn't change.

you enter the number "99999" into the text box and click the Redisplay button, as shown in figure 1.10.

Don't worry about the text of the error messages—in your own applications you can customize it. The important point is that in both cases, when the form was submitted the associated JavaBean property wasn't modified.

If you click the Goodbye button, you see the goodbye.jsp page, shown in figure 1.11. Even though this is an entirely different page, the value of the JavaBean property is displayed. JSF components can reference a JavaBean living in any application scope.

Our Hello, world! example is a standard Java web application, as specified by the Servlet API (it does require the standard Faces libraries, though). All five of these figures were generated with two JSPs. Let's look at them in detail.

1.5.1 Dissecting hello.jsp

Our main page, hello.jsp, provides the interface for figures 1.7 to 1.10. JSF is integrated with JSP through the use of custom tag libraries. The JSF custom tags enable JSPs to use Faces UI components. Tools will often allow you to design JSF pages by dragging and dropping JSF components from a palette. As a matter of

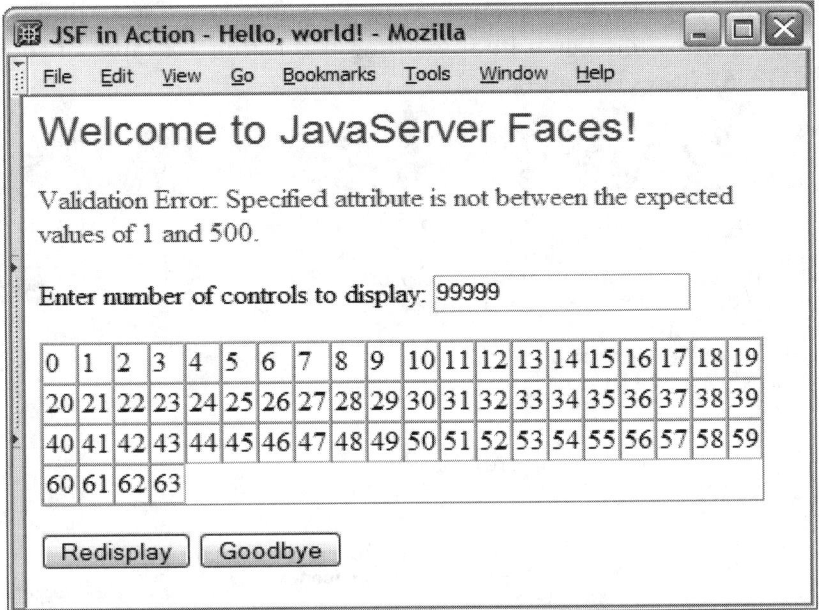

Figure 1.10 The Hello, world! application after you enter in the value "99999" into the text box and click the Redisplay button. The field only accepts numbers between 1 and 500, so a validation error is shown. Because a validation error occurred, the value of the associated JavaBean property didn't change.

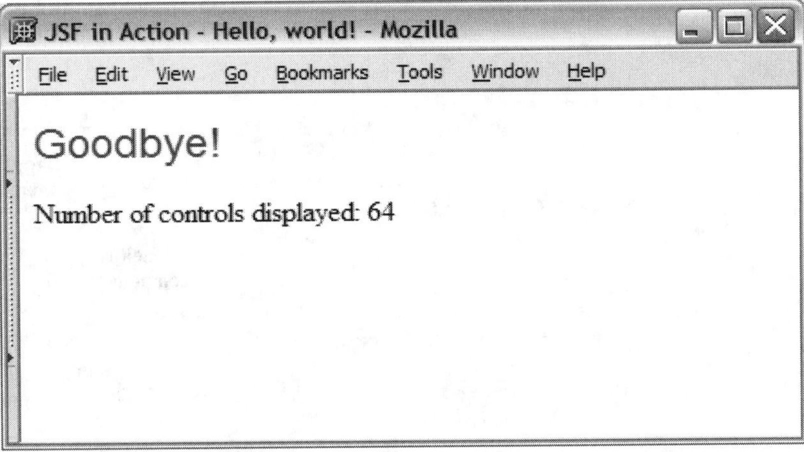

Figure 1.11 The Hello, world! application after you click the Goodbye button. Note that the JavaBean property, which was synchronized with the text box of the first page, is displayed on this page.

fact, figures 1.1 to 1.3 are screen shots of designing hello.jsp in different IDEs. These IDEs ultimately generate something like listing 1.1 (and, of course, you can create JSF pages by hand).

Listing 1.1 hello.jsp: opening page of our Hello, world! application (browser output shown in figures 1.7–1.10)

```
<!DOCTYPE HTML PUBLIC "-//W3C//DTD HTML 4.01 Transitional//EN">

<%@ taglib uri="http://java.sun.com/jsf/core" prefix="f" %>
<%@ taglib uri="http://java.sun.com/jsf/html" prefix="h" %>

<f:view>
  <html>
    <head>
      <title>
        JSF in Action - Hello, world!
      </title>
    </head>
    <body>
      <h:form id="welcomeForm">
        <h:outputText id="welcomeOutput"
                 value="Welcome to JavaServer Faces!"
                 style="font-family: Arial, sans-serif; font-size: 24;
                 color: green;"/>
        <p>
          <h:message id="errors" for="helloInput" style="color: red"/>
        </p>
        <p>
          <h:outputLabel for="helloInput">
            <h:outputText id="helloInputLabel"
                       value="Enter number of controls to display:"/>
          </h:outputLabel>
          <h:inputText id="helloInput" value="#{helloBean.numControls}"
                     required="true">
            <f:validateLongRange minimum="1" maximum="500"/>
          </h:inputText>
        </p>
        <p>
          <h:panelGrid id="controlPanel"
                     binding="#{helloBean.controlPanel}"
                     columns="20" border="1" cellspacing="0"/>
        </p>
        <h:commandButton id="redisplayCommand" type="submit"
                       value="Redisplay"
                      actionListener="#{helloBean.addControls}"/>

        <h:commandButton id="goodbyeCommand" type="submit" value="Goodbye"
                      action="#{helloBean.goodbye}" immediate="true"/>
      </h:form>
```

Annotations:
1. JSF tag libraries
2. Tag enclosing all JSF tags
3. HtmlForm component
4. HtmlOutputText component
5. HtmlMessage component
6. HtmlOutputLabel with child HtmlOutputText
7. HtmlInputText component
8. HtmlPanelGrid component
9. HtmlCommandButton components

```
    </body>
  </html>
</f:view>
```

❶ First, we import the core JavaServer Faces tag library. This library provides custom tags for such basic tasks as validation and event handling. Next, we import the basic HTML tag library, which provides custom tags for UI components like text boxes, output labels, and forms. (The prefixes "f" and "h" are suggested, but not required.)

❷ The `<f:view>` custom tag must enclose all other Faces-related tags (from both the core tag library and the basic HTML tag library).

❸ The `<h:form>` tag represents an `HtmlForm` component, which is a container for other components and is used for posting information back to the server. You can have more than one `HtmlForm` on the same page, but all input controls must be nested within a `<h:form>` tag.

❹ The `<h:outputText>` tag creates an `HtmlOutputText` component, which simply displays read-only data to the screen. This tag has an `id` attribute as well as a `value` attribute. The `id` attribute is optional for all components; it's not required unless you need to reference the component somewhere else. (Components can be referenced with client-side technologies like JavaScript or in Java code.) The `value` attribute specifies the text you want to display.

❺ The `<h:message>` tag is for the `HtmlMessage` component, which displays validation and conversion errors for a specific component. The `for` attribute tells it to display errors for the control with the identifier `helloInput`, which is the identifier for the text box on the page (❼). If no errors have occurred, nothing is displayed.

❻ The `<h:outputLabel>` tag creates a new `HtmlOutputLabel` component, which is used as a label for input controls. The `for` property associates the label with an input control, which in this case is `helloInput` (❼). `HtmlOutputLabels` don't display anything, so we also need a child `HtmlOutputText` (created by the nested `<h:outputText>` tag) to display the label's text.

❼ The `<h:inputText>` tag is used to create an `HtmlInputText` component that accepts text input. Note that the `value` property is `"#{helloBean.numControls}"`, which is a JSF Expression Language (EL) expression referencing the `numControls` property of a backing bean, called `helloBean`. (The JSF EL is a based upon the EL introduced with JSP 2.0.)

Faces will automatically search the different scopes of the web application (request, session, application) for the specified backing bean. In this case, it will find a bean stored under the key `helloBean` in the application's session. The value of the component and `helloBean`'s `numControls` property are synchronized so that if one changes, the other one will change as well (unless the text in the `HtmlInputText` component is invalid).

Input controls have a `required` property, which determines whether or not the field must have a value. In this case, `required` is set to `true`, so the component will only accept non-empty input. If the user enters an empty value, the page will be redisplayed, and the `HtmlMessage` (❺) component will display an error message, as shown in figure 1.9.

JSF also supports validators, which are responsible for making sure that the user enters an acceptable value. Each input control can be associated with one or more validators. The `<f:validateLongRange>` tag registers a `LongRange` validator for this `HtmlInputText` component. The validator checks to make sure that any input is a number between 1 and 500, inclusive. If the user enters a value outside that range, the validator will reject the input, and the page will be redisplayed with the `HtmlMessage` (❺) component displaying the error message shown in figure 1.10.

Whenever the user's input is rejected, the object referenced by the `HtmlInputText` component's `value` property will not be updated.

❽ An `HtmlPanelGrid` component is represented by the `<h:panelGrid>` tag. `HtmlPanelGrid` represents a configurable container for other components that is displayed as an HTML table.

Any JSF component can be associated directly with a backing bean via its JSP tag's `binding` attribute. (Some tools will do this automatically for all of the components on a page.) The tag's `binding` attribute is set to `"#{helloBean.controlPanel}"`. This is a JSF EL expression that references `helloBean`'s `controlPanel` property, which is of type `HtmlPanelGrid`. This ensures that `helloBean` always has access to the `HtmlPanelGrid` component on the page.

❾ The `<h:commandButton>` specifies an `HtmlCommandButton` component that's displayed as an HTML form button. `HtmlCommandButtons` send action events to the application when they are clicked by a user. The event listener (a method that executes in response to an event) can be directly referenced via the `actionListener` property. The first `HtmlCommandButton`'s `actionListener` property is set to `"#{helloBean.addControls}"`, which is an expression that tells JSF to find the `helloBean` object and then call its `addControls` method to handle the event. Once the method has been executed, the page will be redisplayed.

The second `HtmlCommandButton` has an `action` property set instead of an `actionListener` property. The value of this property, `"#{helloBean.goodbye}"`, references a specialized event listener that handles navigation. This is why clicking on this button loads the goodbye.jsp page instead of redisplaying the hello.jsp page. This button also has the `immediate` property set to `true`, which tells JSF to execute the associated listener before any validations or updates occur. This way, clicking this button still works if the value of the input control is incorrect.

That's it for hello.jsp. Listing 1.2 shows the HTML output after a validation error has occurred (the browser's view is shown in figure 1.10).

Listing 1.2 The HTML output of hello.jsp (this code is the source for figure 1.10)

```
<html>
   <head>
     <title>
       JSF in Action - Hello, world!
     </title>
   </head>
   <body>
     <form id="welcomeForm" method="post"
           action="/jia-hello-world/faces/hello.jsp"
           enctype="application/x-www-form-urlencoded">      ❶ HtmlForm component

       <span id="welcomeForm:welcomeOutput"
             style="font-family: Arial, sans-serif; font-size: 24
                    color: green;">Welcome to
JavaServer Faces!</span>                                       HtmlOutputText component
       <p>
        <span id="welcomeForm:errors" style="color: red">
Validation Error: Specified attribute is not between the expected values
 of 1 and 500.</span>                                          ❷ HtmlMessage component
       </p>
       <p>
         <label for="welcomeForm:helloInput">
           <span id="welcomeForm:helloInputLabel">
Enter number of controls to display:</span>                    HtmlOutputLabel with HtmlOutputText
         </label>
         <input id="welcomeForm:helloInput" type="text"
                name="welcomeForm:helloInput" value="99999"/>  HtmlInputText component
       </p>
       <p>
         <table id="welcomeForm:controlPanel" border="1" cellspacing="0">
           <tbody>
             <tr>
               <td><span style="color: blue"> 0 </span></td>
            ...
               <td><span style="color: blue"> 19 </span></td>
             </tr>
            <tr>
              <td><span style="color: blue"> 20 </span></td>   ❸ HtmlPanelGrid component
                ...
              <td><span style="color: blue"> 39 </span></td>
            </tr>
```

```
          <tr>
            <td><span style="color: blue"> 40 </span></td>
            ...
            <td><span style="color: blue"> 59 </span></td>
         </tr>
          <tr>
            <td><span style="color: blue"> 60 </span></td>
            ...
            <td><span style="color: blue"> 63 </span></td>
          </tr>
         </tbody>
       </table>
     </p>
     <input id="welcomeForm:redisplayCommand" type="submit"
            name="welcomeForm:redisplayCommand" value="Redisplay" />

     <input id="welcomeForm:goodbyeCommand" type="submit"
            name="welcomeForm:goodbyeCommand" value="Goodbye" />
     ...
   </form>
 </body>
</html>
```

❸ **HtmlPanelGrid component**

HtmlCommandButton components

You can see from the listing that every component defined in the JSP has a representation in the displayed HTML page. Note that the `<h:form>` tag (❶), which represents an `HtmlForm` component, has an `action` attribute that actually points back to the calling JSP but with the preface "faces". This is an alias for the Faces servlet, which is defined in the application's deployment descriptor. Redisplaying the calling page is the default behavior, but a Faces application can also navigate to another page (which is what happens when the user clicks the Goodbye button).

The output of the `HtmlMessage` component (❷) is the text "Validation Error: Specified attribute is not between the expected values of 1 and 500." As you might expect, this message was generated by the `LongRange` validator we registered in the JSP page. When the validator rejected the attempt to post an incorrect value, the validator created a new error message and the framework refrained from updating the associated JavaBean property's value.

Each HTML element that maps to a JSF component has an `id` attribute that's derived from the `id` specified in the JSP (if no `id` is specified, one will be created automatically). This is called the *client identifier*, and it's what JSF uses to map an input value to a component on the server. Some components also use the `name` attribute for the client identifier.

The output of the `HtmlPanelGrid` component (❸) is an HTML table. Note that the `border` and `cellspacing` properties specified in the JSP were passed through directly to the HTML. (Most of the standard HTML components expose HTML-specific properties that are simply passed through to the browser.) Each cell in the table is the output of an `HtmlOutputText` component that was added to the `HtmlPanelGrid` in Java code, in response to a user clicking the Redisplay button. (In the real HTML, there are 64 cells because that's the number that was entered into the text box; we left some of them out of the listing because, well, that's a lot of lot of extra paper!)

We'll examine the Java code soon enough, but let's look at goodbye.jsp first.

1.5.2 Dissecting goodbye.jsp

The goodbye.jsp page, shown in figure 1.11, is displayed when the user clicks the Goodbye button. The page (listing 1.3) contains some of the same elements as the hello.jsp page: imports for the JSF tag libraries, an `HtmlForm` component, and `HtmlOutputText` components. One of the `HtmlOutputText` components references the same `helloBean` object as the previous page. This works fine because the object lives in the application's session and consequently survives between page requests.

Listing 1.3 goodbye.jsp: Closing page of our Hello, world! application (the browser output is shown in figure 1.11)

```
<!DOCTYPE HTML PUBLIC "-//W3C//DTD HTML 4.01 Transitional//EN">

<%@ taglib uri="http://java.sun.com/jsf/core" prefix="f" %>
<%@ taglib uri="http://java.sun.com/jsf/html" prefix="h" %>

<f:view>
  <html>
    <head>
      <title>
        JSF in Action - Hello, world!
      </title>
    </head>
    <body>
      <h:form id="goodbyeForm">
        <p>
          <h:outputText id="welcomeOutput" value="Goodbye!"
                        style="font-family: Arial, sans-serif; font-size: 24;
                        font-style: bold; color: green;"/>
        </p>
        <p>
          <h:outputText id="helloBeanOutputLabel"
                          value="Number of controls displayed:"/>
          <h:outputText id="helloBeanOutput"
                          value="#{helloBean.numControls}"/>
        </p>
```

Same backing bean as hello.jsp

```
      </h:form>
    </body>
  </html>
</f:view>
```

There's nothing special about the HTML generated by this page that we didn't cover in the previous section, so we'll spare you the details. What's important is that we were able to build a functional application with validation and page navigation with only two simple JSPs. (If we didn't want to show navigation, the first page would have been good enough.)

Now, let's look at the code behind these pages.

1.5.3 Examining the HelloBean class

Both hello.jsp and goodbye.jsp contain JSF components that reference a backing bean called `helloBean` through JSF EL expressions. This single JavaBean contains everything needed for this application: two properties and two methods. It's shown in listing 1.4.

Listing 1.4 HelloBean.java: The simple backing bean for our Hello, world! application

```
package org.jia.hello;

import javax.faces.application.Application;
import javax.faces.component.html.HtmlOutputText;
import javax.faces.component.html.HtmlPanelGrid;
import javax.faces.context.FacesContext;
import javax.faces.event.ActionEvent;

import java.util.List;

public class HelloBean      <-(1) No required superclass
{
  private int numControls;
  private HtmlPanelGrid controlPanel;

  public int getNumControls()
  {
    return numControls;
  }

  public void setNumControls(int numControls)
  {
    this.numControls = numControls;
  }
```

(2) Property referenced on both JSPs

```
    public HtmlPanelGrid getControlPanel()
    {
      return controlPanel;
    }

    public void setControlPanel(HtmlPanelGrid controlPanel)
    {
      this.controlPanel = controlPanel;
    }

    public void addControls(ActionEvent actionEvent)
    {
      Application application =
          FacesContext.getCurrentInstance().getApplication();
      List children = controlPanel.getChildren();
      children.clear();
      for (int count = 0; count < numControls; count++)
      {
        HtmlOutputText output = (HtmlOutputText)application.
                         createComponent(HtmlOutputText.COMPONENT_TYPE);
        output.setValue(" " + count + " ");
        output.setStyle("color: blue");
        children.add(output);
      }
    }

    public String goodbye()
    {
      return "success";
    }
}
```

❸ **Property bound to HtmlPanelGrid**

❹ **Executed by Redisplay HtmlCommandButton**

❺ **Executed by Goodbye HtmlCommandButton**

❶ Unlike a lot of other frameworks, JSF backing beans don't have to inherit from a specific class. They simply need to expose their properties using ordinary JavaBean conventions and use specific signatures for their event-handling methods.

❷ The `numControls` property is referenced by the `HtmlInputText` component on hello.jsp and an `HtmlOutputText` component on goodbye.jsp. Whenever the user changes the value in the `HtmlInputText` component, the value of this property is changed as well (if the input is valid).

❸ The `controlPanel` property is of type `HtmlPanelGrid`, which is the actual Java class created by the `<h:panelGrid>` tag used in hello.jsp. That tag's `binding` attribute associates the component instance created by the tag with the `controlPanel` property. This allows `HelloBean` to manipulate the actual code—a task it happily performs in ❹.

❹ `addControls` is a method designed to handle action events (an *action listener method*); you can tell, because it accepts an `ActionEvent` as its only parameter. The Redisplay `HtmlCommandButton` on hello.jsp references this method with its `actionListener` property. This tells JSF to execute the method when handling the action event generated when the user clicks the Redisplay button. (Associating a component with an event listener *method* may seem strange if you're used to frameworks like Swing that always require a separate event listener *interface*. JSF supports interface-style listeners as well, but the preferred method is to use listener methods because they alleviate the need for adapter classes in backing beans.)

When this method is executed, it adds a new `HtmlOutputText` component to the `controlPanel` `numControls` times (clearing it first). So, if the value of `numControls` is 64, as it is in our example, this code will create and add 64 `HtmlOutputText` instances to `controlPanel`. Each instance's value is set to equal its number in the sequence, starting at zero and ending at 64. And finally, each instance's `style` property is set to `"color: blue"`.

Because `controlPanel` is an `HtmlPanelGrid` instance, it will display all of these child controls inside an HTML table; each `HtmlOutputText` component wll be displayed in a single cell of the table. Figure 1.8 shows what `controlPanel` looks like after this method has executed.

❺ Like `addControls`, the `goodbye` method is a type of event listener. However, it is associated with JSF's navigation system, so its job is to return a string, or a logical outcome, that the navigation system can use to determine which page to load next. These types of methods are called *action methods*.

The `goodbye` method is associated with the Goodbye `HtmlCommandButton` on hello.jsp via its `action` property. So when a user clicks the Goodbye button, the `goodbye` method is executed. In this case, `goodbye` doesn't do any work to determine the logical outcome; it just returns `"success"`. This outcome is associated with a specific page in a Faces configuration file, which we cover next.

Because `goodbye` doesn't perform any processing (as it would in a real application), we could have achieved the same effect by hardcoding the text `"success"` in the button's `action` property. This is because the navigation system will either use the literal value of an `HtmlCommandButton`'s `action` property or the outcome of an action method (if the property references one).

1.5.4 Configuration with faces-config.xml

Like most frameworks, Faces has a configuration file; it's called, believe it or not, faces-config.xml. (Technically, JSF supports multiple configuration files, but we'll keep things simple for now.) This XML file allows you to define rules for navigation, initialize JavaBeans, register your own custom JSF components and validators, and configure several other aspects of a JSF application. This simple application requires configuration only for bean initialization and navigation; the file is shown in listing 1.5.

Listing 1.5 faces-config.xml: The Faces configuration file for Hello, world!

```
<?xml version="1.0"?>
<!DOCTYPE faces-config PUBLIC
  "-//Sun Microsystems, Inc.//DTD JavaServer Faces Config 1.0//EN"
  "http://java.sun.com/dtd/web-facesconfig_1_0.dtd">

<faces-config>      <-❶ Encloses all configuration elements

  <managed-bean>
    <description>The one and only HelloBean.</description>
    <managed-bean-name>helloBean</managed-bean-name>
    <managed-bean-class>org.jia.hello.HelloBean
    </managed-bean-class>
    <managed-bean-scope>session</managed-bean-scope>
  </managed-bean>
                                      ❷ Declares HelloBean in the session

  <navigation-rule>
    <description>Navigation from the hello page.</description>
    <from-view-id>/hello.jsp</from-view-id>
    <navigation-case>
      <from-outcome>success</from-outcome>
      <to-view-id>/goodbye.jsp</to-view-id>
    </navigation-case>
  </navigation-rule>
                                      ❸ Declares navigation case

</faces-config>
```

First and foremost, a JSF configuration file is an XML document whose root node is `<faces-config>` (❶). In this file, you can declare one or more JavaBeans for use in your application. You can give each one a name (which can be referenced via JSF EL expressions), a description, and a scope, and you can even initialize its properties. Objects declared in a configuration file are called *managed beans*. In the listing, we have declared the `helloBean` object used throughout the Hello, world! application (❷). Note that the name of the object is "helloBean", which is the same name used in JSF EL expressions on the two JSPs. The class is `org.jia.hello.HelloBean`, which is the name of the backing bean class we examined in the previous section. The managed bean name and the object's class name don't have to be the same.

Declaring navigation is as simple as declaring a managed bean. Each JSF application can have one or more navigation rules. A *navigation rule* specifies the possible routes from a given page. Each route is called a *navigation case*. The listing shows the navigation rule for Hello, world!'s hello.jsp page (❸). hello.jsp has a Goodbye button that loads another page, so there is a single navigation case: if the outcome is `"success"`, the page goodbye.jsp will be displayed. This outcome is returned from `helloBean`'s `goodbye` method, which is executed when a user clicks the Goodbye button.

It's worthwhile to point out that some aspects of JSF configuration, particularly navigation, can be handled visually with tools. Now, let's see how our application is configured at the web application level.

1.5.5 Configuration with web.xml

All J2EE web applications are configured with a web.xml deployment descriptor; Faces applications are no different. However, JSF applications require that you specify the `FacesServlet`, which is usually the main servlet for the application. In addition, requests must be mapped to this servlet. The deployment descriptor for our Hello, world! application is shown in listing 1.6. You can expect some tools to generate the required JSF-related elements for you.

Listing 1.6 web.xml: The deployment descriptor for our Hello, world! application

```
<?xml version="1.0" encoding="UTF-8"?>
<!DOCTYPE web-app PUBLIC "-//Sun Microsystems, Inc.//DTD Web Application 2.3/
  /EN" "http://java.sun.com/dtd/web-app_2_3.dtd">

<web-app>
  <display-name>Hello, World!</display-name>
  <description>Welcome to JavaServer Faces</description>

  <servlet>
    <servlet-name>Faces Servlet</servlet-name>
    <servlet-class>javax.faces.webapp.FacesServlet</servlet-class>
    <load-on-startup>1</load-on-startup>
  </servlet>
  <servlet-mapping>
    <servlet-name>Faces Servlet</servlet-name>
    <url-pattern>/faces/*</url-pattern>
  </servlet-mapping>
</web-app>
```

JSF servlet (annotation for the <servlet> element)

Standard JSF mapping (annotation for the <servlet-mapping> element)

That's it—Hello, world! dissected. You can see that JSF does a lot of things for you—validation, event handling, navigation, UI component management, and so on. As we walk through the various aspects of JSF in more detail, you'll gain a deep understanding of all of the services it provides so that you can concentrate on building the application and avoid that joyous thing they call grunt work.

1.6 Summary

JavaServer Faces (JSF, or "Faces") is a UI framework for building Java web applications; it was developed through the Java Community Process (JCP) and will become part of Java 2 Enterprise Edition (J2EE). One of the main goals of Faces is to bring the RAD style of application development, made popular by tools like Microsoft Visual Basic and Borland Delphi, to the world of Java web applications.

JSF provides a set of standard widgets (buttons, hyperlinks, checkboxes, and so on), a model for creating custom widgets, a way to process client-generated events on the server, and excellent tool support. You can even synchronize a UI component with an object's value, which eliminates a lot of tedious code.

All JSF applications are built on top of the Servlet API, communicate via HTTP, and use a display technology like JSP. JavaServer Faces applications don't *require* JSP, though. They can use technologies like XML/XSLT, other template engines, or plain Java code. However, Faces implementations are required to provide basic integration with JSP, so most of the examples in this book are in JSP.

The component architecture of Faces leverages JavaBeans for properties, fundamental tool support, an event model, and several other goodies. JSF is considered a web application framework because it performs a lot of common development tasks so that developers can focus on more fun things like business logic. One of the key features is support of the Model 2 design pattern, which enforces separation of presentation and business logic code. However, Faces focuses on UI components and events. As such, it integrates quite nicely with the other frameworks like Struts, and overlaps quite a bit with the functionality of higher-level frameworks.

The Hello, world! example demonstrates the basic aspects of a JavaServer Faces application. It shows how easy it is to define a UI with components like text boxes, labels, and buttons. It also shows how Faces automatically handles input validation and updating a JavaBean based on the value of a text control.

In the next chapter, we'll look at the core JSF concepts and examine how the framework masks the request/response nature of HTTP.

2 JSF fundamentals

This chapter covers

- Key terms and concepts
- How JSF processes an incoming request
- The JSF expression language

If you're anything like me, you probably still have a lot of questions about how JavaServer Faces works. But it's hard to understand how something works if you don't know the lingo. You can't even begin to understand how a circuit works if you don't know what an AND or OR gate is. Similarly, construction would be a bit of a mystery without knowledge of terms like "scaffolding." In this chapter, we discuss the key concepts that are essential for building Faces applications. We then walk through how the framework processes a single Hypertext Transfer Protocol (HTTP) request, so you can see how Faces abstracts the low-level details of web development.

2.1 The key pieces of the pie

Like most technologies, Faces has its own set of terms that form a conceptual base for the features it provides. We're talking about such elements as user interface (UI) components, validators, and renderers. You may have a good idea about what they are, but in order to write Faces applications, you must understand what they are *in the JSF world*. In the following sections, we cover these key concepts and explain how they relate to one another.

Eight core terms come into play when you're developing JSF applications (see table 2.1).

Table 2.1 These terms are the key pieces of the JSF pie.

Term	Description
UI component (also called a control or simply a component)	A stateful object, maintained on the server, that provides specific functionality for interacting with an end user. UI components are JavaBeans with properties, methods, and events. They are organized into a view, which is a tree of components usually displayed as a page.
Renderer	Responsible for displaying a UI component and translating a user's input into the component's value. Renderers can be designed to work with one or more UI components, and a UI component can be associated with many different renderers.
Validator	Responsible for ensuring that the value entered by a user is acceptable. One or more validators can be associated with a single UI component.
Backing beans	Specialized JavaBeans that collect values from UI components and implement event listener methods. They can also hold references to UI components.
Converter	Converts a component's value to and from a string for display. A UI component can be associated with a single converter.
Events and listeners	JSF uses the JavaBeans event/listener model (also used by Swing). UI components (and other objects) generate events, and listeners can be registered to handle those events.

continued on next page

Table 2.1 These terms are the key pieces of the JSF pie. *(continued)*

Term	Description
Messages	Information that's displayed back to the user. Just about any part of the application (backing beans, validators, converters, and so on) can generate information or error messages that can be displayed back to the user.
Navigation	The ability to move from one page to the next. JSF has a powerful navigation system that's integrated with specialized event listeners.

Now, let's take a step back and look at how all of these terms are related. Take a look at figure 2.1, which is a Unified Modeling Language (UML) class diagram representing each of the concepts with simplified relationships (we've included "view" and "model object" as additional concepts for completeness). As the figure shows, UI components, which are contained by a view, update backing beans and generate events based on user input. Renderers display components, and can also generate events and messages. Converters translate and format a component's value for display, and generate error messages as well. Validators verify the value of a component and generate error messages.

Backing beans contain event listeners and action methods, which are event listeners that are specialized for navigation. Event listeners consume events and can manipulate the view or execute model objects, which perform the core application

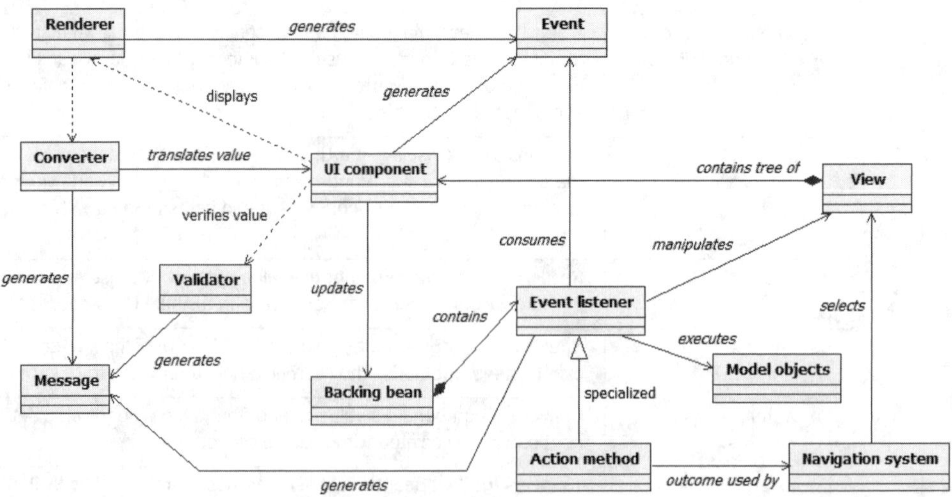

Figure 2.1 A model of how the key JSF concepts relate to one another. They communicate through events and messages.

logic. Action methods can do everything event listeners can, but they also return an outcome that is used by the navigation system. Finally, the navigation system uses this outcome to select the next view to display to the user.

Most of the concepts in this diagram generate a message or an event. This is how JSF applications communicate. Events represent user input or application operations. Messages indicate errors or application notifications.

You may have noticed that events, messages, and model objects are passive from the perspective of JSF. In other words, they don't *do* anything—some other class is always operating on them. This is an important point for model objects, because it means that the model doesn't know about the user interface. This is part of how JSF enforces an MVC-style architecture.

Now that you have an idea about what these terms mean, and how they relate to one another, let's examine each one in detail.

2.1.1 User interface components

User interface (UI) components (also called controls, or simply components) focus on interacting with an end user. Visual Basic has UI components, and so does Swing, so what's unique about Faces components? Like Swing controls, they're built on top of JavaBeans. This means they have properties, methods, and events, plus inherent support for IDEs. Unlike Swing, they're specifically designed for the unique constraints of web applications, and they live on the server side, not the client. This is important, because most web interfaces aren't built with components—they just output markup, like HTML.

Packaging UI elements as a component (like a toolbar or a calendar) makes development easier because the core functions are encapsulated within a reusable piece of code. For example, if you use a calendar control you don't have to develop a complicated combination of HTML, CSS, and graphics to make it look just right. You may have to manipulate some properties, such as the colors, or the default date, but all the hard work has already been completed by the component's developer. There isn't even a need to write a lot of code to integrate it with your application—just associate it with a JavaBean property of a backing bean (described later), and you're done.

If you think about it, there are a bunch of different ways a calendar can be represented. The most common way is to show a month at a time, with a little box for each day of the month. But a calendar could also be represented as three drop-down boxes: one each for the day, month, and year. The way a component looks is how it is *rendered*.

Regardless of how it rendered, a calendar has the same basic functionality and an intrinsic set of properties, like its colors, the default date, and the range of dates you want to display. A calendar component represents what the calendar *does*, not what it looks like. Such behavior is called *renderer neutral*, because it is the same regardless of how the component is rendered. This distinction is key when you're developing components in Java, but as a front-end or application developer, you can use components with interfaces that are tailored for a specific client environment. (For example, an `HtmlInputText` component has HTML-specific properties like `accessKey` and `style`, even though it doesn't technically handle rendering itself.)

One of the key differences between web-based and desktop-based components is that the former never directly interact with the user's machine. If you fill out a form incorrectly in a desktop application and click OK, the page isn't redisplayed—the program just tells you what the errors were (at least you hope it does!). All of the values on the form just stay there. In web applications, the page is often redisplayed with error messages, but the application has to make it *look* as if it wasn't redisplayed at all. In other words, the components have to remember their values, or *state*. JSF components handle this for you automatically.

Faces components can remember their values between requests because the framework maintains a tree of the UI components for a given page. This component tree, called the *view*, is JSF's internal representation of the page, and it allows parent-child relationships, such as having a form that contains a label, a text field, and a panel with two nested buttons, as shown in figure 2.2. Using "view" instead of "page" underscores the fact that the user's representation doesn't always have to be an HTML web page. However, for simplicity, we'll use the two interchangeably.

Each component in the tree is identified with a *component identifier*. The component identifier can be set by a developer; if none is set, it will be generated automatically. In addition, components can be associated with one another via named relationships like "header" or "footer"—these are called *facets*. UI components can also support *accessibility* properties that make them easier to access for users with disabilities.

UI components raise the abstraction bar, bringing a whole new level of flexibility to web development. Building UIs with JSF is more about assembling and configuring components than writing tedious code in different technologies (HTML, CSS, JavaScript, and so on). And all of these components can be referenced and manipulated both in code, via GUI designers, and declaratively (with a display technology like JSP). Faces includes several standard components such

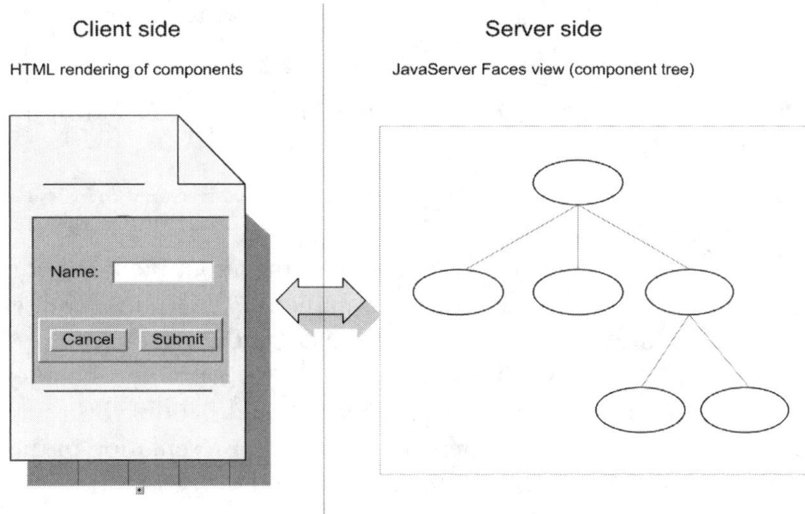

Figure 2.2 UI components are managed on the server in a view, or component tree. The components can be wired directly to the values of JavaBean properties. Components are rendered to the client in HTML (or in some other display language).

as labels, hyperlinks, text boxes, list boxes, checkboxes, radio buttons, panels, and data grids. We cover these in chapters 4 and 5; custom component development is covered in part 4 and online extension part 5.

2.1.2 Renderers

Faces UI components aren't always responsible for their own rendering. When components render themselves, it's called the *direct implementation* model, but JSF also supports the *delegated implementation* model, which allows separate classes to handle the process. Those classes are called, surprisingly enough, *renderers*.

Renderers are organized into *render kits*, which usually focus on a specific type of output. JSF ships with a standard render kit for HTML 4.01, but a render kit could generate a different HTML look and feel (or "skin"), Wireless Markup Language (WML), Scalable Vector Graphics (SVG), or it could communicate with an applet, Java application, or an entirely different type of client.

You can think of a renderer as a translator between the client and the server worlds. On the way from the server, it handles *encoding*, which is the process of creating a representation of a component that the client understands. When JSF receives a response from the user, the renderer handles *decoding*, which is the process of extracting the correct request parameters and setting a component's value based on those parameters.

For example, the following code defines a single `HtmlInputText` component:

```
<h:inputText id="inputText" size="20" maxlength="30"/>
```

When this component is encoded, it is sent to the user as the following HTML snippet:

```
<input id="myForm:inputText" type="text" name="myForm:inputText"
       maxlength="30" size="20" />
```

Let's say that the user enters the text "foo" into this input field. Decoding is the process of taking the form parameters sent in the HTTP response and setting the value of the `HtmlTextInput` component instance on the server to `"foo"`. Behind the scenes, the `Text` renderer in the standard HTML `RenderKit` handles both of these processes. Because all encoding and decoding is handled by a single entity (either the component or its renderer), the visual representation of the component and the underlying protocol for translating between request parameters and objects on the server are nicely self-contained.

When components use the delegated implementation model (as all of the standard components do), changing the entire display of a given page is as simple as changing the render kit. This means that it is quite easy to have the same Faces-compliant template display HTML, WML, or SVG—the components are the same, but displaying a different markup language is just a matter of changing the render kit.

It's worthwhile to note that for average HTML application development tasks, renderers are pretty transparent. All of the standard components are associated with a renderer behind the scenes, so you don't have to worry much about them. However, when you need to dynamically change the appearance of your application, or when you're developing custom components, renderers are an essential and powerful piece of the JSF pie. We cover developing custom renderers in part 4 and online extension part 5.

2.1.3 Validators

One of the joys of developing UIs is making sure the user entered the right thing—which could be as complex as "the correct part identifier from the database" or as simple as "not empty." Often, enforcing the right thing requires a lot of ugly `if` statements written in JavaScript, Java, or both. Moreover, the process of displaying errors is somewhat error-prone if you don't have a framework to help you out.

Faces handles validation in three ways—at the UI component level, via validator methods in backing beans, or in validator classes. UI components generally handle simple validation, such as whether a value is required, or validation logic that's specific to the component itself (and therefore not usable with other components). Validator methods are useful when you need to validate one or more fields on a form (and you don't need to share that logic with other components). External validators are useful for generic cases like the length of a field or a number range; they are pluggable, which means you can attach one or more of them to any component. Validation is handled on the server, because all clients do not support scripting. (JSF components can support validation on the client, but none of the standard components do so.)

When a validator encounters an error, like a string that's too long or an invalid credit card number, it adds an error message to the current message list. This makes it easy to display validation errors back to the user using standard JSF components. Here's an example:

```
<h:inputText>
  <f:validateLength minimum="2" maximum="10"/>
</h:inputText>
```

You can see how easy it is to associate a validator with a component. This defines an `HtmlInputText` component with a `Length` validator that checks to make sure the user's input is between two and ten characters long.

Traditionally, validation can be one of the most tedious web development tasks. Validators provide a powerful framework to help simplify this task. JSF ships with a set of standard validators for such things as the length or range of the input, but you can write your own, and so will third parties. The standard validators are covered in chapter 6, and custom validator development is covered in online extension chapter 20.

2.1.4 Backing beans

In chapter 1, we discussed the Model-View-Controller (MVC) design pattern and how it separates an application into its corresponding model, view, and controller layers. We said that the model consists of application logic and data, the view consists of the UI, and the controller defines the interaction between the two.

In JSF applications, objects that perform the latter role—interaction with the UI and the model—are called *backing beans*. Backing beans generally contain properties you want to retrieve from users and event listener methods (discussed later) that process those properties and either manipulate the UI or perform some sort of application processing. Some development tools will generate backing bean classes automatically when you create a new page. They may also refer to them as "web forms" or "code-behind," which underscores their conceptual similarity to code-behind files in the ASP.NET world (behind the scenes, they're quite different).

JSF allows you to declaratively associate backing beans with UI components. By *declaratively*, we mean with markup instead of code (you can do this in code as well). You associate a component with a backing bean via the JSF expression language (EL), which is similar to the JSP 2.0 and JSTL expression languages. You can use a JSF EL expression to point to a specific backing bean property somewhere in your application. For example, look at this snippet from the Hello, world! example:

```
<h:outputText id="helloBeanOutput"
              value="#{helloBean.numControls}"/>
```

This code snippet hooks up an `HtmlOutputText` component's value directly to the `numControls` property of an object called `helloBean`. Whenever the value of the component changes, the `helloBean.numControls` property changes as well. The same is true if the `helloBean.numControls` property changes first; the two are automatically kept in sync. This a key feature of JSF, and it's how you will typically associate the backing bean properties with the UI component values.

You can also associate, or *bind*, a backing bean property directly with a server-side component instance. This is useful when you want to manipulate a component with Java code, which is the type of processing sometimes performed by event listeners. For example, the Hello, world! application has an `HtmlPanelGrid` component instance that is bound to the `HelloBean` backing bean property:

```
<h:panelGrid id="controlPanel" binding="#{helloBean.controlPanel}"
             columns="20" border="1" cellspacing="0"/>
```

Here, the component's `binding` property uses a JSF EL expression to associate it with the `HelloBean` property `controlPanel`, which is of type `HtmlPanelGrid`. Because the backing bean has a reference to the actual component, it can manipulate it in code:

```
...
List children = controlPanel.getChildren();
children.clear();
...
```

This code, located in a `HelloBean` event listener method, retrieves the child components from `controlPanel` and removes them all. These changes will appear the next time the page is displayed to the user.

BY THE WAY If you're used to thinking that JavaBeans are only useful as Value Objects (objects with only properties), it's important to remember that they can be so much more than that. Backing beans are full-fledged JavaBeans that contain properties, but also contain event listener methods that can act on those properties. They can optionally be associated directly with UI components, so you have the choice of directly manipulating the view if necessary.

A single view can have one or more backing beans, and tools will sometimes automatically create bindings from UI components to their corresponding backing bean properties.

Backing beans will often talk to *model objects*—helper classes, which access services like databases, web services, and EJBs or perform application logic, or represent things like users, user preferences, reports, and trades. Model objects, like backing beans, can be associated directly with a component's value using JSF expressions as well. For example, you may want to associate an input control with a `User` object's `name` property. Model objects aren't bound directly to UI components, though, because they don't know anything about the UI.

So that application developers don't spent a lot of time writing boring code that creates backing beans and model objects, JSF provides a declarative mechanism for creating them, called the *Managed Bean Creation facility*. It allows you to specify which objects will be available throughout the lifecycle of the application. Here's another snippet from Hello, world!:

```
<managed-bean>
  <managed-bean-name>helloBean</managed-bean-name>
  <managed-bean-class>com.virtua.jsf.sample.hello.HelloBean
  </managed-bean-class>
  <managed-bean-scope>session</managed-bean-scope>
</managed-bean>
```

This tells JSF to create an instance of the `HelloBean` class called `helloBean`, and store it in the user's session. This little snippet is all that's required to make an object available for integration with UI components. Any objects that use this facility are called *managed beans*.

Understanding how JSF interacts with backing beans and model objects is an essential part of building Faces applications. One of the framework's primary goals is to ease the burden of integrating the UI with the model, and the more you work with it, the more features you'll find that make that goal a reality.

You can find references to backing beans throughout this book; we develop some in chapter 13.

2.1.5 Converters

When users interact with a JSF application, they interact with the output of renderers, which create specific representations that make sense for a particular client (like a web browser). In order to do this, renderers must have specific knowledge about the components they display. But components can also be associated with backing bean properties. Those properties can be anything—a `String` representing a name, a `Date` representing a birth date, or a `FooBarBazz` representing a `foo` property. Because there are no constraints on the type, a renderer can't know beforehand how to display the object.

This is where *converters* come in—they translate an object to a string for display, and from an input string back into an object. A single converter can be associated with any control. JSF ships with converters for common types like dates and numbers, but you, or third parties, can develop additional ones as well. Renderers (or components themselves) usually use converters internally during encoding or decoding.

Converters also handle formatting and localization. For example, the `DateTime` converter can format a `Date` object in a short, medium, long, or full style. For any given style, it will display the date in a way that makes sense in the user's locale. Here's how you register a converter on an `HtmlOutputText` component:

```
<h:outputText value="#{user.dateOfBirth}">
  <f:convert_datetime type="both" dateStyle="full"/>
</h:outputText>
```

Let's suppose the user's birth date is May 4, 1942. The `HtmlOutputText` component would display the string "05/04/42" if the user is from the United States but display "04/05/42" if the user is from Canada. This is shown graphically in figure 2.3.

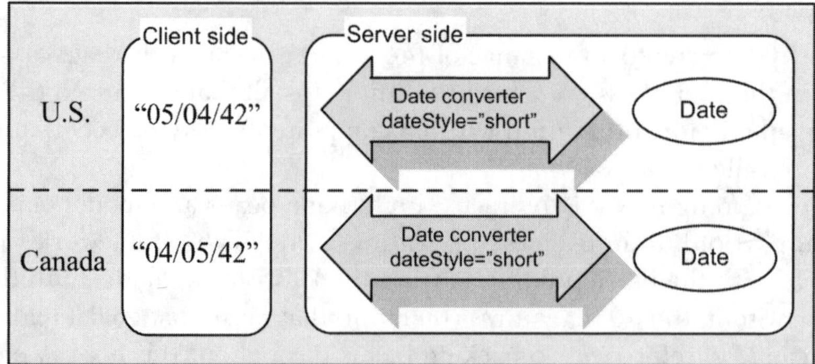

Figure 2.3 A converter translates an object to and from a string for display. It also handles formatting and supports various languages.

Converters are handy because they perform a necessary function—converting an object to a string for display—but provide useful features along the way. Not only do they make it easy to format and localize common data types, but also the architecture allows application developers to do the same for their own model objects. The standard converters are covered in chapter 6, and converter development is covered in chapter 15.

2.1.6 Events and listeners

My wife and I have a few cats. They all eat different types of food, so I feed them a couple of times a day instead of leaving out a feeder. What's funny is that whenever I come downstairs in the morning, or come home later in the day, they start begging for food. This sounds logical, except that no matter when I come downstairs or get home, the cats always beg.

A while ago, I realized the cats are event driven. They aren't necessarily hungry, but certain happenings, such as me entering the room after a long absence, make them think it's time to be fed. Those happenings are significant occurrences that, in their minds, are associated with food.

For UIs, events capture the way the user interacts with UI components. An event could be something like simply clicking on a component, or it could be more complicated, such as executing a specific command. JSF leverages JavaBeans to handle events with event objects and listeners, just like Swing. Any component may fire zero or more events, and developers (or components themselves) can register zero or more listeners to handle those events. I like to think of our cats as *food* listeners—they listen for events that might produce food.

Events are a fundamental shift for web development; more often than not, developing web applications requires that developers think in terms of requests and responses—the mechanism of communication for the underlying stateless protocol, HTTP. Thinking this way is fine for some applications, but for business applications it's unnecessarily complex and ties the application too closely to the protocol.

When you write JSF applications, integrating application logic is a matter of assigning the appropriate listeners to components that generate events that the listeners understand. You don't have to think about requests and responses at all. JSF supports the familiar interface-oriented way of developing event listeners as well as the ability to register an arbitrary method as a listener (as long as it has the proper signature).

There are four standard events: value-change events, action events, data model events, and phase events. *Value-change* events are fired by input controls when a user changes the component's value. *Action* events are generated when a user activates a command component, like a button. *Data model* events are fired when a data-aware component selects a row for processing. And *phase* events execute while JSF processes an HTTP request.

Even though these are the only standard events defined by the framework, there are no limitations on the types of events that are supported. Third-party components, as well as your own, can easily support different types of events.

Value-change events

Value-change events are generated by input controls when the user enters a new value into an input component. You handle value-change events with value-change listeners.

For example, let's say you had `HtmlInputText` and `HtmlPanelGrid` components on the same page:

```
<h:inputText valueChangeListener="#{myForm.processValueChanged}"/>
<h:panelGrid binding="#{myForm.changePanel}" rendered="false">
   ...
</h:panelGrid>
```

Note that for the `HtmlInputText` component, we specify a `valueChangedListener` property with a JSF EL expression. That expression points to a specific value-change listener method in our backing bean: `myForm.processValueChanged`. In addition, the `HtmlPanelGrid` is bound to the backing bean's `changePanel` property so that it can be manipulated in Java code. The grid's `rendered` property is `false`, so that initially it won't be visible to the user.

When a user changes the text in the control and submits the form, JSF will generate a value-change event. It's then up to an event listener method to process this event:

```
public void processValueChanged(ValueChangeEvent event)
{
  HtmlInputText sender = (HtmlInputText)event.getComponent();
  sender.setReadonly(true);
  changePanel.setRendered(true);
}
```

In this example, the event listener method will change the `readOnly` property of the sender (in this case, the `HtmlInputText` component) to `true` so that the user can no longer edit its contents. It will then change the `rendered` property of the `HtmlPanelGrid` component (which is bound to the `changePanel` property) to `true` so that it will be visible when the page is redisplayed. Event listeners can also add messages and perform other JSF operations, as well as execute application logic.

In addition to using listener methods for value-change events, you can register event listener classes that implement an interface. Most of the time, however, associating a specific method with a component is sufficient.

Action events

Action events are triggered when a user interacts with a control that represents a command, or a user gesture. Components that generate action events, also called *action sources*, include controls such as buttons or hyperlinks. Action events are handled by action listeners.

There are two types of action listeners: those that affect navigation, and those that don't. Action listeners that affect navigation typically perform some processing and then return a logical outcome that is used by JSF's navigation system to select the next page (which may actually be the same page that's currently being viewed). Listeners that don't affect navigation usually manipulate components in the current view, or perform some processing that changes model object or backing bean properties, but doesn't alter the current page the user is accessing. Consequently, the page is usually redisplayed after the listener finishes executing.

Technically, all navigation is handled by a single action listener. This listener automatically handles any action events fired by a component, so it doesn't need to be registered manually. By default, this action listener delegates all of its work to *action methods* in your backing beans, so you can have different action methods handle different parts of your application. Typically, most of your application logic will be located in these methods. (The action listener is pluggable, so it's possible to replace it with one that doesn't use action methods at all.)

When a component fires an action event, this default action listener determines its outcome string—`"mainmenu"`, `"success"`, or `"failure"`, for example. There are two basic types of outcomes: static and dynamic. *Static outcomes* are hardcoded strings that are declared with the component or set in code:

```
<h:commandButton type="submit" value="Login" action="success"
                 immediate="true"/>
```

In this example, the static outcome of `"success"` will be generated when the user clicks on this `HtmlCommandButton` and generates an action event—no action method will be called.

Dynamic outcomes are strings returned by action methods themselves—an action method might return a different outcome depending on whatever application logic it performs. The action listener looks for an action method whenever you use a JSF EL expression in the `action` property. Here's an `HtmlCommandButton` that executes an action method instead:

```
<h:commandButton type="submit" value="Login"
                 action="#{loginForm.login}"/>
```

When a user clicks on this button, an action event is fired, and the following method is executed in response to the event:

```
public class LoginForm
{
...
  public String login()
  {
    if (...) // login is successful
    {
       return "success";
    }
    else
    {
       return "failure";
    }
  }
...
}
```

Based on some voodoo application logic, this action method returns an outcome of either `"success"` or `"failure"`. `LoginForm` is a backing bean whose properties are wired up to input control values on the page, and is configured via the Managed Bean Creation facility.

My example has voodoo logic, but your action methods can manipulate JSF components, model objects, or add messages. They can also do other fun tasks, such as performing a redirect, rendering a response (a graphic or some binary type of data), adding events, and talking to databases, EJB servers, or web services. The action listener uses the outcome of an action method to hook into the navigation system and determine what page to choose next.

When you need to execute application logic that is not associated with navigation, you can associate an action listener method with a component. Unlike action methods, action listener methods have access to the component that fired the event as well. Take a look at this example:

```
<h:commandButton id="redisplayCommand" type="submit" value="Redisplay"
                 actionListener="#{myForm.doIt}"/>
```

Like the previous example, when a user clicks on this `HtmlCommandButton`, an action event is fired. This time, however, the action *listener* method is executed instead of the action method:

```
public void doIt(ActionEvent event)
{
```

```
    HtmlCommandButton button = (HtmlCommandButton)event.getComponent();
    button.setValue("It's done!");
  }
```

This method changes the value (label) of the button that fired the event—not terribly useful. What's important, however, is its method signature. Instead of accepting zero parameters and returning an outcome string, action listener methods accept an `ActionEvent` as a parameter and don't return an outcome at all. After this method executes, the page will be redisplayed, incorporating any changes made by the method.

Usually, you use action listener methods for changes that affect the current view. Like value-change listeners, you can also implement an action listener using a Java interface, although in most cases using a method in an existing backing bean is sufficient.

Data model events

Data model events are triggered when a data-aware component processes a row. The most common way to trigger this event is through a component that displays a selectable list of items, such as `HtmlDataTable`, which is the quintessential "data grid" component. Unlike value-change or action event listeners, data model event listeners must implement a Java interface.

Data model events are a little different than the other events because they're not actually fired by a UI component. Instead, they're fired by a `DataModel` instance, which is a model object used internally by data-aware components. `DataModel` objects are wrappers for lists, arrays, result sets, and other data sources. Since the event is technically fired by a model object instead of a component, you can't register a listener on the component itself in JSP. You have to register it in Java code instead:

```
FacesContext facesContext = FacesContext.getCurrentInstance();
dataTable = (HtmlDataTable)facesContext.getApplication().createComponent(
                                       HtmlDataTable.COMPONENT_TYPE);
DataModel myDataModel = new ResultSetDataModel(myResultSet);
myDataModel.addDataModelListener(new DataModelListener()
      {
        public void rowSelected(DataModelEvent e)
        {
          FacesContext.getCurrentInstance().getExternalContext().
                       log("row selected:" + e.getRowIndex());
        }
      });
dataTable.setValue(myDataModel);
```

In this example, we create a new instance of an `HtmlDataTable` component and then create a new `ResultSetDataModel` using a preexisting JDBC ResultSet. Next, we add a new `DataModelListener` (implemented as an inner class) to the `ResultSetDataModel`, and set the data model as the value of the `HtmlDataTable` component. The result is that every time an `HtmlDataTable` iterates through a new row in the data model, our listener will be executed. Usually this happens when the component is being displayed. Since data model events are fired so many times, they're normally used when developing a data-driven component, rather than during application development.

Phase events

Whenever a JSF application receives a request, it goes through a six-step process called the *Request Processing Lifecycle*. During this process, JSF restores the requested view, translates the request parameters into component values, validates input, updates your backing beans or model objects, invokes action listeners, and returns a response to the user. Phase events are generated before and after each step, or *phase*, of this lifecycle. (We cover the Request Processing Lifecycle in detail in section 2.2.)

Phase events are generated by JSF itself rather than by UI components, and require that you implement a Java interface to register event listeners. They're normally used internally by the JSF implementation, but sometimes they can be useful for application development as well. For example, you can use them to initialize a backing bean before it is displayed. (Sun's Java Studio Creator automatically allows backing beans to handle phase events directly.)

Here's an example of registering a phase listener that executes before a view is displayed:

```
lifecycle.addPhaseListener(
  new PhaseListener()
  {
    public void beforePhase(PhaseEvent event)
    {
      priceQuote = QuoteService.getLatestQuote(currentQuoteId);
    }

    public void afterPhase(PhaseEvent event)
    {
    }

    public PhaseId getPhaseId()
    {
      return PhaseId.RENDER_RESPONSE;
    }
  });
```

In this example, we add a new `PhaseListener` instance to a preexisting `Lifecycle` instance (a `Lifecycle` represents the Request Processing Lifecycle). The `phaseId` property of the listener tells the lifecycle when it should process events. In this case, the listener will be executed when the view is rendered (the Render Response phase). The `beforePhase` method will be executed before the view is displayed, and the `afterPhase` method will be executed after it has been displayed. In `beforePhase`, we update the `priceQuote` property based on the latest values from the `QuoteService` class. This updates the `priceQuote` property so that it can be displayed by components in the corresponding view.

As you can see, in JSF applications, there's no need to worry about the details of the protocol—you only need to be concerned with events and listeners. This doesn't mean you don't have to understand how HTTP works, but it makes day-to-day development simpler. (If you like total control, don't worry—you can still access the Servlet API if you want.) Because events and listeners are a fundamental part of developing JSF applications, you'll find examples scattered throughout parts 3 and 4 of this book, but there is specific coverage for application developers in chapter 11.

2.1.7 Messages

All this talk of different JSF concepts is great, but what happens if something goes wrong? One of the biggest issues when developing a UI is properly displaying error messages. They can be split into two major categories: *application* errors (business logic, database, or connection errors, for example) and *user input* errors (such as invalid text or empty fields).

Application errors usually generate a completely different page with the error message on it; input errors usually redisplay the calling page with text describing the errors. Often you'll have the same error message on different pages, and consequently you must make sure that what the user sees is consistent. You don't want to say "Please enter your telephone number" on one page and "Telephone number required" on another page.

JSF provides messages to help deal with these issues. A *message* consists of summary text, detailed text, and a severity level. Messages can also be automatically tailored for the user's current language (assuming your application supports that language). Just about any piece of your application—including UI components, validators, converters, or event listeners—can add messages when processing a request; JSF maintains a list of all the current messages. You can always programmatically get a handle to the current stack of messages through components and application code.

Messages don't necessarily have to indicate errors; they can be informational as well. For example, an action listener method could add a message indicating that a new record was successfully added. The message itself can either be associated with a specific component (for input errors) or no component at all (for application messages).

You can display errors associated with a specific component by using the `HtmlMessage` component. You may remember `HtmlMessage` from the Hello, world! application:

```
<h:message id="errors" for="helloInput" style="color: red"/>
```

This tag displays all errors that were generated for the `helloInput` input component (which must be declared on the same page). You can also display all messages, or those not associated with a specific component, using the `HtmlMessages` component.

Messages provide a convenient way to communicate errors and other happenings to the user. They're an integral part of JSF's validation and type conversion features—any time a validator encounters an incorrect value or a converter processes an incorrect type, it generates an error message. They're also an excellent way for you to communicate information to a user without worrying about how it is being displayed; simply create a new message in your action listener method, and the view will display it for you. You can find out how to customize the standard application messages in chapter 6, and how to create them in Java code in chapter 11.

2.1.8 Navigation

All of the concepts we've discussed so far have been related to interaction on a single page. Writing web applications would be a piece of cake if they were confined to a single page, but in reality that's not the case. Web applications have multiple pages, and we must have some way to move between them. The act of moving from one page to another is called *navigation*.

Faces has a pretty elegant navigation system. The *navigation handler* is responsible for deciding what page to load based on the logical outcome of an action method. For any given page, a *navigation rule* defines what outcomes are understood, and what pages to load based on those outcomes.[1] Each specific mapping between an outcome and a page is called a *navigation case*. The rules are defined

---

[1] This is the way the default navigation handler works. JSF allows you, or other developers, to plug in new ones that behave differently.

in a JSF configuration file. Here is a navigation rule with the two cases for the page login.jsp—the `"success"` and `"failure"` outcomes:

```
<navigation-rule>
  <from-view-id>/login.jsp</from-view-id>
  <navigation-case>
    <from-outcome>success</from-outcome>
    <to-view-id>/mainmenu.jsp</to-view-id>
  </navigation-case>
  <navigation-case>
    <from-outcome>failure</from-outcome>
    <to-view-id>/login.jsp</to-view-id>
  </navigation-case>
</navigation-rule>
```

As you can see, each case maps the outcome to a specific page—no code required. This is a handy feature of JSF that should look familiar if you've used frameworks like Struts. All navigation cases are usually kept in a single place, which means any changes can be made in a central location instead of across several pages. Navigation is covered in detail in chapter 3, and you can find many examples in parts 2 and 3.

Now that we've looked at the key pieces of the JSF pie, let's see how these concepts come into play when the framework processes an incoming request.

2.2 The Request Processing Lifecycle

We've been talking about how JSF simplifies web programming with components, events, listeners, and several other nifty concepts. So why is this section about processing requests? In order for you to understand how the framework masks the underlying request processing nature of the Servlet API, it helps to analyze how Faces processes each request. This will allow you to build better applications because you'll know exactly what operations take place, and when. If you're a front-end developer who tends to avoid such details, you can skip this section. You can always refer back to it if necessary.

In this chapter we describe how JSF responds to requests that Faces generates itself. In other words, the request was generated by a page with JSF components, and the response will have JSF components on it as well. (It's entirely possible to return a page with JSF components on it, even if the initial request wasn't generated by JSF; see chapter 14 for more about different request processing scenarios.)

Figure 2.4 is a state diagram showing what happens when JSF processes an incoming request from a client—the JSF *Request Processing Lifecycle*. This process begins as soon as a request is received by the JSF servlet (remember, JSF is built

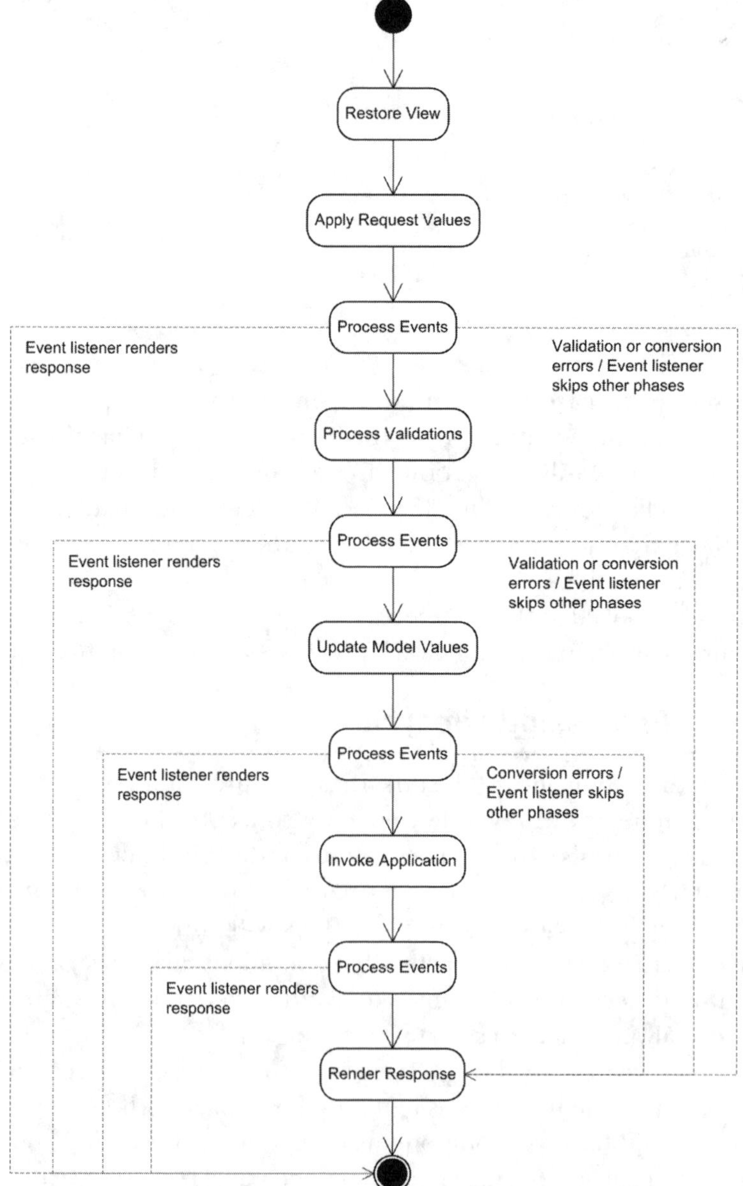

Figure 2.4 The Request Processing Lifecycle. Flows with dotted lines are optional. JSF cycles through several phases as it processes each request. After each phase, event listeners are called. Listeners can either continue as normal, report errors and skip to the Render Response phase, or generate the response themselves.

on top of the Servlet API.) Table 2.2 summarizes each of these phases. There are six primary phases, and events are processed after most of them.

After most phases, JSF will broadcast events to any interested listeners (events can be associated with a particular phase). Event listeners perform application logic or manipulate components; they can also jump to the final phase, Render Response. A listener can even skip the final phase and render a response itself. It might do this if it were returning binary content, performing a redirect, or returning other content that isn't related to JSF, like XML documents or ordinary HTML.

Four of these phases can generate messages: Apply Request Values, Process Validations, Update Model Values, and Invoke Application. With or without messages, it is the Render Response phase that sends output back to the user, unless a listener, renderer, or component has sent the response itself.

The main idea behind this whole process is that by the time the Invoke Application stage has been reached, there is a fully populated component tree, all validations have been completed, and any backing beans or model objects

Table 2.2 JavaServer Faces goes through several phases when it processes a single incoming request.

Phase	Description	Events fired
Restore View	Finds or creates a tree of components for the selected view. Some components, like `HtmlCommandButton`, will generate action events (or other types of events) in this phase.	Phase events
Apply Request Values	Updates the value of the components to equal ones sent in the request, optionally using converters. Adds conversion errors if there is an error. Also generates events from request parameters.	Phase events, data model events, action events
Process Validations	Asks each component to validate itself (which may include using external validators). Validation error messages may be reported.	Phase events, data model events, value-change events
Update Model Values	Updates all the values of backing beans or model objects associated with components. Conversion error messages may be reported.	Phase events, data model events,
Invoke Application	Calls any registered action listeners. The default action listener will also execute action methods referenced by command components (like `HtmlCommandButton`) and choose the next view to be displayed.	Phase events, action events
Render Response	Displays the selected view using the current display technology (like JSP).	Phase events

have been completely updated. In short, JSF does a lot of work for you: It takes the details about a request and translates them into a higher-level view of the world that consists of components and events. It even updates the properties of associated objects for you.

To help make things clearer, we'll use the Hello, world! example to help explain the lifecycle. Specifically, we'll examine the request that generated the output shown in figure 1.8 from chapter 1. The actual HTTP request is shown in listing 2.1.

Listing 2.1 The HTTP request sent from the browser before the Hello, world! application displays figure 1.8

```
POST /jia-hello-world/faces/hello.jsp HTTP/2.1      <-1 URI receiving request
Host: deadlock:8080
User-Agent: Mozilla/5.0 (Windows; U; Windows NT 5.1; en-US; rv:2.2.1)
            Gecko/20021130
Accept: text/xml,application/xml,application/xhtml+xml,text/html;
        q=0.9,text/plain;q=0.8,video/x-mng,image/png,
        image/jpeg,image/gif;q=0.2,text/css,*/*;q=0.1
Accept-Language: en-us, en;q=0.50
Accept-Encoding: gzip, deflate, compress;q=0.9
Accept-Charset: ISO-8859-1, utf-8;q=0.66, *;q=0.66
Keep-Alive: 300
Connection: keep-alive
Referer: http://deadlock:8080/jia-hello-world/faces/hello.jsp   <-2 Same as URI receiving request
Cookie: JSESSIONID=58324750039276F39E61932ABDE319DF   <-3 Session identifier
Content-Type: application/x-www-form-urlencoded
Content-Length: 92

welcomeForm%3AhelloInput=64&
welcomeForm%3AredisplayCommand=Redisplay&
welcomeForm=welcomeForm                              4 Component values
```

We won't get into the details of HTTP requests here, but a few lines in the listing are relevant for our discussion:

1. This request is posting form data to the relative URI "/jia-hello-world/faces/hello.jsp".
2. The *referrer* is the page from which this request was generated. Note that it's the same page that's receiving the request: "/jia-hello-world/faces/hello.jsp".
3. This cookie is used by the servlet container to map this request to a specific session. In this example, JSF uses the servlet session to store the current view. (The view's state can also be stored in a value maintained by the client, like a hidden field.)

❹ This is the important part—these are the actual parameters JSF processes (the ampersand is used to separate parameters, and "%3A" translates to a colon [":"]). The first parameter has a name of "welcomeForm:helloInput" and a value of `"64"`, which is the number entered into the browser. The second parameter has a name of "welcomeForm:redisplayCommand" and value of "Redisplay". The final parameter is simply called "welcomeForm" and has a value of "welcomeForm". We'll see how these parameters are handled in the following sections.

Once JSF receives this HTTP request, it creates and populates an instance of `javax.faces.context.FacesContext`. This class represents the current state of the request, and has hooks to all aspects of the underlying servlet request object. It's where your event listeners can get a handle to the current view, add messages, log events, and so on. JSF uses this object as the basis for the Request Processing Lifecycle. We describe each phase in the following sections.

2.2.1 Phase 1: Restore View

A view represents all of the components that make up a particular page. It can be stored on the client (usually in a hidden field on a browser) or on the server (usually in the session). In this example, it's stored on the server, which is the default. Each view is composed of a tree of components, and has a unique identifier. This *view identifier* is the same as the extra path info for the request.[2] So, for the path referenced by ❶ in listing 2.1, "/jia-hello-world/faces/hello.jsp", the view identifier is "/hello.jsp"—everything after the servlet name.

Because this request was sent when a user clicked on a button in hello.jsp, the page that's sending the request is the same as the page that's receiving it. The process of a page posting back to itself is called *postback*. If you're accustomed to web frameworks like Struts that segregate application code into separate Action classes that are mapped to URLs, this may seem a bit strange. In these types of frameworks, the URL is sort of like a course-grained event that says "perform this action."

JSF events represent more fine-grained events such as "user executed this command" or "user changed the value of this control." The important thing about these events is that they're related to the last page that was requested. When a JSF application receives a request from an existing page, it has to figure out what page sent the request so that it can identify which events the user generated, and then associate them with the components on the sending page.

---

[2] This is how the default JSF implementation works. Some other implementations may use view identifiers differently; for example, the Smile [Smile] open source implementation allows you to map a view identifier to a particular Java class that creates a component tree, rather than a JSP page.

This is the main job of the Restore View phase—to find the current view and apply the user's input to it. In this case, it will look for the view in the user's session. If the view isn't available (the user has never been to this page before), the framework discards the current view (if there is one), and creates a new one based on the requested view identifier. Once the view has been created or retrieved, it is then stored in the current `FacesContext`.

Listing 1.1 in chapter 1 shows the code for hello.jsp in our Hello, world! application. Let's take a look at the component tree that represents this page (see figure 2.5).

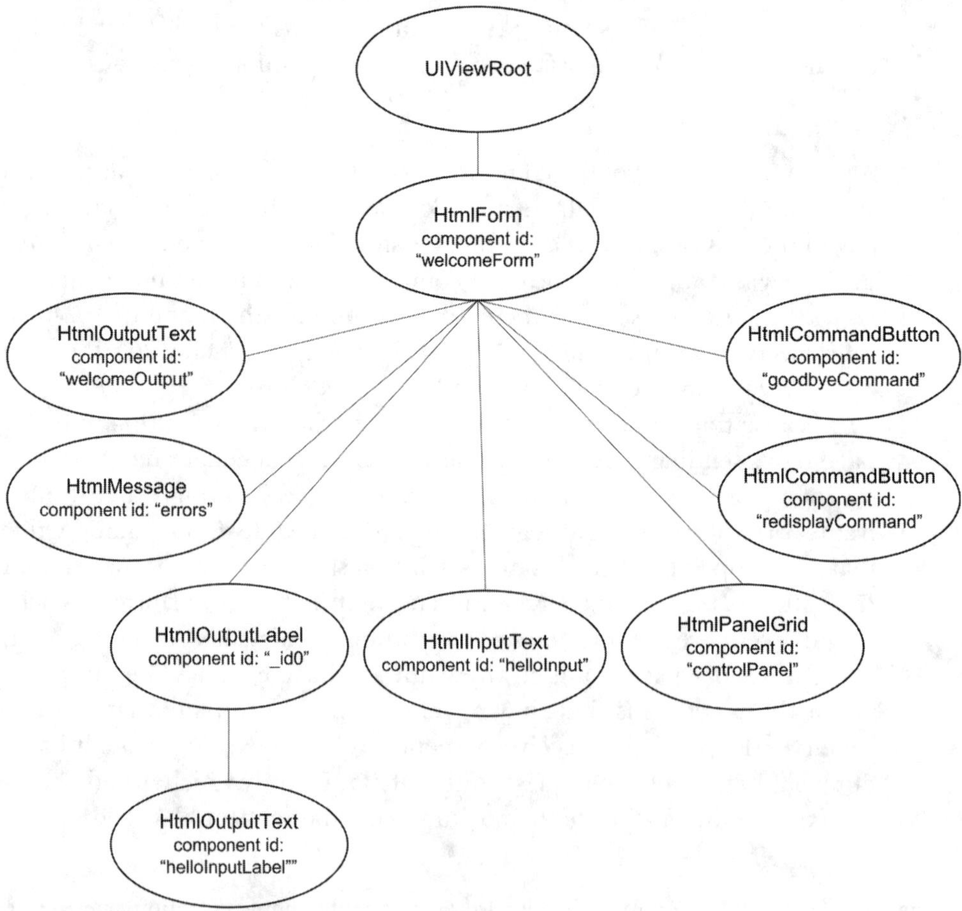

Figure 2.5 The tree of components generated by hello.jsp.

As you can see, the page is represented by a simple component tree. The view starts with a `UIViewRoot` component, which is the container for all of the other controls on the page. It has one child, an `HtmlForm` component with the identifier `welcomeForm`. This form has several children, including an `HtmlInputText` component called `helloInput` and two `HtmlCommandButton` components with the identifiers `redisplayCommand` and `goodbyeCommand`. One of its children is an `HtmlOutputLabel` that has a child `HtmlOutputText` component as well.

Restoring the view also ensures that the component's values, as well as any event listeners, validators, or converters associated with components in the tree, are restored. In this case, the `HtmlInputText` component has a `LongRange` validator associated with it, which is restored with the components in the view. In addition, `redisplayCommand` has an `action` property, and `goodbyeCommand` has an `actionListener` property, both of which are restored.

If any of the components in the tree are bound to a backing bean property, this is where the bean's property and the component instance are synchronized with each other. In this example, the `controlPanel` property of `HelloBean` would be synchronized with the `HtmlPanelGrid` component called `controlPanel` in the view. This allows the backing bean listener methods to manipulate the component in code when they're handling events.

This is also the phase where the language for the view is set, based on the values of the HTTP request sent to the browser. If this request was a postback, JSF will now proceed to the next phase. However, if it is an *initial request* (the first time the user has requested this page), JSF will skip to the Render Response phase, because there is no user input to process.

2.2.2 Phase 2: Apply Request Values

Each UI component that accepts input has a *submitted value* that represents the user's original data from the user. During the Apply Request Values phase, the framework sets that submitted value based on the parameters sent in the request. This process is called decoding.

In hello.jsp, each component was assigned a component identifier like this:

```
<h:inputText id="helloInput" value="#{helloBean.numControls}"
             required="true">
...
</h:inputText>
```

This declares an `HelloInputText` component with the component identifier `helloInput`. When JSF encodes this component as HTML, the identifier sent to the browser is composed of the component's identifier prefixed by the identifier of its parent component. The identifier sent to the browser, which is usually the `id` attribute of an input element, is called the *client identifier*. For example, this `HtmlInputText` component would have the client identifier `welcomeForm:helloInput`, because it's a child of an `HtmlForm` component with the identifier `welcomeForm` (as shown in figure 2.5).

As we saw in the HTTP request in listing 2.1, one of the two parameters had the name `helloInput` and the value `"64"`. In this phase, JSF asks each component to decode itself. The component (or its renderer) does this by first looking for a parameter whose name is the same as its client identifier. Once the parameter has been found, the component's value is set to the value of the parameter. So, in this case, the `HtmlInputText` component will set its submitted value to `"64"`.

Every input control that has an editable value also has an `immediate` property. If this property is set to `true`, validation takes place in this phase instead of the Process Validations phase. The process is the same either way; see the next section for details. (In our example, no control has the `immediate` property set to `true`.) Action sources, like a button or a hyperlink, also have an `immediate` property, and if that property is `true`, they will fire action events during this phase as well. Processing these events early can be pretty handy: for example, you could have a Cancel button that ignores all values on a form, or a hyperlink that only accepts values from a specific control (the `immediate` property for all of these components would be `true`).

Another parameter sent by the request is `"welcomeForm"`, with a value of `"welcomeForm"`. Whenever this parameter exists, the `HtmlForm` component sets its `submitted` property to `true`. This allows you to perform different logic depending on whether the user has submitted the form. (A single view can have multiple forms.)

During this phase, the decoding code can also add events or perform other operations based on the request. In our sample application, this phase is where the other parameter, `"welcomeForm:redisplayCommand"`, is converted into an action event by the `HtmlCommandButton` control with the matching client identifier. Once the action event has been created, it is added to the `FacesContext` for later processing in the Invoke Application phase.

After this phase is completed, any existing events are broadcast to interested listeners. Any renderers, components, or listeners can short-circuit the lifecycle and force control to skip to the Render Response phase, or end processing altogether (if they rendered the entire response themselves). Otherwise, each input component will have properly decoded itself and consequently will have a value that is up-to-date based on the current request. This is the case for our example.

2.2.3 Phase 3: Process Validations

In the Process Validations phase, JSF traverses the component tree and asks each component to make sure its submitted value is acceptable. Because the submitted value of every input component was updated in the Apply Request Values phase, the component now has the most current data from the user. Before validation can occur, the submitted value is converted, by using either the converter registered for the component or a default converter. Validation is then handled either directly by the component or delegated to one or more validators.

If both conversion and validation are successful for all components whose values were submitted, the lifecycle continues onto the next phase. Otherwise, control will skip to the Render Response phase, complete with validation and conversion error messages.

Hello, world! has a single `LongRange` validator that's associated with the `HtmlInputText` component, and the component's `required` property is set to `true`:

```
<h:inputText id="helloInput" value="#{helloBean.numControls}"
             required="true">
<f:validateLongRange minimum="1" maximum="500"/>
</h:inputText>
```

When the view was created, the validator instance was created and associated with the `HtmlInputText` component.

Because the UI component's `required` property is `true`, it will first verify that the submitted value isn't empty. The value is `"64"`, so it's definitely not empty. Next, the submitted value is converted to the type of the `helloBean.numControls` property, which is an `Integer`. The `LongRange` validator is then asked to check the value of its parent component to see if it's valid. In this case, *valid* means that the value is between 1 and 500 (inclusive). Because 64 is indeed in between 1 and 500, this component will be considered valid.

Once the component's submitted value has been validated, its local value is set based on the converted submitted value, which in this case is an `Integer` of 64. If the local value has changed, the component also generates a value-change event.

At this point, value-change events (and any other events associated with this phase) are fired and consumed by the appropriate listeners. These listeners have the option of outputting a response directly or jumping directly to the Render Response phase.

If all submitted values are considered valid, JSF continues on to the next phase of the lifecycle.

2.2.4 Phase 4: Update Model Values

Now that we are sure all of the local values of the components are updated and valid, and of the correct type, it's okay to deal with any associated backing beans or model objects. Because objects are associated with components through JSF EL expressions, this is where those expressions are evaluated, and properties are updated based on the component's local value. Let's look at the `HtmlInputText` declaration once again:

```
<h:inputText id="helloInput" value="#{helloBean.numControls}"
             required="true">
...
</h:inputText>
```

You can see that the `value` property is the expression `"#{helloBean.numControls}"`. JSF will use this to find an instance of a bean stored under the key `helloBean`, searching each of the servlet scopes—request, session, or application (see section 2.4.1 for more about the different scoped variables).[3] In this case, the bean was stored in the session. Once it has been found, the component sets the specified property (`numControls` in this example) to be equal to its local value, which is currently an `Integer` of 64.

Once this phase has completed, the framework will broadcast any events to all interested listeners. As always, a listener could jump to the Render Response phase or return a response itself.

It's important to note that by this point in the lifecycle, we've updated component values based on user input, validated those values, and updated any associated beans without any application code. This is the true power of JSF—it handles a lot of the UI processing tasks for you automatically, because there's more to life than writing tedious, repetitive code.

2.2.5 Phase 5: Invoke Application

Now that the necessary backing beans and model objects are up-to-date, we can get down to business. In the Invoke Application phase, JSF broadcasts events for this phase to any registered listeners. Back in the Apply Request Values phase, an action event was generated for the `redisplayCommand HtmlCommandButton`. So in this phase, JSF will send the action event to any registered action listeners for that component. In this case, there are two: the action listener method restored

[3] The ability to reference a bean regardless of the scope should be familiar to users of frameworks like Struts.

in the Restore View phase, and the default action listener (which is automatically registered for all command components).

Here's the declaration for `redisplayCommand`:

```
<h:commandButton id="redisplayCommand" type="submit" value="Redisplay"
                 actionListener="#{helloBean.addControls}"/>
```

The `actionListener` property is the JSF EL expression `"#{helloBean.addControls}"`. In this phase, JSF evaluates the expression and executes the `addControls` method of a `helloBean` instance stored in the application's session. Here's the method:

```
public void addControls(ActionEvent actionEvent)
{
   Application application =
                        FacesContext.getCurrentInstance().getApplication();
   List children = controlPanel.getChildren();
   children.clear();
   for (int count = 0; count < numControls; count++)
   {
     HtmlOutputText output = (HtmlOutputText)application.
                             createComponent(HtmlOutputText.COMPONENT_TYPE);
     output.setValue(" " + count + " ");
     output.setStyle("color: blue");
     children.add(output);
   }
}
```

This code creates `numControls` instances of `HtmlOutputText` and adds them to `controlPanel`, which is the `HtmlPanelGrid` instance on the page. (The children must be cleared first, or else the list of children would continue to grow each time this method was executed.) Recall that in the Restore View phase, the binding between the view and HelloBean's `controlPanel` property was established. Also, the `numControls` property was updated during the Update Model Values phase.

After this action listener method has executed, JSF will call the default action listener. This listener delegates control to any action methods registered for the component that fired the event, and then chooses the next page based on the action method's logical outcome. In this case, there was an action method registered for `goodbyeCommand` but not `redisplayCommand`, which is the component that fired the event. So the default action listener will simply redisplay the current view.

As we discussed in section 2.1.6, action listeners or action methods can perform a lot of operations, such as rendering the response themselves, adding application messages, generating events, and executing application logic. They can also jump to the Render Response phase in order to avoid any additional application event processing. Action methods are integrated with the navigation system, so they can determine the next page to load.

It's important to point out that even though all of this processing is taking place, this is where your application code lives—you generally don't have to worry about the request at all. Once all the listeners have executed,[4] JSF is ready to display the response to the user.

2.2.6 Phase 6: Render Response

At this point all processing by the framework and the application has taken place. All that's left is to send a response back to the user, and that is the primary goal of the Render Response phase. The secondary goal of this phase is to save the state of the view so that it can be restored in the Restore View phase if the user requests it again. The view's state is saved in this phase because often the view is stored on the client, so it's part of the response that's sent back to the user. In this case, JSF is saving state on the server, so the view would most likely be stored in the user's session.

Remember, JSF isn't tied to a particular display technology. As a result, we have several possible approaches to rendering a response:

- Use only the output from the encoding methods of controls in the view.
- Integrate the output of encoding methods with application code that generates markup.
- Integrate the output of encoding methods with a markup stored in a static template resource.
- Integrate the output of decoding methods with a dynamic resource, like a JSP.

All JSF implementations are required to implement the last approach, which boils down to forwarding the request to the resource represented by the view identifier. In our example, that identifier was `"/hello.jsp"`, so the calling page is just redisplayed. JSF implementations are free to implement the other approaches as well so that they can integrate with other display technologies. See appendix A for examples of using JSF without JSP.

During the encoding process for each component, converters are also invoked to translate the component values into strings for display. So, in our example, the `HtmlInputText` component's `Integer` value of 64 would be converted into a `String`.

[4] If you're good at reading in between the lines, you may have noticed that the Invoke Application phase doesn't do anything but broadcast events. In other words, unlike the other phases, there's no real processing before the events are fired.

That's it. The Render Response phase is the final step in the JSF Request Processing Lifecycle. Once it's complete, the web container physically transmits the resulting bytes back to the user, where it is rendered by the browser. The output of this particular example, displayed in a browser, is shown in figure 1.8, page 23.

Now that you have a thorough understanding of how JSF works, let's look at some other fundamental aspects of developing JSF applications.

2.3 Understanding component and client identifiers

In the previous sections, we've touched on the concept of a client identifier, and we've seen how it's different than the identifier assigned to a component in a JSP. Let's examine this issue a little further.

As we've demonstrated, UI components live in two separate worlds: on the server, where they are represented as an object in a component tree, and on the client, where they can have many representations. The server world is the Java Virtual Machine (JVM), complete with the servlet, JSF, application code, and other supporting libraries. The clients are usually browsers that display markup such as HTML. Browsers live in a world of client-side scripts in languages like JavaScript or VBScript, styling mechanisms like Cascading Style Sheets (CSS), and navigation schemes like anchors and hyperlinks.

Each world needs to way to find a given component. On the server, each component can be found via its *component identifier*. If you assign an identifier to a component, you can use that identifier to access that component in Java code. On the client, each component can be found via its *client identifier*, which is derived from the component identifier. The client identifier allows you to manipulate the component's client-side representation using technologies such as JavaScript, CSS, and the like.

Client identifiers also bridge the gap between the server and the client worlds. When a user submits a form, the client identifier is sent to the server along with data representing the action the user performed on that component. It is then used to map the user's data to the component instance on the server so that its value can be modified, events can be generated, and so on.

This may seem a bit vague, so let's look at an example. Figure 2.6 shows the relationship between components running on the server, their representations on the client, and the types of technologies that use the identifiers. The following JSP code snippet defines the components shown in the figure—an `HtmlOutputText` component and an `HtmlForm` component with two child `HtmlInputText` components:

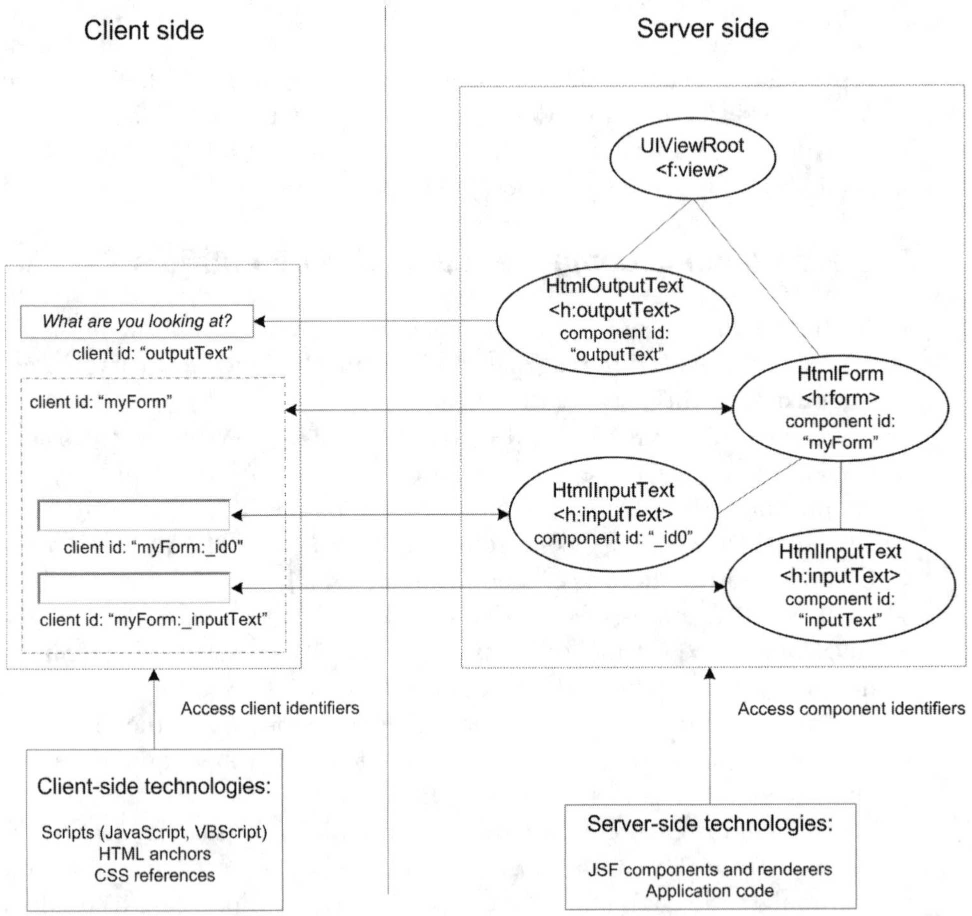

Figure 2.6 Components instances on the server are referenced via component identifiers. On the client, they are referenced by client identifiers. Sometimes the two are the same.

```
<p>
  <h:outputText id="outputText" value="What are you looking at?"/>
</p>
<h:form id="myForm">
  <p>
    <h:inputText/>
  </p>
  <p>
    <h:inputText id="inputText"/>
  </p>
...
</h:form>
```

The first thing to point out is that the id attributes shown here are component identifiers. Also, you'll notice that the first <h:inputText> element has no identifier specified. This is because identifiers are optional—if you don't specify one, JSF will generate one for you.

NOTE Component identifiers must start with a letter or an underscore (_) and be composed of letters, numbers, dashes (-) and underscores. They should also be short in order to minimize the size of responses from the client.

Now, let's look at the corresponding HTML output:

```
<p>
  <span id="outputText">What are you looking at?</span>
</p>
<form id="myForm" method="post"
      action="/jia-standard-components/client_ids.jsf"
      enctype="application/x-www-form-urlencoded">

  <p>
    <input type="text" name="myForm:_id1" />
  </p>
  <p>
    <input id="myForm:inputText" type="text" name="myForm:inputText" />
  </p>
...
</form>
```

The HTML <span> element is displayed by the HtmlOutputText component. Its client identifier, outputText, is the same as the component identifier we defined in JSP. The <form> element is the output of the HtmlForm component; its client identifier is also the same as its component identifier. The client identifiers for all of its children, however, begin with the HtmlForm component's client identifier, myForm. Because the second HtmlInputText component didn't have a component identifier specified, _id0 was assigned to it automatically. (Input controls generally output the client identifier for both the id and name attributes.)

The client identifiers for the HtmlForm component's children begin with HtmlForm's client identifier because the HtmlForm component is a naming container. Conveniently, naming containers are the subject of the next section.

NOTE Component identifiers are usually optional, but they are necessary anytime one component refers to another, or you need to reference a component on the client or the server via a known identifier. If you don't specify one, JSF will generate one for you on the server, but depending on the component, you may not see a client identifier in the rendered markup. If you do specify one, keep component identifiers as short as possible in order to minimize the size of JSF responses.

2.3.1 Naming containers

A *naming container* is a component whose children all have unique component identifiers. So you can't have two components with the component identifier `foo` if they're in the same naming container. The view's root node (`UIViewRoot`), which is the parent of all of the other components on a given page, is not a naming container, but it does require that top-level components in the same view must have different identifiers.

`HtmlForm` is a naming container, so no two components in the same `HtmlForm` can have the same component identifier. This makes sense, because if you had two components named `foo` that were of the same type, it would be impossible to differentiate them from each other. The only other standard component that is a naming container is `HtmlDataTable`. Some third-party components (or ones you write), may also be naming containers.

The client identifier can differ from the component identifier when there is more than one naming container in the control hierarchy. This is because a client identifier must be unique for the whole page, regardless of how many naming containers there are. It must be unique because the client doesn't know about naming containers—it just posts form data back to a JSF application. The application must be able to map that data to specific components, and it needs to differentiate between data for one component and data for another.

To illustrate, let's examine two `HtmlForm` components in the same view. Each one has a child `HtmlInputText` component with the same component identifier.

```
<f:view>
  <h:form id="firstForm">
    <h:inputText id="inputText"/>
    ...
  </h:form>

  <h:form id="secondForm">
    <h:inputText id="inputText"/>
    ...
  </h:form>
<f:view>
```

These two declarations are identical except that each `HtmlForm` component has a different component identifier.

Here is the HTML output:

```
<form id="firstForm" method="post" action="/myapp/client_ids.jsf"
      enctype="application/x-www-form-urlencoded">
  <input id="firstForm:inputText" type="text" name="firstForm:inputText"/>
  ...
</form>

<form id="secondForm" method="post" action="/myapp/client_ids.jsf">
  <input id="secondForm:inputText" type="text" name="secondForm:inputText"/>
  ...
</form>
```

`UIViewRoot` doesn't generate any output; it just marks the beginning of the component tree. What's important, however, is that even though both `HtmlTextInput` components have the component identifier `inputText`, their client identifiers are different. Since the first form's client identifier is `firstForm`, its child input control's client identifier is the `firstForm:inputText`. And since the last form's client identifier is `secondForm`, its child's client identifier is `secondForm:inputText`. As you can see, the client identifier equals the parent naming container's client identifier plus a colon followed by the *component* identifier.

NOTE Because the default separator for client identifiers is `":"`, this can cause problems for CSS stylesheets that try to apply style to components using the client identifier. The workaround is to use the CSS classes style to a component (all of the standard HTML components have a `styleClass` property for this purpose).

You may be wondering how naming containers affect your everyday life as a JSF developer. Knowing which components are naming containers helps you understand what a component's client identifier is. And, if you know the client identifier, you can reference a component on the client and decode it on the server, as we will see next.

2.3.2 Referencing identifiers

So, now we've established the fact that UI components have identifiers on the client and the server, and we know that these identifiers can be different if naming containers are involved. Let's take a look at how you can use these identifiers to reference components on both the client and the server.

On the client

We said earlier that client-side technologies can reference components via their client identifiers. As an example, consider the following JSP code:

```
<h:form id="clientForm">
  <h:outputLabel for="myTextBox"
       onmouseover=
          "document.forms.clientForm['clientForm:myTextBox'].value = '84'"
       onmouseout=
          "document.forms.clientForm['clientForm:myTextBox'].value = ''">
     <h:outputText id="myOutput" value="How old is Memaw?"/>
  </h:output_label>
  <h:inputText id="myTextBox"/>
</h:form>
```

Here we have an `HtmlForm` component with child `HtmlOutputLabel` and `HtmlInputText` components. The child `HtmlOutputLabel` component has a child `HtmlOutput` component. It produces the following HTML:

```
<form id="clientForm" method="post" action="/myapp/client_ids.jsf"
      enctype="application/x-www-form-urlencoded">

   <label for="clientForm:myTextBox"
     onmouseout=
         "document.forms.clientForm['clientForm:myTextBox'].value = ''"
     onmouseover=
         "document.forms.clientForm['clientForm:myTextBox'].value = '84'">
    <span id="clientForm:myOutput">How old is Memaw?</span>
   </label>
<input id="clientForm:myTextBox" type="text" name="clientForm:myTextBox" />
...
</form>
```

The JavaScript in the `onmouseout` and `onmouseover` attributes of the `label` element reference the `input` field by its `name` attribute (`clientForm:myTextBox`), which is also the `HtmlInputText` component's client identifier. When a user mouses over the label, the value of the text box will change to `"84"`. When the user moves the mouse away, it will become empty. This isn't a very useful bit of functionality, but it should get the point across—you can access the text field in JavaScript via its client identifier.

With HTML browsers, the client identifier will usually map to the `name` or `id` attribute of the corresponding HTML element. This means you can also use it within CSS, as an anchor reference, and so on (for a detailed quick HTML reference, see the W3School's site [W3Schools]).

However, keep in mind that JSF isn't limited to HTML applications—you could have a different type of browser, a desktop client, an applet, or something completely different. Regardless of the technology, the code running on the client must think in terms of the client identifier, especially when communicating with the server.

On the server

When you interact with JSF components on the server, the code you write will generally be located in a backing bean event listener method or an event listener class. It could, however, be anywhere you want, as long as you have a reference to a component instance. This is because the base component class, `UIComponent`, has a handy method called `findComponent`. This method searches for components using a special search expression that is similar to a client identifier.

For example, say you had the following form defined in JSP:

```
<h:form id="messageForm">
  <h:outputText id="outputMessage"/>
  <h:commandButton value="Get Message"
                   actionListener="#{testForm.sendMessage}"/>
</h:form>
```

This defines an `HtmlForm` component named `messageForm`, with a child `HtmlOutputText` named `outputMessage` and a child `HtmlCommandButton` with no assigned identifier. The `HtmlCommandButton` references the `testForm.sendMessage` event listener method, which looks like this:

```
public void sendMessage(ActionEvent e)
{
  FacesContext context  = FacesContext.getCurrentInstance();
  UIViewRoot view = context.getViewRoot();
  HtmlOutput output =
      (HtmlOutput)view.findComponent("messageForm:outputMessage");
  output.setStyle("color:blue");
  output.setValue("Who's the Mann?");
}
```

Here, we retrieve the view's root component, and then call `findComponent` using the `HtmlOutputText` component's client identifier. Then, we change its color (using a CSS style) and its value. When a user clicks the button, this method is called, and when the page is redisplayed, the `HtmlOutputText` control displays "Who's the Mann?" in blue. (Backing beans can have direct references to components, especially when generated by an IDE, so this type of lookup may not be necessary.) For more information about the `findComponent` method, see chapter 11. You also need to use client identifiers when you're writing components and renderers in order to map request parameters to component values; see chapter 15 for details.

Now that you know everything there is to know about component and client identifiers, we'll take a look at a fundamental piece of JSF you'll encounter on a daily basis: the JSF expression language.

2.4 Exploring the JSF expression language

So far, you've seen a few examples of the JSF expression language (EL)—you know, all those strings surrounded by a number sign and curly braces ("#{...}"). The main point of the EL is to allow you to reference or update bean properties, or evaluate simple statements, without writing full-fledged Java code. In JSF, expressions are generally used to associate UI component properties with backing beans or model objects in your application. They are evaluated at runtime (usually when a view is being displayed) instead of when your application is compiled.

The JSF EL is based on the EL included in JSP 2.0 (and originally created as part of the Java Standard Tag Library [JSTL] 1.0). It borrows concepts from both ECMAScript (JavaScript) and XPath (a language used to reference parts of an XML document). This means a few things. First, if you're familiar with JSP 2.0, JSTL, JavaScript, XPath, or Struts tags, then the JSF EL should be pretty straightforward. Second, in addition to the ability to reference simple properties such as in the Hello, world! example, there's a syntax for accessing items in maps, collections, and arrays. Third, the EL provides a set of implicit objects that allow you to access request parameters, HTTP headers, and the like. And finally, you can use the EL for logical and mathematical statements as well, and mix literal values with expressions.

Even though the JSF EL is based on JSP 2.0's EL, a few key differences exist:

- JSF uses the number sign (#) to mark the beginning of an expression, as opposed to a dollar sign ($).
- JSF expressions can also be *two-way*. In other words, they can either retrieve a property's value or *update* it.
- The JSF EL also allows you to reference object methods.
- Some JSP-specific features aren't available, like the page scope.
- JSF EL expressions can be evaluated using ordinary Java code (and consequently don't require JSP).
- JSP EL functions are not officially supported.

Table 2.3 lists several examples of JSF EL expressions.

Table 2.3 You can use the JSF EL to wire components to objects that expose JavaBean properties, collections, and simple data types. The EL can also be used to reference methods and create logical or numeric statements. In addition, nested properties are supported.

Example	Description
`#{myBean.value}`	Returns the `value` property of the object stored under the key `myBean`, or the element stored under the key `value` if `myBean` is a `Map`.
`#{myBean['value']}`	Same as `"{#myBean.value}"`.
`#{myArrayList[5]}`	Returns the fifth element of a `List` stored under the key `myArrayList`.
`#{myMap['foo']}`	Returns the object stored under the key `foo` from the `Map` stored under the key `myMap`.
`#{myMap[foo.bar]}`	Returns the object stored under the key that equals the value of the expression `foo.bar` from the `Map` stored under the key `myMap`.
`#{myMap['foo'].value}`	Returns the `value` property of the object stored under the key `foo` from the `Map` stored under the key `myMap`.
`#{myMap['foo'].value[5]}`	Returns the fifth element of the `List` or array stored under the key `foo` from the `Map` stored under the key `myMap`.
`#{myString}`	Returns the `String` object stored under the key `myString`.
`#{myInteger}`	Returns the `Integer` object stored under the key `myInteger`.
`#{user.role == 'normal'}`	Returns `true` if the `role` property of the object stored under the key `user` equals normal. Returns `false` otherwise.
`#{(user.balance - 200) == 0}`	If the value of the `balance` property of the object stored under the key user minus 200 equals zero, returns `true`. Returns `false` otherwise.
`Hello #{user.name}!`	Returns the string "Hello" followed by the `name` property of the object stored under the key `user`. So if the user's name is Sean, this would return "Hello Sean!"
`You are #{(user.balance > 100) ? 'loaded' : 'not loaded'}`	Returns the string "You are loaded" if the `balance` property of the object stored under the key `user` is greater than 100; returns "You are not loaded" otherwise.
`#{myBean.methodName}`	Returns the method called `method` of the object stored under the key `myBean`.
`#{20 + 3}`	Returns 23.

As the table shows, the EL is quite flexible. It can reference properties and methods, and it can also be used for arbitrary boolean and mathematical expressions. You can even mix and match text with EL expressions. It's important to realize, however, that all of the "properties" referenced by the EL must be JavaBean properties. (In other words, a property of `foo` would be implemented by the Java methods `getFoo` and `setFoo`.) To underscore this fact, we'll sometimes refer to objects referenced in EL expressions—backing beans and model objects alike—as simply *beans*.

We can discuss a few examples in the table a bit further. First, when you're using the bracket syntax (`"[]"`), you can embed another expression instead of using a boring old string. So, if you had a `Map` stored under the key `myMap` and you wanted to retrieve an object with the key `foo` from it, the expression would be `"#{myMap['foo']}"`. However, if you don't use the quotes, the text is evaluated as subexpression. So, `"#{myMap[foo]}"` is sort of like `"#{myMap[#{foo}]}"`—`foo` is evaluated first, and that result is then used as a key for `myMap`. So, if `foo` were simply a string with the value `"bar"`, the expression would have the same result as `"#{myMap['bar']}"`.

In addition, you can nest separators. Suppose `"#{myMap['foo']}"` returned a `RandomValue` object. `RandomValue` objects have a `value` property, which you can reference like so: `"#{myMap['foo'].value}"`. If the `value` property were another collection, you could access an element in the collection with `"#{myMap['foo'].value[5]}"`. You can also nest separators for subexpressions, so the expression `"#{myMap[foo.bar.baz]"` is valid as well.

As with JavaScript, you can use either single quotes (`'`) or double quotes ("). In XML-based documents like JSPs,[5] the EL expression and the tag attribute need to use different quote types. So, inside of a tag, these two statements are both valid: `"#{myBean['value']}"` and `'#{myBean ["value"]}'`. However, these two statements are invalid, because the quote types are the same: `"#{myBean ["value"]}"` and `'#{myBean ['value']}'`.

In these examples, we've only touched on some of the operators, like "." and "[]" that the EL supports. As it turns out, it supports a full range of logical and mathematical operators, as shown in table 2.4.

Table 2.4 The JSF EL supports a number of common operators.

Syntax	Alternative	Operation
.		Access a bean property, method, or `Map` entry
[]		Access an array or `List` element, or `Map` entry
()		Creates a subexpressions and controls evaluation order

continued on next page

[5] I say XML-like because JSP has both a true XML syntax (called a JSP document) and a more fluid syntax that is not truly well formed. This statement holds true for either syntax.

Table 2.4 The JSF EL supports a number of common operators. *(continued)*

Syntax	Alternative	Operation
?:		Conditional expression: `ifCondition ? trueValue : falseValue`
+		Addition
-		Subtraction and negative numbers
*		Multiplication
/	div	Division
%	mod	Modulo (remainder)
==	eq	Equals (for objects, uses the `equals()` method)
!=	ne	Not equal
<	lt	Less than
>	gt	Greater than
<=	le	Less than or equal
>=	ge	Greater than or equal
&&	and	Logical AND
||	or	Logical OR
!	not	Logical NOT
empty		Tests for an empty value (`null`, an empty `String`, or an array, `Map` or `Collection` with no values)

So far, we've been talking about expressions that evaluate to a specific property value. These types of expressions, as well as logical ones like `"#{user.demands == 'too much'}"` and mathematical ones like `"#{weather.temp / 32}"`, are considered *value-binding expressions*. Value-binding expressions can be used to associate a UI component's value with a bean property, to bind a UI component to a bean property, or to initialize a UI component's properties.

When you use the EL to reference a bean method, it's called a *method-binding expression*. Method-binding expressions, like `"#{myBean.methodName}"` are used to associate event handler or validation methods with components. Even though no arguments are required in the actual syntax, the component will assume a specific signature depending on the intended use of the method.

From now on, we'll use the specific terms value-binding expression or method-binding expression when necessary. This distinction is important if you're intending to develop JSF application code, since the EL APIs use these terms.

By now, you should have some idea about what the JSF EL looks like, how it is structured, and the kinds of things you can do with it. However, it also has some specific features that make it a harmonious citizen of the web application world. Scoped variable are an essential part of that world, and we discuss them next.

2.4.1 Understanding scoped variables

We've been talking about storing beans under a *key*. But just where are these magical beans located, and what is this key for? Remember that Java web applications have four different scopes of reference: application, session, request, and page.[6] Each one of these scopes can store arbitrary objects under a key. The different scopes are summarized in table 2.5.

Table 2.5 JSF applications support the application, session, and request scopes for referencing variables.

Web application scope	Description	Supported by JSF?
application	Variables stored in this scope are available for the entire life of the application.	Yes
session	Variables stored in this scope are available only during a user's session.	Yes
request	Variables stored in this scope are available only during the current request.	Yes
page	Variables stored in this scope are only available in the current page.	No

Application variables persist during the entire life of the web application; session variables persist during a user's visit; request variables persist while a single request is being processed; and page variables live only while a page is being rendered. Variables stored in these scopes are called *scoped variables*. In our Hello, world! application, we stored `HelloBean` in the session scope.

Because JSF components aren't necessarily tied to the JSP notion of a page, the page scope isn't supported by the EL. It will, however, search all of the other scopes for an object that matches the specified key. So the expression `"#{helloBean.numControls}"` will work properly as long as there is an object stored in the request, session, or application scopes with the key `helloBean` and the property `numControls`.

Because JSF EL expressions search ordinary Java web application scopes, they can reference the same beans as JSP or JSTL expressions, or normal Java code (through the Servlet API). This allows you to mix and match JSTL or JSP

[6] The page scope is actually specific to JSP applications.

expressions on the same JSP page with JSF tags, and generally makes it easier to integrate JSF with existing Java web applications.

In traditional Java web applications, beans are placed in one of these scopes using the raw Servlet API or custom tags (such as the JSTL tags). However, in the world of JSF, they are normally created with the managed bean creation facility or in Java code. The facility is configured in a JSF configuration file; we touched on it in chapter 1. With this facility (which we discuss in the next chapter), you can also use EL expressions to associate different objects with one another.

Now that it's clear what scoped variables are, let's see how you can reference them in the EL.

2.4.2 Using implicit variables

Implicit variables are special EL identifiers that map to specific, commonly used objects. So far, we've been accessing `HelloBean` with expressions like `"#{helloBean.numControls}"`. We know that `HelloBean` is stored in the session scope, so we could use the `sessionScope` implicit variable to reference it like this: `"#{sessionScope.helloBean.numControls}"`. With this expression, JSF will search the session scope only.

There are implicit variables for each of the scopes, but there are some other handy ones as well. They provide convenient access to the typical elements web developers need: request parameters, HTTP header values, cookies, and so on. Table 2.6 lists all of the implicit variables supported by the JSF EL.

Table 2.6 The JSF EL supports implicit variables for accessing commonly used objects. Most of the same variables are supported by the JSP 2.0 EL.

Implicit variable	Description	Example	Supported in JSP 2.0 EL?
applicationScope	A `Map` of application-scoped variables, keyed by name.	`#{application-Scope.myVariable}`	Yes
cookie	A `Map` of cookie values for the current requested, keyed by cookie name.	`#{cookie.myCookie}`	Yes
facesContext	The `FacesContext` instance for the current request.	`#{facesContext}`	No
header	A `Map` of the HTTP header values for the current request, keyed by header name. If there are multiple values for the given header name, only the first is returned.	`#{header['User-Agent']}`	Yes

continued on next page

Table 2.6 The JSF EL supports implicit variables for accessing commonly used objects. Most of the same variables are supported by the JSP 2.0 EL. *(continued)*

Implicit variable	Description	Example	Supported in JSP 2.0 EL?
headerValues	A `Map` of the HTTP header values for the current request, keyed by header name. For each key, an array of `Strings` is returned (so that all values can be accessed).	`#{headerValues['Accept-Encoding'][3]}`	Yes
initParam	A `Map` of the application initialization parameters, keyed by parameter name. (These are also known as servlet context initialization parameters, and are set in the deployment descriptor).	`#{initParam.adminEmail}`	Yes
param	A `Map` of the request parameters, keyed by header name. If there are multiple values for the given parameter name, only the first is returned.	`#{param.address}`	Yes
paramValues	A `Map` of the request parameters, keyed by header name. For each key, an array of `Strings` is returned (so that all values can be accessed).	`#{param.address[2]}`	Yes
requestScope	A `Map` of request scoped variables, keyed by name.	`#{requestScope.userPreferences}`	Yes
sessionScope	A `Map` of session scoped variables, keyed by name.	`#{sessionScope['user']}`	Yes
view	The current view.	`#{view.locale}`	No

We're not going to cover all of these variables here; if you've developed Java web applications before, most of them should be familiar to you. (As a matter of fact, the majority of them are part of the JSP 2.0 EL.) Moreover, there's generally no need to directly reference the current request or HTTP headers (other than for debugging purposes).

A couple of these variables are specific to JSF: `facesContext` and `view`. We introduced the `FacesContext` class in section 2.2. A `FacesContext` instance represents the current request that's being processed. It holds references to the current stack of application messages, the current render kit, and several other useful goodies. It's not useful in generic EL expressions, though—most of its properties weren't designed to be accessed using expressions. A more common use case for this variable is for initializing a bean property with the managed bean creation facility; see chapter 3 for details.

For front-end development, `view` has a few useful properties: `viewId`, `renderKitId`, and `locale`. These values aren't useful for display (unless you're debugging). However, theoretically you could use them in conditional expressions. For example, the expression `"#{view.renderKitId == 'HTML_BASIC'}"` returns `true` if the render kit for the current page is "HTML_BASIC" (the default).

You can also use the `locale` property, perhaps to hide or show certain components depending on the locale. For example, the expression `"#{view.locale != 'en_US'}"` returns `true` if the user speaks U.S. English. Like `facesContext`, the `view` implicit variable is a good candidate for initializing bean properties.

An important point to remember for scoped implicit variables (`requestScope`, `sessionScope`, and `applicationScope`) is that they're normally not necessary unless you're storing a variable. You can store variables using JSF EL expressions in Java code (see chapter 13 for examples).

Now that we've covered the EL syntax, application scopes, and implicit variables, we can take a closer look at how expressions are used in the world of JSF development.

2.4.3 Using the EL with components

The main reason JSF has its own expression language is so that you can dynamically associate UI components with backing beans or model objects. As a matter of fact, you can expect IDEs to help you out with this process (see figure 2.7).

By far, the most powerful use of value binding expressions is associating a bean's property with a component's value. This is how we associated the `HelloBean.numControls` property to the `HtmlInputText` component on hello.jsp in the Hello, world! example. Here's another example: Assume that we have a backing bean stored in the request scope under the key `loginForm`. We could synchronize an `HtmlInputTextArea` control's value with the bean's `comments` property like so:

```
<h:inputTextArea value="#{registrationForm.comments}"/>
```

Whenever the `HtmlInputText` component is displayed to the user, its value will be equal to the registrationForm's `comments` property. Whenever a user types something into the control and submits the form back to the web server, `registrationForm`'s `comments` property will be updated accordingly (assuming it passes validation).

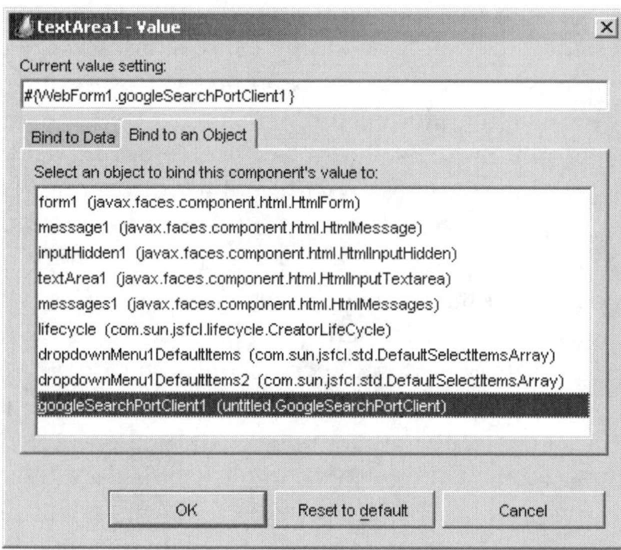

Figure 2.7
Sun's Java Studio Creator provides a dialog box to help you create value-binding expressions for objects accessible via the current backing bean.

You can use the same technique for any type of EL expression that references a bean's property, whether the property is a simple type, a complex object, a `Map`, array, or `List`:

```
<h:graphicImage value="#{user.icons[5]}">
```

In this case, this `HtmlGraphicImage` control will display an image whose URL equals the fifth element of the array or `List` returned by the `user` bean's `icons` property (the actual element is a `String` in this example). The bean could be stored in any of the valid scopes, as long as it's stored under the key `user`.

The last example underscores an important point—`user` represents a business concept, so it is a model object instead of a backing bean like `loginForm`. You can update either one with a value-binding expression, as long as the properties are implemented using JavaBean patterns.

NOTE JSF uses value-binding expressions for internationalization. A special JSP custom tag loads a resource bundle as a `Map`, so localized strings can be referenced like this: `"#{myBundle.welcomeString}"`. See chapter 6 for more about internationalization.

We've been referencing JavaBeans, but it's actually possible to associate a component's value directly with a `List`, `Map`, or a simple type like a `String` or an `Integer`, as long as it's still stored in a scope with a key. Suppose you had a single `String` stored under the key `clientName` in the application scope. You could reference it like this:

```
<h:inputText value="#{clientName}"/>
```

This would associate the control directly to the `String` with the `key` username; it would display and update the `String` directly. If JSF couldn't find an object stored under that key, it would create one and then store it in the request scope.

As we saw in the last chapter, you can also bind a component directly to a backing bean property so that the component can be manipulated in Java code. Some tools will automatically do this when they generate a backing bean class. Here's an example:

```
<h:inputText value="#{registrationForm.comments}"
             binding="#{registrationForm.nameInput}"/>
```

This example will ensure that `registrationForm's` `commentsInput` property references this `HtmlInputText` component, which allows the backing bean to manipulate its properties. Using the `binding` attribute requires that the referenced property be the same type as the component that references the property. So, in this case, the `commentsInput` property must be of type `HtmlInputText` (or one of its superclasses). The backing bean can also choose to initialize the component in its accessor method. Binding components to backing beans property is only necessary when your Java event listeners need to manipulate component properties.

We've also seen the method-binding expressions used to associate UI components with event listener methods:

```
<h:inputText value="#{registrationForm.comments}"
             binding="#{registrationForm.commentsInput}"
             valueChangeListener="#{registrationForm.commentsChanged}"/>
```

This `valueChangeListener` property accepts a method-binding expression that points to the `commentsChanged` method of `registrationForm`. This method must match the signature expected for value-change listener methods. If the value of the control changes, this method will be executed.

You can also use method-binding expressions to associate a UI component with a validator method in a backing bean:

```
<h:inputTextArea value="#{registrationForm.comments}"
                 binding="#{registrationForm.commentsInput}"
                 valueChangeListener="#{registrationForm.commentsChanged}"
                 validator="#{registrationForm.checkSpelling}"/>
```

This associates the `validator` property of this `HtmlInputText` with the `checkSpelling` method of our backing bean. `checkSpelling` must also have a specific signature.

By now, it should be obvious that you can use the EL quite a bit when you're working with UI components on a page. It's an essential part of how you associate components with the rest of the application. But, like Transformers, there's more than meets the eye. You can use value-binding expressions for *any* standard component property. And unlike the use cases we've covered so far, there are no real restrictions, as long as the object you reference is the right type (and is a JavaBean, if necessary). So, let's expand our example to use expressions for other properties:

```
<h:inputTextarea value="#{registrationForm.comments}"
                 binding="#{registrationForm.commentsInput}"
                 valueChangeListener="#{registrationForm.commentsChanged}"
                 validator="#{registrationForm.checkSpelling}"
                 styleClass="#{initParam[commentStyle]}"
                 rows="10"
                 cols="80"
                 title="#{appBundle.commentsTitle}"/>
```

There are a few points here. First, you don't always have to use expressions for component properties—you can freely mix and match them with static values, like the `size` and `width` properties in this example. Second, the expressions used with a specific component don't have to be associated with a single backing bean. For example, the `styleClass` property references a `commentStyle` initialization parameter, which was set in the web application's deployment descriptor. And the `title` property references an `appBundle` object, which is a Java resource bundle that provides localized strings. So the `commentsTitle` property will return a string that's tailored for the user's language. (Resource bundles and internationalization are covered in chapter 6.)

If you're wondering how all this ties to the non-JSP world, don't worry—the APIs for value-binding and method-binding expressions are fully exposed at the Java level. As a matter of fact, it's quite likely you'll *need* to work with them at the Java level—see parts 3 and 4 for examples.

The JSF EL is a fundamental part of JSF application development. You'll see many more examples throughout the rest of this book.

2.5 Summary

Like every technology, JSF has its own lingo—terms and concepts that are make sense when you're developing JSF applications. In this chapter, we examined these fundamental concepts—UI components, renderers, validators, backing beans, converters, events and listeners, messages, and navigation.

UI components, like buttons, text boxes, and panels, are central to JSF—they are full-fledged Java objects that live on the server, but can be displayed to clients in different ways. All UI components have a component identifier, but when they are displayed to a client, a client identifier is used instead. UI components are often displayed by renderers, which also collect input from the user. Renderers are organized into render kits that are usually focused on specific markup like HTML or WML, or a variation of a markup, like a "skin."

User input is collected with backing beans, which can be associated with UI component values, and also handle events. You can also associate component instances with backing beans, which allows you to manipulate them in Java code. These associations are performed by the JSF expression language, which is based on the JSP 2.0 and JSTL expression languages. In addition, the outcome of backing bean action methods is used to control JSF's declarative navigation, which associates those outcomes to specific pages.

The magic of translating an HTTP request into events and updating server-side component values occurs when JSF handles a request—a process called the Request Processing Lifecycle. This lifecycle has six phases: Restore View, Apply Request Values, Process Validations, Update Model Values, Invoke Application, and Render Response.

That's it for the fundamentals of JavaServer Faces. Next, we'll examine configuration, navigation, and the Managed Bean Creation facility, among other things.

3 Warming up: getting around JSF

This chapter covers

- Requirements for building JSF applications
- Application configuration
- Using JSF with JSTL and other JSP custom tags
- Using the Managed Beans Creation facility
- Setting up navigation

When you begin learning how to drive a car, you know the general concept of driving, and you know that every car has things like brakes, headlights, and of course a stereo. But before you speed out of the cul-de-sac, someone normally points out exactly where these things are and how to use them (well, maybe not the stereo). Otherwise, you could easily forget about the parking brake, turn on your brights instead of your normal headlights, brake incorrectly, and generally cause a lot of mayhem.

This chapter covers those little details about JavaServer Faces that would be good to know before you dive into developing a full-fledged JSF application. Covering them now will ensure that you don't waste time later.

3.1 Setting up your JSF environment

So far, we've said a lot about what Faces is and what it does. If you're into details, you may have some additional questions about exactly who provides JSF implementations, what libraries are required, and how configuration works. In the following sections, we'll look into what it takes to get a JSF application up and running.

3.1.1 Basic requirements

As we mentioned in chapter 1, all JSF applications are standard Java web applications, as defined by the Servlet API. This means that they require an installed version of a standard web container like Apache Tomcat [ASF, Tomcat] or New Atlanta's ServletExec [New Atlanta, Servlet-Exec], or a J2EE server like IBM WebSphere Application Server [IBM, WAS], Oracle Application Server [Oracle, AS], or BEA WebLogic [BEA, WebLogic]. For simplicity, we'll refer to them all as web containers.

JSF applications also require that you have installed an implementation of the framework. A JSF implementation is simply compiled Java code that adheres to the JSP specification [Sun, JSF Spec]. All implementations require a web container that supports version 2.3 of the Java Servlet specification [Sun, Servlet] or higher, and version 1.2 of the JSP specification [Sun, JSP] or higher. The examples in this book were developed using Tomcat 5.0.

3.1.2 Choosing a JSF implementation

In order to develop JSF applications, you need a JSF implementation. The reference implementation (RI) is the standard that all other implementations should be measured against (at least in terms of compliance to the specification)—it was developed in conjunction with the specification itself. The RI is freely available with the source code,[1] and will always support the latest version of the specification. All of the examples in this book were developed with version 1.0 of the RI [Sun, JSF RI].

Some J2EE vendors ship their own implementations of JSF, which will most likely have extra features and performance enhancements. Vendors who support JSF (such as IBM, Oracle, Sun, and Borland) will also bundle JSF implementations with their IDEs, and usually give you an option to deploy that implementation into whichever web container you're using. Both Oracle and IBM will be providing JSF implementations in some versions of their IDEs as well as their application servers. If you're currently using a newer version of a J2EE server or IDE that has a complete, stable JSF implementation, you may as well use it. In other words, no additional work is required to begin developing JSF applications.

If, on the other hand, you're using a web container or IDE that doesn't have a JSF implementation (or you're not interested in upgrading to one that does), then the RI is the simplest choice. There are other stand-alone implementations, though, and these can offer advantages such as speed, access to source code, and richer sets of components. These include open-source implementations like MyFaces [MyFaces] and Smile [Smile], and older user interface (UI) frameworks that have announced JSF support, like Kobrix Software's Tag Interface Component Library [Kobrix].

3.1.3 Directory structure

Because JSF applications are standard Java web applications, all of the necessary files must be packaged in a directory structure that is deployed in your web container. Usually, you'll create the physical directory structure (often with a tool) for development and testing, and then deploy it with a web archive (WAR) or enterprise archive (EAR).

The basic directory structure for a JSF application is shown in figure 3.1. As you can see, there are only two special additions: the JAR files for your JSF implementation, and the faces-config.xml file (which is where you typically place all JSF configuration, much like struts-config.xml in Struts applications). Let's take a closer look at what JAR files are used in a typical JSF implementation.

---

[1] The RI has recently been released for "open development" using the Sun Java Research License [Sun, JRL]. Essentially, this means that the source and binaries will be available for free, and you can modify and distribute the source as long as you don't do so commercially, or use it productively internally. If you modify the binaries or the source code for commercial or productive internal use, you must use a commercial license and pass the JSF technology compatibility kit (TCK). You can also submit patches to the JSF RI source code base, and the RI development team plans to accept committers in late 2004.

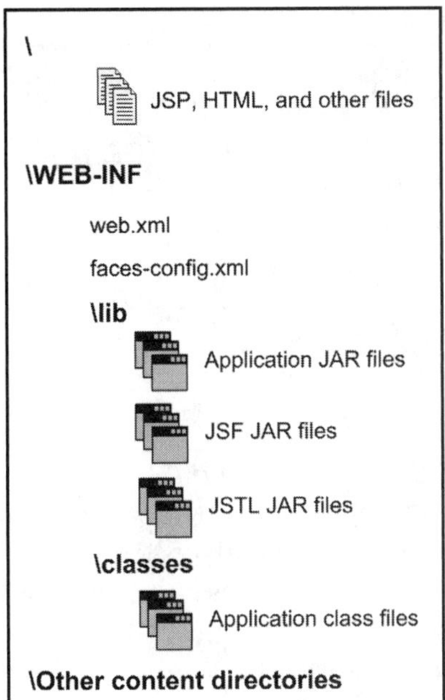

Figure 3.1 Standard directory structure for JSF applications

JSF libraries

One of the main reasons the Java community has different implementations is so that they can compete with added features. Consequently, the actual libraries that a given JSF implementation requires can vary depending on what features have been added. There are, however, a few specific Java archives (JARs) that are required for all JSF applications; these are listed in table 3.1. If you're using an IDE or web container that ships with a JSF implementation, you shouldn't have to worry about them.

Table 3.1 Required JAR files for all JSF applications

Filename in RI	Required? (Name may be different)	Description
jsf-api.jar	Yes	The JSF API classes that are defined in the JSF specification
jsf-impl.jar	Yes	Implementation-specific JSF classes
commons-beanutils.jar	No	Apache Commons bean utilities, for manipulating JavaBeans

continued on next page

Table 3.1 Required JAR files for all JSF applications *(continued)*

Filename in RI	Required? (Name may be different)	Description
commons-collections.jar	No	Apache Commons collections
commons-digester.jar	No	Apache Commons digester, for parsing XML files
commons-logging.jar	No	Apache Commons logging
jstl.jar	Yes	JSTL API classes
standard.jar	Yes	JSTL implementation classes

The most important thing to note is that JSF depends on the JSTL libraries. This doesn't mean that you have to use JSTL in your application, however. If you're using the RI, the JSTL [Sun, JSTL] libraries aren't included, so you may need to download them if your development tool or web container doesn't already have them installed.

Also, note that these names are not required—for example, the MyFaces open-source implementation [MyFaces] currently uses the name myfaces.jar instead of jsf-impl.jar. These files are usually packaged with your web application (in the WEB-INF/lib directory).

Currently, the RI doesn't officially support installation of the JSF libraries as shared classes in your web container. (Shared classes are stored in a single place and made available to all of the web applications in a container; in Tomcat, they are placed is the common/lib directory.) Other JSF implementations may not have this limitation; check the documentation for details.

Once you have a JSF implementation and a web application setup, it's time to move on to configuration.

3.1.4 Configuration

As with all Java web applications, configuration begins with the web application deployment descriptor. In addition, Faces has its own extensive configuration system that supports a range of additional features.

Servlet configuration

JSF applications require a servlet, called `FacesServlet`, which acts as a front controller for the entire application (see chapter 1 for more information on the Model-View-Controller design pattern and controllers). Because servlets are configured in a web application's deployment descriptor file (web.xml), it's no surprise that this is where the JSF servlet must be defined (tools will usually handle this for you when you create a new JSF application). You might remember from our Hello, world! example that we only need to do two things: define the servlet and add a mapping for it. Often you can do this with your IDE's web application configuration editor, but here's an example of the XML:

```
<web-app>
  ...
  <servlet>
    <servlet-name>Faces Servlet</servlet-name>
    <servlet-class>javax.faces.webapp.FacesServlet</servlet-class>
  </servlet>
  <servlet-mapping>
    <servlet-name>Faces Servlet</servlet-name>
    <url-pattern>/faces/*</url-pattern>
  </servlet-mapping>
  ...
</web-app>
```

This example defines a servlet called `Faces Servlet` with the class `javax.faces.webapp.FacesServlet`. You can name the servlet anything you want, but this class name is required. It also maps all requests that start with "/faces/" to this servlet. So, any request to a URL like http://www.sumatra.com/faces/mypage.jsp will be handled by JSF. Mapping the JSF servlet to a URL pattern like this is called *prefix mapping*. You can also specify suffix mapping:

```
<servlet-mapping>
  <servlet-name>Faces Servlet</servlet-name>
  <url-pattern>*.faces<url-pattern>
</servlet-mapping>
```

With *suffix mapping* (also called extension mapping), any page requested with the extension .faces will be handled by the JSF servlet. Your actual pages can use a configurable default suffix (like .jsp). JSF will always look for the filename with the default suffix. So, for example, if you request a resource with the URL http://www.mrcat.org/mypage.faces, the servlet will handle the request with mypage.jsp (assuming that .jsp is your default suffix). For both prefix and suffix mapping, use of the word "faces" is recommended, but you can certainly use something else if you don't want the world to know what technology you're using.

There are also a few JSF-specific parameters that can be configured in web.xml. We cover them next.

Web application parameters

Web applications support application-level parameters via the `<context-param>` element in web.xml. You can use these parameters internally in your own application (a database connection string is a common example), but other libraries that your application uses, like JSF, can use them as well.

Different JSF implementations are likely to have all sorts of parameters to try and differentiate themselves in the marketplace. However, the specification only requires a few parameters, as shown in table 3.2. All of them are optional.

Table 3.2 JSF application configuration parameters

Context Parameter	Description	Default
`javax.faces.CONFIG_FILES`	Comma-delimited list of context-relative JSF configuration resource paths that JSF will load before it loads WEB-INF/faces-config.xml	None
`javax.faces.DEFAULT_SUFFIX`	Default suffix for resources to load when extension mapping is in use	`.jsp`
`javax.faces.LIFECYCLE_ID`	Identifier for the Lifecycle instance to be used when processing JSF requests within this application	The default Lifecycle instance
`javax.faces.STATE_SAVING_METHOD`	Indicates whether to save the state of UI components on the client side (`client`) or server side (`server`)	`server`

The `javax.faces.CONFIG_FILES` parameter contains a comma-delimited list of JSF application configuration files to load. This is useful for cases when your application has several configuration files (perhaps maintained by different teams, or segemented in some other way). See the next section for more information about configuration files.

In the previous section, we talked about suffix mapping, and how JSF uses a default suffix to load the actual page. You configure this suffix with the `javax.faces.DEFAULT_SUFFIX` parameter. The default is .jsp, so if that's what you're using, there's no need to use this parameter. However, if you're using another display technology with a different extension, you would use this parameter.

The `javax.faces.LIFECYCLE_ID` parameter is pretty advanced. It specifies the Lifecycle identifier, which affects the way JSF performs the Request Processing Lifecycle. You won't need to change it in most cases. (See online extension appendix C for more information about how to modify JSF's core functionality.)

JSF has the ability to store the state of the components on a page so that if the page is redisplayed, it remembers the values that the user entered. Component state can either be stored on the client or the server, and this is controlled with the `javax.faces.STATE_SAVING_METHOD` parameter. The possible values are `client` and `server` (the default). Saving state on the client results in less of a load on the server at the expense of additional network traffic (by default, client state is stored as a large hidden `<input>` field in web browsers, much like ASP.NET's view state). Saving state on the client also works better in failover situations because even if the server is down, the state won't be lost. In general, you should make sure your application works with both settings because the person responsible for production configuration may change the parameter at some point.

NOTE If your JSF application saves its state on the server, there is no way for it to know that a view has expired. So if a JSP page changes between requests (possibly because you edited it), there may be inconsistencies between the restored view and the JSP page. In order to avoid this problem, you can either restart the browser or restart your application (so that the session is lost, and JSF will automatically reconstruct the view). The upshot is that it's better to develop with your application configured to save state on the client so that you can avoid this problem.

Here's an example of a configuration file that uses a couple of these parameters:

```
<web-app>
  ...
  <context-param>
    <param-name>javax.faces.STATE_SAVING_METHOD</param-name>
    <param-value>server</param-value>
  </context-param>
  <context-param>
    <param-name>javax.faces.CONFIG_FILES</param-name>
    <param-value>/WEB-INF/navigation.xml,/WEB-INF/RegistrationWizard.xml</
  param-value>
  </context-param>
  ...
<web-app>
```

This tells JSF to save the state on the server, and to look for two additional configuration files: /WEB-INF/navigation.xml and /WEB-INF/RegistrationWizard.xml.

Just so you can get an idea of what additional parameters JSF implementations might provide, tables 3.3 and 3.4 list the parameters for the RI [Sun, JSF RI] and MyFaces [MyFaces].

Table 3.3 RI-specific configuration parameters

Context Parameter	Description	Default
`com.sun.faces.NUMBER_OF_VIEWS_IN_SESSION`	Controls the number of views that are saved in the session when the state saving method is set to `server`	N/A
`com.sun.faces.validateXml`	Tells JSF to validate configuration files against the DTD	`false`
`com.sun.faces.verifyObjects`	Tells JSF to verify that it can create application objects (components, renderers, converters, and so on)	`false`

Now that we've conquered the standard web deployment descriptor, let's take a look at the vast world of JSF-specific configuration.

JSF application configuration

Like many web application frameworks, JSF's configuration information provides a map for your entire application. It handles things like navigation rules, managed beans, and internationalization details. But JSF configuration does a lot more, too. It defines all aspects of the framework—components, renderers, validators, converters, and just about everything else you can think of.

Don't worry, though—you don't need to personally configure all of these things. You only need to worry about the configuration aspects that pertain to the type of work you're doing. Configuration can be broadly partioned into three areas: everyday application development, UI extension development (writing components, renderers, converters, or validators), and advanced development.

Table 3.4 MyFaces-specific configuration parameters[a]

Context Parameter	Description	Default
`myfaces_allow_javascript`	True if components should allow JavaScript	`true`
`myfaces_pretty_html`	Specifies whether or not displayed HTML will be formatted so that it's "human readable" (additional line separators and whitespace will be written that don't influence the HTML code).	`true`
`myfaces_allow_designmode`	Implements design mode using CGLib binary class changes	`false`

[a] *Because open source moves at the speed of lightning (or the speed of molasses, depending on the project), these parameters could change by the time this book is printed.*

So, if you're building an application, you'll be interested in application-oriented details like navigation. If you're developing components, you'll want to know how to register components and renderers. And if you're performing advanced work, like integrating JSF with an existing application or framework, you'll want to learn about configuring pluggable services or factories.

Like most web application frameworks, JSF requires an XML file, called an *application configuration file*. We saw a simple version of this file in the Hello, world! application in chapter 1. If you're not fond of editing XML files, tools are available to help you out. There's a freely available configuration file editor, called the Faces Console [Holmes], that plugs into many popular IDEs and also runs as a stand-alone application (see figure 3.2). Some products, like Sun's Java Studio Creator [Sun, Creator], provide powerful visual editors for some aspects of configuration, such as navigation. You can also expect some IDE vendors to provide direct support for basic JSF configuration elements, as they have for Struts.

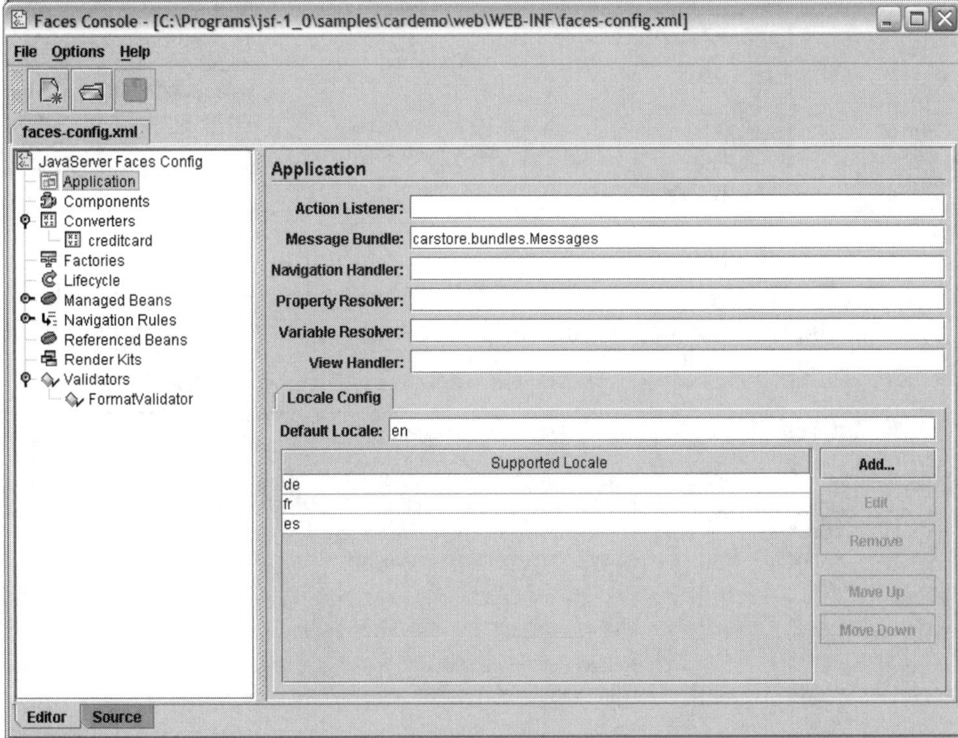

Figure 3.2 James Holmes' Faces Console [Holmes] allows you to visually edit JSF application configuration files.

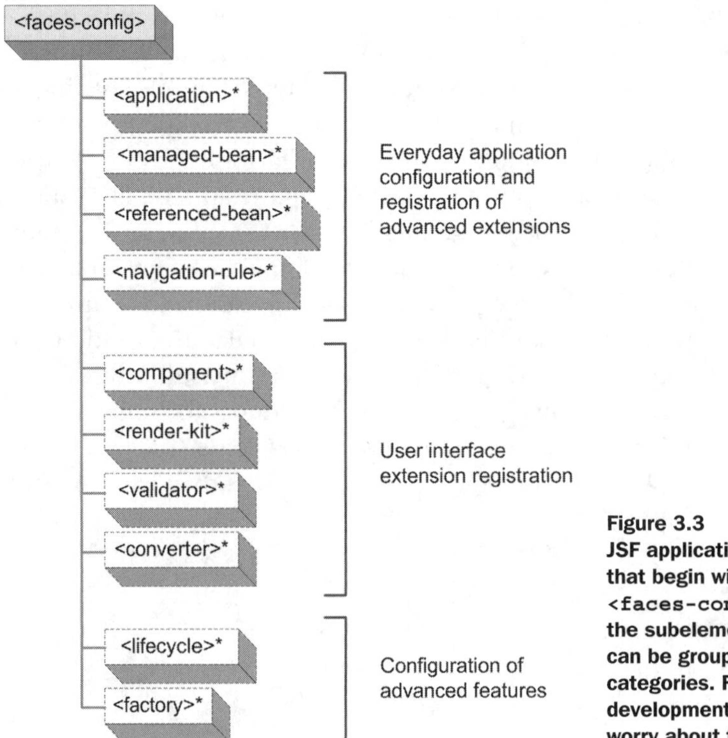

Figure 3.3
JSF application files are XML files that begin with a top-level `<faces-config>` element. All of the subelements are optional, and can be grouped into three major categories. For day-to-day development, you only have to worry about the first category.

All of the elements in an application configuration file are nested under the `<faces-config>` element. Table 3.5 lists the top-level child elements, broken down by the three major categories. The structure is graphically depicted in figure 3.3.

Table 3.5 The three main configuration categories with corresponding XML elements

Category	Feature	XML Element
Everyday application configuration and registration of advanced extensions	Application configuration. Used for specifying supported languages, the location of customized application messages, the default render kit, and advanced pluggable components.	`<application>`
	Managed bean creation facility. Controls automatic creation of objects in a particular scope.	`<managed-bean>`
	Referenced beans. Used to tell an IDE about other objects that may become available.	`<referenced-bean>`
	Navigation rules. Controls flow of application from one page to the next.	`<navigation-rule>`

continued on next page

Table 3.5 The three main configuration categories with corresponding XML elements *(continued)*

Category	Feature	XML Element
User interface extension registration	Component registration. Used to register components with system.	`<component>`
	Render kit and renderer registration. Used to either add renderers to the default render kit or define entirely new render kits.	`<render-kit>`
	Validator registration. Used to register validators with the system.	`<validator>`
	Converter registration. Used to register converters with the system.	`<converter>`
Configuration of advanced features	Phase listener registration. Registers phase listeners for use with the system.	`<phase-listener>`
	Factory configuration. Defines classes for the factories that instantiate the core JSF classes.	`<factory>`

Even though you can define several elements in the configuration file, you'll generally only worry about navigation, managed beans, internationalization, and sometimes UI extensions. As an example, listing 3.1 shows parts of the configuration file included with the RI's CarDemo application. This file also configures a custom validator and a custom converter.

Listing 3.1 Selected portions of the reference implementation CarDemo sample application

```
<?xml version="1.0"?>
<!DOCTYPE faces-config PUBLIC
  "-//Sun Microsystems, Inc.//DTD JavaServer Faces Config 1.0//EN"
  "http://java.sun.com/dtd/web-facesconfig_1_0.dtd">       Configuration
                                                            DTD
<faces-config>
  <application>
    <message-bundle>carstore.bundles.Messages</message-bundle>
    <locale-config>                                          Locales and
      <default-locale>en</default-locale>                    message
      <supported-locale>de</supported-locale>                bundle
      <supported-locale>fr</supported-locale>
      <supported-locale>es</supported-locale>
    </locale-config>
  </application>

  <validator>              Custom
    <description>          validator
```

```
      Registers the concrete Validator implementation,
      carstore.FormatValidator with the validator
      identifier, FormatValidator.
    </description>
    <validator-id>FormatValidator</validator-id>
    <validator-class>carstore.FormatValidator</validator-class>
    <attribute>
      <description>
        List of format patterns separated by '|'.  The validator
        compares these patterns against the data entered in a
        component that has this validator registered on it.
      </description>
      <attribute-name>formatPatterns</attribute-name>
      <attribute-class>java.lang.String</attribute-class>
    </attribute>
  </validator>

  <converter>
    <description>
      Registers the concrete Converter implementation,
      carstore.CreditCardConverter using the ID,
      creditcard.
    </description>
    <converter-id>creditCardConverter</converter-id>
    <converter-class>carstore.CreditCardConverter</converter-class>
  </converter>

...

  <managed-bean>
    <description>
      Causes the default VariableResolver implementation to instantiate
      the managed bean, CustomerBean of the class, carstore.CustomerBean
      in session scope if the bean does not already exist in any scope.
    </description>
    <managed-bean-name> customer </managed-bean-name>
    <managed-bean-class> carstore.CustomerBean </managed-bean-class>
    <managed-bean-scope> session </managed-bean-scope>
  </managed-bean>
  <managed-bean>
    <description>
      The main backing file bean
    </description>
    <managed-bean-name> carstore </managed-bean-name>
    <managed-bean-class> carstore.CarStore </managed-bean-class>
    <managed-bean-scope> session </managed-bean-scope>
  </managed-bean>

  <navigation-rule>
    <from-view-id>/chooseLocale.jsp</from-view-id>
    <navigation-case>
```

Custom validator

Custom converter

Managed beans

Navigation rules

```
      <description>
        Any action on chooseLocale should cause navigation to storeFront.jsp
      </description>
      <from-outcome>storeFront</from-outcome>
      <to-view-id>/storeFront.jsp</to-view-id>
    </navigation-case>
  </navigation-rule>
  <navigation-rule>
    <from-view-id>/storeFront.jsp</from-view-id>              Navigation
    <navigation-case>                                              rules
      <description>
        Any action that returns "carDetail" on storeFront.jsp should
        cause navigation to carDetail.jsp
      </description>
      <from-outcome>carDetail</from-outcome>
      <to-view-id>/carDetail.jsp</to-view-id>
    </navigation-case>
  </navigation-rule>
  ...
</faces-config>
```

We won't delve into the specifics of each element here. Because configuration is an integral part of developing with JSF, you'll see more examples and descriptions throughout this book. And, for reference purposes, the entire document type definition (DTD) is explained in online extension appendix D.

NOTE Depending on your JSF implementation, you may have to reload your application (or redeploy your WAR file) for configuration changes to take effect. (This is true for the reference implementation, for instance.)

It's important to point out that JSF can support *several* configuration files. By default, it will look for a file named WEB-INF/faces-config.xml, and indeed this is where you'll put most of your application configuration. You can also specify additional files with the `javax.faces.CONFIG_FILES` context parameter (described in the previous section). This can be useful in cases where you want to segment your configuration for easier maintenance. For example, two different teams might be working on different modules that have different configuration files. JSF will also search for configuration files named META-INF/faces-config.xml in JAR files (or any other resource path); this allows you to create libraries of components, renderers, validators, and/or converters that are automatically registered by your application.

WARNING Configuration file errors will cause an application to fail during startup. In other words, your application will not run unless all of its configuration files are error-free.

Now that we've taken a look at how configuration works in JSF applications, let's do the same for JavaServer Pages (JSP).

3.2 The role of JSP

As we've said before, JSF applications require some sort of display technology, such as JSP. One of the cool things about JSP is the ability to extend it with custom tags. A *custom tag* is a special XML element, backed by Java code, that can be used in addition to standard JSP elements or HTML elements. A custom tag can do almost anything: display the value of variables, parse XML, conditionally display parts of a page, access a database, and so on.[2] Their main purpose is to keep Java code out of the pages and allow front-end developers to use simple, familiar tags instead. A group of related custom tags forms a *tag library*.

JSF is integrated with JSP using custom tags. All of the JSF tags we've shown so far—`<h:inputText>`, `<h:outputText>`, `<h:form>`, `<f:view>`, and so on—are custom tags. JSF implementations must support JSP with custom tag libraries that provide access to all of the standard components, renderers, validators, and converters. These libraries (included in the JSF JARs) are listed in table 3.6.

All of the tags in these libraries must be named and implemented in a specific manner. This way, your JSP-based applications are guaranteed to be portable across different JSF implementations. Most IDEs, including all of the ones featured in this book, can be used with JSP.

Table 3.6 JSF custom tag libraries

URI	Name	Common Prefix	Description
http://java.sun.com/jsf/core	Core	f	Contains tags that are independent of a particular render kit (like `<f:view>`, `<validator>`, and so on)
http://java.sun.com/jsf/html	HTML	h	Contains tags for all of the standard components and the HTML render kit

[2] Whether or not anyone should be doing all of these things with JSP tags is a question for another day…

Because JSP is the only display technology required for all implementations, we use it for examples throughout this book. If you're not using JSP, don't fret—most of the concepts we present aren't wedded to a specific display technology, and you can read about alternatives in appendix A.

For the most part, using JSF with JSP is just a matter of using the JSF custom tag libraries. There are, however, some nuances you should be aware of, like using JSP includes.

3.2.1 Using JSP includes

One of JSP's key features is the ability to integrate content from multiple JSPs into a single page. This is often used for fun tasks like including a header or a footer. JSP supports two types of includes: dynamic and static. *Dynamic includes* (performed with the `<jsp:include>` tag or the JSTL `<c:import>` tag) access a resource at runtime. In this case, control is forwarded to the included JSP. The response from the included JSP is merged with the response sent back from the calling page. When changes are made to a dynamically included page, they automatically show up in all calling pages.

Static includes integrate the resource at translation time—when the page is morphed into Java code and compiled. The contents of the source page are essentially copied into the calling page. Changes made to the included content generally aren't automatically noticed by calling pages because they already have their own copy of the content. They have to be "touched" so that they can be recompiled with the new content. (JSP 2.0's implicit includes, which can be configured in web.xml, are processed like static includes.)

JSF works with both types of JSP includes. For dynamic includes, there are two requirements:

- Included pages must be enclosed in a JSF `<f:subview>` core tag. This tag can either be in the included page or around the include statement.
- All template text and non-JSF tags inside included pages should be enclosed with the JSF `<f:verbatim>` core tag.

So, let's say we had the following snippet in a JSP page:

```
<f:view>
...
 <jsp:include page="foo.jsp"/>
...
</f:view>
```

Foo.jsp might look like this:

```
<f:subview>
   <h:outputText value="heyah!"/>
    ...
    <f:verbatim>
      <b>Template text.</b>
      <customtag:dothis/>
    </f:verbatim>
</f:subview>
```

As you can see, the entire included page is enclosed in a `<f:subview>` tag, and all non-JSF tags and template text are enclosed in a `<f:verbatim>` tag. Alternatively, we could move the `<f:subview>` tag into the first page, around the `<jsp:include>` tag.

Using a static include is much simpler. There are no restrictions—you don't even have to use the `<f:subview>` tag.

In the last example, we showed a fictitious custom tag, `<customtag:dothis>`, that performs some random task. This underscores an important point: you can use JSF with other JSP custom tags.

3.2.2 Using JSF with JSTL and other JSP custom tags

All of this talk about JSF's custom tag libraries is nice, but what if you have your own custom tags, or third-party ones? Or what if you're using the JSP Standard Template Library (JSTL), which is a set of standard tags that do all of those neat things we just mentioned? For the most part, you can mix and match them with JSF tags. Faces tags can be nested within other tags, and vice versa. Some products, like IBM's WebSphere Application Developer [IBM, WSAD], encourage this approach, while others, like Sun's Java Creator Studio [Sun, Creator], opt for a pure JSF approach. Oracle's JDeveloper [Oracle, JDeveloper], on the other hand, lets you mix and match, but also encourages the pure JSF approach.

> **NOTE** Whenever you nest a JSF tag inside a non-JSF custom tag, you must assign the JSF tag a component identifier (see the previous chapter for more information on component identifiers).

Because JSTL is standard and familiar to many, we'll use it to demonstrate the use of JSF with custom tags. (If you're thirsty for general information on JSTL, check out Shawn Bayern's excellent book, *JSTL in Action* [Bayern].) Let's start with the simple example (shown in listing 3.2) that mixes and matches some JSTL tags with JSF tags. This code imports both JSF tag libraries and the core JSTL tag libraries.

Listing 3.2 Mixing JSTL tags with JSF tags

```
<%@ taglib uri="http://java.sun.com/jsf/core" prefix="f" %>
<%@ taglib uri="http://java.sun.com/jsf/html" prefix="h" %>
<%@ taglib uri="http://java.sun.com/jstl/core" prefix="c" %>

<html>
<head>
  <title>JSF in Action: JSTL Example 1 - Mixing JSF with other custom tags</
   title>
</head>
<body bgcolor="#FFFFFF">

  <f:view>
    <h1>
      <h:outputText value="Example of using JSF tags with other custom
tags"/>
    </h1>
    <p>
      <b>
        <c:out value="Here's the value of your web.xml (don't do this at
home):"/>
      </b>
      <blockquote>
        <f:verbatim>
          <c:import url="WEB-INF/web.xml"/>
        </f:verbatim>
      </blockquote>
    </p>
  </f:view>

</body>
</html>
```

Import of JSF tag libraries (lines 1–2); Import of JSTL core library (line 3); JSF view (`<f:view>`); JSTL tag (`<c:out>`); JSTL tag (`<c:import>`).

In this example, both JSTL and JSF tags are nested within the JSF `<f:view>` tag, which defines the start of the JSF component tree. The example uses the JSF `HtmlOutputText` component (`<h:outputText>`) and the JSTL `<c:out>` tag to display text. A JSTL `<c:import>` tag includes the system's web.xml file in the page (this isn't exactly something you want to share with others, so don't do this on a real server). Because web.xml is an XML file, the `<c:import>` tag is nested in a `<f:verbatim>` tag, which is a JSF `UIOutput` component whose renderer escapes the XML so it can be displayed normally in an HTML page. This example doesn't do much, but it does demonstrate the ability to use different tags on the same page together.

Note that we nested a JSTL tag inside the JSF `<f:verbatim>` tag. In general, it's easier to nest JSF tags inside other tags than vice versa. As a matter of fact, any component that displays its own children, like `HtmlDataTable` and `HtmlPanelGrid`, require that any template text or nested tags be within a `<f:verbatim>` tag. (The `<f:verbatim>` tag is covered in chapter 4.)

What's great about using JSTL tags with JSF tags is that they both use similar expression languages to reference objects (this is true for JSP 2.0's expression language as well). This allows you to easily share data between JSTL and JSF tags in an intuitive manner. To illustrate this point, let's look at another example that allows the user to input a number into an `HtmlInputText` control and then uses that value to display a string repeatedly with a JSTL `<c:forEach>` tag. This code is shown in listing 3.3.

Listing 3.3 Using JSF and JSTL tags together with the same backing bean

```
...
<f:view>
  <jsp:useBean class="org.jia.examples.TestForm" id="exampleBean
             scope="session"/>

  <h1>
   <h:outputText value="Example of using JSF and JSTL expression languages"/>
  </h1>

  <h:form>
    <h:outputLabel for="inputInt">
      <h:outputText value="How many times do you want to repeat
                        the Oracle's prophecy?"/>
    </h:outputLabel>

    <h:inputText id="inputInt"
           value="#{sessionScope.exampleBean.number}"/>
    <h:commandButton value="Go!"/>
    <p>
       <c:if test="${sessionScope.exampleBean.number > 0}">
         <c:forEach begin="0" end="${sessionScope.exampleBean.number - 1}"
                    var="count">
            Queen Tracey will achieve world domination.<br>
         </c:forEach>
       </c:if>
    </p>
  </h:form>
...
</f:view>
...
```

Annotations: **Ordinary JSP tag** (jsp:useBean); **HtmlInputText linked to backing bean** (h:inputText); **JSTL tags that control number of iterations** (c:if / c:forEach).

WARNING If you're using JSP or JSTL expressions with managed beans, you need to ensure that the beans have been created first, either by a JSF expression, Java code, or your own custom tag. This is because these older expression languages don't know about JSF's Managed Bean Creation facility. (See section 3.3 for more about creating managed beans.)

This listing references a JavaBean, called `exampleBean`, that has a `number` property of type `int`. An `HtmlInputText` component is used to update the value of the bean's property based on user input. When the user clicks the Go! button (an `HtmlCommandButton` component), the `number` property is updated and the page is redisplayed. When this happens, the JSTL `<c:forEach>` tag repeats the text displayed by a JSTL `<c:out>` tag `exampleBean.number` times. The `<c:forEach>` tag only executes if `exampleBean.number` is greater than 0; this is controlled by a JSTL `<c:if>` tag.

You *cannot* use JSF component tags inside tags that iterate over their body, like the JSTL `<c:forEach>` tag. The recommended workaround is to use the `HtmlDataTable` component or another component iterates over a data set or collection.

In this example, there are no JSF components nested inside the JSTL `<c:if>` tag. But what happens if a component is displayed once and then hidden by a conditional tag like `<c:if>` when the page is redisplayed? The first time the component is displayed, it will be added to the view. The second time, if the `<c:if>` tag doesn't display the component, JSF will delete it from the view. This means that any input controls will lose their local values, and that you won't be able to reference these components (via client identifiers or in code). As an example, take a look at listing 3.4, which is from the same page as listing 3.3.

The JSTL `<c:if>` tag will execute its body if the value of `exampleBean.number` is greater than 10. If the body is executed, then all of the nested components will be added to the view and displayed. If not, the components will be removed (if they have been added previously). This is shown graphically in figure 3.4. Figure 3.5 shows the output of the JSP page used for listings 3.3 and 3.4.

Listing 3.4 Conditionally displaying JSF components with JSTL tags

```
...
<h:form>
   <h:outputText value="If you entered a number greater than 10,
                        two input controls will display below."/>
    <p>
      <c:if test="${sessionScope.exampleBean.number > 10}">
        <h:outputLabel id="inputStringLabel"for="inputString">
          <h:outputText id="outputStringLabel"
```

```
                         value="Enter in your string. JSF will remember the
    value unless this control is hidden."/>
        </h:outputLabel>
        <h:inputText id="inputString"/>
        <h:commandButton value="Go!"/>
      </c:if>
    </p>
  </h:form>
  ...
```

You can achieve the same effect as the code in listing 3.4 by placing these components in an `HtmlPanelGroup` and setting its `rendered` property to equal the same expression. An `HtmlPanelGroup` is used as a container for multiple components. Here's an example:

```
<h:panelGroup rendered="#{sessionScope.exampleBean.number > 10}">
   <h:outputLabel id="inputStringLabel2"for="inputString">
     <h:outputText id="outputStringLabel2" value="Enter in your string. JSF
   will remember the value."/>
     </h:outputLabel>
   <h:inputText id="inputString2"/>
   <h:commandButton value="Go!"/>
</h:panelGroup>
```

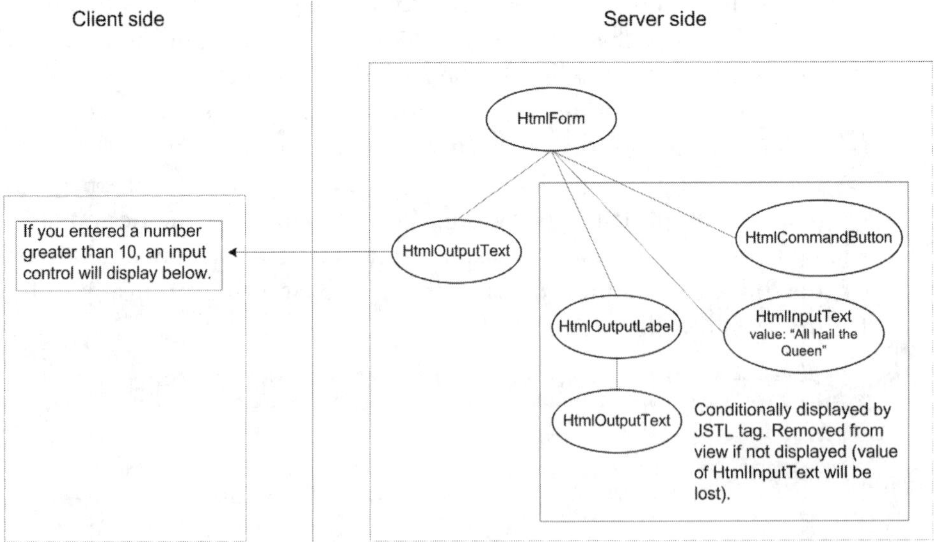

Figure 3.4 If you control visibility of components with JSTL conditional tags (or other custom tags), the components will be removed from the view if they're not displayed. This means that the components will forget their local values as well.

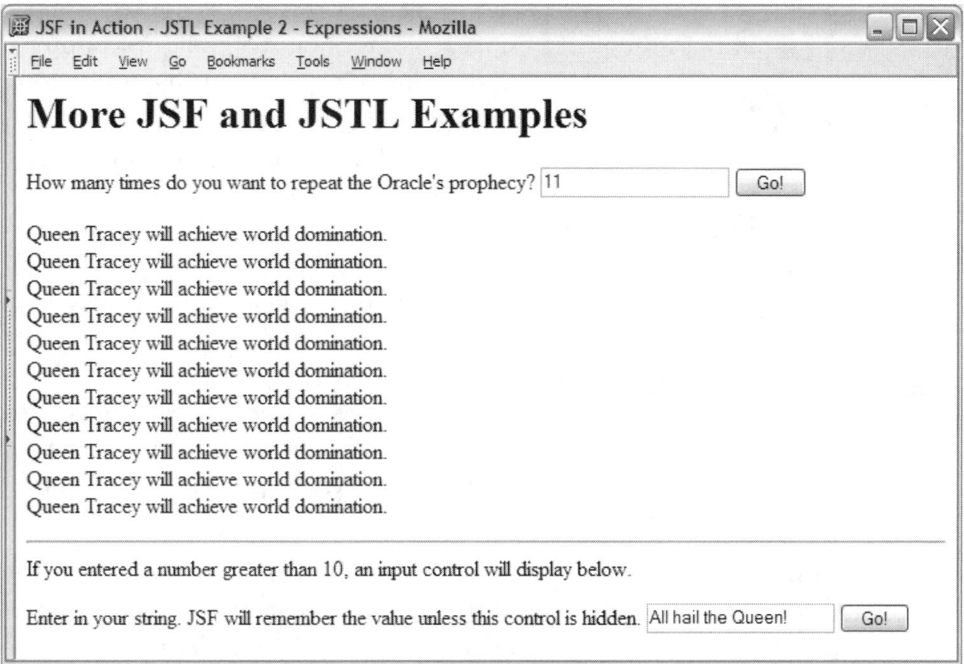

Figure 3.5 The output of the JSP page shown in listings 3.3 and 3.4. The value of the input field at the top (an `HtmlInputText` component) is wired to the `exampleBean.number` backing bean property, which is used by the JSTL `<c:forEach>` tag to display a string `exampleBean.number` times. In the bottom portion of the page, a JSTL `<c:if>` tag shows a form with JSF components if `exampleBean.number` is greater than 10. Otherwise, the components will not be displayed, and they are removed from the view (and the input control will lose its value).

If `exampleBean.number` is greater than 10, this panel becomes visible. In this case, the components *won't* be deleted if they're not displayed. This is a good example of the types of things you can do with pure JSF tags without JSTL.

> **TIP** Even though custom tags like the ones provided by the JSTL provide a lot of functionality, if you're developing from scratch (or refactoring), you should first look to see if you can implement the desired behavior with standard JSF components. Using good components and well-designed backing beans, you can usually avoid the need for many JSTL tags in your pages. You can hide or display entire panels and do all sorts of powerful things with standard JSF.

Here are a few other interoperability constraints for using JSF tags with JSTL internationalization and formatting tags:

- Use of `<fmt:parseDate>` and `<fmt:parseNumber>` is not recommended. You should use the `HtmlInputText` component (covered in chapter 5) with a `DateTime` or `Number` converter (both are covered in chapter 6).
- The `<fmt:requestEncoding>` tag, which is use to determine or specify the character encoding for the page, should not be used. Usually, JSF handles this automatically, and if you need to force a particular encoding, you should use the JSP page directive: `<%page contentType="[content-type];[charset]"%>`.
- The `<fmt:setLocale>` tag shouldn't be used either. Because it doesn't know about JSF, it may cause your JSTL tags to use one locale and your JSF components may use another, which is a recipe for disaster. Instead, you should use JSF's internationalization features (covered in chapter 6). To control the locale for a particular page, use the `locale` property of the `UIViewRoot` component, which is covered in chapter 4. JSF's internationalization features work for both JSF and JSTL.

Combining JSF with the JSTL can be quite powerful. Custom tags that you have developed or obtained from third parties should work with JSF as well as the JSTL tags we've shown here. In general, though, you should stick with JSF tags when possible.

In the next section, we examine how to create and initialize beans, like the `exampleBean` backing bean used in the last example.

3.3 Creating and initializing beans

In the last section, we talked about JSF EL expressions and how you can use them to reference objects in any application scope. In traditional Java web applications, those objects might be created with the `<jsp:usebean>` tag or in Java code. In JSF applications, you can configure and initialize beans in an application configuration file instead. The idea behind this feature, called the *Managed Bean Creation facility*, is simple: any time you reference a bean, the facility will create the bean, initialize it, and store it in the proper application scope if it doesn't already exist. (If the bean already exists, it will be returned.)

Beans that are configured to use the Managed Bean Creation facility are called managed beans. When tools create backing beans for pages that you design, they will typically register the beans in a configuration file for you. But you can also use this feature for any other beans your application uses, including domain objects like a `User`, or model objects like a `RegistrationWizard` or `ShoppingCartBean`.

Using the Managed Bean Creation facility allows you to:

- Declare all of your beans and initialize all of their properties in one central place (an application configuration file).
- Control the scope (application, session, or request) where a bean is stored.
- Change a bean's class or initial property values without changing any code (only a change in the configuration file is necessary).
- Initialize a bean property with value-binding expressions. This has a number of exciting benefits, such as associating a backing bean with business and state-management objects or initializing child objects.
- Access a managed bean using ordinary JSF EL expressions.

Often a back-end developer will be responsible for the initial managed bean configuration. However, a front-end developer or system administrator might be responsible for making changes later.

NOTE You cannot reference a managed bean with the JSTL or JSP 2.0 expression languages unless the bean has already been created, initialized, and stored in an application scope by the Managed Bean Creation facility or some other means (like Java code or the JSP `<jsp:usebean>` tag). Because of this, it's generally safer to use JSF EL expressions whenever possible.

Managed beans can be configured with the `<managed-bean>` XML element in a JSF configuration file. Because they're configured with a JSF configuration file, you can either edit them by hand or with a tool. See section 3.1.4 for more on application configuration and a screenshot of a tool. Even if you have a tool that shields you from editing XML, you should peruse this section so that you understand how managed beans work.

So, if we had a class called `org.jia.examples.UserBean`, we could configure it with the following snippet inside a configuration file:

```
<managed-bean>
  <managed-bean-name>user</managed-bean-name>
  <managed-bean-class>org.jia.examples.UserBean</managed-bean-class>
  <managed-bean-scope>session</managed-bean-scope>
  <managed-property>
    <property-name>firstName</property-name>
    <value>Mark</value>
  </managed-property>
  <managed-property>
    <property-name>lastName</property-name>
    <value>Pippins</value>
```

```
    </managed-property>
  </managed-bean>
```

This configures an instance of the `org.jia.examples.UserBean` class with the key `"user"` in session scope. It also initializes the `firstName` property to `"Mark"` and the `lastName` property to "Pippins".

Now we can access the bean from a UI component using an ordinary JSF EL expression:

```
<h:outputText value="Hello #{user.firstName} #{user.lastName}!"/>
```

This declares an `HtmlOutputText` component whose value includes an EL expression for the `user.firstName` and `user.lastName` properties. The first time this component is initialized, the Managed Bean Creation facility will instantiate a new instance of our `UserBean` class, set the `firstName` property to "Mark" and the `lastName` property to "Pippins", and then store the object in the application's session. If a component references the object after it's already been created, it won't be re-created (assuming it hasn't been removed).

The `HtmlOutputText` component declaration above displays the string "Hello Mark Pippins!" This isn't terribly exciting—normally you wouldn't initialize the `firstName` and `lastName` properties of a user object—but you get the idea.

BY THE WAY If you're pattern-conscious, you may have noticed that the ability to initialize a bean's properties upon creation is the Inversion of Control (IoC) type 2 or Setter Injection pattern [Fowler, Dependency Injection]. The idea is that an external process is in control of configuring the bean—it's *injecting* values into the bean via its setter methods.

In general, it's a good idea to use the Managed Bean Creation facility for any beans that don't need to be created and initialized when your application starts up. Objects that have a potentially long initialization time, such as a data access object that needs to establish a database connection, should be created at application startup (perhaps with a `ServletContextListener;` see chapter 12 for an example). This is because the facility creates objects when they're first referenced, which could cause unexpected delays in the middle of a user's experience for objects with long initialization periods.

At this point we've covered the basics of managed beans, so now let's examine them in more detail.

3.3.1 Declaring managed beans

Any Java class with a no-argument constructor can be declared as a managed bean. All you need to know is the name you want to use as an identifier, the class name, and the scope you'd like to use. The identifier is the name that's actually used in JSF EL expressions, like "user" or "ShoppingCartBean." The class name is the fully qualified Java class name, like `com.foo.bar.ShoppingCart`. The scope can be any valid JSF web application scope: application, session, or request. There's also a fourth scope option, none, which tells the Managed Bean Creation facility to avoid putting the bean in any scope. This is useful when you're associating multiple beans with each other, as we'll see later.

These three pieces of information translate into the `<managed-bean-name>`, `<managed-bean-class>`, and `<managed-bean-scope>` elements in a JSF configuration file. One of each of these elements must be nested within a `<managed-bean>` element. This is depicted in figure 3.6.

Figure 3.6 also shows three optional elements: `<description>`, `<display-name>`, and `<icon>`. Usually you'll just use the `<description>` element to help other developers understand the purpose of a particular managed bean; the others are primarily for use with tools.

Of course, as the example in the previous section shows, you can also configure the bean's properties (and do a lot more). But let's examine a simple declaration:

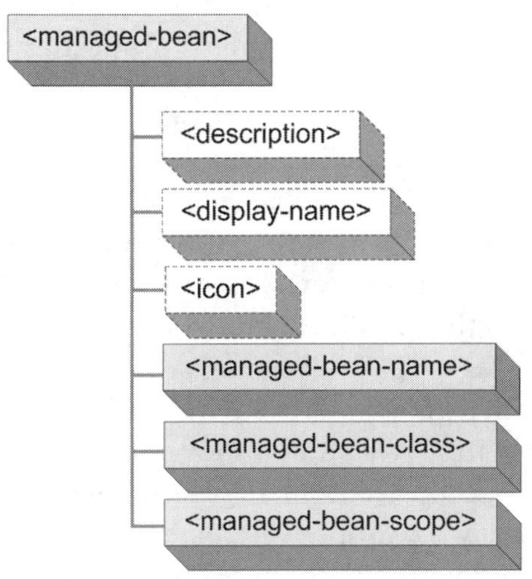

Figure 3.6
To configure a managed bean, you use the `<managed-bean>` element. This element has three optional subelements: `<description>`, `<display-name>`, and `<icon>`. It also requires a `<managed-bean-name>` element, a `<managed-bean-class>` element, and a `<managed-bean-scope>` element.

```
<managed-bean>
   <description>Used for logging and logging out.
   </description>
   <managed-bean-name>authenticationBean</managed-bean-name>
   <managed-bean-class>org.jia.ptrack.web.AuthenticationBean
   </managed-bean-class>
   <managed-bean-scope>session</managed-bean-scope>
</managed-bean>
```

This tells the Managed Bean Creation facility to create a new instance of `org.jia.ptrack.web.AuthenticationBean` and store it in the session under the name `authenticationBean` the first time the bean is accessed. As long as the same session is in use, the same instance of `AuthenticationBean` will be used. This instance can be referenced with the expression `"#{authenticationBean}"`, or, more explicitly, `"#{sessionScope.authenticationBean}"`.

BY THE WAY If you have application code that creates beans itself and stores them in an application scope, you can declare *referenced beans* to tell your JSF IDE when certain objects will be available. This can help the tool generate dialog boxes based on the beans that should be available at different times during the application's life span. Referenced beans are purely for use by IDEs and don't affect the JSF runtime. Configuring referenced beans is similar to configuring managed beans; see appendix D for details.

In some cases, all you need to do is configure the object itself, and there's no need to initialize any properties. However, if you do have properties that you would like to initialize, you can do that as well.

Initializing simple properties

You can initialize any managed bean variable that has been exposed as a JavaBean property (see appendix C for more information on JavaBeans). Only read/write properties (ones with *both* a getter and a setter) will work with the Managed Bean Creation facility. Any properties that aren't explicitly initialized will retain their default values.

At a minimum, you need to specify the property's name and its value. The value can either be `null`, a literal string, or a value-binding expression. Each property is initialized with a `<managed-property>` element (which is nested inside of the `<managed-bean>` element). You specify the property's name with the `<property-name>` element. The value is specified with either the `<value>` element or the `<null-value>` element. These elements are depicted in figure 3.7.

The figure also shows the optional tooling elements—`<description>`, `<display-name>`, and `<icon>`. As usual, most of the time you only need to use the

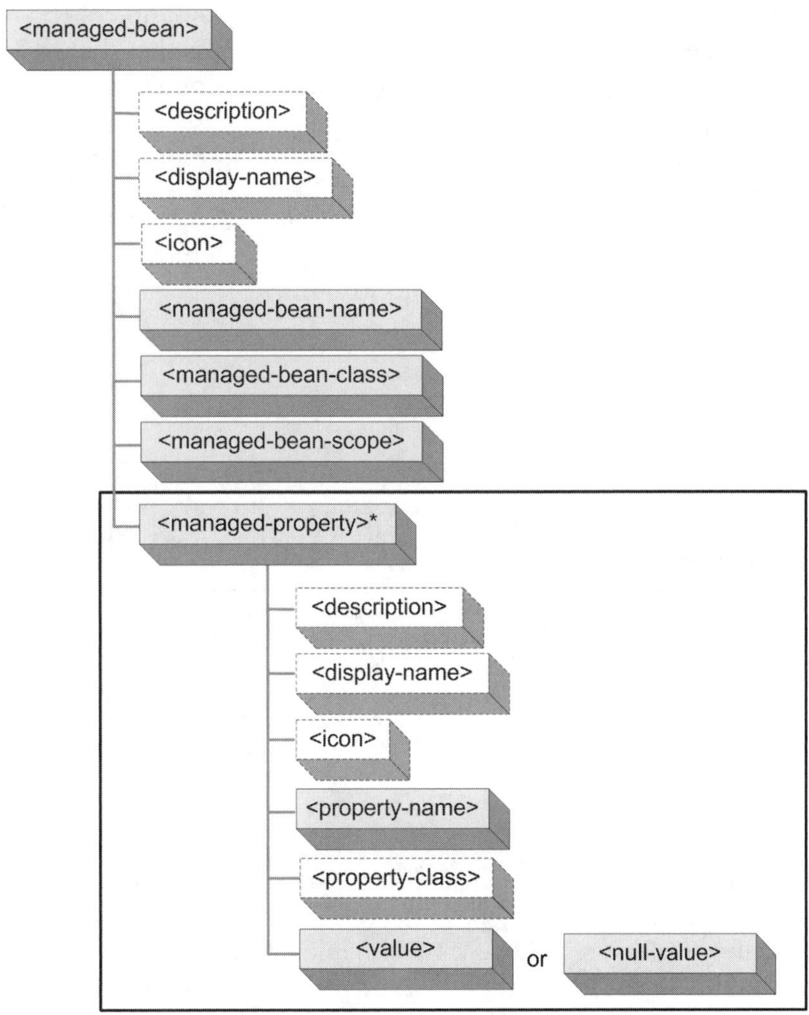

Figure 3.7 You can initialize managed bean properties with the `<managed-property>` element (each `<managed-bean>` element can have zero or more `<managed-property>` elements). Its optional elements are `<description>`, `<display-name>`, `<icon>`, and `<property-class>`. The required elements are `<property-name>` and either `<value>` or `<null-value>`.

`<description>` element. There's another optional element—`<property-class>`—which specifies the property's Java class or primitive type. The Managed Bean Creation facility usually doesn't need this element because it can figure out the property's type on its own. However, some advanced JSF implementations may require them in some situations (such as automatic generation of the managed bean). If you do use the <property-class> element, remember that you can't use the <null-value> element unless <property-class> is an object, rather than a primitive type (like int, boolean, and so on).

Here's an example of configuring a UserBean object and setting some of its properties as well:

```
<managed-bean>
  <managed-bean-name>brokeUser</managed-bean-name>
  <managed-bean-class>org.jia.examples.UserBean
  </managed-bean-class>
  <managed-bean-scope>request</managed-bean-scope>
  <managed-property>
    <property-name>firstName</property-name>
    <value>Joe</value>
  </managed-property>
  <managed-property>
    <property-name>lastName</property-name>
    <value>Broke</value>
  </managed-property>
  <managed-property>
    <property-name>balance</property-name>
    <value>0</value>
  </managed-property>
  <managed-property>
    <property-name>favoriteAnimal</property-name>
    <null-value/>
  </managed-property>
</managed-bean>
```

This snippet creates a new instance of org.jia.examples.UserBean called brokeUser, and stores it in the request scope. The example is similar to the first in that we initialize both the firstName and lastName properties to the literal values "Joe" and "Broke", respectively. We also initialize the balance property, which is an int, to 0. Finally, we set the favoriteAnimal property, which is a String, to null with the <null-value> element. Note that we could not have initialized the balance property to null because it is a primitive type. To access Joe Broke's balance, we can use the expression "#{brokeUser.balance}".

Instead of using static values, we could have associated these properties with other objects using value-binding expressions. We'll get to that soon, but first let's look at initializing properties that are of type List, array, and Map.

Initializing List and array properties

If you have a property that is an array or a List, you can initialize it with default values. If the property is set to null, the facility will create a new List or array and initialize it for you. If it's non-null, the facility will simply add any values you define to the existing collection. Instead of specifying a single value for the property, you specify multiple values. You can configure a List or array property by nesting <value> or <null-value> elements inside a <list-entries> element, which is a child of the <managed-property> element. This is shown in figure 3.8.

WARNING Even if you specify a <property-class> element, if your property is null, JSF will always initialize it with a newly created ArrayList. If, however, the object has already created an object of a different type, JSF won't replace it with an ArrayList.

Let's say our UserBean class also has a favoriteSites property, which is a List of Strings representing the user's favorite sites. If we wanted to provide a default list of values for the favoriteSites property, we could define it like so:

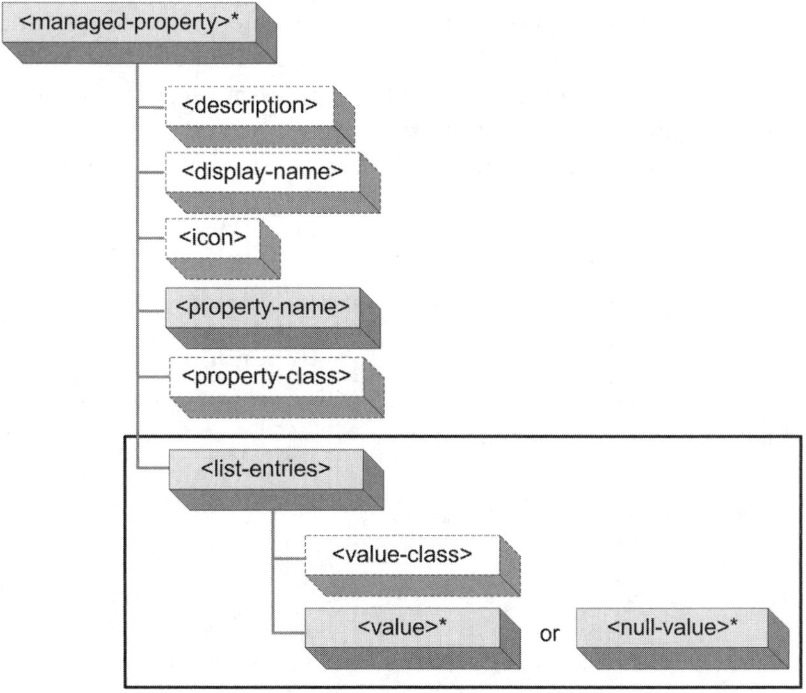

Figure 3.8 To initailize a managed bean property that is a List or array, you use the <list-entries> element and nest zero or more <value> or <null-value> elements in it. Optionally, you can specify the Java class for all of the values with the <value-class> element.

```
<managed-bean>
  <managed-bean-name>user</managed-bean-name>
  <managed-bean-class>org.jia.examples.UserBean</managed-bean-class>
  <managed-bean-scope>request</managed-bean-scope>
  ...
  <managed-property>
    <property-name>favoriteSites</property-name>
    <list-entries>
      <value>http://www.jsfcentral.com</value>
      <value>http://www.theserverside.com</value>
      <value>http://www.ibm.com/developerworks/</value>
      <value>http://otn.oracle.com</value>
      <value>http://www.java.net</value>
      <value>http://www.manning.com</value>
    </list-entries>
  </managed-property>
  ...
</managed-bean>
```

You can see that we have several `<value>` elements nested inside a `<list-entries>` element. Each `<value>` corresponds to a single element that will be added to the list before setting the property. If the `favoriteSites` property hasn't already been initialized, the first item in the list will be "http:/www.jsfcentral.com". This item can be accessed with the JSF EL expression `"#{user.favoriteSites[0]}"`. We could also display the entire list in a table with the `HtmlDataTable` component, which displays tabular data:

```
<h:dataTable value="#{user.favoriteSites}" var="site">
  <h:column>
    <h:outputText value="#{site}"/>
  </h:column>
</h:dataTable>
```

This displays a table with a single column and a row for each item in the list, which looks like this in a browser:

```
http://www.jsfcentral.com
http://www.theserverside.com
http://www.ibm.com/developerworks/
http://otn.oracle.com
http://www.java.net
http://www.manning.com
```

If, however, the `favoriteSites` property were initialized (in the constructor) with a single value, like "http://www.yahoo.com", the list would be:

```
http://www.yahoo.com
http://www.jsfcentral.com
http://www.theserverside.com
http://www.ibm.com/developerworks/
```

```
http://otn.oracle.com
http://www.java.net
http://www.manning.com
```

and the expression `"#{user.favoriteSites[0]}"` would yield "http://www.yahoo.com" instead.

In the previous example, all values were stored as `String` objects, which is the default. If you want all of the values to be converted to a specific type, you can use the `<value-class>` attribute. Here's a `List` property whose values are all `Integers`:

```
<managed-bean>
...
  <managed-property>
    <property-name>favoriteNumbers</property-name>
    <list-entries>
      <value-class>java.lang.Integer</value-class>
       <value>31415</value>
       <value>278</value>
       <value>304</value>
       <value>18</value>
       <value>811</value>
       <value>914</value>
     </list-entries>
   </managed-property>
...
</managed-bean>
```

All of these values will be converted to a `java.lang.Integer` object before being stored in the list. Other than that, the initialization process will be handled in the same manner as the previous example.

In these examples, we've assumed that the properties were `List` objects. They could also be arrays—the configuration and behavior is identical, except that the facility will create an array instead of an `ArrayList`. As a matter of fact, you could change the actual type of the property in Java code, and as long as it was either a `List` or an array, the Managed Bean Creation facility wouldn't even care. (The facility won't resize an array for you, however, so you must be mindful of how such changes will affect your application.)

That's all there is to configuring `List` or array properties. Fortunately, configuring `Map` properties is similar.

Initializing Map properties

You can initialize `Map` properties with the Managed Bean Creation facility as well. If the property is `null` when the object is created, JSF will create a new `HashMap` and populate it for you. Otherwise, it will add entries to the existing `Map`. Initializing a `Map` property requires specifying one or more map entries. Each map entry has a key and a value. In a JSF configuration file, you specify a `<map-entries>` element (as opposed to a `<list-entries>` element) with child `<map-entry>` elements. Each `<map-entry>` element has child `<key>` and `<value>` (or `<null-value>`) elements. This structure is depicted in figure 3.9.

Suppose the list of favorite sites from the previous section is really a `Map` property called `favoriteSitesMap` where each entry's key is the site's name and the value is the actual URL. We could define it like this:

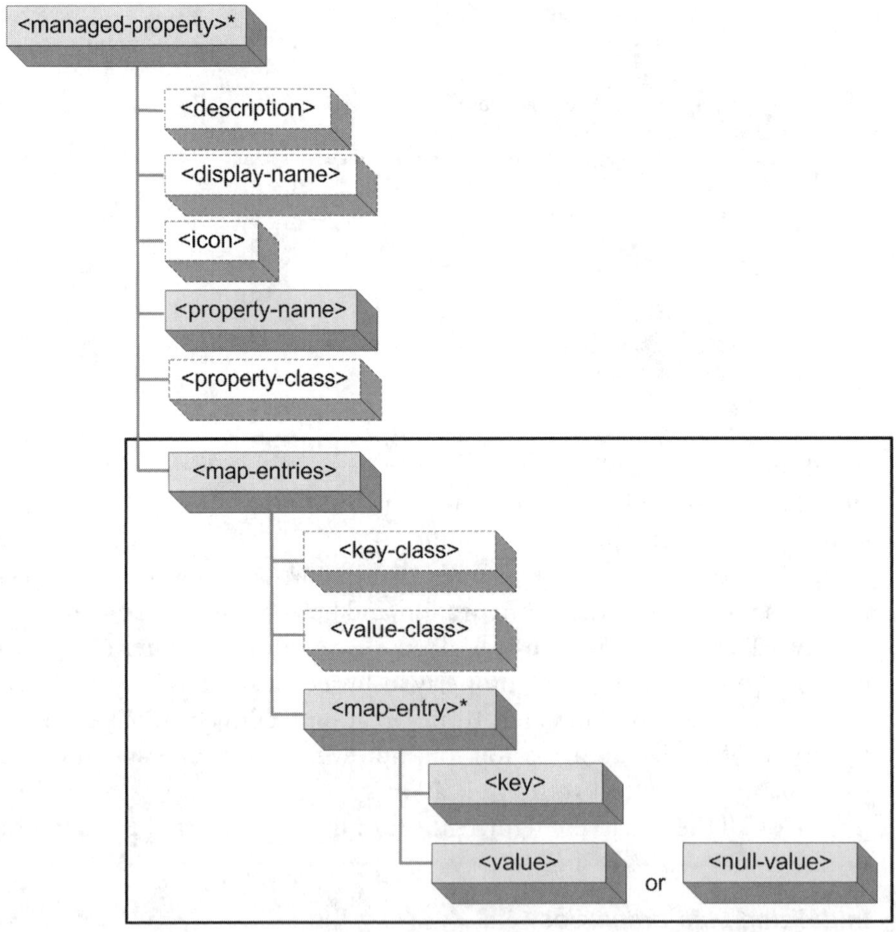

Figure 3.9 To initailize a managed bean property that is a `Map`, you use the `<map-entries>` element and nest one or more `<map-entry>` elements. Each `<map-entry>` can have either a `<value>` or a `<null-value>` element. Optionally, you can specify the Java class for all of the values with the `<value-class>` element.

```
<managed-bean>
  <managed-bean-name>user</managed-bean-name>
  <managed-bean-class>org.jia.examples.UserBean</managed-bean-class>
  <managed-bean-scope>request</managed-bean-scope>
  ...
  <managed-property>
    <property-name>favoriteSitesMap</property-name>
    <map-entries>
      <map-entry>
        <key>JSF Central</key>
        <value>http://www.jsfcentral.com</value>
      </map-entry>
      <map-entry>
        <key>TheServerSide.com</key>
        <value>http://www.theserverside.com</value>
      </map-entry>
      <map-entry>
        <key>IBM DeveloperWorks</key>
        <value>http://www.ibm.com/developerworks/</value>
      </map-entry>
      <map-entry>
        <key>Oracle Technology Network</key>
        <value>http://otn.oracle.com</value>
      </map-entry>
      <map-entry>
        <key>java.net</key>
        <value>http://www.java.net</value>
      </map-entry>
      <map-entry>
        <key>Manning Publications</key>
        <value>http://www.manning.com</value>
      </map-entry>
    </map-entries>
    ...
</managed-property>
```

Instead of using a <list-entries> or <value> element directly under the <managed-property> element, we use the <map-entries> element and child <map-entry> elements to define all of the entries in a Map property. Each <map-entry> element represents a key/value pair that will be added to the Map. If UserBean doesn't initialize this property in its constructor, the facility will create a new HashMap, add each map entry, and then set the property.

With this managed bean configuration, we can access the URL for java.net with the expression "#{user.favoriteSitesMap['java.net']}". We can also display the entire Map with an HtmlOutputText component:

```
<h:outputText value="user.favoriteSitesMap: #{user.favoriteSitesMap}"/>
```

This displays the result of the underlying `Map`'s `toString` method, which looks like this:

```
user.favoriteSitesMap: {IBM DeveloperWorks=http://www.ibm.com/
  developerworks/,
JSF Central=http://www.jsfcentral.com,
Manning Publications=http://www.manning.com,
Oracle Technology Network=http://otn.oracle.com, TheServerSide.com=http://
  www.theserverside.com,
java.net=http://www.java.net}
```

This isn't quite production-ready output, but at least we can see that contents of the `favoriteSitesMap` property match the ones specified in the configuration file. If `UserBean` had already initialized this property, these values would have been added to the `Map`'s existing set of entries.

In the previous example, both the keys and values were `Strings`. This is fine for many cases, but sometimes you need specific types, like a key that's an `Integer`, or a value that's a `Date`. In order to support these situations, you can optionally tell the facility to convert all keys and values to a specific type with the `<key-class>` and `<value-class>` elements, respectively. Here's an example of the `favoriteNumbers` property from the previous section implemented as a `Map`:

```
<managed-bean>
...
  <managed-property>
    <property-name>favoriteNumbersMap</property-name>
    <map-entries>
      <key-class>java.lang.Integer</key-class>
      <map-entry>
        <key>31415</key>
        <value>A pi-like integer.</value>
      </map-entry>
      <map-entry>
        <key>278</key>
        <value>An e-like integer.</value>
      </map-entry>
      <map-entry>
        <key>304</key>
         <value>Tracey's birthday.</value>
      </map-entry>
      <map-entry>
        <key>18</key>
        <null-value/>
      </map-entry>
      <map-entry>
        <key>811</key>
        <null-value/>
      </map-entry>
```

```
      <map-entry>
        <key>914</key>
        <value>Mom's birthday.</value>
      </map-entry>
    </map-entries>
  </managed-property>
  ...
</managed-bean>
```

Here, we specify the <key-class> element to ensure that all keys are converted into java.lang.Integer objects. Any value that can't properly be converted will cause an error. The value, in this case, describes the significance of the number. If you repeat a key, the facility will overwrite the previous value. Note that we use the <null-value> element to indicate a null value (null keys are not allowed).

3.3.2 Declaring Lists and Maps as managed beans

So far, we've talked about declaring JavaBeans as managed beans. You can also declare any List or Map as a managed bean. (Arrays aren't supported as individual managed beans.) All you have to do is specify a concrete type (like an ArrayList or HashMap) and specify the list or map entries instead of individual properties. The elements for a List are shown in figure 3.10.

Here's the infamous favoriteSites list declared as an individual managed bean instead of a property of a UserBean object:

```
<managed-bean>
  <description>List of favorite sites.</description>
  <managed-bean-name>favoriteSites</managed-bean-name>
  <managed-bean-class>java.util.ArrayList</managed-bean-class>
  <managed-bean-scope>application</managed-bean-scope>
  <list-entries>
    <value>http://www.jsfcentral.com</value>
    <value>http://www.theserverside.com</value>
    <value>http://www.ibm.com/developerworks/</value>
    <value>http://otn.oracle.com</value>
    <value>http://www.java.net</value>
    <value>http://www.manning.com</value>
  </list-entries>
</managed-bean>
```

Note that we've specified a concrete List implementation, java.util.ArrayList, with the <managed-bean-class> element. Also, the <list-entries> element and its children are nested within the <managed-bean> element instead of the <managed-property> element. (For more information about initializing lists in general, see the earlier section on initializing List properties.)

The configuration elements for a Map are shown in figure 3.11.

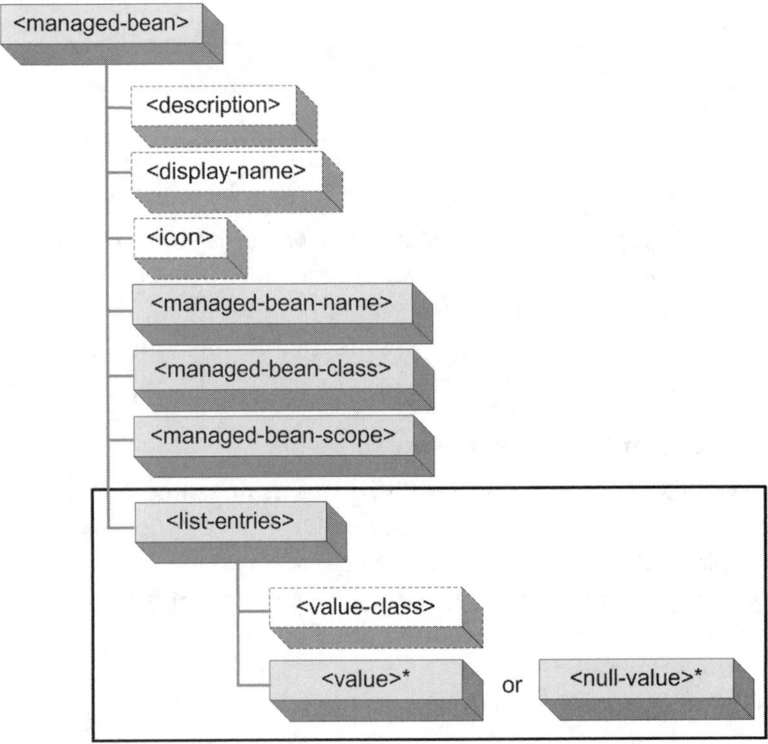

Figure 3.10 To declare a `List` as a managed bean, you must specify a `<managed-bean-class>` that is a concrete List implementation, and use the `<list-entries>` element as a child of the `<managed-bean>` element. Each `<list-entries>` element can have one or more `<value>` (or `<null-value>`) elements and a single `<value-class>` element.

Here's the `favoriteSitesMap` property of `UserBean` configured directly as a managed bean:

```
<managed-bean>
  <description>List of favorite sites, keyed by name.</description>
  <managed-bean-name>favoriteSitesMap</managed-bean-name>
  <managed-bean-class>java.util.HashMap</managed-bean-class>
  <managed-bean-scope>application</managed-bean-scope>
  <map-entries>
    <map-entry>
      <key>JSF Central</key>
      <value>http://www.jsfcentral.com</value>
    </map-entry>
    <map-entry>
      <key>TheServerSide.com</key>
```

```
      <value>http://www.theserverside.com</value>
    </map-entry>
    <map-entry>
      <key>IBM DeveloperWorks</key>
      <value>http://www.ibm.com/developerworks/</value>
    </map-entry>
    <map-entry>
      <key>Oracle Technology Network</key>
      <value>http://otn.oracle.com</value>
    </map-entry>
    <map-entry>
      <key>java.net</key>
      <value>http://www.java.net</value>
    </map-entry>
    <map-entry>
      <key>Manning Publications</key>
      <value>http://www.manning.com</value>
    </map-entry>
  </map-entries>
</managed-bean>
```

You can see that we've specified a concrete `Map` implementation, `HashMap`, with the `<managed-bean-class>` attribute. The `<map-entries>` element is specified as a child of the `<managed-bean>` element, and there are no `<managed-property>` elements. (For more information about initializing Maps in general, see the previous section.)

TIP Don't forget to specify a concrete `List` or `Map` implementation (like `ArrayList`, `Vector`, `HashMap`, and `TreeMap`). JSF can't instantiate a `List` or `Map` directly because they are interfaces.

All of our managed bean examples have included static values—strings and integers. However, the real power of the Managed Bean Creation facility is its ability to initialize properties with value-binding expressions.

3.3.3 Setting values with value-binding expressions

Anytime you specify a managed bean value—whether it's a property, a `List` value, or a `Map` value—you can use a value-binding expression. Because value-binding expressions are JSF EL expressions that reference a JavaBean property or a collection element, they're well suited for initializing managed bean properties—they allow you to wire up objects to each other.

You can, of course, associate objects with each other in Java code, but if you use the facility, you can change these associations without recompiling your application. Also, you may find using the facility simpler than writing Java code, depending on your disposition.

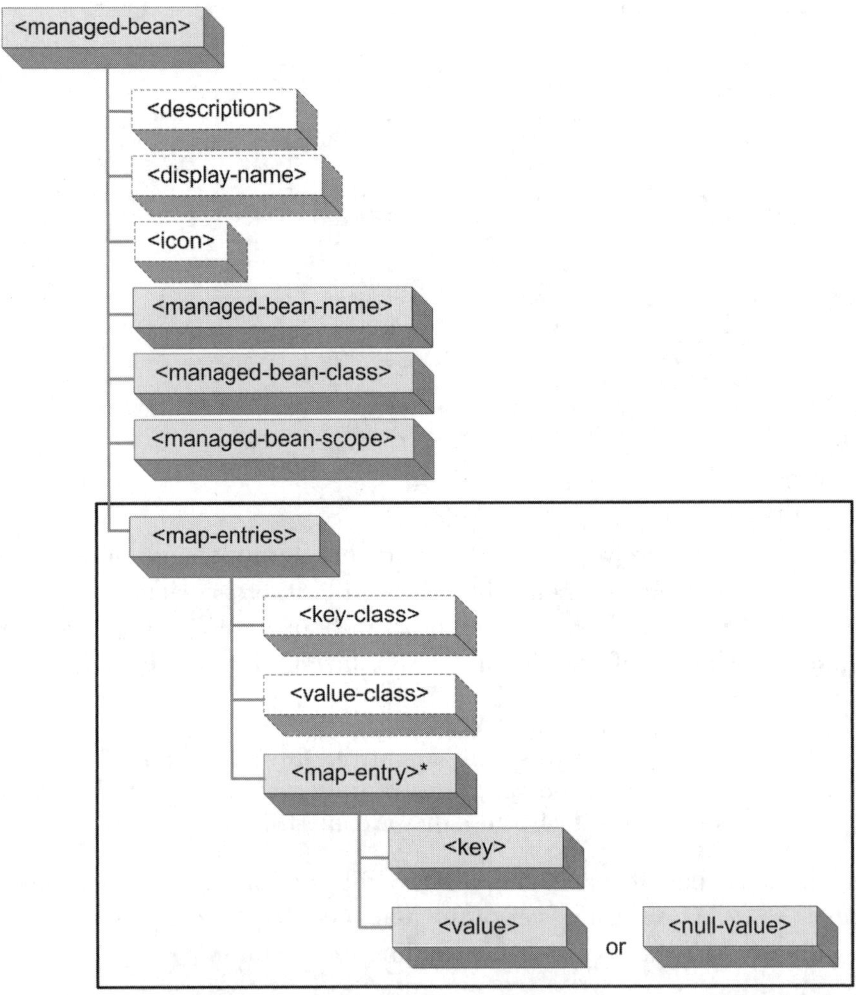

Figure 3.11 To declare a `Map` as a managed bean, you specify the `<managed-bean-class>` element with a value that is a concrete `Map` class and use the `<map-entries>` element as a child of the `<managed-bean>` element. Each `<map-entries>` element can have one or more `<map-entry>` elements, which each have a `<key>` and a `<value>` (or `<null-value>`) element. The `<map-entries>` element can optionally have `<key-class>` and `<value-class>` elements as well.

Listing 3.5 shows the configuration for three managed beans: an `ArrayList` called `defaultFavoriteSites`, a `UserBean` called `newUser`, and a `TestForm` called `exampleForm`. `newUser`'s `favoriteSites` property is stored in the session, and it's associated with `defaultFavoriteSites` through a value-binding expression. Because defaultFavoriteSites is declared in the scope none, it isn't stored anywhere—it's created solely for the purposes of setting newUser's favoriteSites property.

exampleForm is stored in the request scope and has a user property that references newUser via an expression. So, this declaration creates the simple group of related objects shown in figure 3.12: exampleForm references newUser, which references defaultFavoriteSites.

Listing 3.5 Three managed beans that reference each other via JSF EL expressions

```
<managed-bean>
  <managed-bean-name>defaultFavoriteSites</managed-bean-name>
  <managed-bean-class>java.util.ArrayList</managed-bean-class>
  <managed-bean-scope>none</managed-bean-scope>        <— Not stored
  <list-entries>
    <value>http://www.jsfcentral.com</value>
    <value>http://www.theserverside.com</value>
    <value>http://www.ibm.com/developerworks/</value>
    <value>http://otn.oracle.com</value>
    <value>http://www.java.net</value>
    <value>http://www.manning.com</value>
  </list-entries>
</managed-bean>

<managed-bean>
  <description>Default user object.</description>
  <managed-bean-name>newUser</managed-bean-name>
  <managed-bean-class>org.jia.examples.UserBean</managed-bean-class>
  <managed-bean-scope>session</managed-bean-scope>        <— Stored in
  <managed-property>                                            session scope
    <property-name>favoriteSites</property-name>
    <value>#{defaultFavoriteSites}</value>        <— References previous
  </managed-property>                                  managed bean
  <managed-property>
    <property-name>favoriteAnimal</property-name>
    <value>donkey</value>
  </managed-property>
</managed-bean>

<managed-bean>
  <managed-bean-name>exampleForm</managed-bean-name>
  <managed-bean-class>org.jia.examples.TestForm</managed-bean-class>
  <managed-bean-scope>request</managed-bean-scope>        <— Stored in
  <managed-property>                                            request scope
    <property-name>user</property-name>
    <value>#{newUser}</value>        <— References previous
  </managed-property>                    managed bean
</managed-bean>
```

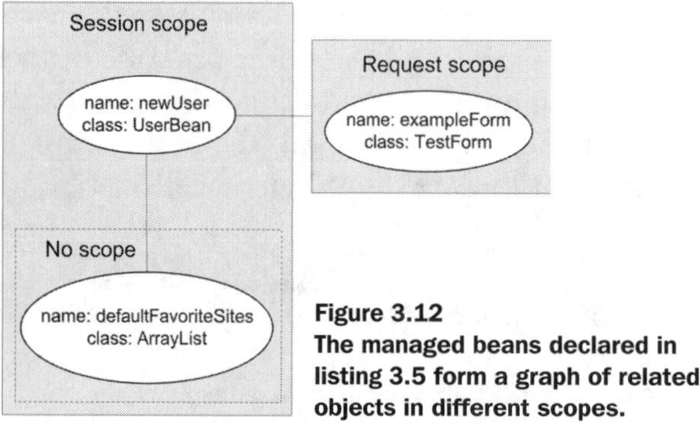

Figure 3.12
The managed beans declared in listing 3.5 form a graph of related objects in different scopes.

In this simple example, the expressions all reference other managed beans. This is certainly not a requirement—you can use any valid value-binding expression, which means you can wire up properties to values derived from implicit objects (like initialization parameters, request parameters, session values, and so on) and mixed-text or expressions that perform arithmetic. (See chapter 2 for more information about value-binding expressions and the JSF expression language.)

We mentioned the scopes for each of these objects in this example because a managed bean can't reference an object with a shorter life span than the managed bean itself. In our example, `exampleForm` references `newUser`. This is okay, because `newUser` is stored in the session and `exampleForm` is stored in the request. In other words, `exampleForm` references an object with a longer life span than it has. When the request is completed and `exampleForm` is removed, `newUser` will continue to live happily. However, `newUser` cannot have a reference to `exampleForm` because `exampleForm` has a much shorter life span; it will be removed long before `newUser` is removed. Table 3.7 explains when it's okay to reference an object in each of the scopes.

Table 3.7 Allowable relationships between managed beans

An object stored in this scope...	Can reference an object stored in this scope...
none	none
application	none, application
session	none, application, session
request	none, application, session, request

NOTE The Managed Bean Creation facility does not support cycles. In other words, you can't have object A reference object B, and also have object B reference object A.

Managed beans are an extremely powerful feature of JSF. Often, tools will hook up backing beans using this facility automatically. However, if you take things a step further, you can configure most of your application objects in a central location. You can even eliminate most of the need to look up objects in particular scopes in your Java code. For more examples of using the Managed Bean Creation facility, see chapter 13.

Managed beans are key feature of JSF that simplify development by eliminating the need for creating and configuring objects in Java code. JSF's navigation system also reduces the amount of code you need to write.

3.4 Navigating the sea of pages

In the first two chapters of this book, we touched on JSF's support for navigating from one page to another. Conceptually, it's similar to Struts' ActionForwards. It doesn't, however, have a catchy name like "ActionForwards," so we'll just call it the JSF navigation system.

The heart of the navigation system is the navigation handler, which is the actual code that decides which page to load next. Throughout this book, we describe the behavior of the default navigation handler. (It's possible to replace or decorate the navigation handler; see appendix C for details.) The navigation handler operates in response to action events,[3] which are usually executed by action sources (components that capture user gestures, like buttons or hyperlinks). An action source is either associated with an action method that performs some application logic and returns a logical outcome, or a hardcoded outcome value.

The navigation handler operates on a set of navigation rules, which define all of the application's possible navigation paths. A navigation rule specifies which pages can be selected from a specific page or set of pages. Each path to a page is represented by a single navigation case. The navigation case is selected based on logical outcome (retrieved from the component itself or its associated action method) and/or the expression for the executed action method itself.

---

[3] Technically, the navigation handler is executed *by* the default action listener, which handles action events.

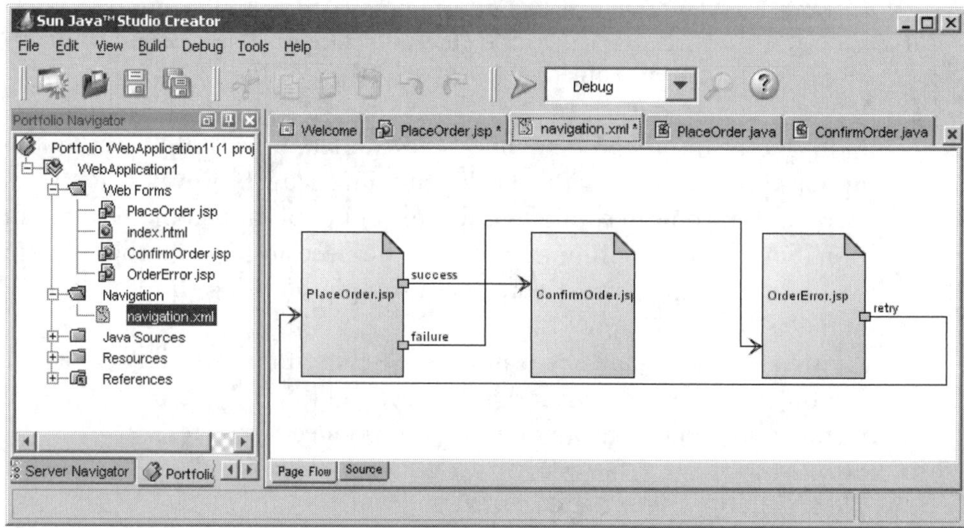

Figure 3.13 Editing page navigation in Sun Java Studio Creator [Sun, Creator]. The XML source is shown in listing 3.6.

Navigation rules are defined in an application configuration file with XML. Some IDEs allow you to visually edit your navigation rules as well. Figure 3.13 shows Sun Java Studio Creator's [Sun, Creator] visual navigation editor. The figure shows three pages: PlaceOrder.jsp, ConfirmOrder.jsp, and OrderEntry.jsp.

There's one rule for navigating from PlaceOrder.jsp with two cases: one that navigates to ConfirmOrder.jsp if the outcome is `"success"`, and one that navigates to OrderEntry.jsp if the outcome is `"failure"`. There are no navigation rules for ConfirmOrder.jsp—it's a dead end. OrderError.jsp has a navigation rule with a single case: return to PlaceOrder.jsp if the outcome is `"retry"`.

Behind the pretty pictures that tools generate, there's an ordinary Faces configuration file with `<navigation-rule>` and `<navigation-case>` elements. Figure 3.14 shows the structure of those elements. Listing 3.6 shows the XML that defines the rules shown in figure 3.13, and figure 3.14 shows the structure of those elements.

Listing 3.6 The XML source for the navigation rules shown in figure 3.13

```
<navigation-rule>
  <from-view-id>/OrderError.jsp</from-view-id>
  <navigation-case>
     <from-outcome>retry</from-outcome>
```

```
    <to-view-id>/PlaceOrder.jsp</to-view-id>
  </navigation-case>
</navigation-rule>
<navigation-rule>
  <from-view-id>/PlaceOrder.jsp</from-view-id>
  <navigation-case>
    <from-outcome>success</from-outcome>
    <to-view-id>/ConfirmOrder.jsp</to-view-id>
  </navigation-case>
  <navigation-case>
    <from-outcome>failure</from-outcome>
    <to-view-id>/OrderError.jsp</to-view-id>
    <redirect/>
  </navigation-case>
</navigation-rule>
```

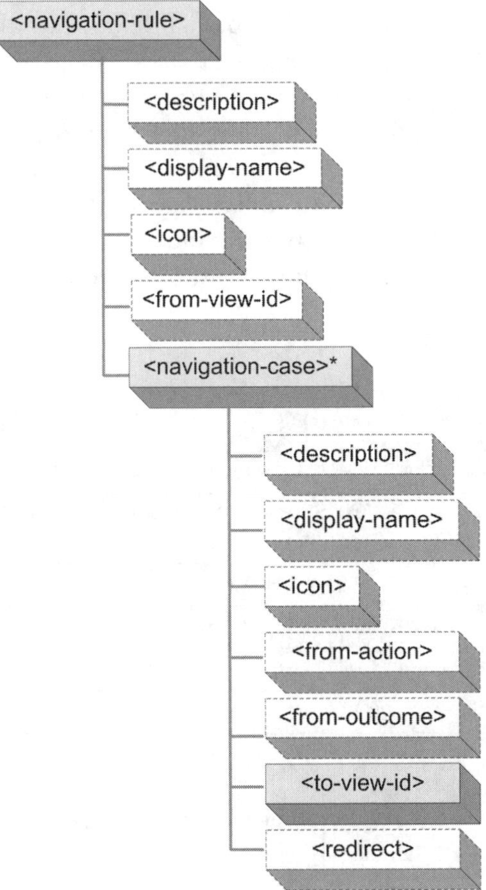

Figure 3.14
Navigation consists of navigation rules, which are defined with the `<navigation-rule>` element in a JSF configuration file. Optionally, a `<navigation-rule>` can specify the page to which it applies with the `<from-view-id>` element. Each `<navigation-rule>` has one or more `<navigation-case>` elements, which must have a `<to-view-id>` element that specifies the next page to load. A `<navigation-case>` can optionally specify an outcome with a `<from-outcome>` element and an action with the `<from-action>` element. If the `<redirect>` element is specified, JSF will send an HTTP redirect instead of forwarding to the view internally. Both the `<navigation-rule>` and `<navigation-case>` elements can optionally have `<description>`, `<display-name>`, and `<icon>` elements which are generally used for tools.

In the listing, JSPs are referenced by the `<from-view-id>` and `<to-view-id>` elements. Every view has an identifier, which is simply the filename.[4] The filename can be either a JSP or any other resource, but it must be relative to the web application's root directory and prefixed with a slash (/). You can have more than one navigation rule with the same `<from-view-id>` value; JSF will treat them all as one big combined navigation rule. This is useful if your application has different configuration files with navigation rules, which could happen if you have different people working on different parts of your application.

The last navigation case specifies the `<redirect>` element, which tells JSF to send an HTTP redirect to send the user to the new view, as opposed to forwarding the user to the view internally. In the world of JSP, this means that the user sees the URL of the page he or she is currently viewing, as opposed to the URL of the previous page (remember, JSF pages post back to themselves). The `<redirect>` element also forces the request for the new view to be handled externally by the web container, which means it will be processed by any additional application logic you may have (like a servlet filter).

Also note that the outcome strings don't map to the specific resources; they're *logical* results. This is key—there's no need for outcomes to be related to a specific resource. If you use outcomes this way, it will be easy to change the actual resource an outcome maps to without changing the meaning of the outcome itself (which means no Java code changes). Table 3.8 shows some common outcome strings.

Table 3.8 Common outcome strings

Outcome	Meaning
success	The operation completed successfully. Move to the next logical page.
failure	The operation did not complete successfully. Show a page that tells users why and what they can do about it.
error	There was a system error of some sort. Show a system error page.
no results	No records matched the user's query. Show the search page again.
login	The user needs to log in first. Show the login page.
logout	Log out of the application. Show the logout page.

[4] The view identifier is a JSP filename by default, but other implementations may provide alternate mappings. For example, a view identifier could map to a Java class that initializes the components in code.

Our order placement example works on the outcomes `"success"`, `"failure"`, and `"retry"`. The first two are dynamic, and they're returned from an action method. OrderEntry.jsp has an `HtmlCommandButton` component:

```
<h:commandButton value="Place Order"
                 action="#{orderManager.placeOrder}"/>
```

When a user clicks this button, the `placeOrder` method is executed, and it returns the string `"success"` or `"failure"`. Action methods can also return `null`; if they do, the current page is just redisplayed. (To learn how to write action methods, see chapter 13.)

Unlike `"success"` and `"failure"`, the `"retry"` outcome is static, so it isn't generated by an action method at all. It's hardcoded as on the OrderError.jsp page:

```
<h:commandButton value="Retry order submission" action="retry"/>
```

The outcome of a user clicking on this button is constant—it will always be `"retry"`.

Even though two of these outcomes are dynamic and one is static, the navigation rules don't make this distinction. This means that you can change the dynamic outcomes to static ones and vice versa without updating the rules.

If you want to make sure that an outcome was generated by a specific action method, you can do that by nesting a `<from-action>` element inside a `<navigation-case>` element:

```
<navigation-case>
 <from-action>#{orderManager.placeOrder}</from-action>
 <from-outcome>success</from-outcome>
 <to-view-id>/ConfirmOrder.jsp</to-view-id>
</navigation-case>
```

This case won't be executed unless the `"success"` outcome was generated by the `orderManager.placeOrder` action method. This is useful in cases where two different action methods produce the same outcome string. You can even omit the `<from-outcome>` element altogether if you want your navigation case to depend solely on the name of the executed action method:

```
<navigation-case>
 <from-action>#{orderManager.placeOrder}</from-action>
 <to-view-id>/ConfirmOrder.jsp</to-view-id>
</navigation-case>
```

This case states that as long as the action method `orderManager.placeOrder` has been executed, the view ConfirmOrder.jsp will be loaded.

The navigation rules we've discussed so far have been for a specific page. You can also set up rules for all pages (like Struts' global ActionForwards), or groups of pages. A navigation rule is global if its `<from-view-id>` element is an asterisk (*):

```
<navigation-rule>
  <from-view-id>*</from-view-id>
  <navigation-case>
   <from-outcome>login</from-outcome>
   <to-view-id>/login.jsp</to-view-id>
  </navigation-case>
  <navigation-case>
   <from-outcome>logout</from-outcome>
   <to-view-id>/logout.jsp</to-view-id>
  </navigation-case>
</navigation-rule>
```

Because in this example the `<from-view-id>` element's value is an asterisk, this rule applies to all pages. Anytime the outcome is `"login"`, the page login.jsp will be loaded; anytime it's `"logout"`, the page logout.jsp will be loaded. We could have achieved the same effect by omitting the `<from-view-id>` element altogether.

Specific groups of pages can be matched by adding a trailing asterisk in the `<from-view-id>` element. (Asterisks aren't supported anywhere else in the string.) So, if you wanted to match all pages that start with "FrogLegs," the element's value would be "FrogLegs*". If there are several rules that start with "FrogLegs", JSF will choose the longest one.

A more common use is associating a rule with an entire directory:

```
<navigation-rule>
  <from-view-id>/corporate/*</from-view-id>
  <navigation-case>
      <from-outcome>about</from-outcome>
    <to-view-id>/corporate/about.html</to-view-id>
  </navigation-case>
  <navigation-case>
    <from-outcome>contact info</from-outcome>
     <to-view-id>/corporate/contact.html</to-view-id>
  </navigation-case>
</navigation-rule>
```

This specifies a rule that applies to all pages within the context-relative directory "corporate". These navigation cases reference pages that are in the same directory, but that's not a requirement.

TIP If your application has a lot of navigation rules, it may make sense to place them in a separate application configuration file instead of placing them inside your main configuration file.

All of the examples we've shown so far leave out a few optional elements that can be applied both at the navigation case and navigation rule level. Namely, these are the <description>, <display-name>, and <icon> elements. Here's the global navigation rule with these elements added:

```
<navigation-rule>
  <description>Global navigation rule. </description>
  <display-name>Global</display-name>
  <icon>
    <small-icon>/images/global_rule.gif</small-icon>
    <large-icon>/images/global_rule_large.gif</large-icon>
  </icon>
  <from-view-id>*</from-view-id>
  <navigation-case>
     <description>
       If the outcome is "login", jump to login.jsp.
      </description>
       <display-name>Login</display-name>
    <from-outcome>login</from-outcome>
     <to-view-id>/login.jsp</to-view-id>
</navigation-case>
<navigation-case>
   <description>
      If the outcome is "logout", jump to logout.jsp.
   </description>
   <display-name>Logout</display-name>
   <from-outcome>logout</from-outcome>
   <to-view-id>/logout.jsp</to-view-id>
</navigation-case>
</navigation-rule>
```

Here, we've added a description, a display name, and an icon to the navigation rule. We've also added a description and a display name to each navigation case (navigation cases can have icons too, but we didn't specify any here). The <description> element can be useful for communicating the purpose of a rule to other developers on your team (or yourself at a later date). The other elements are generally used by tools when they visualize the navigation rules.

TIP It's a good idea to give a navigation rule a description so that other developers understand its purpose.

This concludes our tour of JSF's navigation facilities. You can find more examples as we build the case study in parts 2 and 3.

3.5 Summary

In this chapter, we examined all of the little details that developers like to know about—the requirements for all JSF applications, how configuration works, the role of JSP, managed beans, and navigation. The core requirements for building JSF applications are a JSF implementation and a web container. Configuration is straightforward—JSF applications require a specific servlet, and configuration is handled through a rather expressive XML configuration file, like most Java web frameworks.

JSF was designed to work with many different display technologies, but all implementations must support JSP with custom tags. Fortunately, you can use JSF custom tags inside of JSPs with JSTL or other custom tag libraries. Any beans your application references can also be referenced with JSTL or other mechanisms, but JSF has a powerful facility for creating and configuring beans through its configuration file. Navigation in JSF applications is also controlled through the configuration file.

By now, it should be clear exactly how JSF fits into the current Java web development landscape, what a JSF application is, and how it can be configured. In the next two chapters, we'll take a closer look at all of the standard UI components in detail.

4 Getting started with the standard components

This chapter covers

- UI component basics
- Component development with IDEs
- The standard output components

Now that you understand what JavaServer Faces is and you're familiar with the fundamental concepts, it's time to learn how to use the standard amenities. In this chapter and the next, we cover the standard components that are included with all JSF implementations. They provide the basic set of functionality necessary for building HTML-based web applications. (You can also expect web container vendors, tool vendors, and third-party developers to provide additional components as well.)

In this chapter, we start with an overview of all the components, discuss JSP integration in more detail, and examine components that aren't involved with user input. In the next chapter, we'll focus on the standard input components, and the `HtmlDataTable` component, which displays or edits tabular data from a data source. Our goal with these two chapters is to help you use the components to develop user interfaces (UIs). If you're a front-end developer, these chapters will be indispensable, because you'll be working with these components most of the time. If you're a back-end developer, understanding how these components work will help you develop your own components, and help to ensure smooth integration with your code.

4.1 It's all in the components

The most central feature of JSF is its support for UI components—this is what sets it apart from many other web development frameworks. JSF ships with a standard set of components that are intended to provide support for typical HTML UIs. These include widgets for text display, text entry fields, drop-down lists, forms, panels, and so on. These are listed in table 4.1.

Next to each component name you'll notice a display name column. These are user-friendly names you may see inside IDEs. As you can see, the names may vary by IDE. We haven't listed display names for components that aren't usually shown in a component palette, or for which no examples were available when writing this book. Regardless of what display name an IDE uses, the code it generates will be standard (in other words, any generated JSP or Java code will look like the code in this book).

You may have noticed that many of these components closely resemble standard HTML controls. This is no accident—the intent was to provide enough widgets to build basic HTML UIs. All of the standard components that have a visual representation generate standard HTML 4.01 and integrate well with CSS and JavaScript. (If you were hoping the standard components would support older browsers, you're out of luck—look for third-party alternatives.)

Table 4.1 JSF includes several standard UI components for building HTML views. Related components with similar functionality are organized into families.

Family[a]	Component	Possible IDE Display Names	Description
`Column`	`UIColumn`	N/A	A table column. Used to configure template columns for parent `HtmlDataTable` component.
`Command`	`HtmlCommandButton`	Command – Button, Button	A form button that is an action source and can execute an action method.
	`HtmlCommandLink`	Command – Link, Link Action	A hyperlink that is an action source and can execute an action method.
`Data`	`HtmlDataTable`	Data Grid, Data Table	A data-aware table with customizable headers, footers, and other properties. Can connect to multiple types of data sources.
`Form`	`HtmlForm`	N/A	An input form; must enclose all input components.
`Graphic`	`HtmlGraphicImage`	Image	Displays an image based on its URL.
`Input`	`HtmlInputHidden`	Hidden Field	An input field of type "hidden".
	`HtmlInputSecret`	Secret Field	An input field of type "password".
	`HtmlInputText`	Text Field	An input field of type "text".
	`HtmlInputTextarea`	Multi Line Text Area	A text area (multi-line input field).
`Message`	`HtmlMessage`	Display Error, Inline Message	Displays messages for a specific component.
`Messages`	`HtmlMessages`	Message List	Displays all messages (component-related and/or application-related).

continued on next page

Table 4.1 JSF includes several standard UI components for building HTML views. Related components with similar functionality are organized into families. *(continued)*

Family[a]	Component	Possible IDE Display Names	Description
`Output`	`HtmlOutputFormat`	Formatted Output	Outputs parameterized text.
	`HtmlOutputLabel`	Component Label	A text label for an input field.
	`HtmlOutputLink`	Hyperlink	A hyperlink that's not associated with a user command.
	`HtmlOutputText`	Output Text	Plain text, with optional CSS formatting.
	`UIOutput`	N/A	Plain text (no formatting). Useful for enclosing HTML markup or other custom tags.
`Parameter`	`UIParameter`	N/A	An invisible component used to configure other components.
`Panel`	`HtmlPanelGrid`	Grid Panel	A table with customizable headers, footers, and other properties.
	`HtmlPanelGroup`	Panel – Group Box, Group Box	Groups components together for use inside of other components, and to apply common styles or hide/display a group of components.
`Select-Boolean`	`HtmlSelectBooleanCheckbox`	Check Box, Checkbox	A single checkbox.
`Select-Item`	`UISelectItem`	N/A	Represents a single item or item group for use in SelectMany and SelectOne components.
`Select-Items`	`UISelectItems`	N/A	Represents a collection of items or item groups for use in SelectMany and SelectOne components.

continued on next page

Table 4.1 JSF includes several standard UI components for building HTML views. Related components with similar functionality are organized into families. *(continued)*

Family[a]	Component	Possible IDE Display Names	Description
`Select-Many`	`HtmlSelectManyCheckbox`	Check Box Group	A table with a list of checkboxes, grouped together.
	`HtmlSelectManyListbox`	Multi Select Listbox	A listbox that allows you to select multiple items.
	`HtmlSelectManyMenu`	N/A	A multi-select listbox that shows one available option at a time.
`SelectOne`	`HtmlSelectOneRadio`	Radio Button Group	A table of radio buttons, grouped together.
	`HtmlSelectOneListbox`	Listbox	A listbox that allows you to select a single item.
	`HtmlSelectOneMenu`	Combo Box, Dropdown List	A drop-down listbox that allows you to select a single item.
`ViewRoot`	`UIViewRoot`	N/A	Represents entire view; contains all components on the page.

[a] *Technically, each of the component family names have the prefix "javax.faces." So, the "Form" family is really called javax.faces.Form. Using the full component family name is useful when you're working with renderers or components in Java code.*

Table 4.1 also reveals another aspect of UI components: they're organized into families. A *family* is a group of related UI components that have similar behavior. Families are primarily used behind the scenes to assist with rendering. However, because components in the same family have similar functionality, it's useful to talk about components in the same family together, and that's the approach we'll use in this chapter and the next.

Most of these components have properties specific to HTML—for example, the `HtmlPanelGrid` component has a `cellpadding` property, because it maps to an HTML table. You can manipulate these properties if you're working visually within an IDE, directly with JSP, or in Java code. However, these UI components are subclasses of more generic components that don't have specific properties for the target client. If you're writing Java code or developing custom components, you may prefer to work with the superclasses so that you're not dependent on generating HTML; see parts 3 and 4 for more information.

All of this is fine and dandy, but what is it that makes UI components so important? We touched upon this in chapter 2—they provide stateful, packaged functionality for interacting with the user. For example, the `HtmlTextarea` component handles displaying an HTML `<textarea>` element to the user, updating its value with the user's response, and remembering that value between requests. As we've seen, that value can also be associated directly with a backing bean or model object. UI components also generate events that you can wire to server-side code. `HtmlTextarea` will generate a value-change event whenever the user enters a new value.

UI components also make great use of value-binding expressions—for the most part, *any* component property can be associated with a value-binding expression. This means you can specify all of your component's properties—everything from its `value` to other properties like its `size` and `title`—in some completely different data store. It doesn't really matter where it's stored (or if it's stored at all), as long as it's exposed through a bean.

NOTE In this chapter and the next, we cover the standard components from a front-end development perspective. Consequently, we will only list some properties that accessed exclusively with Java code, and we will not examine the component's methods. See part 3 for more details on writing Java code that interacts with UI components.

As we discussed in chapter 3, JSF is integrated with JSP through custom tags. Tags that are associated with UI components are called *component tags*. The ones that are specific to HTML are in the HTML tag library (usually with the prefix "h"), and the rest of them are in the core tag library (usually with the prefix "f"). The core tag library also has tags for validators, converters, and so on.

4.1.1 Using HTML attributes

All of the standard HTML components have properties that support basic HTML 4.01 attributes. These properties are passed directly through to the web browser, so they're called *pass-through* properties. They're available when you're manipulating a component in an event listener (as we demonstrated in chapter 1), and also in component tags.

In some cases, component tags map directly to an HTML element, so using pass-through properties seems quite logical. For example, this component tag:

```
<h:inputText value="hello" size="30" maxlength="40"
             accesskey="T" tabindex="0"/>
```

maps to this HTML:

```
<input type="text" name="_id1:_id2" value="hello" accesskey="T"
       maxlength="40" size="30" tabindex="0" />
```

The properties marked in bold are passed through to the browser. Even though the `value` property looks as if it were passed through, it was actually checked for validity. This brings up an important point: pass-through properties are *not* checked for validity at all.

As you get a handle on how the component tags map to HTML elements, adding HTML pass-through attributes will become natural. They also make it easy to replace existing HTML tags with JSF component tags. We provide many examples of HTML pass-through attributes throughout the rest of parts 1 and 2.

Using Cascading Style Sheets

One subtle exception to the pass-through rule is the `class` attribute, which is used to associate Cascading Style Sheets (CSS) class names with an HTML element. Due to technical restrictions in JSP, the name "class" can't be used. As a workaround, most UI components have a property called `styleClass`. When you declare a component, you can specify multiple CSS classes by placing a space in between them:

```
<h:myComponent styleClass="style1 style2 style3"/>
```

This specifies three CSS style classes for the fictional `myComponent`. Some IDEs will let you choose an existing class from style sheets that are currently in your project.

Most components also support the CSS `style` property, so you can specify their styles without a class. If you're a CSS expert, you can integrate each component with your style sheets (or styles) manually by simply using the `style` and `styleClass` properties. Some IDEs simplify this process by including basic CSS editors that allow you to modify a component's look and feel without knowing CSS, as shown in figure 4.1. Once you have selected the display properties (font color, background color, border, alignment, and so on), the IDE will create the proper CSS style for you.

4.1.2 Understanding facets

So far, we've seen many examples of parent-child relationships, like an `HtmlInputText` component nested within an `HtmlForm`. JSF also supports named relationships, called *facets*. Facets aren't exactly children, but they're quite similar. They're

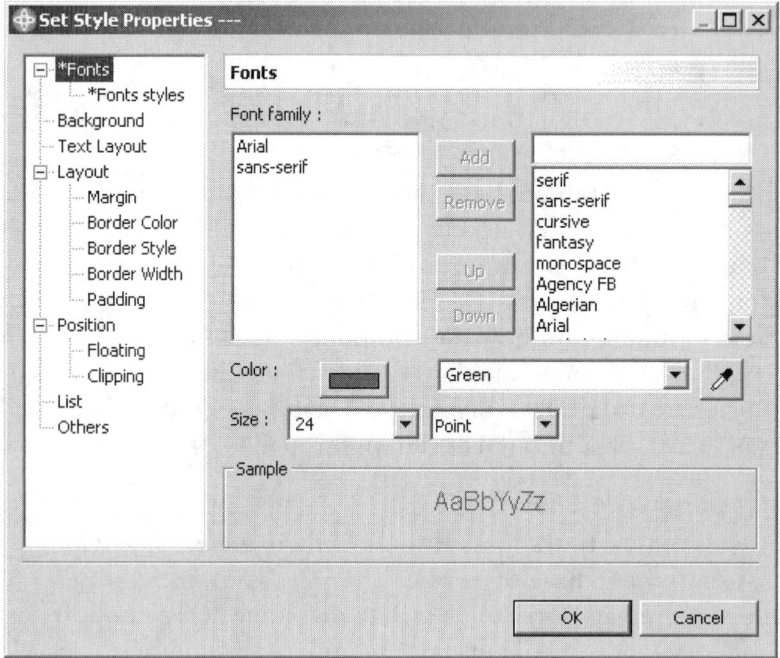

Figure 4.1 WebSphere Application Developer [IBM, WSAD] provides a convenient dialog box for creating new CSS styles that are used by some UI component properties.

used to specify subordinate elements like a header or footer, so they're common in more complicated components like an `HtmlPanelGrid` or an `HtmlDataTable`. Here's an example of the latter:

```
<h:dataTable value="#{defaultUser.favoriteSites}" var="site">
  <f:facet name="header">
    <h:outputText value="Table header"/>
  </f:facet>

  <h:column>
    <f:facet name="header">
      <h:outputText value="Column header"/>
    </f:facet>
    <h:outputText value="#{site}"/>
  </h:column>

  <f:facet name="footer">
    <h:panelGroup>
      <h:commandButton value="Next page" action="#{myBean.nextPage}"/>
      <h:commandButton value="Previous page"
                       action="#{myBean.previousPage}"/>
```

```
    </h:panelGroup>
  </f:facet>
</h:dataTable>
```

This example has three facets: one for the table's header, one for the column header, and one for the table footer. As you can see, the `<f:facet>` tag defines the relationship, but the facet's child is the actual component that's displayed. Each facet can have only one child component, so if you want to include several components, they must be children of another component, like the `HtmlPanelGroup` used to enclose the components in the `footer` facet.

You'll see more facet examples when we explore components, like `HtmlPanelGrid`, that use them. In the meantime, let's take a look at how UI components integrate with development tools—one of JSF's primary goals.

4.1.3 The power of tools

In chapter 1, we talked about the days of Rapid Application Development (RAD) and how the emphasis was on building UIs by dragging and dropping UI components from a palette. That type of functionality is one of the primary goals of JSF. When you use an IDE that has full-fledged support for JSF, there is usually a component palette that includes all of the standard JSF components, and often some nonstandard ones as well. Component palettes are usually small windows that list all of the components with an icon beside them, as shown in figure 4.2. Most tools will also offer proprietary components in addition to standard JSF components, as shown in figure 4.3.

You build the UI by creating or opening a page, dropping the components from the palette into it, and then customizing the component's properties. Usually you'll modify things like the `value` (which is often associated with a backing bean property), the `rendered` property (which controls whether or not the component is visible), and HTML-specific properties like the CSS style. Figure 4.4 should give you an idea what this process looks like.

Because building a UI is largely dependent on the behavior of the UI components, we'll spend some time describing how each of these components behave with different property settings. Moreover, you'll see the raw JSP that these tools often generate (it's quite possible to visually design JSF views without JSP, but tools will initially support only this style of development with JSP).

Knowing how to use the component tags can be useful for cases where you're not using a tool at all, or you prefer to tweak the JSP by hand and immediately see the results while you're working inside an IDE. Most IDEs have *two-way editors*, so any changes you make in the designer will be propagated to the source, and vice versa.

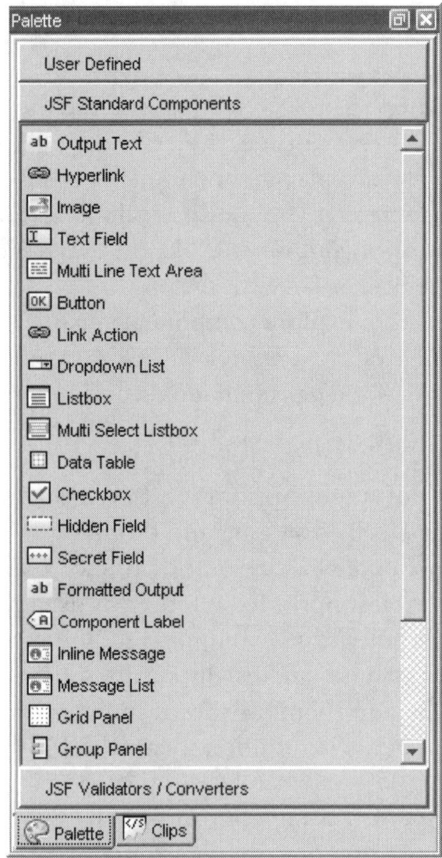

Figure 4.2 Java Studio Creator [Sun, Creator] has a dockable component palette. Note that the display names are different than the actual names of the components, as shown in table 4.1. The display names may vary between IDEs.

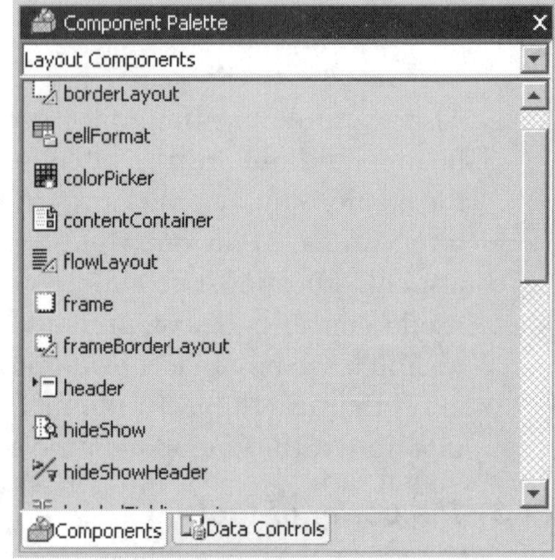

Figure 4.3 Oracle provides a version of JDeveloper [Oracle, JDeveloper] that integrates its extensive palette of UIX components with JSF.

IDEs usually allow you to work with Java code as well—in fact, tools like WebSphere Application Developer [IBM, WSAD] and Oracle JDeveloper [Oracle, JDeveloper] allow you to build applications using a ton of other Java technologies in conjunction with, or instead of, JSF. For details about JSF support in some popular IDEs, see online extension appendix B.

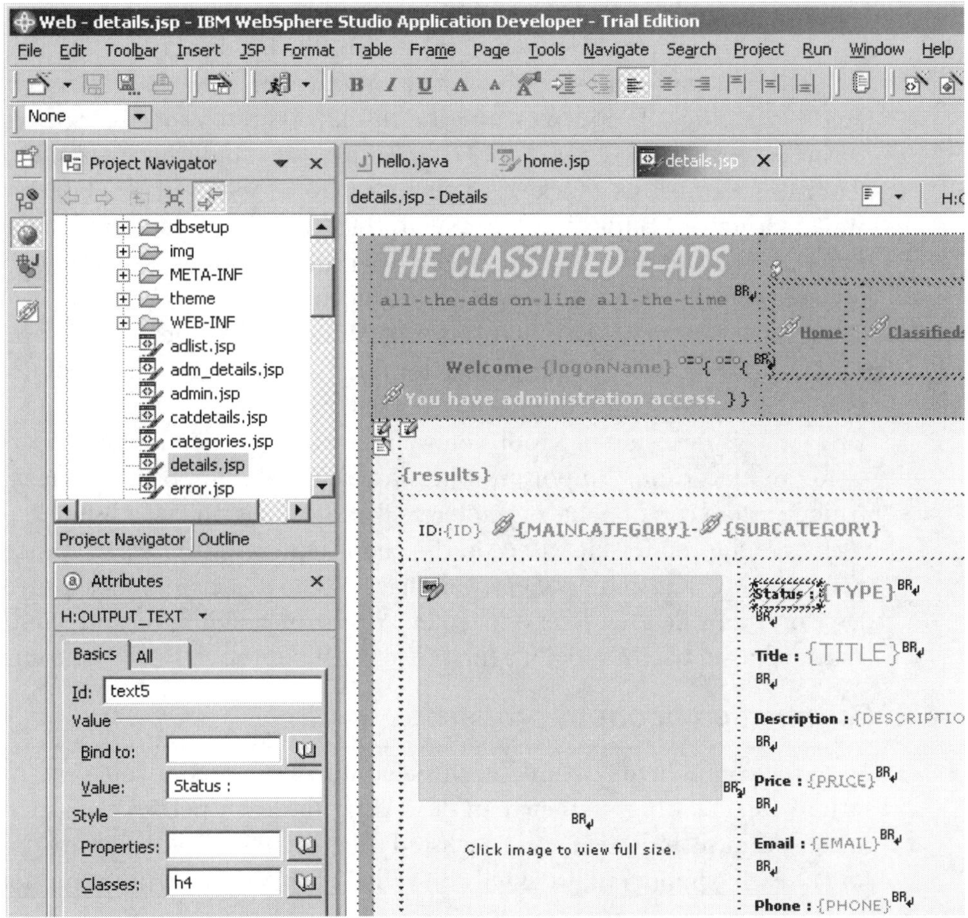

Figure 4.4 Building a JSF page inside of WebSphere Application Developer [IBM, WSAD].

> **TIP** If you want your JSF application to be portable across implementations, stick to these standard components and third-party component suites. Don't rely on nonstandard components bundled with integrated development environments (IDEs) or JSF implementations unless you're sure they can be used in other environments, or vendor lock-in is not a concern.

Now that it's clear how tools are involved, let's take a step back and look at where all the HTML is actually generated.

4.1.4 The render kit behind the scenes

As we said in chapter 2, renderers are responsible for displaying JSF components and setting a component's value based on the user's response. Render kits are logical groupings of renderers, and they usually output a specific type of markup or variants of the same markup. For example, you could have a render kit that generates Extensible Markup Language (XML), Wireless Markup Language (WML), Scalable Vector Graphics (SVG), HTML, or just about any other kind of output. You could also have another render kit that generates HTML but uses a lot of client-side script and browser-specific features.

JSF includes a standard HTML render kit that is responsible for providing HTML encoding and decoding behavior for all of the standard components. The render kit is used behind the scenes, so if you're working exclusively with the standard JSF tags or inside of a tool, you won't need to worry about renderers at all.

Render kits can be important when you're developing back-end Java code or writing custom components or renderers. For example, an event listener may need to change the render kit based on the client type or a user's preference. And if you're writing a new component, you may want to associate it with a specific renderer or write a new renderer altogether. We discuss building custom renderers and components in part 4. Now, it's time to learn about the standard UI components.

4.2 Common component properties

All of the components covered in this chapter share a set of common properties such as `id` and `value`. Rather than describing these properties each time we discuss a specific component, we have listed them all in table 4.2. During our discussion of each component, we'll tell you which of these properties it supports.

Table 4.2 Common properties for UI components discussed in this chapter.

Property	Type	Default Value	Required?	Description
`id`	`String`	None	Yes	Component identifier.
`value`	`Object`	None	Yes	The component's current local value. Can be literal text or a value-binding expression.
`rendered`	`boolean`	`true`	No	Controls whether or not the component is visible.
`converter`	Converter instance (value-binding expression or converter identifier)	None	No	Sets the converter used to convert the value to and from a string for display.

continued on next page

Table 4.2 Common properties for UI components discussed in this chapter. *(continued)*

Property	Type	Default Value	Required?	Description
`styleClass`	`String`	None	No	Name of CSS style class; rendered as an HTML `class` attribute. Multiple classes can be specified with a space in between them.
`binding`	`String`	None	No	A value-binding expression that associates this component with a backing bean property.[a]

[a] *Technically, this is a JSP component tag attribute, and not an actual UI component property. In other words, you can not set this property in Java code.*

4.3 Controlling the page with UIViewRoot

It should be clear by now that all of the components on a page are represented in a tree, and that this tree is called a *view*. `UIViewRoot` is the component at the root of this tree. If there's no `UIViewRoot`, there is no view.

This component is unique because it doesn't display anything, and most tools will automatically add it to your JSP (you usually can't actually drag it from the component palette). Also, you can't bind it directly to a backing bean with the `binding` property.[1] Because it has nothing to do with HTML, it's in the core tag library. `UIViewRoot` is summarized in table 4.3.

Table 4.3 `UIViewRoot` is the container for the entire view.

Component	`UIViewRoot`
Family	`javax.faces.ViewRoot`
Possible IDE Display Names	N/A
Display Behavior	Holds all of the child components for a view. Does not display anything.
Tag Library	Core
JSP Tag	`<f:view>`
Pass-Through Properties	None

continued on next page

[1] You can, however, always access `UIViewRoot` through `FacesContext` in Java code.

Table 4.3 `UIViewRoot` is the container for the entire view. *(continued)*

Property	Type	Default Value	Required?	Description
`locale`	`java.util.Locale`	The user's current locale	No	The locale for the current view

So far, we've seen plenty examples of `UIViewRoot` in use—it's represented by the `<f:view>` tag, as shown in listing 4.1.

Listing 4.1 UIViewRoot must enclose all other UI components on the same page

```
<%@ taglib uri="http://java.sun.com/jsf/core" prefix="f" %>
<%@ taglib uri="http://java.sun.com/jsf/html" prefix="h" %>
<html>
<head>
  <title>UIViewRoot</title>
</head>
<body bgcolor="#ffffff">
<h1>UIViewRoot example</h1>

<f:view>
  <span style="background-color:grey">
     This is template text.
  </span>
  <h:panelGrid columns="2" border="1">
    <h:outputText value="This is an HtmlOutputText component."/>
    <h:graphicImage url="images/hello.gif"/>
  </h:panelGrid>
</f:view>

</body>
</html>
```

In the listing, `UIViewRoot` is used inside of template text (pure HTML). It has UI components nested within it (an `HtmlPanelGrid` with child `HtmlOutputText` and `HtmlGraphicImage` components). It also has raw HTML text nested within it. This is an important point: you can mix and match template text with JSF component tags *inside* the `<f:view>` tag. (If you want to use template text inside any other component, see the `<f:verbatim>` tag, covered in section 4.5.2.) You can't, however, use JSF component tags unless they're nested inside `<f:view>`.

Even though listing 4.1 shows a large amount of HTML in the page, it's certainly not required. In part 2, we'll look at developing views that contain hardly any HTML at all.

The only property exposed in UIViewRoot's component tag is locale, which allows you to specify the language the current page supports. Suppose you wanted to ensure that a particular page always displays in Spanish:

```
<f:view locale="es">
  ...
</f:view>
```

The string "es" is the locale code for Spanish, so this view will always display in Spanish. You can have only one view per page, so the entire page must be in a single language.

Hard-coding the locale isn't terribly useful unless you're creating different pages for each locale; often you'll use a value-binding expression instead. You certainly don't have to set the locale manually—JSF usually sets it automatically. See chapter 6 for more information about internationalization and localization.

4.4 Setting component parameters with UIParameter

Most of the time, when a component displays itself, it knows exactly what to do. But sometimes it needs a little help—some extra information to complete the job. This is the purpose of the UIParameter component: to provide dynamic variables that can be used during the encoding and decoding processes.

UIParameter has no specific HTML equivalent; how it is displayed in a browser depends on the associated component. Three standard components use it: HtmlOutputFormat, HtmlOutputLink, and HtmlCommandLink.

This component's key properties are name and value. The name property is optional, and is only used in cases where the parent component requires a named parameter (for example, HtmlOutputLink requires name, and HtmlOutputFormat doesn't).

Because this component has no direct HTML counterpart, it is part of the core Faces tag library, not the tag library for the HTML render kit. UIParameter is summarized in table 4.4.

Table 4.4 UIParameter is used to add parameters to another component.

Component	UIParameter
Family	javax.faces.Parameter
Possible IDE Display Names	N/A
Display Behavior	None. Adds a parameter to its parent component.

continued on next page

Table 4.4 `UIParameter` is used to add parameters to another component. *(continued)*

Tag Library	Core			
JSP Tag	`<f:param>`			
Pass-Through Properties	None			
Common Properties	`id, value, binding` (see table 4.2)			
Property	**Type**	**Default Value**	**Required?**	**Description**
`name`	`String`	None	No	Name of the parameter. Optional for some components.

Unlike most JSF components, when you use `UIParameter` inside of an IDE, you usually don't drag and drop it off the component palette. Instead, you may be able to edit inside a property inspector. For example, IBM WebSphere Application Developer [IBM, WSAD] lets you add parameters through its attribute view, as shown in figure 4.5. The figure shows two named parameters: one named `operation`, with the value `"update"`, and the other named `id`, with the value `"#{requestScope.id}"`.

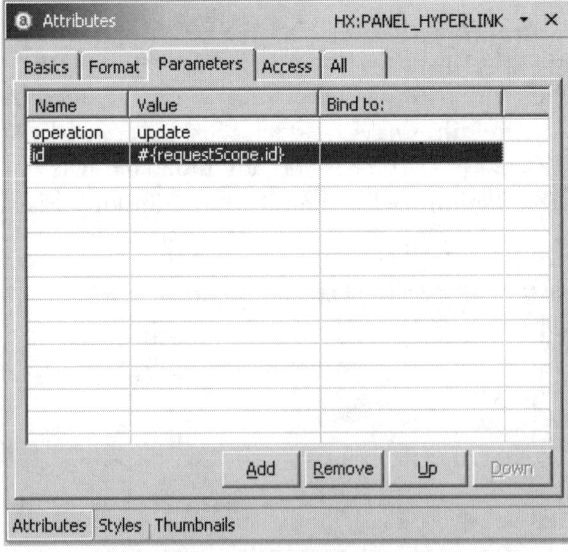

Figure 4.5 WebSphere Application Developer [IBM, WSAD] allows you to edit parameters with its property inspector.

In JSP, you add a parameter to a component by nesting it within the parent component's tag:

```
<h:foobar>
  <f:param name="operation" value="update"/>
</h:foobar>
```

This adds a `UIParameter` named `operation` with the value `"update"` to a fictional component represented by the component tag `<h:foobar>`. The exact behavior the `UIParameter` affects depends on the mysterious purpose of the `Foobar` component.

As shown in the figure, you can also associate a parameter with a value-binding expression. Using the `name` property is optional as well, as long as the component doesn't need a named parameter.

You'll see more examples of using `UIParameter` when we cover components that use it.

4.5 Displaying data with the Output components

A large portion of what web applications do is display data. That's the purpose of the Output components. You can specify explicitly the data that they display or have them display backing bean properties. These components will mind their own business—they are read-only, so they will never modify any associated objects.

JSF provides four components for simple output, all of which are part of the Output component family. The `HtmlOutputText` component is used for displaying plain text but also has properties for CSS styles. For displaying pure text with no formatting, you can use the `UIOutput` component. The `HtmlOutputLabel` component is used for attaching labels to input controls. And finally, the `HtmlOutputMessage` component is used for displaying flexible parameterized strings.

Now, let's take a look at each of these components, their behavior, and their properties. These components are indispensable, so you can find more examples throughout the rest of the book.

4.5.1 Displaying ordinary text with HtmlOutputText

So far you've seen `HtmlOutputText` plenty of times in previous examples; it just displays its value, with optional formatting. Table 4.5 describes this component and its properties.

Table 4.5 `HtmlOutputText` summary

Component	`HtmlOutputText`
Family	`javax.faces.Output`
Possible IDE Display Names	Output Text
Display Behavior	Converts the value to a string and displays it with optional support CSS styles. (If the `id` or `style` property is set, encloses the text in a `<span>` element.)
Tag Library	HTML
JSP Tag	`<h:outputText>`
Pass-Through Properties	`style, title`
Common Properties	`id, value, rendered, converter, styleClass, binding` (see table 4.2)

Property	Type	Default Value	Required?	Description
`escape`	`boolean`	`true`	No	Controls whether or not HTML or XML characters are escaped (displayed literally in a browser).

By default, `HtmlOutputText` displays its value directly with no formatting. That's it. No additives—just the plain value.

Special characters are escaped using the appropriate HTML or XML entities by default, so if you embed any markup characters (HTML or XML), they will be displayed literally. An example is shown in table 4.6.

Table 4.6 `HtmlOutputText` example: Text is escaped by default.

HTML	`What are <i>you</i> looking at?`
Component Tag	`<h:outputText value="What are <i>you</i> looking at?"/>`
Browser Display	What are <i>you</i> looking at?

As the table shows, by default any markup in `HtmlOutputText`'s value will be displayed literally in a browser. If you want to have the markup passed through directly, you can set the `escape` property to `false`, as shown in table 4.7.

Table 4.7 `HtmlOutputText` example: Turning off escaping of text.

HTML	`What are <i>you</i> looking at?`
Component Tag	`<h:outputText value="What are <i>you</i> looking at?" escape="false"/>`
Browser Display	What are *you* looking at?

In this case, the component's value isn't escaped, so it is interpreted by the browser. Turning off escaping is useful whenever you want the component's `value` to pass through directly to the client, but if you have larger sets of text and you don't need to use style sheets or HTML formatting, you should use the `UIOutput` component, covered in the next section, instead.

BY THE WAY If you're familiar with JSTL, you may wonder why anyone would use an `HtmlOutputText` component instead of JSTL's `<c:out>` tag. Using `UIOutput` allows you to take full control of the JSF component model. `HtmlOutputText` components are children of other components in the tree, and you can manipulate their behavior in server-side code. If you use a tag like `<c:out>` that isn't backed by a component, there's no server-side representation of the output—in effect, it's more like template text. It's worthwhile, however, to point out that `<c:out>` is more lightweight, because no server-side component is created.

`HtmlOutputText` is great for displaying simple values (with optional CSS formatting), but it doesn't display its body text (you *must* use the `value` property), and you can't embed custom tags in its body. These are features that the `<f:verbatim>` tag offers.

4.5.2 Using UIOutput with the <f:verbatim> tag

When you want to display literal text without any formatting, or embed other JSP custom tags inside a view, you can use the `UIOutput` component with the `<f:verbatim>` tag. Table 4.8 describes the component and its properties.

Table 4.8 `UIOutput` summary

Component	UIOutput			
Family	javax.faces.Output			
Display Name	N/A			
Display Behavior	Displays its body without formatting, processing any embedded JSP custom tags			
Tag Library	Core			
JSP Tag	<f:verbatim>			
Pass-Through Properties	None			
Property	**Type**	**Default Value**	**Required?**	**Description**
escape	boolean	false	No	Controls whether or not HTML or XML characters are escaped (displayed literally in a browser).

NOTE UIOutput technically has additional properties; this section is limited to the <f:verbatim> tag's use of the component.

As you can see from the table, the <f:verbatim> tag doesn't expose a lot of the common UI component properties like rendered, converter, or binding. If you need to use those properties, you're better off with HtmlOutputText; <f:verbatim> is solely useful for displaying its body content. Unlike HtmlOutputText, the escape property defaults to false.

One of the best uses for <f:verbatim> is escaping and displaying a large block of static text. Suppose we wanted to display this snippet of a JSF configuration file in a page, as shown in table 4.9.

Here, we've placed all of the literal text inside the tag's body, which you can't do with HtmlOutputText. The escape property is also set to true to ensure that all of the XML elements are properly escaped. This example results in properly escaped HTML output without the need to manually type in all of those exciting HTML entities.

The <f:verbatim> tag is also useful for encasing markup or other tags inside components that are containers, like HtmlPanelGrid and HtmlDataTable. This is because these components require that all of their children be JSF components, so you can't nest arbitrary template text or other custom tags inside them. You can, however, use the <f:verbatim> tag.

Table 4.9 `UIOutput` example: Escaping a large block of body text.

HTML

```
<pre>
   &lt;application&gt;
   &lt;message-bundle&gt;CustomMessages&lt;/message-bundle&gt;
   &lt;locale-config&gt;
   &lt;default-locale&gt;en&lt;/default-locale&gt;
   &lt;supported-locale&gt;en&lt;/supported-locale&gt;
   &lt;supported-locale&gt;es&lt;/supported-locale&gt;
   &lt;/locale-config&gt;
   &lt;/application&gt;
</pre>
```

Component Tag

```
<pre>
 <f:verbatim escape="true">
  <application>
    <message-bundle>CustomMessages</message-bundle>
    <locale-config>
      <default-locale>en</default-locale>
      <supported-locale>en</supported-locale>
      <supported-locale>es</supported-locale>
    </locale-config>
  </application>
 </f:verbatim>
</pre>
```

Browser Display

```
<application>
   <message-bundle>CustomMessages</message-bundle>
   <locale-config>
     <default-locale>en</default-locale>
     <supported-locale>en</supported-locale>
     <supported-locale>es</supported-locale>
   </locale-config>
 </application>
```

Suppose we wanted to output a simple two-column table, with the left column displaying a list from a backing bean and the right column displaying normal HTML text. There are only three items in the backing bean list: "www.yahoo.com", "www.javalobby.org", and "www.jsfcentral.com".

You can create HTML tables with the `HtmlPanelGrid` component. We'll cover that component in detail later in this chapter, but for now, let's just use it to generate the preceding table. For the left column, we'll use the JSTL `<c:forEach>` tag. For the right column, we'll just embed literal HTML. The example is shown in table 4.10.

As you can see, the `<c:forEach>` tag and the literal HTML are both embedded in `<f:verbatim>` tags. The `<f:verbatim>` tag is nested inside the `<h:panelGrid>` tag. Only JSF component tags are allowed inside an `<h:panelGrid>`, so using

Table 4.10 `UIOutput` example: Embedding custom tags and markup.

<table>
<tr><td>HTML</td><td><pre>
<table border="1">
  <tbody>
    <tr>
      <td>www.yahoo.com,
          www.javalobby.org,
          www.jsfcentral.com
      </td>
     <td>
        <p>
          <font color="red">This is normal <u>HTML</u>
                             text.</font>
        </p>
     </td>
    </tr>
  </tbody>
</table>
</pre></td></tr>
<tr><td>Component Tag</td><td><pre>
<h:panelGrid columns="2" border="1">
  <f:verbatim>
    <c:forEach items="${user.favoriteSites}" var="site">
      <c:out value="${site}, "/>
    </c:forEach>
  </f:verbatim>
  <f:verbatim escape="false">
    <p><font color="red">This is normal <u>HTML</u>
                         text.</font></p>
  </f:verbatim>
</h:panelGrid>
</pre></td></tr>
<tr><td>Browser Display</td><td><table><tr><td>www.yahoo.com, www.javalobby.org, www.jsfcentral.com,</td><td>This is normal <u>HTML</u> text.</td></tr></table></td></tr>
</table>

`<f:verbatim>` allows us to treat the JSTL tag and the template text like JSF components. Also, note that the `escape` property is set to `false` for the HTML text because we'd like it to be processed by the browser.

`UIOutput` and `HtmlOutputText` are useful components for displaying simple text, but if you need to associate that text with an input control, you must embed them inside an `HtmlOutputLabel` component.

4.5.3 Creating input labels with HtmlOutputLabel

The `HtmlOutputLabel` component is used for associating labels with form elements—it maps directly to the HTML `<label>` element. This allows target devices to be smarter about how text is related with controls on the screen so that they can do such things as highlight a text field when the user clicks on the label. It's also a requirement for creating accessible applications. The component is summarized in table 4.11.

Table 4.11 `HtmlOutputLabel` summary

Component	`HtmlOutputLabel`			
Family	`javax.faces.Output`			
Display Name	Component Label			
Display Behavior	Displays a `<label>` element. Usually has an `HtmlOutputText` and/or other components as its children.			
Tag Library	Core			
JSP Tag	`<h:outputLabel>`			
Pass-Through Properties	HTML attributes for `<label>` element.			
Common Properties	`id, value, rendered, converter, styleClass, binding` (see table 4.2)			
Property	**Type**	**Default Value**	**Required?**	**Description**
`for`	`String`	None	Yes	Component identifier of UI component this label is for.

An `HtmlOutputLabel` component's `for` property is required, and it must be associated with an input control's component identifier. The component doesn't actually display any text—it just renders a `<label>` element (which has no visual representation). To display anything inside that label, you must nest another UI component. (The child component is usually `HtmlOutputText`; some tools will add it automatically when you drag an `HtmlOutputLabel` component from the palette.)

An example of using `HtmlOutputLabel` for an `HtmlInputText` component is shown in table 4.12.

You can see that the `<h:outputLabel>` tag maps directly to the `<label>` tag, and the `accesskey` property is passed through. The `for` property references the `HtmlInputText` component by its component identifier, but the HTML output uses its client identifier (`HtmlOutputLabel` handles this translation for you automatically). This brings up an important point: whenever you're associating

Table 4.12 `HtmlOutputLabel` example: Adding a label to an `HtmlInputLabel` component.

HTML	`<label for="myForm:userNameInput" accesskey="N">`
	`    Enter your name:`
	`</label>`
	`<input id="myForm:userNameInput" type="text"/>`

Component Tag	`<h:outputLabel for="userNameInput" accesskey="N">`
	`  <h:outputText value="Enter your name: "/>`
	`</h:outputLabel>`
	`<h:inputText id="userNameInput"/>`

Browser Display	Enter your name: [text field]

`HtmlOutputLabel` with an input control, you have to specify the input control's identifier. Otherwise, you won't know what value to use as the `for` attribute.

In HTML, you can nest an input element within the label tag and leave out the `for` attribute. With JSF, you can certainly nest an input control one or more components inside of an `<h:outputLabel>` tag, but the `for` attribute is mandatory.

Now that we've examined components that display simple strings (or the result of value-binding expressions), let's look at a component that adds some formatting capabilities.

4.5.4 Using HtmlOutputFormat for parameterized text

`HtmlOutputFormat` displays parameterized text. In other words, you can specify a special string, and the component will insert values (either hardcoded or defined by value-binding expressions) at specific places in the string. You can also use it to repeat variables in a single string of text without having to repeat the same value-binding expression. The component is summarized in table 4.13.

`HtmlOutputFormat` behaves quite similarly to `HtmlOutputText`, except for the fact that you can insert arbitrary parameters in the string that is displayed.

For example, suppose you wanted to display a message to current users that addressed them by their first name, displayed a hardcoded string, and also displayed their browser type. If the person's name was Joe and he was using Mozilla, the output would look something like this:

```
Hey Mark. This is a static value: hardcoded.  Mark, you're using: Mozilla/
  5.0 (Windows; U; Windows NT 5.1; en-US; rv:1.2.1) Gecko/20021130.
```

Table 4.13 **HtmlOutputFormat summary**

Component	HtmlOutputFormat			
Family	javax.faces.Output			
Possible IDE Display Names	Formatted Output			
Display Behavior	Converts its value to a string and displays it, replacing any parameter markers with values retrieved from child UIParameter components. Encloses the value in a <span> element if the id, style, or styleClass property is specified.			
Tag Library	HTML			
JSP Tag	<h:outputFormat>			
Pass-Through Properties	title, style			
Common Properties	id, value, rendered, converter, styleClass, binding (see table 4.2)			
Property	**Type**	**Default Value**	**Required?**	**Description**
escape	boolean	false	No	Controls whether or not HTML or XML characters are escaped (displayed literally in a browser).

Assuming you had a JavaBean stored under the key user, you could generate this output with HtmlOutputText:

```
<h:outputText value="Hey #{user.firstName}. This is a static value: hard-
  coded. #{user.firstName}, you're using: #{header['User-Agent']}."/>
```

This is fine, but you have to use the expression "#{user.firstName}" each time you want to display the user's name. (By the way, header is an implicit EL variable; see chapter 3 for details.)

HtmlOutputFormat simplifies displaying strings with dynamic variables by using message format patterns. A *message format pattern* is a special string with markers that map to parameter values. A *message format element* (not to be confused with an XML or HTML element) is made up of a parameter number surrounded by curly braces ({}). The parameters are specified with nested UIParameter components. (UIParameter is covered in section 4.4.) Table 4.14 shows how to generate our output string with an HtmlOutputFormat component instead of an HtmlOutputText component.

Table 4.14 `HtmlOutputFormat` example: Simple parameter substitution.

HTML	`Hey Mark. This is a static value: hardcoded.  Mark, you're using: Mozilla/5.0 (Windows; U; Windows NT 5.1; en-US; rv:1.2.1) Gecko/20021130.`

Component Tag	`<h:outputFormat value="Hey {0}. This is a static value: {1}. {0}, you''re using: {2}.">`
	`<f:param value="#{user.firstName}"/>`
	`<f:param value="hardcoded"/>`
	`<f:param value="#{header['User-Agent']}"/>`
	`</h:outputFormat>`

Browser Display	Hey Mark. This is a static value: hardcoded. Mark, you're using: Mozilla/5.0 (Windows; U; Windows NT 5.1; en-US; rv:1.7b) Gecko/20040316.

Take a look at the `value` property of the `<h:outputFormat>` tag. This is a message format pattern. Like Java, the parameters start counting with zero: {0}, {1}, {2}, and so on. The first parameter value is substituted everywhere the message format element {0} exists. The second parameter substitutes for {1}, the third for {2}, and so on. If you specify extra parameters, the component ignores them. If you specify too few parameters, it will leave the literal text in the string (like "{1}").

NOTE `HtmlOutputMessage` is often used to parameterize localized text. See chapter 6 for details.

You may have noticed that the string used in the `<h:outputFormat>` tag requires two single quotes to produce the text "you're" and the string in the `<h:outputText>` tag requires only a single quote. This is a specific requirement of the `HtmlOutputMessage`: you must use two single quotes to produce one. If you want to use curly braces inside a string you're displaying, you have to enclose them with single quotes as well.

BY THE WAY If you've ever written Java code using the `MessageFormat` class, you may have noticed that `HtmlOutputFormat` uses the same syntax and abides by similar rules as that class. This is because it uses the `MessageFormat` class internally.

Message format elements

In the last section, we described a message format element as a parameter number surrounded by curly braces—{1}, for example. Most of the time, this is all you need to know. You can, however, format each parameter using a different syntax. After the parameter number, you specify the format type. After the format type, you specify a style or pattern. The parameter number, format type, and format style or pattern are all separated by a comma (,). There are two classes of format types: data type format types (dates, times, and numbers) and choice format types.

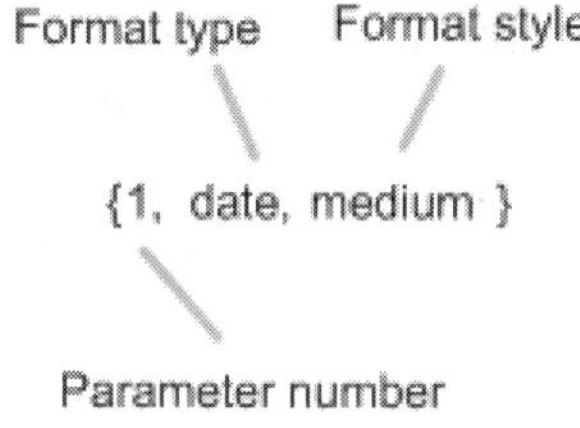

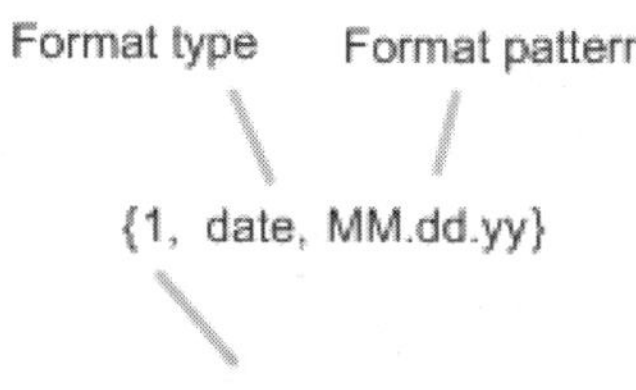

Figure 4.6 Message format elements can specify additional format types. Each format type can have either a style or a pattern. Styles provide some control over formatting, and patterns provide complete control.

Two examples are shown in figure 4.6. The first specifies parameter number one, the date format type, and a format style of medium, which defaults to something like "May 10, 2003". The second example is also a date format pattern for the first parameter, but has a date format pattern, which specifies the specific format for the date. In this case, it would be something like "05.10.03".

Let's say you wanted to display a string using value-binding references for both the name and the date. You could use a message format pattern to format the date property, as shown in table 4.15.

The first parameter uses the normal message element syntax; the second uses the extended syntax for formatting. As the table shows, the `medium` format element displays an abbreviated month with the day and year displayed as a number for U.S. English. For other languages, the actual result may vary.

Table 4.15 `HtmlOutputFormat` example: Using the extended syntax for message format elements, with a specific format type.

HTML	`Hey Mark, you were born on Apr 20, 2004.`

Component Tag	`<h:outputFormat value="Hey {0}, you were born on {1, date, medium}.">`
	`  <f:param value="#{user.firstName}"/>`
	`  <f:param value="#{user.dateOfBirth}"/>`
	`</h:outputFormat>`

Browser Display	Hey Mark, you were born on Apr 20, 2004.

If we hadn't specified the date style, the displayed date would have been "04/20/04 06:04 PM", which is the locale's default format for the `Date` object. For the United States, this includes both the date and time; it may be different in other locales. You can leave out the date style in some cases, but usually it's better to have more control over the output. We cover the specific message format types and patterns as well as internationalization in chapter 6.

Dynamically displaying substrings with choice formats

Sometimes you may want to display part of a string based on the value of a bean property. For example, let's say that you wanted to tell a user whether an account balance was positive without displaying the actual value. You can do this with a choice format. A *choice format* displays one of several values based on a number parameter. It's great when you want to display the plural form of a word instead of a number. Unlike date type formats, choice formats don't have styles; they only have patterns.

A choice format pattern is made up of a set of comparison value/display string pairs. Within each pair, the comparison value and display string are separated by a number sign (#). The comparison value/display string pairs are separated by a pipe separator (|), which stands for "or". This syntax is shown in figure 4.7.

The choice pattern works sort of like a `case` or `switch` statement. The display string whose comparison number is equal to the parameter's value will be displayed. If no comparison number equals the parameter's value, then the display value whose comparison number is the closest but less than the parameter value will be displayed. If the parameter value is less than the first comparison number, the first display string is chosen. If it's greater, the last display string is chosen.

Table 4.16 shows an example. If `user.numberOfTimes` is less than 1, the display string "times" is chosen. If it's equal to 1, the display string "time" is chosen. If it's greater than or equal to 2, the display string "times" is chosen.

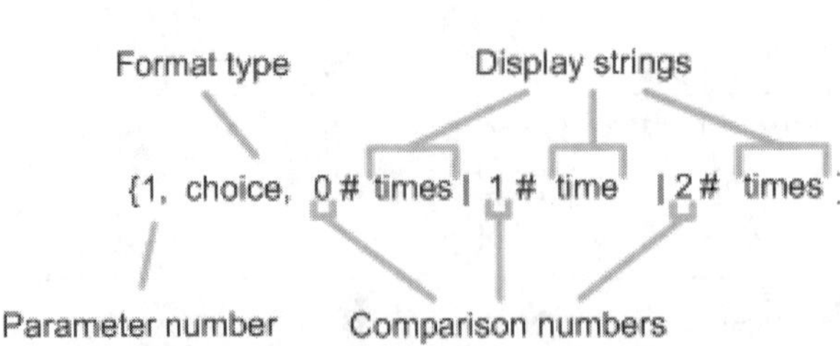

Figure 4.7
A choice format allows you to select one display string depending on how its number compares to the parameter value. This example will choose the display string "times" if the parameter value is less than or equal to 0, or greater than 1. Otherwise (if the value equals 1), the string "time" will be displayed.

Table 4.16 `HtmlOutputFormat` example: Using a choice format for a plural.

HTML (parameter = 0)	`You have visited us 0 times.`
HTML (parameter = 1)	`You have visited us 1 time.`
HTML (parameter = 3)	`You have visited us 3 times.`

Component Tag	`<h:outputFormat`
	`value="You have visited us {0} {0, choice,`
	`0#times|1#time|2#times}.">`
	`<f:param value="#{user.numberOfVisits}"/>`
	`</h:outputFormat>`

Browser Display (parameter = 0)	You have visited us 0 times.
Browser Display (parameter = 1)	You have visited us 1 time.
Browser Display (parameter = 3)	You have visited us 3 times.

Choice formats are a useful tool for displaying complex strings, and don't forget the power of value-binding expressions. You can use them in the value string (with choice or message format patterns), and for the value of any `HtmlOutputFormat` parameters.

4.5.5 Displaying hyperlinks with HtmlOutputLink

The `HtmlOutputLink` component maps to an HTML hyperlink or anchor—an `<a>` element. It can be used to link to either an internal or an external URL. The component's `value` property represents the actual URL, and any nested components will be displayed within the hyperlink. If your web container is using URL rewriting to maintain the session, this component will automatically rewrite the URL for you. Table 4.17 summarizes the component's properties.

Most of the time, you'll want to nest an `HtmlOutputText` component inside an `Html-OutputLink` component to provide the text inside the link. As a matter of fact, some tools, like Sun's Java Studio Creator [Sun, Creator], automatically do this for you. Some tools will also let you select existing pages from within your web application so you don't have to manually type in a relative URL (see figure 4.8).

Let's start with a hyperlink to a relative image, shown in table 4.18.

Table 4.17 HtmlOutputLink summary

Component	`HtmlOutputLink`
Family	`javax.faces.Output`
Possible IDE Display Names	Hyperlink
Display Behavior	Displays an HTML `<a>` element. The `value` property is rendered as the `href` attribute, and any child components are rendered within the `<a>` element.
Tag Library	HTML
JSP Tag	`<h:outputLink>`
Pass-Through Properties	HTML attributes for the `<a>` element
Common Properties	`id, value, rendered, converter, styleClass, binding` (see table 4.2)

Table 4.18 HtmlOutputLink example: Simple link to a relative image.

HTML	`<a href="images/hello.gif">Hello image</a>`

Component Tag	`<h:outputLink value="images/hello.gif">`
	`  <h:outputText value="Hello image"/>`
	`</h:outputLink>`

Browser Display	Hello image

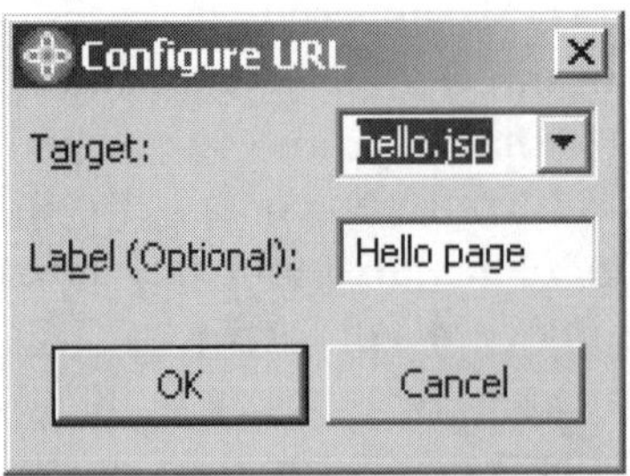

Figure 4.8 WebSphere Application Developer [IBM, WSAD] allows you to select a page in your application and set a label with a simple dialog box.

You can see that the component's value maps to the `href` value of the hyperlink, and the text within the hyperlink is from the nested `HtmlOutputText` component.

Although a single `HtmlOutputText` child component is a really common use case, you can also nest other components, like an `HtmlGraphicImage` component, and even `HtmlPanelGrids`. You can also nest more than one component.

In the real world, you often need to add parameters to the URL, as shown in table 4.19.

Table 4.19 `HtmlOutputLink` example: Passing URL parameters.

HTML	`<a href="http://groups.google.com/groups?group=comp&hl=fr">`
	`  Google Groups - Computers (in French)`
	`</a>`

Component Tag	`<h:outputLink value="http://groups.google.com/groups">`
	`  <h:outputText value="Google Groups - Computers (in French)"/>`
	`  <f:param name="group" value="comp"/>`
	`  <f:param name="hl" value="fr"/>`
	`</h:outputLink>`

Browser Display	Google Groups - Computers (in French)

As you can see, `HtmlOutputLink` will automatically append nested `UIParameter` instances to URL parameters. In this example, two `UIParameter` instances were used to output the parameters at the end of the `href` property. The first parameter tells Google to display all of the newsgroups that start with "comp". The second tells it to use the French language. So, if you click on this link, you'll see all of the comp.* newsgroups in French.

You can use `HtmlOutputLink` this way for external pages as well as other links within your application or site. And remember, `UIParameters`, like most JSF components, can also use value-binding expressions, so the parameters can come from beans in your application.

BY THE WAY If you're wondering why anyone would bother using this `HtmlOutputLink` instead of a normal HTML `<a>` element, there are two good reasons. First, you can't lay out normal HTML elements within panels. So the minute you start using panels for grouping and layout, you must use JSF components. Second, using `UIParameters` allows you to dynamically configure the values being sent to the external URL, which means you can easily sync them up with backing beans.

`HtmlOutputLink` is the last of the Output family of components. Earlier, we used `HtmlGraphicImage` to display an image inside a hyperlink. Let's take a closer look at this component.

4.6 Displaying images with HtmlGraphicImage

Most UIs have images somewhere—little icons that represent menu options, logos, or just something to spice things up. In JSF, images are handled by the

`HtmlGraphicImage` component, a read-only reference to a graphic. The component displays an `<img>` element whose `src` attribute is set to the current value of the component (represented by the `url` property), which should be a static string or value-binding expression for the image's URL. Table 4.20 summarizes this component.

Table 4.20 `HtmlGraphicImage` summary

Component	`HtmlGraphicImage`			
Family	`javax.faces.Graphic`			
Possible IDE Display Names	Image			
Display Behavior	Displays an `<img>` element with the `src` attribute equal to the component's `url` property. Automatically encodes the URL to maintain the session, if necessary.			
Tag Library	HTML			
JSP Tag	`<h:graphicImage>`			
Pass-Through Properties	HTML attributes for the `<img>` element			
Common Properties	`id, value, rendered, styleClass, binding` (see table 4.2)			
Property	**Type**	**Default Value**	**Required?**	**Description**
`url`	`String`	None	No	The URL of the image to be displayed. Can be literal text or a value-binding expression. (This is an alias for the `value` property.)

If your web container is using URL rewriting to maintain the session, `HtmlGraphic-Image` will automatically rewrite the URL for you. Also, if your URL begins with a slash (/), it will be relative to the web application's context root. For example, see table 4.21.

As you can see, the `url` property was rendered as a `src` attribute, prefixed with the application's context root name (no session was active, so the URL was not rewritten). If we had used a relative URL like "images/logo.gif", the context root name would not have been added. All of the other properties were passed through.

Remember that `HtmlGraphicImage`, like most JSF components, supports value-binding expressions. This can be useful for situations where you maintain the URLs for graphics in a central location, like a database or an XML file.

Table 4.21 HtmlGraphicImage example: URL relative to web application root.

HTML	<img src="/jia-standard-components/images/logo.gif" alt="Welcome to ProjectTrack" height="160" title="Welcome to ProjectTrack" width="149" />
Component Tag	<h:graphicImage url="/images/logo.gif" alt="Welcome to ProjectTrack" title="Welcome to ProjectTrack" width="149" height="160"/>
Browser Display	

We present more examples of using `HtmlGraphicImage` in part 2. The topic of the next section, however, is displaying application messages.

4.7 Displaying component messages with HtmlMessage

In chapter 2, we touched on JSF's support for messages that report validation and conversion errors, as well as general-purpose information from the application itself. Zero or more messages can be generated when JSF processes a request. Every message has a severity level as well as summary and detailed information, and the information is usually localized for the user's current language. The severity levels are listed in table 4.22.

Table 4.22 Messages have a severity, which is equal to one of these values.

Severity Level	Description
Info	Represents text you'd like to send back to the user that isn't an error.
Warn	Indicates that an error *may* have occurred.
Error	Indicates a definite error. Recommended for validation messages.
Fatal	Indicates a serious error.

You can probably see where all this is leading—`HtmlMessage` displays application messages. Actually, it displays a *single* message that's associated with a *specific* UI component. It's useful for displaying validation or conversion errors for an input control, and usually the error is displayed next to the component (so the user knows where to correct the problem). If more than one message is registered for a component (which can happen if more than one validator is registered, or if a validator has problems with conversion), HtmlMessage displays only the first one. The component is summarized in table 4.23.

As the table shows, HtmlMessage lets you change the style based on the severity level of the message. This allows you to give the user better visual clues—for example, red text may mean a real problem, but blue text might just be an informational message. In addition, you can control whether or not you want the user to see the summary or detail of the message. Let's start with the example, shown in table 4.24.

Table 4.23 HtmlMessage summary

Component	HtmlMessage			
Family	javax.faces.Message			
Possible IDE Display Names	Display Error, Inline Message			
Display Behavior	Displays the first messages registered for the component referenced by the for property. If the id, a tooltip, or any CSS styles are specified, the text will be wrapped in a <span> element.			
Tag Library	HTML			
JSP Tag	<h:message>			
Pass-Through Properties	style, title			
Common Properties	id, rendered, styleClass, binding (see table 4.2)			
Property	**Type**	**Default Value**	**Required?**	**Description**
for	String	None	Yes	The component identifier of the component for which messages should be displayed.
showDetail	boolean	false	No	Indicates whether or not to show the detail portion of the message.
showSummary	boolean	true	No	Indicates whether or not to show the summary portion of the message.

continued on next page

Table 4.23 `HtmlMessage` summary *(continued)*

Property	Type	Default Value	Required?	Description
`errorClass`	`String`	None	No	CSS class for messages with Error severity.
`errorStyle`	`String`	None	No	CSS style for messages with Error severity
`fatalClass`	`String`	None	No	CSS class for messages with Fatal severity.
`fatalStyle`	`String`	None	No	CSS style for messages with Fatal severity.
`infoClass`	`String`	None	No	CSS class for messages with Info severity.
`infoStyle`	`String`	None	No	CSS style for messages with Info severity.
`warnClass`	`String`	None	No	CSS class for messages with Warning severity.
`warnStyle`	`String`	None	No	CSS style for messages with Warning severity.
`tooltip`	`boolean`	`false`	No	Indicates whether or not the message detail should be displayed as a tooltip. Only valid if `showDetail` is `true`.

In this example, we've associated an `HtmlMessage` component with an `HtmlInputText` that has a `Length` validator and a `LongRange` validator. As we've seen so far, `HtmlInputText` simply collects input. The `Length` validator verifies the length of the input, and the `LongRange` validator checks to make sure the input is an integer in the proper range. (`HtmlInputText` is covered in chapter 5, and validators are covered in chapter 6.)

In this example, the input fails both validators, so two messages are generated. However, `HtmlMessage` displays only the first one.

We actually see the error message twice—once for the summary, and once for the detail. This is sort of a quirk with the RI—both the summary and the detail are the same. Other implementations and custom validators should have a distinctive detail message. For example, if the error was "Invalid credit card number", the detail might be "The expiration date is invalid."

This example also shows use of the style properties that format messages differently based on the severity. The rendered style is "color: red", which is the

Table 4.24 `HtmlMessage` example: Showing summary and detail and applying multiple styles.

HTML (with two validation errors)	`Enter text:`
	`<input id="_id0:myOtherInput" type="text"`
	`name="_id0:myOtherInput" value="this is text" />`
	`<span style="color: red">Validation Error: Value is greater than allowable maximum of '3'. Validation Error: Value is greater than allowable maximum of '3'.`
	`</span>`

Component Tag	`<h:outputLabel for="validatorInput">`
	`<h:outputText value="Enter text:"/>`
	`</h:outputLabel>`
	`<h:inputText id="myOtherInput">`
	`<f:validateLength minimum="0" maximum="3"/>`
	`<f:validateLongRange minimum="1" maximum="100"/>`
	`</h:inputText>`
	`<h:message for="myOtherInput" showDetail="true"`
	`showSummary="true" warnStyle="color: green"`
	`infoStyle="color: blue" errorStyle="color: red"/>`

Browser Display (with two validation errors)	Enter text: [this is text] Validation Error: Value is greater than allowable maximum of '3'. Validation Error: Value is greater than allowable maximum of '3'.

value of the `errorStyle` property. This means that the message's severity level was Error. (All of the standard validation messages have this severity level.) If the message's severity level had been Warn, the `warnStyle` property would have been used; if it had been Info, the `infoStyle` property would have been used.

`HtmlMessage` is designed to display messages for a specific component, and is useful whenever you need to inform the user of a mistake in a particular input control. It's typically used with input controls, but that's not a requirement. If you need to display multiple messages for a page, you should use `HtmlMessages` instead.

4.8 Displaying application messages with HtmlMessages

When JSF processes a request, multiple parts of the application—validators, converters, event listeners, and so on—can generate messages. (See the previous section for a quick overview of messages.) Because messages can be generated from so many sources, it's no surprise that you often end up with multiple messages that need to be displayed to the user. This is the job of the `HtmlMessages` component, which is summarized in table 4.25.

Like HtmlMessage, HtmlMessages lets you change the style based on the severity level of the message. So, if it's displaying several messages, each one can be in a different color. The first message might have the Info severity level and be displayed in blue, the second might have the Error severity level and be displayed in red, and so on.

Because HtmlMessages displays all messages, it doesn't have a for property that limits it to displaying messages for a specific component. You can, however, tell it to display only messages that aren't associated with components with the globalOnly property. This is useful if you want to display messages that were created in application code (like an event listener) as opposed to ones that were created by validators or converters.

Table 4.25 HtmlMessages summary

Component	HtmlMessages			
Family	javax.faces.Messages			
Possible IDE Display Names	Message List			
Display Behavior	Displays all messages if the globalOnly property is false. If globalOnly is true, displays only messages that are not associated with a component (these are usually messages from event listeners). If the layout property is "table", a <table> element will be displayed, with each message on a single row. If the id and tooltip properties, or any CSS styles are specified, the text for each message will be wrapped in a <span> element.			
Tag Library	HTML			
JSP Tag	<h:messages>			
Pass-Through Properties	style, title			
Common Properties	id, rendered, styleClass, binding (see table 4.2)			
Property	**Type**	**Default Value**	**Required?**	**Description**
showDetail	boolean	false	No	Indicates whether or not to show the detail portion of the message.

continued on next page

Table 4.25 `HtmlMessages` summary *(continued)*

Property	Type	Default Value	Required?	Description
`showSummary`	`boolean`	`true`	No	Indicates whether or not to show the summary portion of the message.
`layout`	`String`	"list"	No	Specifies how to display the messages. Possible values are "list", which displays them one after another, and "table", which displays them in table columns.
`errorClass`	`String`	None	No	CSS class for messages with Error severity.
`errorStyle`	`String`	None	No	CSS style for messages with Error severity
`fatalClass`	`String`	None	No	CSS class for messages with Fatal severity.
`fatalStyle`	`String`	None	No	CSS style for messages with Fatal severity.
`infoClass`	`String`	None	No	CSS class for messages with Info severity.
`infoStyle`	`String`	None	No	CSS style for messages with Info severity.
`warnClass`	`String`	None	No	CSS class for messages with Warning severity.
`warnStyle`	`String`	None	No	CSS style for messages with Warning severity.
`tooltip`	`boolean`	`false`	No	Indicates whether or not the message detail should be displayed as a tooltip. Only valid if `showDetail` is `true`.
`globalOnly`	`boolean`	`false`	No	Controls whether or not the component only displays global messages (as opposed to both global messages and messages for a specific component).

Let's start with the simple example, shown in table 4.26. This table shows two sets of output depending on the type of messages available. First, there is the output with two validation messages. These errors happen to be the same two messages generated by the example in table 4.25. The difference is that here, both of them are displayed.

Table 4.26 `HtmlMessages` example: Simple usage with both validation and application messages.

HTML (with two validation errors)	`<span class="errors">Validation Error: Value is greater than allowable maximum of '3'.`
	`</span>`
	`<span class="errors">Validation Error: Value is not of the correct type.`
	`</span>`

HTML (with two application messages)	`<span class="errors">Your order has been processed successfully.`
	`</span>`
	`<span class="errors">Free shipping limit exceeded. </span>`

Component Tag	`<h:messages styleClass="errors"/>`
Browser Display (with two validation errors)	Validation Error: Value is greater than allowable maximum of '3'. Validation Error: Value is not of the correct type.
Browser Display (with two application messages)	Your order has been processed successfully. Free shipping limit exceeded.

The second set of output is for application messages rather than validation messages. The component isn't displaying both types of messages because validation errors usually prevent event listeners from being called. So, in this case, the event listener won't generate any messages unless all of the input is valid.

One subtle point with the last example is that even though the two application messages have different severity levels, they are both displayed with the same CSS class. Because `HtmlMessages` can display several different messages (each of which can have different severity levels), it's generally a good idea to apply different styles so that users can differentiate them.

TIP It's often helpful to place an `HtmlMessages` component at the top of your page during development. This will allow you to see validation and conversion errors that may pop up while you're building the application.

If your views have a lot of forms, you'll be using `HtmlMessage` and `HtmlMessages` quite often. They're key for keeping the user informed about input errors, and they greatly simplify the process of reporting such errors. These components are also handy for displaying messages generated by your application.

4.9 Grouping and layout with the Panel components

If you've worked with Swing, or tools such as Visual Basic or Delphi, then you're probably familiar with the concept of a panel. Panels are often used to group related components. Once you've placed some components inside a panel, you can manipulate them as a single unit simply by interacting with the panel. You can also format the panel with something like a border and hide or display it (and all of its child controls) depending on the application's state.

Panels in JSF are similar to these panels, but they're a little different, too. Their primary goal is to group components together, but sometimes they handle layout as well. As a matter of fact, panels are the only standard way to handle layout within a single view. Using a combination of different panels, you can achieve complex organization of controls on a page.

JSF ships with two panel components: `HtmlPanelGroup` and `HtmlPanelGrid`. `HtmlPanelGroup` simply groups all child components together, and optionally applies CSS styles. `HtmlPanelGrid` can be used for very configurable layouts, sort of like a `GridLayout` in Swing; it renders an HTML `<table>` element.

In the following sections, we examine these components in more detail.

4.9.1 Grouping components with HtmlPanelGroup

The `HtmlPanelGroup` component groups a set of components together so that they can be treated as a single entity. It doesn't map directly to an HTML element. As a matter of fact, the only time it outputs anything is when you specify an identifier or a style, in which case the child components will be enclosed in a `<span>` element. It does, however, display all of its child components without modification. The component is summarized in table 4.27.

Take a look at the simple example shown in table 4.28. In this case, `HtmlPanelGroup` doesn't display anything—the child components are just displayed as is. You'll often use it this way to group together components within a facet; this is quite common, for example, when you're defining the header and footers within an `HtmlPanelGrid` or `HtmlDataTable` (see those sections for more examples).

Table 4.27 `HtmlPanelGroup` summary

Component	`HtmlPanelGroup`
Family	`javax.faces.Panel`
Possible IDE Display Names	Panel – Group Box, Group Box
Display Behavior	All child components are displayed as is. If the `id`, `style`, or `styleClass` properties are specified, encloses all child components in a `<span>` element. Used to group child components together.
Tag Library	HTML
JSP Tag	`<h:panelGroup>`
Pass-Through Properties	`style`
Common Properties	`id, rendered, styleClass, binding` (see table 4.2)

TIP `HtmlPanelGroup` can be useful as a placeholder. Use it when you want to create a blank cell inside a table rendered by `HtmlPanelGrid` or `HtmlDataTable`.

`HtmlPanelGroup` can also be used to add simple formatting to a group of components, as shown in table 4.29.

Table 4.28 `HtmlPanelGroup` example: Grouping three components with no style.

HTML	`<img src="images/inbox.gif" alt="" />Column 1Column 2`

Component Tag	`<h:panelGroup>`
	`  <h:graphicImage url="images/inbox.gif"/>`
	`  <h:outputText value="Column 1"/>`
	`  <h:outputText value="Column 2"/>`
	`</h:panelGroup>`

Browser Display	Column 1Column 2

In this example, the component outputs a `<span>` element with its client identifier and the specified CSS class, providing a nice background and border for the child components. This type of formatting is nice for simple cases, but for laying out components, you should use `HtmlPanelGrid` instead.

Table 4.29 `HtmlPanelGroup` example: Grouping three components with a style.

HTML	`<span id="_id1:myGroup" class="table-background">`
	`   <img src="images/inbox.gif" alt="" />Column 1Column 2`
	`</span>`

Component Tag	`<h:panelGroup id="myGroup" styleClass="table-background">`
	`  <h:graphicImage url="images/inbox.gif"/>`
	`  <h:outputText value="Column 1"/>`
	`  <h:outputText value="Column 2"/>`
	`</h:panelGroup>`

Browser Display	Column 1Column 2

4.9.2 Creating tables with HtmlPanelGrid

`HtmlPanelGrid` is useful for creating arbitrary, static component layouts (it maps to the `<table>` element). You can also configure `header` and `footer` with facets that map to the `<thead>` and `<tfoot>` table subelements, respectively. Table 4.30 summarizes this component.

You can expect tools to render a table for you in real time, as you drag and drop controls into an `HtmlPanelGrid` from a component palette (see figure 4.9). As you can see, a common use of this component is to lay out forms, like a login form.

We'll look at the JSP for more complicated views like a login form in part 2. For now, let's start with a simple three-column, two-row table where each cell contains a single `HtmlOutputText` component. This is shown in table 4.31.

As you can see, child components are organized according to the specified number of columns. Because we specified three columns, the first three components formed the first row (one per column), the next three formed the second row, and so on. The `width`, `border`, and `cellpadding` properties were passed through. Note that unlike with an HTML table, you don't have to explicitly denote columns and rows—you just embed the child components inside the panel, and it will do the rest.

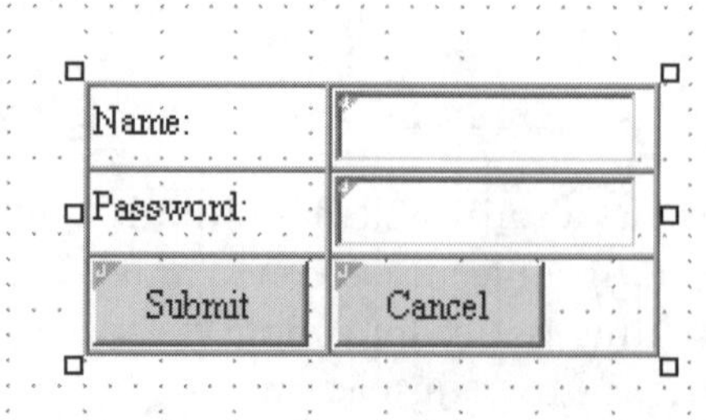

Figure 4.9 Most JSF IDEs, like Java Studio Creator [Sun, Creator], allow you to drag and drop components into an `HtmlPanelGrid` and change the table's layout when you modify the component's properties.

Table 4.30 `HtmlPanelGrid` summary

Component	HtmlPanelGrid			
Family	javax.faces.Panel			
Possible IDE Display Names	Grid Panel			
Display Behavior	Displays an HTML <table> element with the specified number of columns. Lays out one child component per cell, starting a new row after displaying columns components. If the header facet is specified, displays a <thead> element with the contents of the header. If the footer facet is specified, displays a <tfoot> element with the contents of the footer.			
Tag Library	HTML			
JSP Tag	<h:panelGrid>			
Pass-Through Properties	HTML attributes for <table>			
Common Properties	id, rendered, styleClass, binding (see table 4.2)			
Property	**Type**	**Default Value**	**Required?**	**Description**
columns	int	None	No	Number of columns to display.
headerClass	String	None	No	Name of CSS style class for the header facet.
footerClass	String	None	No	Name of CSS style class for the footer facet.
rowClasses	String	None	No	Comma-delimited list of CSS style classes for the rows. You can specify multiple styles for a row by separating them with a space. After each style has been applied, they repeat. For example, if there are two style classes (style1 and style2), the first row will be style1, the second style2, the third style1, the fourth style2, so on.

continued on next page

Table 4.30 `HtmlPanelGrid` summary *(continued)*

Property	Type	Default Value	Required?	Description
columnClasses	String	None	No	Comma-delimited list of CSS style classes for the columns. You can specify multiple styles for a column by separating them with a space. After each style has been applied, they repeat. For example, if there are two style classes (`style1` and `style2`), the first column will be `style1`, the second `style2`, the third `style1`, the fourth `style2`, so on.

Facet	Description
header	Child components displayed as the table's header.
footer	Child components displayed as the table's footer.

Table 4.31 `HtmlPanelGrid` example: A simple three-column, two-row table.

HTML

```
<table border="1" cellpadding="1" width="40%">
  <tbody>
    <tr>
      <td>(1,1)</td>
      <td>(1,2)</td>
      <td>(1,3)</td>
   </tr>
   <tr>
      <td>(2,1)</td>
      <td>(2,2)</td>
      <td>(2,3)</td>
     </tr>
  </tbody>
</table>
```

Component Tag

```
<h:panelGrid columns="3" cellpadding="1" border="1" width="40%">
  <h:outputText value="(1,1)"/>
  <h:outputText value="(1,2)"/>
  <h:outputText value="(1,3)"/>
  <h:outputText value="(2,1)"/>
  <h:outputText value="(2,2)"/>
  <h:outputText value="(2,3)"/>
</h:panelGrid>
```

Browser Display

(1,1)	(1,2)	(1,3)
(2,1)	(2,2)	(2,3)

TIP Currently, there is no guaranteed default number of columns (the RI defaults to one). So, if you want to ensure the same behavior across different implementations, always specify the number of columns.

It's also quite easy to add styles to different columns or rows, and to add a header and footer. Table 4.32 shows how to do this.

Table 4.32 `HtmlPanelGrid` example: A table with a header, a footer, and alternating styles for the columns.

HTML

```
<table class="table-background" border="1" cellpadding="1"
       width="40%">
   <thead>
     <tr>
        <th class="page-header" colspan="4" scope="colgroup">
         <img src="images/inbox.gif" alt="" />This is a sample
header. </th>
     </tr>
   </thead>
   <tfoot>
     <tr>
       <td class="table-footer" colspan="4">This is the footer.
       </td>
     </tr>
   </tfoot>
   <tbody>
     <tr>
       <td class="table-odd-column">(1,1)</td>
       <td class="table-even-column">(1,2)</td>
       <td class="table-odd-column">(1,3)</td>
       <td class="table-even-column">(1,4)</td>
     </tr>
     <tr>
       <td class="table-odd-column">(2,1)</td>
       <td class="table-even-column">(2,2)</td>
       <td class="table-odd-column">(2,3)</td>
       <td class="table-even-column">(2,4)</td>
    </tr>
    <tr>
       <td class="table-odd-column">(3,1)</td>
       <td class="table-even-column">(3,2)</td>
       <td class="table-odd-column">(3,3)</td>
       <td class="table-even-column">(3,4)</td>
    </tr>
  </tbody>
</table>
```

continued on next page

Table 4.32 `HtmlPanelGrid` example: A table with a header, a footer, and alternating styles for the columns. *(continued)*

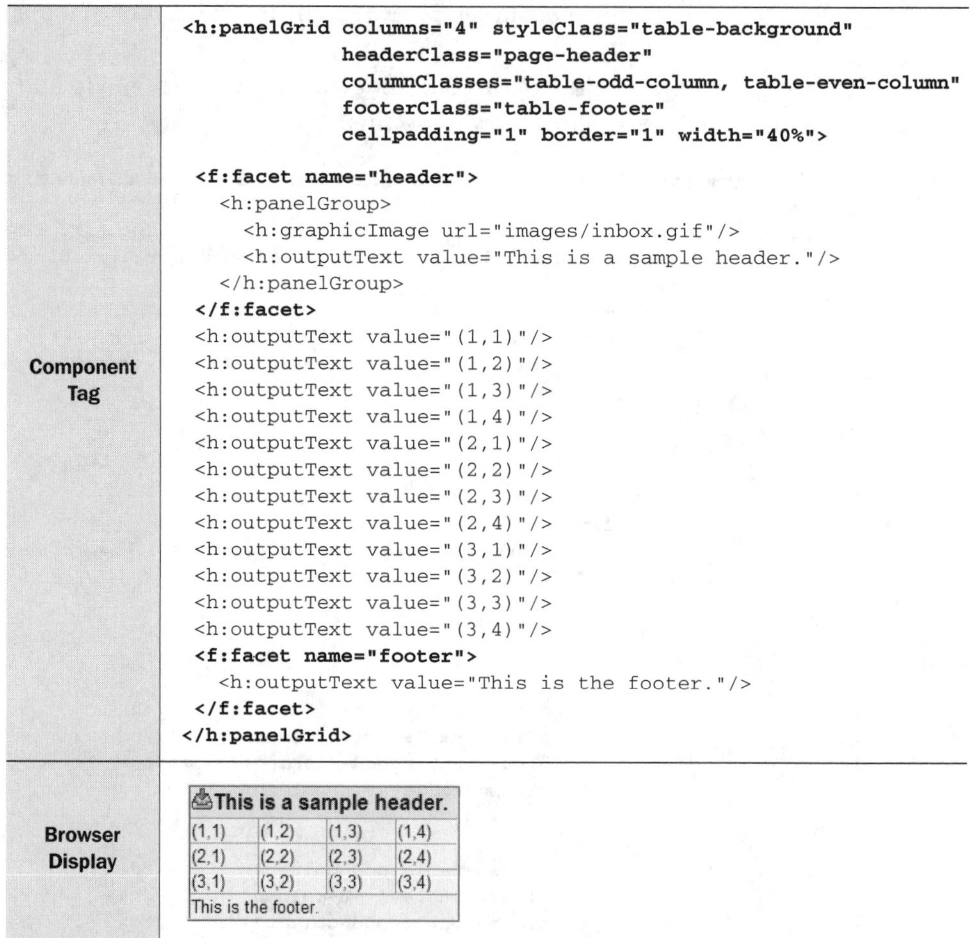

Component Tag

```
<h:panelGrid columns="4" styleClass="table-background"
             headerClass="page-header"
             columnClasses="table-odd-column, table-even-column"
             footerClass="table-footer"
             cellpadding="1" border="1" width="40%">

  <f:facet name="header">
    <h:panelGroup>
      <h:graphicImage url="images/inbox.gif"/>
      <h:outputText value="This is a sample header."/>
    </h:panelGroup>
  </f:facet>
  <h:outputText value="(1,1)"/>
  <h:outputText value="(1,2)"/>
  <h:outputText value="(1,3)"/>
  <h:outputText value="(1,4)"/>
  <h:outputText value="(2,1)"/>
  <h:outputText value="(2,2)"/>
  <h:outputText value="(2,3)"/>
  <h:outputText value="(2,4)"/>
  <h:outputText value="(3,1)"/>
  <h:outputText value="(3,2)"/>
  <h:outputText value="(3,3)"/>
  <h:outputText value="(3,4)"/>
  <f:facet name="footer">
    <h:outputText value="This is the footer."/>
  </f:facet>
</h:panelGrid>
```

Browser Display

This is a sample header.			
(1,1)	(1,2)	(1,3)	(1,4)
(2,1)	(2,2)	(2,3)	(2,4)
(3,1)	(3,2)	(3,3)	(3,4)
This is the footer.			

NOTE You can also style the rows with the `rowClasses` attribute—it works just like `columnClasses`.

You can see that the `styleClass` property specifies the CSS class for the entire table. The class attributes of the table columns alternate between the two values specified in the `columnClasses` properties. There is no limit to the number of classes you can specify. The header is displayed as a single row spanning all columns, and is styled with the CSS class specified by the `headerClass` attribute. The footer also spans all columns, but it is styled with the CSS class specified by the `footerClass` attribute.

Note that the `header` facet uses an `HtmlPanelGroup` component; this is required if you'd like to include several components inside of a facet (you could also use another container, like an additional `HtmlPanelGrid`). The `footer` facet has only one child component, so no nested `HtmlPanelGroup` is necessary.

In this example, we alternated styles for the columns. It's worthwhile to note that you can have more than two different styles. Also, just like `styleClass`, all of the other class properties, including the ones for columns and rows, can support more than one style.

```
<h:panelGrid columns="4"
             headerClass="page-header extra-border"
             columnClasses="table-odd-column extra-border,
                            table-even-column,
                            table-even-column extra-border,
                            table-even-column"
             footerClass="table-footer"
             cellpadding="1" border="1" width="40%">
...
</h:panelGrid>
```

There are two things to note in this example. First, the `headerClass` has two classes—`page-header` and `extra-border`. Both will be applied to the `header` facet. In addition, the `columnClasses` property has classes specified for four rows. The first column has an extra style applied to it, so it will display with both styles combined. The other three columns use a different style, and the second-to-last one has an extra style applied to it as well. If there were more than four columns, these styles would repeat.

You can use the `rowClasses` property just like the `columnClasses` property, and you can use them at the same time. This can lead to some interesting style combinations, which can be a good thing or a bad thing, depending on how your style classes are set up. (If you're not careful, you can have conflicts.)

These simple examples should get you started with `HtmlPanelGrid`. You can accomplish complex layouts by nesting several panels, just as you can with HTML tables. We show more complex examples in part 2. If you need to lay out tabular data retrieved from a data source, `HtmlDataTable` is your component, and it's covered in chapter 5.

4.10 Summary

The core promise of JSF is support for UI components—reusable units of code, like text boxes and data tables, that handle a specific type of interaction with the user. Like other UI component frameworks, JSF components have properties and events, and they're specifically designed to be used inside tools. These tools let you drag and drop UI components from a palette and customize their properties.

JSF includes several standard components that are guaranteed to be available no matter which IDE or implementation you're using. These components are tailored for displaying HTML output, and they're backed by an HTML render kit. Components can also support facets, which are named subordinate elements, like a header or footer.

In this chapter, we covered the nonvisual and read-only standard components. First, we looked at `UIViewRoot`, which contains all of the other components on the page. Next, we examined `UIParameter`, which is used to pass parameters to other components. For example, `HtmlOutputLink` uses it to specify parameters for a hyperlink.

We then moved on to the Output family of components: `HtmlOutputText`, which displays ordinary text; the `<f:verbatim>` tag, which encapsulates JSP tags and template text; `HtmlOutputLabel`, which provides a label for an input field; `HtmlOutputFormat`, which outputs parameterized text; and `HtmlOutputLink`, which displays a hyperlink.

Images in JSF are displayed with the `HtmlGraphicImage` component, and application, validation, and conversion messages are the domain of `HtmlMessage` and `HtmlMessages`. Finally, the Panel components group together components as a single entity. `HtmlPanelGroup` is generally used to group together components, and `HtmlPanelGrid` lays out components in a table, with optional `header` and `footer` facets.

In the next chapter we look at the other side of the coin—the standard input controls and JSF's data grid component, `HtmlDataTable`.

5 Using the input and data table components

This chapter covers

- Registering event listeners
- Text fields, listboxes, and combo boxes
- Buttons and command hyperlinks
- Data grids

Collecting user input is essential for most applications, and JSF's standard component set has the basic components you need for building capable data-entry screens. These controls cover the same feature set as standard HTML forms, so their functionality should be familiar to you. In this chapter, we examine the remaining components, which focus on collecting user input rather than displaying it. We also cover the `HtmlDataTable` component, which allows you to edit data sets or display them in a tabular manner.

As we saw in chapters 1 and 2, input controls generate events—primarily value-change and action events—that can be consumed by event listeners (usually located in backing beans). In this chapter, we'll focus on each component's properties and basic use, and tell you which events they support. In part 2 you'll see more examples of how to integrate event listeners with the user interface (UI), and in part 3 we'll discuss how to write your own event listeners.

Input controls also support validators, which check the user's input for correctness. Validation is covered in chapter 6. And remember that any text entered into an input control that has a `value` property with a value-binding expression will automatically update the referenced bean (for more on value-binding expressions, see chapter 2), as long as the input has been validated.

This chapter builds on some of the concepts introduced in the previous chapter. If you haven't already, you should read the first few sections of chapter 4 first.

Before we study each component, let's first take a closer look at events and event listeners.

5.1 Registering event listeners

The two most important events for everyday JSF development are value-change events and action events. These events are fired by most of the components in this chapter; input controls generate value-change events when their value changes, and action source components generate action events when the user executes them (usually by clicking on them).

Event listeners respond to events, and are written in Java code, either as a backing bean method or as a separate class. Using a backing bean method is more common (and quicker), but implementing a separate interface is useful when a listener needs to be reused in many different contexts.

You can register event listeners either in JSP or in Java code. In this section, we show JSP examples; see part 3 for examples in Java.

5.1.1 Declaring value-change listeners

Any component that collects user input, such as HmtlInputText or HtmlSelectManyCheckbox, generates a value-change event. If you need to execute a listener when the event is generated, you can register a value-change listener method in a backing bean, like so:

```
<h:inputText value="#{editUserForm.name}"
             valueChangeListener="#{editUserForm.nameChanged}"/>
```

This declares an HtmlInputText component associated with the editUserForm.name property. The userBean.nameChanged method will be called whenever the value of the control changes.

If someone has written a value-change listener class instead of a backing bean method, you can register that instead:

```
<h:selectManyCheckbox value="#{preferences.favoriteColors}">
  <f:selectItems value="#{preferences.colors}"/>
  <f:valueChangeListener type="myapp.ColorChangeListener"/>
</h:selectManyCheckbox>
```

This declares an HtmlSelectManyCheckbox associated with the preferences.favoriteColors property. The user will see all of the items returned by preferences.colors, displayed as a set of checkboxes. Whenever they select a different set of checkboxes, the value-change listener ColorChangeListener will be executed.

You can register more than one value-change listener class, and you can combine them with a single value-change listener method:

```
<h:selectManyCheckbox value="#{preferences.favoriteColors}"
                      valueChangeListener="#{preferences.colorsChanged}">
  <f:selectItems value="#{preferences.colors}"/>
  <f:valueChangeListener type="myapp.ColorChangeListener"/>
  <f:valueChangeListener type="myapp.AnyValueChangeListener "/>
</h:selectManyCheckbox>
```

In this example, all three listeners will be called (in the order they were added) whenever the value of the component changes.

5.1.2 Declaring action listeners

Components in the Command family (HtmlCommandButton and HtmlCommandLink) generate action events. If you need to perform an operation when a user clicks on one of these controls (or any third-party action source components), you can register an action listener method in a backing bean, much like a value-change listener method:

```
<h:commandButton value="Update"
                 actionListener="#{editPartForm.updatePrice}"/>
```

This declares an `HtmlCommandButton` component with the label "Update". Whenever a user clicks on this button, it will execute the backing bean method `editPartForm.updatePrice` and redisplay the current view.

As with value-change listeners, you can register individual action listener classes:

```
<h:commandLink>
  <h:outputText value="Next >>"/>
  <f:actionListener type="myapp.NextPageListener"/>
  <f:actionListener type="myapp.NavigationListener"/>
</h:commandLink>
```

This declares an `HtmlCommandLink` component with the text "Next >>". When a user clicks on this link, both `NextPageListener` and `NavigationListener` will be called. You can register zero or more action listener classes but only one action listener method.

As we've mentioned before, you can control navigation by registering an action method instead of an action listener method:

```
<h:commandButton value="Next >>" action="#{wizard.nextPage}"/>
```

In this example, when the user clicks on the button, the action method `wizard.nextPage` is executed, and the logical outcome of that action is used to decide what page to load next. Remember, you can also hardcode the outcome like so:

```
<h:commandButton value="Next >>" action="next"/>
```

This example doesn't execute an action listener per se, but the outcome `"next"` is used by the navigation handler to select the next page (see chapter 3 for more information on navigation).

If you have a lot of processing to perform, you can combine action listener methods, action listener classes, and action methods (or hardcoded `action` properties):

```
<h:commandLink action="#{wizard.nextPage}"
               actionListener="#{wizard.nextPage}"
  <h:outputText value="Next >>"/>
  <f:actionListener type="myapp.NextPageListener"/>
  <f:actionListener type="myapp.NavigationListener"/>
</h:commandLink>
```

When the user clicks on this link, four action listeners will be executed: an action method, an action listener method, and two action listener classes. Registering this many listeners on a regular basis might not be particularly speedy, but it's powerful to be able to associate so much functionality to a specific type of event (an action event, in this case) when necessary.

Now that you understand what events these controls generate, and how to handle them, let's examine each of these components in detail.

5.2 Common component properties

All of the UI components covered in this chapter share a set of common properties, which are listed in table 5.1. Because these components interact with the user, they have a few more properties in common than those in the previous chapter. When we discuss each component, we'll tell you which of these properties it supports. We'll also describe a property again if a component uses it in a special manner.

Table 5.1 Common properties for UI components discussed in this chapter.

Property	Type	Default Value	Required?	Description
`id`	`String`	None	Yes	Component identifier.
`value`	`Object`	None	Yes	The component's current local value. Can be literal text or a value-binding expression.
`rendered`	`boolean`	`true`	No	Controls whether or not the component is visible.
`converter`	Converter instance (value-binding expression or converter identifier)	None	No	Sets the converter used to convert the value to and from a string for display.
`validator`	`String`	None	No	A method-binding expression for a backing bean method that will be called to validate this component's value.
`immediate`	`boolean`	`false`	No	Determines whether or not the component's input should be converted and validated immediately (during the Apply Request Values phase of the Request Processing Lifecycle instead of the Process Validations phase).
`required`	`boolean`	`false`	No	Controls whether or not this component requires a value.
`styleClass`	`String`	None	No	Name of CSS style class; rendered as an HTML `class` attribute. Multiple classes can be specified with a space in between them.

continued on next page

Table 5.1 Common properties for UI components discussed in this chapter. *(continued)*

Property	Type	Default Value	Required?	Description
valueChange-Listener	String	None	No	A method-binding expression for a value-change listener method that will be called when this component's value changes.
binding	String	None	No	A value-binding expression that associates this component with a backing bean property. Must be associated with a property that is the same type as the component (i.e. HtmlInputText) or its superclass.[a]

[a] *Technically, this is a JSP component tag attribute, and not an actual UI component property. In other words, you can not set this property in Java code.*

5.3 Handling forms with HtmlForm

HtmlForm has the same purpose in JSF as the <form> element has in HTML—it has the ability to send all data contained by its child controls back to the server. In order for data to be sent back to the server, an HtmlForm must have at least one child component that can be used to post the form data, like an HtmlCommandButton or HtmlCommandLink, which we cover later in this chapter.

Any time the server needs to process user input, or simply keep track of the state of input controls, those controls must be nested within an HtmlForm. Because of this requirement, sometimes you won't find HtmlForm in a component palette inside of an IDE; tools will typically add it to your JSP automatically when you drop an input component onto a page. JSF does, however, support multiple HtmlForm components on the same page. If a page is simply displaying read-only data or hyperlinks, this component is not required.

HtmlForm is summarized in table 5.2.

Table 5.2 HtmlForm summary

Component	HtmlForm
Family	javax.faces.Form
Display Behavior	Displays an HTML <form> element with the method attribute set to "post". All input controls should be nested inside this form. You can have multiple HtmlForm components on the same page.

continued on next page

Table 5.2 `HtmlForm` summary *(continued)*

Possible IDE Display Names	Form			
Tag Library	HTML			
JSP Tag	`<h:form>`			
Pass-Through Properties	HTML attributes for the `<form>` element (except for `method`, which is always "post")			
Common Properties	`id, rendered, styleClass, binding` (see table 5.1)			
Java-Only Property	**Type**	**Default Value**	**Required**	**Description**
`submitted`	`boolean`	`false`	No	`True` if the form has been submitted; `false` otherwise.

As the table shows, `HtmlForm` doesn't have a value—it's basically a container for other controls. It's also pretty simple to use, as shown in table 5.3.

Table 5.3 `HtmlForm` example: Basic use

<table>
<tr><th>HTML</th><td><pre><form id="_id0" method="post"
      action="/jia-standard-components/scratch.jsf"
      enctype="application/x-www-form-urlencoded"
      title="claimForm">

   Enter some text:

  <input type="text" name="_id0:_id3" />
  <input type="submit" name="_id0:_id4"
         value=" Go! " />[nbsp's?]
  <input type="hidden" name="_id0" value="_id0" />
</form></pre></td></tr>
<tr><th>Component Tag</th><td><pre><h:form title="claimForm">
  <h:outputLabel for="inputText">
    <h:outputText value="Enter some text:"/>
  </h:outputLabel>
  <h:inputText/>
  <h:commandButton value="Go!"/>
</h:form></pre></td></tr>
<tr><th>Browser Display</th><td>Enter some text: [ ] [Go!]</td></tr>
</table>

As you can see, `HtmlForm` displays a simple HTML `<form>` element encasing all child JSF components. The `method` attribute will always be "post", and if you don't specify the `enctype` property, the default is always "application/x-www-form-urlencoded". The `action` is always the view identifier for the current page.

Forms always post back to themselves so that JSF can associate the user's input with controls in the current view (this is called postback, and we discussed it briefly in chapter 2). The `title` property is simply passed through. In addition to the `<form>` element, `HtmlForm` outputs an additional `<input>` element. It uses this field to determine whether or not it has been submitted. (You can check to see if a form has been submitted in a Java event listener.)

In the example, all of the child controls are displayed normally—`HtmlForm` doesn't process them at all. This means that you can nest as many UI components as you want inside an `HtmlForm` without adverse results. (If you're wondering about the origin of the non-breaking spaces in the output, they're generated by `HtmlCommandButton`.)

> **NOTE** Whenever you use any input controls, they must be embedded within an `HtmlForm`. In addition, you must have an action source, like an `HtmlCommandButton` or `HtmlCommandLink`, inside the form so that data can be submitted back to the application.

For more examples of `HtmlForm`, see part 2. Now, let's move on to the basic input controls.

5.4 Handling basic user input

All of the simple user input controls are part of the Input family. These components display a value and also allow the user to change it, updating any associated beans if necessary. The notable exception is `HtmlInputHidden`, which displays an HTML `<hidden>` field and doesn't interact with the user.

There are four components in this family: `HtmlInputText` (for displaying a basic text box), `HtmlInputTextarea` (for displaying a memo field), `HtmlInputSecret` (for showing a password field), and `HtmlInputHidden` (for a hidden input field).

> **NOTE** The Input components (except for `HtmlInputHidden`) are often used with `HtmlOutputLabel` to generate an HTML `<label>` element, which is important for making your application accessible. See chapter 4 for more information about `HtmlOutputLabel`.

In the following sections, we examine these components in more detail.

5.4.1 Declaring basic text fields with HtmlInputText

For basic user input needs, `HtmlInputText` is your component. It maps to a simple text field—the `<input>` element with `type` "text". The component is summarized in table 5.4.

Table 5.4 `HtmInputText` summary

Component	`HtmlInputText`
Family	javax.faces.Input
Display Behavior	Displays an HTML `<input>` element with the `type` attribute set to "text"
Possible IDE Display Names	Text Field
Tag Library	HTML
JSP Tag	`<h:inputText>`
Pass-Through Properties	HTML attributes for the `<input>` element (except for `type`)
Events	Value-change
Common Properties	`id, value, rendered, validator, converter, immediate, required, styleClass, valueChangeListener, binding` (see table 5.1)

Using `HtmlInputText` is similar to using an ordinary HTML `<input>` field, as shown in table 5.5.

Table 5.5 `HtmlInputText` example: Basic use

HTML	`<input type="text" name="_id1:_id3" value="DeathMarch" accesskey="T" maxlength="40" size="30" tabindex="0" />`
Component Tag	`<h:inputText value="#{project.name}" size="30" maxlength="40" accesskey="T" tabindex="0"/>`
Browser Display	DeathMarch

As you can see, `HtmlInputText` generates an `<input>` element that was rendered with type "text". The `size`, `maxlength`, `accesskey`, and `tabindex` properties are passed through. In this example, the component is associated via a value-binding expression with the name property of the project model object. The value of that property is currently "DeathMarch", but if the user enters something else, it will be updated with the new input.

If you want to disable an input control, you can use the standard HTML disabled attribute. HtmlInputText will be one of the most common input controls you'll use, but it's restricted to a single line. If you'd like a multiline input field, use Html-InputTextarea.

5.4.2 Using HtmlInputTextarea for memo fields

HtmlInputTextarea displays a <textarea> element; it's useful for larger memo-style input fields. The component is summarized in table 5.6.

Table 5.6 HtmlInputTextarea summary

Component	HtmlInputTextarea
Family	javax.faces.Input
Display Behavior	Displays an HTML <textarea> element
Possible IDE Display Names	Multi-Line Text Area
Tag Library	HTML
JSP Tag	<h:inputTextarea>
Pass-Through Properties	HTML attributes for the <textarea> element
Events	Value-change
Common Properties	id, value, rendered, validator, converter, immediate, required, styleClass, valueChangeListener, binding (see table 5.1)

Just like their HTML counterparts, using HtmlInputTextarea is similar to using HtmlInputText. Table 5.7 shows an example.

In this example, the value property references a bean property, so any changes made will be automatically synchronized with the bean (assuming everything vali-dates successfully). As shown, the bean's description property already has a value. We are also using several pass-through attributes—accesskey, rows, tabindex, and onmouseout.

Table 5.7 **`HtmlInputTextarea` example: Using a value-binding expression and a JavaScript event**

HTML	`<textarea name="myForm:_id4" accesskey="A" onchange="form.area23.value = this.value" rows="5" tabindex="1">`
	`Keeps track of the number of defects, the amount of feature creep, and the rate of progress for a given project.`
	`</textarea>`

Component Tag	`<h:inputTextarea value="#{project.description}" rows="5" accesskey="A" tabindex="1" onmouseout="document.forms.myForm['myForm:area23'].value =this.value"`
Browser Display	Keeps track of the number of defects, the amount of feature creep, and the rate of progress for a given project.

Don't let `onchange` fool you—it's just a pass-through attribute that happens to reference JavaScript. The JavaScript changes the value of another component on this page whenever the user moves the mouse out of the text area. This isn't a terribly useful thing to do, but it should give you an idea of how you can use pass-through attributes.

Both `HtmlInputText` and `HtmlInputTextarea` show all of their input; if you want to hide what the user types from the person looking over their shoulder, use `HtmlInputSecret`.

5.4.3 Displaying password fields with HtmlInputSecret

The `HtmlInputSecret` component is used to display a password input field, and maps to an `<input>` element of `type` "password". In practice, you use it a lot like `HtmlInputText`; the only difference is that it has a `redisplay` property and, of course, the component tag is different. Take a look at the summary in table 5.8.

Table 5.8 **`HtmlInputSecret` summary**

Component	`HtmlInputSecret`
Family	javax.faces.Input
Display Behavior	Displays an HTML `<input>` element with the `type` attribute set to "password"

continued on next page

Table 5.8 `HtmlInputSecret` summary *(continued)*

Possible IDE Display Names	Secret Field			
Tag Library	HTML			
JSP Tag	`<h:inputSecret>`			
Pass-Through Properties	HTML attributes for the `<input>` element (except for `type`)			
Events	Value-change			
Common Properties	`id, value, rendered, validator, converter, immediate, required, styleClass, valueChangeListener, binding` (see table 5.1)			
Property	**Type**	**Default Value**	**Required?**	**Description**
`redisplay`	`boolean`	`false`	No	Controls whether or not the value is redisplayed if the page is redisplayed. Because this is a potential security risk, the property is `false` by default.

Table 5.9 shows how to use `HtmlInputSecret`.

Table 5.9 `HtmlInputSecret` example: Basic use

HTML	`<input type="password" name="myForm:_id4" value="" maxlength="10" size="10" tabindex="2" />`
Component Tag	`<h:inputSecret value="#{user.password}" size="10" maxlength="10" tabindex="2"/>`
Browser Display	

The `size`, `value`, `maxlength`, and `tabindex` properties are passed through. The `value` attribute will always be empty because the `redisplay` property is `false` by default. This ensures that the field is always cleared, and is generally more secure because it makes it impossible to view the password in the browser. Any text the user types will be displayed using asterisks or some other character (this is up to the browser).

If you want the text to be redisplayed, you can set `redisplay` to `true`. Remember, though, that if someone views the HTML source for the page, they'll be able to see the real password. Also, the password will still be transferred in clear text unless you're using SSL or some other form of encryption. This is why redisplay is set to `false` by default—normally it's not the safest thing to do.

5.4.4 Declaring hidden fields with HtmlInputHidden

Unlike the other components in this section, `HtmlInputHidden` doesn't actually collect any input from the user; it's used for fields that are invisible to the user. Hidden fields are often used to pass variables around from page to page (normally to avoid saving state on the server), and this component is useful for integrating JSF components into application that already use hidden fields. However, if you're building a new JSF application, you generally shouldn't need to use them. (If you really do need to save the state of your beans on the client, some JSF implementations, like MyFaces [MyFaces], have special components that can do this for you.)

`HtmlInputHidden` maps to an HTML `<input>` element of `type` "hidden". It's summarized in table 5.10.

Table 5.10 `HtmlInputHidden` summary

Component	`HtmlInputHidden`
Family	javax.faces.Input
Display Behavior	Displays an HTML `<input>` element with the `type` attribute set to "hidden"
Possible IDE Display Names	Hidden Field
Tag Library	HTML
JSP Tag	`<h:inputHidden>`
Pass-Through Properties	None
Events	Value-change
Common Properties	`id, value, rendered, validator, converter, immediate, required, valueChangeListener, binding` (see table 5.1)

One thing you'll notice is that because `HtmlInputHidden` doesn't actually display anything, there are no HTML pass-through attributes, and no `styleClass` property. An example of using the component is shown in table 5.11.

Table 5.11 `HtmlInputHidden` example: Basic use

HTML	`<input id="myForm:hiddenField" type="hidden" name="myForm:hiddenField" value="hide me!" />`
Component Tag	`<h:inputHidden id="hiddenField" value="hide me!"/>`
Browser Display	N/A

No surprises here—an `<input>` element of type "hidden" is displayed, the `id` attribute is translated to the `name` attribute as normal, and the `value` attribute is the same. Often, you'll use this component with a value-binding expression instead of a hardcoded value.

> **TIP** If you have existing JavaScript code that needs to communicate with back-end application code, the `HtmlInputHidden` component is a good option if the data in question isn't already included in visible fields. (Don't forget to assign an identifier first; the JavaScript will need to access the component via its client identifier.)

That's it for the basic input controls. It's time to move on to UI components that represent boolean values and item lists.

5.5 Using HtmlSelectBooleanCheckbox for checkboxes

As its name implies, `HtmlSelectBooleanCheckbox` represents a single yes/no, or boolean, value. It is displayed as an HTML `<input>` element of `type` "checkbox". The UI component is summarized in table 5.12.

Table 5.12 `HtmlSelectBooleanCheckbox` summary

Component	`HtmlSelectBooleanCheckbox`
Family	javax.faces.SelectBoolean

continued on next page

Table 5.12 `HtmlSelectBooleanCheckbox` summary *(continued)*

Display Behavior	Displays an HTML `<input>` element with the `type` attribute set to "checkbox"
Possible IDE Display Names	Check Box, Checkbox
Tag Library	HTML
JSP Tag	`<h:selectBooleanCheckbox>`
Pass-Through Properties	HTML attributes for the `<input>` element (except for `type`)
Events	Value-change
Common Properties	`id, value, rendered, validator, converter, immediate, required, styleClass, valueChangeListener, binding` (see table 5.1)

Using `HtmlSelectBooleanCheckbox` is straightforward, as shown in table 5.13.

Table 5.13 `HtmlSelectBooleanCheckbox` example: Use with a value-binding expression that evaluates to `false`

HTML	`<input type="checkbox" name="myForm:_id1" tabindex="0"` `title="Registered?" />`
Component Tag	`<h:selectBooleanCheckbox value="#{user.registered}"` `title="Registered?" tabindex="0"/>`
Browser Display	☐

As the table shows, this `HtmlSelectBooleanCheckbox` is associated with the `user.registered` property. In this example, that property is `false`, so the browser shows an empty checkbox. The `title` and `tabindex` attributes are simply passed through.

This component is great for single checkboxes on a form, but if you want to associate multiple checkboxes with a single property, you need to use an `HtmlSelectManyBoolean` component, which is populated with an item list.

5.6 Defining item lists

User interfaces often allow a user to select one or more items from a set of possible choices. In JSF, a selection *item* represents a single choice, and has a value, a description, and a label. Components in the SelectMany and SelectOne families, like `HtmlSelectManyCheckbox` and `HtmlSelectOneListbox`, display lists of items.

Items can be organized into *item groups*, so a list of items may include a group of items as well. For example, consider this list:

- Cats
- Dogs
- Lizards
  - Chameleons
  - Geckos

Here, the first two lines, "Cats" and "Dogs," are items. The third line is an item group called "Lizards" with two items: "Chameleons" and Geckos."

When you're writing event listener code, items are represented by the `javax.faces.model.SelectItem` JSF model object, and item groups are represented by a subclass called `javax.faces.model.SelectItemGroup`. (For more information on these objects from the back-end perspective, see part 3.) On the front end, the `UISelectItem` component represents a single item or item group, and the `UISelectItems` component represents a collection of items or item groups. You use these two components to configure SelectMany or SelectOne components that handle lists of items. (Third-party components may use them as well.)

To make this clearer, we'll take a closer look at `UISelectItem` and `UISelectMany`, and then move on to the components that use them.

5.6.1 Using UISelectItem for single items

A `UISelectItem` component represents a single choice. Typically, several `UISelectItem` instances are displayed as checkboxes, radio buttons, or items in a listbox or drop-down list. The control doesn't display itself—it leaves display to its parent component.

Because `UISelectItem` components are used to display items in a list, they have `itemLabel` and `itemDescription` properties. They also have an `itemValue` property, which is typically associated directly with a bean property. Whenever users select a particular `UISelectItem` component, they are really selecting the `itemValue` property. This component is summarized in table 5.14.

Table 5.14 `UISelectItem` summary

Component	UISelectItem			
Family	javax.faces.SelectItem			
Display Behavior	None. Configures parent component with a single item. (Parent component usually provides a list of items for selection.)			
Possible IDE Display Names	N/A			
Tag Library	Core			
JSP Tag	`<f:selectItem>`			
Pass-Through Properties	None			
Common Properties	`id, binding` (see table 5.1)			
Property	**Type**	**Default Value**	**Required?**	**Description**
`value`	`SelectItem`	None	No	The component's current local value. Must be a `SelectItem` object (or a value-binding expression for a `SelectItem` object). If this property is set, `itemDescription`, `itemLabel`, and `itemValue` are not used. This value will not be updated.
`item-Description`	`String`	None	No	The description of the item—usually longer than the `itemLabel`. Not displayed in any of the standard renderers.
`itemLabel`	`String`	None	No	The short description, or "name" of the item.
`itemValue`	`Object`	None	No	The value of the item; often an object or database table row identifier.
`itemDisabled`	`boolean`	`false`	No	Indicates whether or not this item is disabled.

There are a few things to note from the table. First, because this component isn't displayed, it doesn't have any HTML pass-through properties or the `styleClass` property. Another interesting fact is that you can either use it to specify the `itemDescription`, `itemLabel`, and `itemValue` properties *or* a value-binding expression. Hardcoded values are set like this:

```
<h:foobar>
  <f:selectItem itemValue="0" itemLabel="cats"
                itemDescription="Description not displayed"/>
  <f:selectItem itemValue="1" itemLabel="dogs"/>
  <f:selectItem itemValue="2" itemLabel="birds"/>
  <f:selectItem itemValue="3" itemLabel="hamsters"/>
  <f:selectItem itemValue="4" itemLabel="lizards"/>
  <f:selectItem itemValue="5" itemLabel="snakes"/>
  <f:selectItem itemValue="6" itemLabel="koala bears" />
</h:foobar>
```

Here, we've declared a fictional `foobar` component that presumably displays a list of items. Remember, `UISelectItem` is useless unless it's nested within a component that can make use of it. This example configures it with seven `UISelectItem` instances. Note that the first item has an `itemDescription` property specified. Currently, the standard components don't make use of this property.

If we had an item bean stored under the key `selectHamsters`, we could use it like this:

```
<f:selectItem value="#{selectHamsters}"/>
```

Assuming that selectHamsters is an item bean with the same value as the "hamsters" item in the previous example, this would have the same effect as hardcoding the properties.

To specify a value-binding expression but use default values in case the bean can't be found, you can use the following:

```
<f:selectItem value="#{selectBirds}" itemValue="2"
                         itemLabel="birds"/>
```

In this case, if no bean called `selectBirds` can be found in any scope, the hardcoded values—an `itemValue` of 2 and an `itemLabel` of "birds"—will be used instead. Most of the time, `UISelectItem` represents a single list item. However, if you use a value-binding expression, it can also reference an item group. The usage is the same—the underlying model object is just different. In the previous example, that might mean that the `"#{selectBirds}"` value-binding expression would represent a Birds submenu with five different types of birds. Depending on the type of the parent component, this could be displayed as a nested menu or options list. You'll some examples of how this works later in this chapter.

You can also mix hardcoded values with a value-binding expression:

```
<f:selectItem itemValue="0" itemLabel="cats"/>
<f:selectItem itemValue="1" itemLabel="dogs"
              itemDisabled="#{user.numberOfVisits < 5}"/>
<f:selectItem value="#{selectBirds}" itemValue="2"
           itemLabel="birds"/>
<f:selectItem value="#{selectHamsters}"/>
```

This will result in a combined list, and the user will never know that the items came from different sources. Note that the `itemDisabled` property is set to a value-binding expression; it will be `true` if the user has visited fewer than five times. Remember, you can use value binding for any UI component property.

`UISelectItem` is only useful for single items or item groups, so if you need to display a collection of items (or item groups) from a bean, you should use `UISelectItems` instead, which was designed specifically for that purpose. You can mix `UISelectItem` and `UISelectItems` components together:

```
<f:selectItem itemValue="0" itemLabel="cats"/>
<f:selectItem itemValue="1" itemLabel="dogs"
              itemDisabled="#{user.numberOfVisits < 5}"/>
<f:selectItem value="#{selectBirds}" itemValue="2"
           itemLabel="birds"/>
<f:selectItems value="#{selectAnimals}"/>
```

In this example, the last component is a `UISelectItems` instead of a `UISelectItem` component. This `UISelectItems` component represents a collection of different items. The result will be just like the previous example—they will all be combined into the same list. We cover `UISelectItems` in the next section.

You use `UISelectItem` much the same way regardless of which parent component you're using. (In other words, the examples we just gave will work with all of the components in the SelectMany and SelectOne families.) You can see more examples of `UISelectItem` in the sections on those families—5.6 and 5.7, respectively—as well as in part 2 of this book.

5.6.2 Using UISelectItems for multiple items

Often when you're using a control like a drop-down listbox or a group of checkboxes, you need to associate the contents of the list with a set of dynamic values. These values may come from a data store or back-end business logic. The most common example is populating a listbox from a lookup, or reference data table. `UISelectItems` is designed to add these dynamic values to a parent control, like a combo box or listbox—it has no rendering behavior of its own. It works almost exactly the same as `UISelectItem`, except it can reference either an individual item (or item group) or a collection of items (or item groups).

You can use `UISelectItems` to configure the list of items for components in the SelectMany and SelectOne families (covered in the next two sections). In addition, nonstandard components can use `UISelectItems` as well. `UISelectItems` is summarized in table 5.15.

Table 5.15 `UISelectItems` summary

Component	`UISelectItems`			
Family	javax.faces.SelectItems			
Display Behavior	None. Configures parent component with one or more items. (Parent component usually provides a list of items for selection.)			
Possible IDE Display Names	N/A			
Tag Library	Core			
JSP Tag	`<f:selectItems>`			
Pass-Through Properties	None			
Common Properties	`id, binding` (see table 5.1)			
Property	**Type**	**Default Value**	**Required?**	**Description**
`value`	A single `SelectItem` instance, an array or `Collection` of `SelectItem` instances, or a `Map`	None	No	The component's current local value. Usually specified as a value-binding expression that points to a property of the correct type. If the referenced object is a `Map`, `SelectItem` instances will automatically be created, using the `Map`'s keys for labels and values as `SelectItem` values. This value will not be updated.

Because `UISelectItems` must be associated with a bean, it doesn't have any properties for specifying the item's value, so it can't be hardcoded. You have to use it with a value-binding expression:

```
<h:foobar>
  <f:selectItems value="#{selectItems}"/>
</h:foobar>
```

As you can see, our `UISelectItems` component is nested within a `foobar` component. Because the purpose of `UISelectItems` is to configure another component's list, it must always be nested within another component that displays a list of choices, such as an HtmlSelectOneRadio component.

In this example, we reference a bean stored under the key selectItems, which is a list that has both items and item groups.

If you need to hardcode some values, you can mix and match UISelectItem and UISelectItems:

```
<f:selectItem itemValue="0" itemLabel="cats"/>
<f:selectItem itemValue="1" itemLabel="dogs"/>
<f:selectItem value="#{selectBirds}" itemValue="2"
          itemLabel="asdasd"/>
<f:selectItems value="#{selectAnimals}"/>
```

You can also combine multiple UISelectItems instances:

```
<f:selectItems value="#{selectAnimals}"/>
<f:selectItems value="#{selectMoreAnimals}"/>
```

You use UISelectItems pretty much the same way regardless of which parent component you're using, so these examples will work with any component in the SelectMany and SelectOne families, as well as other components that use UISelectItems. The following sections have additional examples of UISelectItems, as does the case study in part 2.

5.7 Handling multiple-item selections

JSF has several standard components that represent the ability to select many different items from a list. These components are in the SelectMany family, and are rendered as listboxes or checkbox groups. The items within the list are configured with UISelectItem components and/or UISelectItems components (covered in the previous sections). The value of these components is usually associated with a single bean property that represents a collection of possible choices.

There are three standard components in the SelectMany family: HtmlSelectManyCheckbox (for displaying a group of checkboxes), HtmlSelectManyListbox (for displaying a multiselect listbox), and HtmlSelectManyMenu (for selecting a single item from a list but displaying only one item at a time). We cover these components in the following sections.

5.7.1 Using HtmlSelectManyCheckbox for checkbox groups

HtmlSelectManyCheckbox displays all of the child items as checkboxes. It maps to an HTML <table> element with several <input> elements of type "checkbox". It's similar to checkbox group components in other UI frameworks. Table 5.16 summarizes the component.

Table 5.16 `HtmlSelectManyCheckbox` summary

Component	`HtmlSelectManyCheckbox`			
Family	javax.faces.SelectMany			
Display Behavior	Displays all of its items (configured by child `UISelectItem` or `UISelectItems` components) as `<input>` elements of `type` "checkbox" with the item label enclosed inside a `<label>` element. The checkboxes are laid out according to the value of the layout property using a `<table>` element. If one of the items is a group, all of the items in that group are displayed inside another table.			
Possible IDE Display Names	Check Box Group			
Tag Library	HTML			
JSP Tag	`<h:selectManyCheckbox>`			
Pass-Through Properties	HTML attributes for the `<input>` element (except for `type`)			
Events	Value-change			
Common Properties	`id, rendered, validator, converter, immediate, styleClass, valueChangeListener, binding` (see table 5.1)			
Property	**Type**	**Default Value**	**Required?**	**Description**
`value`	`String`	None	No	The component's current local value. Must be a value-binding expression that references an array of objects or primitives, or a `List` of `String`s.
`layout`	`String`	"line-Direction"	No	Specifies how to display the checkboxes. Possible values are "pageDirection", which displays the checkboxes vertically, or "lineDirection", which displays them horizontally.
`enabledClass`	`String`	None	No	Name of CSS style class to use for the label of enabled items.
`disabled-Class`	`String`	None	No	Name of CSS style class to use for the label of disabled items.
Java-Only Property	**Type**	**Default Value**		**Description**
`selected-Values`	`Object[]`	None	No	An array of the currently selected item values (this is a type-safe alias for the `value` property).

Note that this component has properties for styling individual items: `enabledClass` for items that are enabled, and `disabledClass` for items that are not enabled. Table 5.17 shows an example of using `HtmlSelectManyCheckbox`.

Table 5.17 `HtmlSelectManyCheckbox` example: Used with several `UISelectItem` components and the `disabledClass` property.

<table>
<tr><th>HTML</th><td><pre>
<table>
  <tr>
   <td>
     <label>
       <input name="_id1:_id2" value="0" type="checkbox"
              accesskey="C"> cats
       </input>
     </label>
   </td>
  ...
  <td>
    <label class="disabled">
       <input name="_id1:_id2" value="6" type="checkbox"
              disabled="disabled"
              accesskey="C"> koala bears</input>
    </label>
  </td>
 </tr>
</table>
</pre></td></tr>
<tr><th>Component Tag</th><td><pre>
<h:selectManyCheckbox accesskey="C" required="true"
                      disabledClass="disabled">
   <f:selectItem itemValue="0" itemLabel="cats"
                 itemDescription="Description not displayed"/>
   <f:selectItem itemValue="1" itemLabel="dogs"/>
   <f:selectItem itemValue="2" itemLabel="birds"/>
   <f:selectItem itemValue="3" itemLabel="hamsters"/>
   <f:selectItem itemValue="4" itemLabel="lizards"/>
   <f:selectItem itemValue="5" itemLabel="snakes"/>
   <f:selectItem itemValue="6" itemLabel="koala bears"
                 itemDisabled="#{user.numberOfVisits > 20}"/>
</h:selectManyCheckbox>
</pre></td></tr>
<tr><th>Browser Display</th><td>☐ cats ☐ dogs ☐ birds ☐ hamsters ☐ lizards ☐ snakes ☐ koala bears</td></tr>
</table>

As you can see, `HtmlSelectManyCheckbox` outputs quite a bit of HTML for you. All of the items are enclosed in a `<table>` element with only one row (because the `layout` property defaults to "lineDirection"). For each child `UISelectItem` component, the `itemLabel` property is rendered as a `<label>` element and the `itemValue` property is used as the value of an `<input>` element of type "checkbox".

The itemDescription of the first UISelectItem is not displayed at all (which is always the case with HtmlSelectManyCheckbox). The final item is disabled because the value-binding expression "#{user.numberOfVisits > 20}" evaluated to true. Also note that each item has the same client identifier; this is the client identifier of the HtmlSelectManyCheckbox, because it collects all of the selected values.

If one of the child UISelectItem or UISelectItems components references an item group, HtmlSelectManyCheckbox will display all items within that group in a nested table.

In many cases HtmlSelectManyCheckbox is a reasonable way to allow users to select multiple choices. However, if you have more than a few choices, you can end up with an unwieldy number of checkboxes. In such a case, you may want to use a listbox instead, and HtmlSelectManyListbox is perfectly equipped for that job.

5.7.2 Displaying listboxes with HtmlSelectManyListbox

HtmlSelectManyListbox displays child items within a listbox control; it displays an HTML <select> element. You can control the size of the list, allowing as many items to be visible as you see fit. The component is summarized in table 5.18.

Table 5.18 HtmlSelectManyListbox summary

Component	HtmlSelectManyListbox
Family	javax.faces.SelectMany
Display Behavior	Displays a <select> element with the multiple attribute set, and the size attribute set to the value of the size property. All of its items (configured by child UISelectItem or UISelectItems components) are rendered as <option> elements. Any item groups are nested inside an <optgroup> element.
Possible IDE Display Names	Multi-Select Listbox
Tag Library	HTML
JSP Tag	<h:selectManyListbox>
Pass-Through Properties	HTML attributes for the <select> element
Events	Value-change
Common Properties	id, rendered, validator, converter, immediate, required, styleClass, valueChangeListener, binding (see table 5.1)

continued on next page

Table 5.18 **`HtmlSelectManyListbox` summary** *(continued)*

Property	Type	Default Value	Required?	Description
`value`	`Object`	None	No	The component's current local value. Must be a value-binding expression that references an array of objects.
`size`	`integer`	size of the list	No	Specifies the number of items to be displayed. The default is all items.
`enabled-Class`	`String`	None	No	Name of CSS style class to use for the label of enabled items.
`disabled-Class`	`String`	None	No	Name of CSS style class to use for the label of disabled items.
Java-Only Property	**Type**	**Default Value**		**Description**
`selected-Values`	Object[]	None	No	An array of the currently selected item values (this is a type-safe alias for the `value` property).

Let's take a look at an example of using an `HtmlSelectManyListBox` with an item group (see table 5.19).

Table 5.19 **`HtmlSelectManyListbox` example: Used with an item group**

HTML

```
<select name="_id1:_id15" multiple tabindex="5" >
  <option value="0">cats</option>
  <option value="1">dogs</option>
  <optgroup label="lizards">
    <option value="30">chameleons</option>
    <option value="40">geckos</option>
  </optgroup>
</select>
```

Component Tag

```
<h:selectManyListbox tabindex="5">
  <f:selectItem itemValue="0" itemLabel="cats"/>
  <f:selectItem itemValue="1" itemLabel="dogs"/>
  <f:selectItems value="#{animalForm.lizardGroup}"/>
</h:selectManyListbox>
```

Browser Display

cats
dogs
lizards
chameleons
geckos

In this example, the child `UISelectItems` component refers to a backing bean property for an item group instead of an individual item. This group is rendered within an `<optgroup>` element, so it's indented inside the listbox and has a heading, which is the label for the group.

In addition, the `tabindex` property is passed through. Because we didn't specify a size, all of the items are shown.

In cases where using `HtmlSelectManyCheckbox` is not appropriate, `HtmlSelectManyListbox` is usually your best bet. However, if you want to ensure that users only see a single item at a time, use `HtmlSelectManyMenu` instead.

5.7.3 Using HtmlSelectManyMenu for single-item listboxes

`HtmlSelectManyMenu` works almost exactly like `HtmlSelectManyListbox`—it displays child items in a list box, and is rendered as a `<select>` element. The only difference is that the number of items displayed always 1, so the user can only see a single item at a time. The component is summarized in table 5.20.

Table 5.20 `HtmlSelectManyMenu` summary

Component	`HtmlSelectManyMenu`
Family	javax.faces.SelectMany
Display Behavior	Displays a `<select>` element with the `size` attribute set to 1. All of its items (configured by child `UISelectItem` or `UISelectItems` components) are rendered as `<option>` elements of type "checkbox" with the item label enclosed inside a `<label>` element. The checkboxes are laid out according to the value of the `layout` property using a `<table>` element.
Possible IDE Display Names	N/A
Tag Library	HTML
JSP Tag	`<h:selectManyMenu>`
Pass-Through Properties	HTML attributes for the `<select>` element
Events	Value-change
Common Properties	`id, rendered, validator, converter, immediate, required, styleClass, valueChangeListener, binding` (see table 5.1)

continued on next page

Table 5.20 `HtmlSelectManyMenu` summary *(continued)*

Property	Type	Default Value	Required?	Description
`value`	`Object`	None	No	The component's current local value. Must be a value-binding expression that references an array of primitives or objects, or a `List`.
`enabled-Class`	`String`	None	No	Name of CSS style class to use for the label of enabled items.
`disabled-Class`	`String`	None	No	Name of CSS style class to use for the label of disabled items.
Java-Only Property	**Type**	**Default Value**		**Description**
`selected-Values`	`Object[]`	None	No	An array of the currently selected item values (this is a type-safe alias for the `value` property).

As the table shows, this component has all of the same properties and behavior as `HtmlSelectManyListbox`, except for the `size` property. Consequently, the way you use it is similar, as shown in table 5.21.

Table 5.21 `HtmlSelectManyMenu` example: Basic use

HTML

```
<select name="_id1:_id19" multiple size="1"
        title="This is an animal menu">
  <option value="0">cats</option>
  <option value="1">dogs</option>
  <option value="2">birds</option>
</select>
```

Component Tag

```
<h:selectManyMenu title="#{bundle.animalListTile}"
                  immediate="true"
                  styleClass="extra-border">
  <f:selectItem itemValue="0" itemLabel="cats"/>
  <f:selectItem itemValue="1" itemLabel="dogs"/>
  <f:selectItem itemValue="2" itemLabel="birds"/>
</h:selectManyMenu>
```

Browser Display (Mozilla)

birds

Browser display (Internet Explorer)

birds

The `HtmlSelectManyMenu` component was rendered as a `<select>` element with the `size` 1 and the `multiple` attribute set. Unlike most of the other UI components, this one looks different depending on the browser. Note that in Internet Explorer it displays scroll bars, and Mozilla does not. Either way, you can select multiple items. Note that we didn't specify a `size` property—it's always 1. The `title` property's value is a value-binding expression that references a string pulled from a resource bundle. This is how JSF handles internationalization (covered in chapter 6). The actual string pulled from the bundle was the English string "This is an animal menu".

The items referenced by `UISelectItem` components are displayed as `<option>` elements. Because the `immediate` property is set, JSF will process this component before it processes other components on the form. And finally, the `styleClass` property is simply passed through to an enclosing `<select>` element.

Now that we've covered components that accept multiple selections, let's look at controls that allow only one.

5.8 Handling single-item selections

Whereas the SelectMany family of UI components allows a user to select many items from a list, the SelectOne family represents the ability to select a single item from a list. Components in this family are typically rendered as a combo box or a set of radio buttons. As in the SelectMany family, the list is configured with child `UISelectItem` components and/or `UISelectItems` components (covered in section 5.6).

The SelectOne family has three standard components: `HtmlSelectOneRadio` (for displaying a group of radio buttons), `HtmlSelectOneListbox` (for displaying a listbox), and a `HtmlSelectOneMenu` (for displaying a drop-down listbox). These three components are essentially the same as `HtmlSelectOneCheckbox`, `Html-SelectManyListbox`, and `HmtlSelectManyMenu`, except that they allow the user to select only one item. We discuss these components in the following sections.

5.8.1 Using HtmlSelectOneRadio for radio button groups

`HtmlSelectOneRadio` displays all of the child items as a set of radio buttons, so the user can select only one item at a time. It is rendered as a `<table>` element with several `<input>` elements of `type` "radio". This component is summarized in table 5.22.

You can see from the table that using `HtmlSelectOneRadio` is almost identical to using `HtmlSelectManyCheckbox`. The only difference, other than the purpose (selecting a single item as opposed to multiple items), is that `HtmlSelectOneRadio`

Table 5.22 `HtmlSelectOneRadio` summary

<table>
<tr><th>Component</th><td colspan="4"><code>HtmlSelectOneRadio</code></td></tr>
<tr><th>Family</th><td colspan="4">javax.faces.SelectOne</td></tr>
<tr><th>Display Behavior</th><td colspan="4">Displays all of its items (configured by child <code>UISelectItem</code> or <code>UISelectItems</code> components) as <code><input></code> elements of type “radio” with the item label enclosed inside a <code><label></code> element. The radio buttons are laid out according to the value of the <code>layout</code> property using a <code><table></code> element. If one of the items is a group, all of the items in that group are displayed inside another table.</td></tr>
<tr><th>Possible IDE Display Names</th><td colspan="4">Radio Button Group</td></tr>
<tr><th>Tag Library</th><td colspan="4">HTML</td></tr>
<tr><th>JSP Tag</th><td colspan="4"><code><h:selectOneRadio></code></td></tr>
<tr><th>Pass-Through Properties</th><td colspan="4">HTML attributes for the <code><input></code> element (except for <code>type</code>) and <code>border</code> attribute (the number in pixels of the border, just like the <code><table></code> element)</td></tr>
<tr><th>Events</th><td colspan="4">Value-change</td></tr>
<tr><th>Common Properties</th><td colspan="4"><code>id, value, rendered, validator, converter, immediate, required, styleClass, valueChangeListener, binding</code> (see table 5.1)</td></tr>
<tr><th>Property</th><th>Type</th><th>Default Value</th><th>Required?</th><th>Description</th></tr>
<tr><td><code>layout</code></td><td><code>String</code></td><td>“line-Direction”</td><td>No</td><td>Specifies how to display the checkboxes. Possible values are “pageDirection”, which displays the radio buttons vertically, or “lineDirection”, which displays them horizontally.</td></tr>
<tr><td><code>enabled-Class</code></td><td><code>String</code></td><td>None</td><td>No</td><td>Name of CSS style class to use for the label of enabled items.</td></tr>
<tr><td><code>disabled-Class</code></td><td><code>String</code></td><td>None</td><td>No</td><td>Name of CSS style class to use for the label of disabled items.</td></tr>
</table>

has a `border` property, which is passed through to the rendered `<table>` element. This lets you add additional formatting to make your radio group more attractive.

As with `HtmlSelectManyCheckbox`, item groups are displayed using a nested table, with the group's label displayed above the table, as shown in table 5.23.

Table 5.23 `HtmlSelectManyCheckbox` example: Used with an item group

<table>
<tr><td>HTML</td><td>

```
<table>
  <tr>
    <td>
      <label>
        <input name="_id1:radioList" value="0"
               type="radio"> cats
        </input>
      </label>
    </td>
  </tr>
  <tr>
    <td>
      <label>
        <input name="_id1:radioList" value="1"
               type="radio"> dogs
        </input>
      </label>
    </td>
 </tr>
 <tr>
   <td>lizards</td>
 </tr>
 <tr>
   <td>
     <table border="0">
       <tr>
         <td>
           <label>
             <input name="_id1:radioList" value="30"
                    type="radio"> chameleon
             </input>
           </label>
         </td>
       </tr>
       <tr>
         <td>
           <label>
             <input name="_id1:radioList" value="40"
                    type="radio"> gecko</input>
           </label>
         </td>
       </tr>
     </table>
   </td>
 </tr>
</table>
```

</td></tr>
</table>

continued on next page

Table 5.23 `HtmlSelectManyCheckbox` example: Used with an item group *(continued)*

Component Tag	`<h:selectOneRadio id="radioList" layout="pageDirection">`
	`   <f:selectItem itemValue="0" itemLabel="cats"/>`
	`   <f:selectItem itemValue="1" itemLabel="dogs"/>`
	`   <f:selectItem value="#{animalForm.lizardGroup}"/>`
	`</h:selectOneRadio>`

Browser Display	○ cats ○ dogs lizards ○ chameleons ○ geckos

As you can see, the item group is rendered as a nested table. The group's label is displayed on the row above this table. In addition, because we specified "pageDirection" for the `layout` property, all of the radio buttons are in the same column.

`HtmlSelectOneRadio` is a convenient way to collect a single item from a list. However, if you don't want to display all of the items at once, or if you want to take up less space, you can use `HtmlSelectOneListbox` or `HtmlSelectOneMenu`.

5.8.2 Using single-select listboxes with HtmlSelectOneListbox

`HtmlSelectManyListbox` displays its child items within a listbox control with a configurable size and is displayed as a `<select>` element. This is useful for displaying very large lists—you only have to display a few items at a time. Table 5.24 summarizes this component.

Table 5.24 `HtmlSelectOneListbox` summary

Component	`HtmlSelectOneListbox`
Family	javax.faces.SelectOne
Display Behavior	Displays a `<select>` element with the `size` attribute set to the value of the `size` property. All of its items (configured by child `UISelectItem` or `UISelectItems` components) are rendered as `<option>` elements. Any item groups are nested inside an `<optgroup>` element.
Possible IDE Display Names	Listbox
Tag Library	HTML

continued on next page

Table 5.24 `HtmlSelectOneListbox` summary *(continued)*

JSP Tag	`<h:SelectOneListbox>`			
Pass-Through Properties	HTML attributes for the `<select>` element			
Events	Value-change			
Common Properties	`id, value, rendered, validator, converter, immediate, required, styleClass, valueChangeListener, binding` (see table 5.1)			
Property	**Type**	**Default Value**	**Required?**	**Description**
`size`	`integer`	size of the list	No	Specifies the number of items to be displayed. The default is all items.
`enabled-Class`	`String`	None	No	Name of CSS style class to use for the label of enabled items.
`disabled-Class`	`String`	None	No	Name of CSS style class to use for the label of disabled items.

As the table shows, this component is virtually identical to `HtmlSelectManyListbox`, except that a user can select only one item. An example is shown in table 5.25.

Table 5.25 `HtmlSelectManyListbox` example: Used with `UISelectItems`

HTML	`<select name="_id1:_id13" size="2">`
	`   <option value="3">birds</option>`
	`   <option value="4">hamsters</option>`
	`   <option value="99">tree frog</option>`
	`</select>`

Component Tag	`<h:selectOneListbox title="Pick an animal"`
	`                    value="#{animalForm.favoriteAnimal}"`
	`                    size="2">`
	`   <f:selectItems value="#{selectAnimals}"/>`
	`</h:selectOneListbox>`

Browser Display	birds hamsters

The `HtmlSelectOneListbox` component is rendered as a `<select>` element. Because the `size` attribute is set to 2, only two items are displayed at once. The `title` and `tabindex` attributes are passed through. The items referenced by the

UISelect-Items component are displayed as <option> elements. The only difference between the output of this component and that of HtmlSelectManyListbox is that the multiple attribute of the <select> element isn't set, because HtmlSelect-OneListbox allows selection of only a single item. The behavior for handling item groups is almost identical as well.

HtmlSelectOneListbox is a useful way to collect a single response from a list, but if you want to be more economical about space in your views, HtmlSelectOne-Menu may be a better choice.

5.8.3 Declaring combo boxes with HtmlSelectOneMenu

HtmlSelectOneMenu works almost exactly like HtmlSelectOneListbox—it displays its child items in a listbox using the HTML <select> element. The only difference is that the number of items displayed is always one, so the result is a *combo box* (also called a drop-down listbox). Table 5.26 summarizes this component.

Table 5.26 HtmlSelectOneMenu summary

Component	HtmlSelectOneMenu
Family	javax.faces.SelectOne
Display Behavior	Displays a <select> element with the size attribute set to 1. All of its items (configured by child UISelectItem or UISelectItems components) are rendered as <option> elements. Any item groups are nested inside an <optgroup> element.
Possible IDE Display Names	Combo Box, Dropdown List
Tag Library	HTML
JSP Tag	<h:selectOneMenu>
Pass-Through Properties	HTML attributes for the <select> element
Events	Value-change
Common Properties	id, value, rendered, validator, converter, immediate, required, styleClass, valueChangeListener, binding (see table 5.1)

continued on next page

Table 5.26 `HtmlSelectOneMenu` summary *(continued)*

Property	Type	Default Value	Required?	Description
`enabled-Class`	`String`	None	No	Name of CSS style class to use for the label of enabled items.
`disabled-Class`	`String`	None	No	Name of CSS style class to use for the label of disabled items.

Table 5.27 shows how to use `HtmlSelectOneMenu`.

Table 5.27 `HtmlSelectOneMenu` example: Used with item groups

HTML	<select name="claimForm:_id26" size="1" accesskey="F"> <option value="3">birds</option> <option value="4">hamsters</option> <option value="99">tree frog</option> <option value="4">hamsters</option> <optgroup label="lizards"> <option value="30">chameleons</option> <option value="40">geckos</option> </optgroup> </select>

Component Tag	<h:selectOneMenu value="#{user.favoriteAnimal}"
	                styleClass="extra-border"
	                accesskey="F">
	  <f:selectItems value="#{selectAnimals}"/>
	  <f:selectItem value="#{selectHamster}"/>
	  <f:selectItems value="#{animalForm.lizardGroup}"/>
	</h:selectOneMenu>

Browser Display	birds birds hamsters tree frog hamsters *lizards* chameleons geckos

The component is rendered as a `<select>` element with the `size` attribute set to 1 and the `accesskey` attribute passed through. The items referenced by the child `UISelectItem` components are displayed as `<option>` elements. The item group is displayed as an `<optgroup>` element.

This concludes our discussion of JSF's item list support. Next, we'll examine action source components—the ones that actually submit the form.

5.9 Executing application commands

So far, all of the components we've covered either output data or allow for data input. None of them actually tell the application what to do. That's the job of the Command components—they represent an action initiated by the user. Normally they are rendered as a button, a hyperlink, or a menu option.

The other components we've covered in this chapter emit *value-change* events, so that application code can be notified when their value changes. Command components emit *action* events instead, which tell the application that the user wants to perform an operation. Action events are handled by action listeners, which are central to controlling how your application behaves, and can be used to control navigation; see section 5.1 for more information about registering event listeners.

The two standard Command components are `HtmlCommandButton` (for displaying a button) and `HtmlCommandLink` (for displaying a hyperlink). Because they perform the same operation, their usage is quite similar.

5.9.1 Declaring buttons with HtmlCommandButton

`HtmlCommandButton` maps directly to the `<input>` element with a `type` attribute of either "submit" or "reset". If you specify `type` "reset", it works in the same way as the HTML reset button (no server round-trip is made). If you specify `type` "submit" (the default), the form data is submitted and an action event is fired. The `HtmlCommandButton` component is summarized in table 5.28.

Table 5.28 `HtmlCommandButton` summary

Component	`HtmlCommandButton`
Family	javax.faces.Command
Display Behavior	Displays an `<input>` element with the `value` attribute equal to the `value` property, and the `type` ("submit" or "reset") passed through (the default is "submit").
Possible IDE Display Names	Command Button, Button
Tag Library	HTML
JSP Tag	`<h:commandButton>`

continued on next page

Table 5.28 `HtmlCommandButton` summary *(continued)*

Pass-Through Properties	HTML attributes for the `<input>` element
Events	Action
Common Properties	`id, value, rendered, immediate, styleClass, binding` (see table 5.1)

Property	Type	Default Value	Required?	Description
`image`	`String`	None	No	Optionally specifies the URL (absolute or relative) of the image to be displayed for this button. If this property is set, the type "image" will be displayed; otherwise the value will be displayed as the label, and the type will be controlled by the `type` property.
`type`	`String`	"submit"	No	Specifies the type of button to display. If the type is "submit" (the default), an action event will be generated when the user clicks on the button. If the type is "reset", no server round-trip will be made. If the `image` property is set, this property will be ignored.
`action-Listener`	`String`	None	No	A method-binding expression for an action listener method that will be called when the user clicks on this button.

Because the Command components don't actually collect user input, they don't have `converter`, `validator`, or `required` properties. Other than that, the set of properties is similar to the other input controls. Table 5.29 shows a simple example of using `HtmlCommandButton`.

Table 5.29 `HtmlCommandButton` example: Used with a hardcoded action

HTML	`<input type="submit" name="_id1:_id2" value="Next >>" />`
Component Tag	`<h:commandButton value="Next >>" action="next"/>`
Browser Display	Next >>

Here, a single `<input>` element is rendered. The `value` property is displayed as the `value` attribute, and the text ">>" is escaped automatically as ">>". Because no `type` property is specified, the default ("submit") is displayed. When a user clicks this button, the navigation handler executes a navigation rule for the logical outcome "next", which was the value of the `action` property.

NOTE Just as with the HTML `<input>` element, even though you're allowed to specify both the `image` and `type` properties at the same time, only the `image` property will be used. In other words, you can't use an image as a reset button.

If you need to create a Reset button, simply set the `type` attribute to "reset", as you would with a normal HTML button—it will have no effect on the values of input controls on the server.

`HtmlCommandButton` is a great option whenever you need to submit data back to the server, and buttons are useful in many contexts. However, in some cases, you may want to use an ordinary HTML hyperlink to execute a command or pass parameters to the next view, and in those cases, you should use `HtmlCommandLink` instead.

5.9.2 *Creating an action link with HtmlCommandLink*

`HtmlCommandLink` maps to an HTML anchor, or an `<a>` element. It's different than `HmtlOutputLink`, which outputs arbitrary hyperlinks (covered in chapter 4) because it always posts back to the server and executes an action event. It can also support child `UIParameter` components, which gives you the opportunity to send parameters to the associated action method or action listener. Table 5.30 summarizes `HtmlCommandLink`.

Table 5.30 `HtmlCommandLink` summary

Component	`HtmlCommandLink`
Family	javax.faces.Command
Display Behavior	Displays an `<a>` element where the `onclick` event handler has JavaScript that sets a hidden form variable for the `HtmlCommandLink` itself and any child `UIParameter` components, and then submits the form. (The parent `HtmlForm` will output the hidden variable, as well as hidden variables for any nested `UIParameter` components.) Nested `UIGraphic` controls can be used for a background, and `UIOutput` components can be used for text.
Possible IDE Display Names	Command Link, Link Action

continued on next page

Table 5.30 `HtmlCommandLink` summary *(continued)*

Tag Library	HTML			
JSP Tag	`<h:commandButton>`			
Pass-Through Properties	HTML attributes for the `<a>` element (with the exception of `onclick`)			
Events	**Action**			
Common Properties	`id, value, rendered, immediate, styleClass, binding` (see table 5.1)			
Property	**Type**	**Default Value**	**Required?**	**Description**
`action-Listener`	`String`	None	No	A method-binding expression for an action listener method that will be called when the user clicks on this button.

Let's start with the simple example shown in table 5.31.

Table 5.31 `HtmlCommandLink` example: Used with a hardcoded outcome and an action listener class

HTML

```
<a href="#" onclick=
    "document.forms['myForm']['myForm:_id5'].value='myForm:_id5';
     document.forms['myForm'].submit(); return false;">
  Next &gt;&gt;
</a>
<input type="hidden" name="myForm:_id5" />
```

Component Tag

```
<h:commandLink action="next">
  <h:outputText value="Next >>"/>
  <f:actionListener type="myCompany.nextPageListener "/>
</h:commandLink>
```

Browser Display

Next >>

This example outputs an `<a>` element and a hidden field with the same name as the `HtmlCommandLink` component's client identifier. The JavaScript in the `onclick` event handler sets the value for the hidden field and then submits the form. The text of the child `HtmlOutputText` component is simply displayed (and escaped). When the user clicks on this link, the `myCompany.nextPageListener` class is executed, and the navigation case for the hardcoded outcome `"next"` is chosen, resulting in a new page.

The HTML generated by this renderer is emulating the work done with a simple button—submit the form, and execute an action event on behalf of the Command component. In this particular example, this is done by using JavaScript to set the value of a hidden field to the name of the command and then submitting the form. All implementations may not do it exactly this way, but the outcome should be the same—by clicking on a link, the user can submit the form and generate an action event.

NOTE `HtmlCommandLink` always uses JavaScript, so be sure that your target browser can handle it.

`HtmlCommandLink` also lets you nest `UIParameter` components, which can are rendered as hidden form fields. Table 5.32 shows an example of this.

As you can see, the nested `UIParameter` component is rendered as an `<input>` element of type "hidden" by the parent `HtmlForm` component. In the `onclick` client-side event handler, the `value` attribute of that hidden field is set based on `UIParemter`'s `value` property defined in JSP.[1] In the next view, UI components can access these parameters using the `param` implicit variable (see chapter 2 for more information about implicit variables).

The `styleClass` property is rendered as a `class` property (the "button" CSS style was defined elsewhere in the page). The `title` property is simply passed through. This example also has a nested `HtmlGraphicImage`—you can nest several components inside `HtmlCommandLink` and they'll be displayed without modification.

`HtmlCommandLink` is an essential component for executing commands in an attractive manner. Often you'll use it, with several other controls, inside an `HtmlDataTable` component.

5.10 Displaying data sets with HtmlDataTable

All of the components we've covered so far are relatively simple—they output a string, collect data, allow the user to select an item from a list, or submit a form. If there's one complex requisite standard component for any UI framework, it's a data grid. For desktop applications, you'll find several variations on this theme, regardless of whether you're developing in Swing, .NET, or Delphi. (The same is

[1] You may be wondering why the hidden field's value is set in the event handler instead of in the field's declaration. It's set in the event handler so that different `HtmlCommandLink` components on the same form can have the same parameter but different values.

Table 5.32 `HtmlCommandLink` example: Using nested `UIParameter` components

HTML

```
<a id="myForm:inboxLink" href="#" title="Devora's Inbox"
   onclick="document.forms['myForm']['myForm:inboxLink'].value=
              'myForm:inboxLink';
            document.forms['myForm']['showAllColumns'].value=
              'true';
            document.forms['myForm'].submit(); return false;"
   class="button">
  <img src="images/inbox.gif"
       style="border: 0; padding-right: 5px" alt="" />
Devora's Inbox
</a>
<input type="hidden" name="myForm:inboxLink" />
<input type="hidden" name="showAllColumns" />
```

Component Tag

```
<h:commandLink id="inboxLink" action="#{mailManager.loadInbox}"
               styleClass="button"
               title="#{user.firstName}'s Inbox">
  <h:graphicImage url="images/inbox.gif"
                  style="border: 0; padding-right: 5px"/>
  <h:outputText value="#{user.firstName}'s Inbox"/>
  <f:param name="showAllColumns" value="true"/>
</h:commandLink>
```

Browser Display

Devora's Inbox

true for web-based UI frameworks, such as ASP.NET WebForms). In JSF, `HtmlDataTable` is the standard data grid.

Technically, `HtmlDataTable` maps to an HTML `<table>`, like `HtmlPanelGrid`. The key difference is that it's designed to work with data sets backed by database results sets, lists, or arrays. As a matter of fact, you *can't* use it without a dynamic data source. (It is, however, possible to use a list configured via the Managed Bean Creation facility.)

You can use this component simply to display data in a tabular format, or to use input controls to edit the data in your data source. You can also scroll through data sets, displaying a specific number of rows at a time. JSF IDEs provide visual tools for configuring `HtmlDataTable` components, as shown in figure 5.1.

The component is summarized in table 5.33.

Note that this component has more Java-only properties than most. These properties allow you to better manipulate the component in event listeners (see part 3 for more information).

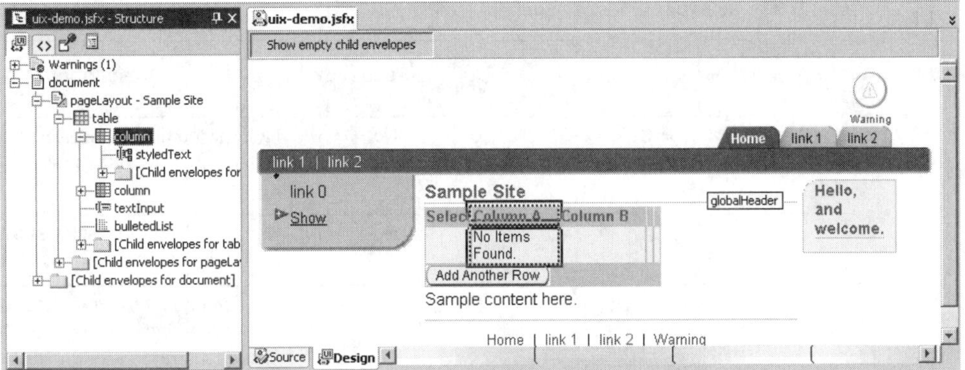

Figure 5.1 Oracle's JDeveloper [Oracle, JDeveloper] lets you visually manipulate the child components in a table, and also view a table's structure in a separate pane.

Table 5.33 also mentions the fact that columns within an `HtmlDataTable` are configured using child `UIColumn` components. Each `UIColumn` acts as a template for a

Table 5.33 `HtmlDataTable` summary

Component	`HtmlDataTable`
Family	javax.faces.Data
Display Behavior	Displays an HTML `<table>`. Columns are specified with child `UIColumn` components. If the `header` facet is specified, displays a `<thead>` element with the contents of the header. If any `UIColumn` components have a `header` facet, those will be displayed in the `<thead>` element as well. For each row, uses the child `UIColumn` components as templates for each column. If the `first` property is specified, starts display with that row. If the `row` property is specified, displays that many rows total (starting with `first`). If the `footer` facet is specified (for this component or child `UIColumn` components), displays a `<tfoot>` element with the contents of the footer(s).
Possible IDE Display Names	Data Grid, Data Table
Tag Library	HTML
JSP Tag	`<h:dataTable>`
Pass-Through Properties	HTML attributes for `<table>`
Common Properties	`id, rendered, styleClass, binding` (see table 5.1)

continued on next page

Table 5.33 `HtmlDataTable` summary *(continued)*

Property	Type	Default Value	Required?	Description
`first`	`int`	0	No	First row number in dataset to display. Change this property to begin displaying a new set of rows.
`rows`	`int`	0	No	Number of rows to display at a time. If set to 0 (the default), all rows are displayed.
`value`	`Object`	None		The component's current local value. Must be a value-binding expression that references an array, a `List`, JDBC `ResultSet`, JSTL `ResultSet`, or any other type of object. (Other objects are represented as one row).
`var`	`String`	None	No	Name of a request-scoped variable under which the current row's object will be stored. Use this value in JSF EL expressions for child components that refer to the current row. (For example, if `var` is "currentUser", a child component might use the expression `"#{currentUser.name}"`.)
`headerClass`	`String`	None	No	Name of CSS style class for the `header` facet.
`footerClass`	`String`	None	No	Name of CSS style class for the `footer` facet.
`rowClasses`	`String`	None	No	Comma-delimited list of CSS style classes for the rows. You can specify multiple styles for a row by separating them with a space. After each style has been applied, they repeat. For example, if there are two style classes (`style1` and `style2`), the first row will be `style1`, the second `style2`, the third `style1`, the fourth `style2`, so on.
`column-Classes`	`String`	None	No	Comma-delimited list of CSS style classes for the columns. You can specify multiple styles for a column by separating them with a space. After each style has been applied, they repeat. For example, if there are two style classes (`style1` and `style2`), the first column will be `style1`, the second `style2`, the third `style1`, the fourth `style2`, so on.

continued on next page

Table 5.33 `HtmlDataTable` summary *(continued)*

Java-Only Property				
`rowCount`	`int`	None	No	Returns the total number of available rows (read-only); returns -1 if the total number is not known.
`rowIndex`	`int`	None	No	Returns the index of the currently selected row (-1 if there is no selected row).
`rowData`	`Object`	None	No	Returns the currently selected row, if available (read-only).
`row-Available`	`boolean`	None	No	Returns `true` if `rowData` is available at the current `rowIndex` (read-only).
Facet	**Description**			
`header`	Child components displayed as the table's header.			
`footer`	Child components displayed as the table's footer.			

specific column; its contents are repeated for each row that is displayed. This component also has `header` and `footer` facets, and it's summarized in table 5.34.

Table 5.34 `UIColumn` summary

Component	`UIColumn`
Family	javax.faces.Column
Display Behavior	None (used to define a column in `HtmlDataTable`)
Possible IDE Display Names	N/A
Tag Library	HTML
JSP Tag	`<h:column>`
Pass-Through Properties	None
Common Properties	`id, rendered, binding` (see table 5.1)

continued on next page

Table 5.34 `UIColumn` summary *(continued)*

Facet	Description
`header`	Child components displayed as the table's header.
`footer`	Child components displayed as the table's footer.

`UIColumn` only has three properties, and although it can be used in third-party components, the only standard component that utilizes it is `HtmlDataTable`.

`HtmlDataTable` is the most powerful standard component, so it's no surprise that there are a lot of ways you can use it. Let's start with the simple example shown in table 5.35.

Table 5.35 `HtmlDataTable` example: Creating a simple read-only table

HTML

```
<table border="1" cellspacing="2">
  <thead>
    <tr>
      <th scope="col">First Name</th>
      <th scope="col">Last Name</th>
      <th scope="col">Balance</th>
    </tr>
  </thead>
  <tbody>
    <tr>
      <td>Devora</td>
      <td>Shapiro</td>
      <td>$32,495.00</td>
    </tr>
    <tr>
      <td>John</td>
      <td>Mann</td>
      <td>$1,200.00</td>
    </tr>
    <tr>
      <td>Joe</td>
      <td>Broke</td>
      <td>$0.00</td>
    </tr>
    <tr>
      <td>MW</td>
      <td>Mann</td>
      <td>$5,050.00</td>
    </tr>
   </tbody>
</table>
```

continued on next page

Table 5.35 `HtmlDataTable` example: Creating a simple read-only table *(continued)*

<table>
<tr><td>Component Tag</td><td>

```
<h:dataTable value="#{userList}" var="user" border="1"
             cellspacing="2">
  <h:column>
    <f:facet name="header">
      <h:outputText value="First Name"/>
    </f:facet>
    <h:outputText value="#{user.firstName}"/>
  </h:column>
  <h:column>
    <f:facet name="header">
      <h:outputText value="Last Name"/>
    </f:facet>
    <h:outputText value="#{user.lastName}"/>
  </h:column>
  <h:column>
    <f:facet name="header">
      <h:outputText value="Balance"/>
    </f:facet>
    <h:outputText value="#{user.balance}">
      <f:convertNumber type="currency"/>
    </h:outputText>
  </h:column>
</h:dataTable>
```

</td></tr>
<tr><td>Browser Display</td><td>

First Name	Last Name	Balance
Devora	Shapiro	$32,495.00
John	Mann	$1,200.00
Joe	Broke	$0.00
MW	Mann	$5,050.00

</td></tr>
</table>

Here, we have a simple HTML table with First Name, Last Name, and Balance columns. The data comes from a list that currently has four `User` objects. In the `HtmlDataTable` declaration, child `UIColumn` components are used to define templates for each column in the output. So, the `header` facet of each `UIColumn` is displayed within the table's header, and the contents of each `UIColumn` are repeated for every row in the list.

`HtmlDataTable` and its child `UIColumn` components output the structure of the table, iterating through the rows in the list. The `cellpadding` and `border` properties of the `HtmlDataTable` are passed through. However, the `var` property is used as the name of a request-scoped variable that can be used by child components—`HtmlOutputText` components in this case. This is why the child components can reference a bean called `user`—the `HtmlDataTable` is making the current row available under that name. Also, note that we used a converter for the last `HtmlOutputText` component; this allows us to format the `user.balance` property as a currency (see chapter 6 for more on converters).

`HtmlDataTable` is useful for displaying data sets in a tabular format, but its real power is the ability to edit those data sets. All you need to do is place input and Command controls inside the table, and associate the Command controls with backing bean methods, as shown in table 5.36.

This example does a lot, so let's start by comparing it to the previous one. There are a few major changes:

- The `HtmlDataTable` component has several style-related properties for the `header` and `footer` facets, and the even and odd rows. These CSS styles are defined in a separate stylesheet included on the page, and spruce up the overall appearance.
- The `HtmlDataTable` component's `binding` property references `userEditForm.userDataTable`. This allows `userEditForm` to access the component on the server.
- We've added a `header` and `footer` facet for the `HtmlDataTable`. The `header` facet has a single `HtmlOutputText` component. The `footer` facet has two `HtmlCommandButton` components—one simply submits the data (and doesn't call any action listeners), and the other resets the form data.
- We replaced the `HtmlOutputText` components for the columns in the previous example with `HtmlInputText` columns so that the user can edit bean properties.
- We added a third Registered column that simply displays the value of the `user.registered` property.
- We added a fourth column with an `HtmlCommandLink` component that allows the user to delete the current row by calling the action listener method `userEditForm.deleteUser`. Internally, this method accesses the list through the `HtmlDataTable` component (which it can access because of the component's `binding` property).

The result is that you can edit the first name, last name, or balance of any of the listed users and JSF will update the underlying rows when you click the Submit button automatically. If you click the Reset button, the browser will reset the input fields to their original values (because the last update)—no server roundtrip will be made. Clicking the Delete button deletes the associated row from the data set *and* updates any other rows that may have been edited; the actual work of removing the item is performed by the `editUserForm.deleteUser` method, and everything

Table 5.36 `HtmlDataTable` example: Using nested Input and Command components to edit a data set

<table>
<tr><td>HTML</td><td>

```
<table class="table-background" cellpadding="5" cellspacing="5">
  <thead>
    <tr>
      <th class="headers" colspan="5" scope="colgroup">
        <span class="table-header">Edit user information
        </span>
      </th>
    </tr>
    <tr>
      <th class="headers" scope="col">First Name</th>
      <th class="headers" scope="col">Last Name</th>
      <th class="headers" scope="col">Balance</th>
      <th class="headers" scope="col">Registered?</th>
      <th class="headers" scope="col"></th>
    </tr>
  </thead>
  <tfoot>
    <tr>
      <td class="table-footer" colspan="5">
        <input type="submit" name="_id1:_id20:_id37"
               value="Submit" />
        <input type="reset" name="_id1:_id20:_id38"
               value="Reset" />
      </td>
    </tr>
  </tfoot>
  <tbody>
    <tr class="table-odd-row">
      <td>
        <input id="_id1:_id20:0:inputName" type="text"
               name="_id1:_id20:0:inputName" value="Devora" />
      </td>
      <td>
        <input type="text" name="_id1:_id20:0:_id26"
               value="Shapiro" />
      </td>
      <td>
        <input type="text" name="_id1:_id20:0:_id29"
               value="$32,495.00" />
      </td>
      <td>false</td>
      <td>
        <a href="#"
           onclick="document.forms['_id1']['_id1:_id20:0:_id34'].
                            value='_id1:_id20:0:_id34';
                    document.forms['_id1'].submit();
                    return false;">Delete
        </a>
      </td>
    </tr>
...
    <tr class="table-even-row">
      <td>
        <input id="_id1:_id20:3:inputName" type="text"
               name="_id1:_id20:3:inputName" value="MW" />
      </td>
      <td>
        <input type="text" name="_id1:_id20:3:_id26"
               value="Mann" />
      </td>
      <td>
        <input type="text" name="_id1:_id20:3:_id29"
               value="$5,050.00" />
      </td>
      <td>false</td>
      <td>
        <a href="#"
           onclick="document.forms['_id1']['_id1:_id20:3:_id34'].
                            value='_id1:_id20:3:_id34';
                    document.forms['_id1'].submit();
                    return false;">Delete
        </a>
      </td>
    </tr>
  </tbody>
</table>
```

</td></tr>
</table>

continued on next page

Table 5.36 `HtmlDataTable` example: Using nested Input and Command components to edit a data set *(continued)*

<table>
<tr><td>Component Tag</td><td>

```
<h:dataTable value="#{userList}" var="user"
             styleClass="table-background"
             headerClass="headers" footerClass="table-footer"
             rowClasses="table-odd-row, table-even-row"
             cellspacing="5" cellpadding="5"
             binding="#{userEditForm.userEditTable}">
    <f:facet name="header">
      <h:outputText value="Edit user information"
                    styleClass="table-header"/>
    </f:facet>
    <h:column>
      <f:facet name="header">
        <h:outputText value="First Name"/>
      </f:facet>
      <h:inputText id="inputName" value="#{user.firstName}"/>
    </h:column>
    <h:column>
      <f:facet name="header">
        <h:outputText value="Last Name"/>
      </f:facet>
      <h:inputText value="#{user.lastName}"/>
    </h:column>
    <h:column>
      <f:facet name="header">
        <h:outputText value="Balance"/>
      </f:facet>
      <h:inputText value="#{user.balance}">
        <f:convertNumber type="currency"/>
      </h:inputText>
    </h:column>
    <h:column>
      <f:facet name="header">
        <h:outputText value="Registered?"/>
      </f:facet>
      <h:outputText value="#{user.registered}"/>
    </h:column>
    <h:column>
      <h:commandLink actionListener="#{userEditForm.deleteUser}">
        <h:outputText value="Delete"/>
      </h:commandLink>
    </h:column>
    <f:facet name="footer">
     <h:panelGroup>
        <h:commandButton value="Submit"/>
        <h:commandButton value="Reset" type="reset"/>
     </h:panelGroup>
    </f:facet>
 </h:dataTable>
```

</td></tr>
<tr><td>Browser Display</td><td>

Edit user information

First Name	Last Name	Balance	Registered?	
Devora	Shapiro	$32,495.00	false	Delete
John	Mann	$1,200.00	false	Delete
Joe	Broke	$0.00	false	Delete
MW	Mann	$5,050.00	false	Delete

Submit Reset

</td></tr>
</table>

else is handled by JSF. Because the Command components don't have the `action` property set, no navigation takes place—the view is always redisplayed.

We are leaving out a piece of the puzzle—the Java code for `editUserForm.deleteUser`. For more information on writing Java code that interacts with `HtmlDataTable`, see chapter 13. Even though some Java code is required, `HtmlDataTable` does a lot of work on its own—using the proper child components, you can display and edit data without code. It can even scroll through a data set, displaying parts of it at a time; see chapter 10 for a real-world example.

5.11 Summary

In this chapter, we examined all of the remaining standard components, starting with basic form input controls, and ending with the quintessential data grid component, `HtmlDataTable`. We began our survey of components with `HtmlForm`, which represents a form that contains input controls. We then moved on to the basic text fields that are supported with components from the Input family: `HtmlInputText` for text boxes, `HtmlInputTextarea` for text areas, `HtmlInputSecret` for password fields, and `HtmlInputHidden` for hidden fields. For simple checkboxes, `HtmlSelectBooleanCheckbox` is also available.

Next, we looked at the SelectMany components, which allow users to select several item from a list, and the SelectOne family, which allow users to select a single item. These components can display both individual items and nested groups (which display as submenus). Individual items are configured as `UISelectItem` or `UISelectItems` components. SelectMany contains `HtmlSelectManyCheckbox` for checkbox groups, `HtmlSelectManyListbox` for multiselect listboxes, and `HtmlSelectManyMenu` for single-item listboxes. SelectOne has `HtmlSelectOneRadio` for radio groups, `HtmlSelectOneListbox` for listboxes, and `HtmlSelectOneMenu` for combo boxes.

We then examined the Command components, which generate action events that event listeners can consume. These components actually submit form data. `HtmlCommandButton` is displayed as a button, and `HtmlCommandLink` is displayed as a hyperlink; both can be associated with action methods and/or action listeners.

Finally, we examined `HtmlDataTable`, which allows you to display tabular data from a data source. This component lets you scroll through a list of items, edit items in a data source, or simply display dynamic data in an easy-to-read format.

By this point, you should be familiar with all of JSF's standard components and have a good handle on how things work. All of the remaining basic topics, including internationalization, validation, and type conversion, are covered in the next chapter.

6 Internationalization, validators, and converters

This chapter covers

- Internationalizing and localizing JSF applications
- Using the standard validators
- Using the standard converters
- Customizing messages

By now you should have a firm understanding of the standard components provided by JavaServer Faces. This set of basic widgets is a good start, but professional-quality applications require more. Sure, you can easily output text with an Output component, but what if that text needs to be displayed in 12 languages? And how do you ensure that the data collected by an input control is valid? What about dates and numbers, which have particular nuances that vary in different cultures—how do you ensure that they're processed correctly?

We're talking about support for internationalization, validation, and type conversion. *Internationalization* is the ability to support different languages. *Validation* enables you to control what input is accepted by your application and ensure that no objects will be updated if the data is not valid. *Type conversion* ensures that the user sees a logical representation of an object and that the application can create an object based on user input. In this chapter, we show you how to use all of these features with the standard JSF components.

6.1 Internationalization and localization

It's not a small world anymore—people and corporations interact with each other on a global scale. There are a lot of nuances to this interaction—you can't always fly over to a different country and start rambling in your native tongue. If the people speak a different language, an individual may look at you like you're crazy, humor you with the five words they know, or speak to you in your own language (if you're really lucky). Regardless, you'll probably make a lot of social blunders, like wearing boots in a Japanese temple or holding up your middle finger in the United States.

Even when the languages are the same, there are a lot of differences in culture and the words used. This is evident to anyone who has bounced between the United States and the United Kingdom—two countries that speak different versions of the same language, each with unique words and phrases that are foreign outside the country's borders. In software development, the culture, political preferences, and language of a region make up a *locale*. In Java, a locale is a country and language combination.

Enabling an application to support multiple locales is called *internationalization*. Even though an application may be internationalized, someone still has to do the work of customizing it for a particular locale. Text strings have to be translated, different graphics may be used, and sometimes an entire page layout may change (especially if some of the supported languages read left-to-right and others read right-to-left). The process of modifying an application to support a locale is called *localization*.

DEFINITION Internationalization is often abbreviated as *i18n*, because there are 18 letters in between the "i" and the "n", and, well, many programmers hate typing out long words. (I'm definitely an exception to that rule.) Localization is often abbreviated as *l10n* (10 characters between the "l" and the "n").

JSF has rich support for internationalization and localization. As a matter of fact, some implementations, like the reference implementation [Sun, JSF RI] provide localized messages for validator and converter errors.[1] So if your user's locale is set to French, error messages will automatically display in French. JSF also does well with numbers, dates, and other objects accessed through the expression language—converters handle localization for you.

If you want the rest of the text in your application to adapt to different locales, however, you will need to do a little bit of work. First, you'll need to tell JSF which locales you want to support. Next, you'll need to create at least one resource bundle, which is a group of localized strings. Then, once you load the resource bundle (often with a JSP tag), you can reference localized strings with normal value binding expressions.

TIP Even if your application isn't going to support multiple languages, you may want to use resource bundles so that you can place all of your strings in one place and enforce consistency. (For example, if your application displays a specific phrase on several pages, you can centralize the phrase in a resource bundle and reference it from multiple pages.)

6.1.1 Looking into locales

So, a locale represents a language and country combination,[2] but what does that mean in the world of JSF? First, let's delve a little deeper into how the Java platform handles locales. A locale is represented as a string with two parts: a language code and a country code.

Language codes are lowercase, two-letter strings defined by the International Organization for Standardization (ISO). For example, *pl* represents Polish, and *en* represents English. Country codes are uppercase, two-letter strings, also defined

---

[1] Currently, the reference implementation supports English, French, and German.

[2] Technically, there is another element, called a *variant*, which represents a vendor and browser-specific code like "WIN" for Windows, "MAC" for Macintosh, and "POSIX" for POSIX. It's not used too often, so we won't cover it here.

by ISO. *PL* is the country code for Poland, and *GB* is the code for the United Kingdom (All of the ISO language and country codes are listed in online extension appendix E.)

The country is optional, so *en* alone is a valid locale string for the English language, regardless of country. Including the country requires adding the country code to the end of the string, and using an underscore in between the language and the country codes. So, *en_GB* means English in the U.K., and *pl_PL* means Polish in Poland.

When you're localizing a JSF application, you'll need to use the proper locale for the languages and countries that you'd like to support. In some cases, simply using the language code is enough, but it's better to be precise in other cases, such as when you're dealing with currencies. (Both the United States and the United Kingdom speak English, but the currencies are completely different.)

Now that it's clear how Java represents locales, let's look at how to make sure your JSF application supports them.

Configuring locales

The first step toward supporting multiple languages is to tell your JSF application which locales it should support. You specify the supported locales with the `<locale-config>` element in a Faces configuration file, under the `<application>` node:

```
<application>
  <locale-config>
    <default-locale>en</default-locale>
    <supported-locale>en</supported-locale>
    <supported-locale>es</supported-locale>
  </locale-config>
  <message-bundle>CustomMessages</message-bundle>
</application>
```

The letters "en" and "es" stand for English and Spanish, respectively. So this tells our application to support both English and Spanish, and to use English as the default. Of course, we could be more specific:

```
<application>
  <locale-config>
    <default-locale>en</default-locale>
    <supported-locale>en</supported-locale>
    <supported-locale>en_US</supported-locale>
    <supported-locale>es_ES</supported-locale>
  </locale-config>
  <message-bundle>CustomMessages</message-bundle>
</application>
```

This tells our application to support English, the United States variant of English, and Spain's variant of Spanish, but to use plain-old English as the default. Even if you specify country-specific locales, it's generally a good idea to also support the language by itself.

NOTE If you don't specify locales in a JSF configuration file, you can't guarantee that your application will support anything other than the default locale of the application's Java virtual machine. (Some JSF implementations may work with other locales, but it's not guaranteed as per the specification.) Therefore, we highly recommend that you configure locales appropriately.

Defining what locales your application supports is one thing, but determining which locale the application is *currently* using is a different story.

Determining the user's current locale

The user's current locale is determined based on a client application's locale settings and the locales supported by the application itself. Web browsers send an HTTP header that specifies the languages they support. So, for JSF HTML applications, the user's locale is selected based on the union of their browser's locales and the application's supported locales.

For example, if your browser's primary language is Spanish (es_ES), and you access a JSF application that supports French (fr or fr_FR) as the default *and* Spanish, you'll see Spanish text. But, if the JSF application doesn't support Spanish, you'll see French instead. As another example, suppose your browser is configured to support U.K. English, Kazakh Russian (kz_RU), and Mexican Spanish (es_MX) (in that order). If you're accessing a JSF application that supports Khazak Russian, Mexican Spanish, and French, you'll see Kazakh Russian text.

You can override the locale JSF selects by `locale` property of the view. You can do this either in JSP with the `<f:view>` tag (see chapter 4), or with Java code in a backing bean. In either case, make sure that you use one of the locales configured for your application.

6.1.2 Creating resource bundles

Once you've configured your JSF application to support different locales, you have to place locale-specific versions of your application's text strings in resource bundles. Resource bundles aren't a JSF feature—they're a fundamental part of the way Java handles internationalization and localization. If you've already worked with them before, you can skip ahead to the next section. Otherwise, read on.

Resource bundles are simply property files[3] with key/value pairs. Each string has a key, which is the same for all locales. So the key `welcomeMessage` would point to the string that represents the welcome message, whether it's in English, French, Russian, or Swahili. Once you've created one or more resource bundles, all you have to do is make sure that your JSF components use the string in the bundle instead of a hardcoded text value (all of the previous examples in this book have used hardcoded values). Listing 6.1 shows an example resource bundle, called LocalizationResources_en.properties.

Listing 6.1 LocalizationResources_en.properties: An example resource bundle

```
halloween=Every day is like Halloween.
numberOfVisits=You have visited us {0} time(s), {1}. Rock on!
toggleLocale=Translate to Spanish
helloImage=../images/hello.gif
```

You can see that the values aren't always simple strings for display. The second line is parameterized, and can accept two parameters that can either be hard-coded or retrieved from an object at runtime. So if the two parameters were "23" and "Joe", the user would see "You have visited us 23 time(s), Joe. Rock on!" The last line is the path for a GIF file. With this resource bundle, we can support English. The Spanish version of the file is shown in listing 6.2.

Listing 6.2 LocalizationResources_es.properties—An example resource bundle in Spanish (translated from the resource bundle in listing 6.1)

```
halloween=Todos los días son como el Día de las Brujas.
numberOfVisits=Nos ha visitado {0} veces, {1}. ¡que buena onda!
toggleLocale=Traducir a Ingles
helloImage=../images/hola.gif
```

You can see that the keys in listing 6.1 and listing 6.2 are the same, but the values in the latter are localized for Spanish.

WARNING You can't use the "." character in resource bundle keys used with JSF. This character is a reserved character in the JSF EL.

---

[3] Technically, they are subclasses of the `ResourceBundle` class. However, unless someone in your group has written a custom Java class, you will probably be working with the property files.

You may have noticed that we named the first file LocalizedResources_en.properties and the second one LocalizedResources_es.properties. The last two letters of the name—"en" and "es"—are the language codes for English and Spanish, respectively.

Every internationalized application should also have a resource bundle with no special ending—a default in case no key is found in the localized versions. In this case, that file would be LocalizedResources.properties. Often this file will be the same as one of the localized ones—English in our case. It can also be used to store strings that are constant across different locales, or for strings that are only localized sometimes. You can also place all of the strings for your default language in this bundle and eliminate the specific bundle for your default language altogether.

After you have created a localized properties file (with whatever character coding is appropriate for that language), you must convert it to use Unicode characters. This can be done with the native2ascii tool included with the Java Development Kit (JDK). See the API docs for `PropertyResourceBundle` for more information. When the system looks for a resource bundle, it starts with the most specific bundle it can find—one that matches language *and* country. If it can't find a key in that bundle (or if the bundle doesn't exist), it searches for the bundle with just the language. It does this for the desired locale, and if that doesn't work, it tries the default locale. If it still can't find one, it uses the default bundle. After you have created a localized properties file (with whatever character coding is appropriate for that language), you must convert it to use Unicode characters. This can be done with the native2ascii tool included with the Java Development Kit (JDK). See the API docs for `PropertyResourceBundle` for more information.

So, if the user's selected locale is Spanish in Spain (es_ES) and the default locale is English in the United States (en_US), and the base resource bundle name is LocalizationResources, the system will search for the following bundles in this order:

```
LocalizationResources_es_ES.properties
LocalizationResources_es.properties
LocalziationResources_en_US.properties
LocalizaitonResources_en.properties
LocalizationResources.properties
```

To keep things simple in our examples, we left out the top-level ones (the ones that end in "es_ES" and "en_US"). That's okay, because the system will simply start with the ones ending in "es" and "en".

So, to review, we have three separate versions of our resource bundle: LocationResources_en.properties, LocationResources_es.properties, and LocationResources.

properties. This gives us an English set of strings, a Spanish set of strings, and a default set of strings, respectively.

These files can be placed anywhere in the web application's classpath. The easiest thing to do is to place them right inside the WEB-INF/classes directory. However, it often makes sense to place them inside a specific package. Also, remember that you don't have to put all of your resources in one bundle—you can group them however you want. In a real application, you may have different bundles for different modules, or even topics.

NOTE This section gave you a brief overview of how to create resource bundles in Java, and should be enough to get you started internationalizing and localizing JSF applications. You can also create resource bundles programmatically, and like most things in Java land, there's even more you can do, such as map binary values to keys. For more information on internationalization and localization from a programmer's perspective, see the Sun Java Tutorial [Sun, i18ln].

6.1.3 Using resource bundles with components

Using a resource bundle in a JSF application is as simple as using a value-binding expression. All you have to do is load the proper resource bundle and make it accessible in an application scope. For JSP, there's a JSF core tag, `<f:loadBundle>`, that loads the bundle and stores it in the request scope automatically.[4] Here's how you use it:

```
<f:loadBundle basename="LocalizationResources" var="bundle"/>
```

The `basename` attribute specifies the name of the resource bundle, prefixed by its location in your classpath. Because our bundles were placed in WEB-INF/classes, no prefix is needed. However, if we had nested them deeper, like in the WEB-INF/classes/org/jia directory, the `basename` would be "org.jia.LocalizationResources". The variable's name is specified by the `var` attribute, and that's the value you'll use for the `bundle` attribute in your JSF component tags. Both attributes are required.

In some cases, it might make sense to set up bundles programmatically instead of using custom tags. This way, front-end developers don't have to use the `<f:loadBundle>` tag, although they'll still need to know the bundle variable name.

Once the bundle has been loaded, whenever you want to access a particular string from that bundle, you can grab it with an ordinary value-binding expression. So, now that we've loaded LocalizationResources under the key `bundle`,

---

[4] Technically, it creates a special `Map` backed by the specified `ResourceBundle`.

we can access value of the key `halloween`, with the value-binding expression `"#{bundle.halloween}"`.

TIP If you're developing a prototype (without backing Java code) first, it's generally best to start out hardcoding values. You can then pull strings out into resource bundles when the application is more mature. We show this technique in part 2.

Let's move on to some specific examples. Figures 6.1 and 6.2 show some JSF components displaying our localized strings in English and Spanish, respectively.

The first example in the figure uses an `HtmlOutputText`. With our LocalizationResources bundle configured under the variable name `bundle`, we can reference a localized string like this:

```
<h:outputText value="#{bundle.halloween}"/>
```

This displays the string stored under the key `halloween` in our resource bundle, which is referenced under the variable name `bundle`. If the user's locale is English, this is the string "Everyday is like Halloween" from LocalizationResources_en.properties, as shown in figure 6.1. If the language is Spanish, the string "Todos los días son como el Día de las Brujas", taken from LocalizationResources_es.properties, as shown in figure 6.2, is displayed.

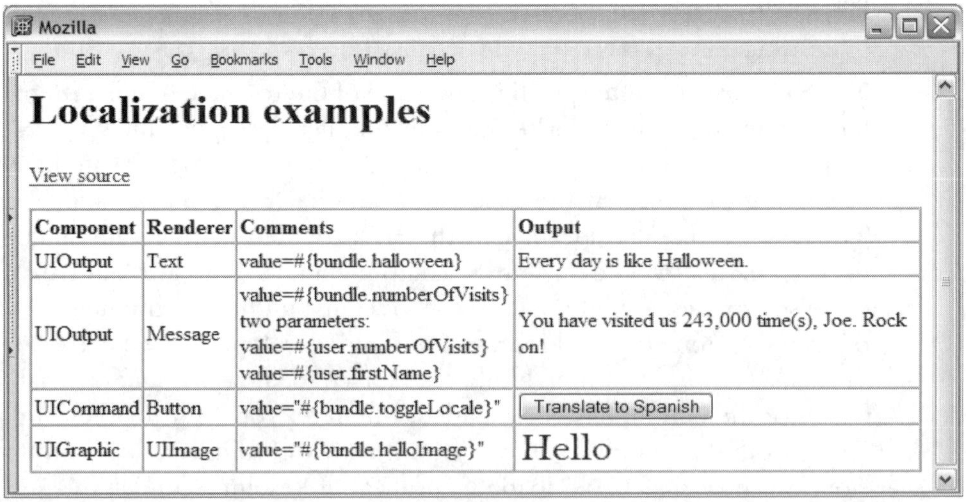

Mozilla

File Edit View Go Bookmarks Tools Window Help

Localization examples

View source

Component	Renderer	Comments	Output
UIOutput	Text	value=#{bundle.halloween}	Every day is like Halloween.
UIOutput	Message	value=#{bundle.numberOfVisits} two parameters: value=#{user.numberOfVisits} value=#{user.firstName}	You have visited us 243,000 time(s), Joe. Rock on!
UICommand	Button	value="#{bundle.toggleLocale}"	Translate to Spanish
UIGraphic	UIImage	value="#{bundle.helloImage}"	Hello

Figure 6.1 Examples of text localized in English with different JSF components.

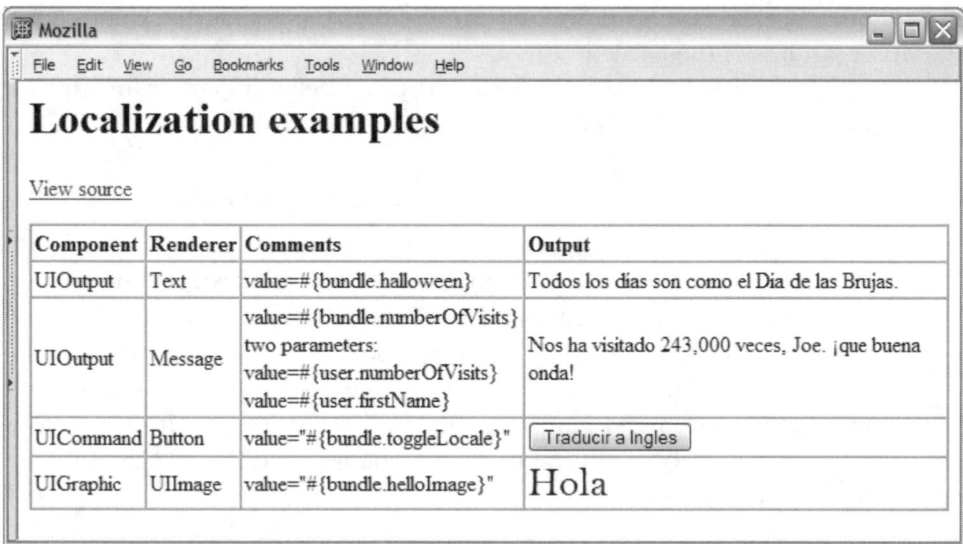

Figure 6.2 Examples of text localized in Spanish with different JSF components.

NOTE If the resource bundle can't find a key, it will return the string "???<key>???" instead. So, in this example, the value displayed would be "???halloween???".

Using the `HtmlOutputFormat` component allows you to have parameterized strings that work in different locales. The values of the parameters, which come from model objects, may or may not be localized themselves—that's up to the object's developer. Often, it's okay if they're not because the values are simple things like a person's name, or numbers:

```
<h:outputFormat value="#{bundle.numberOfVisits}">
  <f:param value="#{user.numberOfVisits}"/>
  <f:param value="#{user.firstName}"/>
</h:outputFormat>
```

This code displays the string stored under the key `numberOfVisits`. That string uses a message format pattern, which is a special pattern that `HtmlOutputFormat` understands (see chapter 4 for details). The string has two placeholders for parameters, which are replaced with two `UIParameter` components—one for the user's number of visits, and the other for their first name. If the user's name is Joe, and they have visited 243 times, this would display "You have visited us 243 time(s), Joe. Rock on!" for English, and "Nos ha visitado 243 veces, Joe. ¡que buena onda!" for Spanish. You can see that the parameter values are the same regardless of the locale in this case.

Button labels need to be localized too—"Submit" and "Go" aren't universal words. Here's an example:

```
<h:commandButton value="#{bundle.toggleLocale}"
                 actionListener="#{testForm.toggleLocale}"/>
```

For English, this displays a button with the label "Translate to Spanish"; for Spanish, it displays the text "Traducir a Ingles". In this case, the `actionListener` property is used to launch server code that changes the locale. Because `actionListener` references a backing bean method, there's no need to internationalize it.

Web user interfaces often use graphics to display text, especially when simple fonts and colors aren't good enough. In these cases, and in situations where an image has a specific cultural meaning, you will need to display different images for different locales:

```
<h:graphicImage value="#{bundle.helloImage}"/>
```

For English, this selects the image "images/hello.gif"; for Spanish, it selects "images/hola.gif". Take a look at figures 6.1 and 6.2 to see the graphics themselves—they're sure to be the envy of designers everywhere.

These examples are only the tip of the iceberg. Basically, anywhere a component accepts a value-binding expression, you can use a localized string instead of hardcoded text. This means you can localize any component property. Just make sure the resource bundle has been loaded, and that you're using the proper variable name (`bundle`, in this case).

TIP If you're manipulating a component in Java code, the same principle applies as long as a resource bundle has been loaded and made accessible. You can access a localized string with a value-binding expression.

6.1.4 Internationalizing text from back-end code

All of this business about linking component textg to resource bundle keys is useful, but so far we've only shown examples of constant values. What about situations where the text is dynamic and comes from backing beans or business objects (and perhaps ultimately a database)? In some cases you can still use resource bundles, but at the Java level instead. This could also be something handled in the database as well, in which case the actual implementation would be dependent on your database design. We show the simpler, non-database approach in chapter 13.

6.2 Input validation

A popular phrase in software development is "garbage in–garbage out." Having a system that spits out garbage isn't good for anybody's professional image, so it pays to keep users from inputting garbage in the first place. That's precisely why *validation*—the ability to block bad input—is so important, and that's why JSF has extensive support for it. Faces supports this through validator methods on backing beans and validators.

NOTE There is no explicit support for client-side validation in JSF's validation model. In other words, any validator methods you write in backing beans, as well as the standard validators (or custom validators you write), will *not* generate JavaScript to check a component's value on the client. You can write support client-side validation in your own validators, and you can also expect third-party component vendors, as well as tool vendors, to provide this capability.

Either approach checks the value of a control see if its current value is acceptable. If so, the `valid` property of the component is set to `true`, and the associated object is updated accordingly (if one is associated with the component's value via a value-binding expression). If the value isn't accepted, an error message is generated for that specific component, and the associated object is not modified. These error messages can then be displayed back to users so that they can correct their erroneous input. (Validation messages are displayed with either the `HtmlMessage` or `HtmlMessages` component, both of which are covered in chapter 4).

6.2.1 Using validator methods

An input control can also be associated with a single validation method on a backing bean. Validator methods are generally used for application-specific validation and aren't necessarily reusable for different applications. Validators, on the other hand, are generic and designed for use in different types of applications.

Suppose we had a backing bean called `registrationBean` and a validation method called `validateEmail`. With JSP, we could associate an input control with this method like so:

```
<h:inputText id="emailInput"
            validator="#{registrationBean.validateEmail}"
            value="#{registrationBean.email}/>
```

Now, anytime a user enters a value into this component, the `validateEmail` method will check to make sure it's valid. If so, the backing bean property `registrationBean.email` will be updated; otherwise, an error message will be generated instead.

For more examples of using validator methods, see part 2. For details on how to write validator methods, see part 3.

6.2.2 Using validators

For any input control, you can register one or more validators. (Custom or third-party components may validate themselves instead, but the standard components don't.) Both validators and converters are generally accessible in the component palette of IDEs that support JSF, as shown in figure 6.3.

There are two ways to register a validator with a component in JSP:

- Nest the validator's custom tag inside a component tag
- Nest the core `<f:validator>` tag with the validator's identifier inside the component tag

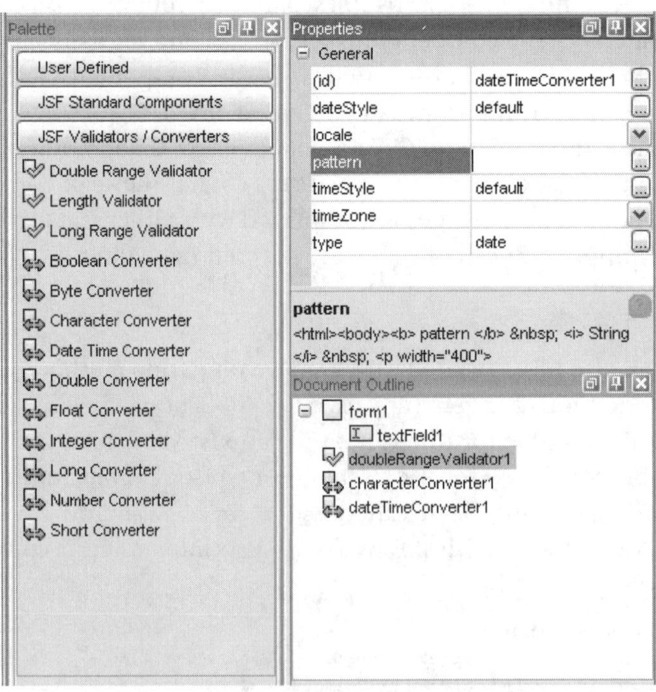

Figure 6.3 JSF-enabled IDEs, like Java Studio Creator [Sun, Creator], will usually allow you to drag and drop validators and converters from a component palette, much like components. They are nonvisual, but they will usually show up in document outlines.

To declare a validator, you nest the validator tag inside the component tag:

```
<h:inputText id="SSNInput" value="#{user.ssn}">
   <jia:validateRegex expression="\\d{3}[-]\\d{2}[-]\\d{4}"/>
</h:inputText>
```

This snippet registers a RegularExpression validator for this input control. The expression property tells the validator to check for a valid U.S. social security number. If a user enters a value that matches the expression, the user.ssn property is updated. Otherwise, an error message is generated.

The RegularExpression validator is a custom validator covered in online extension chapter 20, and you use it the same as any other validator. It's also possible to use both a validation method in conjunction with one or more validators.

If you or someone on your team has developed a custom validator, you can also register it on a component with the <f:validator> tag from the JSF core tag library. This is only useful for validators that don't require any properties. Here's an example for a hypothetical email address validator:

```
<h:inputText>
  <f:validator validatorId="Email"/>
</h:inputText>
```

This would register an Email validator on this HtmlInputText control. (You can configure a custom validator by name in a Faces configuration file; see chapter 1 for an example.) Theoretically, this validator will not accept any strings that aren't valid email addresses. Using the generic tag makes sense for this type of validator, because it's unlikely to have any additional properties.

This tag is only useful for internal development or testing; professional component libraries and IDEs are likely to have to have specific custom tags, as should any validators developed for internal distribution.

You can also register validators on components programmatically; see chapter 11 for details. JSF includes several standard validators, which we cover in the next section.

6.2.3 Using the standard validators

Because validation is a pretty common task, JSF includes a few standard validators right out of the box. Table 6.1 lists all of the standard validators and their corresponding tags, which are located in the core JSF tag library.

Table 6.1 The standard validators and their custom tags, which are located in the JSF core tag library.

Validator	JSP Custom Tag	Java Class (package `javax.faces.validator`)	Properties	Behavior
Double-Range	`<f:validate-DoubleRange>`	`Double-Range-Validator`	`minimum`, `maximum`	Ensures that the control's value can be converted to a `double` (a number with a decimal point), and is greater than or equal to `minimum` (if specified) and less than or equal to `maximum` (if specified). Use this when dealing with money or fractional values.
Length	`<f:validate-Length>`	`Length-Validator`	`minimum`, `maximum`	Ensures that the length of the control's value is greater than or equal to `minimum` (if specified) and less than or equal to `maximum` (if specified).
Long-Range	`<f:validate-LongRange>`	`LongRange-Validator`	`minimum`, `maximum`	Ensures that the control's value can be converted to a `long` (a large integer), and is greater than or equal to `minimum` (if specified) and less than or equal to `maximum` (if specified).

For the validators shown in table 6.1, you can set the `minimum` property, the `maximum` property, or both. Whichever property you omit won't affect the validation process. (In other words, there is no default; the validator just won't worry about that end of the range.) If you want to guarantee that an input control has a value, use the component's `required` property, because these validators happily accept empty values.

Validators can only be accepted by input controls. Figure 6.4 shows examples of the standard validators, and use of the `required` property with different input controls.

NOTE The components in the SelectMany family don't work with the standard validators because their `value` properties, which are arrays of objects, cannot be converted to a type that the validators understand.

You can see that the right-hand side of the figure displays the error messages generated by the validator. We examine each of the standard validators briefly here; see part 2 for examples within a real application.

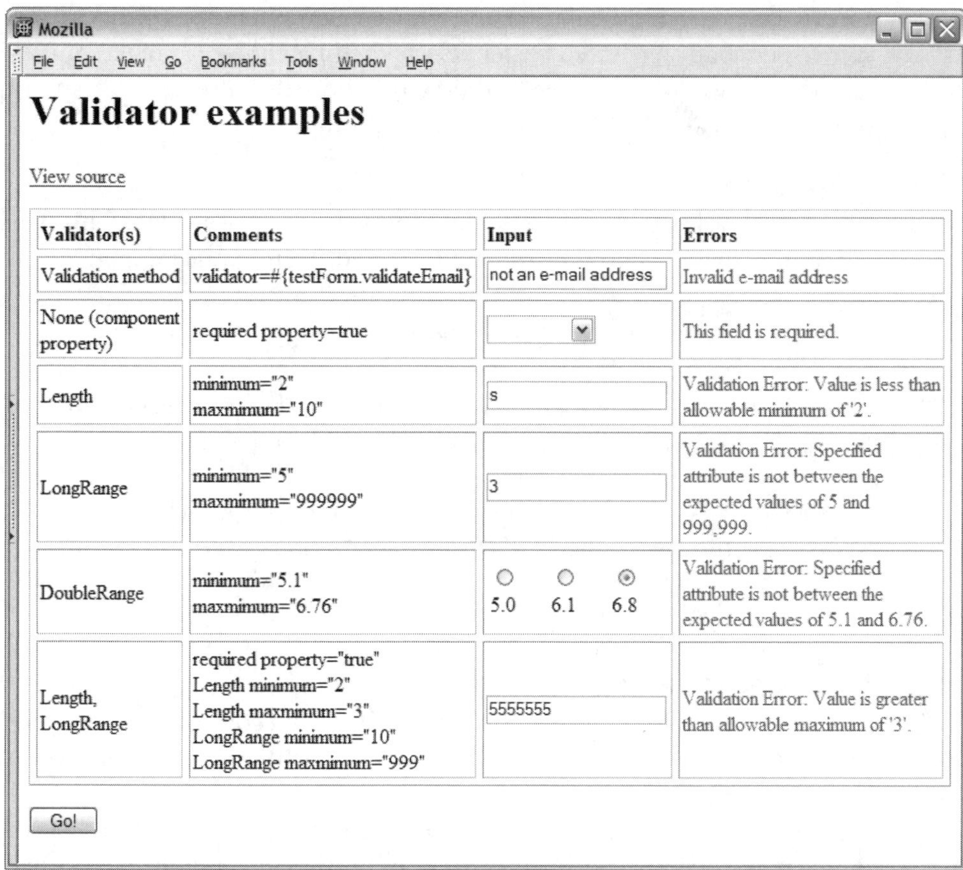

Figure 6.4 Examples of using the standard validators with different input controls.

Requiring an input value

Every input component has a `required` property, which, if `true`, forces the component to reject empty values (the default is `false`). This isn't exactly a standard validator, but it is validation behavior handled by the input components themselves. Here's an example:

```
<h:selectOneMenu id="RequiredInput" required="true">
  <f:selectItem itemValue="" itemLabel=""/>
  <f:selectItem itemValue="1" itemLabel="dogs"/>
  <f:selectItem itemValue="2" itemLabel="birds"/>
  <f:selectItem itemValue="3" itemLabel="hamsters"/>
</h:selectOneMenu>
```

In this case, the user has four choices: an empty choice (the default), "dogs", "birds", or "hamsters". If the user selects the first choice (or makes no selection at all), the component will reject the value and generate an error message. The other options are not blank, so they are all valid.

Length validator

The `Length` validator verifies the length of the control's value. This is useful for enforcing any limits on the size of a text field. Here's an example:

```
<h:inputText id="LengthInput">
  <f:validateLength minimum="2" maximum="10"/>
</h:inputText>
```

This ensures that the text entered by the user is always between 2 and 10 characters long. Any values outside of this range will be rejected.

TIP As a general rule, you should use the `Length` validator even if you've set the size of the field (for instance with the `maxsize` property of `Html-InputText`). This allows you to enforce the length of the field both on the client and on the server.

LongRange validator

The `LongRange` validator ensures that the value of a control is of type `long` (a large integer) and is within a specified range. Use it whenever you want to control the range of numbers a user is entering, and the number can't have any decimal points. If the value is a `String`, it will try and convert into a `Long`, so it will reject any non-numeric values, or numeric values that contain decimal points. Here's an example:

```
<h:inputText id="LongRangeInput">
   <f:validateLongRange  minimum="5" maximum="999999"/>
</h:inputText>
```

This code will reject any values that are not integers between 5 and 999,999.

DoubleRange validator

The `DoubleRange` validator is used to verify that a double value (a number with a decimal point) is within a specified range. This is especially useful for monetary values. Here's an example:

```
<h:selectOneRadio id="DoubleRangeInput">
  <h:selectItem itemValue="5.0" itemLabel="5.0"/>
  <h:selectItem itemValue="6.1" itemLabel="6.1"/>
  <h:selectItem itemValue="6.8" itemLabel="6.8"/>
```

```
<f:validateDoubleRange minimum="5.1" maximum="6.76"/>
</h:selectOneRadio>
```

In this example, only values between 5.1 and 6.76 are allowed. The user has a choice between three possible values: 5.0, 6.1, and 6.8. If the user selects 5.0 or 6.8, an error message is generated. If the user selects 6.1, which is in the proper range, no error is reported and the value is accepted.

6.2.4 Combining different validators

Validators don't have exclusive control of a component; any number of them can be associated with a single component. At the very least, you'll often use the `required` property in addition to one of the standard validators. If you use custom or third-party validators, you can mix them with the standard ones. When you have multiple validators registered for a control, the control's value will be considered invalid if *any* one of the validators rejects it.

Let's say we wanted to require that a user enter a value that's either two or three characters long and between the numbers 10 and 999. Because this is a required field, we can use the control's `required` property. We can enforce the string's length with the `Length` validator, and the specific number values with a `LongRange` validator. Here's all three together:

```
<h:inputText id="MultiInput" required="true">
  <f:validateLength minimum="2" maximum="3"/>
  <f:validateLongRange  minimum="10" maximum="999"/>
</h:inputText>
```

This snippet ensures that the control's value is not empty, that it is between 2 and 3 characters long, and that its numeric value is between 10 and 999. (Validators are executed in the same order they were added.) If the value entered by the user doesn't match all of these requirements, it will be rejected, and an error message will be generated. Otherwise, no message will be generated, and the value will be accepted. (Technically, the `Length` validator isn't required because `LongRange` implicitly validates length.)

That's it for the standard validators. We cover developing custom validators in chapter 15. Now, let's examine JSF's built-in type conversion abilities.

6.3 Type conversion and formatting

When users see an object on the screen, they see it in terms of recognizable text, like "May 10th, 2003". Programs don't think of objects that way, though. A `Date` object is more than just the string "May 10th, 2003"—it has a single property, time, and useful methods like before, after, and compareTo. In order for user interfaces to display objects in terms that users understand, the objects must be converted into strings for display.

Those strings may change based on a number of factors, such as the user's locale (dates are displayed differently in different countries) or simply the constraints of the page (a shorter date format might make more sense in a certain part of a page). That's the purpose of JSF converters—to create a string representation of an object, and to create an object representation of a string. If for some reason a value can't be converted, an error message will be generated. These messages can then be displayed back to the user. (Conversion error messages are displayed with either the HtmlMessage or HtmlMessages components, which are covered in chapter 4.)

JSF provides a set of standard converters to satisfy your basic type conversion needs. You can also write your own converters, and third-party vendors will provide them as well. Converters can be registered both by type and by identifier. For example, there is a converter associated with the Date object, but it can also be referenced by its identifier, which is DateTime.

You can associate a converter with almost any component that displays a simple value—especially input components. Table 6.2 lists the standard components that support converters. Whenever that component's value is displayed, it will be translated into a String by the converter. Conversely, whenever a user enters data into the component, the user's input will be converted into an Object by the converter.

Table 6.2 Converters are supported by these components (and their superclasses).

Component	JSP Component Tag
HtmlOutputText	<h:outputText>
HtmlOutputFormat	<h:outputFormat>
HtmlOutputLink	<h:outputLink>
HtmlOutputLabel	<h:outputLabel>
HtmlInputText	<h:inputText>
HtmlInputTextarea	<h:inputTextarea>
HtmlInputHidden	<h:inputHidden>
HtmlInputSecret	<h:inputSecret>

continued on next page

Table 6.2 Converters are supported by these components (and their superclasses). *(continued)*

Component	JSP Component Tag
`HtmlSelectBooleanCheckbox`	`<h:selectBooleanCheckbox>`
`HtmlSelectManyCheckbox`	`<h:selectManyCheckbox>`
`HtmlSelectManyListbox`	`<h:selectManyListbox>`
`HtmlSelectManyMenu`	`<h:selectManyMenu>`
`HtmlSelectOneRadio`	`<h:selectOneRadio>`
`HtmlSelectOneListbox`	`<h:selectOneListbox>`
`HtmlSelectOneMenu`	`<h:selectOneMenu>`

If you don't specify a converter, JSF will pick one for you. The framework has standard converters for all of the basic Java types: `BigDecimal`, `BigInteger`, `Boolean`, `Byte`, `Character`, `Integer`, `Short`, `Double`, `Float`, and `Long`. So, for example, if your component is associated with a property of type `boolean`, JSF will choose the `Boolean` converter. These converters provide basic conversion functionality. For example, if a `Boolean`'s value is `true`, the string "true" will be displayed. (Primitive types are automatically converted to their object counterparts.) This isn't anything worth emailing home about, but in many cases it's all you need.

For converting `Date` objects and providing fine-grained number formatting, there are two powerful assistants you can employ: `DateTime` and `Number`. These converters provide considerable flexibility for displaying dates and numbers in different ways, respectively. And, unlike the other converters, they have numerous properties that you can configure to help them do their jobs.

It's important to remember that a converter is a two-way street. They're great for tweaking the way objects are displayed to users. But if you use them in conjunction with an input control, the user's input must be in the format specified by the converter. For example, if you've converted your date into the string "May 23, 2003 04:55EST", your user would have to enter a valid date in the same format, right down to the "EST" at the end. This isn't something that you can necessarily expect from most users, so you'd be better off with a simpler format, like "05/23/03".

These standard converters are nice, but what about objects that aren't standard Java types? By default, the object's `toString` method is used. This works in some cases, but the method isn't terribly flexible. Fortunately, you're not limited to using the standard converters. If they don't satisfy your needs and there are no suitable third-party ones, you or someone on your team can develop custom ones. (If you are so inclined, see chapter 15 for more information.) Whether you use a custom converter or a standard one, the usage is the same.

6.3.1 Using converters

Converter registration can be performed declaratively with a display technology such as JSP, or you can register converters programmatically. (If you're interested in registering converters with Java code, see chapter 11.) Converters can also be manipulated inside a JSF IDE in the same manner as components and validators (refer back to figure 6.3).

You can register a converter using JSP in one of three ways:

- Specify the converter identifier with a component tag's `converter` property.
- Nest the `<f:converter>` tag with the converter's identifier inside the component tag.
- Nest the converter's custom tag inside a component tag.

WARNING Be careful assigning more than one converter to the same object. This can happen if, for example, you have two input fields that have a registered converter and use the same value-binding expression. If the two controls are on the same form, the converters will step over each other (in other words, the first converter's result will be overwritten by the last one's result).

If the converter has its own tag, it's better to use it. The following employs the `User` converter we develop later in this book:

```
<h:inputText value="#{user}">
  <jia:userConverter style="lastName_FirstName" showRole="true"/>
</h:inputText>
```

This example assumes that we've imported the converter's tag library with the prefix "jia." The snippet registers a new User converter on the `HtmlInputText` control and configures its `style` and `showRole` properties. These settings tell the converter to expect the user's name to be in the style "LastName, FirstName" and also to display the user's role.

In most cases, you'll use the converter's tag as shown in the previous example. The other two methods are useful only if you don't need to set your converter's properties (or it's property impoverished to begin with). Suppose we had a credit card converter that translates between a string of digits and a string with a hyphen (-) or space separating the different segments of the number. So, if a user entered the string “5555-5555-5555-5555”, the converter would translate it into “5555555555555555”. If this converter’s identifier was `creditcard`, we could use it like this:

```
<h:outputText value="#{user.creditCardNumber}"
              converter="creditcard"/>
```

This code registers a new `creditcard` converter for an `HtmlOutputText` component without setting any converter properties. Instead of using the converter’s identifier, we could also have used a value-binding expression that referenced a converter instance. You can achieve the same result by using the `<f:converter>` tag (from the core JSF library), which accepts only the converter’s identifier. This converter’s identifier is `creditcard` so we can register it this way as well:

```
<h:outputText value="#{user.creditCardNumber }">
  <f:converter converterId="creditcard"/>
</h:outputText>
```

Usually it’s better to use the identifier because it insulates you against package or class name changes. Converter identifiers are set up in a JSF configuration file. All of the standard converters already have identifiers configured; see chapter 15 to learn how to write and configure your own.

Registering converters this way usually isn’t necessary unless you’re using a custom converter that doesn’t have its own JSP tag. Generally speaking, if there’s a JSP custom tag for the converter, it will usually support its own properties. (Otherwise, it’s easier to just use one of the other two methods.)

These registration methods will work with any type of converter, but let’s delve into the details of using the standard ones.

6.3.2 Working with the standard converters

The only standard converters that you’ll typically use explicitly are the `DateTime` and `Number` converters. `DateTime` can be used for formatting a `Date` object, showing the date, the time, or both. The `Number` converter can be used for formatting any type of number, including currency and percentages. These two converters are listed in table 6.3. (Because the other converters are called implicitly by JSF and have no properties, we won’t discuss them here.)

Table 6.3 The standard converters and their custom tags. All tags are located in the core JSF tag library.

Converter	JSP Tag	Java Class (package `javax.faces.convert`)	Properties	Description
`DateTime`	`<f:convertDateTime>`	`DateTimeConverter`	`type, dateStyle, locale, timeStyle, timeZone, pattern`	Displays the date formatted for the specified type (`date`, `time`, or `both`) or for a date format pattern specified by the `pattern` property. If the type is specified, the display of the date can be controlled with the `dateStyle` property, and the time can be controlled with the `timeStyle` property. The output will be localized for the current locale unless the `locale` property is used.
`Number`	`<f:convertNumber>`	`NumberConverter`	`type, currencyCode, currencySymbol, groupingUsed, locale minFractionDigits. maxFractionDigits, minIntegerDigits, maxIntegerDigits, pattern`	Displays the number formatted for the specified type (`number`, `currency`, or `percentage`) or the decimal format pattern specified by the `pattern` property. The number will be formatted for the current locale unless the `locale` property is used.

In the following sections, we examine each of these converters in detail.

Using the DateTime converter

Whenever you want to associate a `Date` object with a UI component, you should use the `DateTime` converter. If you don't, JSF will use the `toString` method of the `Date` object, so you'll end up with something like "Sep 14 13:33:43 GMT-05:00 2003", which may not be the most readable format for your users.

You specify the formatting by either supplying the `type` property (`date`, `time`, or `both`) or specifying a date format pattern with the `pattern` property. Other properties that affect the conversion process are listed in table 6.4.

In the simplest case, you can use `DateTime` with the default values:

```
<h:outputText value="#{user.dateOfBirth}">
  <f:convertDateTime/>
</h:outputText>
```

Table 6.4 `DateTime` converter properties.

Property name	Type	Description
`dateStyle`	`String`	Specifies the formatting style for the date portion of the string. Valid options are `short`, `medium` (the default), `long`, and `full`. Only valid if the `type` property is set.
`timeStyle`	`String`	Specifies the formatting style for the time portion of the string. Valid options are `short`, `medium` (the default), `long`, and `full`. Only valid if the `type` property is set.
`timeZone`	`String`	Specifies the time zone for the date. If not set, Greenwich mean time (GMT) will be used. See online extension appendix E for a list of time zones.
`locale`	`String` or `Locale`[a]	The specific locale to use for displaying this date. Overrides the user's current locale.
`pattern`	`String`	The date format pattern used to convert this number. Use this *or* the `type` property.
`type`	`String`	Specifies whether to display the date, time, or both.

[a] *The `locale` property of the `DateTimeConverter` class must be a `Locale` instance. The JSP tag, however, can accept a locale string (like "ru" for Russian) instead.*

This is the same as specifying a `type` of `date` and a `dateStyle` of `medium`:

```
<h:outputText value="#{user.dateOfBirth}">
  <f:convertDateTime type="date" dateStyle="medium"/>
</h:outputText>
```

This code would display something like "March 20, 1972" for the U.S. locale. For other locales, the `DateTime` converter is smart enough to adjust accordingly. Table 6.5 lists some examples of different `dateStyle` values with two different locales.

Table 6.5 Possible values for the `dateStyle` property. The `DateTime` converter uses the `dateStyle` property to easily specify date formats that are portable across locales.

Value	Example (U.S.)	Example (Canada)
`short`	5/23/03	23/05/03
`medium (default)`	May 23, 2003	23-May-2003
`long`	May 23, 2003	May 23, 2003
`full`	Friday, May 23, 2003	Friday, May 23, 2003

You can see from table 6.5 that sometimes the date may be formatted the same in different locales even when using different `dateStyle` values. However, the values closer to `short` have mostly numbers, and those closer to `full` have more text. This is a general rule that works in most locales.

Let's look at another example that uses the `dateStyle` property:

```
<h:outputText value="#{user.dateOfBirth}">
  <f:convertDateTime type="both" dateStyle="full"/>
</h:outputText>
```

The `dateStyle` in this example is `full`, but this time the type is set to `both`, so the date and the time will be displayed. For U.S. English, this displays a string formatted like this one: "Saturday, May 10, 2003 6:00:00 PM". The time portion of the string is formatted using the default `timeStyle` value, which is `medium`. Like `dateStyle`, `timeStyle` has a few possible values, and will automatically adjust for the current locale. These values are listed in table 6.6, with examples in two different locales.

Table 6.6 Possible values for the `timeStyle` property. The `DateTime` converter uses the `timeStyle` property to easily specify time formats that are portable across locales.

Value	Example (U.S.)	Example (Canada)
`short`	5:41 PM	5:41 PM
`medium (default)`	5:41:05 PM	5:41:05 GMT-03:00 PM
`long`	5:41:05 PM GMT-03:00	5:41:05 GMT-03:00 PM
`full`	5:41:05 PM GMT-03:00	5:41:05 o'clock PM GMT-03:00

Like `dateStyle`, the actual displayed value can change quite a bit depending on the locale, but sometimes it's the same.

The previous example displayed both the date and the time. You can display only the time by setting the `type` property to `time`:

```
<h:outputText value="#{user.dateOfBirth}">
  <f:convertDateTime type="time" timeStyle="full"/>
</h:outputText>
```

For the U.S, this would display "6:50:41 PM GMT-05:00".

Let's move on to something a little more interesting. The following example specifies both date and time styles, as well as a time zone:

```
<h:inputText value="#{user.dateOfBirth}" size="25">
  <f:convertDateTime type="both" dateStyle="short"
```

```
                              timeStyle="short"
                              timeZone="Europe/Moscow"/>
</h:inputText>
```

For the U.S. locale, this displays something like "2/13/04 2:58 AM" in a text box. If the user inputs a value that is not in this format, a conversion error will be generated, and `user.dateOfBirth` will not be updated. The actual displayed date, however, will be adjusted depending on how many hours ahead or behind the time zone "Europe/Moscow" is from the JSF application's default time zone. So, if the application were running on a machine in the Eastern time zone in the United States, the displayed date would be eight hours ahead of the value of the associated `Date` object, because that is the difference between the two time zones.

For example, suppose the value of `user.dateOfBirth` equals January 5, 2004, at 12:00 A.M. The displayed date, adjusted for the "Europe/Moscow" time zone, would be January 5, 2004, at 8:00 A.M.—a difference of eight hours. Remember—the conversion works both ways. `DateTime` would convert the user's input back into the application's time zone as well.

We didn't pull the string "Europe/Moscow" out of a hat—there are hundreds of possible values for the `timeZone` property, all defined by the `java.util.TimeZone` class (which is used behind the scenes). You can write some Java code to get them all from the `TimeZone` class, but they're listed in online extension appendix E in case you don't have the time.

If you want to override the user's current locale, you can specify the `locale` property as well:

```
<h:outputText value="#{user.dateOfBirth}">
  <f:convertDateTime type="both" dateStyle="long" timeStyle="full"
                     timeZone="Europe/Moscow" locale="ru"/>
</h:outputText>
```

This would display a string like "13 Февраль 2004 . 3:13:58 MSK" ("Февраль" is "February" in English). Be careful specifying the locale—usually it's better to let the converter adjust according to the user's current locale.

For most cases, using the `type` property with `dateStyle` and/or `timeStyle` is sufficient. For precise control, however, you'll need to use a date format pattern.

Using the DateTime converter with date format patterns

When you need more control over the formatting than the `dateStyle` and `timeStyle` properties provide, it's time to use a date format pattern. A *date format pattern* is a special string that gives you complete control over the format of the display string—everything from how many characters to display for a year to the number of days in the year and whether to use short or long month names. You can place literal values in the text as well.

> **NOTE** Date format patterns can also be used with the `HtmlOutputFormat` component inside a message format pattern. The format type is either `date` or `time`.

A date format pattern works by interpreting special characters that are replaced by values derived from the associated `Date` object. To use a date format pattern with the `DateTime` converter, you specify the `pattern` property instead of the `type` property. Table 6.7 describes all of these characters.

Table 6.7 Symbols that can be used in a date format pattern.

Date Format Pattern Symbol	Meaning	Presentation	Example Pattern	Example Display
G	Era designator	Text	G	AD
y	Year	Number	yyyy	1996
			yy	96
M	Month in year	Text (if three or more symbols)	MMMM	April
		Number (if less than three symbols)	MM	04
d	Day in month	Number	dd	10
h	Hour in am/pm (1~12)	Number	hh	12
H	Hour in day (0~23)	Number	H	8
			HH	08
m	Minute in hour	Number	mm	15
s	Second in minute	Number	ss	55
S	Millisecond	Number	SSS	978
E	Day in week	Text	EEEE	Friday
			EEE	Fri
D	Day in year	Number	DD	45
			DDD	045

continued on next page

Table 6.7 Symbols that can be used in a date format pattern. *(continued)*

Date Format Pattern Symbol	Meaning	Presentation	Example Pattern	Example Display
F	Day of week in month	Number	FF	07
w	Week in year	Number	w	27
W	Week in month	Number	W	2
a	Am/pm marker	Text	a	AM
k	Hour in day (1~24)	Number	k	9
			kk	09
K	Hour in am/pm (0~11)	Number	K	0
z	Time zone	Text	zzzz	Eastern Standard Time
			z	EST
'	Escape for text		'literal'	literal
''	Single quote		''	'

When using date format pattern symbols, keep in mind a few rules:

- When the symbol is presented as a number, the number is padded to equal the number of characters specified. So, if the number of seconds is 4, the pattern 's' displays '4', but the pattern 'sss' displays "004". (The symbol 'y', for year, is an exception—it is truncated to two digits unless you specify four digits with 'yyyy'.)
- When the symbol is presented as text, the abbreviated value is displayed if the symbol is repeated less than four times; otherwise, the long version is displayed. So, the patterns 'E', 'EE', and 'EEE' all display "Fri" and the pattern 'EEEE' displays "Friday".
- Any characters other than lowercase and uppercase letters, like ':', '.', '#' and '@', will automatically be escaped even if they have no single quotes around them.

Let's look at some examples. The pattern "MM/dd/yyyy (hh:mm a)" displays something like "05/23/2003 (07:24 PM)". The pattern "yy.dd.MM - hh:mm:ss a zz" displays something like "03.24.05 - 07:24:28 PM EST". Here's a more complex example using literals: "EEEE, MMM dd, 'day' DDD 'of year' yyyy GG". This displays something like “Fri, May 23, day 143 of year 2003 AD”. You don’t have to include the date and time in every format; here’s one with just the time: “hh ‘o’‘clock’ a zzzz”. It looks something like this: “07 o’clock AM Korea Standard Time”.

BY THE WAY If you’ve worked with date formats in Java before, you may have noticed that the date format pattern is the same pattern used by the `java.util.SimpleDateFormat` class.

Here’s how you use the `DateTime` converter with one of the date format pattern examples:

```
<h:inputText value="#{user.dateOfBirth}">
  <f:convertDateTime pattern="MM/dd/yyyy (hh:mm a)"/>
</h:inputText>
```

This would display something like “05/23/2003 (07:24 PM)”, but inside a text box. If the user inputs a value that is not in this format, a conversion error will be generated, and `user.dateOfBirth` will not be updated.

You can’t use the `dateStyle` or `timeStyle` properties with the `pattern` property, but you can use the `locale` and `timeZone` properties. Here’s an example that uses the `timeZone` property:

```
<h:inputText size="35" value="#{user.dateOfBirth}">
  <f:convertDateTime pattern="yy.dd.MM - hh:mm:ss a zz"
                     timeZone="Asia/Seoul"/>
</h:inputText>
```

This code converts the date to the “Asia/Seoul” time zone, and displays something like “03.24.05 - 07:24:28 AM KST” inside an input control. If a user doesn’t enter a value using this exact format—including the “AM KST”—the value will be rejected and an error message will be generated.

`DateTime` is a powerful converter—it takes full advantage of Java’s support for locale-aware date and time management features. The `Number` converter does the same thing for any type of number.

Using the Number converter

The `Number` converter is useful for displaying numbers in basic formats that work for the user’s locale. It’s generally more forgiving than the `DateTime` converter; it’s more likely to reformat a user’s input rather than complain about it. As with `DateTime`, you tell `Number` how to handle the associated component’s value with either the `type` or `pattern` property.

The `type` property has three possible values: `number`, `percentage`, and `currency`. The `pattern` property uses a decimal format pattern, which is similar conceptually to the date format patterns we discussed in the last section. `Number` also has several other properties, as shown in table 6.8.

WARNING Make sure you use the correct value for the `type` property. Some JSF tag libraries may not check the value, so if you mistype it, you'll get unexpected results.

Table 6.8 Number converter properties.

Property Name	Type	Description
`currencyCode`	`String`	Specifies a three-digit international currency code when the type is `currency`. Use this *or* `currencySymbol`. See online extension appendix E for a list of currency codes.
`currency-Symbol`	`String`	Specifies a specific symbol, like "$", to be used when the `type` is `currency`. Use this *or* `currencyCode`.
`groupingUsed`	`boolean`	True if a grouping symbol (like "," or " ") should be used. Default is `true`.
`integerOnly`	`boolean`	True if only the integer portion of the input value should be processed (all decimals will be ignored). Default is `false`.
`locale`	`String` or `Locale`[a]	The specific locale to use for displaying this number. Overrides the user's current locale.
`minFraction-Digits`	`integer`	Minimum number of fractional digits to display.
`maxFraction-Digits`	`integer`	Maximum number of fractional digits to display.
`minInteger-Digits`	`integer`	Minimum number of integer digits to display.
`maxInteger-Digits`	`integer`	Maximum number of integer digits to display.
`pattern`	`String`	The decimal format pattern used to convert this number. Use this *or* the `type` property.
`type`	`String`	The type of number; either `number` (the default), `currency`, or `percentage`. Use this *or* `pattern`.

[a] *The `locale` property of the `NumberConverter` class must be a `Locale` instance. The JSP tag, however, can accept a locale string (like "ru" for Russian) instead.*

These properties allow for precise control over how a number is displayed. And, unless you specify a locale-specific property like `currencySymbol`, `currencyCode`, or `locale`, the number will automatically be formatted for the current locale. Table 6.9 shows some examples for the `type` property in two different locales. For the United States and the United Kingdom, there isn't much difference, except that the symbol for British currency (pounds sterling) is different than the symbol for U.S. currency (dollars).

Table 6.9 Possible values for the `Number` converter's `type` property.

Property Value	Example (U.S.)	Example (U.K.)
`percentage`	293,423%	293,423%
`currency`	$2,934.23	£2,934.23
`number`	2,934.233	2,934.233

NOTE If you specify both `currencyCode` and `currencySymbol`, `currencyCode` will take precedence unless you're using a version of the Java Runtime Environment (or Java Development Kit) before 1.4.

The simplest way to use the `Number` converter is not to specify any properties at all:

```
<h:inputText id="NumberInput1">
  <f:convertNumber/>
</h:inputText>
```

This is exactly the same as setting `maxFractionDigits` to 3 and `groupingUsed` to `true`:

```
<h:inputText>
  <f:convertNumber maxFractionDigits="3" groupingUsed="true"/>
</h:inputText>
```

This will display the number with a grouping separator and three decimal points, like "4,029.345", rounding the last digit if necessary. In this case, a comma was the grouping separator, but it could just as easily been a space or something else, depending on the locale. When using the `Number` converter with an input control like this example, users don't have to worry too much about how their input is formatted, as long as they enter in a number with the proper separators.

Here's how you use the `Number` converter with percentages:

```
<h:inputText value="#{user.balance}">
  <f:convertNumber type="percent" maxFractionDigits="2"/>
</h:inputText>
```

If the user's balance was 4,029.3456, this would display "402,934.56%". This is the same as multiplying the value times 100 and adding a percent sign. Because we set `maxFractionDigits` to 2, two decimal points were displayed. The default (when the `type` property is set to `percent`) is not to show any decimal points, so if we had left out the `maxFractionDigits` property, "402,935%" would have been displayed instead.

When updating an object's value, the converter translates the number back into its original value. So if you entered "55%" into the input control, the `user.balance` property would be set to .55. Note that the percentage sign (or the locale's equivalent) is required, or the converter will generate an error and no properties will be updated.

Formatting percentages is useful, but currency formatting is essential. Here's an example using the `type` of `currency`:

```
<h:inputText value="#{user.balance}">
  <f:convertNumber type="currency" currencyCode="KZT"/>
</h:inputText>
```

Here we specify the `currencyCode` property, which formats the number according to a specific currency. (Currency codes, like language and country codes, are defined by the International Organization for Standardization. You can find a complete list in online extension appendix E.) The currency code "KZT" stands for tenge, which is the currency of Kazakhstan. This would display the string "KZT4,029.35". Specifying the currency code usually results in displaying the code as the currency sign.

If we hadn't specified the `currencyCode`, and the locale was U.S. English (en_US), this would display "$4,029.35", using the default currency symbol for the United States. If a user entered in a value without the dollar sign, the converter would report an error and the associated object wouldn't be updated (leaving out the comma will not generate an error).

NOTE In order for the `Number` converter to display the proper currency sign, you must specify support for the language *and* country in an application configuration file. So, in order for a user to see a dollar sign ($), your application must support the locale en_US. If it only supports en, the international currency symbol (¤) will be used instead.

Here's a more complicated example:

```
<h:outputText id="CurrencyDigitsInput" value="#{user.balance}">
  <f:convertNumber type="currency" minIntegerDigits="2"
                   maxIntegerDigits="5" maxFractionDigits="2"
                   currencySymbol="$"/>
</h:outputText>
```

Here we specify a minimum of 2 integer digits and a maximum of 5 digits, as well as a two decimals and a currency symbol of "$". So, for the number 12345678.9876, the converter will display $45,678.99. The numbers to the left of the fifth integer digit—123—will be truncated. Also, only two of the fractional digits will be displayed, and the last one will be rounded. And finally, a dollar sign will be added. Any input converted with these settings would be handled similarly, but would require that the user enter the dollar sign.

You can achieve quite a bit of control over the formatting of your application's numbers with these properties. If, however, there's something you can't handle by specifying `type` and a few other properties, the `pattern` property provides a large amount of flexibility.

Using the Number converter with decimal format patterns

For those cases when you need precise control over things, you can use the `Number` converter's `pattern` property. This is a special string, called a *decimal format pattern,* that controls such things as the number of decimals, how to display negative numbers, and the number of digits to display.

> **NOTE** Number format patterns can also be used with the `HtmlOutputFormat` component inside a message format pattern. The format type is `number`.

Decimal format patterns have two parts—a positive subpattern and a negative subpattern—that are separated by a semicolon. The negative subpattern is optional; if you leave it out, negative numbers will be displayed using the positive subpattern, with the localized minus sign in front ("-" in most cases).

Each subpattern consists of literal and special characters that specify the formatting for the number with an optional prefix and suffix. Some of the special characters can only be used in the number portion of the subpattern; others can be used in either the prefix or the suffix. These characters are summarized in table 6.10.

Here are some examples that don't have a prefix or suffix. The pattern "###,###" for the number 40404 displays "40,404" in the U.S. locale. The pattern "#,###" and "######,###" also display "40,404", but "###, #####", "#,#####", and "######,####" display "4,0404"—the grouping separator closest to the right always wins.

For the number -40404, both "#,###" and "#,###;-#,###" display "-40,404", but the pattern "#,###;(#,###)" displays "(40,404)". You use a "0" when you want to display a specific number of digits—for example, for the number 99, the pattern "0000" displays "0099". The same pattern for the number 99999 displays "9999"—note that last digit has been lopped off.

Table 6.10 Special characters that can be used in a number format pattern.

Number Format Pattern Symbol	Meaning	Location
0	Digit.	Number
#	Digit, but zero is not displayed.	Number
,	Decimal separator or monetary decimal separator for the current locale.	Number
-	Localized minus sign.	Number
,	Localized grouping separator. Only the last separator is used. So, "###,###" is the same as "#########,###" and "#,###". They all mean "place a grouping separator after every three digits."	Number
;	Separates positive and negative subpatterns.	In between subpatterns
%	Multiply by 100 and show as a percentage (with localized percentage symbol).	Prefix or suffix
¤	Localized currency sign (this character is replaced with the proper symbol). If this character appears twice in a row, the international currency code is used—this is useful if you want to be very specific about the type of currency (for example, "USD" is displayed instead of "$"). Whenever this character is used in a subpattern, the monetary decimal separator is used. The unicode character (\u004A) can be used in Java code instead of the actual character.	Number
'	Used to escape special characters—use this if you want to display a character, such as "#".	Number

The most common prefixes you'll use will be for displaying percentages or currency. Whether it's a prefix or suffix depends on where you put the symbol. For example, the number .99 converted with the pattern "###0.00%" displays as "99.00%". In this case, "%" counts as a suffix.

For the number 40404, the pattern "¤#,##0.00;(¤#,##0.00)" displays "$40,404.00" in the United States. For -40404, it would display "($40,404.00)". In the U.K., "£40,404.00" and "-£40,404.00" would be displayed, respectively.

You can also use the international currency symbol, which eliminates symbol ambiguity (for example, "$" could mean U.S. dollars, but it could also mean Canadian dollars or any currency in any other country uses has a dollar). The only difference is that you use two currency symbols: "¤¤#,##0.00;(¤¤#, ##0.00)". For the same number, this would display USD40,404.00 for the United States, and CAD40, 404.00 for Canada.

TIP Don't forget to use the localized currency symbol ("¤") if you want your formatting to be automatically localized. If you use "$", it will be treated as a literal, which means all users will see a dollar sign even if their currency isn't a dollar!

You can also add literals to the prefix or suffix. For instance, the number 40404 formatted with the pattern "'#'# baby!" displays "#40404 baby!". Notice that the "#" character was surrounded with two single quotes so that it would be displayed literally. All special characters must be escaped this way if you want the converter to display them instead of interpreting them as part of the pattern.

BY THE WAY Decimal format patterns can also format numbers as exponents, infinity, and the like. All of the ins and outs are covered in the Java API docs for the `java.text.NumberFormat` class, which this converter uses behind the scenes.

Once you understand how to use decimal format patterns, they're pretty easy to use with the `Number` converter. All you need to do is specify the `pattern` property with the appropriate pattern:

```
<h:inputText value="#{user.balance}">
  <f:convertNumber pattern="###,###.##;(###,###.##)"/>
</h:inputText>
```

For the number 4029, this would display "4,029" inside a textbox for the U.S. locale. Any data collected from the user would have to be in the same format (with or without the grouping separator). This is similar to using the `type`, `maxIntegerDigits`, `maxFractionDigits`, and `groupingUsed` properties, like this:

```
<h:inputText value="#{user.balance}">
  <f:convertNumber type="number" maxIntegerDigits="6"
                   maxFractionDigits="2" groupingUsed="true"/>
</h:inputText>
```

The only difference between the results of these two declarations is how they handle negative numbers. The first one displays them in parenthesis: "(4029)". The latter uses the locale's negative symbol (the U.S. in this case): "-4029".

Here's another example:

```
<h:inputText value="#{user.balance}">
  <f:convertNumber pattern="¤¤#,##0.00;
                            (¤¤#,##0.00)"/>
</h:inputText>
```

For the number -4029 in the Canada locale, this displays "(CAD4,029.00)" inside a textbox. If the number is negative, the user's input must be surrounded by parentheses. The input must also have the proper country currency code (like "CAD" or "USD"), but the grouping separator is optional.

By leveraging the power of Java's number formatting features, the `Number` converter makes formatting numbers in JSF both simple and powerful. We haven't given any thought to the types of error messages these converters display, though. In the next section, we discuss validation and conversion error messages, and how to make them user-friendly.

6.4 Customizing application messages

Validators (and sometimes components) generate error messages when a user's input is not acceptable, and converters generate error messages whenever there's a problem during the conversion process. These messages are handled by JSF's normal application message queue, and can be displayed with the `HtmlMessages` and `HtmlMessage` components we covered in chapter 4.

Messages have summary text, detailed text, and a severity level. The severity levels are Info, Warning, Error, and Fatal. All of the standard validators and converters have default messages (with the Severity level info) that are usually localized for a few different languages. For example, the reference implementation [Sun, JSF RI] includes support for English, French, and German. These messages are configured using a normal Java resource bundle with one extra rule for handling the detailed text. We'll call these specialized resource bundles *message bundles*.

Here's an example from the reference implementation:

```
javax.faces.validator.NOT_IN_RANGE=Validation Error: Specified
    attribute is not between the expected values of {0} and {1}.
javax.faces.validator.NOT_IN_RANGE_detail=The value must be
    between {0} and {1}.
```

These two lines define both the summary and detail for a standard error message used by the `DoubleRange` validator. The first line represents the message summary, and the second line represents the detail. Note that the key for the last line is the same as the first line, but with the string "_detail" at the end.

Each JSF application can be associated with a single message bundle, which is defined in a JSF configuration file. Here's how you configure the application's message bundle:

```
<application>
   <message-bundle>CustomMessages</message-bundle>
  <locale-config>
```

```
    <default-locale>en</default-locale>
    <supported-locale>en</supported-locale>
    <supported-locale>es</supported-locale>
  </locale-config>
</application>
```

This snippet configures a message bundle called CustomMessages. The bundle's properties file should be accessible somewhere in the application's classpath. This snippet also configures support for the English and Spanish locales. In general, you should have one localized bundle for each locale the application supports.

Once you've defined a message bundle for your application, you can selectively override some of the standard error messages as long as you use the proper key. Table 6.11 lists all of the standard keys along with default messages that are included with the reference implementation. The actual message your JSF implementation uses may differ.

Table 6.11 Standard JSF error message keys and default text.

Message Bundle Key	Default Value (in reference implementation)
`javax.faces.validator.NOT_IN_RANGE`	Validation Error: Specified attribute is not between the expected values of {0} and {1}.
`javax.faces.validator.NOT_IN_RANGE_detail`	The value must be between {0} and {1}.
`javax.faces.validator.DoubleRangeValidator.LIMIT`	Validation Error: Specified attribute cannot be converted to proper type.
`javax.faces.validator.DoubleRangeValidator.MAXIMUM`	Validation Error: Value is greater than allowable maximum of "{0}".
`javax.faces.validator.DoubleRangeValidator.MINIMUM`	Validation Error: Value is less than allowable minimum of "{0}".
`javax.faces.validator.DoubleRangeValidator.TYPE`	Validation Error: Value is not of the correct type.
`javax.faces.validator.LengthValidator.LIMIT`	Validation Error: Specified attribute cannot be converted to proper type.
`javax.faces.validator.LengthValidator.MAXIMUM`	Validation Error: Value is greater than allowable maximum of "{0}".
`javax.faces.validator.LengthValidator.MINIMUM`	Validation Error: Value is less than allowable minimum of "{0}".
`javax.faces.component.UIInput.CONVERSION`	Conversion error during model data update

continued on next page

Table 6.11 Standard JSF error message keys and default text. *(continued)*

Message Bundle Key	Default Value (in reference implementation)
`javax.faces.component.UIInput.REQUIRED`	Validation Error: Value is required.
`javax.faces.component.UISelectOne.INVALID`	Validation Error: Value is not valid.
`javax.faces.component.UISelectMany.INVALID`	Validation Error: Value is not valid.
`javax.faces.validator.RequiredValidator.FAILED`	Validation Error: Value is required.
`javax.faces.validator.LongRangeValidator.LIMIT`	Validation Error: Specified attribute cannot be converted to proper type.
`javax.faces.validator.LongRangeValidator.MAXIMUM`	Validation Error: Value is greater than allowable maximum of "{0}".
`javax.faces.validator.LongRangeValidator.MINIMUM`	Validation Error: Value is less than allowable minimum of "{0}".
`javax.faces.validator.LongRangeValidator.TYPE`	Validation Error: Value is not of the correct type.

As you can see, these aren't the friendliest messages on Earth. Most users don't quite know what to make of a message like "Specified attribute cannot be converted to proper type." So, depending on your user base and the quality of your JSF implementation's default messages, it may make sense to customize the standard error messages.

BY THE WAY If you're wondering why the component names in this file start with "UI" instead of "Html", it's because they refer to the superclasses of the concrete HTML components we covered in the previous chapters. For simplicity, you can think of them as keys for families. So, the key `javax.faces.component.UIInput` is for the Input family, the key `javax.faces.component.UISelectMany` is for the SelectMany family, and the key `javax.faces.component.UISelectMany` is for the SelectMany family. (See chapter 11 for more information about the component hierarchy.)

Listing 6.3 shows the CustomMessage message bundle, which customizes some of the standard messages and also defines text for an application message.

Listing 6.3 CustomMessages.properties: Sample message bundle that customizes some of the standard validation messages and also adds an application message.

```
javax.faces.component.UIInput.REQUIRED=This field is required.
javax.faces.component.UIInput.REQUIRED_detail=Please fill in
  this field.
javax.faces.validator.UIInput.MINIMUM=Sorry, this number must be
  greater than {0}.
javax.faces.validator.UIInput.MAXIMUM=Sorry, this number must be
  less than {0}.
javax.faces.component.UIInput.CONVERSION=Sorry, your input is not
  in the right format. Please try again.
javax.faces.component.UIInput.CONVERSION_detail=There was an
  error converting your input into a format the application
  understands.
invalid_Email=This e-mail address is invalid. Please
  try again.
```

All of the messages in listing 6.3 except for the last one have keys that are defined in table 6.11. They also have the same number of parameters. Whenever a JSF component, validator, or converter looks for an error message, it will look for them in this bundle first. So, instead of getting the message "Conversion error during model data update," the user will see something that makes a little more sense: "Sorry, your input is not in the right format. Please try again."

Also, note that some of the messages have details defined, and some don't. This is fine—the detail isn't required. However, if the default message has detailed text, you should define details as well; otherwise you could end up with a customized summary and the default detailed text, which may not be exactly what you intended.

The message on the last line (with the key `invalid_Email`) is an application-specific message rather than a validation or conversion error message. You can use the message bundle for defining custom application messages as well. This is generally only useful if you're adding messages in backing beans. You can put other localized text in this bundle too, but for larger applications it might make sense to put ordinary text strings in separate resource bundles.

In our sample configuration file, we specified support for both English and Spanish. Consequently, we should customize the messages for both languages. The Spanish version is shown in listing 6.4. As you can see, all the keys are the same, but the values are localized for Spanish.

Listing 6.4 CustomMessages_es.properties: Sample message bundle that customizes some of the standard validation messages and also adds an application message

```
javax.faces.component.UIInput.REQUIRED=Se requiere este dato.
javax.faces.component.UIInput.REQUIRED_detail=Por favor, complete
  este dato.
javax.faces.validator.UIInput.MINIMUM=Disculpa, se requiere un
  número mayor que {0}.
javax.faces.validator.UIInput.MAXIMUM=Disculpa, se requiere un
  número menor que {0}.
javax.faces.component.UIInput.CONVERSION=Disculpa, el formato
  de su entrada no es correcto.  Por favor intentarlo de nuevo.
javax.faces.component.UIInput.CONVERSION_detail=Había un errór
  en convertir su entrada en el formato del programa.
myapp.Invalid_Email=No se reconoce como dirección de correo
  electrónico. Por favor intentarlo de nuevo.
```

That's all the work that's required to add or customize application messages—simply define the application's message bundle and create a new bundle for each locale your application supports.

6.5 Summary

In this chapter, we covered JSF's support for multiple languages (internationalization), rejecting incorrect input (validation) and displaying or formatting data types (type conversion). We examined how internationalizing a JSF application starts with configuring support for one or more locales, which represent language/country combinations. For each locale, you create a standard Java resource bundle, which is a property file with name/value pairs (this process is called localization). Once the bundle has been loaded (either with a JSP tag or programmatically), you can easily reference localized strings with ordinary value references.

We then looked at how validation is handled by separate classes that can be registered on any input component. The standard validators are `DoubleRange`, `Length`, and `LongRange`. (Input controls also have a `required` property, which disallows empty input.) For any given component, you can register one or more validators. If any validator rejects the user's input, an error message is generated, and no associated objects are updated.

Next, we examined type conversion, which is also handled by separate classes, called converters. Converters translate back-end objects into strings for display, and translate user input back into the right type of object. Each component that supports type conversion can be registered with a single converter. JSF has implicit converters for all of the standard Java types. It also has the `DateTime` and `Number` converters, which provide a high level of flexibility for converting and formatting dates and numbers.

Validators and converters generate application error messages that can be displayed with the `HtmlMessage` and `HtmlMessages` components. Finally, we discussed how you can customize the standard error messages or define new application messages by creating a message bundle, which is a specialized resource bundle.

Now that we've covered the basic JSF concepts, the world of the standard components, and other goodies like internationalization and validators, it's time to look at how these pieces fit together to build real applications. In the next two parts, we'll develop our case study application—ProjectTrack.

Part 2

Building user interfaces

In part 1, we examined the fundamentals of JSF, as well as its standard functionality. In part 2, we use this knowledge to build a real-world application, step by step. We begin with prototypical screens, and finish with a working application that is fully integrated with back-end logic.

7 Introducing ProjectTrack

This chapter covers

- An overview of ProjectTrack, our case study
- The system's requirements and analysis
- The hypothetical development team

Now that we've studied the architecture of JavaServer Faces and surveyed the standard components, it's time to develop a real application; we'll call it ProjectTrack. The purpose of this application is to provide a high-level view of a project as it moves through the development lifecycle. Each project has a state (such as proposal or beta testing), and different users can promote a project to the next state or demote it to the previous one. The system keeps track of all of the projects under development, their current state, and comments from managers (such as the project and development managers) along the way. In this chapter, we examine ProjectTrack's requirements and look at how the development team might be structured. Then, in chapter 8, we start building its user interface (UI).

7.1 Requirements

One of the biggest issues with software development projects is maintaining a macro-level view of their progress. A hypothetical consulting company, DeathMarch Development, is losing track of its projects, and this is causing problems for its customers. Projects are often late and poorly managed, and upper management has no way to see what's going on. The company handles many projects at once, with managers assigned to different parts of the development lifecycle.

DeathMarch would like a system, called ProjectTrack to track the status of its projects. Managers should know when it is their responsibility to work with a project and what they are expected to do. For instance, a QA manager should know when a particular project is ready for beta testing. The manager should also be able to say that the testing was successful, or that it failed, and why. In other words, the system should manage the project's workflow. For each project, the company would like to have a history of the stages through which the project has passed, and when.

DeathMarch would also like to know what artifacts have been completed for a project. They're interested in tracking documentation artifact managers that cover such topics as requirements, architecture, and deployment. They also want to know the type of project and who initiated it.

For security reasons, the company has requested a simple name- and password-based login. Each user should have a specific role—development manager, for example. The states of a project must be assigned to *roles* instead of *user accounts*, so that if someone leaves the company, any other person in the same role can handle the project.

Because this is a small company, all users work with the same projects—if there are three users in the project manager role, then all three users will see the same set of projects. Users should be able to view the projects currently waiting for their attention, as well as other projects. In addition, there should be an upper management role that can view all of the projects but that can't modify any of them.

Finally, the company has some clients and employees who prefer to speak in Russian instead of English.

Now that we have a handle on DeathMarch's list of requirements, let's break them down into specifics. It's clear that the system must do the following:

- Provide a login based on user name and password.
- Associate a role with each user.
- Support projects that have a specific state.
- Provide a list of projects awaiting approval or rejection for a particular role.
- Allow users to approve or reject (with comments) a project that is waiting for them (this results in the project moving to the next state or a previous state).
- Allow users to view all projects.
- Allow users to manipulate projects details, such as the artifact types completed for a project.
- For a given project, provide a history of previous approvals and rejections.
- Support both English and Russian.

DeathMarch Development has provided a list of the specific roles the system needs to support, as shown in table 7.1.

Table 7.1 ProjectTrack must support several roles for users that participate in the software development lifecycle.

Role	Description
Project Manager	Coordinates the whole project
Development Manager	Manages the development team
Business Analyst	Drives the requirements process
QA Manager	Manages the testing process
Systems Manager	Manages deployment and maintenance
Upper Manager	Higher-level company employee who needs macro view of all projects

A project goes through 12 states before it is considered complete. For each state, only users with a specific role can approve it (move it to the next state) or reject it (move it to the previous state). Table 7.2 lists the actual states of a project, with their associated roles.

Every time someone logs in, that individual will see all of the projects whose state is associated with his or her role. We'll call this the person's *inbox*. For example, when a user in the Development Manager role logs in, his or her inbox will contain a list of all projects that are in the Architecture, Core Development, and Final Development states.

Table 7.2 Each project must go through several states. Only users in a specific role can accept or reject it.

State	Description	Responsible Role
Proposal	Project initiated; may or may not contain formal proposal.	Project Manager
Requirements/Analysis	Business requirements distilled, and analysis made of the problem domain.	Business Analyst
Architecture	Requirements and analysis turned into architectural artifacts.	Development Manager
Core Development	Development begins. This includes alpha releases and minor iterations.	Development Manager
Beta Testing Deployment	Installation into an environment for beta testing.	Systems Manager
Beta Testing	Application feature complete and alpha testing complete. Ready for final testing.	QA Manager
Final Development	Final development—mostly bug fixes.	Development Manager
Acceptance Testing Deployment	Installation into an environment for acceptance testing.	Systems Manager
Acceptance Testing	All bugs believed to be fixed. Final user testing begins.	QA Manager
Production Deployment	Installation into a production environment.	Systems Manager
Completion	Project completed.	Project Manager
Closed	Project closed.	Project Manager

DeathMarch has confirmed that projects progress in sequential order as indicated by table 7.2. However, rejection is a more complicated affair, primarily because when someone rejects a project, it doesn't return to a deployment state. For example, if the QA manager rejects a project in the Acceptance Testing state, it

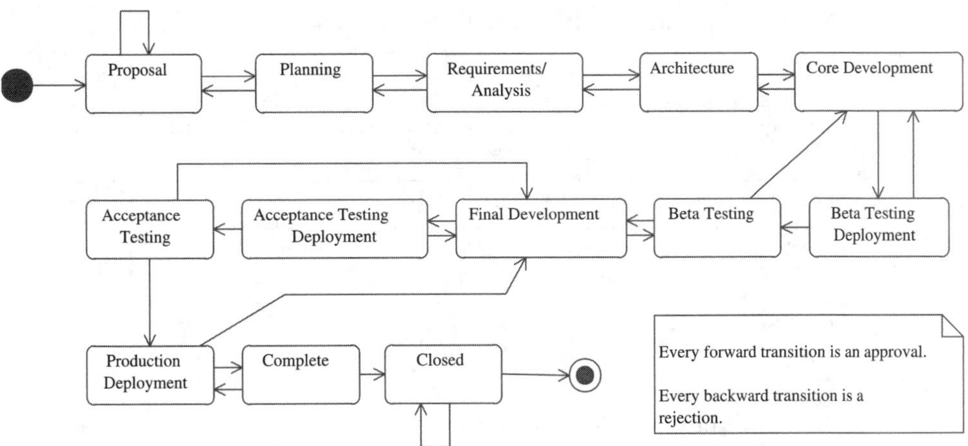

Figure 7.1 A state diagram representing the states of a project. Each project moves forward sequentially through the states. However, when a project is rejected, it may move more than one step back.

shouldn't go back to the Acceptance Testing Deployment state; rather, it should go to the Final Development state. To visualize this, take a look at the diagram shown in figure 7.1.

Now that we have a good handle on what the system needs to do, let's break it down into more granular concepts.

7.2 The conceptual model

From the requirements, we can identify the following entities for this system: User, Role, Project, Project Type, Status, Artifact, and Operation. These are listed in table 7.3.

Table 7.3 These entities are ProjectTrack's primary actors.

Entity	Notes	Properties
User	A company's employee.	name, password
Role	A User's function in relation to Projects in the company.	name
Project	Represents a job for a client.	name, type, initiatedBy, requirements contact, requirements contact e-mail, list of Artifacts, list of Operations

continued on next page

Table 7.3 These entities are ProjectTrack's primary actors. *(continued)*

Entity	Notes	Properties
Project Type	Represents the type of a Project (application development, database changes, etc.).	name
Status	Represents the state of a Project.	name, nextStatus, rejectionStatus
Artifact	An element created during the development process—usually a document.	name
Operation	Created when a Project changes its Status. All of the Operations for a Project make up its history.	timestamp, fromStatus, toStatus, comments

Here's how these entities are related:

- A User has a single Role.
- Users can view, approve, edit, or reject Projects.
- Projects have a single Status, a single Project Type, many Artifacts, and a list of Operations.
- A Status is associated with a Role.

The different entities, and their relationships, are shown in figure 7.2.

So far, we know that Projects can have Project Types and Artifacts, but we don't know what the possible values are for either one. These are shown in table 7.4.

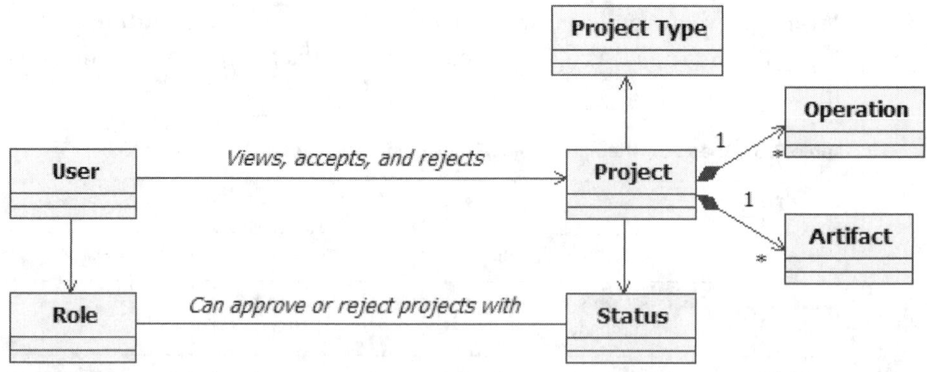

Figure 7.2 A conceptual class diagram of ProjectTrack entities. A User views, accepts, and rejects a Project whose Status is associated with the User's Role. A Project also has a Project Type, one or more Operations, and one or more Artifacts.

Table 7.4 There are several possible values for Project Types and Artifacts.

Entity	Possible Values
Artifacts	▪ Proposal document ▪ Architecture specification ▪ Test plan ▪ Deployment guidelines ▪ Maintenance documentation ▪ User documentation
Project Types	▪ Internal database ▪ External database ▪ External web application ▪ Internal web application ▪ Internal desktop application ▪ External desktop application

So, now we have a conceptual model of the system. We'll use these concepts as we discuss the system in this part of the book and the next. These concepts will also serve as the basis of ProjectTrack's *business model* (also called a *domain model*), which we discuss in chapter 12. When we develop backing beans for the system, they will make calls to classes in the business model.

This is all useful information, but some insight into how the UI works would be nice as well, so let's examine that now.

7.3 User interface

Additional talks with the overworked folks at DeathMarch reveal that the system should have the following views:

- Login
- Inbox
- Show All Projects
- Project Details
- Create a Project
- Approve a Project
- Reject a Project

When a user logs in, the default page should be the Inbox page, unless the user is an upper manager, in which case it should be the Show All Projects page. On every page except Login, we need a toolbar that provides navigation to the Inbox,

Show All Projects, and Create a Project pages, plus the ability to log out. From the Inbox page, a user should be able to access the Approve a Project, Reject a Project, and Project Details pages. From the Show All Projects page, a user should be able to access the Project Details page. All of the functions and their corresponding pages are shown in table 7.5.

Table 7.5 ProjectTrack supports several functions that are accessible only from specific pages.

Function	Display Page	Comments
Login	Inbox	All users except Upper Managers
	Show All Projects	Upper Managers only
View Inbox	Inbox	All users except Upper Managers
View All Projects	Show All Projects	
View Project Details	Project Details	
Create a Project	Create a Project	Project Managers only
Approve a Project	Approve a Project	Allow users to check off completion of Artifacts and add comments
Reject a Project	Reject a Project	Allow users to check off completion of Artifacts and add comments
Logout	Login	

All of the navigation paths we just discussed are visualized in figure 7.3.

That's it for the requirements and analysis of ProjectTrack. We now have a basic idea of the system's functional requirements, its conceptual model, and its UI. Now, let's look at the hypothetical team developing this application.

7.4 Development team

As we step through the development of this project in the following chapters, we'll assume that we have a two-person team: a front-end developer, and an application, or back-end, developer. Our front-end developer will concentrate on creating views with JSP, navigation rules, and integrating views with backing beans and model objects. The application developer will work on everything else—backing beans, managed bean configuration, integration with the domain logic, and so on.

These two roles certainly aren't a requirement for building JSF applications—different projects can vary substantially. JSF works well in environments in which

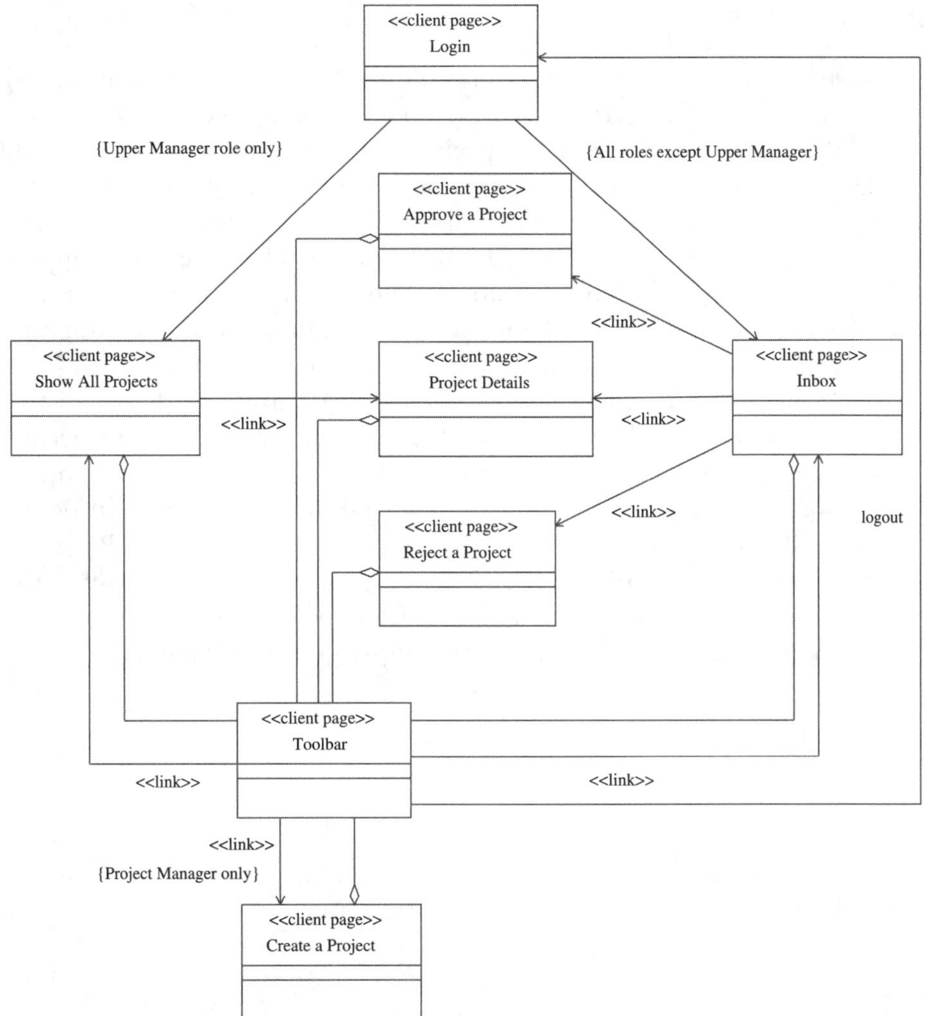

Figure 7.3 A class diagram representing navigation between pages in ProjectTrack.

roles are segregated, but it works equally well in development teams where the lines are more blurry or even nonexistent, and in small one-person projects. Different tools cater to different types of teams better than others.

ProjectTrack is based solely on JSF and JSP, with some use of the Servlet API, such as an authentication filter. We assume that the two people are working independently at first but communicating at key integration points (remember, this is one of the key benefits of JSF and other MVC-style frameworks).

7.5 Summary

In this chapter, we briefly introduced ProjectTrack, a case study designed to help you understand what it's like to develop a real JSF application. ProjectTrack is an application that keeps track of a project's state and allows users to push it forward to the next state or back to the previous one. For each project, it maintains basic information (a description, who started the project, and so on), and a history of approvals and rejects performed on the project. The system will support several roles, simple password-based authentication and both English and Russian.

In parts 2 and 3 of this book, we will build ProjectTrack, starting with the UI and then moving to backing beans, model objects, and additional application functionality such as internationalization and localization. Chapters 8 through 10 will focus on building the UI from the front-end developer's perspective. Chapters 11 through 14 will look at JSF development from the application developer's perspective, touching on all of the core JSF APIs, backing bean development, event listeners, and more. Every chapter won't deal directly with ProjectTrack, but most of them will. ProjectTrack will also take advantage of UI extensions (custom components and validators) that we develop in online extension part 5.

In the next chapter, we begin building ProjectTrack's login page.

8 Developing a user interface without Java code: the Login page

This chapter covers

- Basic application configuration
- Building a login page with JavaScript, CSS, validators, and custom messages
- Using `HtmlPanelGrid` for layout

Now that we've introduced the case study, ProjectTrack, and its system requirements, let's start building the application. In this chapter and the next, we'll develop ProjectTrack's user interface (UI) with JavaServer Faces. Our goal is to have an interactive interface *without* any application logic. This concept should be familiar to rapid application development (RAD) developers—with tools like AWT/Swing IDEs, Delphi, and Visual Studio .NET, it's quite easy to lay out the entire UI with basic navigation and validation but no real code. Integrating the real meat of the application later is fairly straightforward. The closest thing to this for web developers is typically a set of static HTML pages that eventually get thrown away or converted into application templates and then maintained separately.

Like UIs developed with the tools we just mentioned, the one we develop in this chapter will provide basic navigation and will be the basis for the final version. The main difference is that instead of integrating the UI with application logic and model objects, we'll start with static text and hardcode the navigation rules. Even though JSF tools allow you to work visually and generate a lot of the code for you, we'll show all of the examples in raw JSP so that you can get a feel for what vanilla Faces development is like.

If you're not particularly interested in the JSP aspects of these chapters, bear in mind that the behavior of the standard components is the same even if you use another display technology; the mechanism for declaring the view would be the primary difference.

Developing the UI separately gives us two main benefits:

- The front-end developer can initially work independently from the application developer. We're not suggesting that the two work in a vacuum; however, communication can be limited to discussions of interface points. (See chapter 10 for a discussion of the integration process.)
- The working UI can serve as a prototype that can be quickly modified based on user input; this saves time that would otherwise be wasted creating separate sets of HTML.

We'll start with the basic configuration for the web application. Next, we'll assemble the Login page step by step, examining the fundamental aspects of constructing a JSF page. Then, in the next chapter, we'll develop the remaining pages of ProjectTrack.

8.1 Getting started

Even though we're not writing any Java code in this chapter, we need to create a JSF application so the framework can do its magic. All JSF applications are standard Java web applications. All that's required is a properly configured deployment descriptor and an installed JSF implementation. (This will either be included with your application server or installed separately, as is the case with the reference implementation [Sun, JSF RI].) However, most applications also require the JSF configuration file, faces-config.xml, and this one is no different.

Web applications have a specific directory structure. (Tools will often create the basic structure for you.) ProjectTrack's initial directory structure, complete with the basic files, is shown in figure 8.1. You may have noticed that this is a specific instance of the basic directory structure shown in chapter 3 (figure 3.1, page 91).

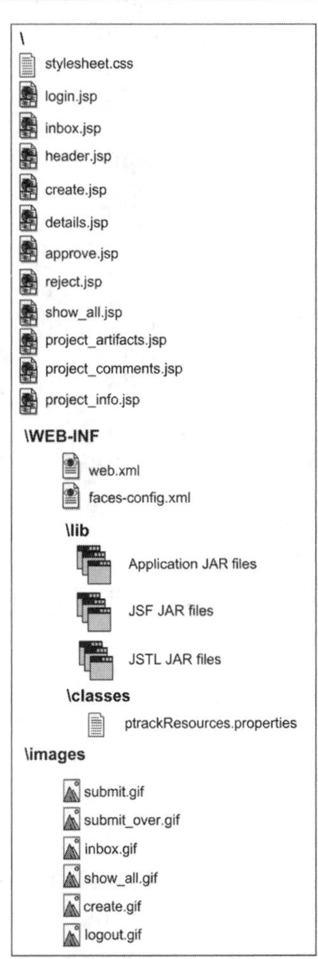

Figure 8.1 ProjectTrack is a web application, whose directory structure includes JSPs, libraries, images, and configuration files.

All JSPs will be placed in the root directory. The deployment descriptor (web.xml) and faces-config.xml are both placed in the WEB-INF directory (no file in this directory is visible to users). The code is placed in the WEB-INF/lib directory. Usually, the JSF libraries will be in this directory as well. The structure also includes a directory for images; we listed all of the image filenames based on the assumption that a wildly productive graphic designer has already created them all. The ptrackResources.properties will be used to customize application messages and perform localization.

Now that we know where the files will go, let's move on to configuration.

8.1.1 Setting up web.xml

Every Java web application has a deployment descriptor called web.xml. You can do a lot with this file—specify event handlers for the servlet lifecycle (which is separate from the JSF Request Processing Lifecycle), configure security, integrate with EJBs, and all sorts of other fun things that we don't discuss in this book. All that's necessary for a simple JSF application like ProjectTrack is a declaration of the `FacesServlet` and the appropriate URL mapping, as shown in listing 8.1. (We added a default page for good measure.)

Listing 8.1 Deployment descriptor (web.xml) for UI development

```
<?xml version="1.0" encoding="UTF-8"?>
<!DOCTYPE web-app PUBLIC
          "-//Sun Microsystems, Inc.//DTD Web Application 2.3//EN"
          "http://java.sun.com/dtd/web-app_2_3.dtd">
<web-app>
  <display-name>ProjectTrack</display-name>
  <description>JavaServer Faces in Action sample application.
  </description>
  <servlet>
    <servlet-name>Faces Servlet</servlet-name>
    <servlet-class>javax.faces.webapp.FacesServlet</servlet-class>
    <load-on-startup>1</load-on-startup>
  </servlet>
  <servlet-mapping>
    <servlet-name>Faces Servlet</servlet-name>
    <url-pattern>/faces/*</url-pattern>
  </servlet-mapping>
  <welcome-file-list>
    <welcome-file>faces/login.jsp</welcome-file>
  </welcome-file-list>
</web-app>
```

The `<welcome-file-list>` element is used to specify the default pages for the web application. For ProjectTrack, the default page is login.jsp. Note the "faces/" prefix—this ensures that the `FacesServlet` handles the request for the page.

You may have noticed that this deployment descriptor looks a lot like the one for the Hello, world! example from the first chapter. Other than the welcome file, only the name and description are different; the basic requirements are always the same.

8.1.2 Setting up faces-config.xml

In chapter 3, we explained how to configure navigation rules. Listing 8.2 defines a single rule for navigating from login.jsp (which is the page we'll develop in this chapter).

Listing 8.2 faces-config.xml: ProjectTrack's configuration file with a single navigation rule

```
<?xml version="1.0"?>

<!DOCTYPE faces-config PUBLIC
  "-//Sun Microsystems, Inc.//DTD JavaServer Faces Config 1.0//EN"
  "http://java.sun.com/dtd/web-facesconfig_1_0.dtd">

<faces-config>
  <navigation-rule>
    <from-tree-id>/login.jsp</from-tree-id>
    <navigation-case>
      <from-outcome>success</from-outcome>
      <to-tree-id>/inbox.jsp</to-tree-id>
    </navigation-case>
    <navigation-case>
      <from-outcome>failure</from-outcome>
      <to-view-id>/login.jsp</to-view-id>
    </navigation-case>
  </navigation-rule>

</faces-config>
```

This navigation rule simply says "For login.jsp, if the outcome is `'success'`, display inbox.jsp; if the outcome is `'failure'`, redisplay login.jsp." When we build inbox.jsp page in this chapter, we'll hardcode the outcome `"success"` for our Submit button so that navigation will work without any application code. We'll continue the process of adding navigation rules and hardcoding outcomes as we walk through additional pages in the next chapter. Then, in chapter 10, we'll update our component declarations to reference action methods instead.

There's a lot more to JSF configuration than just navigation rules. As we build ProjectTrack, we'll define managed beans and configure custom validators, converters, and components. If you want to know more about setting up a JSF environment or configuration in general, see chapter 3.

8.2 Creating the Login page

Let's get started with the Login page: login.jsp. We'll build this page step by step, examining various aspects of JSF as we go. We'll then apply knowledge gained from this process as we build the remaining pages.

The page simply displays a welcome graphic and the name of the application, accepts the username and password for input, and has a single Submit button (because we display only two fields, we have no real need for a Clear button). The

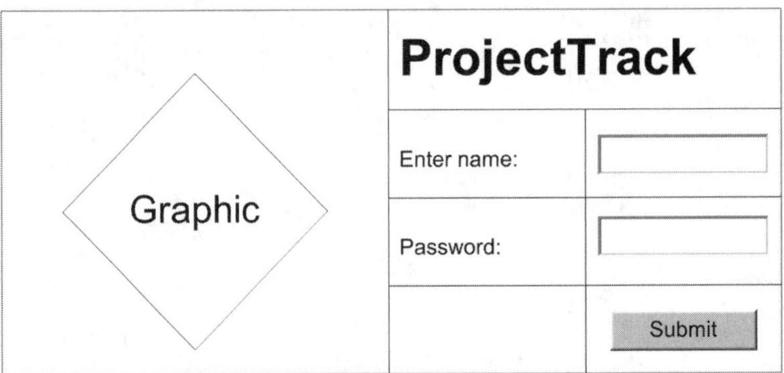

Figure 8.2 Mock-up of the Login page.

password field shouldn't display the text to the user—it should render as a standard HTML password input control so that the browser will show users asterisks instead of the actual text the user types. Figure 8.2 is a rough mock-up of the page.

Structurally, you can think of this design as having a table with one row and two columns: one for the graphic and one for a smaller, embedded table that contains all of the other controls. The embedded table has four rows. The first row has one column and simply contains the title. The second and third rows have two columns that contain a text label and an input field. The final row has two columns: the first is empty, and the second contains a single Submit button.

Now that we have our application configured, and a mock-up of the page, let's get started.

8.2.1 Starting with HtmlGraphicImage and HtmlOutputText components

We'll begin by creating a basic page that just has the graphic and the text "ProjectTrack" in a large font, as shown in figure 8.3. The JSP is shown in listing 8.3.

Listing 8.3 The JSP source for the Login page with only a graphic and the text "Project Track"

```
<!DOCTYPE HTML PUBLIC "-//W3C//DTD HTML 4.01 Transitional//EN">

<%@ taglib uri="http://java.sun.com/jsf/core"      ❶ Core JSF tag library
           prefix="f"%>

<%@ taglib uri="http://java.sun.com/jsf/html"      ❷ JSF HTML tag library
           prefix="h"%>
```

```
<f:view>                                    ❸ View tag that
<html>                                        encloses all
                                              components
<head>
  <title>
    <h:outputText value="ProjectTrack"/>    ❹ HtmlOutputText
  </title>                                    component
</head>

<body>

<table>                                     ❺ Table for
  <tr>                                        layout
   <td>
     <h:graphicImage url="/images/logo.gif"
            alt="Welcome to ProjectTrack"       ❻ HtmlGraphicImage
            title="Welcome to ProjectTrack"       component
            width="149" height="160"/>
   </td>
   <td>
     <font face="Arial, sans-serif"             ❼ Format for
           size="6">                              the heading

       <h:outputText value="ProjectTrack"/>     ❽ Another
     </font>                                      HtmlOutputText
   </td>                                          component
  </tr>
</table>

</body>
</html>
</f:view>
```

Figure 8.3
Our Login page with only `HtmlGraphicImage` and `HtmlOutputText` components.

❶ All JSP-based JSF pages must import the core JSF tag library, which includes tags without rendering functionality, like `<f:view>`, and the various validator and converter tags. If we were using a render kit other than the standard one included with JSF, we would still include this tag library.

❷ We'll be using the standard HTML components for this application, which is referenced by this tag library.

❸ All Faces tags must be enclosed in a `<f:view>` tag.

❹ Here we create an `HtmlOutputText` component with the text "ProjectTrack".

❺ For now, we'll use standard HTML tables for all of our layout.

❻ Here we create an `HtmlGraphicImage` component that references the image located at /images/logo.gif. Because the image URL has a leading slash, it will be rewritten to be relative to the web application's root ("/projects" in this case). The additional properties—`alt`, `title`, `width`, and `height`—are passed through to the HTML output (which is the `<img>` tag in this case). Most of the tags in the standard HTML tag library behave in this way.

❼ For now, we'll use a standard HTML `<font>` tag to format our heading.

❽ This is another `HtmlOutputText` component with the text "ProjectTrack". Because it's enclosed in the `<font>` tag described in ❼, it will appear in a larger font.

The corresponding HTML output is shown in listing 8.4.

Listing 8.4 Output of the Login page with only HtmlGraphicImage and HtmlOutputText components

```
<!DOCTYPE HTML PUBLIC "-//W3C//DTD HTML 4.01 Transitional//EN">

<html>
  <head>
    <title>
      ProjectTrack          <-- HtmlOutputText component
    </title>
</head>
<body>

<table>
  <tr>
   <td>
     <img src="/projects/images/logo.gif"       HtmlGraphicImage
          title="Welcome to ProjectTrack">      component
   </td>
   <td>
     <font face="Arial, sans-serif" size="6">
       ProjectTrack          <-- HtmlOutputText component
     </font>
   </td>
```

```
    <tr>
  </table>

  </body>
  </html>
```

This was a good start. Let's move on to the meat of the page.

8.2.2 *Adding a form*

Now we'll add the basic form elements so that we can capture the login name and password. These include an `HtmlInputText` component for the username, an `HtmlInputSecret` component for the password, and an `HtmlCommandButton` component for the Submit button. All of these elements will be placed within an `HtmlForm` so that JSF knows it will be sending the data back to the server. This page uses nested tables to achieve the layout shown in figure 8.2. Figure 8.4 shows the resulting page, displayed in a browser.

The JSP source is shown in listing 8.5.

Figure 8.4 The Login page with input components and a table layout.

Listing 8.5 The JSP source for the Login page with input components and a table layout

```
<!DOCTYPE HTML PUBLIC "-//W3C//DTD HTML 4.01 Transitional//EN">

<%@ taglib uri="http://java.sun.com/jsf/core" prefix="f"%>
<%@ taglib uri="http://java.sun.com/jsf/html" prefix="h"%>

<f:view>
<html>

<head>
  <title>
    <h:outputText value="ProjectTrack"/>
  </title>
</head>

<body>

<h:form>   <-- (1) HtmlForm containing input controls
<table cellpadding="0" cellspacing="0">   <-- (2) Table-based layout
  <tr>
   <td>
     <h:graphicImage url="/images/logo.gif"
                     alt="Welcome to ProjectTrack"
                     title="Welcome to ProjectTrack" width="149"
                     height="160"/>
   </td>
   <td>
     <table cellpadding="5" cellspacing="3">
       <tr>
         <td colspan="2">
           <font face="Arial, sans-serif" size="6">
             <h:outputText value="ProjectTrack"/>
           </font>
         </td>
       </tr>
        <tr>
          <td>
            <h:outputLabel for="userNameInput">      | (3) HtmlOutputText
             <h:outputText                           |     rendered as a label
                value="Enter your user name:"/>      |
            </h:outputLabel>
          </td>
          <td>
            <h:inputText id="userNameInput" size="20"     | (4) HtmlInputText
                         maxlength="30"/>                 |     with an id
          </td>
         </tr>
         <tr>
           <td>
```

```
                <h:outputLabel for="passwordInput">
                  <h:outputText value="Password:"/>
                </h:outputLabel>
              </td>
              <td>
                <h:inputSecret id="passwordInput"        ❺ HtmlInputSecret
                               size="20"
                               maxlength="20"/>
              </tr>
            </tr>
            <tr>
              <td/>
              <td>
                <h:commandButton action="success"       ❻ HtmlCommandButton
                                 title="submit"
                                 value="Submit"/>
              </tr>
          </table>
        </td>
      </tr>
    </table>

    </h:form>

    </body>
    </html>
    </f:view>
```

❶ We start by declaring an `HtmlForm` component. This will serve as a container for all of the Input and Command components on the page.

❷ The table layout matches the layout of the mock-up in figure 8.2, a large table with a single row and two columns. The graphic is in the first column, and a nested table containing the other controls is in the second column.

❸ Here we use the `<h:outputLabel>` tag to render all embedded components as a label for the control with the identifier "userNameInput". Any component referenced by the `for` property of this tag must have a human-specified identifier. The embedded component is an `HtmlOutputText` instance that has the text "Enter your user name:". So this code outputs an HTML label for a component called "userNameInput" with the value "Enter your user name:". The same method is used for labeling the password field in the page.

❹ This code creates a simple `HtmlInputText` component for accepting the user's login name. This component has been assigned an identifier so that it can be referenced elsewhere (such as with the label described in ❸).

5. This code creates another `HtmlInputText` component for the password, except we use the `<h:inputSecret>` tag, which renders as an HTML `<input>` tag of `type` "password". This way, no one will be able to slyly stand over the user's shoulder and see the password. This component has been assigned an identifier so that it can be referenced elsewhere, as in the `<h:outputLabel>` tag.
6. Submitting a form requires a Command component. This line declares an `HtmlCommandButton` component, which generates an `ActionEvent` with the hardcoded outcome `"success"`. Hardcoding the action value tells JSF to bypass any application code and simply look for a matching outcome in the page's navigation rule. Fortunately, in listing 8.2 we set up the navigation rule for this page so that the outcome `"success"` will always load inbox.jsp.

The output of the JSP is shown in listing 8.6.

Listing 8.6 The HTML output for the Login page with input components and a table layout

```
<!DOCTYPE HTML PUBLIC "-//W3C//DTD HTML 4.01 Transitional//EN">

<html>
<head>
  <title>
    ProjectTrack
  </title>
</head>

<body>

<form id="_id1" method="post"                          Output of
  action="/projects/faces/login.jsp"                   HtmlForm
  enctype="application/x-www-form-urlencoded">

<table cellpadding="0" cellspacing="0">
  <tr>
   <td>
     <img src="/projects/images/logo.gif"
          alt="Welcome to ProjectTrack" height="160"
          title="Welcome to ProjectTrack" width="149" />
   </td>
   <td>
     <table cellpadding="5" cellspacing="3">
       <tr>
         <td colspan="2">
           <font face="Arial, sans-serif" size="6">
             ProjectTrack
           </font>
         </td>
       </tr>
```

```
        <tr>
          <td>
            <label for="_id1:userNameInput">

              Enter your user name:
            </label>
          </td>
          <td>
            <input id="_id1:userNameInput"
                   type="text"
                   name="_id1:userNameInput"
                   maxlength="30"
                   size="20" />
          </td>
        </tr>
        <tr>
          <td>

              Password:

          </td>
          <td>
            <input id="_id1:passwordInput" type="password"
                   name="_id1:passwordInput" value=""
                   maxlength="20" size="20" />
          </tr>
        </tr>
        <tr>
          <td/>
          <td>
            <input type="submit" name="_id1:_id8" value="submit"
                   title="Submit" />
        </tr>
      </table>
    </td>
  </tr>
</table>

<input type="hidden" name="_id1" value="_id1" />
</form>

</body>
</html>

</form>

</body>
</html>
```

HtmlOutputText label

HtmlInputText for the username

HtmlInputSecret for the password

HtmlCommandButton

More output of HtmlForm

If you're wondering why `HtmlForm` has a `<hidden>` field at the end of the page, it's because the component processes that field in order to set its `submitted` property, which returns `true` if that field exists. This isn't something you usually have to worry about. Also note that the form posts back to itself, which, as we mentioned in the first part of this book, is called *postback*. This is the norm for JSF applications because the framework needs to associate events with the current view.

At this point, we have a working page. If you click the Submit button, you'll get an error page saying that inbox.jsp can't be found. (The obscurity of the message, however, will depend on your web container.) This is a good sign—it means that the navigation rule is configured correctly.

8.3 Sprucing things up

Okay, now we have a basic working Login page. But real applications are often a little nicer-looking than figure 8.4. The `<font>` tag and plain-old form buttons are so '90s. Fortunately, you can use familiar HTML development tricks to make JSF applications look a little more modern (if you consider HTML modern, that is). What we're aiming for is something like figure 8.5, which uses JavaScript for a rollover effect on the button and Cascading Style Sheets (CSS) for formatting the title (instead of the `<font>` tag).

Figure 8.5 The Login page with an image for a button, JavaScript for a rollover, and CSS for formatting.

8.3.1 Using an image for the button

An obvious way to spice things is to use a graphic for the button. This can be done by changing the <h:commandButton> tag as follows:

```
<h:commandButton action="success"
    image="#{facesContext.externalContext.requestContextPath}
          /images/submit.gif"/>
```

You may have noticed that the `image` property looks just like HTML. As a matter of fact, it is just passed through to the rendered HTML. Most of the components support these pass-through properties.

Pass-through properties do, however, support value-binding expressions, which is what we have in this example. The expression `"#{facesContext.externalContext.requestContextPath}"` references the application's context path, which is "/projects" in this case. This is necessary for `HtmlCommandButton` because the `image` property isn't automatically prefixed with the context path (as it is for `HtmlGraphicImage`). This is a feature that we hope will be added in a future version of JSF. In the meantime, you can either use a value-binding expression or use an `HtmlCommandLink` instead.

This expression references the `externalContext` property of `FacesContext`, which provides access to properties of the servlet or portlet environment. See chapter 11 for more information about this class.

By the way, this expression is also equivalent to the JSP expression `"<%= request.getContextPath() %>"`. To keep things consistent, it's usually better to use JSF expressions instead. We'll also use this expression to communicate the context path to JavaScript code.

8.3.2 Integrating with JavaScript

The pass-through HTML properties also allow us to integrate with client-side JavaScript quite easily. Although JSF components will often render JavaScript for you, it's quite likely that somewhere along the line you'll need to manually integrate with scripts, especially if you're converting an existing application.

For the Login page, we'll add a simple JavaScript function to create a standard "rollover" so our graphical button will appear to change the color of its text when a user places the mouse over it. We can do this by adding the following JavaScript to the <head> section of our page:

```
<script language="JavaScript">

   function set_image(button, img)
   {
```

```
        button.src = img;
    }

</script>
```

The code for the button itself must be changed as follows:

```
<h:commandButton action="success" title="Submit"
     image="#{facesContext.externalContext.
               requestContextPath}/images/submit.gif"
     onMouseOver="set_image(this,
            '#{facesContext.externalContext.requestContextPath}
            /images/submit_over.gif')"
     onMouseOut="set_image(this,
            '#{facesContext.externalContext.requestContextPath}
            /images/submit.gif');"/>
```

If you do a lot of front-end development, this sort of code should look pretty familiar to you. We use the standard client-side HTML event handlers to call our little function when the user places the mouse over the button (`onMouseOver`) or moves it away from the button (`onMouseOut`). The function receives a reference to the button element (which will be rendered as a standard `<input>` element of type "image") by using this identifier. It also receives a string with the name of the graphic we'd like the browser to display for that button. In the HTML 4 document object model (DOM), this element has an `src` property, which is what we set to equal the new image name in the `set_image()` function. The graphic submit_over.gif looks exactly like submit.gif, except that the color of the text is black. Consequently, while the user's mouse is over the button, the text color appears to change to black; it turns back to green when the user moves the mouse away.

Note that we've prepended the image URL with the value-binding expression for the web application's context path, which is "/projects" in this case. This way, we ensure that the images use an absolute URL instead of a relative URL. This allows us to change the context root without worrying about hardcoded absolute paths.

This simple example demonstrates the fact that integrating JavaScript into JSF applications is as easy as integrating JavaScript into standard JSP applications. Generally speaking, if the custom tag you're using for the component has an HTML property, you can be sure it's going to be in the HTML rendering of the component. This allows you to attach JavaScript event handlers to any component tag that accepts the proper properties. You can also put script elements and references in JSF pages just as you can with any other JSP page.

Client-side tasks like rollovers are extremely common and often require lots of little bits of JavaScript code—sometimes way more than should be necessary. This makes them perfect candidates for JSF components that handle all of the

JavaScript for you. In this example, it'd be much nicer to just specify both image filenames as properties of the `<h:commandButton>` tag and forget about all of the event handling and JavaScript. We develop a renderer with this functionality in online extension chapter 17.

Adding an image to the button makes things look a little better, but we could use some additional formatting as well.

8.3.3 Adding Cascading Style Sheets

Just as we added JavaScript by using pass-through HTML properties, we can also add Cascading Style Sheets (CSS). In the previous listings, we formatted the text "ProjectTrack" using the HTML `<font>` element. Most sites these days use CSS for formatting HTML elements, and we have been using this approach throughout the book.

Some IDEs will give you tools for creating CSS styles without any knowledge of CSS (see figure 4.1 for a screen shot), but most web developers are quite familiar with it already. Let's start by creating a file, stylesheet.css, and then place it in the root of the web application directory. The first style will be the one used to format the name of the application (replacing the `<font>` tag):

```
.login-heading
{
  font-family: Arial, sans-serif;
  font-size: 26pt;
}
```

Next we can add the style sheet reference to our Login page:

```
<head>

...

  <link rel="stylesheet" type="text/css"
        href="stylesheet.css"/>

...

</head>
```

Now we can replace the `<font>` tags:

```
<h:outputText value="ProjectTrack" styleClass="login-heading"/>
```

Most of the components display the `class` property as an HTML `<span>` element. The previous code fragment renders to the following HTML:

```
<span class="login-heading">ProjectTrack</span>
```

That's all there is to it. Every tag in the standard HTML tag library that supports style sheets has a special property called `styleClass`. Panels and `HtmlDataTable` are a little more complicated (they have styles for different rows and columns) but any property ending in "Class" is used to reference a CSS style.

We've now achieved the more attractive page shown in figure 8.5. But a page alone isn't all that exciting.

8.4 Adding validators

Even though our page works as is, it's not being used as much more than a standard web form with no logic. No matter what you type in the input fields, clicking the Submit button always forwards you to the inbox.jsp page. Because JSF has built-in support for validation, it makes sense to add validators so that the interface feels a little more interactive to users. Adding validation during UI prototyping also helps users and developers get a shared vision of how the application should behave.

In chapter 4, we showed you how to use `HtmlMessage` and `HtmlMessages` to display validator error messages. However, our page design has no place for reporting such errors. We need to report errors for both fields, which means adding another column to the nested table. The revised mock-up of the page is shown in figure 8.6. You can see that we've included a new column that is used to display error messages—one cell for each input field. If no errors are present, the column should be empty (in other words, the page should look like the original mock-up in figure 8.1, page 289).

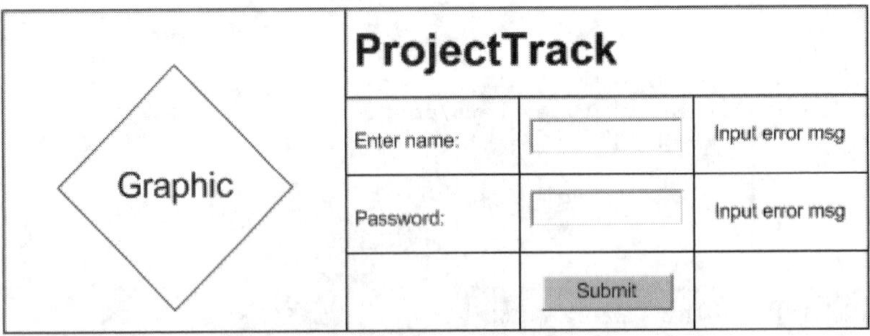

Figure 8.6 A mock-up of the Login page with a column for errors.

These error messages should grab the user's attention, so we'll add a new CSS class to our style sheet for them:

```
.errors {
  color: red;
}
```

No rocket science here; this just ensures that our error message show up in red.

Now that we know where to put the error messages and what they'll look like, let's take a look at the requirements for these two fields. Because both the username and password are necessary to validate the user, both fields are required. They must be at least five characters long. The maximum length of the name field is 30; the maximum length of the password field is 15. This translates to setting the `required` property to true, and adding a `Length` validator, respectively. The relevant portions of the code, changed to add validation, is shown in listing 8.7.

Listing 8.7 Adding validation to the Login page

```
...
<table cellspacing="0" cellpadding="0">
  <tr>
   <td>
     <h:graphicImage url="/images/logo.gif" alt="Welcome to ProjectTrack"
                      title="Welcome to ProjectTrack" width="149"
                      height="160"/>
   </td>
   <td>
     <table cellpadding="5" cellspacing="3">
       <tr>
         <td colspan="3">                          <-- Additional column for errors
           <h:outputText value="ProjectTrack"
                         styleClass="login-heading"/>
         </td>
       </tr>
      <tr>
        <td>
          <h:outputLabel for="userNameInput">
           <h:outputText value="Enter your user name:"/>
          </h:outputLabel>
        </td>
        <td>
          <h:inputText id="userNameInput" size="20" maxlength="30"
                       required="true">            <-- Require input
            <f:validateLength minimum="5"
               maximum="30"/>                      <-- Length validator
          </h:inputText>
```

```
          </td>
          <td>
            <h:message for="userNameInput"
                       styleClass="errors"/>
          </td>
        </tr>
        <tr>
          <td>
            <h:outputLabel for="passwordInput">
              <h:outputText value="Password:"/>
            </h:outputLabel>
          </td>
          <td>
            <h:inputSecret id="passwordInput" size="20" maxlength="20"
                           required="true">
              <f:validateLength minimum="5" maximum="15"/>
            </h:inputSecret>
          </td>
          <td>
            <h:message for="passwordInput" styleClass="errors"/>
          </td>
        </tr>
        <tr>
          <td/>
          <td>
        <h:commandButton action="success" title="Submit"
               image="#{facesContext.externalContext.requestContextPath}
                /images/submit.gif"
               onMouseOver="set_image(this,
            '#{facesContext.externalContext.requestContextPath}
                 /images/submit_over.gif')"
               onMouseOut="set_image(this,
                '#{facesContext.externalContext.requestContextPath}
                 /images/submit.gif');"/>
          </tr>
          <td/>
        </tr>
      </table>
    </td>
  </tr>
</table>
...
```

HtmlMessage component

Now that we've added validators, the `HtmlMessage` components on the page will display error messages if there are any, as shown in figure 8.7.

With validators on the page, JSF now will automatically handle validation, remembering the value of the input controls even if the value is incorrect. The actual text of the error messages could use some help, so let's tackle that task now.

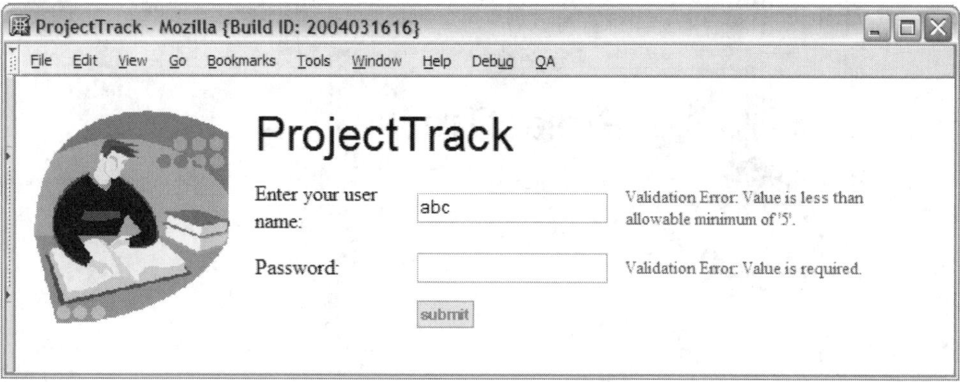

Figure 8.7 The Login page with validation errors.

8.4.1 Customizing validation messages

The validation error messages shown in figure 8.7 are the standard messages that ship with Sun's JSF RI [Sun, JSF RI]. Other implementations may have nicer messages, but because this one doesn't, we'll make some changes.

In the directory listing shown in figure 8.1, we had a simple file called ptrackResources.properties in the WEB-INF/classes directory. This is a resource bundle—a file is for customizing error messages and also localizing other application strings. During prototyping, we can use it to make our validation errors look a little more user-friendly. In part 3, we'll use resource bundles for localization as well.

The file ptrackResources.properties is a standard Java properties file, which has just plain text and name/value pairs. As long as we use the proper validation message key, we can change the value. Listing 8.8 shows the changes necessary for the two validation messages used in the login page.

Listing 8.8 Customized validation error messages

```
javax.faces.component.UIInput.REQUIRED=This field is required.
javax.faces.component.UIInput.REQUIRED_detail=
  Please fill in this field.
javax.faces.validator.LengthValidator.MAXIMUM=
  This field must be less than {0} characters long.
javax.faces.validator.LengthValidator.MINIMUM=
  This field must be at least {0} characters long.
```

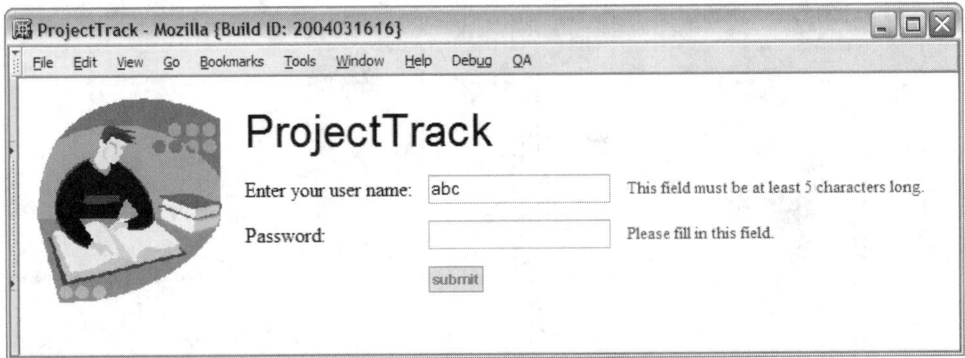

Figure 8.8 The login page with customized validation errors.

This customizes the summary and detail text for input controls with the `required` property set to `true`, and the summary text for the `Length` validator (no detail text has been specified).

All we have to do now is tell JSF about this file so that it will use it for validation error messages. This can be done by adding an `<application>` node to faces-config.xml:

```
<application>
  <message-bundle>ptrackResources</message-bundle>
</application>
```

Note that we don't use the extension ".properties" here—JSF will automatically append it as necessary. After making this change (and restarting the application), we get the friendlier messages shown in figure 8.8, which make the page a little more like a real application. For more information on validation and customizing error messages, see chapter 6.

The page is now pretty complete, but we can still play with the layout.

8.5 Improving layout with HtmlPanelGrid

You may have noticed that even though our page has a decent amount of JSF components, the layout is still handled by standard HTML tables. Another approach is to use multiple `HtmlPanelGrid`s for layout. This component is the closest thing JSF has to Swing's layout managers (as far as standard components go).

Using `HtmlPanelGrid` allows you to work more exclusively with JSF components, which means you can spend less time dealing with the nuances of HTML. In other words, you won't waste time trying to figure out where that missing `<td>`

element went. Well-developed components are also intimately familiar with HTML standards and can change their output depending on the browser type, which saves you the effort of doing so yourself.

So, let's modify our page. The goal is to duplicate the structure shown in figure 8.6: a main two-column table with the image on the left, and a nested table on the right. The nested table will have a heading with the text "ProjectTrack", followed by rows that have input fields, buttons, and output components.

`HtmlPanelGrid` is the perfect choice for this because it lays out components in tables without the need for a value-binding expression. The component displays an HTML table, so just as we had one HTML table nested inside another, we'll have one `HtmlPanelGrid` nested inside another. Our completed login page, revised to use panels, is shown in listing 8.9.

Listing 8.9 The JSP source for our completed Login page using an HtmlPanelGrid for component layout

```
<!DOCTYPE HTML PUBLIC "-//W3C//DTD HTML 4.01 Transitional//EN">

<%@ taglib uri="http://java.sun.com/jsf/core" prefix="f"%>
<%@ taglib uri="http://java.sun.com/jsf/html" prefix="h"%>

<f:view>
<html>
  <head>
    <title>
      <h:outputText value="ProjectTrack"/>
    </title>

    <link rel="stylesheet" type="text/css"
          href="/projects/stylesheet.css"/>

    <script language="JavaScript">

       function set_image(button, img)
       {
         button.src = "/projects" + img;
       }

    </script>
  </head>

<body>

<h:form>

  <h:panelGrid columns="2" border="0" cellpadding="3"
               cellspacing="3">
```

```
<h:graphicImage url="/images/logo.gif"
                alt="Welcome to ProjectTrack"
                title="Welcome to ProjectTrack"
                width="149" height="160"/>

<h:panelGrid columns="3" border="0"
             cellpadding="5"
             cellspacing="3"
             headerClass="login-heading">          ❷ Nested HtmlPanelGrid
                                                      for input components
   <f:facet name="header">
     <h:outputText value="ProjectTrack" />         ❸ Header
   </f:facet>                                         facet

   <h:outputLabel for="userNameInput">
    <h:outputText value="Enter your user name:"/>
   </h:outputLabel>
   <h:inputText id="userNameInput" size="20" maxlength="30"
                required="true">
     <f:validateLength minimum="5" maximum="30"/>
   </h:inputText>
   <h:message for="userNameInput"/>

   <h:outputLabel for="passwordInput">
     <h:outputText value="Password:"/>
   </h:outputLabel>
   <h:inputSecret id="passwordInput" size="20" maxlength="20"
                  required="true">
     <f:validateLength minimum="5" maximum="15"/>
   </h:inputSecret>
   <h:message for="passwordInput"/>

   <h:panelGroup/>   <-❹ HtmlPanelGroup placeholder
  <h:commandButton action="success" title="Submit"
        image="#{facesContext.externalContext.requestContextPath}
         /images/submit.gif"
        onMouseOver="set_image(this,
     '#{facesContext.externalContext.requestContextPath}
          /images/submit_over.gif')"
        onMouseOut="set_image(this,
         '#{facesContext.externalContext.requestContextPath}
          /images/submit.gif');"/>
   <h:panelGroup/>

</h:panelGrid>

     </h:panelGrid>
   </h:form>

   </body>
```

```
</html>
</f:view>
```

❶ First, we add an enclosing HtmlPanelGid. This component uses the columns property to determine the number of columns to display. It works by rendering its child components in order, based on the number of columns. Because two columns have been specified it will display two child components in each row (one per column). It will display them in order: the first component will be displayed in column one, row one. The second will be displayed in row one, column two. The third will be displayed in row two, column one. The fourth will be displayed in row two, column two, and so on.

We've specified only two child components: an HtmlGraphicImage and another HtmlPanelGrid, which is used to lay out additional controls. Consequently, this will render as a table with a single row and two columns; the left column will display an image tag, and the right will have a nested table rendered by the nested HtmlPanelGrid.

❷ This nested HtmlPanelGrid will lay out all of the other components on the form. The headerClass property specifies the CSS style for the header row. The columns property is set to 3, so every group of three child components will make up a single row (one per column). There are three groups: one for entering the name, one for entering the password, and one for the Submit button.

❸ In order to display the text "ProjectTrack" as a single header row with a single column, we can place an HtmlOutputText inside of the header facet. The headerClass property of the parent HtmlPanelGrid will be used to style it appropriately.

❹ If you look at figure 8.6, the bottom row of the nested table has two empty cells (the first and last). In our HTML table, we achieved this effect with the infamous empty cell (<td/>). When using HtmlPanelGrid, we must to do the same thing to ensure that Faces places the button in the middle column. This can be done with the HtmlPanelGroup, which is a panel with no visual representation. If we left this out, the component would place the next component (an HtmlCommandButton) underneath the password input label. This isn't the desired behavior—we want the buttons to be under the password input field itself.

We've now successfully modified the page to use panels for layout. It looks exactly as it did in figure 8.5, because the table structure rendered by the two HtmlPanelGrid components is the same. The generated HTML is shown in listing 8.10

Listing 8.10 The Login page HTML output with layout generated by two HtmlPanelGrids

```
<!DOCTYPE HTML PUBLIC "-//W3C//DTD HTML 4.01 Transitional//EN">

<html>
<head>
  <title>ProjectTrack</title>
  <link rel="stylesheet" type="text/css" href="stylesheet.css">
  <script language="JavaScript" type="text/javascript">

       function set_image(button, img)
       {
         button.src = img;
       }

  </script>
</head>

<body>
  <form id="_id1" method="post"
        action="/projects/faces/login.jsp"
        enctype="application/x-www-form-urlencoded">
    <table border="0" cellpadding="3"
           cellspacing="3">                          ❶ Main HtmlPanelGrid
      <tbody>
        <tr>
          <td>
            <img src="/projects/images/logo.gif"
                 alt="Welcome to ProjectTrack" height="160"
                 title="Welcome to ProjectTrack" width="149">
          </td>

          <td>
            <table border="0"                        ❷ Nested HtmlPanelGrid
                   cellpadding="5"
                   cellspacing="3">

              <thead>
                <tr>
                  <th class="login-heading"
                      colspan="3"                    ❸ Header facet
                      scope="colgroup">
                    ProjectTrack
                  </th>
                </tr>
              </thead>

              <tbody>
                <tr>
                  <td>
                   <label for="_id1:userNameInput">
```

```
    Enter your user name:
   </label>
  </td>

  <td>
    <input id="_id1:userNameInput" type="text"
           name="_id1:userNameInput" maxlength="30"
           size="20">
  </td>

  <td></td>   <-- (4) HtmlPanelGroup placeholder
</tr>

<tr>
  <td>
    <label for="_id1:passwordInput">
      Password:
    </label>
  </td>

  <td>
    <input id="_id1:passwordInput"
           type="password" name="_id1:passwordInput"
           value=""
           maxlength="20" size="20">
  </td>

  <td></td>
</tr>

<tr>
  <td></td>

  <td>
    <input type="image"
      src="/projects/images/submit.gif"
      name="_id1:_id13"
      onMouseOut="set_image(this,
         '/projects/images/submit.gif');"
      onMouseOver="set_image(this,
         '/projects/images/submit_over.gif')"
      title="Submit">

  </td>

  <td></td>
</tr>
</tbody>
</table>
</td>
```

```
        </tr>
      </tbody>
    </table>

    <input type="hidden" name="_id1" value="_id1">
  </form>
</body>
</html>
```

❶ This is the primary table, rendered by the first `<h:panelGrid>` tag. You can see that the HTML pass-through properties were indeed passed through. You may also have noticed that the order of the properties is different than the order in the original JSP code. Components don't necessary guarantee the order of pass-through properties; they just guarantee the content.

❷ This is the nested table, rendered by the second `<h:panelGrid>` tag.

❸ This is the nested `HtmlPanelGrid`'s `header` facet. You can see that it's a single row that spans all three columns, and the CSS class is the same as the parent `HtmlPanelGrid`'s `headerClass` property.

❹ `HtmlPanelGroup` doesn't have a visual representation, so it just outputs empty cells.

We now have a Login page, complete with JavaScript, CSS, validation, custom error messages, and a panel-based layout. We covered each and every step of building this page for a good reason—this way, we can skip the topics explained here when we describe the other pages, so you can focus on the unique aspects of the other pages.

8.6 Summary

In this chapter, we built a static Login page, step by step, with JSF and JSP. We began by examining each element of the Login page, one by one. The first step was to create the page, importing the proper tag libraries and adding `HtmlGraphicImage` and `HtmlOutputText` components. We then added a form for collecting the username and password. Next, we spiced up things up with a button image, Cascading Style Sheets, and a little bit of JavaScript for an image rollover. (Bear in mind that JSF will typically limit the amount of required JavaScript, because components should generate it themselves.)

We then added validators to the Login page, making sure we had enough room for displaying the error messages. This is key—if you add validation and you want to redisplay the page with errors, you must allow space for those errors to be displayed. Next, we customized those error messages with a resource bundle.

Finally, we demonstrated a powerful technique: laying out components with panels as opposed to HTML tables. This technique lets you focus on the conceptual view of the layout as opposed to the specifics of HTML.

In the next chapter, we'll build the rest of the UI using the techniques learned in this chapter.

9 Developing a user interface without Java code: the other pages

This chapter covers

- Working with JSP includes
- Using panels to simulate data tables
- Creating input forms
- Creating static navigation flows

In this chapter, we'll continue developing a static, user interface (UI) prototype for ProjectTrack. We'll build on the concepts introduced in the previous chapter: using `HtmlForm`, `HtmlOutputText`, `HtmlInputText`, `HtmlCommandButton`, and `HtmlCommandLink` components; validation; and `HtmlPanelGrids` for layout. This chapter will also walk through pages that use `HtmlSelectOneListbox` for a combo box, and `HtmlSelectManyCheckbox` for a checkbox group.

By the end of this chapter, you should have a solid understanding of how to build an interactive UI with JSF and no application logic. As we said in chapter 8, building a prototype in JSF allows you to communicate with users effectively and easily transition into a full-fledged application.

For all of these prototypical views, we'll assume the role of a Project Manager, because this is the only role that can access all of the features. In the next chapter, we'll disable certain functionality based on the user's role.

9.1 Building the header with a custom component

One of ProjectTrack's chief requirements is that all of the pages (other than the Login page) have a header at the top to provide navigation. Consequently, the header seems like a good place to start. We'll develop it as a separate JSP and include it as a dynamic resource in all of the other pages. That way, we'll be able to make changes in a single place, and have it automatically affect the rest of the application.

NOTE In our case study, we use JSP includes for layout and reusable page elements. For more complex applications, you may want to use something like Tiles [ASF, Tiles] or SiteMesh [OpenSymphony, SiteMesh]. Both of these, and any other JSP-friendly technologies, should work fine with JSF (as a matter of fact, we discuss Tiles in chapter 14).

Figure 9.1 shows a mock-up of this page. It's basically a series of elements: first the text "ProjectTrack," followed by four graphic/link description pairs and a combo box. At the far right the username is displayed, and the whole header is enclosed in a box to separate it from the rest of the view. This box should stretch to cover the entire length of the page.

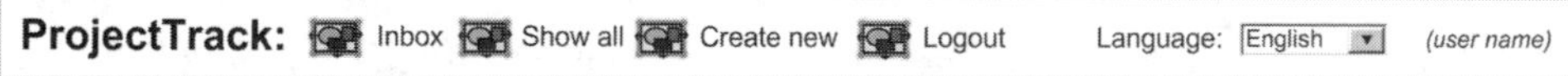

Figure 9.1 Mock-up of the header. This page will be included in all of the other pages (except for the Login page). It provides navigation to different views in the system, and allows the user to change the language on the fly.

So, how do we lay this out with panels? The most important point is that we need one `HtmlPanelGrid` that serves as the main container and that will stretch horizontally across the page. It should have three components: another `HtmlPanelGrid` that contains the "ProjectTrack" text and the header buttons, an `HtmlPanelGroup` that contains the combo box and its label, and an `HtmlOutputText` that displays the user's name. This way, we can use the embedded panel to control the layout of the "ProjectTrack" text and the graphic/link description pairs independently of the username text and the rest of the header.

It may seem more intuitive to use a single `HtmlPanelGrid`. The problem is that you lose explicit control of the text and the graphic/link description pairs. They would have to be rendered with the same properties as the combo box and username text, which would essentially be a single table with even spacing for all elements. This isn't what figure 9.1 shows—headers normally don't have their buttons evenly spaced across the top of the page; usually all the buttons are left- or right-justified.

NOTE This page, and the rest of the ones covered in this chapter, reference additional styles that are defined in stylesheet.css. We'll spare you the details in these pages, but you can examine them electronically from the book's web site (http://www.manning.com/mann).

The JSP source for the header is shown in listing 9.1.

Listing 9.1 header.jsp: ProjectTrack's header

```
<%@ taglib uri="http://java.sun.com/jsf/core" prefix="f"%>
<%@ taglib uri="http://java.sun.com/jsf/html" prefix="h"%>

<f:subview id="header">   <-- 1 Required for JSP includes

  <h:form>   <-- 2 Separate form

    <h:panelGrid columns="3"
                 cellspacing="0"
                 cellpadding="0"
                 styleClass="header"
                 width="100%">          3 Primary container

      <h:panelGrid id="header" columns="9"
                   cellpadding="4"
                   cellspacing="0"
                   border="0">          4 Child panel
```

```
  <h:outputText value="ProjectTrack:"
                styleClass="header-header"/>

  <h:commandLink action="inbox">
    <h:graphicImage
        url="images/inbox.gif"
        styleClass="header-icon"
        alt="Inbox"/>
    <h:outputText value="Inbox"
        styleClass="header-command"/>
  </h:commandLink>

  <h:commandLink action="show_all">
    <h:graphicImage url="images/show_all.gif"
                    styleClass="header-icon"
                    alt="Show all projects"/>
    <h:outputText value="Show all"
                  styleClass="header-command"/>
  </h:commandLink>

  <h:commandLink action="create">
    <h:graphicImage url="images/create.gif"
                    styleClass="header-icon"
                    alt="Create a new project"/>
    <h:outputText value="Create new"
                  styleClass="header-command"/>
  </h:commandLink>

  <h:commandLink action="logout">
    <h:graphicImage url="images/logout.gif"
                    styleClass="header-icon"
                    alt="Logout"/>
    <h:outputText value="Logout"
                  styleClass="header-command"/>
  </h:commandLink>

</h:panelGrid>

<h:panelGroup>
  <h:outputLabel for="languageSelect">
    <h:outputText value="Language:"
         styleClass="language-select"/>
  </h:outputLabel>
  <h:selectOneListbox
        id="languageSelect"
        size="1"
        styleClass="language-select">
    <f:selectItem itemLabel="English"
                  itemValue="English"/>
    <f:selectItem itemLabel="Russian"
                  itemValue="Russian"/>
```

5 **Header text**

6 **Header buttons**

7 **Language combo box**

```
    </h:selectOneListbox>
    <h:commandButton value="Go!"
         styleClass="language-select-button"/>
  </h:panelGroup>

  <h:outputText value="proj_mgr"
                styleClass="user-name"/>

  </h:panelGrid>
 </h:form>
</f:subview>
```

7 **Language combo box**

8 **Username**

1. If you're intending to include a JSP page with dynamic includes (either the `<jsp:include>` or `<c:import>` tags), you must enclose the page in the `<f:subview>` tag. (See chapter 3 for more information on JSP includes and other custom tags.)
2. We enclose the entire header in an `HtmlForm`, which is required for the header buttons and combo box. We can still use a separate form in the page that includes the header—the two forms will be processed independently.
3. We use an `HtmlPanelGrid` component as the primary container. Because no rows or columns attributes were specified, it will display a single row. The style "header" is the basic style for the whole page. Because this style sets the background color to light blue, we satisfy the requirement of enclosing the header in a box. The `width` attribute will be passed through to the rendered HTML table to ensure that the header stretches horizontally across the page.
4. The embedded `HtmlPanelGrid` allows us to lay out the header text "ProjectTrack" and the links to the other pages. We've specified five columns: one for the header text, and one for each header button. The lack of a `rows` attribute indicates that the component should display a single row. The `cellpadding`, `cellspacing`, and other attributes will be passed through to the displayed table.
5. We use a simple `HtmlOutputText` component with the style "header-header" for the header text "ProjectTrack."
6. The header buttons are represented by `HtmlCommandLink` components with child `HtmlGraphicImage` and `HtmlOutputText` components. Both the child `HtmlGraphicImage` and `HtmlOutputText` components have specific styles applied to them; this is required to allow the images to have different styles than the text. For now, all of the `HtmlCommandLink` components have hardcoded action outcomes. We'll map these values to specific navigation cases in the next section, so that navigation works in the prototype. Then, in chapter 10 we'll change the `action` properties to reference the action methods instead.
7. Here, we specify an `HtmlSelectOneListbox` component that allows users to select their language. (One of ProjectTrack's requirements is to support both English

Figure 9.2 header.jsp: The header shown in a browser.

and Russian.) For now, we'll just hardcode the values. In order to make this component useful, we also need an `HtmlOutputLabel` and an `HtmlCommandButton` (to submit the form). Because there's no logic for changing the language currently, we won't set the button's `action` property right now; we'll do that in chapter 9. Note that we've also defined styles for the `HtmlOutputText` and `HtmlSelectOneListbox` components. All of these components are grouped together so that the enclosing `HtmlPanelGrid` will put them in a single column.

8 The username is displayed with a `HtmlOutputText` component, with the style "user-name". For now, the name "proj_mgr" is hardcoded. In chapter 10, we'll integrate it with the model so that it displays the real user's name.

The header, displayed in a browser, is shown in figure 9.2. You can see that a single background color (style "header-background") is used for the whole header, but the heading text and the links appear left-justified. This is because the main panel is stretched across the page but the embedded panel is not.

9.1.1 Using a custom toolbar component

Using an embedded `HtmlPanelGrid` for our header is useful, and works well in most cases. However, it's tedious to specify three components—an `HtmlCommandLink`, an `HtmlGraphicImage`, and an `HtmlOutputText` component—for every single header button. Also, it would be nice if we could configure the buttons dynamically from a model object, or highlight a button once it's been selected. These types of features can be implemented with a custom header component.

As luck would have it, online extension chapter 19 shows you how to build such a component, so we won't go into all of the details here. The component is called `UINavigator`, and its output is almost identical to our custom `HtmlPanelGrid`; however, you can associate it with a model object or hardcode the button values. And best of all, if you hardcode the button values, it requires just one tag.

We can easily replace the header `HtmlPanelGrid` with our custom component. In listing 9.2, we show a modified version of header.jsp that uses `UINavigator`.

Listing 9.2 header.jsp: Header modified to use custom toolbar component

```
<%@ taglib uri="http://java.sun.com/jsf/core" prefix="f"%>
<%@ taglib uri="http://java.sun.com/jsf/html" prefix="h"%>
<%@ taglib uri="jsf-in-action-components" prefix="jia"%>
```

```
<f:subview id="header">

  <h:form>

    <h:panelGrid columns="3" cellspacing="0" cellpadding="0"
                 styleClass="header" width="100%">

      <jia:navigatorToolbar id="header"
           layout="horizontal"
           headerClass="header-header"
           itemClass="header-command"
           selectedItemClass="header-command"
           iconClass="header-icon"
           immediate="false">

        <f:facet name="header">
          <h:outputText value="ProjectTrack:"/>
        </f:facet>

        <jia:navigatorItem name="inbox"
           label="Inbox"
           icon="/images/inbox.gif"
           action="inbox"/>
        <jia:navigatorItem name="showAll" label="Show All"
           icon="/images/show_all.gif"
           action="show_all"/>
        <jia:navigatorItem name="createNew" label="Create New"
           icon="/images/create.gif"
           action="create"/>
        <jia:navigatorItem name="logout" label="Logout"
           icon="/images/logout.gif"
           action="logout"/>

      </jia:navigatorToolbar >

      <h:panelGroup>
        <h:outputLabel for="languageSelect">
          <h:outputText value="Language:"
                        styleClass="language-select"/>
        </h:outputLabel>
        <h:selectOneListbox size="1" styleClass="language-select">
          <f:selectItem itemLabel="English" itemValue="English"/>
          <f:selectItem itemLabel="Russian" itemValue="Russian"/>
        </h:selectOneListbox>
        <h:commandButton value="Go!"
                         styleClass="language-select-button"/>
      </h:panelGroup>

      <h:outputText value="proj_mgr" styleClass="user-name"/>

    </h:panelGrid>
```

UINavigator component

```
  </h:form>
</f:subview>
```

Using `UINavigator` this way yields the same functionality and appearance as listing 9.4. If that's the case, why bother? Well, first of all, using this component is less effort. In the first example, we had to spend time thinking about how the layout was supposed to appear, how to use the CSS classes properly, and how to create the appearance of a header button with an icon and a label. With `UINavigator`, the choices are more explicit: it has specific properties such as `layout` (either "horizontal" or "vertical"), `immediate` (which indicates whether it should be processed before other input controls), and `style` properties for the header, icon, and individual items. Each button is represented by a single `NavigatorItem`, which has properties such as `icon`, `label`, `action`, and so on. In short, all of the guesswork has been eliminated; all we have to do is declare the component and specify the necessary items.

Another benefit of `UINavigator` is that it can be associated with model objects; so the individual header buttons could either be configured using the Managed Bean Creation facility, with Java code, or pulled from a data store. We don't use these features in ProjectTrack, but they can be useful in other applications.

Now that we've finished with header.jsp, let's make it *do* something.

9.1.2 Configuring the navigation rule

In listing 9.2, each `NavigatorItem` has an `action` property. This works just like the `action` property for `HtmlCommandButton` components—it can reference either a hardcoded logical outcome or an action method. In order for these outcomes to move the user from one page to the next, we need to define a navigation rule. Because the header is included in every page, we must make this rule work for *every* page. In order to do this, we'll add the navigation rule in listing 9.3 to faces-config.xml.

Listing 9.3 faces-config.xml: Navigation rule for toolbar buttons in header

```
<navigation-rule>
  <description>Navigation for the toolbar.</description>
  <from-view-id>/*</from-view-id>
  <navigation-case>
    <from-outcome>inbox</from-outcome>
    <to-view-id>/inbox.jsp</to-view-id>
  </navigation-case>
  <navigation-case>
```

```
    <from-outcome>show_all</from-outcome>
    <to-view-id>/show_all.jsp</to-view-id>
  </navigation-case>
  <navigation-case>
    <from-outcome>create</from-outcome>
    <to-view-id>/create.jsp</to-view-id>
  </navigation-case>
  <navigation-case>
    <from-outcome>logout</from-outcome>
    <to-view-id>/login.jsp</to-view-id>
  </navigation-case>
</navigation-rule>
```

The first thing to note here is that the `<from-view-id>` element's value is "/*", which indicates that this rule applies to all pages. Also note that the value of the `<from-outcome>` elements match the values of the `NavigatorItem` `action` properties in listing 9.2.

We've kept things simple: each outcome has the same name as the corresponding view (with the exception of the .jsp extension). This works quite well in prototype situations. When we integrate these rules with real code, the outcomes may change, but the resulting view won't.

Our header is now complete, with basic navigation functionality. Let's move on to the first pages the user sees: the Inbox and Show All pages.

9.2 Prototyping data tables with panels

There are two views in ProjectTrack that list projects—the Inbox and Show All pages. Because the application is database driven, this list should be pulled from a bean, and consequently it should be dynamic. The best control for displaying dynamic lists of data is `HtmlDataTable`. However, this is a prototype without any Java code, and `HtmlDataTable` *must* be associated with a bean of some sort. So, if we're not writing any beans, how do we prototype these pages?

There are two choices:

- Configure a `List` of `Maps` with the Managed Bean Creation facility and associate it with an `HtmlDataTable`.
- Use `HtmPanelGrid` components.

The benefit of the first approach is that it's closer to the final application. The downside, however, is that it's more time-consuming to configure sample managed beans. Also, some front-end developers aren't anxious to configure objects in XML (although some tools like James Holmes's JSF Console [Holmes] simplify this process).

The second approach's primary benefit is that it's quick and easy. It's straightforward to change an `HtmlPanelGrid` declaration into an `HtmlDataTable` declaration when it's time to integrate with the back end. The downside is that if you're showing the same sample data on multiple pages, you will have to cut and paste from one page to the next, and then keep the pages in sync. This is fine for a couple of pages, but not for dozens.

Because ProjectTrack only has a couple of pages that list projects, we'll select the latter method.

9.2.1 The Inbox page

The first thing most ProjectTrack users will see is the Inbox. (Upper Managers will see the Show All page instead, and won't be able to access this page at all.) The Inbox is the page that shows all of the projects waiting for processing, and it's the one that users will typically interact with the most. Users can view details, approve, or reject any projects on this page. A mock-up is depicted in figure 9.3.

As you can see in figure 9.3, this view has a page header and a panel that contains the main content for the page. The panel has a header that states the name of the page, a row for optional application messages, and a section that comprises the main content of the page. Application messages will be displayed only if a backing bean creates a message for this page, which could happen if the user tries to approve a project that was just approved by someone else, for example.

The inner panel simulates a data table. The first row has column headers for the project fields we want to display: the project name, type, and status. The user

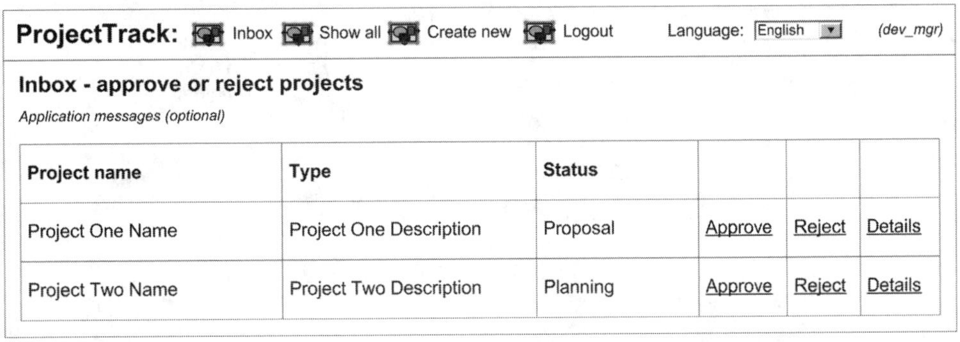

ProjectTrack: Inbox Show all Create new Logout Language: English (dev_mgr)

Inbox - approve or reject projects

Application messages (optional)

Project name	Type	Status			
Project One Name	Project One Description	Proposal	Approve	Reject	Details
Project Two Name	Project Two Description	Planning	Approve	Reject	Details

Figure 9.3 Mock-up of the Inbox page. This page lists all projects currently waiting for users, and allows them to approve, reject, or view the details of each project.

should be able to click on any of these column headers in order to re-sort the list by that column. The other rows cycle through the list of projects waiting for this user, with links for the three primary operations: approve, reject, and view details. This page is shown in listing 9.4.

Listing 9.4 Inbox.jsp: JSP source

```
<!DOCTYPE HTML PUBLIC "-//W3C//DTD HTML 4.01 Transitional//EN">

<%@ taglib uri="http://java.sun.com/jsf/core" prefix="f"%>
<%@ taglib uri="http://java.sun.com/jsf/html" prefix="h"%>

<f:view>
<html>
  <head>
    <title>
      <h:outputText value="ProjectTrack - Inbox"/>
    </title>
    <link rel="stylesheet" type="text/css"        ❶ Style sheet
          href="stylesheet.css"/>                    import
  </head>

<body class="page-background">   ❷ Background style

<jsp:include page="header.jsp"/>   ❸ Page header
                                      include
<h:form>

  <h:panelGrid headerClass="page-header"        ❹ Main
      styleClass="table-background"               panel
      columns="1" cellpadding="5">

    <f:facet name="header">                             ❺ Main panel
      <h:outputText                                        header
          value="Inbox - approve or reject projects"/>
    </f:facet>

    <h:outputText                          ❻ Messages
        value="Application messages."        placeholder
        styleClass="errors"/>
    <h:panelGrid columns="6"                              ❼ Inner
        styleClass="table-background"                       panel
        rowClasses="table-odd-row,table-even-row"
        cellpadding="3">

      <h:commandLink styleClass="table-header">          ❽ Column
        <h:outputText value="Project name"/>                headers
      </h:commandLink>
      <h:commandLink styleClass="table-header">
```

```
        <h:outputText value="Type"/>
      </h:commandLink>

      <h:commandLink styleClass="table-header">
        <h:outputText value="Status"/>
      </h:commandLink>
      <h:panelGroup/>
      <h:panelGroup/>
      <h:panelGroup/>

      <h:outputText
          value="Inventory Manager v2.0"/>
      <h:outputText
          value="Internal Desktop Application"/>
      <h:outputText
           value="Requirements/Analysis"/>
      <h:commandLink action="approve">
        <h:outputText value="Approve"/>
      </h:commandLink>
      <h:commandLink action="reject">
        <h:outputText value="Reject"/>
      </h:commandLink>
      <h:commandLink action="details">
        <h:outputText value="Details"/>
      </h:commandLink>

      <h:outputText value="TimeTracker"/>
      <h:outputText value="Internal Web Application"/>
      <h:outputText value="Requirements/Analysis"/>
      <h:commandLink action="approve">
        <h:outputText value="Approve"/>
      </h:commandLink>
      <h:commandLink action="reject">
        <h:outputText value="Reject"/>
      </h:commandLink>
      <h:commandLink action="details">
        <h:outputText value="Details"/>
      </h:commandLink>

    </h:panelGrid>

  </h:panelGrid>
</h:form>

</body>
</html>
</f:view>
```

❽ **Column headers**

❾ **Project rows**

❶ Import the CSS style sheet. We'll use the same style sheet for every other page.

2. This whole page should have a pleasant light-blue background, so we'll use a CSS style for the HTML `<body>` element.
3. We include the header with a dynamic JSP include tag.
4. This is the main panel, declared with the popular `HtmlPanelGrid` control. Because we want the heading to be large and bold, we add a CSS style for the header with the `headerClass` attribute. This panel is basically a container for the inner panel, so it has only one column.
5. Here, we specify the main panel's header, which serves as the title of the page.
6. This `HtmlOutputText` will serve as a placeholder for application messages. In chapter 10, we'll replace this with an `HtmlMessages` component. (We use `HtmlOutputText` now because `HtmlMessages` won't show anything unless there are actually messages, and because there's no back-end code in our prototype, there aren't any application messages yet.)
7. This is the inner panel, which is where all of the action takes place. It's an `HtmlPanelGrid` that simulates an `HtmlDataTable`. There are six columns, and we specify two styles for the rows so that the component will alternate between the two when it displays the rows.
8. These are the column headings. You may have noticed that these make up a *row* in the table, even though they're used as headings. Laying the components out this way allows the headings to line up in the same columns with the content in subsequent rows. Because the `HtmlPanelGrid` displays headings as a single column, this would not be possible if the components were part of a heading. (When we convert this into an `HtmlDataTable`, we'll use `UIColumn` components, which have `header` facets.)

   The first three columns are `HtmlCommandLink` components, so that we can resort the table's data when the user clicks on a column heading. In this prototype, the `action` property isn't set, so clicking on the header just redisplays the page without changes. The final three columns are simply `HtmlPanelGroup` components, which are used to create blank headings.
9. This is the actual data of the inner panel. Our prototype has only two rows, so it looks like there are two projects in the user's inbox. The first three columns display different project fields with `HtmlOutputText` components. The final three columns represent the commands you can perform on that project with `HtmlCommandLink` components. We'll create navigation cases for each of the outcomes specified by the `action` properties in the next section. Then, in chapter 10, we'll integrate them with real action methods. Once this section is integrated with the model, these rows will come from model objects instead of static data.

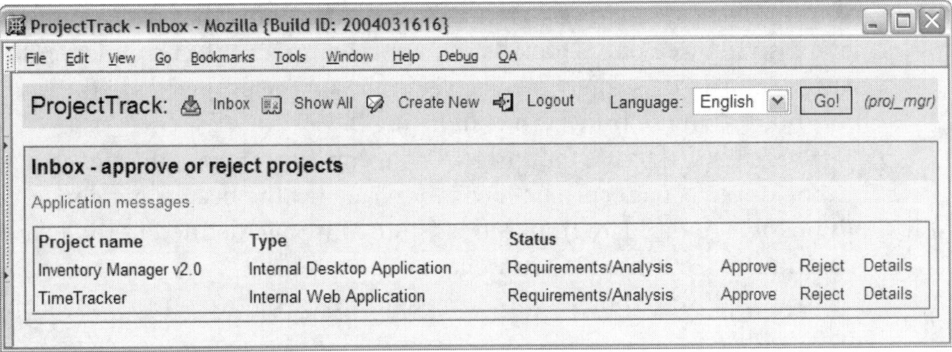

Figure 9.4 inbox.jsp: Displayed in a browser.

The output of this page is shown in figure 9.4. You can see that the header is seamlessly integrated. The use of style sheets for colors and fonts enhances the look of the page.

We have now created an attractive Inbox page. It's time to create a navigation rule for it.

9.2.2 *Configuring the navigation rule*

Each project row in the inbox has three links that perform operations for the project displayed that row. In the JSP, we specified specific outcomes for those links (we'll change this in chapter 10). Listing 9.5 shows the navigation rule that maps these outcomes to specific pages.

Listing 9.5 faces-config.xml: Navigation rule for inbox.jsp

```
<navigation-rule>
  <from-view-id>/inbox.jsp</from-view-id>
  <navigation-case>
    <from-outcome>details</from-outcome>
    <to-view-id>/details.jsp</to-view-id>
  </navigation-case>
  <navigation-case>
    <from-outcome>approve</from-outcome>
    <to-view-id>/approve.jsp</to-view-id>
  </navigation-case>
  <navigation-case>
    <from-outcome>reject</from-outcome>
    <to-view-id>/reject.jsp</to-view-id>
  </navigation-case>
</navigation-rule>
```

Nothing terribly exciting here. This rule just states that we can navigate from inbox.jsp to three pages (details.jsp, approve.jsp, or reject.jsp) depending on the outcome. All of these outcomes are set in the `action` properties of the `HtmlCommandLink` buttons in the project rows of listing 9.7.

Remember, the rule for any given page is the union of all rules that match the `<from-view-id>` pattern. The navigation rule for the header matches all pages, so it's possible to navigate from inbox.jsp to any page defined in the header's navigation rule (see listing 9.3) as well.

Now that we've built the Inbox page, we can move on to Show All, which is quite similar.

9.2.3 *The Show All page*

The Show All page is displayed to users when they want to see all of the projects, not just the ones in their own inbox. It's also the only way upper management can get to projects, because they don't have an inbox. Functionally, the page is almost exactly the same as the Inbox page, with two main differences: it displays *all* projects, and you can only view project details from the page (in other words, you can't approve or reject projects). The first point doesn't matter for our discussion right now; it will be important when we integrate the view with the back end later.

Technically, the code for Show All is almost the same except there's an extra "Waiting for" column. This column wouldn't make sense on the Inbox page, because a project is always waiting for the person who sees it listed on that page. In addition to the extra column, the buttons for approving and rejecting projects have been removed. Rather than modify the Inbox page to work for both cases, we'll take a simple approach and create a separate JSP for this page. This gives us the flexibility to vary the pages independently. Because the code isn't much different, there's no need to examine it in detail; figure 9.5 shows the page.

Now, let's take a look at this page's navigation rule.

9.2.4 *Configuring the navigation rule*

The navigation rule for the Show All page is a subset of the rule for the Inbox page; there is a single navigation case for the outcome `"details"`. The rule is shown in listing 9.6.

Listing 9.6 faces-config.xml: Navigation rule for the Show All page

```
<navigation-rule>
  <from-view-id>/show_all.jsp</from-view-id>
  <navigation-case>
```

```
      <from-outcome>details</from-outcome>
      <to-view-id>/details.jsp</to-view-id>
    </navigation-case>
  </navigation-rule>
```

We have now successfully created the two project listing pages. Next, let's examine views that allow you to create and edit projects.

9.3 Creating input forms

All of the pages we've built so far are read-only; they don't actually modify any projects. There are three views in ProjectTrack that can manipulate projects: Approve a Project, Reject a Project, and Create a Project. The Approve a Project and Create a Project pages display project information, but only allow you to update the list of completed artifacts; the Create a Project page contains input controls for all of the properties of a project. Because these pages share some functionality, some portions can be reused. Let's start by examining the Approve a Project page.

9.3.1 The Approve a Project page

When users click the Approve button on the Inbox page, they are shown an approval page for the selected project. This page displays all of the necessary details about the project, and allows them to check or uncheck completed artifacts and add a comment to the project's history. Once they've filled out the form,

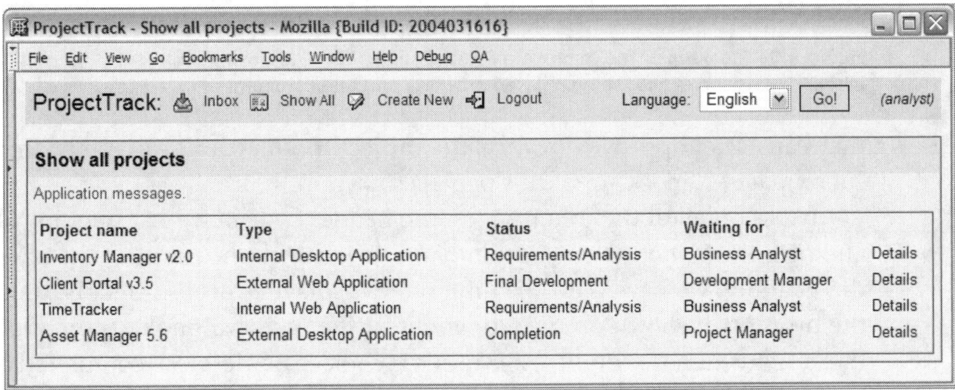

Figure 9.5 show_all.jsp: The Show All page, which lists all projects currently in the system, shown in a browser.

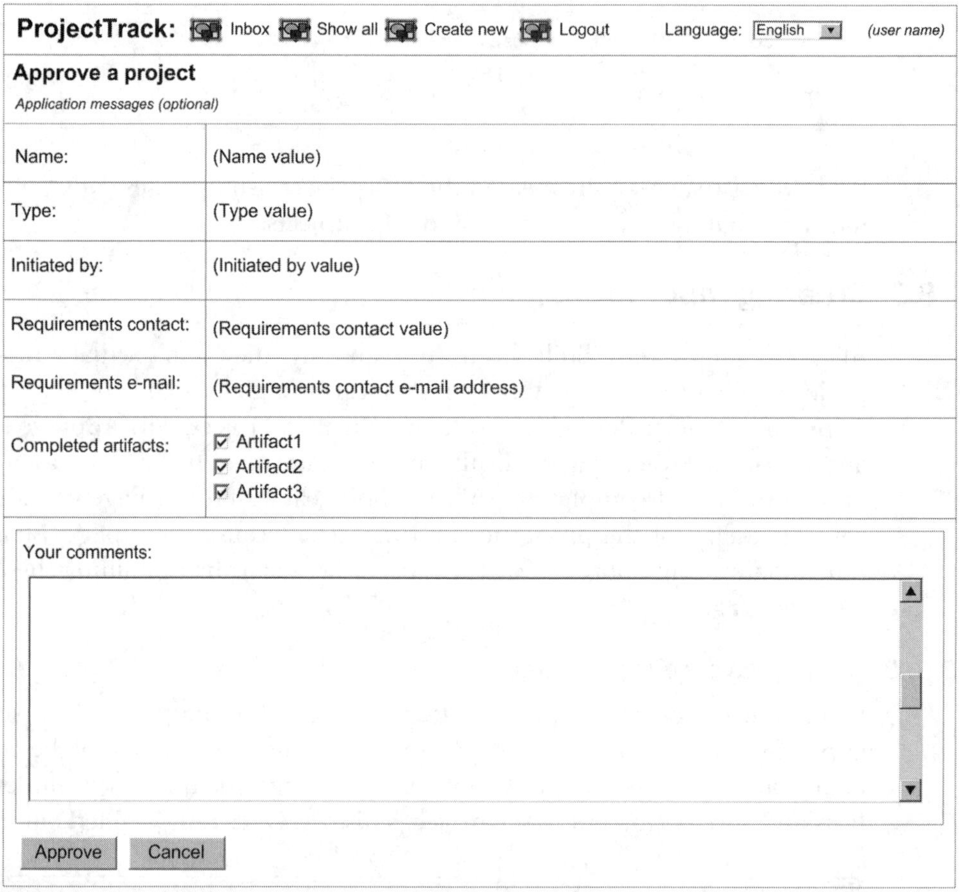

ProjectTrack: Inbox Show all Create new Logout Language: English (user name)

Approve a project

Application messages (optional)

Name:	(Name value)
Type:	(Type value)
Initiated by:	(Initiated by value)
Requirements contact:	(Requirements contact value)
Requirements e-mail:	(Requirements contact e-mail address)
Completed artifacts:	☑ Artifact1 ☑ Artifact2 ☑ Artifact3

Your comments:

Approve Cancel

Figure 9.6 Mock-up of the Approve a Project page. When approving a project (accessible from the Inbox), the user can choose completed artifacts and add comments.

they can either approve or cancel the project. Both actions will return them to the Inbox page. A mock-up of this page is shown in figure 9.6.

Just as on all of the other pages, the header is displayed at the top. This page also uses the standard convention of a title bar with the name of the page. Below the heading, we have a two-column table displaying project details; the name of the property is shown on the left, and its value is shown on the right. Only one of these fields accepts input—the user can select or deselect completed artifacts, represented via checkboxes. Below the details section, there's a text area where a user can add comments. Finally, there are two buttons—one for approval and one to cancel input—located at the bottom of primary table.

Once again, we'll use nested `HtmlPanelGrid` components to achieve this layout. The page header will be handled through a JSP include, and is separate from the rest of the layout. The rest of the screen can be handled with a main panel that has a header, a footer, and two columns. The header is used for the "Approve a project" text. The middle section will be filled with `HtmlOutputText` and `HtmlInputText` components. The footer is composed of two `HtmlPanelGrids`—one for the comments section and one for the two buttons—both contained within an `HtmlPanelGroup` so they'll be treated as a single footer element. The source is shown in listing 9.7.

Listing 9.7 approve.jsp: JSP source for the Approve a Project page

```
<!DOCTYPE HTML PUBLIC "-//W3C//DTD HTML 4.01 Transitional//EN">

<%@ taglib uri="http://java.sun.com/jsf/core" prefix="f"%>
<%@ taglib uri="http://java.sun.com/jsf/html" prefix="h" %>
<f:view>
<html>
  <head>
    <title>
      <h:outputText value="ProjectTrack - Approve a Project"/>
    </title>
    <link rel="stylesheet" type="text/css" href="stylesheet.css"/>
  </head>

<body class="page-background">

<jsp:include page="header.jsp"/>

<h:form>

  <h:panelGrid columns="2" cellpadding="5"
      headerClass="page-header"
      footerClass="project-background"
      styleClass="project-background"
      rowClasses="project-row">

     <f:facet name="header">
       <h:panelGrid columns="1"
           width="100%" cellpadding="3"
           styleClass="project-background"
           headerClass="page-header">
         <f:facet name="header">
           <h:outputText value="Approve a project"/>
         </f:facet>
         <h:outputText
             value="Application messages."
             styleClass="errors"/>
       </h:panelGrid>
     </f:facet>
```

❶ **Main panel** (annotates the `<h:panelGrid columns="2" …>` lines)

❷ **Header for main panel** (annotates the `<f:facet name="header">` block)

```
<h:outputText value="Name:"/>
<h:outputText value="Inventory Manager 2.0"
              styleClass="project-data"/>

<h:outputText value="Type:"/>
<h:outputText value="Internal Web Application"
              styleClass="project-data"/>

<h:outputText value="Initiated by:"/>
<h:outputText value="Rip Van Winkle"
              styleClass="project-data"/>

<h:outputText value="Requirements contact:"/>
<h:outputText value="Joan TooBusy"
              styleClass="project-data"/>

<h:outputText value="Requirements contact e-mail:"/>
<h:outputText value="toobusy@deathmarch.com"
              styleClass="project-data"/>

<h:outputText value="Initial comments:"/>
<h:outputText value="The first version
  is horrible and completely unusable.
  It's time to rewrite it."
              styleClass="project-data"/>

<h:outputLabel for="artifactSelect">
  <h:outputText value="Completed artifacts:"/>
</h:outputLabel>
<h:selectManyCheckbox
    id="artifactSelect"
    layout="pageDirection"
    styleClass="project-input">
  <f:selectItem itemValue="0"
      itemLabel="Proposal document"/>
  <f:selectItem itemValue="1"
      itemLabel="Requirements document"/>
  <f:selectItem itemValue="2"
      itemLabel="Architecture specification"/>
  <f:selectItem itemValue="3"
      itemLabel="Test plan"/>
  <f:selectItem itemValue="4"
      itemLabel="Deployment guidelines"/>
  <f:selectItem itemValue="5"
      itemLabel="Maintenance documentation"/>
  <f:selectItem itemValue="6"
      itemLabel="User documentation"/>
</h:selectManyCheckbox>

<f:facet name="footer">
```

❸ **Project info display**

❹ **Artifact selection**

```
      <h:panelGroup>   <-(5) Group for footer components

        <h:panelGrid columns="1" cellpadding="5"
            styleClass="table-background"
            rowClasses="table-odd-row,
                        table-even-row">
          <h:outputLabel for="commentsInput">
            <h:outputText value="Your comments:"/>      (6) Panel for comments
          </h:outputLabel>
          <h:inputTextarea id="commentsInput"
              rows="10" cols="80"/>
        </h:panelGrid>

        <h:panelGrid columns="2"
           rowClasses="table-odd-row">
          <h:commandButton value="Approve"
             action="approve"/>
          <h:commandButton value="Cancel"                (7) Panel for buttons
             action="cancel"
             immediate="true"/>
        </h:panelGrid>
      </h:panelGroup>

    </f:facet>

  </h:panelGrid>

</h:form>

</body>
</html>
</f:view>
```

❶ This is the main panel. Note that we've specified several CSS styles to control the panel's appearance. The rendered table will have two columns, as per our mock-up.

❷ There's currently no JSF equivalent to the `colspan` attribute of an HTML table row, so in order to have both the header text "Approve a project" and the application messages placeholder span all of the columns, they must be in a `header` facet. We group them in an `HtmlPanelGrid` component to make sure that each component is in a separate row, control spacing, and ensure that styles apply to the whole row (as opposed to just the component's text). We also emphasize the entire `header` with a border, courtesy of the "project-background" style.

It may seem like an `HtmlPanelGroup` would work fine here, too, but you can't control the layout of the child components with `HtmlPanelGroup`. If we had used it, the header text and the application messages would have displayed right after each other, rather than in separate rows.

❸ These components display the project's details—for each pair, there will be one row with an `HtmlOutputText` component in each column. Note that we apply a style to the second component in each row; this is to ensure that the property's value is a different color than its description. For example, the text "Requirements contact:" will be in a different color than its value, which is "Joan TooBusy".

As it turns out, this whole section can be reused in the Reject a Project and Project Details pages. In order to avoid repeating this work, we can separate it into a separate file called project_info.jsp and include it with a static include:

```
<%@ include file="project_info.jsp"%>
```

❹ Unlike the other project properties, the artifacts can be changed during the approval process. This section specifies an `HtmlSelectManyCheckbox` instance, which displays a set of checkboxes so that users may select or deselect any of the listed artifacts. When we integrate this page with the application, we'll pull the items from a model object instead of hardcoding them in the JSP.

Like the project info section, this too can be reused; as a matter of fact, we can reuse it in the Reject a Project and Create a Project pages. We'll factor it out into a separate JSP called project_artifacts.jsp and include it in these pages:

```
<%@ include file="project_artifacts.jsp"%>
```

❺ This panel groups the footer components.

❻ This panel is used for displaying the `HtmlOutputText` and `HtmlInputText` components for gathering comments. It uses an `HtmlPanelGrid` with a single column, so that the `HtmlOutputText` component will be the first row, and the `HtmlInputText` (rendered as a text area) will be the second row. Because two different CSS classes are specified for the `rowClasses` attribute, the row will alternate styles.

This section can also be moved into an external JSP and included in the other project pages:

```
<%@ include file="project_comments.jsp"%>
```

❼ This `HtmlPanelGrid` is used to lay out the two `HtmlCommandButtons` in a single row of two columns. Note that the Cancel button has the `immediate` property set to `true`. For our prototype, this makes no difference, but in the real application, this will ensure that JSF bypasses validation and simply jumps back to the inbox. In general, Cancel buttons should have the `immediate` property set to `true`, because the goal is normally to bypass input processing.

The output of this page is shown in figure 9.7. There are two buttons on this page, so now we need to configure navigation cases for them.

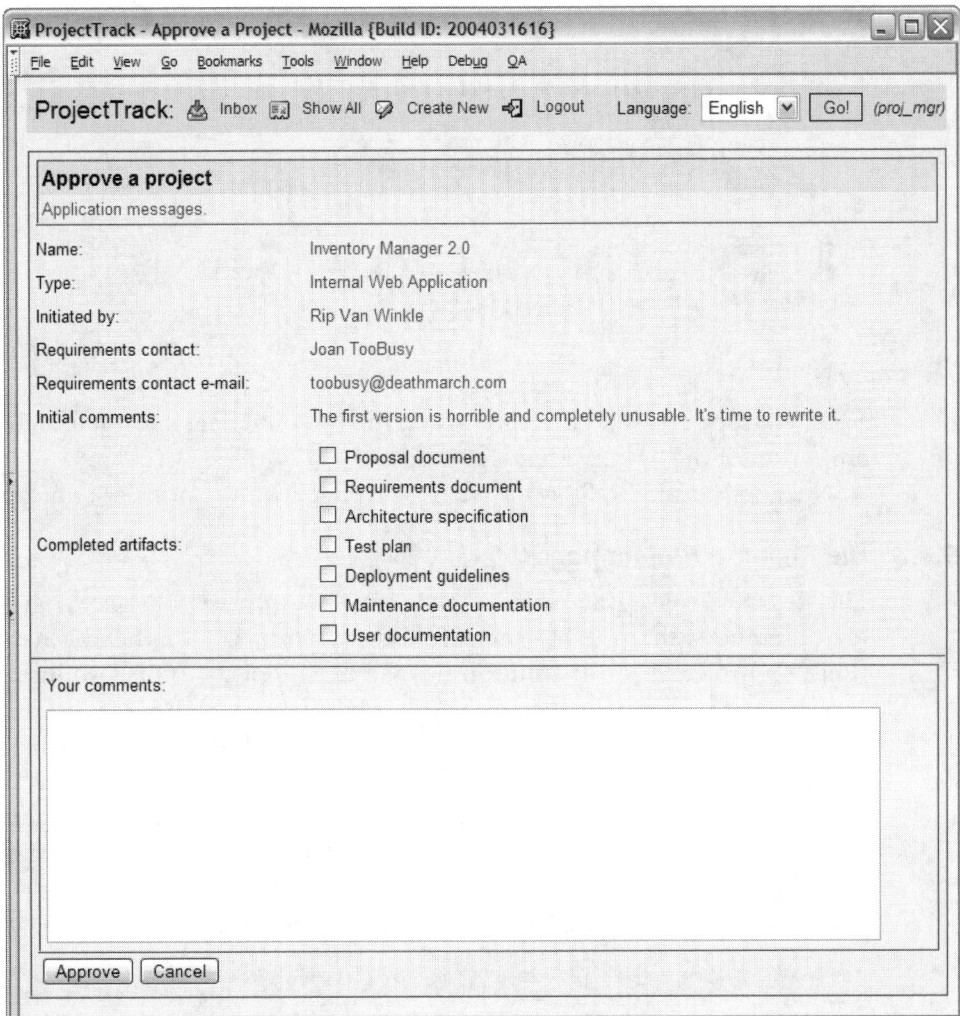

Figure 9.7 approve.jsp: The Approve a Project page in a browser

9.3.2 Configuring the navigation rule

The navigation rule for Approve a Project is pretty simple—the outcomes from both buttons return to inbox.jsp. The rule is shown in listing 9.8.

Listing 9.8 faces-config.xml: Navigation rule for approve.jsp

```
<navigation-rule>
  <from-view-id>/approve.jsp</from-view-id>
  <navigation-case>
    <from-outcome>approve</from-outcome>
    <to-view-id>/inbox.jsp</to-view-id>
  </navigation-case>
  <navigation-case>
    <from-outcome>cancel</from-outcome>
    <to-view-id>/inbox.jsp</to-view-id>
  </navigation-case>
</navigation-rule>
```

Note that the specified outcomes match the two outcomes specified in the `action` properties of the two `HtmlCommandButtons`.

Next, let's examine Reject a Project—a page with the opposite functionality.

9.3.3 The Reject a Project page

The Reject a Project page looks exactly like the Approve a Project page with two key differences: the title has the text "Reject a project," the header has the text "Reject a project," and the button has the text "Reject." (Once we integrate the application functionality, the pages will call different action methods as well.) For simplicity, we won't parameterize the Approve a Project page to make these changes. However, we will include the JSPs factored out of the Approve a Project page. This approach has the added benefit of allowing the overall look and feel of each page to vary independently, while ensuring consistency for specific sections.

The JSP code, with common sections included, is shown in listing 9.9. Lines that are different than approve.jsp are marked in bold.

Listing 9.9 reject.jsp: JSP source for the Reject a Project page

```
<!DOCTYPE HTML PUBLIC "-//W3C//DTD HTML 4.01 Transitional//EN">

<%@ taglib uri="http://java.sun.com/jsf/core" prefix="f"%>
<%@ taglib uri="http://java.sun.com/jsf/html" prefix="h"%>

<f:view>
<html>
  <head>
    <title>
      <h:outputText value="ProjectTrack - Reject a Project"/>
    </title>
    <link rel="stylesheet" type="text/css"
```

```
          href="stylesheet.css"/>
  </head>

<body class="page-background">
<jsp:include page="header.jsp"/>

<h:form>

  <h:panelGrid columns="2" cellpadding="5"
      footerClass="project-background"
      styleClass="project-background"
      rowClasses="project-row">

    <f:facet name="header">
      <h:panelGrid columns="1" width="100%" cellpadding="3"
                   styleClass="project-background"
                   headerClass="page-header">
        <f:facet name="header">
          <h:outputText value="Reject a project"/>
        </f:facet>
        <h:outputText value="Application messages."
                      styleClass="errors"/>
      </h:panelGrid>
    </f:facet>

    <%@ include file="project_info.jsp"%>
    <%@ include file="project_artifacts.jsp"%>

    <f:facet name="footer">
      <h:panelGroup>

        <%@ include file="project_comments.jsp"%>

        <h:panelGrid columns="2" rowClasses="table-odd-row">
          <h:commandButton value="Reject" action="reject"/>
          <h:commandButton value="Cancel" action="cancel"
                           immediate="true"/>
        </h:panelGrid>

      </h:panelGroup>
    </f:facet>

  </h:panelGrid>

</h:form>

</body>
</html>
</f:view>
```

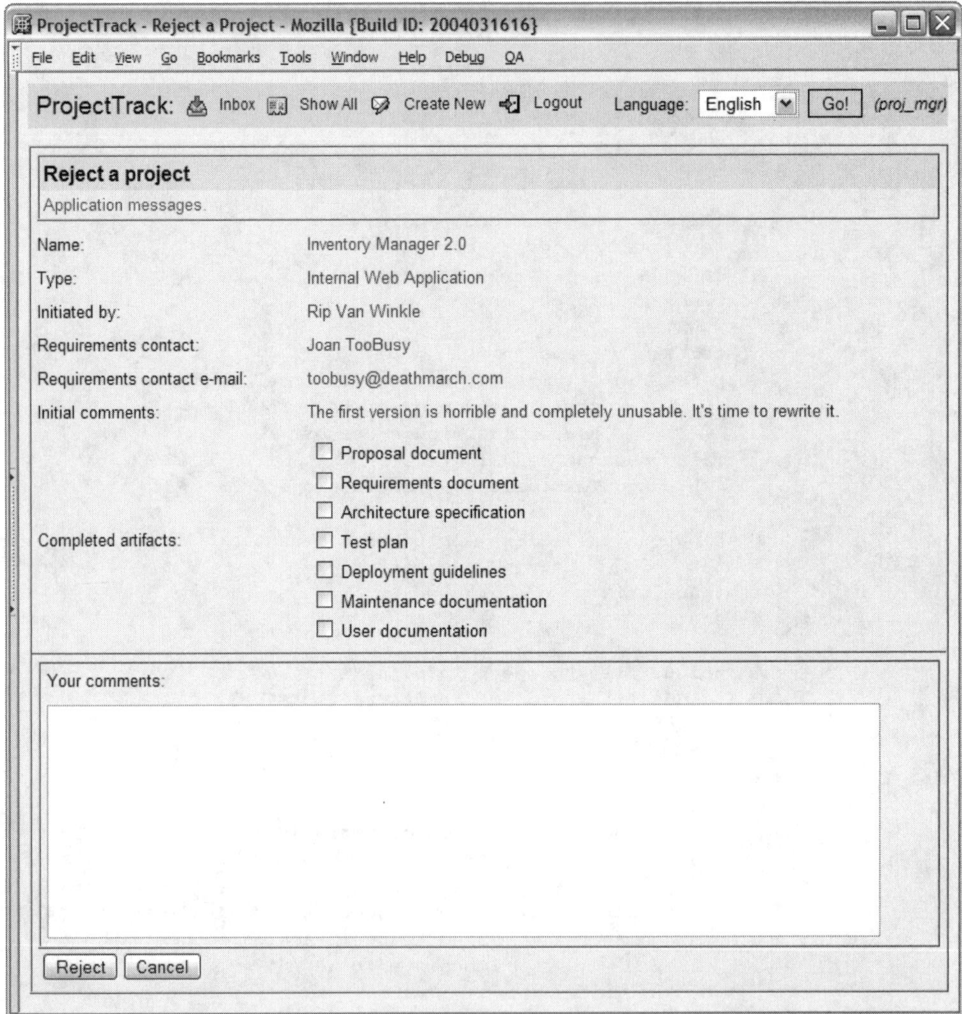

Figure 9.8 reject.jsp: The Reject a Project page in a browser. This page is similar to Approve a Project, and can be accessed from the Inbox. The user can select completed artifacts and add comments before rejecting the project.

The output of this page is shown in figure 9.8.

Like Approve a Project, the navigation rule for this page is quite simple.

9.3.4 Configuring the navigation rule

There are two buttons on the Reject a Project page, so there are two navigation cases in the page's navigation rule, as shown in listing 9.10.

Listing 9.10 faces-config.xml: Navigation rule for the Reject a Project page

```
<navigation-rule>
  <from-view-id>/reject.jsp</from-view-id>
  <navigation-case>
    <from-outcome>reject</from-outcome>
    <to-view-id>/inbox.jsp</to-view-id>
  </navigation-case>
  <navigation-case>
    <from-outcome>cancel</from-outcome>
    <to-view-id>/inbox.jsp</to-view-id>
  </navigation-case>
</navigation-rule>
```

As you can see, both cases send the user back to the Inbox page.

Now let's examine a page with several input controls.

9.3.5 The Create a Project page

The Create a Project view allows Project Managers to construct a new project; it's accessible from the toolbar in the header. It's similar to the Approve a Project and Reject a Project pages. The main difference is that the user can edit all of the properties of the project. Because the page uses validators, it also has space for validation errors. The comments section refers to the initial set of comments, as opposed to comments that are part of the project's history. A mock-up of this page is shown in figure 9.9.

From a layout perspective, the main difference between this page and the Approve and Reject pages is the extra column for displaying errors. The Initial comments field has been removed as well, because the comments entered on this for *are* the initial comments. We'll use `HtmlInputText` components for all of the fields, and keep the `HtmlSelectManyCheckbox` component for the completed artifacts section. We'll also attach validators to some of the fields, including a custom validator. Because the comments field for this page has a different purpose, we won't reuse project_comments.jsp. The source is shown in listing 9.11; we will only discuss elements that are different than the previous two pages.

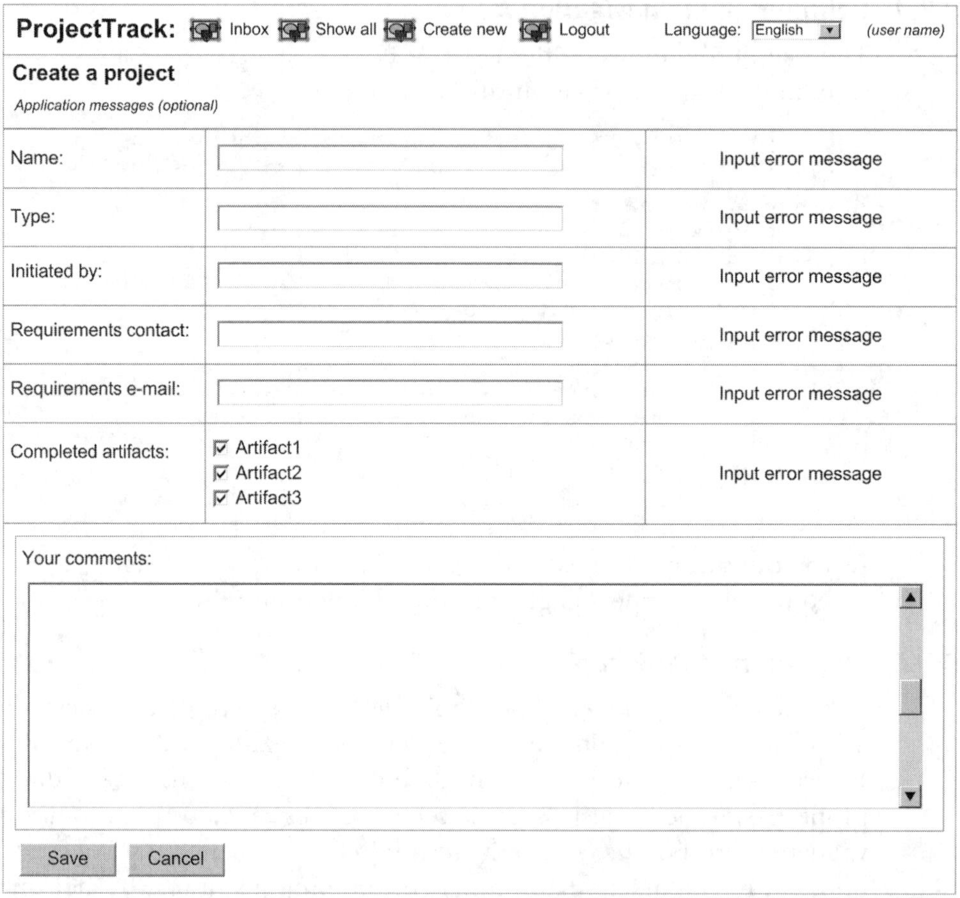

ProjectTrack: Inbox Show all Create new Logout Language: English *(user name)*

Create a project

Application messages (optional)

Name:		Input error message
Type:		Input error message
Initiated by:		Input error message
Requirements contact:		Input error message
Requirements e-mail:		Input error message
Completed artifacts:	Artifact1 Artifact2 Artifact3	Input error message

Your comments:

Save Cancel

Figure 9.9 Mock-up of the Create a Project page. In this page, the user can initialize all of the project's fields.

Listing 9.11 JSP source for the Create a Project page

```
<!DOCTYPE HTML PUBLIC "-//W3C//DTD HTML 4.01 Transitional//EN">

<%@ taglib uri="http://java.sun.com/jsf/core" prefix="f"%>
<%@ taglib uri="http://java.sun.com/jsf/html" prefix="h"%>
<%@ taglib uri="jsf-in-action-components"
           prefix="jia"%>

<f:view>

<html>
  <head>
    <title>
```

❶ **Custom validator import**

```
      <h:outputText value="ProjectTrack - Create a new project"/>
    </title>
    <link rel="stylesheet" type="text/css"
          href="stylesheet.css"/>
  </head>

<body class="page-background">

<jsp:include page="header.jsp"/>

<h:form>
  <h:panelGrid columns="3" cellpadding="5"
      footerClass="project-background"
      styleClass="project-background"
      rowClasses="project-row"
      columnClasses=",project-input">

    <f:facet name="header">
      <h:panelGrid columns="1" width="100%" cellpadding="3"
                   styleClass="project-background"
                   headerClass="page-header">
        <f:facet name="header">
          <h:outputText value="Create a project"/>
        </f:facet>
        <h:outputText value="Application messages."
                      styleClass="errors"/>
      </h:panelGrid>
    </f:facet>

    <h:outputLabel for="nameInput">
      <h:outputText value="Name:"/>
    </h:outputLabel>
    <h:inputText id="nameInput" size="40"
                 required="true">
      <f:validateLength minimum="5"/>
    </h:inputText>
    <h:message for="nameInput"
               styleClass="errors"/>

    <h:outputLabel for="typeSelectOne">
      <h:outputText value="Type:"/>
    </h:outputLabel>
    <h:selectOneMenu id="typeSelectOne"
         title="Select the project type"
         required="true">
      <f:selectItem  itemValue="" itemLabel=""/>
      <f:selectItem  itemValue="0"
         itemLabel="Internal Database"/>
      <f:selectItem  itemValue="5"
         itemLabel="External Database"/>
      <f:selectItem  itemValue="10"
         itemLabel="Internal Web Application"/>
```

2 Main panel with extra column

3 Project info edit fields with validators

```
  <f:selectItem  itemValue="15"
     itemLabel="External Web Application"/>
  <f:selectItem  itemValue="20"
     itemLabel="Internal Desktop Application" />
  <f:selectItem  itemValue="25"
     itemLabel="External Desktop      Application"/>
</h:selectOneMenu>
<h:message for="typeSelectOne" styleClass="errors"/>

<h:outputLabel for="initiatedByInput">
  <h:outputText value="Initiated by:"/>
</h:outputLabel>
<h:inputText id="initiatedByInput"
    size="40" required="true">
  <f:validateLength minimum="2"/>
</h:inputText>
<h:message for="initiatedByInput"
    styleClass="errors"/>

<h:outputLabel for="requirementsInput">
  <h:outputText
      value="Requirements contact:"/>
</h:outputLabel>
<h:inputText id="requirementsInput"
      size="40"/>
<h:panelGroup/>

<h:outputLabel for="requirementsEmailInput">
 <h:outputText value="Requirements contact e-mail:"/>
</h:outputLabel>
<h:inputText id="requirementsEmailInput" size="40">
  <jia:validateRegEx
      expression="\\w+([-+.]\\w+)*@\\w
                 +([-.]\\w+)*\\.\\w+([-.]\\w+)*"
      errorMessage="Please enter a
            valid e-mail address."/>
</h:inputText>
<h:message for="requirementsEmailInput"
    styleClass="errors"/>

<%@ include file="project_artifacts.jsp" %>
<h:panelGroup/>

<f:facet name="footer">

   <h:panelGroup>

    <h:panelGrid columns="1" cellpadding="5"
                 styleClass="table-background"
                 rowClasses="table-odd-row,table-even-row">
      <h:outputLabel for="commentsInput">
        <h:outputText value="Your comments:"/>
      </h:outputLabel>
```

3 Project info edit fields with validators

```
          <h:inputTextarea id="commentsInput" rows="10" cols="80"/>
        </h:panelGrid>

        <h:panelGrid columns="2" rowClasses="table-odd-row">
           <h:commandButton value="Save" action="save"/>
           <h:commandButton value="Cancel" action="cancel"
                            immediate="true"/>
         </h:panelGrid>
         <h:panelGroup/>

       </h:panelGroup>

    </f:facet>

  </h:panelGrid>

</h:form>

</body>
</html>
</f:view>
```

❶ This line imports the tag library for the custom validator.

❷ This is the main panel; it has three columns, the last of which is for displaying validation errors.

❸ These tags specify the input fields with an `HtmlSelectOneMenu` component and several `HtmlInputText` components. The `size` property is passed through to the HTML. All of the components were assigned `id` attributes so that they can be referenced by validators and labels.

The fields that have validation requirements each have one or more validators attached, and the required ones have the `required` property set to `true`. For the `HtmlSelectOneMenu` component, the default item has an empty value and label. Because the component's `required` property is `true`, this means that it will consider the value to be empty unless the user selects something else.

Some of the components have length requirements as well, so they use the `Length` validator. The `HtmlInputText` component for the requirement contact's email uses a custom `RegularExpression` validator to make sure the email address is in the correct format. The validator's `expression` property tells it which pattern to match, and the `errorMessage` property tells it which error message to display if the validation fails. (For more information about this validator, see online extension chapter 20.)

Validation errors are displayed in the extra column with `HtmlMessage` components, whose `for` property matches the component identifier of the associated input control. For components that don't have any validators, an empty panel group is used as a placeholder for the third column.

The `HtmlSelectOneMenu` component's items are hardcoded currently, but they will come from the model in the final application.

Figure 9.10 shows the page with some validation errors. As you can see, they are displayed in the right column. Note that the error messages are friendlier than the defaults; this is because we customized them in chapter 8. The navigation rule for this page isn't much different than the other pages.

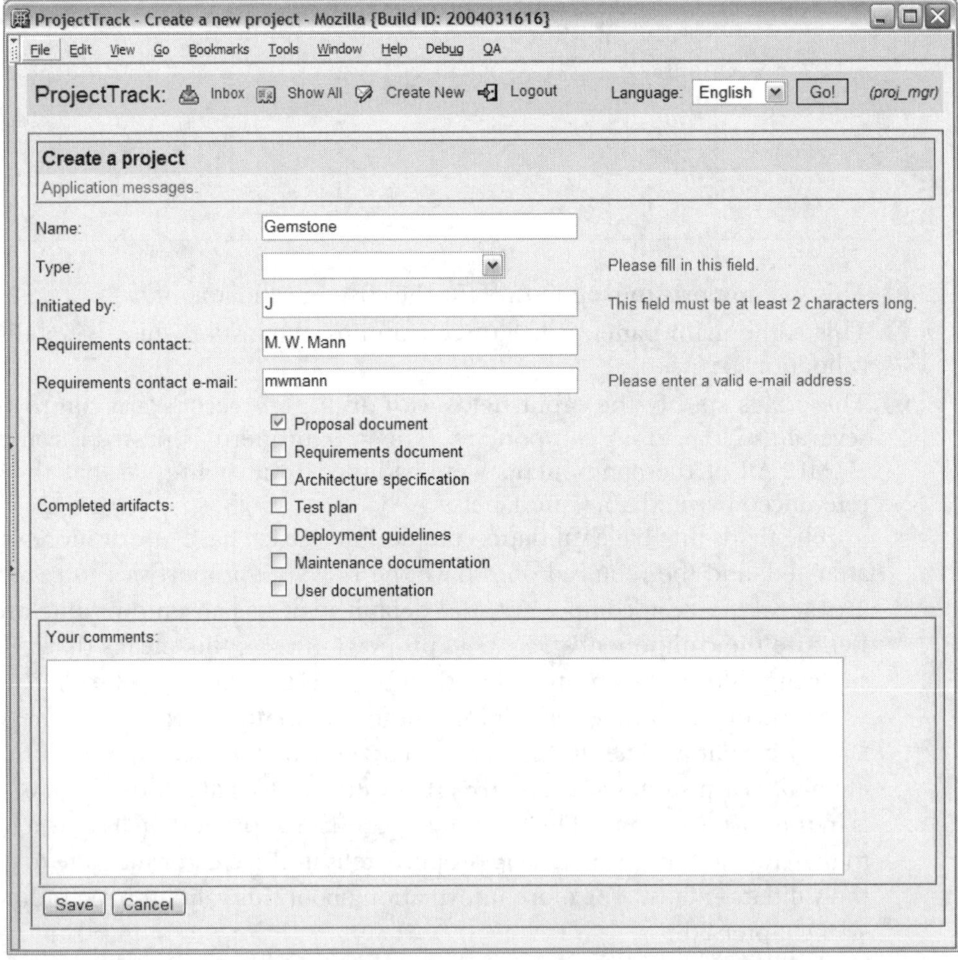

Figure 9.10 create.jsp: The Create a Project page in a browser, with validation errors. The Type field was left blank, the Initiated by field is too short, and the email address is invalid. The other fields passed validation.

9.3.6 Configuring the navigation rule

The two buttons on this page—Save and Cancel—both return the user to the inbox.jsp page. In the real application, we'll modify the rule so that the Save button returns the user to the page from which they arrived—either the Inbox or the Show All page. The navigation rule is shown in listing 9.12.

Listing 9.12 faces-config.xml: Navigation rule for the Create a Project page

```
<navigation-rule>
  <from-view-id>/create.jsp</from-view-id>
  <navigation-case>
    <from-outcome>save</from-outcome>
    <to-view-id>/inbox.jsp</to-view-id>
  </navigation-case>
  <navigation-case>
    <from-outcome>cancel</from-outcome>
    <to-view-id>/inbox.jsp</to-view-id>
  </navigation-case>
</navigation-rule>
```

Now, let's finish the prototype with one last page that displays all of a project's properties and its history.

9.4 The Project Details page

The Project Details page displays all of the project's information, as well as its history. The history keeps track of each operation (approval or rejection), when it was performed, who performed it, and the user's comments. This page is somewhat similar to the Approve and Reject a Project pages, except that there are no input fields, and it displays the history instead of collecting comments. Because this view doesn't perform any work, there's only one button. Figure 9.11 shows a mock-up of this page.

Because this page displays the same set of project information as the Approve a Project and Reject a Project pages, we can reuse the same JSP include used in those pages. However, because the artifact listing isn't included in that include we must add that that section.

The interesting part of this page is the history. In our prototype, we'll just include two fictitious entries, but in the real application there could be several (one for every time the project is approved or rejected). This means that the history is the perfect candidate for an `HtmlDataTable`; however, we'll prototype it with an `HtmlPanelGrid`, as we did for the Inbox and Show All pages. The JSP

ProjectTrack: Inbox Show all Create new Logout Language: English (user name)

Project details

Name:	(Name value)
Type:	(Type value)
Initiated by:	(Initiated by value)
Requirements contact:	(Requirements contact value)
Requirements e-mail:	(Requirements contact e-mail address)
Initial comments:	(Comments from when project was created)
Completed artifacts:	Artifact1 Artifact2 Artifact3

History

(Date operation was performed) (From status) -> (To status) (User who performed operation)

Comments:

(Comments from when project was approved or rejected.)

(Date operation was performed) (From status) -> (To status) (User who performed operation)

Comments:

(Comments from when project was approved or rejected.)

OK

Figure 9.11 Mock-up of the Project Details page, which displays all of the project's properties, as well as its history. The history includes entries for every time the project was approved or rejected.

source is shown in listing 9.13; only portions that are different than the previous pages are annotated.

Listing 9.13 details.jsp: JSP source for the Project Details page

```
<!DOCTYPE HTML PUBLIC "-//W3C//DTD HTML 4.01 Transitional//EN">

<%@ taglib uri="http://java.sun.com/jsf/core" prefix="f"%>
```

```
<%@ taglib uri="http://java.sun.com/jsf/html" prefix="h"%>

<f:view>
<html>
  <head>
    <title>
      <h:outputText value="ProjectTrack - Project details"/>
    </title>
    <link rel="stylesheet" type="text/css"
          href="stylesheet.css"/>
  </head>
<body class="page-background">

<jsp:include page="header.jsp"/>

<h:form>

  <h:panelGrid id="projectPanel" columns="2" cellpadding="5"
      footerClass="project-background"
      columnClasses=",project-data"
      styleClass="project-background"
      rowClasses="project-row">
    <f:facet name="header">
      <h:panelGrid columns="1" width="100%"
                   cellpadding="3"
                   styleClass="project-background"
                   rowClasses="page-header">
          <h:outputText value="Project details"/>
      </h:panelGrid>
    </f:facet>

    <%@ include file="project_info.jsp" %>

    <h:outputText value="Completed artifacts:"/>
    <h:panelGrid columns="1"
               rowClasses="project-data"
               cellpadding="0" cellspacing="0">
      <h:outputText value="Proposal document"/>
      <h:outputText value="Project plan"/>
    </h:panelGrid>

    <f:facet name="footer">
     <h:panelGroup>
      <h:panelGrid columns="1" cellpadding="5"
                   styleClass="table-background">

         <f:facet name="header">
           <h:outputText value="History" styleClass="table-header"/>
         </f:facet>
```

❶ Header without messages

❷ JSP include for project info

❸ Artifacts display

❹ Groups panels for footer

❺ Panel for history

```
<h:panelGrid columns="1" width="100%" border="1"
      styleClass="table-even-row">

 <h:panelGrid columns="3" cellpadding="7"
      styleClass="table-even-row">
   <h:outputText
     value="Tuesday, March 4,
            2003 04:30 PM"/>
   <h:outputText
      value="Proposal -> Planning"/>
   <h:outputText
      value="(Project Manager)"/>
 </h:panelGrid>

 <h:panelGrid columns="1"
     cellpadding="3"
     styleClass="table-odd-row"
     width="100%">
   <h:outputText value="Comments:"/>
   <h:outputText
       value="Funding has been
         approved. The users are
         excited about the
         prospect of having
         something they can use."
       styleClass="project-data"/>
 </h:panelGrid>
</h:panelGrid>
```

❻ **Panel for history entry**

```
<h:panelGrid columns="1" width="100%" border="1"
              styleClass="table-even-row">

 <h:panelGrid columns="3" cellpadding="7"
    styleClass="table-even-row">
   <h:outputText value="Monday, August 11, 2003 08:30 PM"/>
   <h:outputText value="Planning -> Requirements/Analysis"/>
   <h:outputText value="(Project Manager)"/>
 </h:panelGrid>

 <h:panelGrid columns="1" cellpadding="3"
    styleClass="table-odd-row" width="100%">
   <h:outputText value="Comments:"/>
  <h:outputText value="Initial resources have been allocated and a
                        rough plan has been developed."
               styleClass="project-data"/>
 </h:panelGrid>
 </h:panelGrid>
</h:panelGrid>

<h:commandButton value="OK" action="inbox"
                  style="margin-top: 5px"/>
```

❼ **Single button**

```
            </h:panelGroup>
      </f:facet>

    </h:panelGrid>

  </h:form>

  </body>
  </html>
  </f:view>
```

❶ This page doesn't perform any processing, so there's no need to display application messages. Consequently, the `header` facet is a little simpler than the previous pages. It's an `HtmlPanelGrid` with a single row, which contains an `HtmlOutputText` component with the text "Project details". Why place it in a panel at all? We need to place it in some type of panel in order to place a box around it; that panel must be an `HtmlPanelGrid` to ensure that that the box is stretched the entire length of the enclosing table. (`HtmlPanelGroup` doesn't offer this level of control, because it renders to a `<span>` element.)

❷ Here, we include the JSP that was factored out of the Approve a Project page. This page displays all of the basic project properties.

❸ Unlike the previous pages, we only display the completed artifacts.

❹ This panel groups two child components for the `footer` facet—an `HtmlPanelGrid` and an `HtmlCommandButton`.

❺ This `HtmlPanelGrid` groups together all of the history entries. This component will be replaced with an `HtmlDataTable` in chapter 10.

❻ Each history entry is enclosed in another `HtmlPanelGrid`, which has two nested `HtmlPanelGrid` components. This is necessary to ensure that the two sections—the history entry's header information (date stamp, username, etc.) and the comments—are laid out separately.

❼ This page has a single button, so there's no need to use another panel to lay out two buttons, as we did in the previous pages. We do, however, specify a `style` property to ensure that there's a reasonable amount of space above the button. This space was created by the button panel in the other pages.

Figure 9.12 shows the Project Details page in a browser.

Last but not least, let's examine this page's navigation rule.

9.4.1 Configuring the navigation rule

In our prototype, there's only one path from the Project Details page: the Inbox. The `action` property of the view's solitary `HtmlCommandButton` is `"inbox"`, which

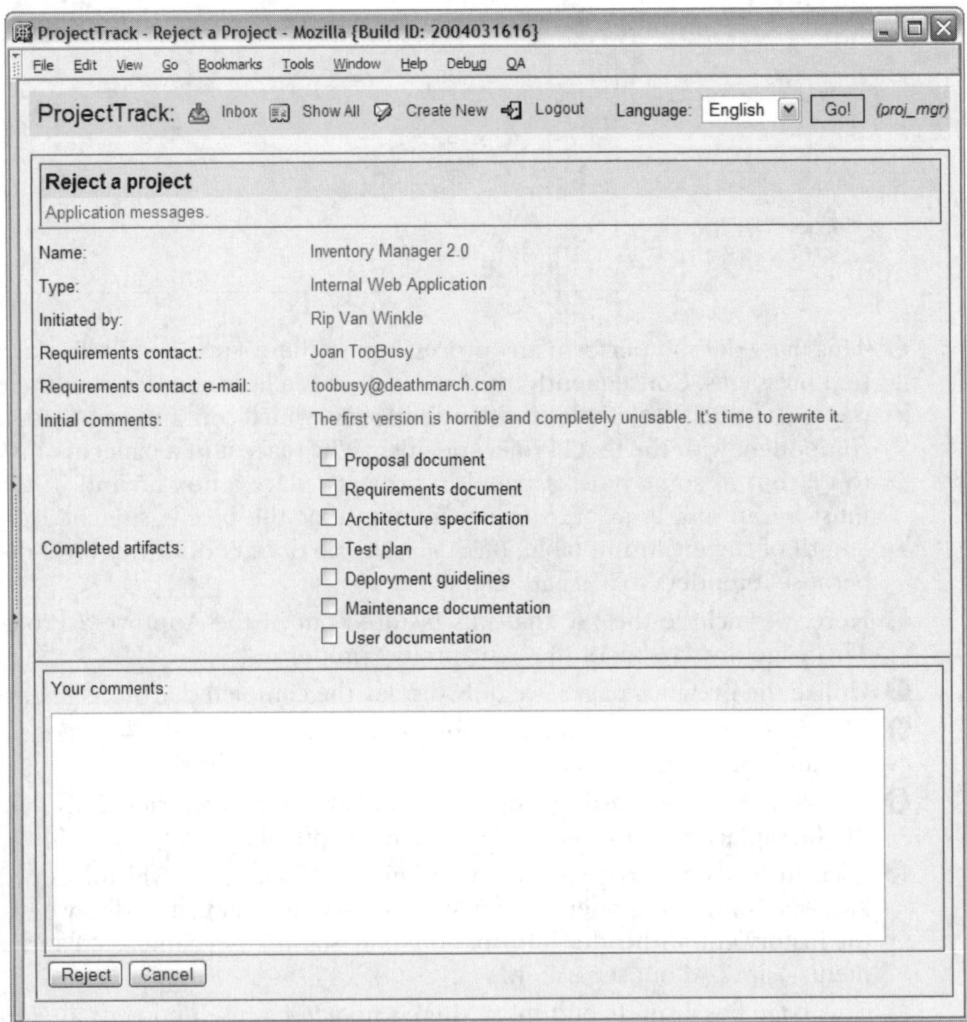

Figure 9.12 details.jsp: The Project Details page shown in a browser.

happens to be one of the global outcomes we handled in listing 9.3. In that navigation rule, which we defined for the toolbar's navigation, the outcome of `"inbox"` is mapped to inbox.jsp. Because this case has already been handled, there's no need to create a new navigation rule.

In the real application, we'll make sure that users return to either the Inbox or the Show All page, depending on how they accessed the Project Details page.

9.5 Summary

Using the techniques learned in our detailed discussion of the login page, we built the other pages of the application, starting with the header. The header can be included in all of the other pages. After we built an initial version of the toolbar portion of the header (which provides navigation), we then incorporated a custom toolbar component from online extension part 5 of this book. Next, we built the Inbox and Show All pages—these are the main pages of the application. These pages used `HtmlPanelGrid` components to create a static prototype of tables that will eventually be generated by `HtmlDataTable` with a dynamic data source.

We then moved on to pages that are built for data input—the Approve, Reject, and Create a Project pages. All of them are similar, allowing you to modify properties of a project and then submit the changes back to the server. The Create a Project page, however, allows you to modify all of the project's fields and make use of validators. We even used a custom regular expression validator from online extension part 5. Finally, we built the Project Details page, which displays all of the project's properties as well as history of all previous approvals and rejections.

At this point, we've created a fully navigational, interactive user interface, with a custom component, a custom validator, and use of the standard validators. All of ProjectTrack's views have been developed. The screens may present static data, but they show exactly what the application will look like. It's certainly possible to create an interactive demo with pure HTML and CSS. However, integrating that demo with the application involves basically rewriting every single page, tediously integrating Java scriplets or (we hope) tag libraries like JSTL. Using JSF to do your prototype makes integration much easier—once your beans have been developed, you simply wire all of the components up to the proper objects. And guess what? That's the subject of the next chapter.

10 Integrating application functionality

This chapter covers

- Different JSF front-end development approaches
- Integrating prototypical pages with back-end objects
- Converting static `HtmlPanelGrid`s into dynamic `HtmlDataTable`s
- Internationalizing and localizing the UI

We spent the last two chapters building a prototypical JSF user interface (UI) without any application code. (If you haven't yet read chapters 8 and 9, we highly suggest that you take a look at them first.) Now it's time to bring that UI to life. In this chapter, we'll integrate it with backing beans and model objects developed by the application developer.

For the most part, this work simply requires wiring up UI component values with backing bean properties and attaching UI components to event listener methods. It's something that can be done iteratively, integrating a single page at a time. This means that your prototype can spring to life over time, in response to user feedback. Once we've finished creating a fully functional application, we'll internationalize it and then localize it for English and Russian.

Integrating the UI with ProjectTrack's back-end requires an understanding of backing beans and model objects that have been created by the application developer. Before we examine those objects, let's take a look at some other JSF development approaches that don't require a full object model on the back-end.

10.1 Understanding JSF development approaches

With RAD-style tools like Visual Studio .NET, Visual Basic, or Delphi, you often build forms with UI components that interact directly with data source objects. In this approach, you don't necessarily have to have a full object model of your application; you can simply connect each view to a data source, such as a database or a web service. This form-centric style of development, as shown in figure 10.1, is certainly possible with JSF.

The basic idea behind this approach is that each view is associated with a single backing bean, and that backing bean has objects that represent data sources for that page. You can then wire up components on the view directly to the data sources through the backing beans, and the application developer can write action methods that perform any operations (which usually update the data store

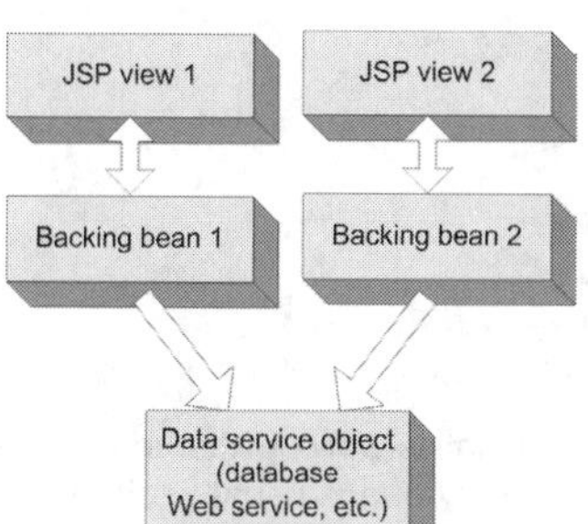

Figure 10.1
Form-centric development associates backing beans directly with data sources, and usually has one backing bean per view.

directly). This is fundamentally the same as using "data-aware" controls, which in tools like Delphi are associated directly with an underlying data source. Some tools, like Sun's Java Studio Creator [Sun, Creator], make this approach easy by allowing you to easily browse for data sources and then add them to your backing bean.

The form-centric approach works well for small applications. For larger systems, and those that need to be maintained over a long time period, JSF supports a more object-oriented approach that is more familiar to Struts developers and users of other frameworks. This approach requires developing model objects that represent the business domain, and then backing beans that work with the view and access the model objects.

In this approach, a backing bean may be associated with one or more views, and the source of the data is abstracted from the front-end developer, as shown in figure 10.2. (The figure leaves out the application layer objects, which are invisible to the UI; we discuss these in chapters 12 and 13.) Of course, it's possible to combine the two approaches. For example, there could be a `User` object that is available for the life of the user's session, even though UI components are wired directly to data service objects.

NOTE IDEs will often generate one backing bean per page. This approach is certainly easy to handle (especially for tools), and works well in many cases. JSF can support much more complicated scenarios, however. And, in some cases, it is useful to associate the same backing bean with more than one page.

For ProjectTrack, we take the object-based approach, largely because it's more familiar to users of other Java web frameworks, and also because it exhibits the high level of flexibility that JSF provides. Regardless of the approach, integration of the UI is similar—you wire up components to backing bean properties and event listeners. The key difference is that in the form-based approach, the backing bean property might be a data source object, like a JDBC `RowSet`; in the

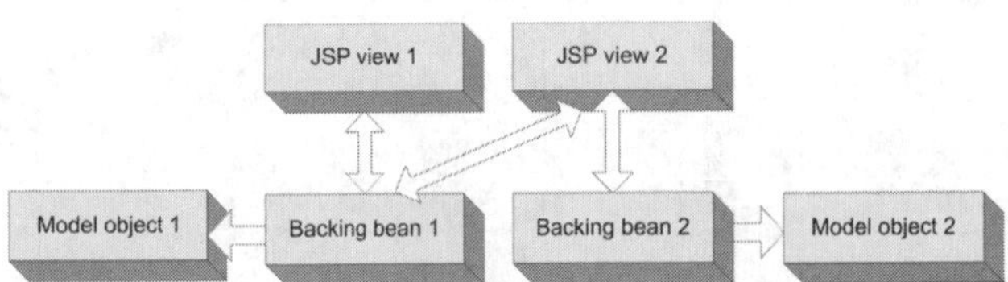

Figure 10.2 An object-based approach to development associates views with one or more backing beans, which expose model objects as properties. These backing beans usually talk to a separate application layer, but that world is invisible to the UI.

object-based approach, the backing bean property might be a `List` of `Project` objects. (JSF's EL syntax is so flexible that you can sometimes change the approach without affecting the UI; in chapter 13, we'll examine this capability.)

Before we begin the integration process, let's take a look at the ProjectTrack's back-end objects.

10.2 Exploring the application environment

Throughout most of this book, I've been talking about all of the services that JSF provides to make building web applications easier. When web application developers write application code, their goal is to provide services—in the form of objects—that make it easy to build the UI. This is what we call the *application environment*, and it consists of backing beans, event listeners, and model objects.

ProjectTrack's environment is segmented into several key backing beans, which expose model object properties such as `User` and `Project`. These objects will be configured by the application developer as managed beans in the faces-config.xml file. The process of writing and configuring beans (and other application objects) is covered in part 3.

During the integration process, you shouldn't be concerned about which Java class was used to implement the bean. What's important is what the bean represents, what properties and event listener methods it has, and the key and scope you can use to access it. Table 10.1 summarizes the beans for ProjectTrack. Armed with this information, you can intelligently construct JSF EL expressions that hook up the objects to your components.

Table 10.1 ProjectTrack's application environment includes these objects. Since they're stored under a key in a given scope, they can be easily accessed through JSF EL expressions.

Backing Bean Name	Description	Scope	Properties	Action Methods	Action Listener Methods
`visit`	Provides access to objects that are valid only during the user's session. Contains properties for the current user, the current project, and the user's locale.	session	`user`, `currentProject`, `locale`, `supported-LocaleItems`		

continued on next page

Table 10.1 ProjectTrack's application environment includes these objects. Since they're stored under a key in a given scope, they can be easily accessed through JSF EL expressions. *(continued)*

Backing Bean Name	Description	Scope	Properties	Action Methods	Action Listener Methods
authenticationBean	Collects login form values, provides login and logout, and checks for access to specific functions.	session	name, password, createNewAuthorized, inboxAuthorized	login, logout	
selectProjectBean	Lists projects and allows user to select one for approval, rejection or viewing of details.	request	inboxProjects, allProjects, projectTable	approve, reject, details	sort
updateProjectBean	Approves or rejects the current project.	request	comments, artifactSelectMany	approve, reject	
createProjectBean	Creates a new project and adds it to the data store.	request	projectSelectOne	create, add	
showHistoryBean	Allows users to scroll through the project's history	request	currentProjectHistory, firstRow, rowsToDisplay	next, previous	
selectItems	Provides access to lookup lists for artifacts, project types, and roles for use with SelectMany and SelectOne components.	application	artifacts, projectTypes, roles		

As you can see, ProjectTrack has seven backing beans. Each bean has properties that a UI component may reference, such as the currently selected projects, or the user's comments when approving or rejecting a project. Some backing beans also have event listener methods—action methods and action listener methods. The names that end in *Bean* represent functionality for one or more specific views; the other two objects—`visit` and `selectItem`—are used by many different views. Table 10.2 shows which views access which beans.

Table 10.2 Most of ProjectTrack's views access a specific backing bean, but some access more than one. Also, sometimes two different views interact with the same backing bean.

Views	Backing Bean Name
Header, Create a Project, Approve a Project, Reject a Project, Project Details	`visit`
Login, Header	`authenticationBean`
Inbox, Show All Projects	`selectProjectBean`
Approve a Project, Reject a Project	`updateProjectBean`
Header, Create a Project	`createProjectBean`
Project Details	`showHistoryBean`
Create a Project, Approve a Project, Reject a Project	`selectItems`

ProjectTrack's model objects are exposed as properties of these backing beans; this is how it implements the object-based development strategy (shown in figure 10.2). In the rest of this chapter, we'll modify each view to use JSF EL expressions that associate its components with these backing beans. For pages that reference action methods, we'll also need to make modifications to the navigation rules.

You may be thinking that it's quite unlikely that you would ever get complete documentation about the application environment when you begin integration. After all, half of these objects may not even be written when the project manager asks to see a working login page. In reality, integration can be performed in a somewhat ad hoc manner—display of a given page is dependent only on the objects it requires. So the entire application doesn't have to be finished in order to integrate the login page with the database—it only requires `authenticationBean`.

TIP An easy way to provide documentation for front-end developers is to generate JavaDocs for backing beans (assuming, of course, that there are JavaDoc comments to begin with).

Now that it's clear what the application environment looks like, let's begin the integration process.

10.3 Reorganizing pages for security

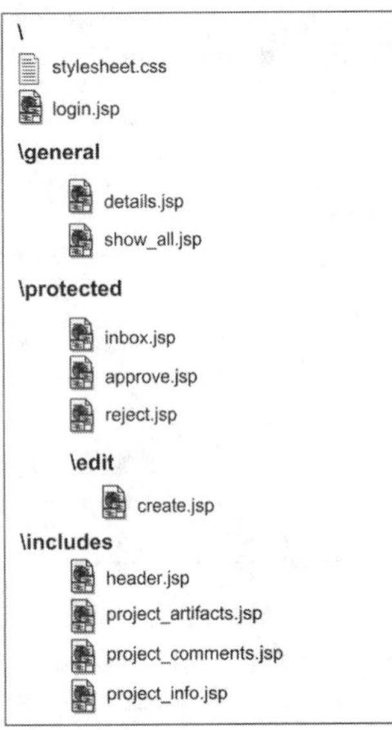

Figure 10.3 Our new directory structure for ProjectTrack JSPs with directories required by the authentication filter. All other directories are the same as in figure 8.1, page 289.

One back-end object we didn't cover in the previous section is the authentication filter, which controls access to pages in the application based on the user's role. The only effect the filter has on the integration process is the requirement of a specific directory structure.

Pages that are accessible by all authenticated users should be in a /general directory, pages specifically for those who can create projects are in the /protected/edit directory, and all other pages are in the /protected directory. The Login page will remain in the root directory, since it's accessible to people who haven't yet logged in. The filter controls access to our JSP pages based on these directory names. Because we have to move the files around, it makes sense to place all of the includes into a central directory, since they're accessed by multiple pages; we'll use an /includes directory for this purpose. The new JSP file locations are shown in figure 10.3.

As we update each of the pages shown in the figure, and their corresponding navigation rules, we'll add the appropriate directory name.

10.4 The Login page

Let's start with the first page users see—the Login page. This page is backed by `authenticationBean`, which is summarized in table 10.3.

Table 10.3 `authenticationBean` summary

Backing Bean	`authenticationBean`
Description	Provides login, logout, and access-control functionality.
Scope	Session

continued on next page

Table 10.3 `authenticationBean` summary *(continued)*

Property	Type	Description
`login`	`String`	Specifies the user's login name.
`password`	`String`	Contains the user's password.
`createNew-Authorized`	`boolean`	Specifies whether or not the user can create a new project.
`inboxAuthorized`	`boolean`	Specifies whether or not the user has an inbox.
Action Method	**Outcomes**	**Description**
`login`	`"success_readonly"`, `"success_readwrite"`, `"failure"`	Logs the user into the system. Returns `"success_readonly"` if the user's role is Upper Manager, `"success_readwrite"` if it's any other role, and `"failure"` if the login is incorrect. Sets the `visit.user` property.
`logout`	`"success"`	Logs the user out of the system (invalidates the session).

NOTE ProjectTrack uses custom security with `AuthenticationBean`, but JSF also works well with container-based security. See chapter 13 for more information.

This view uses the `loginName` and `password` properties, as well as the `login` action method. Four integration tasks come to mind:

- Add the context path to the stylesheet reference.
- Wire up the input controls to the `loginName` and `password` properties.
- Associate the single `HtmlCommandButton` with the `login` action method.
- Add an `HtmlMessages` component to display messages generated by the `authenticationBean.login` action method.

Listing 10.1 shows login.jsp updated to integrate with `authenticationBean`.

Listing 10.1 login.jsp: Fully integrated with authenticationBean

```
<!DOCTYPE HTML PUBLIC "-//W3C//DTD HTML 4.01 Transitional//EN">

<%@ taglib uri="http://java.sun.com/jsf/core" prefix="f"%>
<%@ taglib uri="http://java.sun.com/jsf/html" prefix="h"%>

<f:view>
<html>
```

```
<head>
  <title>
    <h:outputText value="ProjectTrack"/>
  </title>

  <link rel="stylesheet" type="text/css"
    href="<%= request.getContextPath() %>          <-- 1 Add context path
          /stylesheet.css"/>

  <script language="JavaScript">

    function set_image(button, img)
    {
      button.src = img;
    }

  </script>
</head>

<body>


<h:form>

  <h:panelGrid columns="2" border="0" cellpadding="3" '
               cellspacing="3">

     <h:graphicImage url="/images/logo.gif"
          alt="Welcome to ProjectTrack"
       title="Welcome to ProjectTrack" width="149" height="160"/>

       <h:panelGrid columns="3" border="0"
            cellpadding="5" cellspacing="3"
            headerClass="login-heading">

          <f:facet name="header">
              <h:outputText value="ProjectTrack"/>
          </f:facet>

          <h:messages globalOnly="true"
               styleClass="errors"/>                2 New row for
          <h:panelGroup/>                              application
          <h:panelGroup/>                              messages

          <h:outputLabel for="userNameInput">
             <h:outputText value="Enter your user name:"/>
          </h:outputLabel>
          <h:inputText id="userNameInput" size="20" maxlength="30"
                       required="true"
                      value="#{authenticationBean.loginName}">
            <f:validateLength minimum="5" maximum="30"/>
```

```
            </h:inputText>
            <h:message for="userNameInput" styleClass="errors"/>

            <h:outputLabel for="passwordInput">
              <h:outputText value="Password:"/>
            </h:outputLabel>
            <h:inputSecret id="passwordInput" size="20" maxlength="20"
                           required="true"
                           value="#{authenticationBean.password}">
              <f:validateLength minimum="5" maximum="15"/>
            </h:inputSecret>
            <h:message for="passwordInput" styleClass="errors"/>

            <h:panelGroup/>
            <h:commandButton action="#{authenticationBean.login}"
                title="Submit"
                image="#{facesContext.externalContext.
                         requestContextPath}/images/submit.gif"
                onmouseover="set_image(this,
                      '#{facesContext.externalContext.
                         requestContextPath}/images/submit_over.gif')"
                onmouseout="set_image(this,
                      '#{facesContext.externalContext.
                         requestContextPath}/images/submit.gif');"/>
            <h:panelGroup/>

          </h:panelGrid>

     </h:panelGrid>
   </h:form>

   </body>
   </html>
   </f:view>
```

We added the web application's context path in ❶ so that stylesheet references will work properly regardless of the directory the page is in. Note that we didn't use a JSF expression here, because the stylesheet link is ordinary template text that doesn't accept JSF expressions.[1] We'll make this change in every other page as well.

With these changes, the page is now fully functional. When the user types in his or her username and password, the `login` action will execute, and it will log the user into the system. If the action method succeeds, the user will see the next page. If the `login` action fails, it will generate a message (the most common message

[1] In JSP 2.0, you can embed JSP expressions anywhere in the template text (in JSP 2.1, slated for release in mid-2005, JSF and JSP expressions will work together).

says that the username and/or password is invalid). This message will be displayed by the new `HtmlMessages` component we added to the page in ❷. We're not interested in displaying errors for a specific component (that's what `HtmlMessage` components are for), but we are interested in displaying general errors that aren't associated with a specific component. This is why the `HtmlMessage` component's `globalOnly` property is set to `true`.

> **TIP** If you get an `EvaluationException` when displaying your page, it means that there is a problem executing your EL expression. If the message itself doesn't make sense, be sure to check your web container's logs; often you'll find the actual root of the problem there.

That's it—four changes. Now, let's update the navigation rule.

10.4.1 Updating the navigation rule

The `login` action has three possible outcomes: `"success_readonly"` if the user is an Upper Manager or `"success_readwrite"` for any other role; otherwise, it will return `"failure"`. When the `login` action returns `"success_readonly"`, the user should be sent to the Show All Projects page, and when the outcome is `"success_readwrite"`, the user should see the Inbox page. Otherwise, the Login page should redisplay so that the user can see any messages generated by the `login` action.

The original navigation rule for this page only had a `"success"` outcome defined. We'll need to replace that navigation case with ones for `"success_readonly"` and `"success_readwrite"`. Technically, we don't have to set up a rule for the `"failure"` outcome because if an outcome isn't defined in the navigation rule for the page, JSF will simply redisplay the page. However, if you know all of the possible outcomes, it's better to be explicit about the navigation cases. This way, you can tell from the configuration files what the outcomes are, and it'll be easier to change things later (for example, if you added a special error page). The updated navigation rule, with the changes in bold, is shown in listing 10.2.

Listing 10.2 faces-config.xml: Updated navigation rule for login.jsp

```
<navigation-rule>
  <from-view-id>/login.jsp</from-view-id>
  <navigation-case>
     <from-outcome>success_readonly</from-outcome>
     <to-view-id>/includes/show_all.jsp</to-view-id>
  </navigation-case>
  <navigation-case>
     <from-outcome>success_readwrite</from-outcome>
```

```
      <to-view-id>/protected/inbox.jsp</to-view-id>
   </navigation-case>
   <navigation-case>
      <from-outcome>failure</from-outcome>
      <to-view-id>/login.jsp</to-view-id>
   </navigation-case>
</navigation-rule>
```

Note that for all of these navigation cases, we use the new directory names shown in figure 10.3.

Now it's time to convert the header page, which is included in every other page except Login.

10.5 The header

The primary goal of the header is to provide navigation to the most common sections of the site—the Inbox, Show All Projects, and Create a Project pages. The header page also displays the user's name, and allows the user to change the current locale. In order to accomplish these tasks, it uses three different backing beans: `authenticationBean`, `visit`, and `createProjectBean`. We discussed `authenticationBean`, which provides login and logout functionality, in the previous section; it's summarized in table 10.3.

The `visit` bean provides access to objects that are valid only during the user's session (after the `authenticationBean.login` action method is executed, and before `authenticationBean.logout` is executed). These objects are the current user, the current project, and the user's locale. Table 10.4 summarizes this bean.

Table 10.4 `visit` summary

Backing Bean	`visit`	
Description	Provides access to the current user, project, and locale	
Scope	session	
Property	**Type**	**Description**
`user`	`User`	The current user
`currentProject`	`Project`	The currently select project
`locale`	`Locale`	The user's current locale
`supportedLocales`	`List` of `SelectItems`	Lists all of the locales that the application supports

The header uses the `user`, `locale`, and `supportedLocale` properties. The `user` property is a `User` object, which has a few properties of its own, as shown in table 10.5.

Table 10.5 The properties for `User` model objects.

Property	Type	Description
`login`	`String`	Name used to log into the system
`firstName`	`String`	The user's first name
`lastName`	`String`	The user's last name
`password`	`String`	The user's password
`role`	`RoleType`	The user's role

The header also uses the `create` action method of the `createProjectBean`, which creates a new project for the `visit.currentProject` property for use by the Create a Project page. (We'll discuss the other properties of this bean later.)

Recall from chapter 9 that we used a custom `UINavigator` component (developed in online extension part 5) for the toolbar that provides navigation. Each `UINavigator` has several child `NavigatorItems`, each of which has an `action` property (much like the Command components), and a `disabled` property to indicate whether or not a user can click on it. We need to make four changes to these items:

- Enable or disable the Inbox item based on the `authenticationBean.allowInbox` property.
- Enable or disable the Create New item based on the `authenticationBean.createNewAuthorized` property.
- Associate the Create New item with the `createProjectBean.create` action method.
- Associate the Logout item with the `authenticationBean.logout` action method.

For the rest of the page, there are two additional integration tasks:

- Associate the `HtmlOutputText` component that displays the user's name with the `visit.user.login` property.
- Associate the `HtmlSelectOneListbox` for selecting the user's locale with the `visit.locale` and `visit.supportedLocales` properties.

These changes are shown in listing 10.3.

Listing 10.3 header.jsp: Integrated with authenticationBean, visit, and createProjectBean

```
<%@ taglib uri="http://java.sun.com/jsf/core" prefix="f"%>
<%@ taglib uri="http://java.sun.com/jsf/html" prefix="h"%>
<%@ taglib uri="jsf-in-action-components" prefix="jia"%>

<f:subview id="header">

  <h:form>

    <h:panelGrid columns="3" cellspacing="0" cellpadding="0"
                 styleClass="header" width="100%">

      <jia:navigatorToolbar id="toolbar" layout="horizontal"
             headerClass="toolbar-header" itemClass="toolbar-command"
             selectedItemClass="toolbar-command"
             iconClass="toolbar-icon" immediate="false">

        <f:facet name="header">
          <h:outputText value="ProjectTrack:"/>
        </f:facet>

        <jia:navigatorItem name="inbox" label="Inbox"
               icon="/images/inbox.gif"
               action="inbox"
               disabled=
                 "#{!authenticationBean.
                     inboxAuthorized}"/>      Expression used for disabled property
        <jia:navigatorItem name="showAll" label="Show All"
               icon="/images/show_all.gif"
               action="show_all"/>
        <jia:navigatorItem name="createNew" label="Create New"
               icon="/images/create.gif"
               action="#{createProjectBean.create}"
               disabled="#{!authenticationBean.createNewAuthorized}"/>
        <jia:navigatorItem name="logout" label="Logout"
               icon="/images/logout.gif"
               action="#{authenticationBean.logout}"/>

     </jia:navigatorToolbar>

      <h:panelGroup>
        <h:outputLabel for="languageSelect">
          <h:outputText value="Language:"
              styleClass="language-select"/>
        </h:outputLabel>
        <h:selectOneListbox id="languageSelect" size="1"
              styleClass="language-select"
              value="#{visit.locale}">
```

```
            <f:selectItems
                 value="#{visit.
                       supportedLocaleItems}"/>        ❶ List populated
         </h:selectOneListbox>                            with SelectItems
         <h:commandButton value="Go!"
              styleClass="language-select-button"/>
      </h:panelGroup>

      <h:outputText value="(#{visit.user.login})"
           styleClass="user-name"/>

    </h:panelGrid>
  </h:form>
</f:subview>
```

As you can see, the changes are minor. What's interesting is that we have initialized the `disabled` property of two of `NavigatorItems` with a JSF EL expression. The expression `"#{!authenticationBean.inboxAuthorized}"` returns `true` if the user does not have an inbox, and the expression `"#{!authenticationBean.createNewAuthorized}"` returns `true` if the user cannot create a new project. Remember, you can use a value-binding expression for any standard component property, and often for properties in custom components, as is the case here.

Another interesting change is the replacement of two static `UISelectItem` components with a single `UISelectItems` component in ❶. Populating the item list with the `visit.supportedLocaleItems` property (which is a list of `SelectItem` objects) ensures that the list will always contain the locales that the application currently supports. It also ensures that the proper value is used when the parent `HtmlSelectOneListbox` component updates its value, which is now set to `visit.locale`. These two properties were designed to work together. The list of supported locales is defined in an application configuration file; see section 10.10.3, page 402 for details.

TIP If the backing bean you referenced doesn't show up, there are a few possibilities: (1) your reference is incorrect, (2) the object isn't there, or (3) the value of the property is empty. A handy trick is to output the object itself: `<h:outputText value="#{visit}"/>`. If you see a string like "org.jia.ptrack.web.Visit@1ba5839" (the output of the default `toString` method) then you know JSF found the object, and at least the first part of your expression is correct (which eliminates possibility #1).

We now have a working header page that disables some toolbar items for particular users, can create a new project and log users out, and allows users to change their locale. It also provides basic navigation (as it did in the prototype) and displays the user's login name. Let's examine the view's navigation rules.

10.5.1 Updating the navigation rule

This page references two action methods (`createProjectBean.create` and `authenticationBean.logout`), both of which return the outcome `"success"`. Since the outcome is the same, we need to specify the `<from-action>` element so that JSF knows the action method for which to look. These two navigation cases replace the ones defined in the prototype for the `"create"` and `"logout"` outcomes, respectively. We also need to update the `<to-view-id>` nodes to include the new directories that have been added. The updated rule is shown in listing 10.4.

Listing 10.4 faces-config.xml: Updated global navigation rule

```
<navigation-rule>
  <description>Navigation for the toolbar.</description>
  <from-view-id>*</from-view-id>
  <navigation-case>
     <from-outcome>inbox</from-outcome>
     <to-view-id>/protected/inbox.jsp</to-view-id>
  </navigation-case>
  <navigation-case>
     <from-outcome>show_all</from-outcome>
     <to-view-id>/includes/show_all.jsp</to-view-id>
  </navigation-case>
  <navigation-case>
     <from-action>#{createProjectBean.create}</from-action>
     <from-outcome>success</from-outcome>
     <to-view-id>/protected/edit/create.jsp</to-view-id>
  </navigation-case>
  <navigation-case>
     <from-action>#{authenticationBean.logout}</from-action>
     <from-outcome>success</from-outcome>
     <to-view-id>/login.jsp</to-view-id>
  </navigation-case>
</navigation-rule>
```

Now that we've completed the header page, let's move on to the meat of the application—the project selection pages.

10.6 Integrating data grids

The Inbox and Show All pages let a user select a project from a table. The table also has `HtmlCommandLink` components users can click on to perform specific functions like viewing details, approving the project, or rejecting the project. For each page, we need to change the existing `HtmlPanelGrid` into an `HtmlDataTable` and integrate it (and its child components, which include the `HtmlCommandLink` components) with the appropriate backing bean. Let's start with the Inbox page.

10.6.1 The Inbox page

The Inbox page is essentially ProjectTrack's main menu—it's the first page seen by all of the users who can participate in the process flow, and it lists all of the projects currently waiting for them to process. This view is backed by `inboxBean`, whose properties and methods are described in table 10.6.

Table 10.6 `inboxBean` and `showAllBean` summary

Backing Bean	`inboxBean` or `showAllBean`	
Description	Lists current projects waiting for a user, or all projects.	
Scope	Request	
Component Binding Property	**Type**	**Description**
`projectTable`	`HtmlDataTable`	Property for the table that lists all of the projects. Must be set so the bean can determine which row was selected.
Property	**Type**	**Description**
`inboxProjects`	`List`	List of all of projects in the current user's inbox.
`allProjects`	`List`	List of all projects.
Action Methods	**Outcomes**	**Description**
`approve`	`"success"`, `"failure"`, `"error"`	Loads the selected project for approval and makes it available through `visit.currentProject`. Returns `"success"` if the project loaded properly, `"failure"` if there was a nonfatal error, and `"error"` if there was a fatal error.
`reject`	`"success"`, `"failure"`, `"error"`	Loads the selected project for rejection and makes it available through `visit.currentProject`. Returns `"success"` if the project loaded properly, `"failure"` if there was a nonfatal error, and `"error"` if there was a fatal error.

continued on next page

Table 10.6 `inboxBean` and `showAllBean` summary *(continued)*

Action Methods	Outcomes	Description
`details`	`"success"`, `"failure"`, `"error"`	Loads the selected project for viewing of details and makes it available through `visit.currentProject`. Returns `"success"` if the project loaded properly, `"failure"` if there was a nonfatal error, and `"error"` if there was a fatal error.
Action Listener Methods		
`sort`		Sorts the list according to the selected column.

As the table shows, `inboxBean` has exactly the same properties and methods as `showAllBean`, which is used by the Show All page (because they're two instances of the same object). Note that this bean has a component-binding property that's intended to be associated with the `HtmlDataTable` that lists the projects. Also note that this bean has an action listener method, which is used to sort the project list. We'll be registering that method with the column headings, which are `HtmlCommandLink` components.

Integrating the Inbox with the application objects requires the following steps:

- Update the paths for the JSP includes.
- Change the `HtmlPanelGrid` used to display projects to an `HtmlDataTable`.
- Wire input controls to the corresponding `visit.currentProject` properties.
- Replace the `HtmlOutputText` at the top of the page with an `HtmlMessages` component.
- Associate `HtmlCommandLink` components for the column headers with an action listener.
- Associate `HtmlCommandLink` components for the functions with action methods.

Because changing an `HtmlPanelGrid` into an `HtmlDataTable` is a common task with a few nuances, let's examine that process first. The main issue is thinking in terms of columns instead of rows. `HtmlPanelGrid` groups a set of components together as a row, while `HtmlPanelTable` uses `UIColumn` components to specify columns. Let's look at the original `HtmlPanelGrid` declaration and the new `HtmlDataTable` declaration side by side (changes related to component layout are marked in bold):

<table>
<tr><th>Prototype JSP</th><th>Integrated JSP</th></tr>
<tr><td>
<pre>
<h:panelGrid columns="6"
     styleClass="table-background"
     rowClasses="table-odd-row,
                 table-even-row"
     cellpadding="3">

<%-- Header (technically the first
row) --%>

  <h:commandLink
       styleClass="table-header">
    <h:outputText
         value="Project name"/>
  </h:commandLink>
  <h:commandLink
      styleClass="table-header">
    <h:outputText value="Type"/>
  </h:commandLink>
  <h:commandLink
       styleClass="table-header">
    <h:outputText value="Status"/>
  </h:commandLink>
  <h:panelGroup/>
  <h:panelGroup/>
  <h:panelGroup/>

  <%-- Static data row 1 --%>

  <h:outputText
     value="Inventory Manager v2.0"/>
  <h:outputText
      value="Internal Desktop
             Application"/>
  <h:outputText
      value="Requirements/Analysis"/>
  <h:commandLink action="approve">
    <h:outputText value="Approve"/>
  </h:commandLink>
  <h:commandLink action="reject">
    <h:outputText value="Reject"/>
  </h:commandLink>
  <h:commandLink action="details">
    <h:outputText value="Details"/>
  </h:commandLink>

  <%-- Static data row 2 --%>
</pre>
</td><td>
<pre>
<h:<b>dataTable</b>
     styleClass="table-background"
     rowClasses="table-odd-row,
                 table-even-row"
     cellpadding="3"
     value="#{inboxBean.
              inboxProjects}"
     var="project"
     binding="#{inboxBean.
                projectTable}">

  <h:column>
    <f:facet name="header">
      <h:commandLink
          styleClass="table-header"
          actionListener=
            "#{inboxBean.sort}">
        <h:outputText
            value="Project name"/>
        <f:param name="column"
             value="name"/>
      </h:commandLink>
    </f:facet>
    <h:outputText
      value="#{project.name}"/>
  </h:column>

  <h:column>
    <f:facet name="header">
      <h:commandLink
           styleClass="table-header"
           actionListener=
             "#{inboxBean.sort}">
        <h:outputText value="Type"/>
        <f:param name="column"
            value="type"/>
      </h:commandLink>
    </f:facet>
    <h:outputText
        value="#{project.type}"/>
  </h:column>

  <h:column>
    <f:facet name="header">
      <h:commandLink
          styleClass="table-header"
          actionListener=
</pre>
</td></tr>
</table>

continued on next page

<table>
<tr><th>Prototype JSP</th><th>Integrated JSP</th></tr>
<tr><td><pre>
  <h:outputText value="TimeTracker"/>
  <h:outputText
       value="Internal Web
              Application"/>
  <h:outputText
      value="Requirements/Analysis"/>
  <h:commandLink action="approve">
    <h:outputText value="Approve"/>
  </h:commandLink>
  <h:commandLink action="reject">
    <h:outputText value="Reject"/>
  </h:commandLink>
  <h:commandLink action="details">
    <h:outputText value="Details"/>
  </h:commandLink>

</h:panelGrid>
</pre></td><td><pre>
              "#{inboxBean.sort}">
      <h:outputText value="Status"/>
<f:param name="column"
                      value="status"/>
     </h:commandLink>
   </f:facet>
   <h:outputText
       value="#{project.status}"/>
 </h:column>

 <h:column>
   <h:commandLink
        action="#{inboxBean.
                approve}">
     <h:outputText value="Approve"/>
   </h:commandLink>
 </h:column>

 <h:column>
   <h:commandLink
       action="#{inboxBean.reject}">
     <h:outputText value="Reject"/>
   </h:commandLink>
 </h:column>

 <h:column>
   <h:commandLink
     action="#{inboxBean.details}">
     <h:outputText value="Details"/>
   </h:commandLink>
 </h:column>

</h:dataTable>
</pre></td></tr>
</table>

There are several changes in the column on the right; for now, let's discuss the ones in bold, which are related to the conversion from an `HtmlPanelGrid` to an `HtmlDataTable`. We started by simply changing the `<h:panelGrid>` tags to `<h:dataTable>` tags, and then adding specific `HtmlDataTable` properties.

The `value` property references `inboxBean.inboxProjects`, which returns a list of all of the projects in the user's inbox. The component will cycle through each row in this list and expose a request-scoped variable called `projects` (set by the `var` property), displaying each column. The `binding` property binds the component to the `inboxBean.projectTable` property, so that this component can be manipulated in code. Note that we were able to keep the several properties that are common between the two components.

The main change is that all of the columns are split into individual columns and grouped inside a `UIColumn` component. `HtmlDataTable` requires this—all of its children must be either `UIColumns` or facets.

> **TIP** A common mistake when converting a panel to a table is to forget to enclose the child components in a `header` or `footer` facet, or inside a `UIColumn`. If you forget to do this, your child components won't be displayed.

Also, note that we've moved the three header columns into `header` facets for the individual `UIColumn` components. Remember, each column can have its own header or footer, in addition to a header or footer for the entire table. Because each column acts as a template for each row, we need to specify the column only once—it'll be repeated for each row returned by `inboxBean`. This is different than the prototype, which explicitly specified two static rows of data.

We glossed over the value-bindings that were added to the page. All of the components that are children of the `HtmlDataTable` reference the `projects` variable. This object is of type `Project`, which is one of the key model objects in our application. Its properties are shown in table 10.7.

Table 10.7 The properties for `Project` model object (usually accessed through `visit.currentProject`).

Property	Type	Description
`artifacts`	`List` of `ArtifactTypes`	All of the artifacts this project has completed. Use when listing artifacts.
`history`	`List` of `Operations`	All of the operations (approvals or rejections) that have been performed on this project.
`initialComments`	`String`	Initial comments entered by a user when the project was created.
`initiatedBy`	`String`	The name of the individual responsible for starting the project.
`name`	`String`	The project's name.
`requirementsContact`	`String`	The name of the contact for requirements.
`requirementsContactEmail`	`String`	The email address of the requirements contact.

continued on next page

Table 10.7 The properties for `Project` model object (usually accessed through `visit.currentProject`). *(continued)*

Property	Type	Description
`status`	`StatusType`	The current status (Proposal, Requirements/Analysis, Deployment, etc.).
`type`	`ProjectType`	The project type (Internal Desktop Application, External Web Application, etc.).

It's important to note that the `status` and `type` properties can be displayed without any explicit conversion. Now that we know more about the `Project` object, let's examine the updates to the entire page in listing 10.5.

Listing 10.5 inbox.jsp: Integrated with the inboxProjects backing bean

```
<!DOCTYPE HTML PUBLIC "-//W3C//DTD HTML 4.01 Transitional//EN">

<%@ taglib uri="http://java.sun.com/jsf/core" prefix="f"%>
<%@ taglib uri="http://java.sun.com/jsf/html" prefix="h"%>

<f:view>
<html>
  <head>
    <title>
      <h:outputText value="ProjectTrack - Inbox"/>
    </title>
    <link rel="stylesheet" type="text/css"
          href="<%= request.getContextPath() %>/stylesheet.css"/>
  </head>

<body class="page-background">

<jsp:include page="/includes/header.jsp"/>

<h:form>

  <h:panelGrid headerClass="page-header"
       styleClass="table-background"
       columns="1" cellpadding="5">

    <f:facet name="header">
      <h:outputText value="Inbox - approve or reject projects"/>
    </f:facet>

    <h:messages globalOnly="true" styleClass="errors"/>   <-- (1) HtmlOutputText replaced with HtmlMessages
```

```
<h:dataTable styleClass="table-background"
     rowClasses="table-odd-row,table-even-row" cellpadding="3"
     value="#{inboxBean.inboxProjects}"
     var="project"
     binding="#{inboxBean.projectTable}">

  <h:column>
    <f:facet name="header">
      <h:commandLink id="name"
           styleClass="table-header"
           actionListener=
             "#{inboxBean.sort}">
        <h:outputText
          value="Project name"/>
      </h:commandLink>
    </f:facet>
    <h:outputText value="#{project.name}"/>
  </h:column>

  <h:column>
    <f:facet name="header">
      <h:commandLink id="type"
           styleClass="table-header"
           actionListener=
             "#{inboxBean.sort}">
        <h:outputText value="Type"/>
      </h:commandLink>
    </f:facet>
    <h:outputText value="#{project.type}"/>
  </h:column>

  <h:column>
    <f:facet name="header">
      <h:commandLink id="status"
           styleClass="table-header"
           actionListener="#{inboxBean.sort}">
        <h:outputText value="Status"/>
      </h:commandLink>
    </f:facet>
    <h:outputText value="#{project.status}"/>
  </h:column>

  <h:column>
    <h:commandLink action="#{inboxBean.approve}">
      <h:outputText value="Approve"/>
    </h:commandLink>
  </h:column>

  <h:column>
    <h:commandLink action="#{inboxBean.reject}">
      <h:outputText value="Reject"/>
```

2 Action listener method for sorting by name

3 Action listener method for sorting by type

4 Action listener method for sorting by status

```
      </h:commandLink>
    </h:column>

    <h:column>
      <h:commandLink action="#{inboxBean.details}">
        <h:outputText value="Details"/>
      </h:commandLink>
    </h:column>

  </h:dataTable>

</h:panelGrid>

</h:form>

</body>
</html>
</f:view>
```

Note that in ❶ we've replaced the static `HtmlOutputText` from the prototype with an `HtmlMessages` component that displays application messages. Such messages may be generated by `inboxBean` when a user executes one of its action methods (if a user tries to reject a message that has just been rejected by someone else, for example).

The `HtmlCommandLink` component used for each column's titles has been associated with the `inboxBean.sort` method (❷, ❸, ❹), which will sort the list by the column. All three columns execute the same action, and they differentiate themselves with by assigning different identifiers to the `HtmlCommandLink` components.

The Inbox page is now fully integrated with the application. Let's see how this affects its navigation rule.

Updating the navigation rule

All three action methods used on this page (`inboxBean.approve`, `inboxBean.reject`, and `inboxBean.details`) return one of the following outcomes:

- `"success"`, which indicates successful completion.
- `"falure"`, which indicates a nonfatal error executing the update.
- `"error"`, which indicates a serious database error.

However, these action methods should send the user to completely different pages. Unsurprisingly, these pages are approve.jsp, reject.jsp, and details.jsp. As before, we can have different navigation cases for the same outcomes if we use the `<from-action>` element. In the prototype, the expected outcomes had the same name as the page itself, so that will have to be changed as well. The updated rule is shown in listing 10.6.

Listing 10.6 faces-config.xml: Updated navigation rule for approve.jsp

```
<navigation-rule>
  <from-view-id>/protected/inbox.jsp</from-view-id>
  <navigation-case>
     <from-action>#{inboxBean.details}</from-action>
     <from-outcome>success</from-outcome>
     <to-view-id>/includes/details.jsp</to-view-id>
  </navigation-case>
  <navigation-case>
     <from-action>#{inboxBean.approve}</from-action>
     <from-outcome>success</from-outcome>
     <to-view-id>/protected/approve.jsp</to-view-id>
  </navigation-case>
  <navigation-case>
     <from-action>#{inboxBean.reject}</from-action>
     <from-outcome>success</from-outcome>
     <to-view-id>/protected/reject.jsp</to-view-id>
  </navigation-case>
</navigation-rule>
```

Note that we also changed the path for the `<from-view-id>` elements; we'll have to do this for every page.

That's it for the Inbox page. Let's take a look at the Show All page.

10.6.2 *The Show All page*

The Show All page is almost exactly like the Inbox page. Other than static display text (like the title and heading of the page), the only changes are that it has an additional column, it displays *all* projects, and the user can't approve or reject projects. This boils down to the following differences:

- There is an additional `UIColumn` called "Waiting for" that retrieves its value from `"#{project.status.role}"`.
- The `HtmlDataTable` uses the value-binding expression `"#{inboxBean.all-Projects}"` instead of `"#{inboxBean.inboxProjects}"`.
- There are no columns for the Approve and Reject buttons.

Other than that, all of the integration steps are the same, including the navigation rule changes.

10.7 Integrating input forms

The operation pages—Approve a Project and Reject a Project—allow users to view information about a project, add or remove completed artifacts, and submit comments to be added to the project's history. The pages are pretty similar, but they execute different action methods. The Create a Project page allows a user to create a new project, and is conceptually similar to the other two pages, but is backed by a different bean. Because these pages display or edit several properties of the current project, the main task is simply integrating controls with the correct property.

TIP If a page redisplays unexpectedly, make sure you're not getting a conversion or validation error—place an `HtmlMessages` component at the top of the page to display any possible errors.

10.7.1 Updating the includes

In chapter 9, we defined three JSP includes that were used by these pages: project_info.jsp, project_artifacts.jsp, and project_comments.jsp. The input controls on the first two of these pages need to be wired to properties of the current project (`visit.currentProject`). This is a `Project` model object, whose properties are listed in table 10.7. Listings 10.7 and 10.8 show how it is integrated with these pages.

Listing 10.7 project_info.jsp: Integrated with visit.currentProject

```
<h:outputText value="Name:"/>
<h:outputText value="#{visit.currentProject.name}"
              styleClass="project-data"/>         <!>

<h:outputText value="Type:"/>
<h:outputText value="#{visit.currentProject.type}"
              styleClass="project-data"/>

<h:outputText value="Initiated by:"/>
<h:outputText value="#{visit.currentProject.initiatedBy}"
              styleClass="project-data"/>

<h:outputText value="Requirements contact:"/>
<h:outputText value="#{visit.currentProject.requirementsContact}"
              styleClass="project-data"/>

<h:outputText value="Requirements contact e-mail:"/>
<h:outputText value="#{visit.currentProject.
                          requirementsContactEmail}"
              styleClass="project-data"/>
```

```
<h:outputText value="Initial comments:"/>
<h:outputText value="#{visit.currentProject.initialComments}"
              styleClass="project-data"/>
```

Listing 10.8 project_artifacts.jsp: Integrated with visit.currentProject and selectItems.artifacts

```
<h:outputLabel for="artifactSelect">
  <h:outputText value="Completed artifacts:"/>
</h:outputLabel>
<h:selectManyCheckbox id="artifactSelect" layout="pageDirection"
                      styleClass="project-input"
                      value="#{visit.currentProject.artifacts}"
                      converter="ArtifactType">
  <f:selectItems
      value="#{selectItems.artifacts}"/>
</h:selectManyCheckbox>
```

❶ Global list of SelectItems

As you can see, for the most part, integration is straightforward—simply replace static values with value-binding expressions. Note that for project_artifacts.jsp (❶), we've changed several `UISelectItem` components into a single `UISelectItems` component that references `selectItems.artifacts`, which provides a list of all of possible artifact types. The `selectItems` backing bean has three properties that can be used to populate lists for SelectMany and SelectOne components. This bean is summarized in table 10.8.

Table 10.8 `selectItems` summary

Backing Bean	`selectItems`	
Description	Provides access to global, static lookup lists for use with SelectMany or SelectOne components.	
Scope	application	
Property	**Type**	**Description**
`artifacts`	`List` of `SelectItems`	List of all of the artifact types.
`roles`	`List` of `SelectItems`	List of all of the different roles.
`projectTypes`	`List` of `SelectItems`	List of project types.

Whenever we encounter a SelectMany or SelectOne component that requires one of these lists, we'll reference `selectItems`.

The last include, project_comments.jsp, is associated with `updateProjectBean`, which is used for both the Approve a Project and Reject a Project pages. This bean is summarized in table 10.9.

Table 10.9 `updateProjectBean` summary

Backing Bean	`updateProjectBean`	
Description	Provides action methods for approving or rejecting a project.	
Scope	request	
Property	**Type**	**Description**
`comments`	`List` of `SelectItems`	List of all of the artifact types.
Action Methods	**Outcomes**	**Description**
`approve`	`"success_readonly"`, `"success_readwrite"`, `"failure"`, `"error"`	Approves the project, moving it to the next status and adding a new approval operation to its history. Returns `"success_readonly"` or `"success_readwrite"` if the update operation is successful, and `"failure"` otherwise. The `"error"` outcome is returned if there is a data store error.
`reject`	`"success"`, `"failure"`, `"error"`	Rejects the project, moving it to the previous status and adding a new rejection operation to its history. Returns `"success"` if the update operation is successful, and `"failure"` otherwise. The `"error"` outcome is returned if there is a data store error.
`cancel`	`"cancel_readonly"`, `"cancel_readwrite"`	Returns `"cancel_readonly"` if this is a read-only user (Upper Manager), or `"cancel_readwrite"` for other users.

The only property used by project_comments.jsp is the `comments` property, which needs to be wired to the `HtmlInputTextarea` control on the page. The updated page is shown in listing 10.9.

Listing 10.9 project_comments.jsp: Integrated with updateProjectBean

```
<h:panelGrid columns="1" cellpadding="5"
             styleClass="table-background"
             rowClasses="table-odd-row,table-even-row">
  <h:outputLabel for="commentsInput">
    <h:outputText value="Your comments:"/>
  </h:outputLabel>
```

```
    <h:inputTextarea id="commentsInput" rows="10" cols="80"
                     value="#{updateProjectBean.comments}"/>
  </h:panelGrid>
```

That's all we needed to change—just the value of one `HtmlInputTextarea` control.

With these includes integrated, the changes to the actual input forms are minor. Let's examine those changes now.

10.7.2 The Approve a Project page

The purpose of the Approve a Project page is to do just what it says—approve the current project. Part of the approval process is to collect comments and update the list of completed artifacts; these are functions that are performed by the JSP includes we discussed in the previous section. The view leverages `updateProject-Beand` to perform its work. These are the only changes necessary for the page itself:

- Update the paths for the JSP includes.
- Replace the `HtmlOutputText` at the top of the page with an `HtmlMessages` component.
- Associate the Approve `HtmlCommandButton` with the `updateProjectBean.approve` action method.

The updated page is shown in listing 10.10.

Listing 10.10 approve.jsp: Integrated with updateProjectBean

```
<!DOCTYPE HTML PUBLIC "-//W3C//DTD HTML 4.01 Transitional//EN">

<%@ taglib uri="http://java.sun.com/jsf/core" prefix="f"%>
<%@ taglib uri="http://java.sun.com/jsf/html" prefix="h" %>
<f:view>
<html>
  <head>
    <title>
      <h:outputText value="ProjectTrack - Approve a Project"/>
    </title>
    <link rel="stylesheet" type="text/css"
          href="<%= request.getContextPath() %>/stylesheet.css"/>
  </head>

<body class="page-background">
```

```
<jsp:include page="/includes/header.jsp"/>
<h:form>

  <h:panelGrid columns="2" cellpadding="5"
      footerClass="project-background"
      styleClass="project-background"
      rowClasses="project-row">

    <f:facet name="header">
      <h:panelGrid columns="1" width="100%" cellpadding="3"
          styleClass="project-background"
          headerClass="page-header">
        <f:facet name="header">
          <h:outputText value="Approve a project"/>
        </f:facet>
        <h:messages globalOnly="true"
             styleClass="errors"/>     <-- (1) HtmlOutputText replaced
      </h:panelGrid>                           with HtmlMessages
    </f:facet>

    <%@ include file="/includes/project_info.jsp"%>
    <%@ include file="/includes/project_artifacts.jsp"%>

    <f:facet name="footer">

      <h:panelGroup>

        <%@ include file="/includes/project_comments.jsp"%>

        <h:panelGrid columns="2" rowClasses="table-odd-row">
          <h:commandButton value="Approve"
                           action="#{updateProjectBean.approve}"/>
          <h:commandButton value="Cancel"
                           action="#{createProjectBean.cancel}"
                           immediate="true"/>
        </h:panelGrid>
      </h:panelGroup>

    </f:facet>

  </h:panelGrid>

</h:form>

</body>
</html>
</f:view>
```

If `updateProject.approve` has a problem updating the database, it will add the appropriate error messages to the JSF message queue, and return `"failure"`. Any such messages will be displayed by the `HtmlMessages` component added in ❶.

With these changes, we now have a complete working page. It displays all of the project's properties, and allows the user to add artifacts or comments. When the user clicks on the Approve `HtmlCommandButton`, the `updateProject.approve` method is executed, the current project moves to the next status, and a new approve operation is added to the project's history. When viewing the project later with the Project Details page, the user will see a record of this operation.

Next, we examine the view's navigation rule.

Updating the navigation rule

The `updateProjectBean.approve` method has four possible outcomes:

- `"success_readonly"`, which indicates successful completion for Upper Managers.
- `"success_readwrite"`, which indicates success for other users.
- `"failure"`, which indicates a nonfatal error executing the update.
- `"error"`, which indicates a serious database error.

The prototype only had the positive outcome `"success"`, which was mapped to inbox.jsp. We'll update that navigation case to map to the outcome `"success_readwrite"`, and add a new navigation case for `"success_readonly"` that maps to show_all.jsp because read-write users (i.e., Upper Managers) don't have an inbox.

For the `"failure"` outcome, we want the page to redisplay so that the user can see error messages. Originally, we didn't define a navigation case for this outcome, and because JSF redisplays the page for unknown outcomes, this is our desired behavior. It's generally better to be explicit, though, so we'll add a navigation case for `"failure"` as well. The `"error"` outcome was handled by the global navigation rule shown in listing 10.2.

The Cancel button calls the `updateProjectBean.cancel` method, which returns `"cancel_readonly"` for Upper Managers and `"cancel_readwrite"` for everybody else. This is so that Upper Managers can be sent to the Show All page, and everybody else will see the Inbox page. We'll change the `"cancel"` navigation case so that it expects `"cancel_readwrite"`, and add a new case for `"cancel_readonly"`.

We'll also make sure that all of the cases include the new directories that we've added. The updated navigation rule is shown in listing 10.11.

Listing 10.11 faces-config.xml: Updated navigation rule for approve.jsp

```
<navigation-rule>
    <from-view-id>/protected/approve.jsp</from-view-id>
    <navigation-case>
       <from-outcome>success_readonly</from-outcome>
       <to-view-id>/protected/show_all.jsp</to-view-id>
    </navigation-case>
    <navigation-case>
       <from-outcome>success_readwrite</from-outcome>
       <to-view-id>/protected/inbox.jsp</to-view-id>
    </navigation-case>
    <navigation-case>
       <from-outcome>failure</from-outcome>
       <to-view-id>/protected/approve.jsp</to-view-id>
    </navigation-case>
    <navigation-case>
       <from-outcome>cancel_readonly</from-outcome>
       <to-view-id>/protected/show_all.jsp</to-view-id>
    </navigation-case>
    <navigation-case>
       <from-outcome>cancel_readwrite</from-outcome>
       <to-view-id>/protected/inbox.jsp</to-view-id>
    </navigation-case>
 </navigation-rule>
```

Now, when a user leaves the Approve a Project page, he or she will return to either the Inbox or Show All page, or see the Approve a Project again with error messages. Next, let's examine the Reject a Project page.

10.7.3 The Reject a Project page

Integrating the Reject a Project page can be performed in exactly the same manner because most of the page is composed of the JSP includes project_info.jsp, project_artifacts.jsp, and project_comments.jsp, which are shared by the Approve a Project page. Both pages use the `updateProject` bean, but the Reject a Project page uses the `reject` action method instead. As you've probably guessed, this action method moves the project's status backward (as opposed to forwards, like the `approve` action method), but still creates an operation entry in the project's history, which can be displayed on the Project Details page.

Because the `reject` action method has exactly the same outcomes as the `approve` action method, the changes to the navigation rule are identical as well.

Let's move on to something a bit more complicated: the Create a Project page.

10.7.4 *The Create a Project page*

The Create a Project page collects all of the information necessary for adding a new project to the data store. It's backed by `createProjectBean`, which has two action methods: `create`, which the header uses to create a new project, and `add`, which adds the current project to the database. The backing bean is summarized, in table 10.10.

Table 10.10 `createProjectBean` summary

Backing Bean	`createProjectBean`	
Description	Provides action methods for creating a new project and adding it to the data store.	
Scope	request	
Component Binding Property	**Type**	**Description**
`reqContactEmail`	`HtmlInputText`	Property for the control used to collect the requirements contact e-mail. Used by the `validateReqContact` method.
`projectSelect-One`	`UISelectOne`	Property for `HtmlSelectOneListbox` or `HtmlSelectOneMenu`, or `HtmlSelect OneRadio` control in the view that's used to select the project type. This property allows the bean to configure a converter for the control.
Validator Methods	**Description**	
`validateReq-Contact`	Requires that an e-mail address be entered into the control bound to `reqCon-tactEmail` if the validated control is not empty. Used to ensure that if someone enters a requirement contact's name, they also enter an e-mail address.	
Action Methods	**Outcomes**	**Description**
`add`	`"success_readonly"`, `"success_readwrite"`, `"failure"`, `"error"`	Adds `visit.currentProject` to the database. Returns `"success_readonly"` or `"success_readwrite"` if successful; `"failure"` for non-fatal errors, and `"error"` for major problems.
`create`	`"success"`	Creates a new `Project` object and makes it available through `visit.currentProject`. Should be called before loading the Create a Project page.
`cancel`	`"cancel_readonly"`, `"cancel_readwrite"`	Returns `"cancel_readonly"` if this is a read-only user (Upper Manager), or `"cancel_readwrite"` for other users.

As the table shows, this backing bean has a component binding property. This allows the bean to initialize the component as it sees fit. In ProjectTrack, `createProjectBean` sets the `UISelectOne`'s properties, and configures a converter in order to show this can be done in code. In your applications, the backing bean can do just about anything when it initializes a component—configure properties, add child components, and so on.

The table also shows that the `create` action method creates a new `Project` object for the `visit.currentProject` property. This means that if we wire up all of the controls on this page to `visit.currentProject`, we'll be modifying the new project, because the header executes the `create` action method before this page is loaded. The properties of `Project` model objects are summarized in table 10.7.

Integration the Create a Project page involves:

- Update paths of the JSP includes.
- Changing the `HtmlOutputText` for displaying messages to an `HtmlMessages` component.
- Wiring input controls to the corresponding `view.currentProject` properties.
- Wire input controls to component binding properties.
- Setting the `validator` property of `HtmlInputText` that collects a requirement contact's name.
- Associating the `HtmlCommmandButtons` with the appropriate action methods.

The updated page is shown in listing 10.12.

Listing 10.12 create.jsp: Integrated with visit.currentProject and createProjectBean

```
<!DOCTYPE HTML PUBLIC "-//W3C//DTD HTML 4.01 Transitional//EN">

<%@ taglib uri="http://java.sun.com/jsf/core" prefix="f"%>
<%@ taglib uri="http://java.sun.com/jsf/html" prefix="h"%>
<%@ taglib uri="jsf-in-action-components" prefix="jia"%>

<f:view>

<html>
  <head>
    <title>
      <h:outputText value="ProjectTrack - Create a new project"/>
    </title>
    <link rel="stylesheet" type="text/css"
          href="<%= request.getContextPath() %>/stylesheet.css"/>
  </head>
```

```
<body class="page-background">

<jsp:include page="/includes/header.jsp"/>

<h:form>
  <h:panelGrid columns="3" cellpadding="5"
      footerClass="project-background"
      styleClass="project-background"
      rowClasses="project-row"
      columnClasses=",project-input">

    <f:facet name="header">
      <h:panelGrid columns="1" width="100%" cellpadding="3"
                   styleClass="project-background"
                   headerClass="page-header">
        <f:facet name="header">
          <h:outputText value="Create a project"/>
        </f:facet>
        <h:messages globalOnly="true" showDetail="true" styleClass="errors"/>
      </h:panelGrid>
    </f:facet>

    <h:outputLabel for="nameInput">
      <h:outputText value="Name:"/>
    </h:outputLabel>
    <h:inputText id="nameInput" size="40" required="true"
                 value="#{visit.currentProject.name}">
      <f:validateLength minimum="5"/>
    </h:inputText>
    <h:message for="nameInput" styleClass="errors"/>

    <h:outputLabel for="typeSelectOne">
      <h:outputText value="Type:"/>
    </h:outputLabel>
    <h:selectOneMenu
         binding="#{createProjectBean.
                    projectSelectOne}">
      <f:selectItems value="#{selectItems.projectTypes}"/>
    </h:selectOneMenu>
    <h:message for="typeSelectOne" styleClass="errors"/>

    <h:outputLabel for="initiatedByInput">
      <h:outputText value="Initiated by:"/>
    </h:outputLabel>
    <h:inputText id="initiatedByInput" size="40" required="true"
                 value="#{visit.currentProject.initiatedBy}">
      <f:validateLength minimum="2"/>
    </h:inputText>
    <h:message for="initiatedByInput" styleClass="errors"/>
    <h:outputLabel for="requirementsInput">
      <h:outputText value="Requirements contact:"/>
```

Bind to bean for initialization

```
    </h:outputLabel>
    <h:inputText id="requirementsInput" size="40"
         value="#{visit.currentProject.requirementsContact}"
         validator="#{createProjectBean.validateReqContact}"/>    <-- Add validator method
    <h:panelGroup/>

  <h:outputLabel for="requirementsEmailInput">
    <h:outputText value="Requirements contact e-mail:"/>
  </h:outputLabel>
  <h:inputText id="requirementsEmailInput" size="40"
       value="#{visit.currentProject.
                 requirementsContactEmail}"
       binding="#{createProjectBean.reqContactEmailInput}">   <-- Bind to bean for use with validator method
    <jia:validateRegEx
          expression=
           "\\w+([-+.]\\w+)*@\\w+([-.]\\w+)*\\.\\w+([-.]\\w+)*"
           errorMessage="Please enter a valid e-mail address."/>
  </h:inputText>
  <h:message for="requirementsEmailInput" styleClass="errors"

  <%@ include file="\includes\project_artifacts.jsp" %>

  <h:panelGroup/>

   <f:facet name="footer">

       <h:panelGroup>

        <h:panelGrid columns="1" cellpadding="5"
                     styleClass="table-background"
                     rowClasses="table-odd-row,table-even-row">
          <h:outputLabel for="commentsInput">
            <h:outputText value="Your comments:"/>
          </h:outputLabel>
          <h:inputTextarea id="commentsInput" rows="10" cols="80"
               value="#{visit.currentProject.initialComments}"/>
        </h:panelGrid>

         <h:panelGrid columns="2" rowClasses="table-odd-row">
           <h:commandButton value="Save"
                            action="#{createProjectBean.add}"/>
           <h:commandButton value="Cancel"
                            action="#{createProjectBean.cancel}"
                            immediate="true"/>
         </h:panelGrid>
         <h:panelGroup/>

       </h:panelGroup>
   </f:facet>
  </h:panelGrid>
```

```
    </h:form>

    </body>
    </html>
    </f:view>
```

Fortunately, the page with the most input controls was fairly straightforward to integrate—just hook up the value-bindings, and voilà! One integrated page.

Updating the navigation rule

This view references two action methods: `createProjectBean.approve` and `createProjectBean.cancel`. As luck would have it, these two methods have the exact same set of outcomes as the action methods referenced by the Approve a Project and Reject a Project pages, so the navigation rule changes are the same. See section 10.7.2, page 382 for details.

10.8 The Project Details page

The Project Details page is a read-only view of everything there is to know about a project. Most of its components are similar to the ones used in the Approve a Project and Create a Project pages, except that all of them (other than a single `HtmlCommandButton`) are output components. The model object we're interested in here is `visit.currentProject`, whose properties we listed earlier in table 10.7. This view also uses a backing bean called `showHistoryBean` to allow the user to page through the list of previous operations. That bean is summarized in table 10.11.

Table 10.11 `showHistoryBean` summary

Backing Bean	`showHistoryBean`	
Description	Allows the user to page through the current project's history.	
Scope	request	
Component Binding Property	**Type**	**Description**
`historyDataTable`	`HtmlDataTable`	Property for the table that lists the project history. Must be set so that the table will page through the history.

continued on next page

Table 10.11 `showHistoryBean` summary *(continued)*

Property	Type	Description
`currentProject-History`	`List`	List of operations that represent the current project's history.
`firstRow`	`int`	First row to display for the current page.
`rowsToDisplay`	`int`	Number of rows to display for each page.
Action Methods	**Outcomes**	**Description**
`next`	`"success"`, `"failure"`	Scrolls to the next page (changes the value of `firstRow`). Always returns `"success"` unless the last page has already been reached.
`previous`	`"success"`, `"failure"`	Scrolls to the previous page (changes the value of `firstRow`). Always returns `"success"` unless the first page has already been reached.
`cancel`	`"cancel_readonly"`, `"cancel_readwrite"`	Returns `"cancel_readonly"` if this is a read-only user (Upper Manager), or `"cancel_readwrite"` for other users.

As you can see, this bean exposes a `currentProjectHistory` property to contain the list of operations, and then exposes other properties that integrate well with an `HtmlDataTable` component. We'll use the `next` and `previous` action methods for buttons at the bottom of the history table.

Most of the integration work involves the simple process of adding value-bindings to the input controls, as usual; however, there are few anomalies. The steps are

- Update the paths for the JSP includes.
- Wire input controls to the corresponding `view.currentProject` properties.
- Change the `HtmlPanelGrid` used to display artifacts to an `HtmlDataTable`.
- Change the `HtmlPanelGrid` that displays project history to an `HtmlDataTable`, and associate it with `showHistoryBean`.
- Change the Ok `HtmlCommandButton` to reference an action method.

Note that two of these steps involve changing `HtmlPanelGrids` into `HtmlDataTables`, as we did in section 10.6. The translation is fairly simple, but it involves the same shift we discussed earlier—changing from a row-oriented layout of `HtmlPanelGrid` to a column-based layout of `HtmlDataTable`. The table for displaying the project's history will be associated with `showHistoryBean` and also require an additional footer with buttons for moving forward and backward in the history list; these buttons will be wired to the `next` and `previous` action methods of `showHistoryBean`. The updated page is shown in listing 10.13.

Listing 10.13 details.jsp: Integrated with visit.currentProject and showHistoryBean

```
<!DOCTYPE HTML PUBLIC "-//W3C//DTD HTML 4.01 Transitional//EN">

<%@ taglib uri="http://java.sun.com/jsf/core" prefix="f"%>
<%@ taglib uri="http://java.sun.com/jsf/html" prefix="h"%>

<f:view>
<html>
  <head>
    <title>
      <h:outputText value="ProjectTrack - Project details"/>
    </title>
    <link rel="stylesheet" type="text/css"
          href="<%= request.getContextPath() %>/stylesheet.css"/>
  </head>

<body class="page-background">

<jsp:include page="/includes/header.jsp"/>

<h:form>

  <h:panelGrid id="projectPanel" columns="2" cellpadding="5"
      footerClass="project-background"
      columnClasses=",project-data"
      styleClass="project-background"
      rowClasses="project-row">

    <f:facet name="header">
      <h:panelGrid columns="1" width="100%" cellpadding="3"
                   styleClass="project-background"
                   rowClasses="page-header">
          <h:outputText value="Project details"/>
      </h:panelGrid>
    </f:facet>

    <%@ include file="/includes/project_info.jsp" %>

    <h:outputText value="Completed artifacts:"/>
    <h:dataTable
        value="#{visit.currentProject.artifacts}"
        var="artifact" rowClasses="project-data"
        cellpadding="0" cellspacing="0">
      <h:column>
```

❶ Convert HtmlPanelGrid to HtmlDataTable

```
    <h:outputText value="#{artifact}"/>
  </h:column>
</h:dataTable>

<f:facet name="footer">

<h:panelGroup>
  <h:dataTable cellpadding="5"
       styleClass="table-background"
       value="#{showHistoryBean.
                currentProjectHistory}"
       var="operation"
       binding="#{showHistoryBean.
                  historyDataTable}"
       rows="#{showHistoryBean.
               rowsToDisplay}">

     <f:facet name="header">
       <h:outputText value="History" styleClass="table-header"/>
     </f:facet>

     <h:column>
       <h:panelGrid columns="1" width="100%" border="1"
                    styleClass="table-even-row">

        <h:panelGrid columns="3" cellpadding="7"
                     styleClass="table-even-row">
          <h:outputText value="#{operation.timestamp}">
            <f:convertDateTime
                 dateStyle="full"
                 timeStyle="short"/>
          </h:outputText>
          <h:outputText value=
           "#{operation.fromStatus} -> #{operation.toStatus}"/>
      <h:outputText value="(#{operation.user.role})"/>
        </h:panelGrid>

        <h:panelGrid columns="1" cellpadding="3"
                     styleClass="table-odd-row" width="100%">
          <h:outputText value="Comments:"/>
          <h:outputText value="#{operation.comments}"
                        styleClass="project-data"/>
        </h:panelGrid>
       </h:panelGrid>
     </h:column>

     <f:facet name="footer">
       <h:panelGroup>
         <h:commandLink action="#{showHistoryBean.previous}"
              rendered="#{showHistoryBean.showPrevious}"
                        style="padding-right: 5px;">
```

❷ Convert HtmlPanelGrid to HtmlDataTable

❸ Add converter for date value

❹ Add footer for scrolling buttons

```
                <h:outputText value="Previous"/>
              </h:commandLink>
              <h:commandLink action="#{showHistoryBean.next}"
                   rendered="#{showHistoryBean.showNext}">
                <h:outputText value="Next"/>
              </h:commandLink>
            </h:panelGroup>
          </f:facet>

        </h:dataTable>

        <h:commandButton value="Ok"
             action="#{showHistoryBean.cancel}"
             immediate="true" style="margin-top: 5px"/>    <-5 Set immediate
                                                               to true
      </h:panelGroup>
      </f:facet>

    </h:panelGrid>

  </h:form>

  </body>
  </html>
  </f:view>
```

❶ In this section, we change the artifact list from an `HtmlPanelGrid` with static data to an `HtmlDataTable` with dynamic data. In the updated code, we replaced the `<h:panelGrid>` tag with the `<h:dataTable>` tag, and were able to keep the `rowClasses` property as well as the HTML pass-through properties. The prototype had two hardcoded example `HtmlOutputText` components, which we replaced with a single component with a value-binding expression. This component is nested within a `UIColumn` so that the `HtmlDataTable` will use it as a template column. Because there's only one column in this table, this has the effect of showing all of the artifacts for the project—one per row.

❷ In this case, we replace the static `HtmlPanelGrid` with an `HtmlDataTable` for showing the project's history, which can consist of several operations (approvals or rejections). The new `HtmlDataTable` is bound to the `showProjectHistory` bean, which provides scrollable access to the project's history. The component's `rows` property is set to the `rowsToDisplay` property of the bean. We were able to keep the `cellpadding` and `styleClass` properties from the previous `HtmlPanelGrid` declaration.

All of the child panels remain the same, except for the addition of value-binding expressions for the `operation` variable (which represents the current row) and removal of the extra static row. These panels are explicitly grouped inside a single `UIColumn` component because there is only one column.

❸ Here we configure a `DateTime` converter for the `operation.timestamp` property. In our prototype, timestamps are hardcoded in text and look like this: "Tuesday, March 4, 2003 04:30 PM". But once we set use the value-binding expression `"#{operation.timestamp}"`, which is of type `Date`, the output looks more like this: "Tue Mar 4 16:30:23 EDT 2003". We could just leave it that way, but users have an uncanny way of expecting everything to look just like the prototype. Instead, we can achieve the same formatting as the prototype with a `DateTime` converter that has a `dateStyle` attribute set to `full` and a `timeStyle` attribute set to `short`.

❹ In order to control scrolling, we need Next and Previous buttons, which are bound to the `showHistoryBean`'s `next` and `previous` action methods. These methods update the values of the `currentProjectHistory`, `firstRow`, and `rowsToDisplay` properties as necessary. (These properties are bound to the `HtmlDataTable` component in ❷). The buttons, which are `HtmlCommandButton` components, are grouped inside the footer using an `HtmlPanelGroup` component.

❺ In the prototype, we didn't set the `immediate` property because there were no other input controls on the page. However, now that we've added other `HtmlCommandButtons`, it's prudent to ensure that cancellation happens before any other processing takes place. This is generally a good idea for cancel buttons anyway, regardless of the other components on the page. (Even though the button says Ok, it functions more like a cancel button, so we associated with the `showHistoryBean.cancel` action method.)

Now that we've dissected the changes to this view, let's see what needs to be done with the navigation rule.

10.8.1 Updating the navigation rule

In the prototype, we didn't define a navigation rule for the Project Details page because it returned an outcome that was defined in the toolbar's navigation rule. In our integrated page, there's a single `HtmlCommandButton` component that calls the `showHistoryBean.cancel` method, which returns either the `"success_readonly"` or `"success_readwrite"` outcomes. The new navigation rule is shown in listing 10.14.

Listing 10.14 faces-config.xml: New navigation rule for details.jsp

```
<navigation-rule>
<from-view-id>/includes/details.jsp</from-view-id>
<navigation-case>
  <from-outcome>cancel_readonly</from-outcome>
  <to-view-id>/includes/show_all.jsp</to-view-id>
   </navigation-case>
   <navigation-case>
```

```
      <from-outcome>cancel_readwrite</from-outcome>
    <to-view-id>/protected/inbox.jsp</to-view-id>
  </navigation-case>
  </navigation-rule>
```

When users click the page's Ok button, they will be sent to either the Show All or the Inbox page.

We're almost there. This is the last page from chapters 8 and 9 that we need to integrate. With a quick set of relatively minor changes, we were able to fully integrate it with our backing beans, resulting in a fully functional application. Well, it's fully functional except for things like an error page and internationalization.

10.9 Adding an error page

Now that we have a fully working application, the question of the day is: what do we do if something goes *wrong*? We haven't configured an error page for our web application, and although some action methods return an `"error"` outcome, we haven't defined a navigation case to handle it. So, let's make a simple error page and then let the rest of our application know about it. The page is shown in listing 10.15.

Listing 10.15 error.jsp: Simple JSP error page (with no JSF controls)

```
<!DOCTYPE HTML PUBLIC "-//W3C//DTD HTML 4.01 Transitional//EN">

<html>
  <head>
    <title>ProjectTrack - Error"</title>
    <link rel="stylesheet" type="text/css"
          href="stylesheet.css"/>
  </head>

<body class="page-background">

<span class="error-heading">
 Sorry, a fatal error has occurred. The error has been logged.
</span>
<p>
  <a href="<%= request.getContextPath()%>">Please log in again.</a>
</p>

</body>
</html>
```

The one odd thing about this page is that it doesn't reference any JSF components. Why not? Because if there's a problem with the JSF implementation itself, the error page wouldn't work. It's entirely possible to create one error page with JSF components that's referenced in your navigation rules, and another one without JSF components that's referenced in web.xml, but then you have to maintain two files. Another option is to define a single page in web.xml and then have your actions throw exceptions—this way, it will catch errors. This approach doesn't allow you to specify different error pages for different actions, as you can with JSF navigation rules. So, we'll define this page both in the deployment descriptor and in the navigation rules.

10.9.1 Updating web.xml

To add the error page, we can add the following three lines to ProjectTrack's deployment descriptor (web.xml):

```
<web-app>
...
  <error-page>
    <location>/error.jsp</location>
  </error-page>
...
</web-app>
```

Now, if there's ever a fatal error that our application doesn't handle, or in the JSF implementation itself, this page will be displayed.

10.9.2 Updating the navigation rule

For cases where our application catches its exceptions (as it should), we must define a new navigation case. The outcome we're going to handle is `"error"`, which is returned by several ProjectTrack action methods. In order to ensure that it's always handled, we can add it to our global navigation rule:

```
<navigation-rule>
  <description>Navigation for the toolbar.</description>
  <from-view-id>*</from-view-id>
...
  <navigation-case>
     <from-outcome>error</from-outcome>
     <to-view-id>/error.jsp</to-view-id>
  </navigation-case>
...
</navigation-rule>
```

That's it for the error page. A real application would most likely have something a little more sophisticated, possibly with different error pages for different outcomes or views.

Now, let's make this application speak another language.

10.10 Internationalizing and localizing the UI

At this point, we have a complete, working application. However, when we defined ProjectTrack's requirements in chapter 7, we specified support for English *and* Russian. So far, we've been dealing exclusively with English text. Since we've hardcoded all of this English text in every page, supporting another language will take a bit of work.

That bit of work is called *internationalization*—the ability to support more than one language. Fortunately, it's a onetime affair. Once we've internationalized ProjectTrack, it will be fairly easy to add other languages, or *localize,* the application (assuming the language isn't different enough to force different layouts).

TIP If your prototype is fairly complicated, it can save time to internationalize it first, even if it only supports one language.

Internationalization and localization are covered in detail in chapter 6, but the process is pretty straightforward. The first step is to add the proper text to a resource bundle.

10.10.1 Externalizing text into the resource bundle

In order to internationalize ProjectTrack, we need to pull out all of our display strings into a resource bundle and then change all hardcoded text to value-binding expressions that reference that bundle. In general, this means *every* string that the user sees. Having all of the strings in one or more resource bundles not only makes localization possible, it also makes it easier to change the text the application displays, especially if you have the same text in more than one place.

In chapter 8, we created a resource bundle for ProjectTrack's messages called ptrackResources.properties, placed it in the WEB-INF/classes directory and added it to faces-config.xml. All we need to do now is centralize all of the application's display strings in this file, as shown in listing 10.16.

Listing 10.16 ptrackResources.properties: Text strings from the UI

```
...
# Login
LoginCaption=Enter your user name:
PasswordCaption=Password:
SubmitButtonImage=/images/submit.gif

# Header
AppNameHeader=ProjectTrack
InboxToolbarButton=Inbox
ShowAllToolbarButton=Show All
CreateNewToolbarButton=Create New
LogoutToolbarButton=Logout
LanguageCaption=Language
LanguageButton=Go!

# Inbox
InboxHeader=Inbox - approve or reject projects

# Show All
ShowAllHeader=Show all projects
ProjectWaitingForHeader=Waitingfor

# Inbox and Show All
ProjectNameHeader=Project name
ProjectTypeHeader=Type
ProjectStatusHeader=Status

# Create a Project
CreateProjectHeader=Create a project

# Approve a Project
ApproveProjectHeader=Approve a project

# Reject a Project
RejectProjectHeader=Reject a project

# Project Details
ProjectDetailsHeader=Project details
ProjectHistoryHeader=History
ProjectHistoryCommentsCaption=Comments

# Create a Project, Approve a Project, Reject a Project,
# Project Details
ProjectNameCaption=Name
ProjectTypeCaption=Type
ProjectInitiatedByCaption=Initiated by
ProjectReqContactCaption=Requirements contact
ProjectReqContactEmailCaption=Requirements contact e-mail
ProjectArtifactsCaption=Completed artifacts
```

```
ProjectComments=Your comments
...
```

Note that we organized the entries by page, and that some entries are used by several pages. If one day we decide the "Requirements contact" label, which is displayed on four pages, should be replaced with the text "The person responsible for this mess," we could make the change once in ptrackResources.properties instead of each page.

That takes care of step one. Step two is actually modifying the pages.

10.10.2 Internationalizing the header

Once we've externalized the text and placed it in a resource bundle, we need to modify all of the views to use value-binding expressions instead of hardcoded text. We can load this resource bundle with the `<f:loadBundle>` tag. Let's take a look at a modified version of the header (listing 10.17) that's fully internationalized and that uses the ptrackResources.properties bundle we defined in the previous section.

Listing 10.17 header.jsp: Internationalized

```
<%@ taglib uri="http://java.sun.com/jsf/core" prefix="f"%>
<%@ taglib uri="http://java.sun.com/jsf/html" prefix="h"%>
<%@ taglib uri="jsf-in-action-components" prefix="jia"%>

<f:loadBundle basename="ptrackResources"          Load bundle as request-
    var="bundle"/>                                scoped variable

<f:subview id="header">

  <h:form>

    <h:panelGrid columns="3" cellspacing="0" cellpadding="0"
                 styleClass="header" width="100%">

      <jia:navigatorToolbar id="toolbar" layout="horizontal"
          headerClass="toolbar-header" itemClass="toolbar-command"
          selectedItemClass="toolbar-command"
          iconClass="toolbar-icon"
          immediate="false">  <!>

        <f:facet name="header">
          <h:outputText value="#{bundle.AppNameHeader}:"/>
        </f:facet>
```

```
        <jia:navigatorItem name="inbox"
                           label="#{bundle.InboxToolbarButton}"
                           icon="/images/inbox.gif"
                           action="inbox"
                           disabled="#{!authenticationBean.
                                        inboxAuthorized}"/>
        <jia:navigatorItem name="showAll"
                           label="#{bundle.ShowAllToolbarButton}"
                           icon="/images/show_all.gif"
                           action="show_all"/>
        <jia:navigatorItem name="createNew"
                           label="#{bundle.CreateNewToolbarButton}"
                           icon="/images/create.gif"
                           action="#{createProjectBean.create}"
                           disabled="#{!authenticationBean.
                                        createNewAuthorized}"/>
        <jia:navigatorItem name="logout"
                           label="#{bundle.LogoutToolbarButton}"
                           icon="/images/logout.gif"
                     action="#{authenticationBean.logout}"/>
    </jia:navigatorToolbar>

      <h:panelGroup>
        <h:outputLabel for="languageSelect">
          <h:outputText value="#{bundle.LanguageCaption}:"
                        styleClass="language-select"/>
        </h:outputLabel>
        <h:selectOneListbox id="languageSelect" size="1"
                            styleClass="language-select"
                            value="#{visit.locale}">
          <f:selectItems value="#{visit.supportedtLocaleItems}"/>
        </h:selectOneListbox>
        <h:commandButton value="#{bundle.LanguageButton}"
                         styleClass="language-select-button"/>
      </h:panelGroup>

      <h:outputText value="(#{visit.user.login})"
                    styleClass="user-name"/>
    </h:panelGrid>
  </h:form>
</f:subview>
```

This page will look exactly the same as it did before, except that now any display text will be changed in ptrackResources.properties instead of in header.jsp.

All of the other ProjectTrack pages can be internationalized in exactly the same way. However, in order for them to display another language, we need to localize the application for that language as well.

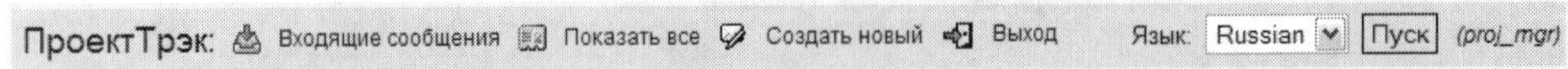

Figure 10.4 The header localized for Russian.

10.10.3 Localizing for Russian

In section 10.10.1, we created an English resource bundle. Note that the name—ptrackResources.properties—doesn't contain a locale or country code. We could have used ptrackResources_en.properties to specify English; leaving out the suffix means that this bundle is the default—the text that will be seen if all else fails. That's fine, because our default language really is English. It's time to make another resource bundle, however, for Russian—the other language that ProjectTrack must support. After we've created this resource and configured the application, we'll get the lovely browser output shown in figure 10.4.

The first step is to copy ptrackResources.properties into a new file called ptrackResources_ru.properties. The suffix "ru" means that the bundle supports Russian. Note that this is generic Russian, rather than the Russian spoken in a particular country. (See appendix E for a list of language and country codes). Next, we change all of the values to Russian (the keys remain the same). The result is shown in listing 10.18.

Listing 10.18 ptrackResources_ru.properties: All strings translated to Russian

```
# Standard messages
javax.faces.component.UIInput.REQUIRED=
  необходимое поле
javax.faces.component.UIInput.REQUIRED_detail=
  Пожалуйста, заполните поле
javax.faces.validator.LengthValidator.MAXIMUM=
  Поле должно быть короче, чем {0} знак[а/ов]
javax.faces.validator.LengthValidator.MINIMUM=
  Поле должно быть не короче, чем {0} знак[а/ов]

# Login
LoginCaption=Введите имя пользователя
PasswordCaption=Пароль
SubmitButtonTitle=отправит
SubmitButtonImage=/images/submit_ru.gif
SubmitButtonOverImage=/images/submit_over_ru.gif

# Header
AppNameHeader=ПроектТрэк
InboxToolbarButton=Входящие сообщения
ShowAllToolbarButton=Показать все
CreateNewToolbarButton=Создать новый
LogoutToolbarButton=Выход
```

```
LanguageCaption=Язык
LanguageButton=Пуск

# Inbox
InboxHeader=Подтвердить или отменить проекты

# Show All
ShowAllHeader=Показать все проекты
ProjectWaitingForHeader=Ожидание

# Inbox and Show All
ProjectNameHeader=Название проекта
ProjectTypeHeader=Тип
ProjectStatusHeader=Статус

# Create a Project
CreateProjectHeader=Создать проект

# Approve a Project
ApproveProjectHeader=Подтвердить проект

# Reject a Project
RejectProjectHeader=Отменить проект

# Project Details
ProjectDetailsHeader=Детали проекта
ProjectHistoryHeader=История
ProjectHistoryCommentsCaption=Комментарии

# Create a Project, Approve a Project,
# Reject a Project, Project Details

ProjectNameCaption=Название
ProjectTypeCaption=Тип
ProjectInitiatedByCaption=Кем создано
ProjectReqContactCaption=Запрос контакта
ProjectReqContactEmailCaption=Запрос адреса электронной почты
ProjectArtifactsCaption=Завершение артефакта
ProjectComments=Ваши комментарии
...
```

This file is exactly the same as the one in listing 10.16 except for the Russian text, and a different image file name for the Submit button.

NOTE After you have created a localized properties file (with whatever character coding is appropriate for that language), you must convert it to use Unicode characters. This can be done with the native2ascii tool included with the Java Development Kit (JDK). See the API docs for `PropertyResourceBundle` for more information.

The last step is to update faces-config.xml.

Updating faces-config.xml

In order for JSF to support a new locale, it must be configured in faces-config.xml under the `<application>` node. By default, JSF chooses the default locale of the current Java Virtual Machine (JVM). We'd like ProjectTrack to support English (as the default) and Russian as well. We're interested in the locales only (no country codes are required). This boils down to the addition to faces-config.xml shown in listing 10.19.

Listing 10.19 faces-config.xml: Adding language support

```
...
<application>
  <locale-config>
    <default-locale>en</default-locale>
    <supported-locale>en</supported-locale>
    <supported-locale>ru</supported-locale>
  </locale-config>
  <message-bundle>ptrackResources</message-bundle>
</application>
...
```

As you can see, all we've added is the `<local-config>` element, specifying support for both en and ru, with en being the default.

That's it—we've walked through turning a simple prototype into a fully internationalized, integrated application localized for both English and Russian.

10.11 Summary

Once you've built an eye-catching set of screens with JSF components, it's fairly easy to integrate them with back-end objects. First, you need to understand the application's environment—the specific backing beans, event listeners, and model objects that make it tick. What's most important is that you know what properties are exposed, and how the different objects relate to one another and the event listeners. For ProjectTrack, UI components interact with backing beans that expose properties, model objects, and event listeners. You don't need to know the entire object model before you can start integrating—you only need to know the objects that are necessary to make a particular page interactive.

After you understand the application's environment, integrating each page is mostly a matter of hooking up UI components to backing beans with value-binding expressions. Command components often need to be associated with actions via method-binding expressions as well. Sometimes, you'll encounter situations where the dynamic nature of the data may require changing components (for instance, changing from an `HtmlPanelGrid` to an `HtmlDataTable`) or using a converter to format a date or a number.

In this chapter, we applied these techniques to ProjectTrack and walked through integrating each prototypical page developed in the previous two chapters. The end result is a fully integrated version of the application, which, amazingly enough, looks almost exactly like the prototype (that's why we left out the screen shots). We also added an error page and localized the application for Russian. In the next part, we move from front-end development to the back-end, and explore the Java classes that make JSF tick. In the process, we'll peer into the black boxes that make up the application's environment and explain how to write the actual Java code for ProjectTrack.

Part 3

Developing application logic

Part 2 examined how to build a user interface using JSF components, and how to integrate those components with back-end logic. In part 3, we show you how to build that back-end logic. We start with an overview of the Faces API, and then move on to build backing beans and other objects that were used in part 2. Finally, we show you how to integrate JSF with Struts and other frameworks. This part of the book is primarily intended for application developers.

11 The JSF environment

This chapter covers

- Evaluating JSF EL expressions in code
- The `FacesContext` class
- Events and event listener classes
- Key UI component classes
- Other core classes in the JSF API

Whenever you're writing an application that runs within a particular framework, there is a set of classes that you use on a daily basis. These classes form the API to the environment—the world in which your application runs. In this chapter, we discuss the classes that you'll encounter in day-to-day JavaServer Faces development, and take a close look at its component model.

11.1 From servlets to JSF

If you've done servlet programming before, you're probably familiar with the basic servlet classes like `HttpServlet`, `HttpSession`, `HttpRequest`, `HttpResponse`, and `ServletContext`. (The Portlet API, which you can also use with JSF, has extremely similar classes that are based on the Servlet API.) `HttpServlet` has the primary servlet entry point—the `service` method.[1] This is where you actually process the user's request. It has two parameters: an `HttpServletRequest` instance for input, and an `HttpServletResponse` object for output. You can store attributes in those two objects, as well as in the `HttpSession` object (which represents the same user between requests).

Application-wide attributes and methods are available via the `ServletContext`. The user's response is dependent on how you process the `HttpServletResponse` object; you can write to an output stream directly, but usually you delegate to a display technology like JSP or Velocity [ASF, Velocity] after you've grabbed parameters from the `HttpServletRequest` object and processed them accordingly.

The servlet model is pretty tightly coupled with HTTP, and consequently low level by nature. In other words, it's tedious. With frameworks like Struts [ASF, Struts], things are easier—instead of worrying about subclassing `HttpServlet`, you subclass `Action` classes, which process specific requests. `Action`s access (or contain) your application logic, and usually forward to another resource, such as a JSP or a template (resources are managed externally, like JSF). You still have to use the other servlet classes, though, because the framework doesn't shield you from the Servlet API.

JSF has its own set of classes that you'll encounter when building applications, and they provide a more high-level, event-oriented view of the world. The framework as a whole has quite a few classes; here we focus only on the ones necessary

1 This is an oversimplification. Technically, the default service method dispatches to `doGet`, `doPost`, `doPut`, or `doTrace`, depending on the type of HTTP request (GET, POST, PUT, or TRACE). Usually the real code goes in `doGet` and `doPost`.

for application development. Of course, you can still get a handle to the servlet or portlet environment, but in many cases, you won't need to.

From an application development perspective, JSF's classes can be organized into four main categories: application, context, event handling, and UI components. Application classes are split into two areas. First, there is the `Application` class. Conceptually, this class is similar to `ServletContext` because it represents the web application as a whole. In practice, it provides access to many JSF-specific features, such as JSF EL evaluation and factory methods for JSF objects. This group also includes your application logic, organized into backing beans. Since backing beans don't require a superclass and manage data and events, they are sort of a hybrid of Struts' `Action` classes and `ActionForms`. Backing bean properties and methods are made accessible through the JSF EL.

Context-related classes provide access to current request data, a handle to the outside environment, and entry to objects in other categories. In many ways, classes in this category replace `HttpServletRequest`. However, they represent a larger concept—the state of the application while it's processing a set of user-generated events.

Event-handling classes are responsible for processing user gestures, such as clicking on a button or changing the value of an input field. In servlets, the request *is* the event. In JSF, request parameters are translated into event objects, and you can write listeners for processing those events.

As we've discussed, views in JSF are entirely composed of UI components, which can be manipulated with Java code. Because neither servlets nor Struts have a full-fledged component model, they have no true equivalent.

Figure 11.1 is a high-level class diagram that shows the primary classes in each of these areas. In the group of application-related classes, the `Application` class provides access to supported locales, factory methods for UI components, and access to the default message resource bundle. It's also responsible for creating `ValueBinding` and `MethodBinding` instances, which can be used to evaluate JSF EL expressions in code. These expressions usually reference properties and methods in your backing beans.

The context-related classes center around the venerable `FacesContext` class, which provides access to `FacesMessages`, `FacesEvents`, and the `ExternalContext`. The event-handling classes provide three sets of event/listener pairs—one for action events, one for value-change events, and one for phase events. In addition, there's a default `ActionListener` that delegates to action methods. (There is technically no concrete class defined for the default `ActionListener`, but it does have required behavior.)

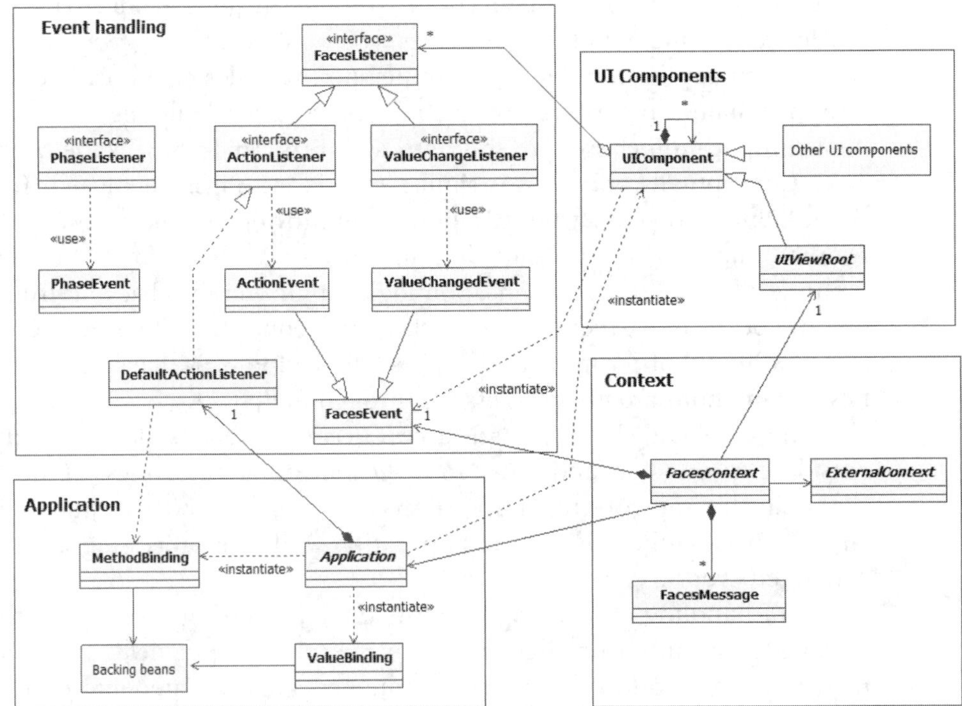

Figure 11.1 A high-level class diagram of JSF's application-related classes. These classes can be categorized into four general areas: event handling (for processing user input), component management (for manipulating components on a page), application (for factory methods and configuration information), and context (for handling the current request and accessing other resources).

All UI components extend the `UIComponent` abstract class. Views are implemented by the `UIViewRoot` class, which is the container for all of the `UIComponent` instances on a page, and can be retrieved from the `FacesContext`. However, because components often have child-parent relationships, any `UIComponent` instance can contain other `UIComponents`.

In the following sections, we'll survey the classes in each of these categories and show you the key methods of their interfaces. We won't explain every method in detail—that's why they invented JavaDocs—but we will give you a sense of what the methods do and where you might use them. If you haven't looked at chapter 2 in a while, we recommend that you review the section "The Request Processing Lifecycle" on page 57 before reading this chapter. If you're not interested in surveying each of these classes individually right now, skip ahead to chapter 12 to see how they're used in a real application. You can always refer back to this chapter later.

BY THE WAY You may have noticed that there's no mention of renderers in this section. That's because they're largely transparent to your application code. If you want to learn more about them, see chapter 15.

11.2 The application foundation

Every JSF application is made up of quite a few sets of objects: UI components, backing beans, converters, validators, events, listeners, and so on. In order to make sense of this world, there must be some classes that help tie them together. These are the application-related classes. At the core is the `Application` instance itself; on the periphery are classes that evaluate JSF EL expressions, which associate different objects in an application: `ValueBinding` and `MethodBinding`. These three classes are summarized in table 11.1.

Table 11.1 The `Application` instance provides access to global resources.

Class or Interface	Package	Where to Get a Reference	Description
`Application`	`javax.faces.application`	`FacesContext.getApplication()`	Provides access to supported locales, default render kit, and factory methods for creating UI components, converters, validators, and value-binding expressions
`ValueBinding`	`javax.faces.el`	`Application.createValueBinding()`, `UIComponent.getValueBinding()`	Represents a value-binding expression, and provides the ability to set or evaluate that expression
`MethodBinding`	`javax.faces.el`	`Application.createMethodBinding()`	Represents a method-binding expression, and provides the ability to set or evaluate that expression

In the following sections, we cover these classes.

11.2.1 Application

If you've done client-server development with Borland Delphi or Microsoft .NET, the notion of an `Application` class should seem familiar to you. In those environments, a single `Application` instance runs the main Windows message loop and provides a number of utility methods for such tasks as managing threads and accessing the startup directory.

In JSF applications, there is no message loop, and a lot of the user-oriented types of methods are available via the `FacesContext` or the `ExternalContext` (covered later in this chapter). The JSF `Application` class (located in the `javax.faces.application` package), does, however, serve two important purposes. First, it provides access to configured parameters, like the set of supported locales, and the application's message bundle. Second, it provides factory methods for creating `ValueBindings`, `MethodBindings`, `UIComponents`, `Validators`, `Converters`, and so on.

You can retrieve a new `Application` instance from the `FacesContext`:

```
Application app = facesContext.getApplication();
```

In many cases, your code will have a reference to the current `FacesContext` instance, and if not, there is a static method that will return it for you (see section 11.3.1).

Let's start with the `supportedLocales` property, which keeps track of all the locales that the application currently supports:

```
public Iterator getSupportedLocales();
```

Support for locales is configured in a JSF configuration file; you cannot guarantee that your application will support any locale that hasn't been configured to support. The `supportedLocales` property has some interesting possibilities, like dynamically populating an item list and allowing users to select their current locale—see chapter 12 for such an example.

As we've discussed, you can also configure an application-wide resource bundle that can be used for messages and other strings. You can retrieve the name of this bundle with the `messageBundle` property:

```
public String getMessageBundle();
```

JSF uses this bundle internally to override default validation and conversion messages. You can also use it to create your own messages or localize other strings through this bundle. To do this, however, you'll need to create a new `java.util.ResourceBundle` instance yourself, since `getMessageBundle` just returns the base name:

```
String bundleName = application.getMessageBundle();
ResourceBundle bundle =
  ResourceBundle.getBundle(bundleName, locale);
```

In most cases, it's practical to create utility methods for working with resource bundles and creating messages; we show this technique in chapter 13.

Every JSF application has a default render kit whose identifier is exposed through the `renderKitId` property:

```
public String getDefaultRenderKitId();
public void setDefaultRenderKitId(String renderKitId);
```

This value is configured in a JSF configuration file, and the default is "HTML_BASIC" (which is represented by the RenderKitFactory.HTML_BASIC_RENDER_KIT constant). You normally won't need to reference this property, but it can be useful in cases where you're not sure what the default render kit is.

WARNING If you're using the JSF RI [Sun, JSF RI] 1.0 or 1.1, do not call setDefaultRenderKit after JSF has processed its first request because the implementation cannot support multiple render kits at the same time. We hope this will change in a future release.

One of JSF's most powerful features is the ability to manipulate JSF EL expressions in code. The Application class has utility methods to facilitate this process, which you will often use:

```
public ValueBinding createValueBinding(String ref)
                              throws ReferenceSyntaxException;
public MethodBinding createMethodBinding(String ref, Class[] params)
                              throws ReferenceSyntaxException;
```

Value-binding expressions are encapsulated by the ValueBinding class, and method-binding expressions are encapsulated by the MethodBinding class. Any time you need to evaluate either one, you can call one of these factory methods to retrieve an instance. Once you have retrieved it, you can access its value, set its value, and find out more about it. See section 11.1.2 for more information about these classes.

The Application class also has factory methods for creating several other types of objects, including UI components:

```
public UIComponent createComponent(String componentType)
                              throws FacesException;
public UIComponent createComponent(
                            ValueBinding componentBinding,
                            FacesContext context,
                            String componentType)
                              throws FacesException;
```

The first method is simple—it just creates a new UI component based on its type. What is its type? Basically, it's an identifier the component was given in a JSF configuration file; you can map this identifier to a specific class name. For example, you could register the class name com.my.SillyComponent with the type "SillyComponent". Subsequent calls to getComponent with that type would return a new instance of your class. All of the standard components are registered this way, and they expose their type through a constant called `COMPONENT_TYPE`. Here's an example:

```
HtmlOutputText outputText = application.createComponent(
                                HtmlOutputText.COMPONENT_TYPE);
```

JSF uses similar conventions for validators and converters as well. This means that you can register your own classes as well as override the defaults; regardless, these factory methods will work the same.

The second `createComponent` method gives a backing bean the opportunity to create and initialize a new UI component instance. The `componentBinding` parameter should point to a backing bean property that returns the proper UI component instance. If the property returns `null`, this method creates a new instance based on the component's type and uses it to set the backing bean property. This is how JSF handles component bindings internally, but you may want to call this method in rare cases when you need such factory-like functionality in code. See chapter 12 for more information about component binding properties.

The following method creates new `Validator` instances:

```
public Validator createValidator(String validatorId)
                             throws FacesException;
```

A validator class's identifier is made available through the `VALIDATOR_ID` constant. You may want to create a new `Validator` instance if you're initializing a UI component in code. Validators can only be registered on components that implement the `EditableValueHolder` interface; see section 11.5.4 for more information.

The following two methods can be used to create new `Converter` instances:

```
public Converter createConverter(String converterId);
public Converter createConverter(Class targetClass);
```

You may remember from chapter 6 that converters can be registered by identifier or by type (`Integer`, `Date`, `boolean`, and so on). The first method creates a new `Converter` based on its identifier, and the latter creates a new instance based on its type. More often than not, you'll use the first method because JSF handles the second case for you automatically. Converter classes usually have a `CONVERTER_ID` constant that equals their identifier. They can only be used with UI components that implement the `ValueHolder` interface; see section 11.5.3 for more information.

Whenever you need to create a new instance of these classes, you should use these methods rather than create the objects manually. If you declare your user interface with a display technology, as shown in this book with JSP, you usually won't need to create `Converter`, `Validator`, and `UIComponent` instances in Java code unless you're initializing a new UI component through a component binding property, or modifying a view based on user input.

BY THE WAY We've only scratched the surface of the `Application` class's functionality because this discussion is constrained to possible everyday application development usage. In many ways, it's the programmatic interface to your application's configuration. It contains mappings between identifiers and classes for all of JSF's core objects. It also exposes a lot of the framework's pluggable functionality, such as the default `ActdionListener` as well as classes that are used for navigation, creating views, and so on. See appendix C for more information about JSF's internals and some of its advanced customization opportunities.

Throughout the rest of this book, you'll see many references to the `Application` class, primarily for its factory methods. The following sections elaborate on two of the classes returned by those methods—`ValueBinding` and `MethodBinding`.

11.2.2 Evaluation expressions

Most of our discussions about JSF's EL have centered around the syntax and semantics, as well as use within JSP. As it turns out, you can programmatically create and evaluate expressions using the same APIs that JSF uses internally. The `ValueBinding` class represents value-binding exceptions, and the `MethodBinding` class represents method binding expressions.

BY THE WAY `ValueBinding` and `MethodBinding` use other classes to perform their actual work. These classes are pluggable, so you can swap in different implementations, and you can also add additional functionality, such as your own implicit variables. See appendix C for more information about the classes behind the EL.

ValueBinding

`ValueBinding` is a class in the `javax.faces.el` package that represents a specific value-binding expression. It has five methods:

```
public String getExpressionString();
public Object getValue(FacesContext facesContext)
                            throws PropertyNotFoundException;
public void setValue(FacesContext facesContext,
                                Object object)
                         throws PropertyNotFoundException;
```

```
public boolean isReadOnly(FacesContext facesContext)
                          throws PropertyNotFoundException;
public Class getType(FacesContext facesContext)
                     throws PropertyNotFoundException;
```

With these methods, you can determine the value or type of the object to which the expression evaluates, as well as set the object and find out if the expression is read-only. Also, you can retrieve the original expression using the `expressionString` property.

Usually, you'll just use `getValue` to retrieve the referenced object:

```
User user = (User)app.createValueBinding("#{sessionScope.user}").
                      getValue(facesContext);
```

or `setValue` to set it:

```
app.createValueBinding("#{sessionScope.user}").
    setValue(facesContext, user);
```

`PropertyNotFoundException` is a runtime exception; you're not forced to catch it.

This is generally how you retrieve or set an object in one of the application's scopes rather than using servlet methods because the `ValueBinding` instance automatically uses the Managed Bean Creation facility, which creates managed beans that are defined in a JSF configuration file (if they don't already exist).

When you write custom components, you will tend to work with `ValueBinding` instances more often.

MethodBinding

Method-binding expressions in the JSF EL are represented by the `MethodBinding` class, also located in the `javax.faces.el` package. `MethodBinding` has three methods:

```
public String getExpressionString();
public Object invoke(FacesContext context,
                     Object[] params)
                  throws EvaluationException,
                         MethodNotFoundException;
public Class getType(FacesContext context)
                     throws MethodNotFoundException;
```

The `getType` method returns the class of the method's return type.

When you're developing applications, your use of `MethodBinding` will be somewhat limited. You may, however, use it to set an action listener method, value-change listener method, or validator method on a specific UI component that you are manipulating in code:

```
MethodBinding mBinding =
   app.createMethodBinding("#{myBean.myActionListener}",
```

```
                                new Class[] { ActionEvent.class } );
myUICommand.setActionListener(mBinding);
```

This snippet creates a new `MethodBinding` instance for the `myActionListener` method of the backing bean `myBean`, and then uses it to set a `UICommand` instance's `actionListener` property. This registers the `myActionListener` method to handle any action events `UICommand` may fire, and is equivalent to the following JSP:

```
<h:commandButton ...
    valueChangeListener="#{myBean.myActionListener"}/>
```

This is the most common use case for `MethodBinding` during ordinary application development. If you develop custom components, however, you may wish to expose event listener properties that are of type `MethodBinding`, and consequently you'll work with them more heavily. See chapter 15 for details.

The `Application` class, `ValueBinding`, and `MethodBinding` are the backdrop of the JSF environment. `FacesContext`, however, is the gateway.

11.3 It's all in the context

Context is a popular term in modern APIs. It's all over the place in Java—`EJBContext`, `ServletContext`, `NamingContext`, and so on. If you go to Dictionary.com and look up *context*, you'll find this definition: "The circumstances in which an event occurs; a setting." In the world of JavaServer Faces, that event is something the user does with the UI like clicking on a hyperlink or expanding a node in a tree control. Once event processing has begun, you have access to the application's setting, or state. This state is encapsulated in the `FacesContext` class, from which you can access messages and the external context (which is provided by the servlet or portlet container). This state is fleeting; it exists only while events are being processed.

Table 11.2 lists all of the context-related classes.

Table 11.2 Context-related JSF classes represent the application's current user-related state.

Class or Interface	Package	Where to Get a Reference	Description
`FacesContext`	`javax.faces.context`	Either passed in, or via `FacesContext.getCurrentInstance()`	Represents the state of the current request. You can get access to the current view, add a new message, control the lifecycle, and so on. This is the main entry point into the JSF API when you're developing an application.

continued on next page

Table 11.2 Context-related JSF classes represent the application's current user-related state. *(continued)*

Class or Interface	Package	Where to Get a Reference	Description
`FacesMessage`	`javax.faces.application`	`FacesContext.getMessages()`	Represents a message for the current request (normally used to report errors). `FacesContext` keeps a list of messages. Messages can be displayed with an `HtmlMessage` or `HtmlMessages` component.
`External-Context`	`javax.faces.context`	`FacesContext.getExternal-Context()`	Provides access to the hosting environment, which is either a servlet or portlet container. From here, you can get access to the underlying session, request, response objects, and so on.

We cover all of these classes in the following sections.

11.3.1 FacesContext

The window into the soul of a JSF application is the `FacesContext`. Technically, it represents the state of the current HTTP request. Conceptually, you can think of it as the class that has all the stuff you need to interact with the UI and the rest of the JSF environment. The JSF implementation will either create a new instance for each request or choose one from a pool of available instances. Either way, there will be an instance available to you any time your application is interacting with a user.

WARNING Do not access `FacesContext` from any thread other than the one servicing the request. In other words, don't spawn a new thread and try to use a `FacesContext` instance—this behavior is not supported.

`FacesContext` is a class in the `javax.faces.context` package. In action methods and other places in your code, you may not have access to the current instance. If that's the case, there's a static method you can use to access it:

```
public static FacesContext getCurrentInstance();
```

This method returns the `FacesContext` instance for the current thread.

While an event is being processed, this class manages a list of the messages relating that event. These are typically validation error messages, converter error messages, and any messages your event listeners generate. Five methods are available for working with these messages:

```
public FacesMessage.Severity getMaximumSeverity();
public Iterator getClientIdsWithMessages();
public Iterator getMessages();
public Iterator getMessages(String clientId);
public void addMessage(String clientId, FacesMessage message);
```

These methods manipulate the current list of `FacesMessage` instances; the list is cleared after the response has been sent back to the user. Messages are used for both errors and information, so each one has a severity level. By using `getMaximumSeverity`, you can see if there are any serious errors. Messages can be registered for a specific component (as is usually the case with validation or conversion errors), or for the whole page.

Components are identified by their client identifier, which is the identifier rendered in the view (see chapter 2). Specifying `null` as the first parameter to `addMessage` tells JSF that the message relates to the entire view. Using `null` also works when you're retrieving messages with `getMessages`. If no messages are available, you'll get an empty `Iterator`. If you want to determine which components have messages waiting for them, call `getClientIdsWithMessages`. See the next section for more information about messages.

Each JSF view is represented by a tree of components. You can use the `FacesContext` to access the view with these methods:

```
public UIViewRoot getViewRoot();
public void setTree(UIViewRoot tree);
```

Use `getViewRoot` to access or remove existing components on the current page, or add new components. Use `setViewRoot` to tell JSF to display an entirely different page altogether. We cover `UIViewRoot` and related classes in section 11.4.

You can control the JSF Request Processing Lifecycle with these methods:

```
public void renderResponse();
public void responseComplete();
```

Use `renderResponse` to jump to the Render Response phase, which displays the currently selected view back to the user. This effectively skips all further event processing and all phases in between the current phase and the Render Response phase. Use `responseComplete` if you've already sent an entire response back to the user; it skips all subsequent event processing and phases, *including* the Render Response phase.

JSF application code usually doesn't send output directly to the user; after all, that's the whole point of display technologies like JSP as well as component renderers. However, two methods are available that provide access to the underlying output stream:

```
public ResponseStream getResponseStream();
public ResponseWriter getResponseWriter();
```

These methods are useful if you need to return binary data (like an image file) or add direct output to the beginning of a response. Use `getResponseStream` for outputting binary data and `getResponseWriter` for character data (`ResponseWriter` has some useful methods for outputting markup). You have to use either one or the other; you can't output both binary and character data.[2] If you use these methods to generate the entire response, then you also need to call `responseComplete` so that JSF won't attempt to send a response as well.

You can access the Servlet API you know and love (or hate), as well as the Portlet API, with the `getExternalContext` method:

```
public ExternalContext getExternalContext();
```

The `ExternalContext` provides a wrapper for just about every Servlet or Portlet API method you can think of, and direct access to specific objects (like `HttpRequest`) if necessary. Most of the time, you won't need to use the `ExternalContext`, but it's particularly handy for migrating existing applications to JSF, and for performing tasks that the JSF APIs can't handle, such as invalidating the session. We cover this class in section 11.3.3.

Those are all of the essential `FacesContext` methods for application development. Typically you'll find that retrieving the `FacesContext` is the first thing your event-handling code will do. From there, you'll typically retrieve objects from it, or add messages to it. Now, let's examine the message-related classes.

11.3.2 FacesMessage

Whenever you need to report an application error or another type of message back to the UI, you can do so by adding a `FacesMessage` instance to the current `FacesContext`.

`FacesMessage` is a class in the `javax.faces.application` package. It has three properties: `summary`, `detail`, and `severity`:

```
public String getDetail();
public void setDetail(String detail);

public String getSummary();
public void setSummary(String summary);

public FacesMessage.Severity getSeverity();
public void setSeverity(FacesMessage.Severity severity);
```

[2] This is due to a limitation in the Servlet API 2.3.

The summary property is a short version of the message, like "This value is out of range"; the detail property is a longer message like "The value you entered is greater than the maximum value of 5." The severity property provides an additional level of information about the message. It returns an instance of FacesMessage.Severity, which is a type-safe enumeration. The possible values are shown in table 11.3. In application code, you may want to check the severity level of any current messages, and then act accordingly if something is wrong. You can even get the maximum security level at any given time with the FacesContext.getMaximumSeverity method.

Table 11.3 Every FacesMessage instance has a severity property, which is equal to one of these values.

Severity Level Constant	Description
FacesMessage.SEVERITY_INFO	Represents text you'd like to send back to the user that isn't an error. Recommended for validation messages.
FacesMessage.SEVERITY_WARN	Indicates that an error *may* have occurred.
FacesMessage.SECURITY_ERROR	Indicates a definite error.
FacesMessage.SECURITY_FATAL	Indicates a serious error.

Note that these constants map to the strings "info", "warn", "error", and "fatal" that are used by the HtmlMessage and HtmlMessages components to display messages back to the user (see chapter 4).

You can create FacesMessage instances directly using one of four constructors:

```
public FacesMessage();
public FacesMessage(String summary);
public FacesMessage(String summary, String detail);
public FacesMessage(FacesMessage.Severity severity,
         String summary, String detail);
```

Here's an example of creating a new FacesMessage instance and adding to the FacesContext:

```
FacesContext facesContext = FacesContet.getCurrentInstance();
facesContext.addMessage(null,
              new FacesMessage(FacesMessage.SEVERITY_WARN,
                   "This project no longer exists.",
                   "The project is not in the data store."));
```

This adds a new FacesMessage instance to the current message list. When the page is redisplayed, this message can be displayed with an HtmlMessages component.

In this case, the first parameter of `addMessage` is `null`, so the message isn't assigned to a component identifier, and it can be displayed only by an `HtmlMessages` component (which can display all errors for the view). If we had associated it with a client identifier, it could be displayed either by `HtmlMessages` or `HtmlMessage` (which displays only one message for a specific UI component).

The example code previously discussedis fine if you're not internationalizing your application. As we discussed back in chapter 6, JSF can create messages from resource bundles, and you can even override the default messages. However, there is no standard API for creating `FacesMessage` instances from resource bundles, so you'll either have to use nonstandard solutions provided by your JSF vendor or roll your own. We show how to do this in chapter 13 (you'll find other examples of using this class in that chapter as well).

Those are the basics of message handling in JSF. Next, we examine the gateway to the container in which JSF applications live: the `ExternalContext`.

11.3.3 ExternalContext

The `ExternalContext` provides access to the world outside of JSF—its external environment. Usually, this is a web or portlet container. You won't need to worry about this class unless you have to do something that the JSF API doesn't support (such as accessing resource paths), or you're integrating with non-JSF content or applications.

`ExternalContext` is a class in the `javax.faces.context` package; its interface is somewhat generic because it supports both servlets and portlets. Using this class usually requires some knowledge of the Servlet or Portlet API innards.

The main point of `ExternalContext` is to provide convenience wrappers around the typical methods you may want to use, whether they're related to the application as a whole, to the current request, or to the current response. In most cases where attributes are available (`session`, `request`, and `application`), the class provides a `Map` to make things easier. For example, in addition to providing a `getSession` method to return the user's session, there is a `getSessionMap` method, which is used just for adding, retrieving, and removing objects from the session scope. This is handy because most of the time that's what people do with the session anyway.

The following methods are related to the application as a whole:

```
public Map getApplicationMap();
public Set getResourcePaths(String path);
public InputStream getResourceAsStream(String path);
public String getInitParameter(String name);
public Map getInitParameterMap();
public URL getResource(String path) throws MalformedURLException
```

These methods wrap the corresponding ServletContext or PortletContext methods. You can get a reference to the context itself via the following method:

```
public Object getContext();
```

Using this method requires a cast to the appropriate context object—either ServletContext or PortletContext. Consequently, it's usually best to use the wrapper methods if you want your JSF application to work in both environments without a lot of unnecessary instanceof calls.

You can use the following methods to access the HttpSession or PortletSession object and its attributes:

```
public Object getSession(boolean create);
public Map getSessionMap();
```

Retrieving the session directly is useful if you need to invalidate it:

```
HttpSession session = (HttpSession)facesContext.getExternalContext().
                                   getSession(false);
if (session != null)
{
  session.invalidate();
}
```

In this snippet, we simply grab the ExternalContext from the FacesContext, call getSession, and then call HttpSession.invalidate. Note that getSession, like getContext, requires a cast to the appropriate object.

The ExternalContext also provides several useful methods for handling the request directly:

```
public Object getRequest();
public Map getRequestMap();
public Map getRequestParameterMap();
public Map getRequestParameterValuesMap();
public Iterator getRequestParameterNames();
public Map getRequestHeaderMap();
public Map getRequestHeaderValuesMap();
public Map getRequestCookieMap();
public Locale getRequestLocale();
public Iterator getRequestLocales();
public String getRequestPathInfo();
public String getRequestContextPath();
public Cookie[] getRequestCookies();
```

These are wrappers for standard servlet and portlet methods, so we won't cover them in detail here. It's worthwhile to note, however, that there are often JSF-specific ways of performing the same functions as these methods. For example, UIViewRoot.getLocale can be used instead of getRequestLocale. Also, you can retrieve

HTTP request headers, parameters, and cookies using value-binding expressions instead of these methods. So this call:

```
String agent = (String)externalContext.getRequestHeaderMap().
                   get("User-Agent");
```

is equivalent to this call:

```
String agent = (String)application.
                   getValueBinding("#{header['User-Agent']}").
                   getValue(facesContext);
```

The same holds true for most of the methods listed earlier—see chapter 2 for more about implicit value-binding expression variables.

Even though you can access these attributes via value-binding expressions, it's convenient to have access to specific methods with compile-time checking, especially if most of your application is already using these methods (as is the case if you're migrating an existing application to JSF). However, if you're accessing managed objects, using value-binding expressions is the only way to hook into the Managed Bean Creation facility.

`ExternalContext` also wraps the servlet and portlet authentication methods, which are usually found in their request objects:

```
public String getAuthType();
public String getRemoteUser();
public Principal getUserPrincipal();
public boolean isUserInRole(String role);
```

The `getAuthType` method returns the current authentication scheme, which is one of these constants: `ExternalContext.BASIC_AUTH`, `ExternalContext.CLIENT_CERT_AUTH`, `ExternalContext.DIGEST_AUTH`, or `ExternalContext.FORM_AUTH`. Note that these are the same constant names you'll find in the `HttpServletRequest` class; you should, however, use the `ExternalContext` versions instead. (We discuss the different authentications schemes briefly in chapter 13.) The other methods let you check to see who the current user is and if they have a specific role, just as they do in servlet and portlet environments.

Unlike the multitude of methods for obtaining information about the request, there's a single method for retrieving the response:

```
public Object getResponse();
```

This returns a `ServletResponse` or `PortletResponse` object, depending on which environment you're using. If all you need to do is access an output stream, use the `FacesContext.getResponseStream` or `FacesContext.getResponseWriter` instead.

And, if you've finished outputting the entire response, don't forget to call `FacesContext.responseComplete`.

If you want to redirect the user to another URL, you can use this method:

```
public void redirect(String url) throws IOException;
```

This method will send an HTTP redirect to your user for the given URL (which can be either absolute or relative), and then call `FacesContext.responseComplete`. This is one of the few `ExternalContext` methods that does something in addition to calling the external environment's API.

To forward control of the request to a URI in the external environment, use `dispatch`:

```
public void dispatch(String requestURI)
                     throws IOException, FacesException;
```

For servlets, this is equivalent to `RequestDispatcher.forward`. For portlets, it uses the `RequestDispatcher.include` method instead. It makes sense to use `dispatch` when you're integrating with non-JSF resources in the same web application. If you want to forward to another JSF view, use `FacesContext.setViewRoot` instead.

`ExternalContext` also provides some methods for encoding URLs, which means rewriting them so they'll work properly within servlet or portlet environments:

```
public String encodeActionURL(String url);
public String encodeResourceURL(String url));
public String encodeURL(String url);

public String encodeNamespace(String aValue);
```

You generally won't need to use these for application development because encoding is handled automatically by components or their renderers. (They're quite useful for developing components and renderers, however.) If you're outputting markup directly, however, they're a necessity. Use `encodeActionURL` anytime you're outputting a URL for an action, `encodeResourceURL` for other links within a page (like an image), and `encodeURL` for any other URLs. Most of time, these methods just call `HttpServletResponse.encodeURL`, but their general purpose is to make sure that the web container and portlet container properly understand the URL.

Last but not least, `ExternalContext` wraps the container's logging methods as well:

```
public void log(String message);
public void log(String message, Throwable exception);
```

These methods can be used whenever you want to log a message or an error, and you would like to use the logging facilities of the container, which are usually configurable.

> **TIP** You may have noticed that the methods in this class, unlike `FacesContext`, are tied much more closely to HTTP. This is because the underlying Servlet and Portlet APIs are built that way. Because JSF is intended to promote higher-level programming, it's generally better to use methods on the `FacesContext` class if possible.
>
> Also, if you need to store objects in one of the application scopes, it's generally better to use a `ValueBinding` (which can be retrieved from the `Application` class) instead of accessing the maps directly from the `ExternalContext`. This is because the `ValueBinding` class is hooked into the Managed Bean Creation facility, unlike the vanilla `Maps` you can retrieve from the `ExternalContext`.

This concludes our tour of the context-related JSF classes. As you begin developing real-world JSF applications, these classes will become second nature. Usually you'll access them inside event listeners, which we cover next.

11.4 Event handling

We've been saying throughout this book that JSF is event driven, like Swing and other Rapid Application Development (RAD) environments. All this means is that interaction with the user interface is represented as event objects that know what event occurred and which component sent it. This happens during the decoding process—during the Apply Request Values phase of the Request Processing Lifecycle, components (or their renderers) may create events and add them to the current `FacesContext` instance. This saves you the trouble of reading request parameters to attempt to decipher what the user did. The two standard UI events are *action events*, which represent user commands, and *value-change events*, which represent a change in a component's value. (It's nice when names make sense, isn't it?)

JSF has two other event types that are not related to the UI: *phase events*, which are generated during the Request Processing Lifecycle, and *data model events*, which are generated by `DataModel` objects. (`DataModel` objects are used by `HtmlDataTable` components internally.) We won't cover data model events here, since they're not likely to be used in everyday application development.

Events are handled by event listeners. All UI event listeners extend the `javax.faces.event.FacesListener` interface, which in turn extends the `java.util.EventListener` interface. `EventListener` is a marker interface [Grand], so it defines no methods of its own, and neither does `FacesListener` (although subclasses must have a no-argument constructor). Other non-UI listeners extend `EventListener` directly.

The event and listener features of JSF are based on the JavaBeans naming patterns. So, a `kaplow` event would have an event class named `KaplowEvent` and a listener class named `KaplowListener`. Any `UIComponent` that wants to support this event would have `addKaplowListener(KaplowListener listener)` and `removeKaplowListener (KaplowListener listener)` methods for registering and unregistering listeners, respectively.

In addition to the concrete listener classes, some components support method bindings to associate event listeners with a single method in an arbitrary object (usually a backing bean). This is the preferred method for developing application-related event listeners.

These event classes and their listeners are summarized in table 11.4.

Table 11.4 Common event classes and listener interfaces.

Class or Interface	Method Binding Signature	Description
`FacesEvent`	N/A	Base class for UI-oriented events.
`ActionEvent`	N/A	Represents a user-initiated action, sent from an `ActionSource`.
`ActionListener`	`public void myListener (ActionEvent e)`	Handles action events. A single `ActionListener` instance is registered for the application, but you can also register your own on components that fire them, like a `UICommand`.
Any (normally a backing bean; no superclass required)	`public String myAction()`	Primary application-level event listeners. The default `ActionListener` instance calls `action` methods based on the `action` property of the `ActionSource` that fires action events.
`ValueChangeEvent`	N/A	Represents a change in an input control's value.
`ValueChangeListener`	`public void myListener (ValueChangeEvent e)`	Handles value-change events. Must be registered for any input controls whose state you'd like to monitor.
`PhaseEvent`	N/A	Represents execution of a particular phase in the Request Processing Lifecycle.

continued on next page

Table 11.4 Common event classes and listener interfaces. *(continued)*

Class or Interface	Method Binding Signature	Description
`PhaseListener`	N/A	Handles phase events—has methods that are executed before and after a given phase.

You or third parties can, of course, define new event/listener pairs as well; this would typically be done in conjunction with developing custom components.

We cover the standard events and listeners in the following sections. For examples of registering listeners in JSP, see chapter 5.

11.4.1 FacesEvent

In JSF, all UI events are represented by subclasses of the class `javax.faces.event.FacesEvent`, which, in turn subclasses the same `java.util.EventObject` class that is used for Swing events. `FacesEvent` has a type-safe version of `EventObject`'s `sender` property:

```
public UIComponent getComponent();
```

This simply returns the `UIComponent` that fired the event.

Events also control when they should execute:

```
public PhaseId getPhaseId();
public void setPhaseId(PhaseId phaseId)
```

Each `PhaseId` instance is a type-safe enumeration that maps to a particular phase in the Request Processing Lifecycle. An event is always broadcast *after* the phase has been completed. The possible values are shown in table 11.5. If a particular phase is skipped (by calling `FacesContext.responseComplete`, for instance), an event registered for that phase won't be broadcast.

Table 11.5 The possible `PhaseId` values. `FacesEvent` instances are executed after a particular phase.

PhaseId Value	Event Will Be Broadcast...
`PhaseId.ANY_PHASE`	Whenever the event type is fired on the registered component, regardless of the phase.
`PhaseId.RESTORE_VIEW`	After the Restore View phase has completed. This is particularly useful if you want to bypass application of request values (or change the request values before they're applied to components).

continued on next page

Table 11.5 The possible `PhaseId` values. `FacesEvent` instances are executed after a particular phase. *(continued)*

PhaseId Value	Event Will Be Broadcast...
`PhaseId.APPLY_REQUEST_VALUES`	After the Apply Request Values phase has completed. This is useful for adding additional validators or skipping validation altogether.
`PhaseId.PROCESS_VALIDATIONS`	After the Process Validations phase has completed.
`PhaseId.UPDATE_MODEL_VALUES`	After the Update Model Values phase has completed.
`PhaseId.INVOKE_APPLICATION`	After the Invoke Application phase has completed. Action listeners are typically executed during this phase.
`PhaseId.RENDER_RESPONSE`	After the Render Response phase has completed. This is a good place to clean up objects associated with a specific view.

Events are fired from specific components, and they're broadcast to listeners that are registered for the component that fires the event. So, if you had a single `HtmlCommandButton` instance, you might register a listener in JSP like so:

```
<h:commandButton value="Go!" action="go">
  <f:actionListener type="foo.bar.GoListener"/>
</h:commandButton>
```

This registers an `ActionListener` that will consume any action events generated by the component.

`FacesEvent` has a method that ensures it is processed by a particular listener:

```
public void processListener(FacesListener listener);
```

This would typically be used by a component to process events for a particular listener, as opposed to within application code.

You can also check to see if an event can be consumed by a particular listener instance:

```
public boolean isAppropriateListener(FacesListener listener)
```

And, to register an event for later broadcasting, you can call the `queue` method:

```
public void queue()
```

These last three methods are used more often during UI component development.

Next, let's look at action events and listeners.

11.4.2 *Handling action events*

A user command is represented via an instance of the `ActionEvent` class. `UIComponents` that implement the `ActionSource` interface (covered in section 11.5.2) fire an `ActionEvent` when the user interacts with them, usually by clicking a button or a hyperlink. `HtmlCommandButton` and `HtmlCommandLink` are the only standard components that fire `ActionEvents`, but that doesn't mean you or third parties can't write ones that fire them as well. The `ActionEvent` class is located in the `javax.faces.event` package and subclasses the `FacesEvent` class, but it doesn't add any new properties or methods.

Action listeners

`ActionEvents` are consumed by implementations of the `javax.faces.event.ActionListener` interface. This interface extends `FacesListener` and adds a single method:

```
public void processAction(ActionEvent event)
               throws AbortProcessingException;
```

This method is the entry point into an `ActionListener` instance—it's where you put logic for handling the action event. Because action listeners aren't associated with JSF's navigation handler, they're typically used to execute logic that affects what the user sees, such as manipulating a data set or changing the state of UI components in the view. You can, however, combine them with action methods (which do affect navigation).

The `ActionEvent` parameter can be inspected to see which component sent the event through the `ActionEvent.getComponent` method. If you need to get a handle to the `FacesContext`, use the static method `FacesContext.getInstance`. Throwing an `AbortProcessingException` stops JSF from processing this particular event; it doesn't affect the Request Processing Lifecycle as a whole. Using this exception is a somewhat greedy act—it prevents any other listeners from consuming the current event.

You can achieve the same functionality as an `ActionListener` with an action listener *method* on any backing bean. Action listener methods don't require a particular class or interface—they just need to be available via method-binding expressions. For example, suppose you had a class called `Foo`:

```
public class Foo
{
  public void nextPage(ActionEvent actionEvent)
  {
```

```
        // go to next page
    }
  }
```

As long as an instance of `Foo` is available as a scoped variable, you could register the `nextPage` method as an action listener for any action source. Action listener methods can throw `AbortProcessingExceptions` as well—it's a runtime exception, so it does not have to be declared.

`ActionListener` classes are arguably more useful for component development than application development, because most of your application logic will be in backing beans, which can easily expose action listener methods. However, you can register only *one* action listener method with an action source, and you can register any number of `ActionListener` instances. `ActionListener` instances are also easier to reuse across completely different applications, so they're good for operations like logging.

Applications will typically have several action sources, so manually registering an `ActionListener` with all of them would be a bit tedious. Consequently, JSF has a single `ActionListener` instance registered with the `Application` that is automatically registered for `UICommand` components. This instance is executed during the Invoke Application phase regardless of how many other `ActionListeners` you have registered.

Action methods

The default `ActionListener` instance invokes action methods based on the `action` property of the UI component firing the event. Remember, the `action` property can be a method-binding expression that refers to a method in any bean living in one of the application scopes.

Once the `ActionListener` finds the correct action method, it invokes that method, and then sends the action method's outcome to the navigation handler. If the `action` property of the source component is a literal value instead of a method-binding expression, that value is used as the outcome. The navigation handler uses the outcome to set the proper page for JSF to display next (by default, this is based on the navigation rules defined in a JSF configuration file).

Action methods are where you place any logic that affects navigation, and they are typically located in backing beans that collect values from a form (or a set of forms). This means they can access the bean's properties easily.

Any class can have an action method, as long as it has this signature (you can substitute any name you like for `myAction`):

```
public String myAction();
```

The signature doesn't include a reference to a `FacesContext` instance, so if you need a reference to the `FacesContext`, use `FacesContext.getInstance`. The `String` returned from this method should be the logical outcome of the work performed—something like `"success"` or `"failure"`. This outcome can then be mapped to a specific page with a navigation case defined in a JSF configuration file.

Most of the application logic in ProjectTrack is written using action methods and action listener methods, and this will be true of your applications as well.

Now that we've covered action events and their listeners, let's look at value-change events and their listeners.

11.4.3 Handling value-change events

When the local value of an input component changes and passes all validations, it fires an instance of the `javax.faces.event.ValueChangeEvent`. This occurs *before* any model objects have been updated, but after conversion and validation have taken place. `UIComponents` that implement the `ValueHolder` interface (covered in section 11.5.3) are responsible for firing these events, although third-party or custom components or renderers can fire them as well.

Unlike action events, a single view could generate several value-change events—one for every UI component whose value changes. (Action events are usually generated by a single UI component in a view.)

`ValueChangeEvent` implements `FacesEvent` and adds two new properties:

```
public Object getOldValue();
public Object getNewValue();
```

You can use these two read-only properties to determine what the value of the component was before, and what the current (new) value is.

Value-change listeners

`ValueChangeListeners` consume `ValueChangeEvent` objects. You typically write a `ValueChangeListener` whenever you want to perform some action based on the altered state of the UI. `ValueChangeListener`, which is located in the `javax.faces.event` package, implements the `FacesListener` interface and adds a single method:

```
public void processValueChange(ValueChangeEvent event)
            throws AbortProcessingException;
```

This method is where you place any logic for handling a value-change event. You can use the `event` parameter to find the component that fired the event. If you need to get a handle to the `FacesContext`, use the static method `FacesContext.getInstance`. As with any `FacesListener`, throwing an `AbortProcessingException` aborts processing of the event but doesn't affect the Request Processing Lifecycle as a whole. Use this exception sparingly, since it prevents any other listeners from consuming the event.

Instead of implementing the `ValueChangeListener` interface, you can write a value-change listener *method* in any backing bean. The method must have the same signature as the interface's method (sans the exception):

```
public class Foo
{
  ...
  public void valueChange(ValueChangeEvent event)
  {
    // logic here
  }
  ...
}
```

This method can still throw an `AbortProcessingException`, since it is a runtime exception (and consequently doesn't have to be declared). In the course of application development, value-change listener methods are preferable, because they give you access to bean properties and don't require implementing a specific interface. However, you can register only one value-change listener method with a `ValueHolder` component, and you can register multiple `ValueChangeListener` instances.

> **TIP** Write a `ValueChangeListener` when a component's value affects the state of the UI or indicates that some operation should occur. If you want to fire an event when the value of a model property changes, then your model objects should have their own events and listeners that don't know anything about the UI. That way, your design will continue to separate the presentation layer from the application layer.

Action and value-change events are the only standard UI events; however, you may find yourself working with phase events as well.

11.4.4 Handling phase events

Phase events are generated during each phase of the Request Processing Lifecycle. On a daily basis, you won't need to worry about them. However, in situations where you want processing to occur before a view is displayed, or manipulate the lifecycle in some other way, handling them can be useful.

Phase events are represented by the `javax.faces.event.PhaseEvent` class, which subclasses `java.util.EventObject` directly (as opposed to `FacesEvent`). It has two properties:

```
public FacesContext getFacesContext();
public PhaseId getPhaseId();
```

The facesContext property is a type-safe alias for EventObject's source property. The phaseId property returns the phase this event is for, just as it does for FacesEvent instances. PhaseId is a type-safe enumeration of the different phases; its values are listed in table 11.5.

Phase listeners

You handle phase events with implementations of the javax.faces.event.PhaseListener class, which extends the java.util.EventListener interface (as opposed to FacesListener) and the java.io.Serializable interface. PhaseListeners indicate which phase they're interested in by exposing a phaseId property:

```
public PhaseId getPhaseId();
```

Processing can be performed before and after the phase executes with these methods:

```
public void afterPhase(PhaseEvent event);
public void beforePhase(PhaseEvent event);
```

Implementations of these methods can use the facesContext property of the event parameter to manipulate the lifecycle directly, or access the view, if necessary.

You register PhaseListener instances with the java.faces.lifecycle.Lifecycle instance, which is responsible for actually executing each phase. This class has three methods for handling phase listeners:

```
public void addPhaseListener(PhaseListener listener);
public void removePhaseListener(PhaseListener listener);
public PhaseListener[] getPhaseListeners();
```

You can retrieve the current Lifecycle instance from the LifecycleFactory:

```
LifecycleFactory factory = (LifecycleFactory)
   FactoryFinder.getFactory(FactoryFinder.LIFECYCLE_FACTORY);
Lifecycle = factory.getLifecycle(
                    LifecycleFactory.DEFAULT_LIFECYCLE);
```

FactoryFinder is a convenience class for finding factory classes, which is necessary because JSF allows you to plug in different factory implementations (see appendix C for details).

Phase listeners can be useful for initializing objects that you want to make available for a particular view. This can be done in a backing bean like so:

```
public class MyBean()
{
```

```
    public MyBean()
    {
      LifecycleFactory lifecycleFactory = (LifecycleFactory)
        FactoryFinder.getFactory(FactoryFinder.LIFECYCLE_FACTORY);
      Lifecycle lifecycle = lifecycleFactory.getLifecycle(
                              LifecycleFactory.DEFAULT_LIFECYCLE);
      lifecycle.addPhaseListener(
        new PhaseListener()
        {
          public void beforePhase(PhaseEvent event)
          {
            refreshList();
          }

          public void afterPhase(PhaseEvent event)
          {
          }

          public PhaseId getPhaseId()
          {
            return PhaseId.RENDER_RESPONSE;
          }
        });
    }

    protected void refreshList()
    {
      ...
    }
  ...
  }
```

This code registers a new `PhaseListener` instance (implemented as an anonymous inner class) for the Render Response phase that will execute the `refreshList` method before the phase begins. Presumably, `refreshList` performs some sort of processing that will update properties of `MyBean` that views use. This effectively saying "execute `refreshList` before a view is rendered."

You can use this approach to register event listeners on behalf of any backing beans for any phase you like; it is effectively equivalent to event handlers available in ASP.NET WebForms [Microsoft, ASP.NET]. If you need to register global phase listeners before JSF begins displaying views, you can use do so within a `ServletContextListener`, which is executed when the web application is loaded. `ServletContextListeners` are part of the Servlet API.

This isn't the only way you can use `PhaseListeners`. They are useful any time you want to manipulate the lifecycle—you can even terminate processing or output the response directly.

That's all we're going to say about events and listeners for now; you'll see more examples as we build our case study in the next couple of chapters. Now it's time to take a closer look at UI components.

11.5 Components revisited

One of JSF's primary benefits is the ability to manipulate the components in a view with code, like Swing and other desktop-based UI component frameworks. Even though JSF user interfaces are usually declared with templates such as JSPs, sometimes you may need to retrieve or change the state of a component or add new components to the page altogether. Some JSF implementations, such as the open-source Smile project [Smile], even allow you to construct all of your views in code (see appendix A for an example).

Throughout this book, we've been talking about concrete HTML components—`HtmlInputText`, `HtmlSelectMany`, `HtmlDataTable`, and so on. These are the components that the standard JSP component tags create, and they're also easy to explain. As it turns out, the HTML components are subclasses of more generic classes, which are really the backbone of JSF's component hierarchy, and can be used for clients other than HTML browsers. They all implement specific interfaces as well, which are shown in table 11.6.

Table 11.6 Interfaces used by UI components. All of them are in the `javax.faces.component` package.

Interface	Description
`StateHolder`	Indicates that state should be saved in between requests. Implemented by all standard components, validators, and converters.
`NamingContainer`	Indicates that a component is responsible for naming its children. (See chapter 3 for more information on naming containers.)
`ActionSource`	Represents a UI component that sends action events.
`ValueHolder`	Represents a UI component that has a value.
`EditableValueHolder`	Represents a UI component that has a value that can be changed. Sends value-change events.

Your application code may come into contact with UI components that implement the `ActionSource` interface (which fires action events), the `ValueHolder` interface (which contains a value), or the `EditableValueHolder` interface (which contains an editable value and sends value-change events). In practice, the other two interfaces, `StateHolder` and `NamingContainer`, are mostly used for component development.

In chapter 4, we introduced component families and said that they grouped similar components together. This grouping is particularly useful for renderers, because it allows them to treat components of the same family in similar ways. Families also happen to map directly to the base UI component classes. Table 11.7 lists all of these classes with their family names and HTML-specific subclasses.

Table 11.7 The base UI component classes, and their HTML subclasses. All of them are in the `javax.faces.component` package.

Class	Family[a]	HTML Subclasses	Description
`UIComponent`	N/A	N/A	The abstract base abstract class for all components.
`UIComponentBase`	N/A	N/A	Abstract base class with basic implementations of almost all `UIComponent` methods.
`UIColumn`	Column	N/A	A table column. Used to configure template columns for the parent `UIData` component.
`UICommand`	Command	`HtmlCommandButton`, `HtmlCommandLink`	A user command.
`UIData`	Data	`HtmlDataTable`	Represents a data-aware component that cycles through rows in the underlying data source and exposed individual rows to child components. Requires child `UIColumn` components.
`UIForm`	Form	`HtmlForm`	An input form; must enclose all input components.
`UIGraphic`	Image	`HtmlGraphicImage`	Displays an image based on its URL.
`UIInput`	Input	`HtmlInputHidden`, `HtmlInputSecret`, `HtmlInputText`, `HtmlInputTextarea`	A component that displays its output and collects input.
`UIMessage`	Message	`HtmlMessage`	Displays messages for a specific component.
`UIMessages`	Messages	`HtmlMessages`	Displays all messages (component-related and/or application-related).

continued on next page

Table 11.7 The base UI component classes, and their HTML subclasses. All of them are in the `javax.faces.component` package. *(continued)*

Class	Family[a]	HTML Subclasses	Description
`UIOutput`	Output	`HtmlOutputFormat`, `HtmlOutputLabel`, `HtmlOutputLink`, `HtmlOutputText`	Holds a read-only value and displays it to the user.
`UIParameter`	Parameter	N/A	Represents a parameter for a parent component.
`UIPanel`	Panel	`HtmlPanelGrid`, `HtmlPanelGroup`	Groups together a set of child components.
`UISelectBoolean`	Checkbox	`HtmlSelectBoolean-Checkbox`	Collects and displays a single boolean value.
`UISelectItem`	SelectItem	N/A	Represents a single item or item group. Usually used with `UISelectMany` or `UISelectOne`.
`UISelectItems`	SelectItems	N/A	Represents multiple items or item groups. Usually used with `UISelectMany` or `UISelectOne`.
`UISelectMany`	SelectMany	`HtmlSelectMany-Checkbox`, `HtmlSelectMa-nyListbox`, `HtmlSelectManyMenu`	Displays a set of items, and allows the user to select zero or more of them.
`UISelectOne`	SelectOne	`HtmlSelectOneRadio` `HtmlSelectOneList-box` `HtmlSelectOneMenu`	Displays a set of items, and allows the user to select only one of them.
`UIViewRoot`	ViewRoot	N/A	Represents entire view; contains all components on the page.

[a] *The standard family names technically have the prefix javax.faces.*

Note that the component hierarchy starts with `UIComponent`, which is the abstract base class for all UI components, and `UIComponentBase`, which provides default implementations of `UIComponent` methods.

You may have noticed that this table is similar to table 4.1 back in chapter 4, which lists all of the HTML component classes. Some of the components that are listed, like `UIViewRoot`, don't have an HTML equivalent, so the listing in this table is pretty much the same. For the others, there is a key difference: the description.

The descriptions are more generic, and don't specify how the component is displayed or other types of HTML-specific behavior. This is because the base UI components don't know anything about HTML at all.

So, what do the HTML components add to the superclasses? To answer this question, we need to discuss one feature provided by the `UIComponent`: attributes. Attributes are arbitrary name/value pairs registered for a `UIComponent` instance that can be used by renderers, converters, and validators when they interact with UI components. Renderers use render-dependent attributes to help them do their work. For example, the standard HTML renderers use attributes such as `cellpadding`, `title`, `border`, and so on.

But when you're working with a UI component in code, attributes are cumbersome to manipulate, and they're not type-safe.

```
myUIPanel.getAttributes().put("cellpadding", "0");
```

This is fine, as long as you happen to know all of the attributes and you never misspell anything. The concrete HTML components are the solution; they expose renderer-dependent attributes as strongly typed properties:

```
myHtmlPanelGrid.setCellpadding("0");
```

That's it—that's the only difference.

When you're writing backing beans that manipulate UI components in code, it's helpful to know about the base classes. This will allow you to write backing beans that are more flexible—for example, a component binding property of type `UISelectOne` can be associated with an `HtmlSelectOneListbox`, `HtmlSelectOneMenu`, or `HtmlSelectOneRadio` component, which is useful if the front-end developer changes the component tag.

The same principal applies to event listener code as well. If your event listener expects an `HtmlDataTable` but your application also supports WML (via a third-party `WmlDataTable`), you had better use the superclass, `UIData`. Some IDEs do, however, encourage you to work with the HTML components.

Figure 11.2 shows how all of the base UI component classes and interfaces are related.

Throughout the rest of this book, we'll often refer to the base component class in our discussions, rather than concrete HTML subclasses. You are free, however, to use whichever one fits your needs, and in many cases, the HTML component classes are sufficient. Regardless of which route you choose, there are some key interfaces and classes, like `UIComponent`, with which you will interact. We cover these in the following sections.

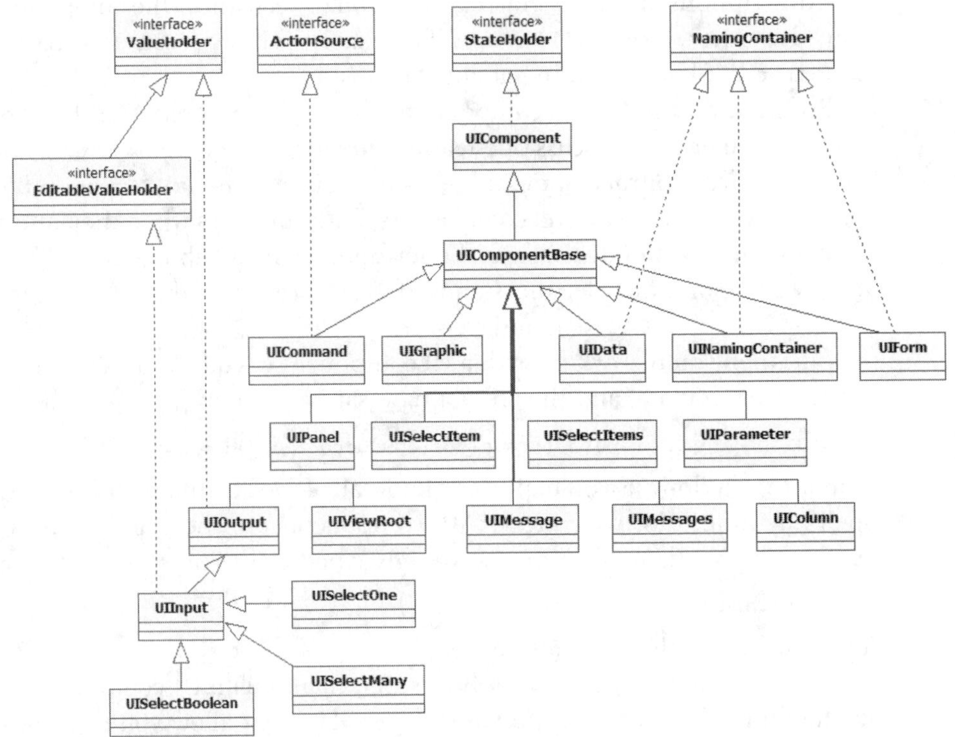

Figure 11.2 A class diagram of the base UI component classes. All components descend from `UIComponent` (which implements the `StateHolder` interface). `UIOutput` components implement the `ValueHolder` interface, and `UIInput` components implement the `EditableValueHolder` interface. Also, `UIData` and `UIForm` implement the `NamingContainer` interface. (`UINamingContainer` is a convenience class that implements the interface.)

11.5.1 UIComponent

All UI components must extend the abstract class `javax.faces.component.UIComponent`. Like any base class, `UIComponent` has several useful properties in methods, including ones for finding child components, identifiers, facet management, and so on. Let's start our tour with the component identifier, which is accessible through the `id` property:

```
public String getId();
public void setId(String id);
```

This identifier is specified when the component is created (either in code or declaratively). If no `id` is specified when the component is created, JSF generates one automatically. Usually the only time you have to specify an identifier is if the component must be referenced by other components or validators, or your code is looking for a specific component it knows about beforehand. For more on component identifiers, see chapter 2.

In addition to an identifier, every component has a *type,* which is a unique string that represents the component's specific set of functionality. The component's type isn't a property, but it is used to register a specific class name with JSF. This registration is performed in a JSF configuration file, which means that you can change the implementation for a particular UI component type (see appendix D). From an application development perspective, the type is useful for creating a component instance using a factory method of the `Application` class:

```
projectSelectOne = (HtmlSelectOneMenu)getApplication().
        createComponent(HtmlSelectOneMenu.COMPONENT_TYPE);
```

As you can see, `HtmlSelectOneMenu` returns its type through a constant field called `COMPONENT_TYPE`—this is the same for all UI components.

A component's attributes can be accessed with this single method:

```
public Map getAttributes();
```

You can manipulate this `Map` normally, but you can't add a `null` key, and all keys must be `Strings`. You can use it to retrieve a specific attribute, set an attribute, or retrieve all of the attributes for the current component.

Attributes are used by converters, renderers, and validators when they need configuration values that are associated with a specific component. This is useful because unlike `UIComponent` instances, other objects may be stateless, which means that they need a place to store component-related information necessary to perform their work. You can also use attributes to store any application-specific objects that you'd like to associate with a given component. If you do so, however, the objects must implement the `java.io.Serializable` interface if you have client-side state saving enabled.

All component properties can also be accessed through this `Map`. So, for example, the `id` property can also be retrieved with `getAttributes.get("id")`. If you're accessing a property through this `Map`, however, there are some additional restrictions: you can't call `remove`, and `containsKey` always returns `false`. Also, `get` and `put` wrap the getters and setters for the property (respectively), and will throw an exception if the corresponding method doesn't exist. Note that the `containsKey` rule implies that a call to `getAttributes().getKeySet` returns only keys for attributes, excluding property names.

You can associate or retrieve a value-binding expression for any attribute or property with these methods:

```
public void setValueBinding(String name,
                            ValueBinding binding);
public ValueBinding getValueBinding(String name);
```

The following snippet sets the value-binding expressions for the `value` and `title` properties of an `HtmlInputText` component:

```
userNameInputText.setValueBinding("value",
        application.createValueBinding("#{myBean.userName}"));
userNameInputText.setValueBinding("title",
        application.createValueBinding("#{myBundle.userNameTitle}"));
```

This is equivalent to the following JSP snippet:

```
<h:inputText value="#{myBean.userName}"
             title="#{myBundle.userNameTitle}"/>
```

Any property or attribute that supports value-binding expressions is called *value-binding enabled*. All of the properties and attributes of the standard UI components are value-binding enabled, and this will be the case for most third-party components you encounter. (We show how to do this in your own components in chapter 15.) Whenever you retrieve a property or attribute, the component will first check for a normal value (set with a mutator or through the `attributes` property); if the value is `null`, it will then check for a `ValueBinding` instance and evaluate it (if found). In other words, value-binding expressions are evaluated only if the property's or attribute's value is `null`.

The `rendered` property indicates whether a component is currently visible:

```
public boolean isRendered();
public void setRendered(boolean rendered);
```

This property is handy when you want to hide a part of the screen based on user input or access level. If you hide a component that's a container for others, its children will be hidden as well. By default, this property is set to `true`.

SOAPBOX I find "rendered" to be sort of a strange property name. Whatever happened to "visible"?

A view's structure is implemented using the Composite design pattern [GoF], which basically means that the view is a tree where every node is implemented using the same interface, and each node provides navigation capabilities. This is why `UIViewRoot` is a `UIComponent`, even though the user can't directly interact with it.

JSF component trees don't have any true leaves; any `UIComponent` instance can have children. However, the component or its renderer may ignore them, so check the component or renderer documentation to be sure children are recognized before you add them.

`UIComponent` has several methods for accessing and manipulating its children, accessing its parent, and finding child components::

```
public UIComponent getParent();
public UIComponent getChild(int index);
public List getChildren();
public UIComponent findComponent(String expr);
```

These methods allow you to find components in the view as well as add or remove ones from it. Note that if you add or remove a `UIComponent` from the `List` returned by `getChildren`, the `parentId` property will be set automatically by the `List` (a `UIComponent` cannot be the child of more than one component). Also, you cannot add any object to the `List` that is not a `UIComponent` instance.

NOTE If you're going to be adding new components to the tree, use the `Application.createComponent` method instead of creating the `UIComponent` manually.

At first glance, it may seem like `findComponent` is the optimal way to find the component on a page—you could simply retrieve a `UIViewRoot` instance from the `facesContext` and then search for the desired component. However, it's often easier to associate a component to your backing bean with a component binding; this way, you have direct access to the necessary component, and you don't have to know its identifier (see chapter 12 for examples).

Every `UIComponent` can have *facets*, which are special, named subordinate components such as `header` and `footer`. Because they aren't technically children of the component, there is a separate set of methods for accessing and manipulating them:

```
public Map getFacets();
public UIComponent getFacet(String name);
public Iterator getFacetsAndChildren();
```

Often, facets are components that contain children, like a `UIPanel`; however, you shouldn't make that assumption—it could be a single component, such as `UIOutput`. The `Map` returned by `getFacets` works just like the one returned by `getChildren`. Just as with child components, you probably won't need to add or remove facets programmatically—usually you'll just need to find and update existing ones.

Also, remember that most components don't support facets, even though they don't restrict you from adding them.[3]

These are all of the `UIComponent` methods and properties we think you may encounter during everyday application development. However, the interface has quite a few more that are necessary for component development—see chapter 15 for details.

`UIComponent` does a lot, but sometimes you'll still need to cast to the appropriate subclass and work with that class's or interface's own properties and methods. In the next sections, we cover a few common interfaces and classes that you will encounter. For overviews of all of the standard components (including coverage of supported facets), see chapters 4 and 5.

11.5.2 UIViewRoot

The components in a JSF view are organized into a tree structure with an instance of the `javax.faces.component.UIViewRoot` class at the root. There are basically three things you can do with a `UIViewRoot`: set or retrieve the current render kit, set or retrieve the view's locale, and set or retrieve its `viewId` property. Also, because `UIViewRoot` implements `UIComponent`, you can access all the child components in the current view using ordinary `UIComponent` methods like `getChildren`.

You can retrieve the current `UIViewRoot` with the `facesContext.getViewRoot` method. Once you have a handle to the current instance, you can access the view's identifier with the `viewId` property:

```
public String getViewId();
```

If JSP is being used for the view, the `viewId` is the extra path information of the request, which is the part of the URI after the servlet name but before any request parameters. So, for the request http://www.something-funny.com/faces/kindafunny.jsp, the `viewId` is /kindafunny.jsp. If the request was http://www.something-funny.com/faces/really_funny/hysterical.jsp, the `viewId` would be /really_funny/hysterical.jsp.

You can use a view identifier to create a new `UIViewRoot` instance. Creating a new view isn't a common application development activity, but you may need to do it in cases when you want to bypass the navigation system and control the next page that will be displayed:

```
String myViewId = "/foobar.jsp";
UIViewRoot view = (UIViewRoot)app.getViewHandler().
```

[3] Technically, displaying facets is up to the renderer. This is why you can arbitrarily add them to a `UIComponent`—a component doesn't know what facets its renderer supports.

```
                    createView(facesContext, myViewId);
facesContext.setViewRoot(view);
```

This snippet of code ensures that JSF will display foobar.jsp next, and the newly created `UIViewRoot` instance's `viewId` will be /foobar.jsp.

BY THE WAY The `ViewHandler` class is used internally by JSF to create new `UIViewRoot` instances. This class is pluggable, so you can either decorate it or write an entirely new implementation—this is how JSF can support display technologies other than JSP. See appendix C for more information.

You can set or retrieve the view's locale with the `getLocale` and `setLocale` methods:

```
public Locale getLocale();
public void setLocale(Locale locale);
```

JSF handles most of the localization duties for you (see chapter 6), so you normally won't need to use these methods directly unless you're setting your users' locale based on their input, or you need to make a decision programmatically based on their language or country. ProjectTrack, for instance, lets users change their locale:

```
public void setLocale(String locale)
{
  FacesContext.getCurrentInstance().getViewRoot().
                 setLocale(new Locale(locale));
}
```

This property is bound to the value of an `HtmlSelectOneListbox` component. JSF carries over the `locale` property from the previous view, so once you set it for the current view, you don't need to set it again (unless you want to change it again).

The two methods for handling the current render kit are

```
public String getRenderKitId();
public void setRenderKitId(String string);
```

These methods let you retrieve or change the current render kit. Each render kit has its own unique identifier, which is usually specified in a JSF configuration file (the identifier for the standard render kit is stored in the `RenderKitFactory.HTML_BASIC_RENDER_KIT` constant). For basic HTML applications, you normally won't need to change it—the standard render kit will be enough. However, if you have multiple render kits available—perhaps an additional kit for a mobile device and one for enhanced JavaScript and DHTML—you can change the render kit depending on the user's preference (or client type).

WARNING The JSF RI [Sun, JSF RI] versions 1.0 and 1.1 cannot dynamically changing the render kit, so use of `setRenderKitId` is not recommended. We hope this will be addressed in a future release, but other JSF implementations may support this capability sooner.

Most of your interaction with the `UIViewRoot` class will probably involve finding, and/or modifying, `UIComponent` instances in the page, and perhaps adding new `UIComponent` instances to the page.

Now, let's move on to a core interface for interacting with users—`ActionSource`.

ActionSource

Any component that fires an `ActionEvent` implements the `ActionSource` interface. The only standard component that implements this interface is `UICommand` (and its subclasses `HtmlCommandButton` and `HtmlCommandLink`), but it's not uncommon to develop a custom component that implements this interface as well (`UINavigator`, covered in online extension chapter 19, is such a component).

The most familiar feature of the `ActionSource` interface is the `action` property, which is used by the default `ActionListener` instance to determine the next page to display:

```
public MethodBinding getAction();
public void setAction(MethodBinding methodbinding);
```

The method referenced by this `MethodBinding` instance must be an action method. You can create a new instance through the `Application` instance:

```
MethodBinding mBinding =
   app.createMethodBinding("myBean.processClaims", new Class[] {} );
myUICommand.setAction(mBinding);
```

Here, we create a new `MethodBinding` instance for the `processClaims` action method of `myBean`, and set the `action` property of a `UICommand` (which implements `ActionSource`).

When a user executes an action event through an `ActionSource` instance, the event is normally processed during the Invoke Application phase. You can force JSF to execute the event in the Apply Request Values phase, before validation even takes place, with the immediate property:

```
public boolean isImmediate();
public void setImmediate(boolean immediate);
```

Usually this is used for things like Cancel or Previous buttons on a form. This property is usually initialized to `false`.

ActionSources are associated with ActionListener instances. (UICommand automatically adds the application's default ActionListener instance.) In order to support ActionListener instances, the ActionSource interface exposes three methods:

```
public void addActionListener(ActionListener listener);
public ActionListener[] getActionListeners();
public void removeActionListener(ActionListener listener);
```

This allows you to add or remove ActionListener instances in code:

```
UICommand command = (UICommand)application.
            createComponent(UICommand.COMPONENT_TYPE);
command.addActionListener(
     new ActionListener()
    {
      public void processAction(ActionEvent event)
                    throws AbortProcessingException
      {
        FacesContext.getCurrentInstance().getExternalContext().
            log("User fired action for component id " +
                event.getComponent());
      }
    });
```

This should look pretty familiar to you if you've ever worked with Swing. First, we create a new UICommand using the Application instance, and then we add an ActionListener instance (implemented as an anonymous inner class). This simple ActionListener just writes to the container's log file—kind of a poor man's way to audit what a user does.

ActionSource also supports an actionListener property, which allows a component to specify a method binding expression for handling action events:

```
public MethodBinding getActionListener();
public void setActionListener(
             MethodBinding methodbinding);
```

You can use this property just like the action property, except the referenced method must be an action listener method.

That's all you need to know about ActionSource. Next, let's examine ValueHolder.

11.5.3 *ValueHolder*

Any UIComponent that has a value implements the ValueHolder interface, located in the javax.faces.component package. Components that implement this interface include UIOutput, and its subclasses: UIInput, UISelectOne, UISelectMany, and UISelectBoolean. In other words, any component that displays or collects data implements ValueHolder.

You can retrieve and update the component's value with these methods:

```
public Object getValue();
public void setValue(Object value);
```

In section 11.5.1 we talked about how all of the standard component properties are value-binding enabled. The `value` property is handled just like any other—if it has been set by `setValue`, `getValue` will return that value. Otherwise, `getValue` will check for an associated `ValueBinding` instance and return the result of its evaluation if found, and `null` otherwise.

If you don't want the component to check for a `ValueBinding` instance, you can use `getLocalValue` instead:

```
public Object getLocalValue();
```

This method always returns the value that has been set for this component without looking for `ValueBinding` instances.

In order to support type conversion, every `ValueHolder` instance can be associated with a single converter, whose job is to translate the component's `value` property to and from a `String` value, and optionally provide formatting or localization. Usually the converter is set declaratively in the page template, but the following methods allow you to retrieve or set the converter in code:

```
public Converter getConverter();
public void setConverter(Converter converter);
```

You can create a `Converter` instance from the `Application` class using a `converter` identifier, which is configured in a JSF configuration file. Each `Converter` class has a constant with its identifier:

```
myUISelectOne.setConverter(application.createConverter(
                           DateTimeConverter.CONVERTER_ID));
```

This registers a new `DateTimeConverter` instance with a `UISelectOne` component. This is equivalent to the following JSP:

```
<h:selectOneListbox ....>
  <f:convertDateTime/>
</h:selectOneListbox>
```

The standard converters are covered in chapter 6. To learn how to write custom converters, see chapters 12 and 15.

As you can see, `ValueHolder` adds a few necessary methods for handling component values. `EditableValueHolder` builds on this base to provide capabilities for manipulating those values.

11.5.4 *EditableValueHolder*

The `EditableValueHolder` interface, located in the `javax.faces.component` package, adds support for validation and value-change events. As figure 11.2 shows, it extends `ValueHolder` and is implemented by `UIInput` (and consequently all input controls).

An `EditableValueHolder` can have one or more `Validator` instances, which are managed by these methods:

```
public void addValidator(Validator validator);
public Validator[] getValidators();
public void removeValidator(Validator validator);
```

As with `Converters`, you can create new `Validator` instances through the `Application` class:

```
LongRangeValidator myValidator = (LongRangeValidator)
       application.createValidator(LongRangeValidator.VALIDATOR_ID);
myValidator.setMinimum(0);
myValidator.setMaximum(555);
myUIInput.addValidator(myValidator);
```

This registers a `LongRange` converter with a `UIInput` control, and is equivalent to the following JSP component tag declaration:

```
<h:inputText ...>
  <f:validateLongRange minimum="0" maximum="555"/>
</h:inputText>
```

For details about the standard validators, see chapter 6. To learn how to write your own validators, see part 4.

Support for validator methods in backing beans is provided by the `validator` property, which is of type `MethodBinding`:

```
public MethodBinding getValidator();
public void setValidator(MethodBinding validatorBinding);
```

An `EditableValueHolder` instance can be associated with only one validator method, which must have the following signature:

```
public void myValidatorMethod(FacesContext facesContext,
                              UIComponent component,
                              Object objectToValidate)
              throws ValidatorException
```

We show an example of implementing a validator method in chapter 13.

`EditableValueHolder` components also have a `required` property, which is a simple type of validation:

```
public boolean isRequired();
public void setRequired(boolean required);
```

If this property is `true`, empty input for this control will not be valid.

This interface is also a source of value-change events, and support is implemented with these methods:

```
public void addValueChangeListener(ValueChangeListener listener);
public ValueChangeListener[] getValueChangeListeners();
public void removeValueChangeListener(ValueChangeListener listener);
```

Note that these methods are quite similar to those used for `ActionSource` to handle `ActionListener` instances.

If you want to register a single backing bean method instead of a whole class, you can use the `valueChangeListener` property:

```
public MethodBinding getValueChangeListener();
public void setValueChangeListener(MethodBinding valueChangeMethod);
```

The method referenced by this `MethodBinding` instance must be a value-change listener method. Most of the time, you'll set the `valueChangeListener` property instead of implementing the `ActionListener` interface, because backing bean methods have direct access to form values.

A component's `value` is only valid once all converters and validators have completed successfully. You can check the validity with the `valid` property:

```
public boolean isValid();
```

If you access this property in an event listener, be cognizant of the phase for which your event listener is registered. If it executes before the end of the Process Validations phase, the `valid` property could be further manipulated by later phases. (Remember, even action methods and action listeners can run during the Apply Request Values phase if the `ActionSource`'s `immediate` property is set to `true`.)

`EditableValueHolders` also have an `immediate` property, which forces conversion and validation to take place during the Apply Request Values phase:

```
public boolean isImmediate();
public void setImmediate(boolean immediate);
```

This property is usually initialized to `false`. You may want to set it to `true` if you need to access the value of a component even if validation of other controls in the same form fails.

We have now completed our whirlwind tour of the most common component interfaces and classes you'll interact with during day-to-day development. Next, let's examine a few classes that some components may use internally.

11.5.5 SelectItem and SelectItemGroup model beans

In chapter 5, we discussed item lists and how they are used to populate UISelectOne and UISelectMany components. Item lists are configured with UISelectItem and UISelectItems components, which are basically wrappers for SelectItem model objects. UISelectItem will either create a SelectItem instance itself based on its own properties, or retrieve it from an associated value-binding expression. UISelectItems must be associated with a value-binding expression that points to a SelectItem instance or an array, List, or Collection of SelectItem instances. (UISelectItems can also be associated with a Map, which is subsequently converted into SelectItem instances.)

SelectItem is a simple class in the javax.faces.model package with label, value, description, and disabled properties:

```
public String getLabel();
public void setLabel(String label);
public Object getValue();
public void setValue(Object value);
public String getDescription();
public void setDescription(String description);
public boolean isDisabled();
public void setDisabled(boolean disabled);
```

The label property is what users see in the item list, and the value property is what your application actually cares about. The value property requires a converter so that the user's selection(s) can be translated to and from the proper type. If you stick to standard Java data types, JSF will automatically use one of the standard converters. However, if you use your own class, you will need to write your own converter (see chapter 12 for an example).

The description property should be a more detailed version of the label, but it isn't displayed by the standard renderers. The disabled property determines whether or not a user can currently select this item; it is often grayed out when displayed.

SelectItem also has several constructors:

```
public SelectItem();
public SelectItem(Object value);
public SelectItem(Object value, String label);
public SelectItem(Object value, String label, String description);
public SelectItem(Object value, String label, String description,
                  boolean disabled);
```

So, to create a single item, you can use one of these constructors:

```
SelectItem chameleons = new SelectItem("30", "chameleons");
myUISelectItem.setValue(chameleons);
```

Here, we create a new `SelectItem` instance and set it as the value of a `UISelectItem` component.

To create a list of several items, we can use an array, `List`, or `Collection`:

```
SelectItem[] items = new SelectItem[2];
items[0] = new SelectItem("30", "chameleons");
items[1] = new SelectItem("40", "geckos");
myUISelectItems.setValue(items);
```

This creates a list of two items, and sets it as the value of a `UISelectItems` component.

You can represent subgroups with an item group. Item groups are represented by the `SelectItemGroup` class, which is a subclass of `SelectItem`. `SelectItemGroup` adds a single property:

```
public SelectItem[] getSelectItems();
public void setSelectItems(SelectItem[] selectItems);
```

The `selectItems` property is an array of additional `SelectItem` instances. Technically, the objects in the array can also be `SelectItemGroups`, but the standard components cannot display nested groups (due to limitations of HTML). In addition, the `value` property of a `SelectItemGroup` instance is usually ignored during rendering.

This class also adds some additional constructors:

```
public SelectItemGroup(String label)
public SelectItemGroup(String label, String description,
                       boolean disabled, SelectItem[] selectItems);
```

Using these constructors, we could create a group using the array defined in the previous snippet:

```
SelectItemGroup lizardGroup =
  new SelectItemGroup("lizards", null, false, items);
```

This creates a new `SelectItemGroup` with the label "lizard" that includes all of the `SelectItem` instances in the array items.

Most of the time, you'll create one or more `SelectItem` instances in code and expose them as a backing bean property, intended to be bound to the value of a `UISelectItem` or `UISelectItems` component (we show how to do this in chapter 12). Sometimes these values will be hardcoded, but you can also create `SelectItem` instances with values retrieved from a database. See chapter 6 for more information about these components (as well as `UISelectOne` and `UISelectMany` subclasses).

11.6 Summary

Whenever you're building an application with a framework, there is always a core set of classes that you need to understand in order to get any work done. For JSF applications, those classes can be grouped into four primary areas: application, context, event handling, and UI components.

Application-related classes include your backing beans, and classes that evaluate JSF EL expressions. They also include the `Application` class, which provides access to configuration information like the locale, and factory methods for creating new components, validators, and renderers, and so on.

Context-related classes provide access to the current state of interaction with a user, which is available while processing events. This state is encapsulated in the `FacesContext` class, which provides access to messages, events, and a wide variety of additional data. `Messages` are used to convey information to the user, and you can retrieve localized `Messages` through the `MessageResources` class. The `ExternalContext` provides access to the hosting servlet or portlet environment.

Event-handling classes manage the interaction between the user interface and the rest of the application. When a user interacts with a JSF application, one or more events will be fired from the component with which the user interacts. Events are consumed by listener classes. There are two standard event types: `ActionEvents`, which are consumed by `ActionListeners`, and `ValueChangeEvents`, which are consumed by `ValueChangeListeners`. In addition, there is a default `ActionListener` instance that delegates work to specific action methods. Usually, your true application logic will be written in action methods. In addition to UI-related events, there are also phase events, which are executed during different stages of the Request Processing Lifecycle.

UI component classes allow you to manipulate the individual controls on a page. All components extend the `UIComponent` class. You can access an entire view through the `UIViewRoot` class, and there are also interfaces for sending action events and working with values.

Now that you have an understanding of the classes you need to build an application, in the next chapter let's take a look at the steps involved in building a real-world JSF application.

12

Building an application: design issues and foundation classes

This chapter covers

- How to build layered applications
- Writing bean properties
- Adapting business objects
- Writing a base backing bean class

In the first two parts of this book, we covered all of the basic JSF building blocks and examined what it's like to build the front-end of our case study, ProjectTrack, using JSP. In chapter 11, we surveyed the JSF environment from an application developer's perspective to help you understand JSF's coding model. Now it's time to look at what Java code is necessary to make ProjectTrack a fully functional application using the concepts, techniques, and knowledge presented in the earlier portions of this book. (If you haven't looked at the previous three chapters, we suggest you do so now; some of the configuration for this application takes place in chapter 10.)

First, we'll examine how to design applications using a layered approach, and how ProjectTrack's classes fit into different layers. Next, we'll take a look at the requirements for developing objects that interact with JSF components. Once we've finished examining the design possibilities, we'll inspect the system's business layer, and then begin writing backing beans and other classes, examining how they integrate with faces-config.xml and JSPs every step of the way.

12.1 Layers of the pie

In chapter 10, we discussed different development approaches for JSF applications from the front-end perspective. We said that there were two primary options: form-based development, and object-based development. From an application development perspective, we can look at these options in terms of layers.

Layered architectures are a key aspect of well-designed web applications [Husted], and that's why they are enforced by most web frameworks, including Struts and JSF. The idea is that you divide your application into different distinct layers, and each layer can interact only with adjacent layers. So, by keeping distinct parts of your applications separated and dependencies limited, you ensure that your applications will be more maintainable and less brittle. When you start building JSF applications, it's important to understand what the layers are, and where to use them.

In the simplest case, there are only two layers: the *UI layer*, which consists of JSF views, and an application layer, which talks directly to the data store, as shown in figure 12.1. JSF is responsible for separating these two layers. In this scenario, your backing beans would contain business logic and data store access logic (using APIs such as Java Database Connectivity, or JDBC). When you develop JSF applications this way, the front-end is developed using the form-based approach we discussed in chapter 10. There are no business-specific objects in your system;

UI components and backing beans interact directly with data service objects, like JDBC `RowSets`.

This approach can work for small applications, especially if there is little or no business logic. However, it can become messy fast. Intermixing application, business, and data access logic is usually a scary proposition, because it's hard to separate the different concerns. If you can't separate the concerns, then it's fragile and difficult to read and test. Technically, this isn't much of a layered approach—all of your code is muddled together in one layer.

A better approach is to split up your application into different layers that concentrate on specific tasks. In addition to the UI layer, there is still an application layer, which consists of backing beans and other objects that interoperate with JSF. However, the application layer doesn't know much about the business, or the data store. Instead, it counts on the *business layer* to deal with those things. The business layer doesn't know much about the application layer, but it does know a lot about the business. As a matter of fact, it has objects that *model* the business (called model or business objects), so in the case of ProjectTrack, it includes `User` and `Project` objects. The business layer can be implemented using plain old Java objects (POJOs), Enterprise JavaBeans (EJBs), or web services.

The business layer, however, doesn't know anything about the database—it lets the *integration layer* handle that work. The integration layer is responsible for accessing databases like Oracle or SQL Server, but it can also access other services, such as EJB servers or web services. This design approach (see figure 12.1) is much more powerful, and is generally easier to maintain and test.

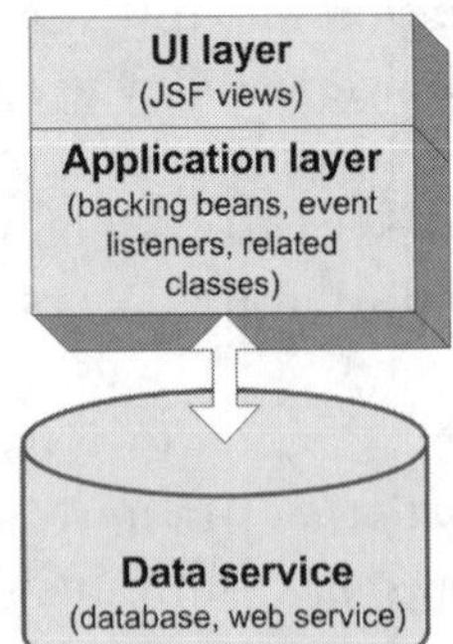

Figure 12.1
A simple JSF application only has two layers: a UI layer, which consists of JSF views, and an application layer, which consists of backing beans that have both business logic, and data-access code.

NOTE Even though figure 12.2 implies that JSF would never interact with the business layer, this isn't necessarily true. You may have a business object, like a `User`, that has a property (like `name`) that you want to synchronize with a UI component. The application layer is then responsible for exposing the business object to the UI component and invoking the business layer to process the updated object. If this sounds anti-MVC, remember that JSF is acting as a controller, mediating between the UI and the business objects.

Of course, the real world isn't always so cut and dry. You may have an application that uses both approaches. For example, your application layer may have a couple of business objects, but still interact directly with data service objects. Those data service objects could also even be retrieved from an integration layer. And, in ProjectTrack, backing beans talk to the integration layer to retrieve business objects. The key is consistency—the more inconsistent your application's architecture is, the harder it will be to maintain.

ProjectTrack uses multiple layers, and that is what we recommend for most applications. In this chapter and the next, we'll place great emphasis on the application layer, since it interacts with JSF. However, the layered design will be evident in the way the application layer is written. For example, action methods delegate most of their work to the business layer. If you're interested in the simpler approach, don't worry—we show how to integrate UI components with a JDBC `ResultSet` in chapter 13.

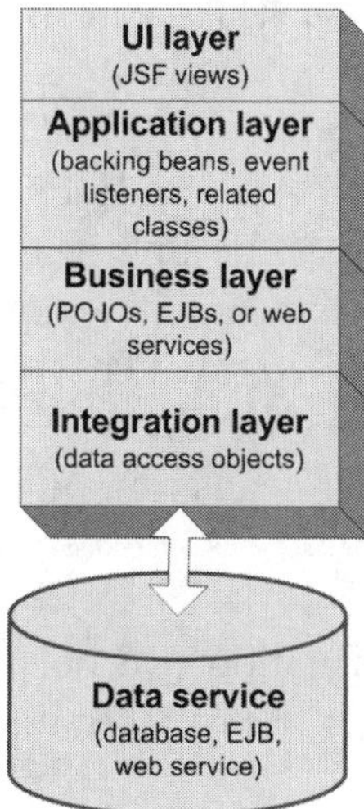

Figure 12.2
A better approach is to separate your application into different layers. The UI layer consists of JSF views, the application layer has backing beans, the business layer has business objects, and the integration layer talks to the data store.

Now that you know about the layered design of a JSF application, let's take a look at the design requirements for classes that interact with the framework.

12.2 Roasting the beans

Any object you develop that you want to integrate with JSF should expose JavaBean properties. This not only includes backing beans that interact directly with a view, but also any business objects, like a `Report`, that you'd like to wire up to JSF components. We're not saying that you should design your classes around JSF. There are, however, some things that make it easier for JSF to interact with them.

If you're working with existing business objects that aren't JavaBeans, you can always create adapters [GoF]—JavaBeans that delegate behavior to the original business object. If you don't have a full-fledged business domain model and you're wiring up UI components directly to data service objects (like a JSP Standard Tag Library, or JSTL, `Result`), this discussion is only relevant for properties that your backing beans expose.

Technically, a JavaBean simply requires a no-argument constructor (it can have other constructors as well). However, they usually publish properties in a specific manner, as we will discuss shortly. A no-argument constructor allows JSF to create a bean automatically with the Managed Bean Creation facility. If your object isn't going to be created in that way, a no-argument constructor isn't necessary. You may not want one in cases where you want more control over how the object is initialized. Objects without a no-argument constructor aren't officially JavaBeans, but as long as they publish properties properly, JSF can still interact with them.

If business objects and backing beans are both JavaBeans, what's different about them? Remember, business objects represent concepts and operations in the business domain, which have nothing to do with JSF. Backing beans, on the other hand, are designed to work with JSF forms, and can contain action listener or value-change listener methods, as well as action methods. They may even manipulate UI component instances in a view, and they usually have code that accesses the JSF API. Often, tools will generate backing beans for you when you create a new view. You can think of backing beans as adapters between the world of JSF and your business objects.

In the following sections we cover the basic information you need to write backing beans and business objects for JSF applications. We'll elaborate on these concepts as we discuss ProjectTrack's application layer.

TIP When you're designing the application layer, think of the front-end developer as an end user (even if you are the front-end developer). Pick property, class, and managed bean names that make sense to the person or people responsible for integrating the UI with your code.

12.2.1 The importance of toString

One of the handy features of JSF is its support for type conversion. When displaying the value of a bean property to the user, JSF will automatically convert it to a `String` for display. If no converter is registered on the UI component associated with the property, JSF will use the converter that is registered for that type. For example, `Integers` are usually converted using the `IntegerConverter` class. JSF has converters for all of the standard Java types (see chapter 6 for details).

For your own objects, you can write a custom converter, which can be registered by type (so that it's called automatically) or by name (so that it can be explicitly registered with UI components). However, there's an easier way—just use Java's standard `String` conversion feature: the `toString` method. If JSF can't find a converter for your object, it will call this method.

If `toString` isn't overridden, the default `toString` method on the `Object` class will be used. For example, let's look at a property of the `Project` class:

```
public ProjectType getType()
{
  return type;
}
```

This returns the project's `type` property, which is a `ProjectType` object. Here's a reference to this property on the Project Details JSP from chapter 10:

```
<h:outputText value="#{project.type}"/>
```

This converts the `type` property to a `String` and displays it. If `ProjectType` didn't override the `toString` property, it would look something like this: "org.jia.ptrack.domain.ProjectType@2f6684." This may be useful for debugging, but it sure isn't pretty. Fortunately, `EnumeratedType`, `ProjectType`'s super class, overrides the `toString` method:

```
private String description;
...
public String toString()
{
  return description;
}
```

This just returns the `ProjectType` instance's `description` property, which is already a `String`. So, instead of the ugly output without the `toString` method, we get something a little more palatable, like "Internal Web Application." Of course, we could have referenced the `description` property directly:

```
<h:outputText value="#{project.type.description}"/>
```

This would have worked fine. But normally all anyone cares about is the `description` property, so why require the extra work? In a sense, `toString` can be used as the default property for beans.

This technique is useful for just about any object you expect to be referenced by the UI. Every ProjectTrack business object has a basic `toString` method, including `Project`. For `Project`, this returns the `name` property. Returning the name is useful for front-end development because simple value-binding expressions such as this work:

```
<h:outputText value="#{project}"/>
```

This displays the project's name, like "Inventory Manager 2.0," which is pretty intuitive.

Of course, this approach won't work in cases where you're dealing with existing beans that already use `toString` in a different way, when you want to add parameterized formatting or localization during the conversion process, or if you need to *update* a property with an input control. That's when you need to write a custom converter; we show how to do this in section 12.4.4, and cover the process thoroughly in chapter 15.

12.2.2 Serialization for breakfast

ProjectTrack's beans implement the `java.io.Serializable` interface. This is required for any objects you want to be shared across application server instances or persisted to disk when the server shuts down (in other words, objects that are stored in session scope). This usually applies to business objects like `User` or `Project`, but also to any other objects you might be using to manage state, like a `ShoppingCart` object or a `RegistrationWizard` object. In short, make sure both your business objects and backing beans are serializable.

12.2.3 It's all in the properties

As we've mentioned before, JSF expects all objects accessed through value-binding expressions to expose their properties using the JavaBeans patterns. If you've developed applications with Struts or other bean-based frameworks, this should seem familiar to you.

JavaBeans properties are accessed through getters (also called *accessors*) and setters (also called *mutators*). Here's an example from ProjectTrack's `AuthenticationBean` class:

```
public class AuthenticationBean implements Serializable
{
  private String loginName;
  private String password;

  public AuthenticationBean()
  {
  }

  public void setLoginName(String loginName)
  {
    this.loginName = loginName;
  }

  public String getLoginName()
  {
    return loginName;
  }

...

}
```

This snippet has a single no-argument constructor, and exposes a single property called `loginName`. If the bean is stored under the key `authenticationBean` in some application scope, this property can be referenced easily with the value-binding expression `"#{authenticationBean.loginName}"`. Here's a declaration of an `HtmlInputText` component that uses this property:

```
<h:inputText value="#{authenticationBean.loginName}"/>
```

This associates the `value` property of the `HtmlInputText` component to with the `loginName` property of an `AuthenticationBean` instance. Any changes made by the user through the input control will update the property, and vice versa.

The same property can also be accessed in Java code:

```
FacesContext context = FacesContext.getCurrentInstance();
Application app = context.getApplication();
String loginName =
  (String)app.createValueBinding("#{authenticationBean.loginName}").
            getValue(context);
```

Boolean properties, which are required by UISelectBoolean, can have an is method instead of a get method. Here's another AuthenticationBean method that returns true if a user cannot access the Inbox:

```
public boolean isInboxAuthorized()
{
  return getVisit().getUser().
                   getRole().equals(RoleType.UPPER_MANAGER);
}
```

This property is used in the header JSP like so:

```
<jia:navigatorItem name="inbox" label="#{bundle.InboxToolbarButton}"
                   icon="/images/inbox.gif"
                   action="inbox"
                   disabled="#{!authenticationBean.inboxAuthorized}"/>
```

Here, we disable the Inbox toolbar button if the user is not authorized to access it. In this case, we're referencing the property as part of a JSF EL expression used for a UI component property other than value. If you're associating a property with an input component's value, as in the first example, it must be a read/write property. Read/write properties have both an accessor and mutator, like our loginName property.

If you want a property to be read-only, just don't write an accessor, as shown with the inboxAuthorized property. Keep in mind, however, that read-only properties can't be used as the value of input controls because their values can't be updated.

If you write a property that's intended to be associated with a UI component's value, you also have to make sure it's the proper type; otherwise, the component won't know how to handle it. So far, we've looked at just String and boolean properties. For most UI components, such as UIInput, UIOutput, and their subclasses, just about any type of object will do, as long as it can aesthetically be converted to a String, either with a converter or via the object's toString method.

Table 12.1 lists all of the standard components and the types they accept for the value property. Note that we're listing the renderer-independent superclasses; the same rules apply to the subclasses, like HtmlOutputText.

Table 12.1 Each component knows how to handle specific data types. In many cases, you can count on converters (either standard or custom) to handle differences for you.

UI Component	Accepted Types for value Property
UIInput, UIOutput, UISelectOne	Any basic or primitive types that have converters, or custom types (often with custom converters).

continued on next page

Table 12.1 Each component knows how to handle specific data types. In many cases, you can count on converters (either standard or custom) to handle differences for you. *(continued)*

UI Component	Accepted Types for `value` Property
`UIData`	An array of beans, a `List` of beans, a single bean, `java.sql.ResultSet`, `javax.servlet.jsp.jstl.Result`, or `javax.faces.model.DataModel`.
`UISelectBoolean`	A `boolean` or `Boolean`.
`UISelectItem`	A single `SelectItem` instance.
`UISelectItems`	A single `SelectItem` instance, an array of `SelectItem`s, a `Collection` of `SelectItem`s, or a `Map` whose key/value pairs (converted to `String`s) will be used as the label and value of `SelectItem` instances.
`UISelectMany`	An array of any basic or custom type with a converter, or a `List` of `String`s.

As the table shows, the rules are pretty simple: in some cases, the component expects only specific types, and in other cases, any type with a valid converter (or `toString` method) will do. You'll see examples of bean properties that work with most of these components, and a situation that requires a custom converter, as we discuss ProjectTrack in detail.

What's a little tricky, though, is dealing with the SelectOne and SelectMany components, and `UISelectItem` and `UISelectItems`. It's tricky because these are the only components that require specific JSF model objects—`javax.faces.model.SelectItem` and its subclass, `javax.faces.model.SelectItemGroup`. (`UIData` uses a `DataModel` object internally, but you can associate it with several other types.)

Working with SelectMany and SelectOne components

As we discussed in chapter 5, SelectMany components (represented by the `UISelectMany` superclass) are responsible for selecting one or more items from a list. SelectOne components (represented by the `UISelectOne` superclass) are responsible for selecting a single item from a list. So far, so good. Those lists, however, are specified with `UISelectItem` and `UISelectItems` components, which are essentially wrappers for `SelectItem` model objects (for an overview of `SelectItem`, see chapter 11).

The list of items can be configured statically in the UI, as we did in chapter 5. But if you plan to dynamically configure the list, you must wite a property that

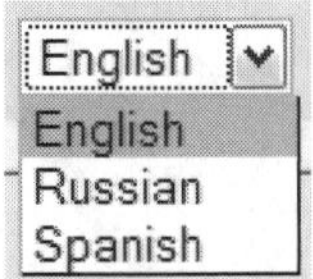

Figure 12.3
ProjectTrack's header has an `HtmlSelectOneListbox` component for different locales.

returns a collection of `SelectItem` instances, and make sure that the property that the component updates has the same type as the `itemValue` property of the `SelectItem` instances. (Instead of `SelectItem` instances, your property can return a `Map` whose key/value pairs will be converted into `SelectItem` instances.)

> **NOTE** Your business objects should never contain properties that return `SelectItem` instances (or any other JSF-specific object, for that matter). If you need to expose objects from the business tier in an item list, write an adapter method in a backing bean, as shown in section 12.4.4.

Let's look at a simple example. ProjectTrack's header has a drop-down listbox that allows the user to select his or her current locale from a list, as shown in figure 12.3. (In the real application, there are only two supported locales, and the JSP is slighlty different, but we've modified things for this example.)

This listbox, which is an `HtmlSelectOneListbox` component, references the `visit.locale` property, which represents the user's selected locale:

```
<h:selectOneListbox id="languageSelect" size="1"
                    styleClass="language-select"
                    value="#{visit.locale}">
  <f:selectItems value="#{visit.supportedLocaleItems}"/>
  <f:selectItem value="#{visit.extraLocaleItem}"/>
</h:selectOneListbox>
```

The `locale` property is defined as a follows (the implementation isn't relevant to our discussion):

```
public String getLocale(){ ... }
public void setLocale(String locale) { ... }
```

The listbox has a child `UISelectItems` component that references the `supportedLocaleItems` property, which is defined like so:

```
public SelectItem[] getSupportedLocaleItems()
{
  SelectItem[] localeItems = new SelectItem[2];
  localeItems[0] = new SelectItem("en", "English");
  localeItems[1] = new SelectItem("ru", "Russian");
  return localeItems;
}
```

This method was designed to be referenced by `UISelectItems` components, so it returns an array of `SelectItem` instances. The first parameter of the constructor is the item's value, which is the value passed into the `setLocale` method when the `HtmlSelectOneListbox` updates the `locale` property.

The `extraLocaleItem` property returns a single `SelectItem` instance:

```
public SelectItem getExtraLocaleItem()
{
  return new SelectItem("es", "Spanish");
}
```

Because this method returns a single `SelectItem` instance, it can be used as the value for either a `UISelectItem` component (as in this example) or a `UISelectItems` component.

The important point is that the value of the `SelectItem` instances are designed to work with the property referenced by the listbox, which is the `locale` property in this case. The `setLocale` method understands the values "en", "ru", and "es".

BY THE WAY Hardcoding a list of locales isn't the best way to do things. The real application creates `SelectItem` instances dynamically based on the locales the application supports. See section 12.5 for details.

Things get slightly more complicated when you're not using `Strings`. If the `locale` property were defined as an `Integer`, the value of the `SelectItem` objects would have to be an `Integer` as well. Suppose that the `locale` property was defined like this:

```
public Integer getLocale(){ ... }
public void setLocale(Integer locale) { ... }
```

Our previous versions of `getSupportedLocaleItems` and `getExtraLocaleItem` would have to be updated, because the values "en", "ru", and "es" can't be converted to an `Integer`:

```
public SelectItem[] getSupportedLocaleItems()
{
  SelectItem[] localeItems = new SelectItem[2];
  localeItems[0] = new SelectItem(new Integer(0), "English");
  localeItems[1] = new SelectItem(new Integer(1), "Russian");
  return localeItems;
}

public SelectItem getExtraLocaleItem()
{
  return new SelectItem(new Integer(3), "Spanish");
}
```

- [ ] Deployment guidelines
- [ ] Architecture specification
- [ ] Maintenance documentation
- [x] Proposal document
- [ ] User documentation
- [ ] Test plan
- [x] Project plan

Figure 12.4
Several ProjectTrack views allow the user to select one or more artifacts from a list with an `HtmlSelectManyCheckbox` component.

The bottom line is that the value of `SelectItem` instances must be the same type as the property being set by the `HtmlSelectOneListbox` component.

The same rule applies to SelectMany components, except for the fact that they can accept several selected values from a user. Properties associated with Select-Many component values must return an array of primitives or objects instead of a single object. They can also return a `List`, but the `List` can only contain `Strings`.

As an example, consider the list of artifacts shown in several project pages (figure 12.4).

Here's the declaration of this `HtmlSelectManyCheckbox` component:

```
<h:selectManyCheckbox id="artifactSelect" layout="pageDirection"
                      styleClass="project-input"
                      value="#{visit.currentProject.artifacts}">
  <f:selectItems value="#{selectItems.artifacts}"/>
</h:selectManyCheckbox>
```

The `HtmlSelectManyCheckbox` updates the `artifacts` property of the current project, which looks like this:

```
public void setArtifacts(ArtifactType[] artifacts) {...}
public ArtifactType[] getArtifacts() {...}
```

As you can see, it accepts an array of `ArtifactType` objects. The `selectItems` bean returns a `List` of `SelectItem` instances for the list of artifacts. Here's a simplified version of the accessor:

```
public List getArtifacts ()
{
  List artifacts = new ArrayList();
  artifacts.add(
     new SelectItem(ArtifactType.DEPLOYMENT,
                    ArtifactType.DEPLOYMENT.getDescription()));
...
  artifacts.add(
```

```
    new SelectItem(ArtifactType.PROJECT_PLAN,
                   ArtifactType.PROJECT_PLAN.getDescription()));
  return artifacts;
}
```

The static fields `DEPLOYMENT` and `PROJECT_PLAN` return `ArtifactType` instances, and the `getDescription` method returns a `String`. So, once again, the `value` of the `SelectItem` instances is the same type as the property the items will be updating. The only difference is that the property is an array instead of a single value.

We did leave out one piece of this puzzle. Because `ArtifactType` isn't supported by the standard JSF converters, we need a custom converter. Fortunately, the SelectMany components are smart enough to use the converter for all of the elements in the array. All that's necessary is to associate the proper converter with the UI component. (We develop this converter in section 12.4.4.) This isn't necessary for types that JSF converts automatically (see chapter 6).

Next, let's see how to write properties that are bound directly to a component instance.

Using component bindings

We've touched on the ability to bind a UI component instance to a backing bean. This is different than binding a UI component's `value` property to a backing bean. A component binding gives a backing bean access to an instance of the UI component. This can be useful in cases where you need to dynamically create or manipulate controls in the view, as we did in the Hello, world! application. You can also use component bindings to influence the logic of action methods, or to initialize a UI component. Using component bindings and binding a property to the component's value aren't mutually exclusive endeavors; sometimes you may use both approaches with the same UI component.

ProjectTrack's `SelectProjectBean` has a property that is bound to the `UIData` component in the associated view:

```
import javax.faces.component.UIData;
...
private UIData projectTable;
...
public UIData getProjectTable()
{
  return projectTable;
}
public void setProjectTable(javax.faces.component.UIData projectTable)
{
  this.projectTable = projectTable;
}
```

Because this class doesn't manipulate any HTML-specific properties, we use the superclass for data table components, `UIData`, rather than its HTML-specific subclass, `HtmlDataTable`. This bean is exposed as a request-scoped variable named `inboxBean`, and is referenced in the Inbox view like so:

```
<h:dataTable styleClass="table-background"
             rowClasses="table-odd-row,table-even-row" cellpadding="3"
             value="#{inboxBean.inboxProjects}"
             var="project"
             binding="#{inboxBean.projectTable}">
...
</h:dataTable>
...
<h:commandLink action="#{inboxBean.approve}">
  <h:outputText value="Approve"/>
</h:commandLink>
```

This declaration binds a `UIData` component to the `inboxBean`'s `projectTable` property. This view also references an action method, which uses the `UIData` instance to help perform its work:

```
public String approve()
{
  ...
  Project project = (Project)projectTable.getRowData();
  ...
}
```

This line retrieves the currently selected row of the `UIData` component, which is a `Project` instance. This is an example of binding to a UI component solely to assist with performing application-level processing. In this case, JSF created the actual instance of the component.

Instead of letting JSF do your dirty work, you can create and initialize a UI component in the property's accessor. For example, the Create a Project page uses the `CreateProjectBean` to initialize the `HtmlSelectOneListbox` for project types:

```
<h:selectOneMenu binding="#{createProjectBean.projectSelectOne}">
```

In `CreateProjectBean`, the `htmlProjectSelectOne` property is defined like this:

```
import javax.faces.component.html.HtmlSelectOneListbox;
...
private HtmlSelectOneListbox projectSelectOne;
...
public HtmlSelectOneListbox getProjectSelectOne()
{
  if (projectSelectOne == null)
  {
```

```
        projectSelectOne = (HtmlSelectOneListbox)getApplication().
            createComponent(HtmlSelectOneListbox.COMPONENT_TYPE);
        projectSelectOne.setId("typeSelectOne");
        projectSelectOne.setTitle("Select the project type");
        projectSelectOne.setRequired(true);
        projectSelectOne.setValueBinding("value", getApplication().
            createValueBinding("#{visit.currentProject.type}"));
        projectSelectOne.setConverter(getApplication().
            createConverter(ProjectTypeConverter.CONVERTER_TYPE));
    }

    return projectSelectOne;
}
```

Here, we create a new `HtmlSelectOneListbox` instance using the `Application` class's factory method. Next, we set a few properties and create a `ValueBinding` instance for its `value` property. We also register a new custom converter instance for the component. This is equivalent to the following declaration in JSP:

```
<h:selectOneMenu id="typeSelectOne" title="Select the project type"
                 required="true"
                 value="#{visit.currentProject.type}">
                 converter="ProjectType"/>
```

The JSP is decidedly more terse, which is the appeal of creating the UI declaratively. However, in some cases, you may want to initialize UI component properties this way, especially if you're building a graph of components dynamically.

In this example, the `projectSelectOne` property is a concrete HTML component class, which is ideal if you're going to be manipulating a lot of HTML-specific properties. However, if you're not, we recommend you use the component's superclass as in the previous example. Using the superclass has the added benefit of allowing the view to change the JSP tag without affecting the code. So, if this property had been declared as a `UISelectOne` instead, the Create a Project page could use the `<h:selectOneListbox>`, `<h:selectOneMenu>`, or `<h:selectOneRadio>` JSP component tags. The HTML-specific property `title`, which is used by all three renderers, could be initialized like so:

```
projectSelectOne.getAttributes().put("title",
                                     "Select the project type");
```

This works because the different tags use separate renderers, and all of the renderers understand the `title` attribute.

12.2.4 Exposing beans

By now, the guidelines for JavaBeans used in JSF applications should be clear. Once you've written the beans, the last step is to make sure your application can access them. All you have to do is expose the bean as a scoped variable, and JSF EL expressions will be able to find them.

Because the Managed Bean Creation facility handles this for you automatically, the typical pattern is to configure backing beans as managed beans, and expose any business objects through those backing beans. The business objects themselves may or may not be managed beans, depending on your application. Remember, the facility is great for initializing object properties, so you could use it to create instances of business objects and set them as properties of backing beans. Here's an example of registering the `SelectProjectBean`, which is responsible for selecting a single project from a list, with the Managed Bean Creation facility:

```
<managed-bean>
  <description>Loads a Project from the ProjectCoordinator.
  </description>
  <managed-bean-name>inboxBean</managed-bean-name>
  <managed-bean-class>org.jia.ptrack.web.SelectProjectBean
  </managed-bean-class>
  <managed-bean-scope>request</managed-bean-scope>
  <managed-property>
    <property-name>visit</property-name>
    <value>#{sessionScope.visit}</value>
  </managed-property>
  <managed-property>
    <property-name>projectCoordinator</property-name>
    <value>#{applicationScope.projectCoordinator}</value>
  </managed-property>
  <managed-property>
    <property-name>statusCoordinator</property-name>
    <value>#{applicationScope.statusCoordinator}</value>
  </managed-property>
  <managed-property>
    <property-name>userCoordinator</property-name>
    <value>#{applicationScope.userCoordinator}</value>
  </managed-property>
</managed-bean>
```

Here, we declare an instance of `org.jia.ptrack.web.SelectProjectBean` as a request-scoped variable with the name `inboxBean`. We also specify four properties to initialize when the bean is created. Note that each property is initialized with a value-binding expression that refers to an existing scoped variable. The expressions marked in bold reference business objects; the other expression, `"#{sessionScope.visit}"`, refers to a backing bean that manages session information for a user.

Value-binding expressions aren't required; you can also initialize properties to static values. (See chapter 3 for a detailed discussion of managed beans.)

This bean can now be referenced with the expression `"#{inboxBean}"`. Here's an example from inbox.jsp:

```
<h:dataTable styleClass="table-background"
             rowClasses="table-odd-row,table-even-row" cellpadding="3"
             value="#{inboxBean.inboxProjects}"
             var="project">
...
</h:dataTable>
```

This binds the `value` property of this `dataTable` with the `SelectProjectBean.inboxProjects` property, which returns a `List` of `Project` objects. `Project` is a business object, and `SelectProjectBean` internally uses its `projectCoordinator` property, set with the Managed Bean Creation facility, to retrieve that list.

You can also expose beans using the `ValueBinding` objects in code. Here's an example from the `AuthenticationBean`'s `login` method:

```
Visit visit = new Visit();
...
visit.setUser(newUser);
visit.setAuthenticationBean(this);
...
application.createValueBinding("#{sessionScope.visit}").
    setValue(facesContext, visit);
```

Here, we create a new `Visit` object, set some properties, and then create and set a new value-binding expression. Now, our newly created object will be available as a session-scoped variable under the key `visit`. The header references this object like so:

```
<h:outputText value="(#{visit.user.login})" styleClass="user-name"/>
```

This `HtmlOutputText` component displays the user's login name, retrieving the current user from the `Visit` object.

Now that we're clear on how to write beans, let's take a step back and look at the objects that make up ProjectTrack's business layer.

12.3 Exploring the business layer and data layers

Before we start writing the application layer, let's briefly examine ProjectTrack's business layer. Rather than build each class here, we'll take a high-level tour and assume that the work has already been completed and unit-tested independently. (We don't cover the unit tests here, but they're included with the downloadable

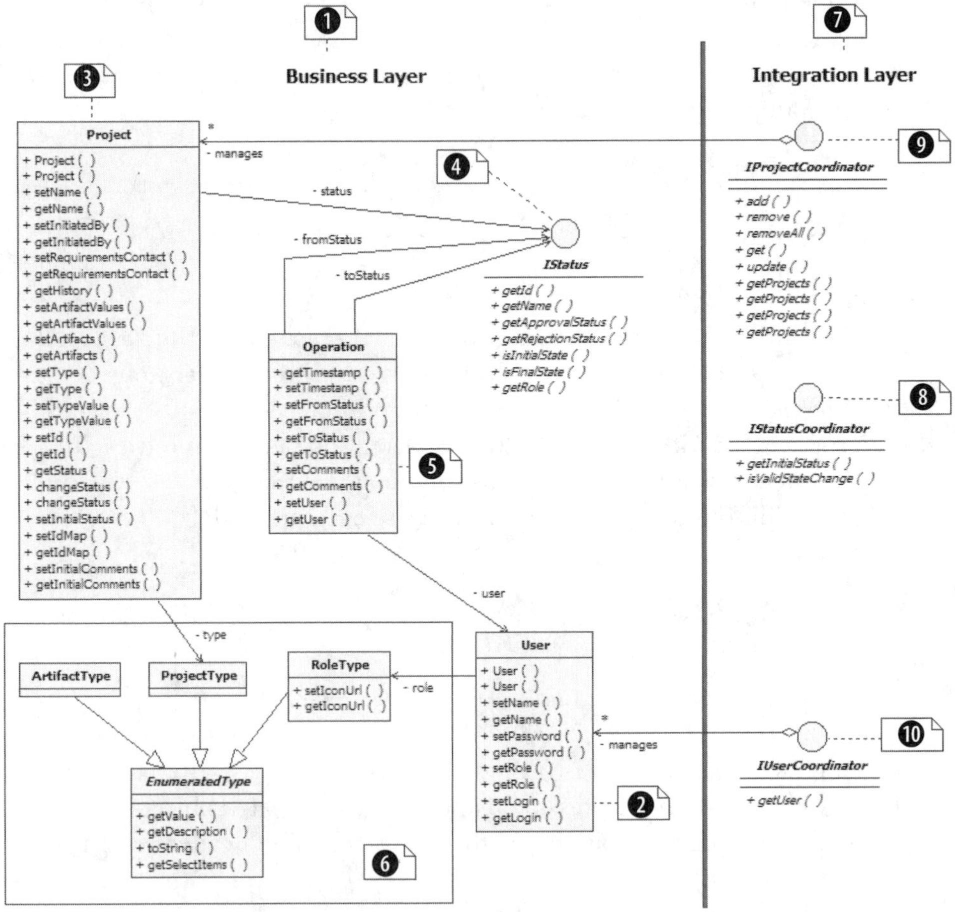

Figure 12.5 A class diagram of ProjectTrack's business layer.

source to ProjectTrack, available at http://www.manning.com/mann.) Remember—these classes concentrate on business logic and data access, and don't know anything about JSF, or even the Web, for that matter.

> **TIP** Business objects aren't aware of the JSF environment, so they're easy to unit-test. The online code for ProjectTrack includes JUnit test cases for the classes mentioned here.

In chapter 7, we talked about ProjectTrack's conceptual model, which includes entities like Project and User, and their relationships. To recap, the application centers on a Project. Projects have a status, like "Proposal" or "Deployment." They have a type, such as "Internal Web Application" or "External Desktop Application." They have artifacts, like "Project plan" and "Architectural document." They're also created by Users.

Users have different roles, like "Project Manager" and "Development Manager." A Project's status is associated with a specific role. Users in that role can promote or demote Projects to a different status, as shown in figure 7.1. Each time a user does this, it's called an Operation. From this conceptual model, we can derive ProjectTrack's object model, which is shown in figure 12.5. All of the business objects we mentioned—`Project`, `ProjectType`, `ArtifactType`, `IStatus`, `User`, `RoleType`, and `Operation` are depicted. There's also a second set of objects that are responsible for loading these objects from a data store.

❶ The business objects represent the main entities that make up the system; these are the ones that JSF components will directly display and modify. Most of them are simple JavaBeans—they have a no-argument constructor, and expose all of their properties via getter and setter methods, as we described in section 12.2.3. This is key, because JavaBean properties are accessible via JSF value-bindings.

❷ The `User` object represents a user during his or her interaction with the system. It has `login`, `name`, `password`, and `role` properties. The `role` property, represented as a `RoleType` object, is used to help decide which `Projects` a user can modify.

❸ The `Project` class is the center of the ProjectTrack universe. It has a ton of simple properties, like `name`, `description`, `initiatedBy`, and `requirementsContact`. It also has a `status` property, which represents its current state, and can be manipulated with the `changeStatus` method. A `Project`'s `history` property is a collection of `Operation` objects; new `Operations` are added via by the `changeStatus` method, as well. `Artifacts` are maintained as a collection of `ArtifactType` objects, and there is a single `type` property, which is represented by a `ProjectType` object.

❹ The `Project` class's `status` property is represented by the `IStatus` interface. An `IStatus` has simple `id` and `name` properties. It is associated with a single `RoleType` instance via the `role` property—only `Users` with that `RoleType` should be able to manipulate a `Project`. The `approvalStatus` property returns the next `IStatus` instance in the project workflow; the `rejectionStatus` property returns the previous `IStatus` instance. You can think of an `IStatus` instance as a node in a doubly linked list. If it's the first object in the list, the `isInitialState` property is set to `true`; if it's the last, the `isFinalState` property is set to `true`.

❺ An `Operation` represents the act of changing from one status to another. Each `Operation` is initiated by a `User`, and has `timestamp` and `comment` properties. The previous and current status are represented by the `fromStatus` and `toStatus` properties, which are `IStatus` instances.

6. Like many Java developers, I have my own version of an enumerated type class, with the terribly uncreative name `EnumeratedType`.[1] All of the `Type` classes in the system—`ArtifactType`, `ProjectType`, and `RoleType`, descend from this class. Each class has several public static instances (with private constructors) and handy methods for dealing with them. For example, the `ArtifactType` class has instances whose names match the different artifact types: `PROPOSAL`, `ARCHITECTURE`, and so on.
7. The objects in the integration layer are responsible for retrieving objects from a data store. They aren't accessed directly from UI components, although they will often be accessed via event listeners. All of them are singletons—there's only one instance per application.

   You may have noticed that we've left out the concrete classes that implement these interfaces. Since ProjectTrack is a small sample application, these are POJOs that talk to some data store (there are also memory-only implementations, which we use here). However, they could delegate their work to EJBs if the requirements demanded it. Since the interfaces would remain the same regardless of the data store, the concrete classes were omitted for simplicity.
8. `IStatusCoordinator` is responsible for managing `IStatus` instances. In practice, it acts as a factory for the first `IStatus` via its `initialStatus` property.
9. `IProjectCoordinator` is responsible for managing `Project` objects. It has basic database operations like `add`, `remove`, `removeAll`, and `get`.
10. `User` objects are managed by the `UserCoordinator`. Because you can't add users in ProjectTrack currently, it has one important method: `getUser`.

ProjectTrack's integration layer also defines a simple exception hierarchy with three classes: `BaseException`, `DataStoreException` (which subclasses `BaseException`), and `ObjectNotFoundException` (which subclasses `DataStoreException`). You'll see backing beans catch these exceptions, log the error, and generate JSF messages when necessary.

This concludes our tour of the business layer. As we build the rest of the application, you'll see how event listeners delegates all business logic calls to this layer. Without further ado, let's introduce the application layer.

12.4 Developing the application layer

Now that we've covered the classes that make up the JSF environment, discussed how to write backing beans, and examined the business objects that provide ProjectTrack's

[1] You have no idea how long I've been waiting for enumerated types to be added to Java—thankfully, JDK 1.5 adds this feature.

core functionality, we can build the application layer. The bulk of the code will be backing beans that expose properties and action methods. These will be the meat of the application, and they're the classes that we'll be hooking up to UI components.

There are two other categories of classes—utility and adapter classes. Utility classes provide helper methods and constants, initialize business layer objects, and help out with authentication and authorization. Adapter classes expose business object properties in a way that makes sense to UI components.

All of ProjectTrack's application layer classes are listed in table 12.2.

Table 12.2 ProjectTrack's application model includes several classes.

Class	Category	Description
`Constants`	Utility	Static class that contains `String`s for keys and outcomes.
`Utils`	Utility	Static class with simple utility methods for logging and retrieving values.
`Initializer`	Utility	`ServletContextListener` that initializes singletons.
`Authentication-Filter`	Utility	Filter used for custom authentication.
`EnumItemAdapter`	Adapter	Wraps business layer enumerated types with Faces `SelectItem` instances.
`ArtifactType-Converter`	Adapter	Converts an `ArtifactType` to and from a `String`.
`ProjectType-Converter`	Adapter	Converts a `ProjectType` to and from a `String`.
`Visit`	Application logic	Holds references to session-related objects like the current `User` and the current `Project`. Also used to change the user's current locale.
`BaseBean`	Application logic	Superclass for most backing beans.
`AuthenticationBean`	Application logic	Handles login, logout, and simple authorization duties.
`SelectProjectBean`	Application logic	Selects and loads a `Project` instance.
`UpdateProjectBean`	Application logic	Updates the current `Project` instance.
`CreateProjectBean`	Application logic	Creates and saves a new `Project` instance.
`ShowHistoryBean`	Application logic	Scrolls through `Project`s history.

Now, let's take a detailed look at each of these classes, and see how they cooperate to make ProjectTrack work. For each class, we'll discuss how it's implemented and show what JSF APIs and business layer APIs it uses. We'll also show any related configuration code (in places like web.xml or faces-config.xml), and give you a sense of how it relates to other ProjectTrack classes.

12.4.1 Handling constants

Web application frameworks often use strings for things like keys and navigation. Action methods sometimes need to store or retrieve an object—like a `User`—that's hanging out in some application scope. These objects are stored using a key that is also used to find them by means of value-binding expressions or the `ExternalContext`. Such keys are essential for accessing objects with non-JSF classes like filters or servlet event listeners. Action methods also return an outcome `String` that's used by the navigation handler to choose the next view to display.

Whenever you're building an application that relies on `Strings` to get the job done, it makes sense to store those `Strings` as constants somewhere and use the constant instead of the literal string. If you've developed applications with web frameworks like Struts, you may have seen this approach before. It provides these major benefits:

- Your code is more readable because a constant can say what the `String` *means*, as opposed to what it *is*. For example, the literal string "ptrackResources" isn't as meaningful to someone reading your code as `Constants.BUNDLE_BASENAME`.
- Another advantage is compile-time safety—for example, if you mistype "Constants.BUNDLE_BASENAME", the Java compiler will complain. If you mistype "ptrackResources", you're bound to waste time trying to figure out why your code is retrieving `null` instead of an actual value.
- You can use code-assist features in an IDE to get a list of possible values, which is good for those of us with poor memory.
- If the value changes, you have update it in only one place.

Generally, it's best to put all of these constants in one place so that they're easy to find—ProjectTrack places them all in a class called `Constants`. Usually constants are added as you build the application—for example, if you're writing a new action method that needs to return `"success"`, it's time to add a new constant called `SUCCESS_OUTCOME`. However, to avoid mucking up our other discussions with constant-talk, we'll just add them all right now—see listing 12.1.

Listing 12.1 Constants.java: Stores all application-wide strings

```
package org.jia.ptrack.web;

public class Constants
{
  // Backing bean keys
  public final static String VISIT_KEY_SCOPE = "sessionScope.";
  public final static String VISIT_KEY = "visit";

  // Business object keys
  public final static String CURRENT_PROJECT_SCOPE =
                              "sessionScope.";
  public final static String CURRENT_PROJECT_KEY =
                              "currentProjectAdapter";

  public final static String PROJECT_COORDINATOR_SCOPE =
                              "applicationScope.";
  public final static String PROJECT_COORDINATOR_KEY =
                              "projectCoordinator";

  public final static String STATUS_COORDINATOR_SCOPE =
                              "applicationScope.";
  public final static String STATUS_COORDINATOR_KEY =
                              "statusCoordinator";

  public final static String USER_COORDINATOR_SCOPE =
                              "applicationScope.";
  public final static String USER_COORDINATOR_KEY =
                              "userCoordinator";

  // Authorization
  public final static String ORIGINAL_VIEW_SCOPE = "sessionScope.";
  public final static String ORIGINAL_VIEW_KEY = "originalTreeId";
  public final static String PROTECTED_DIR = "protected";
  public final static String EDIT_DIR = "protected/edit";
  public final static String LOGIN_VIEW = "/faces/login.jsp";

  // Action outcomes
  public final static String SUCCESS_READONLY_OUTCOME =
                              "success_readonly";
  public final static String SUCCESS_READWRITE_OUTCOME =
                              "success_readwrite";
  public final static String SUCCESS_OUTCOME = "success";

  public final static String CANCEL_READONLY_OUTCOME =
                              "cancel_readonly";
  public final static String CANCEL_READWRITE_OUTCOME =
                              "cancel_readwrite";
  public final static String CANCEL_OUTCOME = "cancel";
```

```
    public final static String FAILURE_OUTCOME = "failure";
    public final static String ERROR_OUTCOME = "error";

    // Resource bundle keys
    public final static String BUNDLE_BASENAME = "ptrackResources";
}
```

We won't cover every constant here, but you can see that there are five groups: backing bean keys, model object keys, authentication keys, action method outcomes, and resource bundle keys. There's only one backing bean key, which is for the `Visit` object (we'll discuss that later). This key is used to check for the object's existence and store it for use by other backing beans. The business object keys are used to store a few essential objects after they've been initialized.

Note that each of these beans have two constants—the scope and the key itself. When you're dealing directly with a servlet object like an `HttpSession`, you'll use just the key. If you're using `ValueBindings`, which are part of the JSF API, you may need both. You'll see some examples of this as we discuss other aspects of the system.

Authentication keys are for objects that are also stored in some application scope, but they're used only for authentication and authorization—they're not referenced by UI components or backing beans at all. These keys are specific to the way ProjectTrack implements security. (In a real application, some of these constants would be configurable as servlet initialization parameters.) Action outcomes are returned by action methods. And finally, resource bundle keys are used for loading the resource bundle in code.

This class doesn't have a constant for every single model object key or navigation outcome that ProjectTrack uses—only the ones referenced in code. As a matter of fact, all of these keys and scopes must map to keys and scopes defined in the JSF configuration file (either as managed beans, referenced beans, or navigation rules). You can think of the configuration file as the map of all possible beans and outcomes; `Constants` is like a filter of that map that's restricted to the ones necessary for writing Java code. As we examine the different parts of the system, we'll show the relevant pieces of configuration.

12.4.2 Organizing utility methods

Most real applications require a set of useful, stateless methods that don't fit into a specific class hierarchy. These methods are perfect candidates for static methods in a utility class. In JSF applications, methods for things like getting or setting model object references and logging are good candidates. Like the constants in the previous section, you would generally refactor repetitive code into these methods during the course of development. In order to save time, let's look at the whole class—it's shown in listing 12.2.

Listing 12.2 Utils.java: Houses utility methods for logging and other operations

```
package org.jia.ptrack.web;

import javax.faces.application.FacesMessage;
import javax.faces.context.FacesContext;
import javax.servlet.ServletContext;

public class Utils
{
  public static void log(FacesContext facesContext, String message)
  {
    facesContext.getExternalContext().log(message);
  }

  public static void log(FacesContext facesContext, String message,
                         Exception exception)
  {
    facesContext.getExternalContext().log(message, exception);
  }

  public static void reportError(FacesContext facesContext,
                                 String message,
                                 String detail,
                                 Exception exception)
  {
    facesContext.addMessage(null,
                 new FacesMessage(FacesMessage.SEVERITY_ERROR,
                                  message, detail));
    if (exception != null)
    {
      facesContext.getExternalContext().log(message, exception);
    }
  }

  public static void log(ServletContext servletContext, String message)
  {
    servletContext.log(message);
  }

  protected static void addInvalidStateChangeMessage(
                          FacesContext context, boolean approve)
  {
    String message;
    if (approve)
    {
```

```
      message = "You cannot approve a project with this status.";
    }
    else
    {
      message = "You cannot reject a project with this status.";
    }
    context.addMessage(null,
                       new FacesMessage(FacesMessage.SEVERITY_WARN,
                                        message, ""));
  }

}
```

You can see from the listing that the primary point of these methods is to simplify fairly long statements that are used often. Also, the implementation of these methods can be changed without breaking any existing code.

The `log` methods simply delegate to the `log` method of the `ServletContext`, (which is wrapped by the `log` method of `ExternalContext`). The `reportError` method has the added benefit of adding a new `FacesMessage` instance to the `FacesContext`. Of course, if you're using a logging framework, you may not need all of these methods.

The `addInvalidStateChangeMessage` just adds one of two possible messages to the `FacesContext`'s error list. This is used by both the `SelectProjectBean` and `UpdateProjectBean`, which need to complain when a user tries to move a `Project` to an invalid state.

12.4.3 Initializing singletons

Most of the objects in an application can be created using JSF's handy Managed Bean Creation facility. This is true for all of ProjectTrack's objects, *except* for singletons [GoF] that must live for the lifetime of the application. The Managed Bean Creation facility creates objects when they are requested, which is fine for simple JavaBeans. But if object creation requires initializing external resources like databases or EJB connections, it can be time-consuming. Such operations should be performed at start-up so that users aren't forced to wait for them to occur in the middle of their experience.

NOTE Singletons are often implemented as static properties of a class. We don't use that approach here because the action methods work with interfaces (and consequently shouldn't know the concrete class), and these classes may need configuration information from the `ServletContext`.

In web applications, start-up code can be written with a `ServletContextListener`. These are event listeners that are executed after the web application is first initialized (before it processes requests), and right before it is destroyed. ProjectTrack has a single `ServletContextListener` called `Initializer` that creates instances of the `IProjectCoordinator`, `IStatusCoordinator`, and `IUserCoordinator` interfaces. These are integration layer objects, so they may establish connections to other systems when they are initialized. The code is shown in listing 12.3.

Listing 12.3 Initializer.java: A ServletContextListener for initializing singletons

```
package org.ptrack.web;

import org.ptrack.domain.MemoryProjectCoordinator;
import org.ptrack.domain.MemoryStatusCoordinator;
import org.ptrack.domain.MemoryUserCoordinator;

import javax.servlet.ServletContext;
import javax.servlet.ServletContextEvent;
import javax.servlet.ServletContextListener;

public class Initializer implements ServletContextListener
{

  public Initializer()
  {
  }

  public void contextInitialized(ServletContextEvent event)
  {
    ServletContext servletContext = event.getServletContext();
    Utils.log(servletContext, "Initializing ProjectTrack...");

    servletContext.setAttribute(
      Constants.PROJECT_COORDINATOR_KEY,
      new MemoryProjectCoordinator());

    servletContext.setAttribute(
      Constants.STATUS_COORDINATOR_KEY,
      new MemoryStatusCoordinator());

    servletContext.setAttribute(
      Constants.USER_COORDINATOR_KEY,
      new MemoryUserCoordinator());

    Utils.log(servletContext, "Initialization complete...");
  }
```

❶ **Save in application scope**

```
    public void contextDestroyed(ServletContextEvent sce)
    {
    }
}
```

The `contextInitialized` method is executed once, when the web application is initialized. First, we get a handle to the `ServletContext` instance, which represents the web application. `MemoryProjectCoordinator`, `MemoryStatusCoordinator`, and `MemoryUserCoordinator` are memory-only implementations of the `IProjectCoordinator`, `IStatusCoordinator`, and `IUserCoordinator` interfaces. We call the `ServletContext` instance's `setAttribute` method for each coordinator object, storing each one in application scope using the specified key.

So, the line of code referenced by ❶ saves a new `MemoryProjectCoordinator` instance in application scope under the key `Constants.PROJECT_COORDINATOR_KEY`. This means that the instance can be found with the simple JSF EL expression `"projectCoordinator"`, since that's the value of `Constants.PROJECT_COORDINATOR_KEY`. The other coordinators are stored in the same way.

Once this method has executed, all of the classes in the integration layer will be available to the rest of the web application. If you're wondering why we're using the `ServletContext` explicitly instead of getting a `ValueBinding` from the JSF `Application` object, it's because the `getValueBinding` method requires a `FacesContext` instance. Because JSF hasn't started servicing requests yet, no `FacesContext` instance is available.

TIP For all managed beans, it's best to use `ValueBindings` to get and set values. Only use the objects of the Servlet API or `ExternalContext` directly if you don't have a handle to the `FacesContext`, or if you need to remove an object (which you can't do with a `ValueBinding`).

12.4.4 Adapting business objects

In section 12.2.3, we discussed how to write objects so that they work properly with the standard JSF components. Sometimes you'll get to write your objects from scratch, so it'll be easy to follow these guidelines. However, you may have to work with existing objects that don't follow these rules, and can't necessarily be changed by you or your group in the allotted time frame. Also, there are some objects—particularly business objects that shouldn't have to return JSF-specific objects like `SelectItem` instances.

In these cases, it makes sense to use the Adapter pattern [GoF] to develop classes that provide access to your object's properties using the types that JSF components expect. This way the original classes remain unmodified, but your UI components can happily interact with the adapter class which translates between the object's properties and the properties expected by the components. ProjectTrack is a new application, so the need is purely based on the desire to keep JSF out of the business layer. This will make it easier to reuse business objects in non-JSF applications.

In addition to writing adapter classes that return `SelectItem` instances or other component-friendly property types, you may also need to write converters for your business objects. Let's examine both scenarios.

Returning SelectItem instances

The only UI components that require special types for their value-binding properties are `UISelectItems` and `UISelectItem`, which are used by SelectMany and SelectOne components. These controls are used on the Approve a Project, Reject a Project, and Create a Project pages. All three pages use a `UISelectMany` to choose an artifact, and the Create a Project page also uses a `UISelectOne` to select the project type.

Using these components requires two value-binding expressions—one that points to the list of items (for `UISelectItems`), and another that points to the property that needs to be updated (for `UISelectMany` and `UISelectOne`). We can get a list of all of the possible items from the `ArtifactType` and `ProjectType` classes in ProjectTrack business layer. The business object to update is, of course, a `Project` instance. Unfortunately, these classes don't know anything about `SelectItem` instances, which is what the UI select components require. We can combat this by developing an adapter class. (This uses a more sophisticated approach than we showed in section 12.2.3.)

`ArtifactType` and `ProjectType` both inherit from an `EnumeratedType` class, so it makes sense to just develop a single adapter class that can return a list of `SelectItem` instances for either class. There is a third `EnumeratedType` subclass, `RoleType`, which we might as well add to this adapter as well, even though it's not currently used in the user interface. The class, `EnumItemAdapter`, is shown in listing 12.4.

Listing 12.4 EnumItemAdapter.java: Translates EnumeratedType values to SelectItem instances

```
package org.ptrack.web;

import org.ptrack.domain.ArtifactType;
```

```
import org.ptrack.domain.EnumeratedType;
import org.ptrack.domain.ProjectType;
import org.ptrack.domain.RoleType;

import javax.faces.component.SelectItem;

import java.util.ArrayList;
import java.util.HashMap;
import java.util.Iterator;
import java.util.List;
import java.util.Map;

public class EnumItemAdapter
{
  private Map itemLists = new HashMap();     <-- 1

  public EnumItemAdapter()    <-- 2
  {
    addType(ProjectType.class, ProjectType.getEnumManager());
    addType(ArtifactType.class, ArtifactType.getEnumManager());
    addType(RoleType.class, RoleType.getEnumManager());
  }

  protected void addType(Class clazz,                                    3
                   EnumeratedType.EnumManager enumManager)
  {
    Iterator types = enumManager.getInstances().iterator();
    List selectItems = new ArrayList();
    while (types.hasNext())
    {
      EnumeratedType type = (EnumeratedType)types.next();
      SelectItem item = new SelectItem(type,
                                      type.getDescription(),
                                      type.getDescription());
      selectItems.add(item);
    }
    itemLists.put(clazz, selectItems);
  }

  public List getArtifacts()
  {
    return (List)itemLists.get(ArtifactType.class);
  }
                                                               4
  public List getRoles()
  {
    return (List)itemLists.get(RoleType.class);
  }

  public List getProjectTypes()
  {
```

```
        return (List)itemLists.get(ProjectType.class);   ❹
    }
}
```

EnumItemAdapter manages a Map of SelectItem Lists (❶), keyed by the EnumeratedType subclass. In the constructor, the addType method is called for each EnumeratedType subclass (❷). Each EnumeratedType subclass has an EnumManager that returns all of the instances for the class.

For example, the ProjectType class has public final static instances of itself with the names EXTERNAL_WEB, INTERNAL_WEB, INTERNAL_DB, and so on. Its EnumManager will return a list of all of these instances. The addType method (❸) simply gets this list and creates a new SelectItem instance for each EnumeratedType instance. It's really doing all of the adaptation work up-front and storing a List of SelectItem instances for later reference. It's okay to do the work up-front because the EnumeratedTypes don't change dynamically.

All of the properties declared in ❹ are the ones that will be wired to UISelectItems components on the JSP pages. They simply return the proper List of SelectItem instances for the desired EnumeratedType subclass—ArtifactType, RoleType, or ProjectType. So, after we've completed the adaptation work, the properties return the proper types that SelectMany and SelectOne components require.

> **TIP** Even if you don't need an adapter, it still might make sense to have a single object (or small number of objects) responsible for populating lookup lists for SelectMany or SelectOne components. An alternative approach is to expose these properties on the beans that are used for collecting input. This is a little less flexible, however, because two different pages may need to display the same list of items even if they're associated with different beans. (The Visit class, which we discuss in section 12.5, uses the latter approach).

This class, like the data layer classes, is a singleton [GoF]. However, since initialization isn't expensive, we can register it with the Managed Bean Creation facility as an application-scoped object instead of using a ServletContextListener. The configuration file entry is shown in listing 12.5.

Listing 12.5 faces-config.xml: Managed bean configuration for EnumItemAdatper

```
<managed-bean>
  <managed-bean-name>selectItems</managed-bean-name>
  <managed-bean-class>
```

```
    org.jia.ptrack.web.EnumItemAdapter
  </managed-bean-class>
  <managed-bean-scope>application</managed-bean-scope>
</managed-bean>
```

Note that the name for the managed bean is `selectItems`, which is quite different than the class name `EnumItemAdapter`. This is what we mean when we say you should think in terms of the front-end developer. The word "selectItems" is much more intuitive when you're integrating the UI than "EnumItemAdapter."

Writing this adapter is one piece of the puzzle; the other piece is translating user input into custom types, which is the purpose of converters.

Writing a custom converter

In section 12.2.3, we discussed how the Project object's `artifacts` property required a custom converter. Recall that this property returns an array of `ArtifactType` instances:

```
public void setArtifacts(ArtifactType[] artifacts) {...}
public ArtifactType[] getArtifacts() {...}
```

In order for JSF to properly convert the user's input to this array, we need to develop a converter for `ArtifactType`, called `ArtifactTypeConverter`. All this class does is convert an `ArtifactType` instance to and from a `String`. Listing 12.6 shows the source.

Listing 12.6 ArtifactTypeConverter.java: Converts an ArtifactType to and from a String

```
package org.jia.ptrack.web;

import javax.faces.component.UIComponent;
import javax.faces.context.FacesContext;
import javax.faces.convert.Converter;
import javax.faces.convert.ConverterException;

import org.jia.ptrack.domain.ArtifactType;

public class ArtifactTypeConverter                    ❶ Implement Converter
               implements Converter                     interface
{
  public final static String CONVERTER_ID = "jia.ArtifactType";  ❷ Declare standard identifier

  public ArtifactTypeConverter()
  {
```

```
}

public Object getAsObject(FacesContext context,
                          UIComponent component, String value)
{
  if (value == null)
  {
    return null;
  }
  try
  {
    int artifactValue =
         Integer.parseInt(value);
    return ArtifactType.getEnumManager().
           getInstance(artifactValue);
  }
  catch (NumberFormatException ne)
  {
    Utils.log(context,
              "Can't convert to an ArtifactType; value (" +
              value + ") is not an integer.");
    throw new ConverterException(
            "Can't convert to an ArtifactType; value (" +
            value + ") is not an integer.", ne);
  }
  catch (IllegalArgumentException e)
  {
    Utils.log(context,
              "Can't convert ArtifactType; unknown value: " +
              value);
    throw new ConverterException(
              "Can't convert ArtifactType; unknown value: " +
               value, e);
  }
}

public String getAsString(FacesContext context,
                          UIComponent component, Object value)
{
  if (value == null)
  {
    return null;
  }
  if (value instanceof ArtifactType)
  {
    ArtifactType artifact = (ArtifactType)value;
    return String.valueOf(artifact.getValue());
  }
  else
  {
    Utils.log(context,
```

3 Actual conversion to ArtifactType

4 Actual conversion to String

```
                "Incorrect type (" + value.getClass() + "; value = " +
                value + "); value must be an ArtifactType instance");
        throw new ConverterException(
                    "Incorrect type (" + value.getClass() +
                    "; value = " + value +
                    "); value must be an ArtifactType instance");
      }
    }
  }
```

We start by implementing the `Converter` interface (❶). Next, we declare a constant for this converter's standard identifier (❷). This is the same identifier we'll use in a JSF configuration file, and it can also be used to create a new `ArtifactTypeConverter` instance through the `Application` class.

Note that we're converting the `ArtifactType` to and from its numeric `value` property (which every `EnumeratedType` has), rather than its `description` property, which is a readable string. The actual work of converting a `String` to an `ArtifactType` involves only the few lines shown in ❸. If the `String` can't be converted to an `int`, a `NumberFormatException` will be thrown. If the `EnumManager` can't find an `ArtifactType` instance for the `int` value, an `IllegalArgumentException` will be thrown. The rest of the work in the `getAsObject` method is simply logging these exceptions and throwing a new `ConverterException` (which will be translated into a `FacesMessage` by JSF).

The `getAsString` method is the inverse of `getAsObject`, and also only has a few real lines of work (❹). Here, we just check to make sure the object is of the correct type, and if so, we return the `int` value as a `String`. If it's not the correct type, we throw an exception.

That's all there is to writing the actual class. Next, we need to register the converter with JSF, as shown in listing 12.7.

Listing 12.7 faces-config.xml: Registering the ArtifactType converter

```
<converter>
  <converter-id>ArtifactType</converter-id>
  <converter-class>
   org.jia.ptrack.web.ArtifactTypeConverter
  </converter-class>
</converter>
```

All we're doing here is giving is giving the converter an identifier that JSF knows about. This identifier (which is the value of the `ArtifactType.CONVERTER_ID` constant) can now be used to register the converter with any UI components that are associated with an `ArtifactType` property. This work was performed for the project_artifacts.jsp file in chapter 10:

```
<h:selectManyCheckbox id="artifactSelect" layout="pageDirection"
                      styleClass="project-input"
                      value="#{visit.currentProject.artifacts}"
                      converter="ArtifactType">
  <f:selectItems value="#{selectItems.artifacts}"/>
</h:selectManyCheckbox>
```

Voilà! We've adapted our business object to work with JSF.

BY THE WAY We could also have registered this converter by type instead of by its identifier. This would have avoided the need to explicitly register the converter for a UI component, because JSF would find the converter based on its type. However, in this case, registration by type would not have worked, because `ArtifactTypeConverter` converts an `ArtifactType` into an integer, which isn't always the desired effect (sometimes we'd prefer conversion to a descriptive `String`).

ProjectTrack also uses another converter, `ProjectTypeConverter`, similarly in the Create a Project page. Since `ProjectType` is also an `EnumeratedType`, the implementation doesn't reveal anything new, so we'll spare you the details.

This is often how you'll develop simple custom converters for your application. More powerful converters, like the standard JSF converters, require additional work. We examine converter development thoroughly in chapter 15.

12.5 Writing a visit object for session state

Web applications need to keep track of information for the current user. This is the whole motivation between the "session" concept; in a sense, it represents the user's current visit to your application. The typical place to store this information is the servlet session. The problem, however, is that the session doesn't know anything about your application; it just stores name/value pairs. So, if you have several objects to keep track of, you have to remember the key for each object, and then retrieve that object from the session.

This whole process is simpler if you maintain a single `Visit` object that has access to all of the properties your application needs for the current session. You then only have to worry about storing and retrieving the `Visit` object from the session.

ProjectTrack's `Visit` class keeps track of the current `User` and the current `Project` the user is viewing, and also provides methods for manipulating the user's locale. It's shown in listing 12.8.

Listing 12.8 Visit.java: Contains properties for the current user's state

```
package org.jia.ptrack.web;

import javax.faces.context.FacesContext;
import java.util.Locale;
import javax.faces.model.SelectItem;
import javax.faces.application.Application;
import java.util.*;
import org.jia.ptrack.domain.*;

public class Visit implements Serializable
{
  private User user;
  private Project currentProject;
  private List localeItems;
  private AuthenticationBean authenticationBean;

  public Visit()
  {
  }

  public User getUser()
  {
    return user;
  }

  public void setUser(User user)
  {
    this.user = user;
  }

  public Project getCurrentProject()
  {
    return currentProject;
  }

  public void setCurrentProject(Project currentProject)
  {
    this.currentProject = currentProject;
  }

  public AuthenticationBean getAuthenticationBean()
  {
    return authenticationBean;
  }
```

```
   public void setAuthenticationBean(
                AuthenticationBean authenticationBean)
  {
    this.authenticationBean = authenticationBean;
  }

  public List getSupportedtLocaleItems()    <-- 1 Returns list of SelectItem instances for locales
  {
    if (localeItems == null)
    {
      localeItems = new ArrayList();
      Application app = FacesContext.getCurrentInstance().
                        getApplication();
      for (Iterator i = app.getSupportedLocales(); i.hasNext(); )
      {
        Locale locale = (Locale)i.next();
        SelectItem item = new SelectItem(locale.toString(),
                                   locale.getDisplayName());
        localeItems.add(item);
      }
      if (localeItems.size() == 0)
      {
        Locale defaultLocale = app.getDefaultLocale();
        localeItems.add(
              new SelectItem(defaultLocale.toString(),
                             defaultLocale.getDisplayName()));
      }
    }
    return localeItems;
  }

  public String getLocale()
  {
    return FacesContext.getCurrentInstance().
                       getViewRoot().
                       getLocale().toString();
  }

  public void setLocale(String locale)
  {
    FacesContext.getCurrentInstance().getViewRoot().
              setLocale(new Locale(locale));
  }
}
```

2 Includes property for setting locale

This class exposes four properties that are related to the user's current visit: `user`, `currentProject`, `AuthenticationBean`, and `locale` (`AuthenticationBean` is a backing bean that performs login and simple access checking; we discuss it in chapter 13).

`Visit` also contains methods for setting the user's current locale. The `getSupportedLocaleItems` method (❶) returns a `List` of `SelectItem` instances generated dynamically from the list of supported locales returned by the `Application`. These locales come from faces-config.xml; support for both English and Russian were configured in chapter 10. If no locales have been configured, it simply returns a `SelectItem` with the default locale.

The `SelectItem` instances returned by `getSupportedLocaleItems` are used in conjunction with the `locale` property defined in ❷. Note that all `setLocale` does is set the locale for the current view. Once the locale has been set for one view, JSF will always use that locale until it is changed for another view. We examined how this property was integrated with the header in section 12.2.3.

A `Visit` instance's properties aren't initialized with the Managed Bean Creation facility. Instead, a new `Visit` instance is created and initialized by `AuthenticationBean`'s `login` method (that snippet is shown in section 12.2.4). So, when a user logs in, a new `Visit` instance is created, initialized, and stored in the session. Several different UI components in ProjectTrack access properties of the current `Visit` instance using value-binding expressions.

Since the `Visit` instance is accessed often, every backing bean has a reference to it. This reference is initialized with the Managed Bean Creation facility, so that the backing beans don't have to worry about what scope it's stored in, or what its key is. Since this functionality is common, it's part of a base backing bean class, which we discuss next.

12.6 Developing a base backing bean class

One of the most powerful features of JSF is the ability to combine backing beans with the Managed Bean Creation facility. You can use the two together not only to make your beans dynamically available, but also to avoid the necessity of looking up beans you've stored as scoped variables. Instead of looking up these variables, you can define backing bean properties and set them with the Managed Bean Creation facility. This makes development easier because your code isn't bogged down with statements that retrieve a variable, and you can easily change a property's value in a JSF configuration file. This means that if you change the name of a scoped variable, you can change it in a configuration file instead of in Java code.

In order to facilitate this approach, we'll develop a base class that includes common properties that our backing beans will need. These properties can then be initialized when a bean is created by the Managed Bean Creation facility. Placing common properties in a base class give subclasses a sense of what objects they need to carry out their work, and keeps you from defining the same property in multiple backing beans. Listing 12.9 shows the source for the `BaseBean` class.

Listing 12.9 BaseBean.java: Base class for all ProjectTrack backing beans

```
package org.jia.ptrack.web;

import java.io.Serializable;
import javax.faces.context.FacesContext;

import org.jia.ptrack.domain.*;

public class BaseBean implements Serializable
{
  private Visit visit;
  private IProjectCoordinator projectCoordinator;
  private IStatusCoordinator statusCoordinator;
  private IUserCoordinator userCoordinator;

  public BaseBean()
  {
  }

  // Faces objects   <-❶

  public FacesContext getFacesContext()
  {
    return FacesContext.getCurrentInstance();
  }

  public javax.faces.application.Application getApplication()
  {
    return getFacesContext().getApplication();
  }

  // Application objects   <-❷

  public Visit getVisit()
  {
    return visit;
  }

  public void setVisit(Visit visit)
  {
    this.visit = visit;
  }

  // Accessors for business objects   <-❸

  public IProjectCoordinator getProjectCoordinator()
```

```
  {
    return projectCoordinator;
  }

  public void setProjectCoordinator(
               IProjectCoordinator projectCoordinator)
  {
    this.projectCoordinator = projectCoordinator;
  }

  public IStatusCoordinator getStatusCoordinator()
  {
    return statusCoordinator;
  }

  public void setStatusCoordinator(
               IStatusCoordinator statusCoordinator)
  {
    this.statusCoordinator = statusCoordinator;
  }

  public IUserCoordinator getUserCoordinator()
  {
    return userCoordinator;
  }

  public void setUserCoordinator(IUserCoordinator userCoordinator)
  {
    this.userCoordinator = userCoordinator;
  }

  // Common action methods   <-4

  public String cancel()
  {
    if (getVisit().getAuthenticationBean().isReadOnly())
    {
      return Constants.CANCEL_READONLY_OUTCOME;
    }
    else
    {
      return Constants.CANCEL_READWRITE_OUTCOME;
    }
  }

}
```

As listing 12.9 shows, this class has several common properties and a couple of common methods. First and foremost, it has properties for a couple of JSF objects

(❶)—`FacesContext` and `Application`. These are really convenience methods, but since just accessing these two objects is so common, it makes sense to have them has properties in a base class (they're also good candidates for the `Utils` class).

This class also has a property for the current `Visit` object (❷). This object (discussed in the previous section) is session-scoped, and contains everything a backing bean needs to know about the current user's visit. There are also several properties for application-scoped integration layer objects (❸) that were initialized with a `ServletContextListener` in section 12.4.3. Note that for all of the properties defined in ❷ and ❸, we didn't retrieve the objects from a particular scope using `ValueBinding` instances or the `ExternalContext`. Instead, we'll leave that configuration to the Managed Bean Creation facility. Any bean that subclasses `BaseBean` will need to use the facility to initialize these properties as follows:

```
<managed-bean>
...
  <managed-property>
    <property-name>visit</property-name>
    <value>#{sessionScope.visit}</value>
  </managed-property>
  <managed-property>
    <property-name>projectCoordinator</property-name>
    <value>#{applicationScope.projectCoordinator}</value>
  </managed-property>
  <managed-property>
    <property-name>statusCoordinator</property-name>
    <value>#{applicationScope.statusCoordinator}</value>
  </managed-property>
  <managed-property>
    <property-name>userCoordinator</property-name>
    <value>#{applicationScope.userCoordinator}</value>
  </managed-property>
...
</managed-bean>
```

Initializing the properties this way keeps your code from worrying about how to retrieve an object, and makes it easy to change the association later without recompiling code. This is the benefit of the Setter Injection [Fowler, Dependency Injection] pattern that the Managed Bean Creation facility implements. (If you're worried about repeating this bit of XML throughout your configuration file, remember that you could use XML entities to avoid repetition.) We could have initialized the `facesContext` property this way, but since the facility only initializes properties when the object is created, this wouldn't work for beans that live between requests.

Finally, this class contains a common action method (❹). This is useful, since outcomes in ProjectTrack can differ based on the user's role.

BY THE WAY Tools will often create their own backing bean base classes that have convenience properties that access the `FacesContext`, `Application`, and other JSF constructs. For examples, see appendix B.

12.7 Summary

In this chapter, we began examining the process of building a JSF application. Our application takes a layered design approach, separating code into application, business, and integration layers. The business layer includes backing beans, utility methods, and other objects; the business layer contains objects that represent business concepts or perform business functions, like `Project` and `ProjectCoordinator`; the integration layer is responsible for integrating with the data store.

Objects in the application layer and business layer may need to interact with UI components. Any objects that are must interact with JSF components should expose public properties using JavaBeans conventions. In addition, components in the SelectMany and SelectOne families require that properties are written in a certain way.

Using these guidelines we began building ProjectTrack. We started with classes for constants and utility methods. We then developed a `ServletContextListener` to initialize singleton objects. Next, we adapted business objects so that they exposed properties compatible with JSF components, and wrote a custom converter during this process. We also developed a `Visit` object to represent the user's current state, and a base backing bean class.

Now that we've laid the foundation, it's time to move forward with the rest of the application.

13 Building an application: backing beans, security, and internationalization

This chapter covers

- Developing backing beans
- Working with `UIData` and other components
- Working with JDBC `ResultSets`
- Implementing application security
- Internationalizing and localizing text from Java code

In the previous chapter, we laid the foundation for a JSF application. We began with design considerations and examined the business layer. Then, we started building the foundation with utility classes, a business layer adapter, custom converters, a `Visit` bean, and a base backing bean class. In this chapter, we build on top of this foundation. We start with the meat of the application: the concrete backing bean classes and event listeners. Then, we round out the chapter with discussions about security, internationalization, and alternative design choices.

13.1 Writing backing beans

Now that we've laid the groundwork, it's time to develop ProjectTrack's backing beans. Each bean will handle a particular application function, like authentication or loading of a project. Each of these classes will be a JavaBean with properties like `loginName` or `comments` that can be wired to UI components. Each bean will also have event listener methods that use these properties and call the business layer.

For example, `AuthenticationBean` has two properties: `loginName` and `password`. It has two action methods, `login` and `logout`, that use these properties to invoke the `UserCoordinator` data layer object to retrieve a new `User` instance and invalidate the user's session, respectively. (It also has a few other properties that are used for authorization.)

This is the beauty of backing beans: a single class can encapsulate the data and logic necessary to perform a specific set of functionality. This contrasts with frameworks like Struts [ASF, Struts], where the form (`ActionForm`) is separate from the event handler (`Action`). Using backing beans this way is, however, similar to developing ASP.NET Web Forms [Microsoft, ASP.NET],[1] except that you can attach a backing bean to a single view, part of a view, or several different views.

In the following sections, we describe each bean, its managed bean configuration, and snippets of JSP code that reference the bean's properties and methods with JSF EL expressions. For more information, including the full JSP source, navigation rules, and integration in general, see chapter 10.

---

[1] Even though a backing bean can be used in a way that's similar to an ASP.NET web form, they're pretty different under the hood. Whereas backing beans are objects that are used by a view, Web forms *are* the view—each web form holds all of the UI controls for the page, in addition to implementing event handlers.

TIP When designing your applications, try to reduce dependencies between different sets of objects and action methods. This is the benefit of packaging action methods as properties of a backing bean—the action methods operate on properties of the bean, which are usually collected from a form in the view. This doesn't mean that other backing beans can't be related to the same view—you may have a backing bean that's related to a search form, and another that's related to the primary form in the view. However, in each scenario, the backing bean's action methods handle data that the bean collects. Designing applications this way makes front-end development more about composing different objects—a particular page may have a several different backing beans. If a component executes an action method for one backing bean, it won't use properties from another.

Before we get into ProjectTrack's specific classes, it's worthwhile to discuss common development issues you'll face—thread safety and error handling.

13.1.1 Thread safety

Most backing beans will be declared in the request scope, so they'll be created and executed once. However, in some cases, you may want to declare a bean in session or application scope. In these cases, your beans can be accessed by more than one client request at the same time, so they must be thread-safe. If you're used to developing action methods in Struts [ASF, Struts], this should sound familiar—Struts Actions must be thread-safe as well.

The most common possibility for a threading conflict is if a user executes action methods in the same bean repeatedly (for instance, clicking a button several times). As long as there aren't any side effects that occur if this happens, there's no need to synchronize the code. Often, this is the case, because the action methods are simply calling business layer classes. This is certainly the case with ProjectTrack—the backing beans themselves don't have to worry about synchronization; it's all handled by the coordinator classes themselves. However, if there are cases where you are working with a property that could be changed by another thread, you need to use synchronization.

13.1.2 Handling errors

Way back in chapter 2, we said that there are two classes of errors: input errors and application errors. Input errors occur when a user enters the wrong data, and these are the types of errors JSF validators normally handle. Application errors occur when something goes wrong—an object can't be found, or even worse, a request to a database or application server times out.

We've discussed the method signatures required for JSF event listeners. You may have noticed that they don't throw any exceptions. There's a good reason for this—it forces you to catch exceptions and handle them. When you catch the exception, you have two possible choices: create an error message and possibly return a different outcome, or rethrow the exception as a `FacesException`. The benefit of the first approach is that the page the user sees is defined in the JSF navigation rules, and you can display an error message and have the user fill out a form again. Throwing an exception allows the web container to handle the error, but will always take the user to an error page rather than display a friendly message in the original page.

> **TIP** If you find yourself writing code that generates an error if the user's input is incorrect, make sure it's in a validator method instead of an event listener method.

You can return a message to the user by adding a `FacesMessage` instance to the current `FacesContext`. The `AuthenticationBean` class does this to tell users that they entered the wrong username and password:

```
try
{
  newUser = getUserCoordinator().getUser(loginName, password);
}
catch (ObjectNotFoundException e)
{
  facesContext.addMessage(null,
              new FacesMessage(FacesMessage.SEVERITY_WARN,
                      "Incorrect name or password.", ""));
  return Constants.FAILURE_OUTCOME;
}
...
```

If the `UserCoordinator.getUser` method throws an `ObjectNotFoundException`, a new `FacesMessage` instance is added to the `FacesContext` with the message "Incorrect user name or password" (leaving the detail portion of the message blank). The `Constants.FAILURE_OUTCOME` constant is a string with the value "failure". In the navigation rules for ProjectTrack, the `"failure"` outcome simply redisplays the login page:

```
<navigation-rule>
  <from-tree-id>/login.jsp</from-tree-id>
...
  <navigation-case>
    <from-outcome>failure</from-outcome>
```

```
    <to-tree-id>/login.jsp</to-tree-id>
  </navigation-case>
</navigation-rule>
```

The Login page has an `HtmlMessages` component on it, so the user will see this error message when the page is redisplayed, as shown in figure 13.1.

For more serious errors, a separate error page is more appropriate. The `UserCoordinator.getUser` method also throws a `DataStoreException`, which indicates a serious problem at the data store level. You can handle this by reserving one or more outcomes for serious errors:

```
try
{
  newUser = getUserCoordinator().getUser(loginName, password);
}
...
catch (DataStoreException d)
{
  Utils.reportError(facesContext, "A database error has occurred.",
                               "Error loading User object", d);
  return Constants.ERROR_OUTCOME;
}
```

Here, we call the `reportError` method of the `Utils` class, which looks like this:

Figure 13.1 The `AuthenticationBean.login` method returns an error message to the user if no `User` object can be found.

```
public static void reportError(FacesContext facesContext,
                               String message, String detail,
                               Exception exception)
{
  facesContext.addMessage(null,
                 new FacesMessage(FacesMessage.SEVERITY_ERROR,
                 message, detail));
  if (exception != null)
  {
    facesContext.getExternalContext().log(message, exception);
  }
}
```

First of all, the severity of this message is `FacesMessage.SEVERITY_ERROR` instead of `FacesMessage.SEVERITY_WARN`. Second, we log this error—all serious errors should be logged. The outcome we return is `Constants.ERROR_OUTCOME`, which evaluates to the string "error". In the navigation rules in faces-config.xml, there's a global navigation case that maps the `"error"` outcome to the page error.jsp:

```
<navigation-rule>
  <description>Global navigation.</description>
  <from-tree-id>*</from-tree-id>
...
  <navigation-case>
    <from-outcome>error</from-outcome>
    <to-tree-id>/error.jsp</to-tree-id>
  </navigation-case>
</navigation-rule>
```

This way, whenever there's a serious error, our application code handles it, and JSF forwards the user to error.jsp.

An alternate approach for handling serious errors is to simply throw an instance of the `FacesException` class. `FacesException` is a runtime exception, so it can be thrown even if it is not declared in a `throws` clause. Here's an example:

```
try
{
  user = Utils.getUserCoordinator(facesContext).
         getUser(name, password);
}
...
catch (DataStoreException d)
{
   Utils.log(facesContext, d);
   throw new FacesException("Error loading User object", d);
}
```

As you can see, the `FacesException` constructor takes another `Exception` as an argument, so it can keep track of the entire exception stack. This exception will be bubbled up to the web container—if the web application has an error page configured in its deployment descriptor, that page will be displayed. Otherwise, you'll see a default web container error page, which is typically verbose enough to confuse most users.

This approach moves some of the navigation out of the world of JSF and into the servlet world. Consequently, it's difficult to see what error pages are displayed by looking at navigation rules, and you can't have different error pages that map to different outcomes in your application. ProjectTrack uses the previous approach.

> **TIP** Even if you manage error pages using the JSF navigation scheme, you should still configure an error page in web.xml if you don't want the default error page to be displayed when serious errors (with JSF, the web container, or your own code) occur. We show how to do this in chapter 10.

Now that we've covered the fundamentals, let's examine ProjectTrack's backing beans.

13.1.3 Performing authentication

ProjectTrack uses custom authentication and authorization. Logging in and out is handled by the `AuthenticationBean` class. (For more on security in general, see section 13.2.) This bean is used by the Login and Header pages. For this and other backing beans in ProjectTrack, we'll build things pretty much the same way:

- Define public properties for collecting input from UI components.
- Optionally define other properties for use in JSF EL expressions.
- Implement action methods to perform the work, usually delegating to the business layer for any true business logic.
- Implement any action listener, value-change listener, or validator methods.
- Configure the bean via the Managed Bean Creation facility.
- Reference the bean via JSP (for a detailed discussion of how the beans are integrated into the user interface, see chapter 10).

`AuthenticationBean` has two properties that are meant to be wired to a login form: `loginName` and `password`. It also has two action methods: `login` and `logout`. The `login` method performs three primary operations: it gets the `User` object from the `UserCoordinator`, creates and initializes a new `Visit` object and stores it

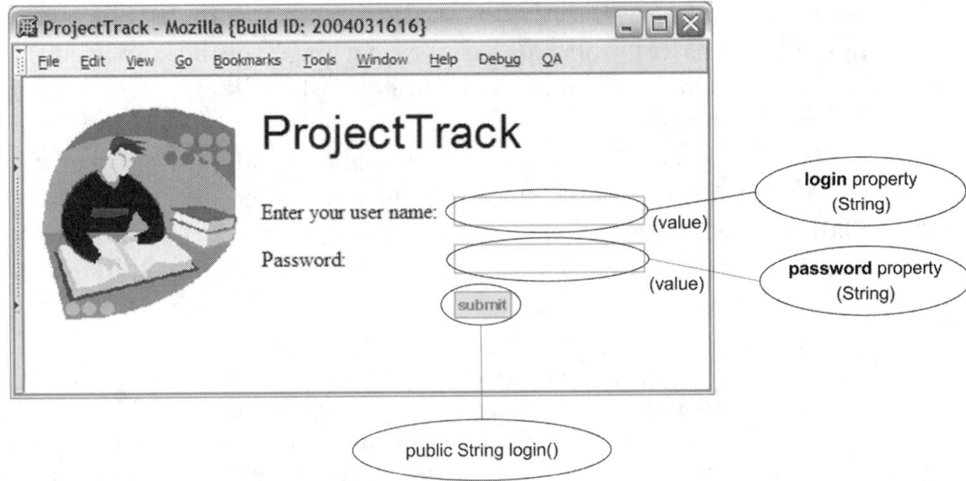

Figure 13.2 The Login page associates `HtmlInputText` components with the `login` and `password` properties. It has a single `HtmlCommandButton` component that executes the `login` action method.

in as a session-scoped variable, and returns the appropriate outcome. There are also a few properties that are used for simple authorization checks. Figure 13.2 shows how the Login page uses this class. The code is shown in listing 13.1.

Listing 13.1 AuthenticationBean.java: This backing bean logs a user in and out, and provides simple authorization duties.

```
package org.jia.ptrack.web;

import javax.faces.application.Application;
import javax.faces.application.FacesMessage;
import javax.faces.context.FacesContext;
import javax.servlet.http.HttpSession;

import org.jia.ptrack.domain.*;

public class AuthenticationBean extends BaseBean   <-(1)
{
  private String loginName;
  private String password;

  public AuthenticationBean()
  {
  }

  public void setLoginName(String loginName)
  {
```

```
    this.loginName = loginName;
  }

  public String getLoginName()
  {
    return loginName;
  }

  public void setPassword(String password)
  {
    this.password = password;
  }

  public String getPassword()
  {
    return password;
  }

  public String login()   <-❷
  {
    FacesContext facesContext = getFacesContext();
    User newUser = null;
    try
    {
      newUser = getUserCoordinator().getUser(loginName, password);
    }
    catch (ObjectNotFoundException e)
    {
      facesContext.addMessage(null,
                    new FacesMessage(FacesMessage.SEVERITY_WARN,
                          "Incorrect name or password.", ""));
      return Constants.FAILURE_OUTCOME;
    }
    catch (DataStoreException d)
    {
      Utils.reportError(facesContext,
                      "A database error has occurred.",
                      "Error loading User object", d);
      return Constants.ERROR_OUTCOME;
    }

    Visit visit = new Visit();
    visit.setUser(newUser);
    visit.setAuthenticationBean(this);
    setVisit(visit);

    getApplication().createValueBinding("#{" +
         Constants.VISIT_KEY_SCOPE +  Constants.VISIT_KEY +
         "}").setValue(facesContext, visit);

    if (newUser.getRole().equals(RoleType.UPPER_MANAGER))
```

```
      {
        return Constants.SUCCESS_READONLY_OUTCOME;
      }

      return Constants.SUCCESS_READWRITE_OUTCOME;
    }

    public String logout()   <-3
    {
       FacesContext facesContext = getFacesContext();
       HttpSession session =
         (HttpSession)facesContext.getExternalContext().
                                  getSession(false);
       session.removeAttribute(Constants.VISIT_KEY_SCOPE +
                               Constants.VISIT_KEY);

       if (session != null)
       {
         session.invalidate();
       }

       return Constants.SUCCESS_OUTCOME;
     }

    public boolean isInboxAuthorized()
    {
      return !getVisit().getUser().getRole().
              equals(RoleType.UPPER_MANAGER);
    }

    public boolean isCreateNewAuthorized()
    {
      return getVisit().getUser().getRole().
              equals(RoleType.PROJECT_MANAGER);                  4
    }

    public boolean isReadOnly()
    {
      return getVisit().getUser().getRole().
              equals(RoleType.UPPER_MANAGER);
    }
  }
```

❶ All of our backing beans subclass the `BaseBean` class, which we developed in chapter 12. This class has common properties and methods useful for all of our backing beans.

❷ The `login` action method is responsible for using the `loginName` and `password` properties to locate a valid `User` object. Its job is to call `UserCoordinator`'s `getUser` method and process its result. If a `User` object is returned, the code creates a new `Visit` instance, sets its `user` and `authenticationBean` properties, and stores it using a scope and key defined in the `Constants`. It then returns the proper outcome based on the user's role.

If the role is Upper Manager, the `Constants.SUCCESS_READONLY_OUTCOME` is returned; otherwise the `Constants.SUCCESS_READWRITE_OUTCOME` is returned. This allows us to display different pages to users based on their roles. If no `User` object is returned from `UserCoordinator.getUser`, a new `FacesMessage` is added to the message error list, and the appropriate outcome is returned.

❸ The `logout` method is a little simpler. It only performs one operation—invalidating the current session. This is one of the cases where accessing the actual servlet session is necessary. This method simply grabs the current `HttpSession` from the `ExternalContext` (which is a property of the `FacesContext`), removes the `Visit` object (which was stored in the `login` method), and then calls its `invalidate` method, which removes any other variables and terminates the session.

❹ These read-only properties are for simple authorization checks. For example, the header uses the `createNewAuthorized` property to determine whether or not the Create New toolbar button is disabled. This method checks the user's `role` property because ProjectTrack uses custom authentication. If we had used container-based authentication, they would execute the `isInUserRole` property of the `ExternalContext`.

What's obvious from `AuthenticationBean` is the basic structure of a backing bean—declare properties for collecting data from the user interface and expose action methods for operating on that data. All such methods delegate most of their work to business layer classes, but handle things like logging, error handling, and navigation.

Now that we've examined the code, let's look at how to integrate it into our application.

Initializing and referencing the bean

As we've discussed, backing beans are usually declared with the Managed Bean Creation facility in faces-config.xml. `AuthenticationBean` is declared as a session-scoped variable because it can be used by different beans for minor authorization duties. The managed bean configuration is shown in listing 13.2.

Listing 13.2 faces-config.xml: Managed bean configuration for AuthenticationBean

```
<managed-bean>
  <description>Used for logging and logging out.
  </description>
  <managed-bean-name>authenticationBean</managed-bean-name>
```

```
  <managed-bean-class>org.jia.ptrack.web.AuthenticationBean
  </managed-bean-class>
  <managed-bean-scope>session</managed-bean-scope>
  <managed-property>
    <property-name>visit</property-name>
    <value>#{sessionScope.visit}</value>
  </managed-property>
  <managed-property>
    <property-name>projectCoordinator</property-name>
    <value>#{applicationScope.projectCoordinator}</value>
  </managed-property>
  <managed-property>
    <property-name>statusCoordinator</property-name>
    <value>#{applicationScope.statusCoordinator}</value>
  </managed-property>
  <managed-property>
    <property-name>userCoordinator</property-name>
    <value>#{applicationScope.userCoordinator}</value>
  </managed-property>
</managed-bean>
```

The code in listing 3.2 will store an instance of the `AuthenticationBean` under the key `authenticationBean`. Note that we initialize the common properties implemented in our `BaseBean` class (which `AuthenticationBean` subclasses). We'll initialize these properties for every other bean as well.

Here's how the Login page references the bean:

```
<h:outputLabel for="userNameInput">
   <h:outputText value="Enter your user name:"/>
</h:outputLabel>
<h:inputText id="userNameInput" size="20" maxlength="30"
             required="true"
             value="#{authenticationBean.loginName}">
  <f:validateLength minimum="5" maximum="30"/>
</h:inputText>
...
<h:outputLabel for="passwordInput">
  <h:outputText value="Password:"/>
</h:outputLabel>
<h:inputSecret id="passwordInput" size="20" maxlength="20"
               required="true"
               value="#{authenticationBean.password}">
  <f:validateLength minimum="5" maximum="15"/>
</h:inputSecret>
...
<h:commandButton action="#{authenticationBean.loginName}"
                 title="Submit"
.../>
```

As you can see, there are two `HtmlInputText` controls whose values references the `loginName` and `password` properties of the `AuthenticationBean` instance. There's also an `HtmlCommandButton` component whose `action` property references `AuthenticationBean`'s `login` action method.

The `logout` action method property is referenced separately by the header, as are two of the authorization properties:

```
<jia:navigatorToolbar ...>

  <jia:navigatorItem name="inbox"
        label="Inbox"
        icon="/images/inbox.gif"
        action="inbox"
        disabled="#{!authenticationBean.inboxAuthorized}"/>
...
  <jia:navigatorItem name="createNew"
         label="Create new"
         icon="/images/create.gif"
         action="#{createProjectBean.create}"
         disabled="#{!authenticationBean.createNewAuthorized}"/>
  <jia:navigatorItem name="logout"
         label="logout"
         icon="/images/logout.gif"
         action="#{authenticationBean.logout}"/>
</jia:navigatorToolbar>
```

The header has a `UINavigator` component, which we will develop in chapter 19. A `UINavigator` has child navigator items, which represent toolbar buttons in this case. The first two buttons are enabled or disabled based on the value of the `inboxAuthorized` and `createNewAuthorized` properties. The last button executes `AuthenticationBean`'s `logout` action method.

That's it for `AuthenticationBean`. Once a user has logged in, he or she is directed to either the Inbox or Show All page, both of which are backed by `SelectProjectBean`.

13.1.4 Listing projects with UIData and parameterizing listeners

The `SelectProjectBean` is responsible for listing projects and allowing a user to approve, reject, or view the details of a project in the list. The class has two properties, `inboxProjects` and `allProjects`, that return a `List` of `Project` instances. The `List` that these properties return can be sorted by the `sort` action listener method. The lists returned by the `inboxProjects` and `allProjects` properties are also intended to be used with a `UIData` component, so `SelectProjectBean` also has a component binding property called `projectTable`, which is meant to be bound to the `UIData` that displays the project list. This property is used by `getProject`, which is the method that performs the real work of loading a project and returning the

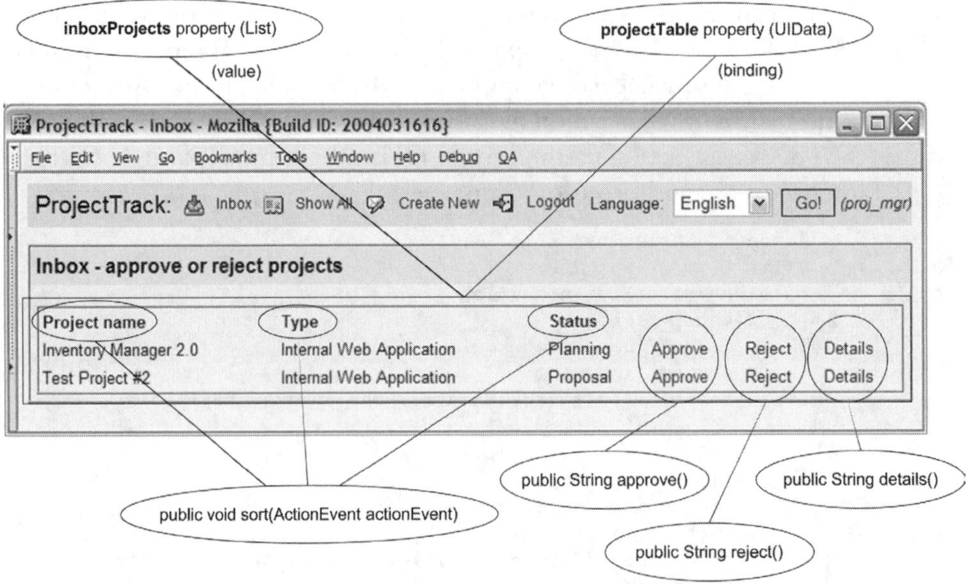

Figure 13.3 The Inbox page associates an `HtmlDataTable` with `SelectProjectBean`'s `getInboxProjects` property. The table is also is bound to the bean via the `projectTable` component binding property. There are three `HtmlCommandLink` components that are used for column headers and call the `sort` action listener method. There are also three `HtmlCommandLink` buttons that are repeated for each project; they call the `approve`, `reject`, and `details` action methods.

proper outcome. `getProject` is called by the `approve`, `reject`, and `delete` action methods, which are referenced by Command components in the JSPs. Figure 13.3 shows how the Inbox page uses `SelectProjectBean` and gives you an idea of how this bean works.

The source for this class is shown in listing 13.3.

Listing 13.3 SelectProjectBean.java: Lists projects and allows users to approve, reject, or delete them

```
package org.jia.ptrack.web;

import java.util.ArrayList;
import java.util.List;
import javax.faces.application.FacesMessage;
import javax.faces.component.UIData;
import javax.faces.context.FacesContext;
import javax.faces.event.ActionEvent;

import org.jia.ptrack.domain.*;
```

```
class CommandType extends EnumeratedType   <-❶
{
  public final static CommandType APPROVE =
    new CommandType(0, "Approve");
  public final static CommandType REJECT =
    new CommandType(10, "Reject");
  public final static CommandType DETAILS =
    new CommandType(20, "Details");

  private CommandType(int value, String description)
  {
    super(value, description);
  }
}

public class SelectProjectBean extends BaseBean
{
  private UIData projectTable;
  private ProjectColumnType sortColumn;   <-❷

  public SelectProjectBean()
  {
  }

  public UIData getProjectTable()
  {
    return projectTable;
  }

  public void setProjectTable(                ❸
              UIData projectTable)
  {
    this.projectTable = projectTable;
  }

  public List getInboxProjects()
             throws DataStoreException         ❹
  {
    try
    {
      return  getProjectCoordinator().getProjects(
              getVisit().getUser().getRole(), sortColumn);
    }
    catch (ObjectNotFoundException e)
    {
      return new ArrayList(0);
    }
  }

  public List getAllProjects()
              throws DataStoreException        ❺
  {
    try
```

```
    {
      return getProjectCoordinator().getProjects(sortColumn);
    }
    catch (ObjectNotFoundException e)
    {
      return new ArrayList(0);
    }
  }

  public void sort(ActionEvent actionEvent)   <-6
  {
    boolean paramFound = false;
    List children = actionEvent.getComponent().getChildren();
    for (int i = 0; i < children.size(); i++)
    {
      if (children.get(i) instanceof UIParameter)
      {
        UIParameter currentParam = (UIParameter) children.get(i);
        if (currentParam.getName().equals("column") &&
            currentParam.getValue() != null)
        {
          String paramValue = currentParam.getValue().toString();
          sortColumn = (ProjectColumnType)ProjectColumnType.
                          getEnumManager().getInstance(paramValue);
          paramFound = true;
          break;
        }
      }
    }
    if (!paramFound)
    {
      throw new FacesException("Expected child UIParameter with " +
      "name 'column' and a value equal to the column name to sort.");
    }
  }

  protected String getProject(                    7
                     CommandType command)
  {
    FacesContext facesContext = getFacesContext();
    Project project = (Project) projectTable.getRowData();
    try
    {
      project = getProjectCoordinator().
                 get(project.getId());
    }
    catch (ObjectNotFoundException e)
    {
      facesContext.addMessage(null,
        new FacesMessage(FacesMessage.SEVERITY_WARN,
               "The project you selected cannot be found",
```

```
                "The project is no longer in the data store."));
        return Constants.FAILURE_OUTCOME;
      }
      catch (DataStoreException d)
      {
        Utils.reportError(facesContext,
                          "A database error has occrred",
                          "Error loading project", d);
        return Constants.ERROR_OUTCOME;
      }

      if (command == CommandType.APPROVE ||
          command == CommandType.REJECT)
      {
        if (!getStatusCoordinator().
            isValidStateChange(project.getStatus(),
                               command == CommandType.APPROVE))
        {
          Utils.addInvalidStateChangeMessage(facesContext,
                  command == CommandType.APPROVE);
          return Constants.FAILURE_OUTCOME;
        }
      }

      getVisit().setCurrentProject(project);

      return Constants.SUCCESS_OUTCOME;
    }

    public String approve()
    {
      return getProject(CommandType.APPROVE);
    }

    public String reject()
    {
      return getProject(CommandType.REJECT);                    ❽
    }

    public String details()
    {
      return getProject(CommandType.DETAILS);
    }
  }
```

❶ This defines an enumerated type called `CommandType` that's used internally to parameterize calls to `getProject` (❼).

❷ `sortColumn` is an internal field that stores the sort order for project lists returned by the `inboxProjects` (❹) and `allProjects` (❺) properties. This field is of type `ProjectColumnType`, which is an enumerated type with static constants for four project columns: `NAME`, `STATUS`, `TYPE`, and `ROLE`. The `sort` action listener method (❻) sets this field based on user input, and then the field is used in subsequent requests for the `inboxProjects` and `allProjects` properties.

❸ This defines the `projectTable` component binding property, which is meant to be bound to the `UIData` component that lists the projects. We use `UIData` as opposed to its HTML-specific subclass, `HtmlDataTable`, because we're not manipulating any HTML-specific properties. This property is used by `getProject` (❼) to determine which row has been selected.

❹ `inboxProjects` is a read-only property that returns a `List` of `Project` instances for the user's inbox. It retrieves this list from the `ProjectCoordinator` class's `getProjects` method, which takes the user's role and the column to use for sorting as parameters. (It needs the user's role because an inbox is technically a list of the projects available for a specific role.)

❺ The `allProjects` property is also read-only, and it returns a `List` of all `Project` instances, sorted by `sortColumn`.

❻ The `sort` action listener method sets the `sortColumn` field based on the column the user clicks on. There can be up to four different columns in the associated view, so we need to tell `sort` which column the user selected. There are few ways to do this:

- Give each column a different action listener method, and have all of them call an internal method, each sending different parameters. This approach is perfectly valid, and we use it for the `getProject` method (❼), which is called by the `approve`, `reject`, and `details` methods (❽). The drawback to this approach is that if we had many columns, we would have to have a separate action listener method for each one.
- Look at the `value` property of the component that executed the action listener. This can work in some situations, but you can't guarantee that the value will remain constant, especially if it's displayed to the user. If it's displayed to the user, as is often the case (because the value is often a label), it could change based on the user's locale.
- Look for a `UIParameter` component that's the child of the event's sender. This is useful if you need to send several parameters to an action listener, but the code is a bit cumbersome:

```
public void sort(ActionEvent e)
{
   boolean paramFound = false;
   List children = e.getComponent().
         getChildren);
   for (int i = 0; i < children.size(); i++)
   {
```

```
      if (children.get(i) instanceof
          UIParameter)
      {
        UIParameter currentParam =
          (UIParameter)children.get(i);
        if (currentParam.getName().
            equals("column") &&
            currentParam.getValue() != null)
        {
          String paramValue = currentParam.
                   getValue().toString();
          sortColumn = (ProjectColumnType)
            ProjectColumnType.getEnumManager().
              getInstance(paramValue);
          paramFound = true;
          break;
        }
      }
    }
    if (!paramFound)
    {
      throw new FacesException(
        "Expected child UIParameter with " +
        "name 'column' and a value equal " +
        "to the column name to sort.");
    }
}
```

Here, we iterate through the child components, looking for a `UIParameter` with the `name` "column". If found, we then use its `value` property to retrieve the proper value from the `ProjectColumnType` class (the `enumManager.getInstance` method just returns the proper `ProjectColumnType` instance based on the value of a string). If no parameter is found, we throw an exception, because the front-end developer tried to call this action listener method without adding the correct `UIParameter`.

The `UIParameter` component could be configured in JSP like so:

```
<h:commandLink styleClass="table-header"
     actionListener="#{inboxBean.sort}">
   <h:outputText value="Type"/>
   <f:param name="column" value="type"/>
</h:commandLink>
```

Here, the sender is an `HtmlCommandLink` instance, and it has a child `UIParameter` with the name "column" and the value "type".

This approach will work, and can be useful in situations where you need to pass several parameters to an action method, but it's not the simplest or the most efficient way to do things.

- Use the `id` property of the component that called the action listener. This is the approach we use in ❻. The value of the sender's identifier maps to a `ProjectColumnType` description, so all we have to do is retrieve the correct instance from the `ProjectType` class. Here's the same JSP for the type column:

```
<h:commandLink styleClass="table-header" id="type"
               actionListener="#{inboxBean.sort}">
  <h:outputText value="Type"/>
</h:commandLink>
```

In general, we recommend either the identifier-based approach or the method-based approach to parameterizing event listeners.

❼ The `getProject` method retrieves the currently selected `Project` instance from the associated `UIData` component via the `projectTable` property (❸). It then uses the object's identifier to load a fresh, new `Project` instance from the `ProjectCoordinator` (this ensures that we have the most recent copy). The `ProjectCoordinator`'s `getProject` method can throw some exceptions; these are handled by creating error messages and returning different outcome, as described in section 13.1.2.

> **NOTE** `UIData` also stores a variable in request scope called "var" that can be used to retrieve the currently selected item.

Projects can't always be approved or rejected. For example, if a `Project` is in the initial state (Proposal), it can't be rejected because there's no state before Proposal. Also, a `Project` can't be approved or rejected if it's in the final state (Closed), because that state indicates that no further action can occur. When a user selects a `Project` for approval or rejection, it's important to make sure the operation is valid before showing them a new screen. Consequently, the `getProject` method performs this check using the `StatusCoordinator.isValidStateChange` method.

If the state change isn't valid, it calls the `Utils.addInvalidStateChange` method and then returns `Constants.FAILURE_OUTCOME` so that the page will redisplay itself with the error message. The `addInvalidStateChange` method simply adds a generic message to the `FacesContext` indicating the specific type of error. This message isn't associated with a specific UI component, so it's applicable to the entire page (the source for `Utils` is shown in chapter 12, listing 12.2).

If the state change is valid and there aren't any errors, the method simply sets this `Project` as the current project with the `visit.currentProject` property, which will be used by subsequent views. It then returns `Constants.SUCCESS_OUTCOME`.

❽ `SelectProjectBean` exposes three action methods: `approve`, `reject`, and `details`. Each method calls `getProject` (❼) with a different `CommandType` (❶) value. This is a different approach to parameterizing access to a method than ❻, and it's better for action methods, because action methods don't have direct access to the component that fired the action event as do action listener methods.

Even though `getProject` is called by all three action methods, we would like them to take the user to different views. `getProject` returns the same outcome regardless of the `CommandType` value that's passed in, so how do we do this? In the navigation rules, we can specify a different view based on the specific action method that's called:

```
<navigation-rule>
  <from-view-id>/protected/inbox.jsp</from-view-id>
  <navigation-case>
     <from-action>#{inboxBean.details}</from-action>
     <from-outcome>success</from-outcome>
     <to-view-id>/general/details.jsp</to-view-id>
  </navigation-case>
  <navigation-case>
     <from-action>#{inboxBean.approve}</from-action>
     <from-outcome>success</from-outcome>
     <to-view-id>/protected/approve.jsp</to-view-id>
  </navigation-case>
  <navigation-case>
     <from-action>#{inboxBean.reject}</from-action>
     <from-outcome>success</from-outcome>
     <to-view-id>/protected/reject.jsp</to-view-id>
  </navigation-case>
</navigation-rule>
```

This is the navigation rule for the Inbox page (there is a `SelectProjectBean` instance stored in the request with the key `inboxBean`). All of the action methods will return `"success"` if they complete without errors, but a different page is chosen depending on the specific action method that's called. So, if an `HtmlCommandButton` references the `details` action method property, details.jsp is displayed upon successful completion; if the `approve` action method property is referenced, the approve.jsp page is displayed; if the `reject` action method property is referenced, the reject.jsp page is displayed.

We've now finished analyzing `SelectProjectBean`'s code. Next, we examine how it's configured, and show some more examples of its use.

Initializing and referencing the bean

This backing bean performs double duty—an instance is stored for the Inbox page and another one for the Show All Projects page. Listing 13.4 shows the managed bean declaration.

Listing 13.4 faces-config.xml: Managed bean configuration for SelectProjectBean

```
<managed-bean>
   <description>Lists projects in the user's inbox and allows
      them to select one for approval, rejection, or details.
   </description>
   <managed-bean-name>inboxBean</managed-bean-name>
  <managed-bean-class>org.jia.ptrack.web.SelectProjectBean
  </managed-bean-class>
  <managed-bean-scope>request</managed-bean-scope>
  <managed-property>
    <property-name>visit</property-name>
    <value>#{sessionScope.visit}</value>
  </managed-property>
  <managed-property>
    <property-name>projectCoordinator</property-name>
    <value>#{applicationScope.projectCoordinator}</value>
  </managed-property>
  <managed-property>
    <property-name>statusCoordinator</property-name>
    <value>#{applicationScope.statusCoordinator}</value>
  </managed-property>
  <managed-property>
    <property-name>userCoordinator</property-name>
    <value>#{applicationScope.userCoordinator}</value>
  </managed-property>
</managed-bean>
<managed-bean>
  <description>Lists all projects and allows the user to select
     one and view its details.
  </description>
  <managed-bean-name>showAllBean</managed-bean-name>
  <managed-bean-class>org.jia.ptrack.web.SelectProjectBean
  </managed-bean-class>
  <managed-bean-scope>request</managed-bean-scope>
  <managed-property>
    <property-name>visit</property-name>
    <value>#{sessionScope.visit}</value>
  </managed-property>
  <managed-property>
    <property-name>projectCoordinator</property-name>
    <value>#{applicationScope.projectCoordinator}</value>
  </managed-property>
  <managed-property>
    <property-name>statusCoordinator</property-name>
    <value>#{applicationScope.statusCoordinator}</value>
  </managed-property>
  <managed-property>
    <property-name>userCoordinator</property-name>
    <value>#{applicationScope.userCoordinator}</value>
```

```
  </managed-property>
</managed-bean>
```

The code in listing 13.4 declares two request-scoped instances of the `SelectProjectBean`: one stored under the key `inboxBean` (for the Inbox page) and one under the key `showAllBean` (for the Show All page). Note that these names don't sound anything like "SelectProjectBean", but they do make sense to the person developing the actual page.

Listing 13.5 shows how this bean is used by the Inbox page.

Listing 13.5 inbox.jsp: SelectProjectBean used with an HtmlDataTable

```
...
<h:dataTable styleClass="table-background"
             rowClasses="table-odd-row,table-even-row"
             cellpadding="3"
             value="#{inboxBean.inboxProjects}"
             var="project"
             binding="#{inboxBean.projectTable}">

  <h:column>
    <f:facet name="header">
      <h:commandLink styleClass="table-header" id="name"
                     actionListener="#{inboxBean.sort}">
        <h:outputText value="Project name"/>
      </h:commandLink>
    </f:facet>
    <h:outputText value="#{project.name}"/>
  </h:column>

  <h:column>
    <f:facet name="header">
      <h:commandLink styleClass="table-header" id="type"
                     actionListener="#{inboxBean.sort}">
        <h:outputText value="Type"/>
      </h:commandLink>
    </f:facet>
    <h:outputText value="#{project.type}"/>
  </h:column>

  <h:column>
    <f:facet name="header">
      <h:commandLink styleClass="table-header" id="status"
                     actionListener="#{inboxBean.sort}">
        <h:outputText value="Status"/>
      </h:commandLink>
    </f:facet>
    <h:outputText value="#{project.status}"/>
```

```
    </h:column>

    <h:column>
      <h:commandLink action="#{inboxBean.approve}">
        <h:outputText value="Approve"/>
      </h:commandLink>
    </h:column>

    <h:column>
      <h:commandLink action="#{inboxBean.reject}">
        <h:outputText value="Reject"/>
      </h:commandLink>
    </h:column>

    <h:column>
      <h:commandLink action="#{inboxBean.details}">
        <h:outputText value="Details"/>
      </h:commandLink>
    </h:column>

  </h:dataTable>
  ...
```

The page in listing 13.5 lists all projects in the user's inbox by accessing the `inboxProjects` property. It has three column headers: Name, Type, and Status. Each of these columns has an `HtmlCommandLink` component with the action listener method `inboxBean.sort` registered, so when a user clicks on a column, this method will re-sort the items.

For each project listed, there is an `HtmlCommandButton` for each of the bean's three action methods. `HtmlDataTable` keeps track of the object related to the row containing the `HtmlCommandButton`; this is why the `getProject` method can retrieve the current `Project` instance with the `UIData.getRowData` method. This is the same JSP that displays the page shown in figure 13.3.

This completes our tour of `SelectProjectBean`, which is the most complicated backing bean in our application. Now, let's examine `UpdateProjectBean`.

13.1.5 Updating projects

Once `SelectProjectBean` has set the `currentProject` property of the `Visit` object, `currentProject` can be modified by other beans. This is the job of the `UpdateProjectBean`. Projects in ProjectTrack aren't edited in the traditional sense—all a user can do is change the status (either approve or reject it). In the process, they can add comments to the history or update the list of artifacts. This bean backs both the Approve a Project and Create a Project pages.

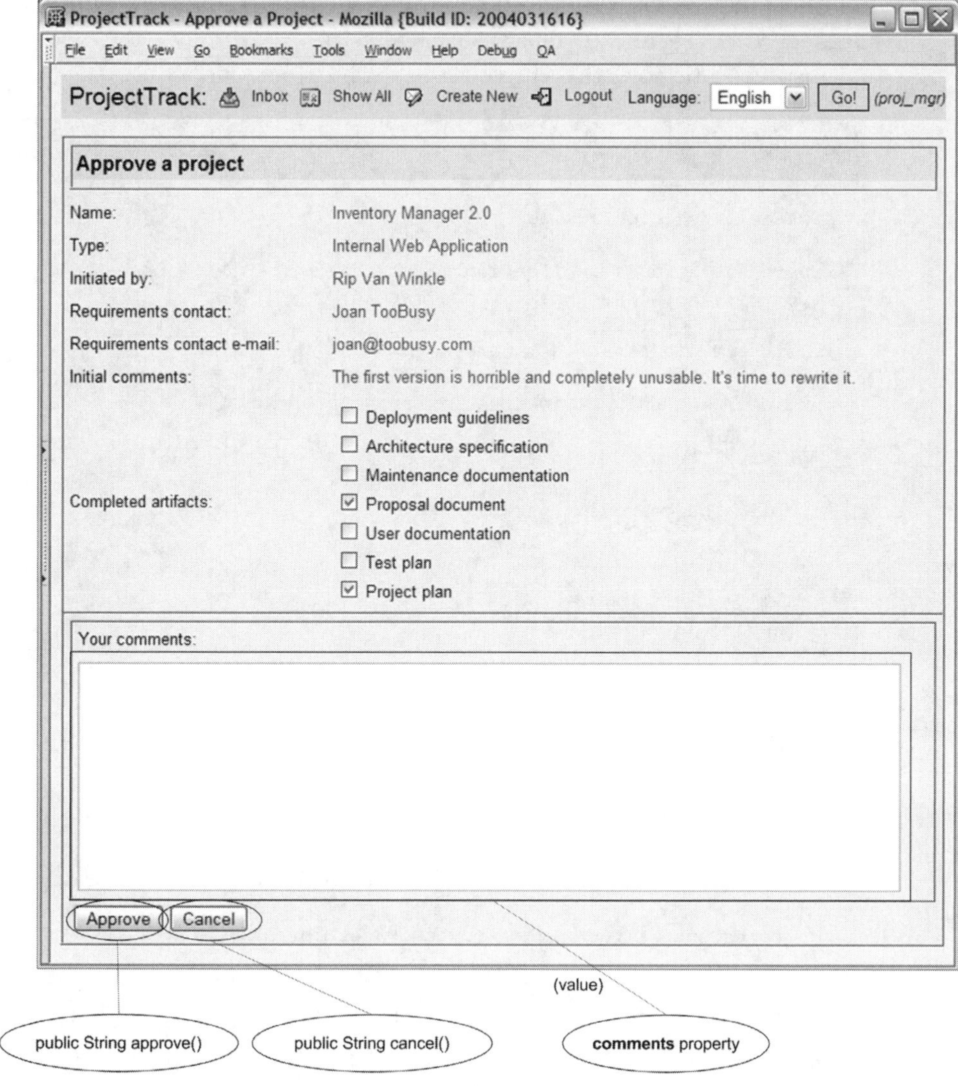

Figure 13.4 The Approve a Project page associates `UpdateProjectBean`'s `comments` property with an `HtmlTextarea` component, and has an `HtmlCommandButton` for both the `approve` and `cancel` action methods. The other fields on the form are associated with `visit.currentProject`.

`UpdateProjectBean` has single property called `comments`; we can edit artifacts by directly manipulating `visit.currentProject`. `UpdateProjectBean` handles approval and rejection with a single parameterized method, `update`, that's called by two separate action methods (`approve` and `reject`). Figure 13.4 shows how the Approve a Project page works with this bean (the `cancel` action method is implemented by `UpdateProjectBean`'s superclass, `BaseBean`).

Listing 13.6 shows the source for `UpdateProjectBean`.

Listing 13.6 UpdateProjectBean.java: Handles the actual approval or rejection of the current project

```
package org.jia.ptrack.web;

import javax.faces.application.FacesMessage;
import javax.faces.context.FacesContext;

import org.jia.ptrack.domain.*;

public class UpdateProjectBean extends BaseBean
{
  private String comments;

  public UpdateProjectBean()
  {
  }

  public String getComments()
  {
    return comments;
  }
                                                          ❶
  public void setComments(String comments)
  {
    this.comments = comments;
  }

  protected String update(boolean approve)             <-❷
  {
    FacesContext facesContext = getFacesContext();

    Visit visit = getVisit();
    boolean projectFound = true;
    Project project = visit.getCurrentProject();
    if (project.changeStatus(approve, getVisit().getUser(), comments))
    {
      try
      {
        getProjectCoordinator().update(project);
      }
      catch (ObjectNotFoundException e)
      {
        projectFound = false;
      }
      catch (DataStoreException d)
```

```
        {
          Utils.reportError(facesContext, "A database error has occurred.",
                            "Error updating project.", d);
          return Constants.ERROR_OUTCOME;
        }
      }
      else
      {
        Utils.addInvalidStateChangeMessage(facesContext, approve);
        return Constants.FAILURE_OUTCOME;
      }

      if (projectFound == false)
      {
        facesContext.addMessage(null,
         new FacesMessage(FacesMessage.SEVERITY_WARN,
               "The project you selected cannot be found",
               "The project is no longer in the data store."));

        return Constants.FAILURE_OUTCOME;
      }

      if (visit.getAuthenticationBean().isReadOnly())
      {
        return Constants.SUCCESS_READONLY_OUTCOME;
      }
      else
      {
        return Constants.SUCCESS_READWRITE_OUTCOME;
      }
    }

    public String approve()
    {
      return update(true);
    }
                                      ❸
    public String reject()
    {
      return update(false);
    }
  }
```

❶ The `comments` property is used in the `update` method (❸) when changing the project's status. Internally, the `Project` creates a new `Operation` instance, using this property for the comment. `Operations` make up a project's history, and are displayed on the Project Details page.

❷ The `update` method performs the actual work of updating the project, and is called by the `approve` and `reject` action methods (❸). It has one `boolean` parameter, `approve`, so that it knows whether this is an approval or rejection. First, the method retrieves the current project. Next, it calls the `Project.changeStatus` method, which performs the actual approval or rejection using the current `User` object and the `comments` property (❶).

If the status change is successful, the `Project` is updated through the `ProjectCoordinator`. If the status change isn't valid (for instance, an attempt to reject a project that's already in the first state), the `Utils.invalidStateChange` method is called (which adds an error message to the `FacesContext`; see listing 12.2), and a `"Constants.FAILURE"` outcome is returned. This indicates that the page should be redisplayed with an error message.

If no project was found, then the current project was deleted from the data store sometime in between the time it was displayed on a page and the time the user tried to update it. In that case, a different error message is added and a failure outcome is returned as well. If there were no errors, the `Constants.SUCCESS` outcome is returned.

❸ The `update` method is executed by two separate action methods—`approve` method calls it with the value of `true`, and the `reject` method passes in `false`. This is similar to the `SelectProjectBean.getProject` method except that we use a `boolean` instead of an `EnumeratedType` subclass. (Unlike `SelectProjectBean`, there's no need to define special navigation cases that take into account the action method, because these two action methods are called from entirely different pages.)

Now that we've examined the code, let's see how to use `UpdateProjectBean` in the rest of the application.

Initializing and referencing the bean

`UpdateProjectBean` doesn't need to remember its state between requests because it's geared toward processing updates performed on a single page, so we'll store it in request scope. The managed bean entry is shown in listing 13.7.

Listing 13.7 faces-config.xml: Managed bean entry for UpdateProjectBean

```
<managed-bean>
  <description>Approves or rejects the current Project.</description>
  <managed-bean-name>updateProjectBean</managed-bean-name>
  <managed-bean-class>org.jia.ptrack.web.UpdateProjectBean
  </managed-bean-class>
  <managed-bean-scope>request</managed-bean-scope>
  <managed-property>
```

```
    <property-name>visit</property-name>
    <value>#{sessionScope.visit}</value>
  </managed-property>
  <managed-property>
    <property-name>projectCoordinator</property-name>
    <value>#{applicationScope.projectCoordinator}</value>
  </managed-property>
  <managed-property>
    <property-name>statusCoordinator</property-name>
    <value>#{applicationScope.statusCoordinator}</value>
  </managed-property>
  <managed-property>
    <property-name>userCoordinator</property-name>
    <value>#{applicationScope.userCoordinator}</value>
  </managed-property>
</managed-bean>
```

The code in listing 13.7 configures an instance of `UpdateProjectBean` in the request scope under the key `updateProjectBean`. All of the configured properties are implemented by `UpdateProjectBean`'s superclass.

This bean is referenced on both the Approve a Project and Reject a Project pages. Here are some snippets from the Approve a Project page and from project_comments.jsp, which it includes:

```
...
<h:panelGrid columns="1" cellpadding="5"
             styleClass="table-background"
             rowClasses="table-odd-row,table-even-row">
  <h:outputLabel for="commentsInput">
    <h:outputText value="Your comments:"/>
  </h:outputLabel>
  <h:inputTextarea id="commentsInput" rows="10" cols="80"
                   value="#{updateProjectBean.comments}"/>
</h:panelGrid>
...
<h:commandButton value="Approve"
                 action="#{updateProjectBean.approve}"/>
 <h:commandButton value="Cancel"
                 action="#{updateProjectBean.cancel}"
                 immediate="true"/>
...
```

The first segment associates the value of an `HtmlInputTextarea` component with `UpdateProjectBean`'s `comments` property. There are also two `HtmlCommandButtons` at the bottom; one of them calls the `approve` action method, and the other calls the `cancel` action method (defined in the superclass). Figure 13.4 shows what this page looks like in a browser.

This bean is used the same way in the Reject a Project page, except that it uses the `reject` action method instead of `approve`.

That's all there is to approving and rejecting a project. Now, let's see the code behind the creation process.

13.1.6 Creating new projects

New projects are added to the system by `CreateProjectBean`, which backs the header and Create a Project views. The bean has a component binding property, `projectSelectOne`, that it uses to initialize a new `HtmlSelectOneMenu` component. It has two action methods: `create` and `add`. The `create` action method is called by the header before navigation to the Create a Project page, to ensure that the bean has a new `Project` instance to work with. Then, once the user has edited the project with the Create a Project page, the `add` method adds the project to the data store.

Figure 13.5 shows how the header and Create a Project pages use `CreateProjectBean`. Note that Create a Project basically edits `visit.currentProject` but executes `CreateProjectBean` action methods, including the `cancel` action method, which is inherited from `BaseBean`. The bean's source is shown in listing 13.8

Listing 13.8 CreateProjectBean.java: Creates a new Project and adds it to the data store

```
package org.jia.ptrack.web;

import javax.faces.application.FacesMessage;
import javax.faces.component.UIComponent;
import javax.faces.component.UIInput;
import javax.faces.component.html.HtmlSelectOneMenu;
import javax.faces.context.FacesContext;
import javax.faces.validator.ValidatorException;

import org.jia.ptrack.domain.DataStoreException;
import org.jia.ptrack.domain.Project;

public class CreateProjectBean extends BaseBean
{
  private HtmlSelectOneMenu projectSelectOne;

  public CreateProjectBean()
  {
  }

  public HtmlSelectOneMenu getProjectSelectOne()
  {                                                    ❶
    if (projectSelectOne == null)
    {
```

```
    projectSelectOne = (HtmlSelectOneMenu)
      getApplication().createComponent(
        HtmlSelectOneMenu.COMPONENT_TYPE);
    projectSelectOne.setId("typeSelectOne");
    projectSelectOne.setTitle(
      "Select the project type");
    projectSelectOne.setRequired(true);
    projectSelectOne.setValueBinding("value",
        getApplication().createValueBinding(
          "#{visit.currentProject.type}"));
    projectSelectOne.setConverter(
        getApplication().createConverter(
          ProjectTypeConverter.CONVERTER_ID));
  }

  return projectSelectOne;
}

public void setProjectSelectOne(
   HtmlSelectOneMenu projectSelectOne)
{
  this.projectSelectOne = projectSelectOne;
}

public UIInput getReqContactEmailInput()
{
  return reqContactEmailInput;
}

public void setReqContactEmailInput(
              UIInput reqContactEmailInput)
{
  this.reqContactEmailInput = reqContactEmailInput;
}

public void validateReqContact(
               FacesContext facesContext,
               UIComponent component, Object newValue)
               throws ValidatorException
{
  if (reqContactEmailInput.getSubmittedValue().toString().equals(""))
  {
    facesContext.addMessage(
           reqContactEmailInput.getClientId(facesContext),
           new FacesMessage("Please fill in this field."));
    throw new ValidatorException(new FacesMessage(
             "E-mail address is required for the contact."));
  }
}

public String create()
```

```
    {
      getVisit().setCurrentProject(new Project());
      return Constants.SUCCESS_OUTCOME;
    }

    public String add()   <-5
    {
      FacesContext facesContext = getFacesContext();
      Project project = getVisit().getCurrentProject();
      project.setInitialStatus(getStatusCoordinator().getInitialStatus());
      try { getProjectCoordinator().add(project); }
      catch (DataStoreException e)
      {
        Utils.reportError(facesContext, "A database error has occurred",
                          "Error adding project", e);
        return Constants.ERROR_OUTCOME;
      }
      return Constants.SUCCESS_OUTCOME;
    }
  }
```

❶ The `projectSelectOne` component binding property is meant to be bound to an `HtmlSelectOneMenu` component on the associated view that selects the project's `type` property. The property's getter method is an example of how you can create and initialize a UI component in code. It sets a few of the component's properties, including its `value` with a `ValueBinding` instance. This is essentially the same work that's done with JSP declarations for other components on the page.

You can initialize a UI component like this whenever it is bound to a backing bean component property. However, this is usually only necessary when the initialization depends on factors that can't be expressed with value-binding expressions. (Technically, there's no need to do this in ProjectTrack, but this *is* a sample application...) For more information on component binding properties, see section 12.2.3, page 462.

❷ The `reqContactEmailInput` component binding property is used by the `validateReqContact` method (❸). It is of type `UIInput`, so it can be bound to any input control.

❸ `validateReqContact` is a validator method that's intended to be used with the field that collects the requirements contact name. This method enforces a very basic rule: if you enter a requirements contact name, you must also enter an email address for that person. So, the method simply checks the `submittedValue` property of the `reqContactEmailInput` component, and if it's empty, it creates a new `FacesMessage` and registers it for that component. It also throws a `ValidatorException` with another `FacesMessage`, which tells JSF that validation has failed. The result is two error messages—one for the input control that collects the

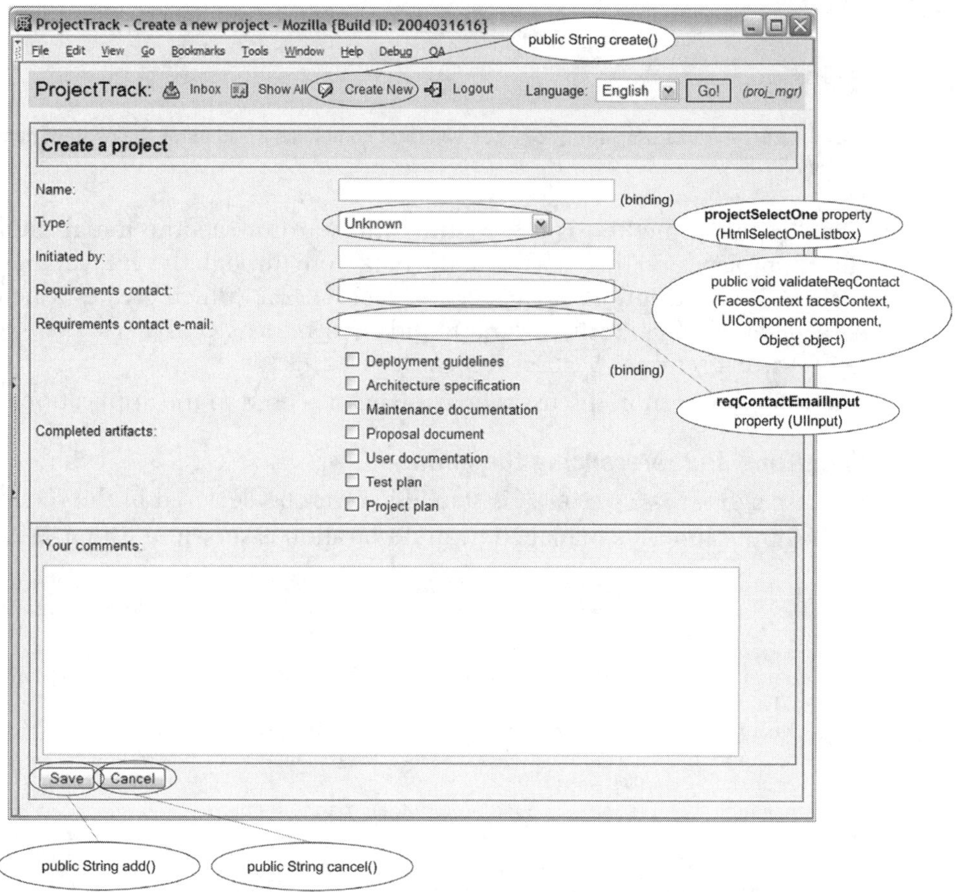

Figure 13.5 The header executes the `CreateProjectBean.create` action method before navigating to the Create a Project page. The Create a Project page associates most properties with `visit.currentProject`, but it also binds an `HtmlSelectOneMenu` component to a `CreateProjectBean` property, and also executes two action methods with `HtmlCommandButton` components. The `cancel` action method is implemented by `CreateProjectBean`'s superclass, `BaseBean`.

requirements contact name (created from the `ValidatorException`), and one for the control that collects the email address (added manually), as shown in figure 13.6.

If the Requirements contact field is empty, this validator isn't called. In other words, it's perfectly valid to leave both fields blank or to enter just the email address.

❹ The `create` action method simply creates a new `Project` instance and sets it as the current project, so that it can be edited and added to the data store on the next page.

Requirements contact:	John A. Mann II	E-mail address is required for the contact.
Requirements contact e-mail:		Please fill in this field.

Figure 13.6 The `validateReqContact` validator complains if you enter the contact name but not the email address.

5 The `add` action method is pretty straightforward; it sets the initial status of the current project, and then adds it to the data store through the `ProjectCoordinator`. If there is an exception, it calls `Utils.reportError` (which creates a new `FacesMessage` and writes to the log file), and then returns `Constants.ERROR_OUTCOME`. Otherwise, it returns `Constants.SUCCESS_OUTCOME`.

The following section discusses how the bean is used in the application.

Initializing and referencing the bean

Because a `CreateProjectBean` is stateless, it can be declared in the request scope of the application. Its managed bean declaration is shown in listing 13.9.

Listing 13.9 faces-config.xml: Managed bean entry for CreateProjectBean

```
<managed-bean>
  <description>Creates and adds a new Project to the data store.
  </description>
  <managed-bean-name>createProjectBean</managed-bean-name>
  <managed-bean-class>org.jia.ptrack.web.CreateProjectBean
  </managed-bean-class>
  <managed-bean-scope>request</managed-bean-scope>
  <managed-property>
    <property-name>visit</property-name>
    <value>#{sessionScope.visit}</value>
  </managed-property>
  <managed-property>
    <property-name>projectCoordinator</property-name>
    <value>#{applicationScope.projectCoordinator}</value>
  </managed-property>
  <managed-property>
    <property-name>statusCoordinator</property-name>
    <value>#{applicationScope.statusCoordinator}</value>
  </managed-property>
  <managed-property>
    <property-name>userCoordinator</property-name>
    <value>#{applicationScope.userCoordinator}</value>
  </managed-property>
</managed-bean>
```

The code in listing 13.9 declares a request-scoped instance of `CreateProjectBean` under the key `createProjectBean`, and then initializes all of the necessary properties inherited from `BaseBean`.

As we stated earlier, this bean is referenced in the header and the Create a Project page. Remember, the header's toolbar is implemented using the `UINavigator` custom component (see online extension chapter 20). One of the component's navigator items (which represents a single button on the toolbar) references the `create` method:

```
<jia:navigatorToolbar ...>
...
  <jia:navigatorItem name="createNew"
        label="Create New"
        icon="/images/create.gif"
        action="#{createProjectBean.create}"
        disabled="#{!authenticationBean.createNewAuthorized}"/>
...
</jia:navigatorToolbar>
```

The outcome of this action (which is always `Constants.SUCCESS_OUTCOME`) is used to load the Create a Project page.

The Create a Project page has a lot of components on it—one for each property a user needs to set when creating a new project. Most of these components are associated with `visit.currentProject`. Several components on the page use `CreateProjectBean`, however:

```
...

<h:outputLabel for="typeSelectOne">
  <h:outputText value="Type:"/>
</h:outputLabel>
<h:selectOneMenu binding="#{createProjectBean.projectSelectOne}">
...

<h:outputLabel for="requirementsInput">
  <h:outputText value="Requirements contact:"/>
</h:outputLabel>
<h:inputText id="requirementsInput" size="40"
             value="#{visit.currentProject.requirementsContact}"
             validator="#{createProjectBean.validateReqContact}"/>
<h:message for="requirementsInput" styleClass="errors"/>

<h:outputLabel for="requirementsEmailInput">
  <h:outputText value="Requirements contact e-mail:"/>
</h:outputLabel>
<h:inputText id="requirementsEmailInput" size="40"
           value="#{visit.currentProject.requirementsContactEmail}"
           binding="#{createProjectBean.reqContactEmailInput}">
...
```

```
</h:inputText>
<h:message for="requirementsEmailInput" styleClass="errors"/>

<h:commandButton value="Save" action="#{createProjectBean.add}"/>
<h:commandButton value="Cancel" action="#{createProjectBean.cancel}"
                 immediate="true"/>
...
```

Note that for the HtmlSelectOneMenu declaration, we don't specify any properties because they're all initialized with createProjectBean.projectSelectOne's getter method. The requirementsInput component has createProjectBean.validateReqContact set as its validator, and the requirementsEmailInput control is bound to the reqContactEmailInput so that the validator method can check its values. The errors are displayed with the HtmlMessages components declared after the controls.

The action methods are referenced, as usual, in the action property of Command components. Figure 13.6 shows what the header and Create a Project pages look like in a browser.

We've now covered backing beans for just about every view in ProjectTrack, except for Project Details.

13.1.7 *Paging through the project history with UIData*

The last of ProjectTrack's backing beans is ShowHistoryBean, which has a simple goal: to allow a UIData component to break up the project's history listing into several pages. Paging through data isn't a core feature of UIData, but it's simple to implement. UIData has a first property, which tells it which row to display first, and a rows property, which tells it how many rows to display. All we have to do is modify the component's first property every time the user wants to move forward or backward in the data set, increasing or decreasing it by rows.

ShowHistoryBean has a component binding property, historyDataTable, that should be bound to the UIData component in the view. (We use HtmlDataTable's superclass, since the bean doesn't access any HTML-specific properties.) It also has a rowsPerPage property, which determines how may rows the component will display at once.

In addition, it has a read-only property called currentProjectHistory, which returns the history for the current Project instance (which is a List of Operation objects). This is the property that should be associated with the UIData component's value property.

This bean is used only by the Project Details view. Figure 13.7 shows how the view uses this bean; note that the cancel action method is implemented in the base class. The source for ShowHistoryBean appears in listing 13.10.

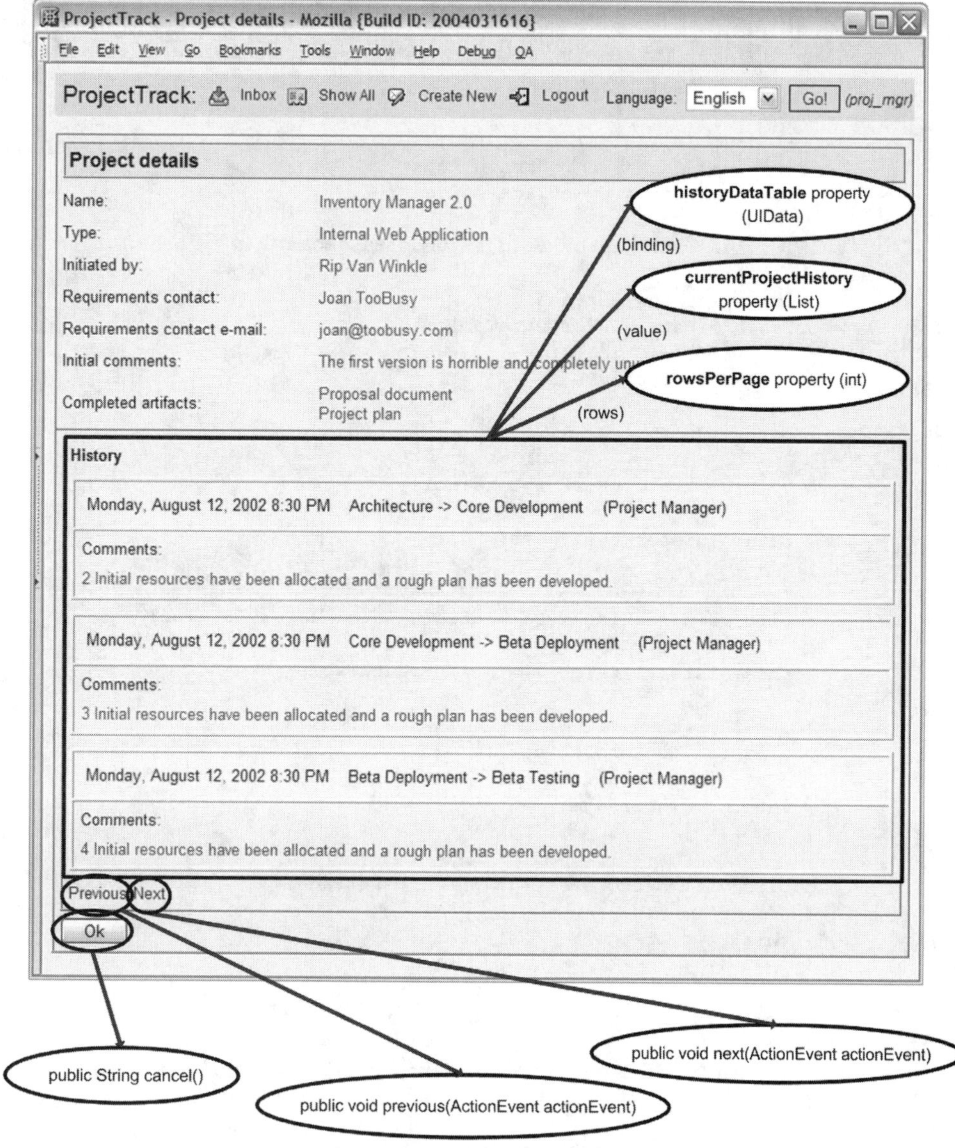

Figure 13.7 The Project Details page uses the `ShowHistoryBean` to display the project's history, and allow the user to page through the data set. The history is displayed with an `HtmlDataTable` component, which is bound to to the `ShowHistoryBean.historyDataTable` property. The table's `rows` property is bound to the bean's `rowsPerPage` property, and its `value` is bound to the bean's `currentProjectHistory` property. Two action listener methods—`next` and `previous`—control paging forward or backward (respectively) in the data set. Also, the Ok button executes the `cancel` action method, which is implemented in the superclass.

Listing 13.10 ShowHistoryBean.java: Displays a project's history and allows the user to page through the operations

```
package org.jia.ptrack.web;

import java.util.List;
import javax.faces.component.UIData;
import javax.faces.event.ActionEvent;

public class ShowHistoryBean extends BaseBean
{
  private int rowsPerPage = 5;
  private UIData historyDataTable;

  public ShowHistoryBean()
  {
  }

  public UIData getHistoryDataTable()
  {
    return historyDataTable;
  }
                                                                    ❶
  public void setHistoryDataTable(UIData historyDataTable)
  {
    this.historyDataTable = historyDataTable;
  }

  public int getRowsPerPage()
  {
    return rowsPerPage;
  }
                                                      ❷
  public void setRowsPerPage(int rowsPerPage)
  {
    this.rowsPerPage = rowsPerPage;
  }

  public List getCurrentProjectHistory()     <-❸
  {
    return getVisit().getCurrentProject().getHistory();
  }

  public boolean getShowNext()
  {
    return (historyDataTable.getFirst() +                 ❹
            rowsPerPage) <
           getCurrentProjectHistory().size();
  }
```

```
    public boolean getShowPrevious()
    {
      return (historyDataTable.getFirst()-
              rowsPerPage) >= 0;
    }

    public void next(ActionEvent actionEvent)
    {
      int newFirst =
        historyDataTable.getFirst() + rowsPerPage;
      if (newFirst <
          getCurrentProjectHistory().size())
      {
        historyDataTable.setFirst(newFirst);
      }
    }

    public void previous(ActionEvent actionEvent)
    {
      int newFirst =
        historyDataTable.getFirst() - rowsPerPage;
      if (newFirst >= 0)
      {
        historyDataTable.setFirst(newFirst);
      }
    }

}
```

❶ The `historyDataTable` property is meant to be bound to the `UIData` component with which our bean will be working. The `next` and `previous` action listener methods (❺) `historyDataTable`'s `first` property, which is the first row the `UIData` will display.

❷ The `rowsPerPage` property sets the number of rows to be displayed on each page. Because a setter method has been exposed, it can be initialized with the Managed Bean Creation facility.

❸ The `currentProjectHistory` property returns the actual `List` of `Operation` objects that the `UIData` will display. It's intended to be bound to the `UIData` component's `value` property.

❹ The `showNext` property returns `true` if there are any more pages to display, and the `showPrevious` property returns `true` if there are previous pages to display. The intention is for these two properties to be bound to the `rendered` properties of the `UICommand` components responsible for moving to the next and previous pages. (In the Project Details page, these are `HtmlCommandLink` components.)

❺ The `next` and `previous` action listener methods perform the actual work of this bean—they either increase or decrease `historyDataTable`'s `first` property by `rowsPerPage` rows, as long as doing so wouldn't make `first` out of the `currentProjectHistory`'s bounds.

When `historyDataTable` is redisplayed, it will begin with the `first` row. For example, let's suppose that `rowsPerPage` was set at 5 (the default), there are 50 items in `currentProjectHistory`, and we are displaying rows 0–4 (so `first` is 0, which is the default). If `next` is executed, `first` will be set to 5, so rows 5–9 will be displayed. If `previous` is executed, `first` will be set back to 0, so rows 0–4 will be displayed again.

We chose to implement `next` and `previous` as action listener methods because they don't affect navigation (the page is always redisplayed). If you're wondering why we chose to manipulate the `historyDataTable.first` property in code instead of using a value-binding expression in JSP, the reason is simple: `ShowHistoryBean` is request-scoped, and consequently stateless. If `ShowHistoryBean` kept track of the `first` property itself, it would have to be stored in the session so that it could remember the value.

TIP Try to write your backing beans to be stateless if possible, so they can be stored in request scope. The easiest way to do this is to push your state onto UI components – either by setting their properties, or adding application-specific attributes. Making beans stateless simplifies development and reduces server load (as opposed to storing beans in the session). If you store your bean in the session, it may need be initialized before a page is displayed, which requires more overhead. (If you really need to initialize a bean when a page is displayed, you can do so with a phase listener; see chapter 11.)

You may have noticed that `ShowHistoryBean` could be reused for other types of lists. As a matter of fact, it is a prime candidate for generalization; for example, you could have a `DataPager` bean that worked with any property of type List, as well as other `UIData`-friendly data types like `java.sql.ResultSet` and `javax.servlet.jsp.jstl.sql.Result`. This property for the data list could be configured with the Managed Bean Creation facility. You can also expect to see third-party components that perform scrolling for you.

Now that we've examined this bean's code, let's look at how the application uses it.

Initializing and referencing the bean

We can configure `ShowHistoryBean` using the Managed Bean Creation facility just like the other beans. The only difference is that we can also set its `rowsPerPage` property so that the number of rows displayed can be modified in faces-config.xml. Listing 13.11 shows the managed bean entry.

Listing 13.11 faces-config.xml: Managed bean entry for ShowHistoryBean

```
<managed-bean>
  <description>Pages through history list.</description>
  <managed-bean-name>showHistoryBean</managed-bean-name>
  <managed-bean-class>
    org.jia.ptrack.web.ShowHistoryBean
  </managed-bean-class>
  <managed-bean-scope>request</managed-bean-scope>
  <managed-property>
    <property-name>rowsPerPage</property-name>
    <value>3</value>
  </managed-property>
  <managed-property>
    <property-name>visit</property-name>
    <value>#{sessionScope.visit}</value>
  </managed-property>
  <managed-property>
    <property-name>projectCoordinator</property-name>
    <value>#{applicationScope.projectCoordinator}</value>
  </managed-property>
  <managed-property>
    <property-name>statusCoordinator</property-name>
    <value>#{applicationScope.statusCoordinator}</value>
  </managed-property>
  <managed-property>
    <property-name>userCoordinator</property-name>
    <value>#{applicationScope.userCoordinator}</value>
  </managed-property>
</managed-bean>
```

As you can see, the entry defines a request-scoped bean called `showHistoryBean` and configures all of the `BaseBean` properties, but it also sets the `rowsPerPage` property to 3. The value 3 is logical, because each entry consumes a decent amount of screen real estate.

This bean is used by the Project Details page because it is the only one that displays a project's history. Here's a snippet from that JSP:

```
<h:dataTable cellpadding="5" styleClass="table-background"
             value="#{showHistoryBean.currentProjectHistory}"
             var="operation"
             binding="#{showHistoryBean.historyDataTable}"
             rows="#{showHistoryBean.rowsPerPage}">
...
```

```
  <h:column>
    <h:panelGrid columns="1" width="100%" border="1"
                 styleClass="table-even-row">
...
        <h:outputText value="#{operation.timestamp}">
          <f:convertDateTime dateStyle="full" timeStyle="short"/>
        </h:outputText>
        <h:outputText
            value="#{operation.fromStatus} -> #{operation.toStatus}"/>
       <h:outputText value="(#{operation.user.role})"/>
...
        <h:outputText value="Comments:"/>
        <h:outputText value="#{operation.comments}"
                      styleClass="project-data"/>
...
    </h:panelGrid>
  </h:column>

  <f:facet name="footer">
    <h:panelGroup>
      <h:commandLink actionListener="#{showHistoryBean.previous}"
                     rendered="#{showHistoryBean.showPrevious}"
                     style="padding-right: 5px;">
        <h:outputText value="Previous"/>
      </h:commandLink>
      <h:commandLink actionListener="#{showHistoryBean.next}"
                     rendered="#{showHistoryBean.showNext}">
        <h:outputText value="Next"/>
      </h:commandLink>
    </h:panelGroup>
  </f:facet>
</h:dataTable>
```

As expected, both the `HtmlDataTable` component and its value are bound to the `ShowHistoryBean` instance. In addition, the component's `rows` property, which indicates the number of rows to display, is bound to the bean's `rowsPerPage` property. The `UICommand` components responsible for executing the action listener methods are `HtmlCommandLink` components, and their `rendered` properties are bound to the `showPrevious` and `showNext` properties, so that they are hidden when no more pages are available. The Project Details page is shown in figure 13.7.

With this simple class, we've added the capability to page through our data set—but what if we were working with JDBC instead of collections?

13.1.8 Working with JDBC ResultSets and UIData

So far, all of our backing beans have treated data layer objects such as `ProjectCoordinator` as black boxes; all we know is that they work with `Projects`, which implies that they perform some sort of persistence mechanism such as object/

relational mapping (ORM), either with custom code or with a library like Hibernate [JBoss, Hibernate] or Java Data Objects (JDO) [Sun, JDO]. This works great for a pure object-oriented approach. In some cases, however, you may want to hook up UI components directly to a data service object, like a JDBC `ResultSet`. Let's take another look at `SelectProjectBean` from that perspective, and then talk about how the rest of ProjectTrack would be different.

`SelectProjectBean` uses a `UIData` component to list project information for both the Inbox and Show All pages. Recall that `UIData` works with `DataModel` objects exclusively. You can set its `value` property to an array, `java.util.List`, `java.sql.ResultSet`, or `javax.servlet.jsp.jstl.sql.Result`, and `UIData` will automatically create a `DataModel` wrapper for the object using one of several subclasses. (If you use any other type, it will create a `ScalarDataModel` instance as a wrapper, which represents a single row.) So, in the case of the `SelectProjectBean.allProjects` property, which is a `List` of `Project` instances, a `UIData` component would wrap it with a `ListDataModel` interface.

In practical terms, this means that using `UIData` directly with a `ResultSet` is similar to using it with a `List`, an array, and any other data types it supports. It also means that if you create your own `DataModel` subclass (as we do in online extension chapter 18), `UIData` will treat it the same as well. So, as long as `SelectProjectBean` returns a `ResultSet` instead of a `List`, there should be very few modifications (if any) to the associated views.

To examine this scenario, let's assume that the `projectCoordinator` property of `BaseBean` actually returns a class called `ResultSetProjectCoordinator`, which works with `ResultSets` instead of `Lists`. There would be a single instance of this class initialized at startup through the `Initializer` class we covered in chapter 12, just as there is with the `MemoryProjectCoordinator` class.

What we'd like is for `SelectProjectBean`'s `inboxProjects` property to return a `ResultSet`. Here's what that property's accessor currently looks like:

```
public List getInboxProjects() throws DataStoreException
{
  try
  {
    return getProjectCoordinator().
            getProjects(getVisit().getUser().getRole(),
                        sortColumn);
  }
  catch (ObjectNotFoundException e)
  {
    return new ArrayList(0);
  }
}
```

Let's change it to the following:

```
public java.sql.ResultSet getInboxProjects()
        throws DataStoreException
{
   return getProjectCoordinator().
           getProjects(getVisit().getUser().getRole());
}
```

This time, we return a `ResultSet` instead. No `ObjectNotFoundException` is thrown, so there's no need to catch one. We also leave out the `sortColumn` parameter, just to keep things simple.

This `ResultSetProjectCoordinator` class uses a standard SQL query to retrieve all of the projects available for the specified role, as shown in listing 13.12.

Listing 13.12 ResultSetProjectCoordinator.java: Coordinator class that returns a JDBC ResultSet instead of a List of Project instances

```
package org.jia.ptrack.domain;

import java.sql.*;

public class ResultSetProjectCoordinator
{
  private String url;
  private String name;
  private String password;

  public ResultSetProjectCoordinator(String url, String name,
         String password) throws DataStoreException
  {
    try
    {
      Class.forName("org.hsqldb.jdbcDriver");
    }
    catch (Exception e)
    {
      throw new DataStoreException("Error loading JDBC driver", e);
    }
    this.url = url;
    this.name = name;
    this.password = password;
  }

  public ResultSet getProjects(RoleType role)      <- Returns standard ResultSet
          throws DataStoreException
  {
    try
    {
```

```
      Connection conn = DriverManager.getConnection(url,
                                   name, password);
      Statement stmt = conn.createStatement(
          ResultSet.TYPE_SCROLL_INSENSITIVE,   <-(1) Must be
          ResultSet.CONCUR_READ_ONLY);               scrollable

      return stmt.executeQuery(
        "select p.id, p.name as name, pt.description as type, " +
        "s.name as status, r.description as waitingfor " +
        "from projects p, project_type pt, status s, role r " +
        "where p.type = pt.project_type_id " +
        "and   p.status = s.status_id " +
        "and   s.role_id = r.role_id " +
        "and   r.role_id = " + role.getValue());
    }
    catch (SQLException e)
    {
      throw new DataStoreException(
                "Error executing query for loading projects", e);
    }
  }
  ...
}
```

As you can see, all this class does is execute a SQL query and return the results (the tables referenced in the query map to ProjectTrack's Project, Project Type, Status, and RoleType entities). Note, however, that when the `Statement` is created, we set the `ResultSet` type to `ResultSet.TYPE_SCROLL_INSENSITIVE` (1), which means it can move backward and forward through the data, and that the data is generally not sensitive to change.

NOTE In order to use a `javax.sql.ResultSet` instance with a `UIData` component (or, specifically, the `ResultSetDataModel` object that `UIData` uses internally), the `ResultSet` must be scrollable. The valid types for scrollable `ResultSets` are `ResultSet.TYPE_SCROLL_SENSITIVE` and `ResultSet.TYPE_SCROLL_INSENSITIVE`. A `ResultSet`'s type is usually set when executing a query, either through a `Statement` or a `PreparedStatement` object.

The `ResultSetProjectCoordinator` class isn't an example of great design—it doesn't pool connections, use prepared statements, or perform any other intelligent optimizations. It also uses an older mechanism of accessing a JDBC driver, as opposed to the newer `javax.sql.DataSource` class introduced in JDBC 2.0. Even if we had implemented more functionality and used the `DataSource` class, the bottom line would hold true: we're just returning a `ResultSet`. (The same thing goes for `javax.sql.RowSets`, since it subclasses `ResultSet`.)

So, how does this all affect the associated Inbox view, with the `UIData` component? It doesn't affect it at all. To see why, let's examine the view's `UIData` declaration:

```
<h:dataTable styleClass="table-background"
             rowClasses="table-odd-row,table-even-row"
             cellpadding="3"
             value="#{inboxBean.inboxProjects}"
             var="project"
             binding="#{inboxBean.projectTable}">
  <h:column>
...
    <h:outputText value="#{project.name}"/>
...
    <h:outputText value="#{project.type}"/>
...
    <h:outputText value="#{project.status}"/>
...
</h:dataTable>
```

So, the `UIData` component is associated with the `inboxBean.inboxProjects` property. Each row in `inboxBean.inboxProjects` is exposed as a request-scoped variable named `project` that is made available to child components when displaying their rows. So, the expressions `"#{project.name}"`, `"{project.type}"`, and `"{project.status}"` are accessing the `name`, `type`, and `status` properties of the current row.

Previously this worked fine because `inboxProjects` returned a `List` of `Project` instances, and each `Project` has `name`, `type`, and `status` properties. The same JSP declaration works equally well for a `ResultSet` because the `ResultSetDataModel` class, which is used internally by `UIData`, returns a `java.util.Map` for each row, backed by the underlying `ResultSet`.

So, the expression `"#{project.name}"` asks the current row's `Map` for the value of key `name`, which is the same as retrieving the value of the name column for the current row. If you take a look at the SQL query in listing 13.13, you can see that we gave the result columns in the query names that matched the `Project` property's names. Consequently, no changes to the view are necessary.

That's really all there is to it—just associate a `ResultSet` directly to a `UIData` component, and you've finished. Displaying multiple pages of a `ResultSet` is similar to the `ShowHistoryBean` class we discussed in section 13.1.7, except for the fact that you can't retrieve the total row count from a `ResultSet`.

JSF's EL was designed to easily accommodate different types, so you can associate other UI components directly with data service objects that expose

JavaBean-style properties. Some tools, like Java Studio Creator [Sun, Creator], will even allow you to drop `RowSets` into your backing beans and then let you wire up columns to UI components visually. IBM's WebSphere Studio [WSAD] handles this through service data objects (which are being submitted for standardization as JSR 235).

> **TIP** In most cases, we don't recommend creating data service objects, like `ResultSets` and `RowSets`, directly in your backing beans, but this approach can work for small applications. Using a separate class like `ResultSetProjectCoordinator`, which is an implementation of the Data Table Gateway pattern [Fowler, Enterprise], is more flexible because you can unit-test it and reuse it within different backing beans.

So, how would this database-centric view of the world affect the rest of ProjectTrack? Simply put, it wouldn't work with objects. For starters, take a look at the code in `SelectProjectBean` that retrieves the selected `Project` instance from the `UIData` component:

```
Project project = (Project)projectTable.getRowData();
```

This wouldn't work, since `projectTable` is associated with a `ResultSet` instead of a `List` of `Project` instances. As we said earlier, each row is returned as a `Map`, so the equivalent line would be

```
Map projectMap = (Map)projectTable.getRowData();
```

Of course, the rest of the application was designed to work with `Project` instances, so this isn't the only necessary change. The main theme is simple, though: use `Maps` instead of beans and `ResultSets` instead of `Lists`.

13.2 Adding security

So far, we've been oblivious to any possible security issues with ProjectTrack. Web security is a big topic, so we'll leave the exhaustive discussions to experts in that arena. For our purposes, only two words are necessary: authentication and authorization. *Authentication* is the process of validating a user's credentials; *authorization* allows the user to access particular resources.

ProjectTrack has pretty basic requirements—a user is authenticated based on his or her login name and password. Each user has a role, and there are only two different levels of authorization—read-write and read-only access. The only role that has read-only access is the Upper Manager; every other role has read-write access. In addition, only Project Managers can create new projects. In practical terms, this means that Upper Managers can't access the Inbox, Approve a Project, or Reject a Project pages, and only Project Managers can access the Create a Project page.

In order to add basic authentication and authorization capabilities to ProjectTrack, we have two options: traditional web container–based security, and custom security.

13.2.1 Container-based vs. custom security

The basic premise behind web container–based security is that the container handles authentication by checking a username and password against some data store. Exactly which data store is used is up to the web container vendor—most offer a few options ranging from a Lightweight Directory Access Protocol (LDAP) server to a flat XML file or a relational database. Once the user has been authenticated, the container can control which resources the user can access based on his or her role. (The specifics about which resource can be accessed by which role are configured in the application's deployment descriptor.)

All web containers provide four types of authentication: HTTP basic, HTTP digest, client-certificate, and form-based. All of these mechanisms provide the basic functionality described previously, but they interact with the user differently. Basic authentication uses the HTTP protocol to pop up a modal dialog box asking for the username and password. Digest authentication works the same way, except a digest of the password is transferred instead of clear text.

Certificate-based authentication relies on client certificates to identify users, so users are never prompted for their username or password. Form-based authentiation lets you use a custom form (which can be JSP, HTML, or something else). This form must, however, post to a specific URL and contain special form parameters that the web container understands. All of these methods can be used in conjunction with Secure Sockets Layer (SSL), which ensures that the login is encrypted. (For more about servlet security, see *Java Servlet Programming* [Hunter].)

Regardless of which method you'd like to implement, there's one point that's important from the perspective of JavaServer Faces: container-based security requires posting directly to the server, avoiding `FacesServlet`, which handles all JSF requests. In all of these scenarios, the web container does its work before it even thinks about JSF. JSF is implemented as a just another servlet, after all, so it doesn't get any special treatment.

For all of the authentication methods other than form-based, this isn't a problem, because the user doesn't interact with input controls. For these methods, you can use the standard container security features, which are configured via web.xml.

If you want to have a nice form-based login page complete with JSF components and features like validation and action methods, you're out of luck. Because the form-based security requires posting to a specific URL that's processed by the web container before `FacesServlet`, there's no way to use JSF components with form-based container security. There are two choices: use a login page that doesn't have any JSF components, or don't use container-based security at all.

There's nothing wrong with using a non-JSF login page for container-based authorization. If you choose to do so, integration is the same as with any other Java web application. You can access familiar methods like `getUserPrincipal`, `getRemoteUser`, and `isUserInRole` through `ExternalContext` (see chapter 11).

13.2.2 Using custom security

ProjectTrack uses custom security. We've already examined the code for the `AuthenticationBean`, which handles authentication duties. It collects a login and password from JSF components, retrieves a `User` object from the `UserCoordinator` (if possible), creates a new `Visit` object (initializing its `user` property), and then forwards the user either to the Inbox or Show All page (depending on the user's access level)—see section 13.1.3 for details.

`AuthenticationBean` has methods for simple authorization checks, but as ProjectTrack stands, any user can access any page, no matter what access level he or she has. In fact, any user can access pages without even logging in. In order to control access to specific pages, we can use an authorization filter.

Developing an authorization filter

Filters are a standard feature of the Servlet API—they allow you to perform additional processing on a request before and after it's handled by traditional servlets. (The pattern-conscious will note that filters are an implementation of the Intercepting Filter pattern [Alur, Crupi, Malks].) Because JSF is implemented as a servlet, you can use filters to do work before or after JSF processes requests as well.

Filters are commonly used for authorization duties because they can reroute a request if the user isn't authorized to view the requested resource. This is exactly what ProjectTrack's `AuthorizationFilter` does—if there's no `Visit` object stored in the session, it reroutes the request to the Login page. If there is a `Visit` object in the session and the user is an Upper Manager, it denies access to any protected resources (the Inbox, Approve a Project, and Reject a Project pages); if the user is not a Project Manager, it denies access to the Create a Project page. Otherwise, it's business as usual. The source is shown in listing 13.13.

Listing 13.13 AuthorizationFilter.java: Redirects to the login page unauthenticated users and denies access to unauthorized resources

```
package org.jia.ptrack.web;

import java.io.IOException;
import java.text.MessageFormat;
import java.util.ResourceBundle;
import javax.servlet.*;
import javax.servlet.http.*;

import org.jia.ptrack.domain.RoleType;

public class AuthorizationFilter implements Filter
{
  FilterConfig config = null;
  ServletContext servletContext = null;

  public AuthorizationFilter()
  {
  }

  public void init(FilterConfig filterConfig)
              throws ServletException
  {
    config = filterConfig;
    servletContext = config.getServletContext();
  }

  public void doFilter(ServletRequest request,
              ServletResponse response, FilterChain chain)
              throws IOException, ServletException
  {
    HttpServletRequest httpRequest = (HttpServletRequest)request;
    HttpServletResponse httpResponse = (HttpServletResponse)response;
    HttpSession session = httpRequest.getSession();

    String requestPath = httpRequest.getPathInfo();
    Visit visit = (Visit)session.                              ❶
                   getAttribute(Constants.VISIT_KEY);

    if (visit == null)
    {
      session.setAttribute(                          ❸        ❷
              Constants.ORIGINAL_VIEW_KEY,
              httpRequest.getPathInfo());
      httpResponse.sendRedirect(
                 httpRequest.getContextPath() +
                 Constants.LOGIN_VIEW);
    }
    else
    {
```

```
        session.removeAttribute(                    4
          Constants.ORIGINAL_VIEW_KEY);
        RoleType role = visit.getUser().getRole();

        if ((role.equals(
               RoleType.UPPER_MANAGER) &&
             requestPath.indexOf(
               Constants.PROTECTED_DIR) > 0) ||
            (!role.equals(RoleType.PROJECT_MANAGER) &&      5
             requestPath.indexOf(
               Constants.EDIT_DIR) > 0))
        {
          httpResponse.sendError(
             HttpServletResponse.SC_NOT_FOUND,
             "Path " + requestPath + " not found."
        }
        else
        {
          chain.doFilter(request, response);    <-- 6
        }
      }
    }

    public void destroy()
    {
    }
  }
```

The first thing you should notice about the `doFilter` method is that there are no references to the JSF APIs. The `doFilter` method looks for the `Visit` object using the standard Servlet `HttpSession` object rather than a `ValueBinding` (❶). Because a filter executes before JSF processes the request, there is no `FacesContext` instance available. Because the `Application.getValueBinding` method requires a `FacesContext`, it can't be used in filters.

This highlights an important distinction we made in the `Constants` class—for any given key, there's a constant for the scope and a constant for the value itself. For example, for the `Visit` object, there's the `Constants.USER_KEY_SCOPE` and the `Constants.USER_KEY`. In ❶, we simply use `Constants.USER_KEY`, because we're already working with an `HttpSession` instance. In our action method classes, we use both constants, because we're dealing with the `ValueBinding` instance:

```
Visit visit = (Visit)app.getValueBinding(
                          Constants.VISIT_KEY_SCOPE +
                          Constants.VISIT_KEY);
```

This distinction is handy when you're working with code that doesn't know about JSF.

If a `Visit` instance can't be found in the session, the code forwards the user's request to the login page (❷). During this process, it saves the original request path (❸). This can be useful if the login code wants to forward the user to that page after a successful login (the next section explains how to do this).

If a `Visit` can be found, the method first removes the original request path from the session because the user has already seen the first page (❹). If the current user is an Upper Manager who has requested any file in the protected directory, the familiar HTTP "404 Not Found" error appears. The same goes for users who are not Project Managers but try to access the edit directory (where the Create a Project page lives) (❺). Otherwise, the filter chain is executed—this will call any other filters, and then process the request normally (❻).

Note that this filter requires that a `Visit` object be created and stored in the session upon successful login. This work is performed by `AuthenticationBean`, which is executed by the Login page (see section 13.1.2 for more about this class).

BY THE WAY It's also possible to implement authentication using a phase listener that fires at the beginning of the Request Processing Lifecycle. The benefit of this approach is that you can work directly with JSF objects; the drawback is that it will only be executed for resources that are processed by the Faces servlet.

Forwarding to another view

The `AuthorizationFilter` described in the previous section stores the original request path if the user hasn't yet logged in. The idea is that the action method handling the login can retrieve it and forward users to their original page after they have logged in. This is typical of many systems—if a user requests a page within the site but they haven't yet logged in, they see the login page. After successfully logging in, users are sent to the page they originally requested.

This feature doesn't work too well for applications like ProjectTrack, because most of the operations center around selecting a project to approve, reject, or view. If a user just logged in, they haven't selected a project yet, so half of the application won't work properly.

Even though this feature isn't part of ProjectTrack, we'll cover it because it might be useful in your applications. You can, of course, do this with the normal Servlet APIs by calling either `HttpResponse.redirect` or `RequestDispatcher.forward`. However, this can also be done using the JSF APIs. This is the code that would be in the `AuthenticationBean`'s `login` method if ProjectTrack needed to forward to the originally requested page after authentication:

```
Application app = getApplication();
ValueBinding originalViewBinding =
   app.createValueBinding("#{" + Constants.ORIGINAL_VIEW_KEY + "}");
String originalViewId = (String)originalViewBinding.
                           getValue(facesContext);
if (originalViewId != null)
{
   originalViewBinding.setValue(facesContext, null);
   UIViewRoot view = (UIViewRoot)app.getViewHandler().
                     createView(getFacesContext(), originalViewId);
   facesContext.setViewRoot(view);
   facesContext.renderResponse();

   return null;
}
```

The first thing this code does is retrieve the original request path, which is the same as the view ID of the requested page. This was stored by the `AuthenticationBean` (shown in listing 13.1).

If the view identifier isn't `null`, it's okay to forward the user to that tree. You can get a handle to a page through the `Application.createView` method. By default, JSF will display the view whose identifier is specified in the navigation case for the action method's outcome. To bypass this facility, we can set the view identifier explicitly with the `FacesContext.setViewRoot` method. Next, we can skip any further steps of the request processing lifecycle by calling `FacesContext.renderResponse`. This tells JSF to display the newly set view right away and avoid any additional work. We then return `null`; there's no need to return an outcome since the normal navigation behavior will be skipped.

BY THE WAY In this particular scenario, we could have called `ExternalContext.redirect` (for a client-side redirect) or `ExternalContext.dispatch` (to forward the request internally) instead of using the JSF API. However, generally speaking, it's better to use the JSF API, because a view identifier isn't guaranteed to always map to a URL. This is even more important in portlet environments, where you have no control over URL structure.

That's it for ProjectTrack's security, as well as all of its application code. Now, lets look at internationalizing the application.

13.3 Supporting internationalization in code

ProjectTrack works fine as it is, as long as you know English. DeathMarch Development wanted support for Russian as well, so we have some extra work ahead of us. Supporting multiple languages involves two steps. First, you move the text from code into external property files that hook into Java's multilingual support; this is called *internationalization*. Next, you create versions of those files for different languages; this is called *localization*. For more information about internationalization and localization in general, see chapter 6.

> **TIP** If you know you need to support multiple locales, it's better to internationalize your application from the beginning, instead of updating it later—even if you start with support for only one language initially.

In chapter 10, we went through the process of internationalizing the JSPs and localizing them for both Russian and English. We also configured ProjectTrack to support both languages in faces-config.xml. So, now we need to do the same for strings displayed through code.

Two types of strings need to be translated: display strings and messages. Display strings are the text that users typically see on a screen—strings like "Inbox" and "Project Details". Messages are either the result of validation errors or generated by action methods; for example, the `AuthenticationBean` sends a message if the login or password is incorrect, and most of the action methods will send an error message if there is a problem with the database.

13.3.1 Internationalizing text with resource bundles

Display strings are handled through normal Java resource bundles. Almost all of ProjectTrack's display strings are defined in JSP; there are a couple of classes, however—namely `AuthorizationFilter` and `CreateProjectBean`—that have display strings as well. These strings are listed in table 13.1.

Table 13.1 Display strings in Java code that need to be internationalized.

Class	Key	English text
AuthorizationFilter	PathNotFound	Path {0} not found.
CreateProjectBean	ProjectTypeTitle	Select the project type

Note that the text for the `PathNotFound` string has "{0}". This means that the code can substitute a parameter into the string, which is the request path name in this case. Your strings can have any number of parameters. For simplicity, we'll use the same resource bundle that was used in chapter 10—ptrackResources.

In order to support the strings listed in table 13.1, we need to add new name/value pairs to the default resource bundle (WEB-INF/classes/ptrackResources.properties), as shown in listing 13.14.

Listing 13.14 ptrackResources.properties: Text strings for Java classes

```
# AuthorizationFilter
PathNotFound=Path {0} not found.

# CreateProjectBean
ProjectTypeTitle=Select the project type
```

Note that the filename doesn't end with "en" because English is configured as the default language.

Now that we've added the proper strings to the resource bundle, it's time to modify the code. Since retrieving localized display strings is a common operation, we'll add a new method, called `getDisplayString`, to our `Utils` class, as shown in listing 13.15.

Listing 13.15 Utils.java: Updated with a new method to load localized display strings

```
...
import java.text.MessageFormat;
import java.util.ResourceBundle;
import java.util.MissingResourceException;
import java.util.Locale;
...
protected static ClassLoader
                   getCurrentClassLoader(Object defaultObject)     ❶
{
  ClassLoader loader =
         Thread.currentThread().getContextClassLoader();
  if (loader == null)
  {
    loader = defaultObject.getClass().getClassLoader();
  }
  return loader;
}

public static String getDisplayString(
                         String bundleName,
                         String id,                    ❷
                         Object params[],
                         Locale locale)
{
  String text = null;
```

```
    ResourceBundle bundle =
        ResourceBundle.getBundle(bundleName, locale,
                                 getCurrentClassLoader(params));
    try
    {
      text = bundle.getString(id);
    }
    catch (MissingResourceException e)
    {
      text = "!! key " + id + " not found !!";
    }
    if (params != null)
    {
      MessageFormat mf = new MessageFormat(text, locale);
      text = mf.format(params, new StringBuffer(), null).toString();
    }
    return text;
  }
  ...
```

The code starts with a utility method, `getCurrentClassLoader` (❶), that returns either the class loader for the current thread or the class loader of a specified default object. Why do we need this? When you load a resource bundle, the `ResourceBundle` class searches the classpath for files that are resource bundles. In this case, we want it to search our web application's classpath. Utility classes like `Utils` are sometimes loaded from a web application's main classpath with a different class loader, and consequently shared across many different web applications. If we didn't account for this fact, we couldn't guarantee that `getDisplayString` would work properly unless the `Utils` class was in the same WEB-INF directory as the rest of the web application.

The `getDisplayString` method (❷) loads the bundle using the static `ResourceBundle.getBundle` method, passing in the `ClassLoader` instance retrieved from `getCurrentClassLoader`. It then retrieves a string from the bundle for the passed-in identifier, using the `ResourceBundle.getString` method. This method can throw a `MissingResourceException` if the specified identifier wasn't found. We'd prefer to return an error string instead in that case, so we catch the exception. If an array of parameters were passed in, we insert those into a string using the `MessageFormat` class.

We can use the `getDisplayString` method in any code that needs to retrieve a localized display string. Let's start with `AuthorizationFilter`. All we have to do is change the hardcoded error message to use the proper string from the resource bundle:

```
public void doFilter(ServletRequest request,
                     ServletResponse response,
                     FilterChain chain)
             throws IOException, ServletException
{
  ...
  HttpServletRequest httpRequest = (HttpServletRequest)request;
  HttpServletResponse httpResponse = (HttpServletResponse)response;
  HttpSession session = httpRequest.getSession();

  String requestPath = httpRequest.getPathInfo();
  ...

     if ((role.equals(RoleType.UPPER_MANAGER) &&
           requestPath.indexOf(Constants.PROTECTED_DIR) > 0) ||
          (!role.equals(RoleType.PROJECT_MANAGER) &&
           requestPath.indexOf(Constants.EDIT_DIR) > 0))
     {
        String text =
          Utils.getDisplayString(Constants.BUNDLE_BASENAME,
                                 "PathNotFound",
                                 new Object[] { requestPath },
                                 request.getLocale());
        httpResponse.sendError(HttpServletResponse.SC_NOT_FOUND,
                               text);
     }
  ...
}
```

First, note that the `Constants` class declares the name of the resource bundle, avoiding the possibility of mistyping the name. Also, we pass in the current `Locale` directly from the `HttpRequest` object since there is no `FacesContext` yet (filters are executed before JSF begins processing the request). Since the string in the bundle has a parameter in it, we also need to send the `getDisplayString` method `requestPath` as a single parameter (it will replace "{0}" with the value of the `requestPath`).

Now, let's update `CreateProjectBean`. The only display string in this class is the `title` property that's set for the `projectSelectOne` component binding property, so we need to retrieve the localized string in the property's accessor:

```
public HtmlSelectOneMenu getProjectSelectOne()
{
  ...
  projectSelectOne.setTitle(
    Utils.getDisplayString(getApplication().getMessageBundle(),
        "ProjectTypeTitle", null,
        getFacesContext().getViewRoot().getLocale()));
  ...
  return projectSelectOne;
}
```

This time we have access to the JSF APIs, so we retrieve the name of the bundle from the `Application` and the locale from the `ViewRoot`. Note that the `Application.messageBundle` property returns the bundle configured in faces-config.xml, which is primarily for customized messages but can also be used to localize display strings. You can specify only one bundle in faces-config.xml, so if your application has several bundles, you should load them with string constants, as in the previous example. Since this string is not parameterized, we pass in `null` for the parameters.

TIP Resource bundle keys are perfect candidates for centralized constants, since they can easily be mistyped and they're sometimes reused. In ProjectTrack, we could have placed constants for these two strings in the `Constants` class.

With these minor changes, we've internationalized all of the display text that's handled by Java code. The application, however, will behave exactly the same—it will display English text for everything.

Localizing for Russian

To localize these strings for Russian, we just need to add strings to the Russian resource bundle, which has the suffix "ru", which is the ISO Language Code for Russian (see appendix E for a list of all the language codes). The ptrackResources_ru.properties file is shown in listing 13.16.

Listing 13.16 ptrackResources_ru.properties: Updated with Russian text strings for Java classes

```
# AuthorizationFilter
PathNotFound={0} не найдено

# CreateProjectBean
ProjectTypeTitle=выберите тип проекта
```

As soon as we create this file and place it in the WEB-INF/classes directory, these strings will display in Russian (if the user's locale is currently Russian). Now that we've mastered the display text, let's take a look at internationalizing messages.

13.3.2 Internationalizing messages

If you examine each of the ProjectTrack backing beans, you'll find a decent number of messages, both for information purposes and to report errors. These are summarized in table 13.2.

Table 13.2 ProjectTrack contains a number of error and informational messages.

Class	Severity	ID	English Summary	English Detail
`AuthenticationBean`	Info	BadLogin	Incorrect name or password.	
`AuthenticationBean`	Error	ErrorLoadingUser	A database error has occurred.	Error loading User object.
`SelectProjectBean`, `UpdateProjectBean`	Info	ProjectNotFound	The project you selected cannot be found.	The project is no longer in the data store.
`SelectProjectBean`	Error	ErrorLoadingProject	A database error has occurred.	Error loading project.
`CreateProjectBean`	Error	ErrorAddingProject	A database error has occurred.	Error adding project.
`CreateProjectBean`	Info	ContactEmailRequired	E-mail address is required for the contact.	
`UpdateProjectBean`	Error	ErrorUpdatingProject	A database error has occurred.	Error updating project.
`Utils`	Info	CanNotApprove	You cannot approve a project with the status "{0}".	
`Utils`	Info	CanNotReject	You cannot reject a project with the status "{0}".	

Because messages have properties like a severity level, a summary, and detailed messages, JSF handles them slightly differently than ordinary display text. You specify two name/value pairs in the resource bundle—one for the summary and one for the detail. The identifiers are the same, but the detail string's identifier ends with ".detail". This is the same process we used for customizing default messages in chapter 6. Listing 13.17 shows the resource bundle updated to include strings for ProjectTrack's application-generated messages.

Listing 13.17 ptrackResource.properties: Messages string used in Java classes

```
# Messages
BadLogin=Incorrect name or password.
ErrorLoadingUser=A database error has occurred.
ErrorLoadingUser_detail=Error loading User object.
ProjectNotFound=The project you selected cannot be found.
ProjectNotFound_detail=The project is no longer in the data store.
ErrorLoadingProject=A database error has occurred.
ErrorLoadingProject_detail=Error loading project.
ErrorAddingProject=A database error has occurred.
ErrorAddingProject_detail=Error adding project.
ContactEmailRequired=E-mail address is required for the contact.
ErrorUpdatingProject=A database error has occurred.
ErrorUpdatingProject_detail=Error updating project.
CannotApprove=You cannot approve a project with the status "{0}".
CannotReject=You cannot reject a project with the status "{0}".
```

Here, we've defined the identifiers and strings for all of the messages created in our backing beans. For each message, we define its identifier, the summary, and detail (the severity level must still be handled in code). Note that the last two strings, `CannotApprove` and `CannotReject`, accept a single parameter, which should be a string representation of a project's status.

Now that we've defined all the message strings, we need to update the code to use them instead of hardcoded values. In order to do this, we'll write a factory method [GoF] that will load the resource bundle and then construct a new `FacesMessage` instance based on the summary and detail strings in the bundle. We'll place it in our `Utils` class, just like `getDisplayString`, since it can be used by many classes throughout an application (backing beans, validators, converters, and so on). We'll also update the `Utils.reportError` method to use this new method. The source is shown in listing 13.18.

Listing 13.18 Utils.java: Factory method for constructing new FacesMessage instances from a resource bundle

```
...
public static FacesMessage
                getMessage(String messageId,
                           Object params[],
                           FacesMessage.Severity severity)        ❶
{
  FacesContext facesContext = FacesContext.getCurrentInstance();
  String bundleName =
          facesContext.getApplication().getMessageBundle();
  if (bundleName != null)
```

```
  {
    String summary = null;
    String detail = null;
    Locale locale = facesContext.getViewRoot().getLocale();
    ResourceBundle bundle =
        ResourceBundle.getBundle(bundleName, locale,
                                 getCurrentClassLoader(params));
    try
    {
      summary = bundle.getString(messageId);
      detail = bundle.getString(messageId + "_detail");
    }
    catch (MissingResourceException e) {}
    if (summary != null)
    {
      MessageFormat mf = null;
      if (params != null)
      {
        mf = new MessageFormat(summary, locale);
        summary = mf.format(params, new StringBuffer(), null).toString();
      }
      if (detail != null && params != null)
      {
        mf.applyPattern(detail);
        detail = mf.format(params, new StringBuffer(), null).toString();
      }
      return (new FacesMessage(severity, summary, detail));
    }
  }
  return new FacesMessage(severity,
                          "!! key " + messageId + " not found !!",
                          null);
}
...

public static void reportError(
                     FacesContext facesContext,
                     String messageId,                    (2)
                  Exception exception)
{
  FacesMessage message = getMessage(messageId, null,
                         FacesMessage.SEVERITY_ERROR);
  facesContext.addMessage(null, message);
  if (exception != null)
  {
  facesContext.getExternalContext().
    log(message.getSummary(), exception);
  }
}
...
```

The new getMessage method (❶) is similar to getDisplayString in listing 13.16. The difference is that it creates a new FacesMessage instance based on two display strings—the summary and the detail. The only difference between the two identifiers is that the latter one ends in "_detail". This is what JSF does internally for standard messages, as well as custom ones that you define. The listing also shows an updated version of reportError (❷), which uses getMessage to load a message based on its identifier.

BY THE WAY Here, we've created a single factory method that takes a few parameters. It would be nice to have some convenience methods with defaults, so we wouldn't have to specify commonly known parameters like locale and the severity. If you don't want to write these methods yourself, the CarDemo application, included with the JSF RI [Sun, JSF RI], has a MessageFactory class with additional methods, which is free for reuse.

Now that we've defined a new factory method, we can use it in all of the places throughout our code where we created a FacesMessage instance manually. Let's see how to do this by examining the login method of the AuthenticationBean class:

```
public String login()
{
  FacesContext facesContext = getFacesContext();

  User newUser = null;
  try
  {
    newUser = getUserCoordinator().getUser(loginName, password);
  }
  catch (ObjectNotFoundException e)
  {
    facesContext.addMessage(null,
                            Utils.getMessage("BadLogin", null,
                                     FacesMessage.SEVERITY_INFO));
    return Constants.FAILURE_OUTCOME;
  }
  catch (DataStoreException d)
  {
    Utils.reportError(facesContext, "ErrorLoadingUser", d);
    return Constants.ERROR_OUTCOME;
  }
  ...
}
```

The changes are in the exception handling after the method calls getUser. An ObjectNotFoundException is not a major error, so in this case we add a message with the info severity level using our new `getMessage` method with the identifier `BadLogin`. `DataStoreExceptions` are serious errors, though, so we use the updated version of `reportError` with the identifier `ErrorLoadingUser`.

SOAPBOX Creating messages in code is currently too much work—you shouldn't have to write a `FacesMessage` factory method at all; it should be part of the standard API. We hope this will be addressed in a future version of JSF.

With similar changes to the other backing beans, we'll have a fully internationalized version of ProjectTrack. The next step is to add support for Russian.

Localizing for Russian

Now that the messages are internationalized, let's localize them for Russian. All we have to do is update ptrackResources_ru.properties as shown in listing 13.19.

Listing 13.19 ptrackResources_ru.properties: Updated with Russian message text

```
# Messages
InvalidEmail=Введите действующий адрес электронной почты
BadLogin=Неверное имя или пароль
ErrorLoadingUser=Ошибка в базе данных
ErrorLoadingUser_detail=Ошибка в загрузке имени пользователя
ProjectNotFound=выбранный проект не найден
ProjectNotFOund_detail=проект выведен из базы данных
ErrorLoadingProject=Ошибка в базе данных
ErrorLoadingProject_detail=Ошибка в загрузке проекта
ErrorAddingProject=Ошибка в базе данных
ErrorAddingProject_detail=Ошибка в добавления проекта
ContactEmailRequired=Требуется контактный адрес электронной почты
NoProjectAdapter=Системная ошибка
NoProjectAdapter_detail=свойство ProjectAdapter не установлено
ErrorUpdatingProject=Ошибка в базе данных
ErrorUpdatingProject_detail=Ошибка в обновлении проекта
CannotApprove=Вы не можете подтвердить проект со статусом {0}
CannotReject=Вы не можете отменить проект со статусом {0}
```

That's it for internationalizing and localizing ProjectTrack's Java code. Figure 13.8 shows the login page, fully localized for Russian, with a message generated by `AuthenticationBean`.

We've now completed developing a full-fledged JSF application. It's time to talk about what we did and didn't do, and why.

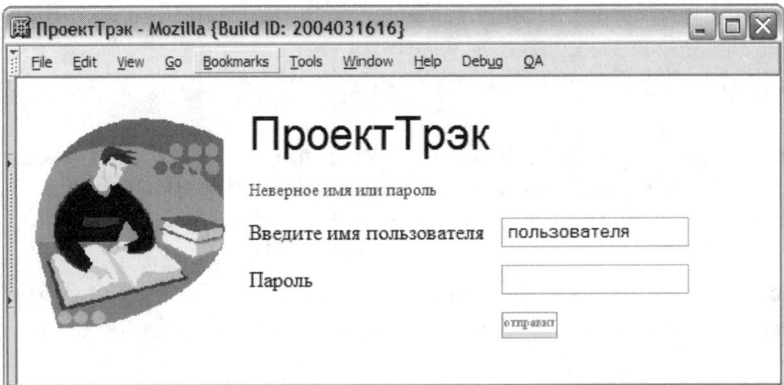

Figure 13.8 The login page localized for Russian

13.4 Design consequences and alternatives

ProjectTrack was designed to demonstrate one possible architecture for a JSF application, and also to help you understand how all of JSF's features can be used in a working piece of software that's more complicated than a typical example. The specific design decisions we made are by no means the only way you can develop a JSF application. Like most things in software development, your optimal solution depends on the specific needs and constraints of your project. In this section, we briefly review the decisions made with ProjectTrack, and talk about some of the alternatives.

13.4.1 Accessing the business layer

In chapter 12 we talked about the different layers of an application. The application layer includes action methods and backing beans like `AuthenticationBean`; the business layer includes objects like `User` and `ProjectCoordinator`.

In practice, this means that the business layer doesn't know anything about JSF and can be unit-tested independently. The application layer, on the other hand, knows about JSF, and can manipulate UI components on based on user input. It's mainly responsible for collecting data, calling the business layer, and then returning a result that JSF uses to select the next view. This type of design is less error-prone and much easier to maintain in the long term, and consequently a necessity for larger projects.

Alternative: implementing business logic and data access in action methods

Even though we highly recommend always using a separate domain layer, it's entirely possible to forgo it entirely and write everything in action methods. This the simple approach we highlighted at the beginning of chapter 12 (see figure 12.1). In this scenario, the action methods perform all of the business logic and talk directly to other systems like databases, web services, or EJB servers. In terms of ProjectTrack, this means that instead of calling the Coordinator objects to get object instances, the action methods would implement this work themselves (or call other methods located in the same class).

WARNING Some tools will default to placing data service objects in backing beans. Be aware of the consequences if you choose to let them do the work for you.

This approach can be faster, so it may work well for prototypes or very small projects. However, it's harder to unit test (because action methods are tied into Faces, which requires different types of testing harnesses), and often less maintainable because the action methods can become bloated. We think of this approach as sort of a slippery slope as the project becomes larger. Even if you want to factor out logic into a separate business layer, the chances of you having the time to do so are slim. Consequently, you could end up with a very brittle application that has data access code, business logic, and application layer code all mixed together.

13.4.2 Organizing beans by function

In ProjectTrack, we took the approach of developing a bean for each class of functions. Each bean manages the data and the action methods for its type of work. The `AuthenticationBean` manages login and logout, the `SelectProjectBean` manages listing and selecting projects (for approval, rejection, or viewing), and so on.

Organizing application code this way means that it's not tied to specific views. For example, `SelectProjectBean` is used by two entirely different pages—Show All and Inbox. The Show All page executes one of the bean's action methods, and the Inbox page executes all three. An entirely different page could easily execute any one of these action methods. There are still constraints—for instance, `SelectProjectBean` expects to be bound to a `UIData` component—but as long as the associated view satisfies those constraints, the backing bean is happy.

This type of organization also makes the system conceptually simple to understand because the code is organized into logical areas of functionality. It's quite obvious, for example, that any functionality related to login and logout should be in the `AuthenticationBean`. What's not so obvious, however, is the relationship between the bean and the view. There's no way you can tell, for example, that `UpdateProjectBean` is associated with both the Approve a Project and Reject a Project pages without looking at the navigation rules.

Alternative: organizing beans by form

An alternative to organizing beans by function is to organize them by form. So, for ProjectTrack, we'd have `LoginForm`, `GetProjectForm`, `ApproveRejectForm`, and so on. This way, each page has an associated form that collects its values (and optionally has associated action methods as well). In this scenario, the emphasis is more on the form that's collecting the values than on the function of the class. The form may or may not expose action methods for operating on those values. Often, IDEs will take this approach—every time you create a new view, they will create a new backing bean for that view.

One possible drawback to this approach is repeated logic for similar pages. You can, of course, combat this with inheritance, but if this happens a lot you could end up with some ugly hierarchies.

Organizing your backing beans by form works well if your action methods are implemented using a service class, which we discuss in the next section.

13.4.3 Action methods implemented by backing beans

Since ProjectTrack's beans are organized around their functionality, each bean exposes one or more action methods that make up the system's functional API. Often it's easier to expose your action methods from backing beans because it allows you to associate data with methods, which is, after all, one of the main features of object-oriented programming. It also avoids the overhead of searching for the bean that holds the data and then calling getter methods to get the data; you can simply use instance variables. In general, we recommend this approach.

The ability to associate action methods directly with data collected from forms is one of the main differences between JSF and Struts. Struts favors separate Action classes and form beans.

Alternative: action methods implemented independently

You can mimic the Struts-style action methods in JSF by writing classes that each have a single action method. This way, the action methods are independent entities that can live in the application scope and are instantiated the first time they're accessed (alternatively, you can initialize them at startup). All backing beans would be completely separate, and the action methods would simply reference the necessary beans.

This approach can yield many tiny classes, as is often the case with Struts Actions. The drawback is that it's not necessarily clear what the relationship is between a view, its backing bean(s), and the action methods. In contrast, when the action method is on the backing bean, it's clear that it was intended to manipulate that bean's properties.

Alternative: action methods implemented by service classes

Another approach is to organize action methods by function. So, you could have a called `ProjectService` class that exposed all of the action methods for the system. You could alternatively have a few service classes that logically grouped different system functions. Each of these services would be registered with the Managed Bean Creation facility (or configured at startup).

This is conceptually similar to the approach ProjectTrack takes, except the service classes would generally be more granular and would not be directly associated with backing bean properties. Instead, they could access backing beans through managed properties or retrieve them with their scoped variable name. In addition, they would probably be application-scoped.

This is roughly equivalent to having a group of Struts Actions at your disposal—the code that performs the work is not directly associated with the values it manipulates. The service's action methods could be stateless, like Struts Actions, or stateful, depending on the needs of your application.

The benefit of this approach is that you have a clear view of your application's functions, and they are well organized. The drawback is the same as using individual action methods: it's hard to see how all of the pieces—views, backing beans, and action methods—are related. This approach is more appealing than creating one class per action method because it's easier to manage (fewer classes) and better organized (several action methods in one class that perform a specific type of work).

13.4.4 Initializing backing bean properties with the Managed Bean Creation facility

ProjectTrack takes a decidedly different approach to associating objects with each other—for the most part, this is done with the Managed Bean Creation facility. Any objects that a backing bean needs are exposed through properties that are configured with the facility. This gives beans strongly typed access to other objects, and severely limits the need to search for related objects in an application scope. The details about what object is available in what scope are managed in a JSF configuration file instead of code.

Because event listeners reference type-safe properties, the code is less error-prone. Also, it's obvious what objects a developer needs to access because they're exposed as properties (through the `BaseBean` class). We highly recommend this approach whenever possible; the only real drawback is the need to edit yet another configuration file and create new properties when you introduce a new dependency.

Alternative: retrieving objects by value-binding expressions

Another option is to use the familiar servlet approach of retrieving objects from different application scopes as necessary. For example, the `Visit` object could be retrieved directly from the session scope, and the coordinator classes could be retrieved from the application scope. There would be no properties to retrieve these objects, but there may be static utility methods that simplify the task.

This approach makes sense to existing servlet developers, and also makes it easy to modify the system when new objects are added to one of the application's scopes. The downside is that you're still forced to worry about where objects are located, and what their keys are—hallmarks of the Servlet API that are somewhat clunky.

If you decide to use this approach, remember to use value-binding expressions when necessary, since they create new object instances for you. So, instead of defining a `visit` property in our `BaseBean` class:

```
Visit visit = getVisit();
```

we would retrieve it through a value binding:

```
Visit visit = (Visit)app.getValueBinding(Constants.VISIT_KEY).
                          getValue(facesContext);
```

Using value bindings ensures that your application code acts in a manner that's consistent with the way UI components retrieve objects.

In general, we highly recommend using strongly typed backing beans and the Managed Bean Creation facility instead of this approach. However, this approach is particularly useful when you're integrating JSF with existing applications that access objects in this way (see chapter 14 for more information on integrating with current applications and Struts).

13.5 Summary

In this chapter, we completed developing ProjectTrack, a full-fledged application based solely on JSF. We began by developing backing beans and action methods—

the core classes that interact with JSF components. We talked about how threading issues may be a concern for beans that aren't stored in request scope, and how action methods should catch and log all exceptions.

Next, we walked through the development of backing beans that handle authentication, as well as loading, updating, and creating projects. For each bean, we examined how they expose properties that are wired to JSF components, and how their action methods used those values to execute classes in the business layer. Each bean was configured via the Managed Bean Creation facility, and we showed examples of using the bean in JSP (from previous chapters).

ProjectTrack's business layer is completely object-oriented, which is the preferred approach for most applications (especially larger ones). However, JSF works equally well with data service objects like JDBC `ResultSets`, so we also examined how ProjectTrack might be implemented if we used `ResultSets` directly instead of objects.

In addition to the application logic, we examined security issues (settling on an authorization filter) and the process of internationalization. Finally, we looked at alternate design choices, like developing a backing bean hierarchy to provide access to common properties, implementing action methods as independent classes, and organizing backing beans by form.

Our tour of ProjectTrack shows how easy it is to develop powerful real-world JSF applications, building on all of the concepts covered earlier in this book. But what if you have an existing application with which you'd like to use JSF's features? If that's the question on your mind, read on to the next chapter. (If not, skip to part 4 to learn how to write custom components, validators, and converters.)

14 Integrating JSF with Struts and existing applications

This chapter covers

- When to use JSF with other frameworks
- Integrating JSF with Struts
- Migrating from Struts to JSF
- Integrating or migrating other types of applications

So far in this book, we've been concentrating on the world of JavaServer Faces. We've looked at what makes a web application a JSF application. We've meticulously surveyed all of the standard components and examined navigation, validation, and type conversion. And we've examined what it's like to build a JSF web application from scratch.

Now it's time to step outside of the box. In the real world, you're likely to have additional concerns like integrating JSF with existing applications and deciding whether you should build new JSF applications in conjunction with another web framework. In this chapter, we examine these issues and provide general guidelines plus detailed instructions for integrating JSF with applications that use Struts [ASF, Struts].

14.1 What integration means

Before we go any further, let's define what we really mean by integration. First, remember that there are two different pieces of the JSF puzzle:

- User interface components, converters, validators, and event handling.
- Application features—navigation, action methods, and so on.

Integration means using either one of these pieces with an application or framework that is not based on a JSF implementation. Usually, your primary interest will be in using the components, and your secondary interest will be integrating the other features.

So, you may have an existing Struts application, but you want to take advantage of JSF components and leave your existing infrastructure (including Struts Actions) intact. Or, you may have a custom-built application that you slowly migrate to JSF, starting with its navigation features and later adding JSF components. Another scenario is developing a new application that uses JSF components and navigation but integrates with another framework for additional features. For example, there is a library that allows you to use JSF in conjunction with Spring [Spring-Faces], which is a framework that focuses more on enterprise application issues.

Now that you know what we mean by "integration," let's look at when it might be necessary.

14.2 When to use JSF with other frameworks

Way back in chapter 1, we talked about all of the Java web application frameworks on the market. You'll recall that we made two main points. The first was that there are too many—frameworks exist in places where there's a hole in the standard platform stack; the Servlet API and JSP have left a hole that dozens of companies and organizations have tried to fill. Second, those frameworks can be broken into two camps: user-interface (UI) frameworks and foundation frameworks.

The main purpose of JSF is to fill this hole so that using another framework isn't a *requirement*. It's primarily a UI framework, but it also has some foundation features, such as page navigation. However, because JSF is new, it may not have all of the bells and whistles your existing toolkit has, so you may want to use the two together. (In chapter 1, figure 1.3 shows the stack of web application features and which of those features are provided by JSF and Struts.)

Okay, so now it's clear that JSF does a lot, but not necessarily everything. It's also clear that JSF has two main features: UI components and basic application infrastructure. So, when should you use something else? Our recommendations are shown in table 14.1.

Table 14.1 Recommendations for when to use JSF with another framework.

Scenario	Recommendation
New small-to-medium scale application	Use JSF by itself. With a standard JSF application, you can still hook into EJBs, web services, databases, and other back-end data sources.
New large-scale application	Build a JSF application but consider another framework for additional services, like template management or client-side validation, if necessary.
Existing framework-based application	Integrate with JSF. The primary benefit of supporting JSF will be third-party components, so look at using UI components first. A safe approach is to simply migrate to using JSF components and then follow the direction of your framework for other services. If, however, you aren't using any advanced framework features, you may want to migrate entirely.
Existing small-to-medium scale application with no framework	Migrate to JSF entirely. This will give you access to JSF components and industry-wide support for core services; you can augment JSF with any additional services your application provides.
Existing large-scale application with no framework	Migrate to JSF entirely, but consider integrating with another framework for additional services, like template management or client-side validation, if necessary.

NOTE Even if you're not a big JSP fan, remember that you can still use JSF without JSP. There's an example of integrating JSF with XUL, Mozilla's XML-based user interface definition language [XUL], in the JSF reference implementation [Sun, JSF RI]. See appendix A for details. You can expect to see more support for JSP alternatives as time moves on.

Now that you know when to integrate JSF with an existing framework or application, let's look at what's involved in such a task.

14.3 The many faces of requests and responses

Throughout this book, we've talked about the Request Processing Lifecycle, which is the set of phases a JSF implementation goes through when it's processing an HTTP request. The goal of this lifecycle is to translate a raw request into events, update components, perform type conversion and validation, and execute application logic. In other words, this lifecycle is what JSF is about: providing a higher-level abstraction for the low-level world of an HTTP request.

This lifecycle is the norm for an application built entirely with JSF. Most requests are Faces requests, and most responses are Faces responses (see the definition for an explanation). But what if you're integrating JSF with an existing application, or you have a JSF event listener or additional servlet that generates its own response (like a dynamically generated image)? In these cases, things get a little more complicated. Your application can receive a Non-Faces request and generate Non-Faces responses as well.

DEFINITION A *Faces request* is any client request that's processed by the normal Request Processing Lifecycle. This means any request that's generated by a JSF `ActionSource` component. A *Faces response* is any response that is generated by the Render View stage of the lifecycle. A *Non-Faces request* is any request that was not initiated by a JSF `ActionSource` component. A *Non-Faces response* is any response that wasn't created by the Render View phase of the request Processing Lifecycle. This would include forwards to non-JSF resources and redirects. Most of the time, a Faces request results in a Faces response.

As it turns out, there are four possible scenarios: a Faces request generates a Faces response, a Faces request generates a Non-Faces response, a Non-Faces request generates a Faces response, and a Non-Faces request generates a Non-Faces response. The different scenarios are depicted in figure 14.1.

It's important to realize that using JSF doesn't limit you to a world of Faces requests and Faces responses. This is essential for integration with other frameworks, because they often have their own request processing lifecycle. If JSF was arrogant enough to require applications to always generate Faces responses, it would be much harder to integrate with those frameworks.

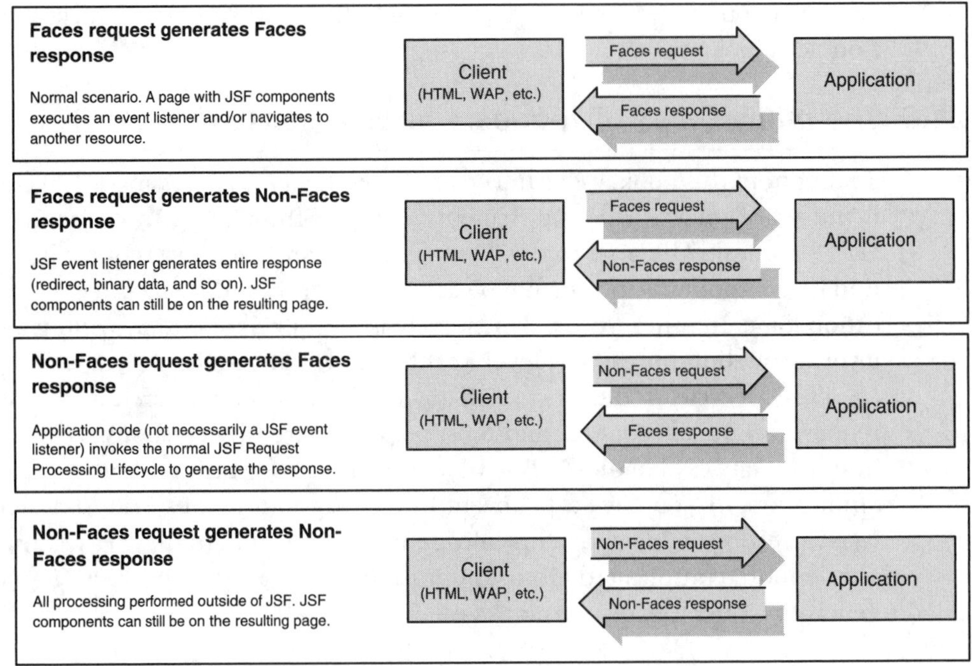

Figure 14.1 The four possible ways that an application can handle requests and responses.

This level of flexibility also allows you to integrate with other, non-JSF servlets in the same web application. As a matter of fact, this is the approach used by the Struts-Faces integration library [ASF, Struts-Faces], which we discuss in the next section. The ability to mix and match JSF processing also makes it easy to migrate your applications over time. Because your existing application and JSF both use the underlying Servlet API, they can access the same application logic.

The best way to understand a concept is with an example, so in the next section, we'll explore integration with Struts, and examine how to combine this approach to make the most out of both frameworks.

14.4 Integrating JSF with Struts applications

Now that we've talked about when to integrate, and how an integrated application differs from a pure JSF application, let's move ahead with a real-world example. There's been a lot of industry speculation about Struts [ASF, Struts] and JSF, and the reality is that you can use the two together today, due to the release of the Struts-Faces integration library [ASF, Struts-Faces]. The library was developed by the original author of Struts and one of the leads for the JSF specification, and, like Struts, is a product of the Apache Software Foundation. This section is primarily geared toward current users of Struts, but even if you're not a Struts user, you may be interested in how the library handles integration of the two technologies.

The primary goal of the library is to provide support for JSF's UI components. This means that you can use JSF components on pages that use normal Struts features like ActionForms, ActionForwards, and Actions. In order to facilitate this process, Struts-Faces includes JSP custom tags, renderers, and UI components that replace existing Struts tags. In most cases, the replacement is extremely straightforward. Most important, you can usually leave your Struts Actions and your application and domain logic untouched.

The library takes the approach of integrating Struts support into the JSF implementation and leaving you access to the traditional Struts `ActionServlet`. This means that Struts-Faces applications can continue to process Struts requests normally, but they can also support all of the combinations of Faces and Non-Faces requests. So, for example, you can have a Faces request that generates a Struts response, as well as a Struts request that generates a Struts response. These options are depicted in figure 14.2.

Struts-Faces supports the different request/response scenarios because it doesn't replace Struts' `ActionServlet` or JSF's `FacesServlet`. It simply allows the two to work together—a Struts-Faces application has an instance of both servlets running.

Faces requests result in Struts responses if the Struts-Faces `<s:form>` tag is used. This is accomplished by replacing JSF's default `ActionListener` implementation with a Struts-Faces `ActionListener`. So, when an `ActionEvent` occurs from a Struts-Faces form, the new `ActionListener` executes a Struts Action instead of a JSF action method. Technically, the Struts Action is executed by a specialized `RequestProcessor` (in Struts, the `RequestProcessor` is responsible for most of the details involved with servicing a request). Figure 14.3 shows this architecture.

In the following sections, we'll examine how to integrate JSF components with an existing Struts application, using JSP as the display technology. Familiarity with Struts and some of its features, like Actions, ActionForms, the Struts Validator, and Tiles, is assumed. (If you're in the market for a book on Struts we highly recommend Ted Husted's *Struts in Action* [Husted].) We'll start with basic steps like adding the proper libraries, and then move on to replacing the old Struts tags with new ones that integrate with JSF. We'll then move on to using Tiles for templating, and take a look at possibilities for integrating Action architectures.

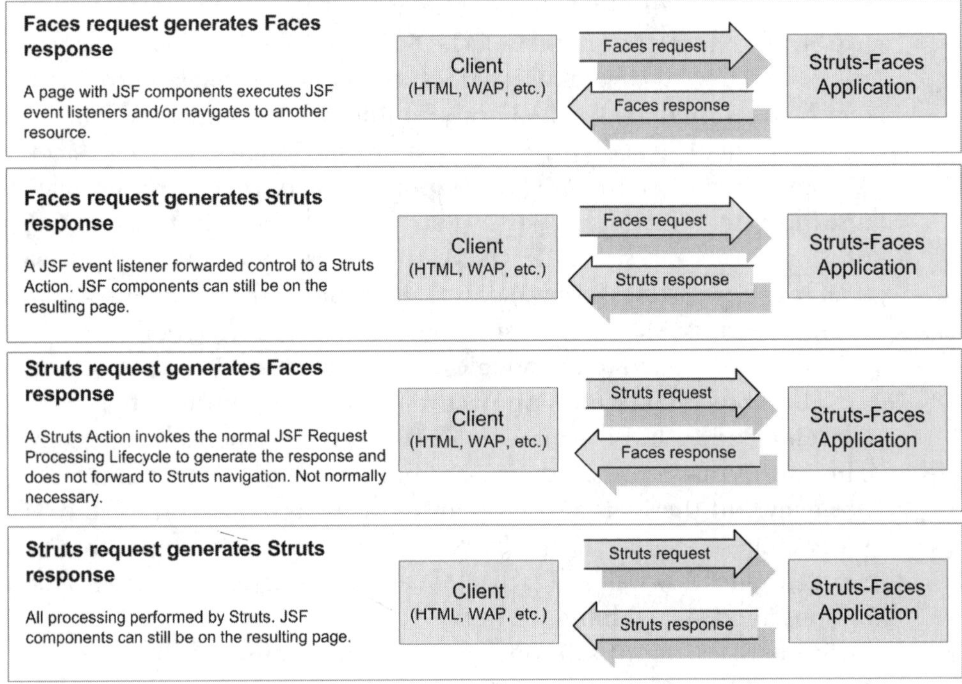

Figure 14.2 The Struts-Faces integration library supports all of the possible scenarios for generating Struts and Faces requests and responses. However, you generally won't genreate a Faces response from a Struts request, unless you're explicitly trying to hook into JSF's navigation features.

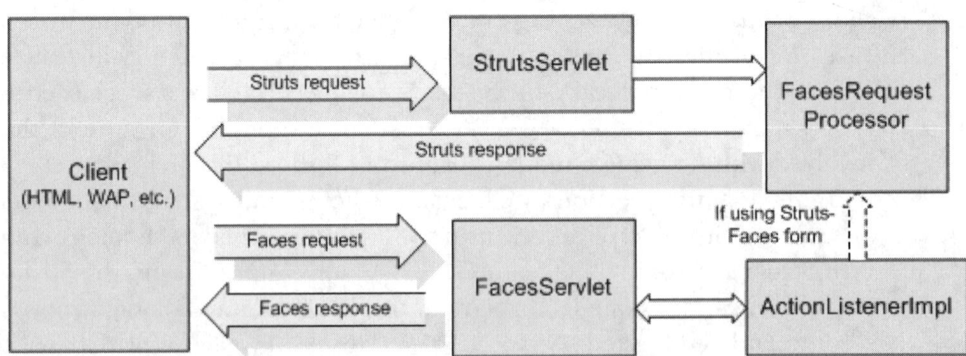

Figure 14.3 The Struts and Faces servlets both work independently; the integration occurs through the Struts-Faces `ActionListener` when using the Struts-Faces form.

If you intend to follow along, you'll need an existing Struts application, the Struts-Faces integration library [ASF, Struts-Faces] and a JSF implementation (either the Sun RI [Sun, JSF RI] or MyFaces [MyFaces]).

NOTE This section is based on Struts-Faces 0.5, which is the most current version at the time of this writing. If you're using a newer version, we recommend that you read the release notes for any changes or updates. Some of the examples in this section are based on the example application included in Struts-Faces, but they may not be exactly the same.

14.4.1 First steps

The first thing you need to do is set up the proper libraries:

1. **Add the Struts-Faces library to your application:** The Struts-Faces library is contained neatly in a single JAR file called struts-faces.jar. Copy this file from the Struts-Faces distribution into your web application's WEB-INF/lib directory.
2. **Add the JavaServer Faces libraries to your application:** If you're using the reference implementation [Sun, JSF RI], the JARs will be called jsf-api.jar and jsf-impl.jar. Copy these two files from your JSF distribution into your application's WEB-INF/lib directory.
3. **Add the JavaServer Pages Standard Template Library (JSTL) to your application:** You can either get these the official JSTL distribution site [Sun, JSTL], or from your JSF implementation. Copy the JSTL JAR files (jstl.jar and standard.jar) into your application's WEB-INF/lib directory.
4. **Add the JSF controller servlet to your web application's deployment descriptor (WEB-INF/web.xml):** This step is also required for any other JSF application:

```
<servlet>
  <servlet-name>Faces Servlet</servlet-name>
  <servlet-class>
    javax.faces.webapp.FacesServlet
  </servlet-class>
  <load-on-startup>1</load-on-startup>
</servlet>
```

Note that `<load-on-startup>` is set to 1 to make sure that `FacesServlet` loads first. Because `FacesServlet` must load first, you must make sure that the Struts servlet, `ActionServlet`, loads second (or even later). This can be done by either omitting the `<load-on-startup>` element from the `ActionServlet` definition, or changing it to 2 or higher:

```
<servlet>
  <servlet-name>Struts Servlet</servlet-name>
    <servlet-class>
          org.apache.struts.action.ActionServlet
  </servlet-class>
  <load-on-startup>2</load-on-startup>
</servlet>
```

5 **Add a servlet mapping for the JSF controller servlet to your web application's deployment descriptor (WEB-INF/web.xml):** Like step 4, this is a normal JSF configuration step:

```
<servlet-mapping>
  <servlet-name>Faces Servlet</servlet-name>
  <url-pattern>/faces/*</url-pattern>
</servlet-mapping>
```

This is an example of prefix mapping; you can also use suffix mapping (see chapter 3 for more about JSF application configuration).

6 **Add the Struts-Faces `RequestProcessor` to your Struts configuration file (WEB-INF/struts-config.xml):** You can do this by adding a `<controller>` element. If you're not using Tiles, use the `FacesRequestProcessor` class:

```
<controller>
  <set-property property="processorClass"
          value="org.apache.struts.faces.
                 application.FacesRequestProcessor"/>
</controller>
```

If you are using Tiles, use the `FacesTilesRequestProcessor`:

```
<controller>
  <set-property property="processorClass"
     value="org.apache.struts.faces.
            application.FacesTilesRequestProcessor"/>
</controller>
```

NOTE If you've developed your own `RequestProcessor`, you'll need to modify it to subclass the appropriate Struts-Faces `RequestProcessor`. Be careful that you don't interfere with any JSF-specific processing (look at the source for the Struts-Faces class first). Of course, if you do this, you must also change the `<controller>` entry in struts-config.xml.

Now that JSF has been added to your Struts application, let's start the integration process.

14.4.2 *Migrating Struts JSP tags*

The JSP custom tags included with Struts-Faces have a single goal: to replace most of the Struts HTML and bean custom tags with equivalents that are based on JSF. The Struts team also advocates replacing the remaining Struts Logic and Bean tag libraries with the equivalent Java Standard Tag Library (JSTL) tags. We won't go into detail about converting your application to use JSTL, but you will see some examples of equivalent tags as we walk through the conversion process. (For information about using JSF with JSTL, see chapter 3.)

The Struts-Faces tags are designed to make conversion a relatively simple process. Some of the tags are direct replacements for Struts tags, and some are intended to be used instead of standard JSF tags. You can import the tag library with the following directive:

```
<%@ taglib prefix="s"
    uri="http://jakarta.apache.org/struts/tags-faces" %>
```

Table 14.2 lists all of the tags with detailed descriptions. Like the standard JSF tags, all attributes of these tags accept value-binding expressions.

Table 14.2 The Struts-Faces integration library includes tags that are replacement for Struts HTML and Bean tags (and a couple of tags that are replacements for standard JSF tags.) All of these tags accept value-binding expressions for attributes.

Struts-Faces JSP Tag	Required Attributes	Optional Attributes	Encoding Behavior
`<s:base>`		`id, rendered, target`	Displays an HTML `<base>` element.
`<s:errors>`		`id, rendered, bundle`	Displays all Struts and JSF messages (if there are any).
`<s:form>`	`action`	`id, rendered, enctype, focus, focusIndex, method, onreset, onsubmit, rendered, style, styleClass, styleId, target`	Displays an HTML `<form>` element associated with a Struts Action.
`<s:html>`		`id, locale, xhtml`	Displays an `<html>` element.
`<s:javascript>`		`cdata, dynamicJava-Script, formName, htmlComment, method, page, src, staticJavascript`	Displays JavaScript validation logic when used in conjunction with the Struts Validator. This doesn't map to a JSF component; it's simply a convenience tag.

continued on next page

Table 14.2 The Struts-Faces integration library includes tags that are replacement for Struts HTML and Bean tags (and a couple of tags that are replacements for standard JSF tags.) All of these tags accept value-binding expressions for attributes. *(continued)*

Struts-Faces JSP Tag	Required Attributes	Optional Attributes	Encoding Behavior
`<s:message>`	`key` or `value`	`id, rendered, styleClass, value, bundle`	Display a localized message from a resource bundle. The key can either be specified literally or retrieved with a value-binding expression via the `value` attribute. You can nest parameters with the JSF `<f:param>` tag.
`<s:loadMessages>`	`var`	`messages`	Stores a `MessageResources` instance (specified by the `message` attribute) as a `Map` in the request scope under the key specified by `var`. This allows the resources to be accessed through value-binding expressions (and JSP 2.0/JSTL expressions); for any key, the `Map` will return the corresponding localized string. If `messages` is not specified, the default `MessageResources` for this Struts application will be used. This tag is the Struts equivalent of the `<f:loadBundle>` tag.
`<s:stylesheet>`	`path`	`id, rendered`	Displays a relative reference to a stylesheet using an HTML `<link>` element.
`<s:subview>`	`id`		Represents a nested JSP fragment (this is equivalent to the JSF `<f:subview>` tag).
`<s:write>`		`id, rendered, value, styleClass, filter`	Displays the specified value (either text or a value-binding expression). If filter is `true` (the default), HTML-sensitive characters will be filtered out.

Table 14.3 lists all of the standard Struts HTML tags and some Struts Bean tags with their Struts-Faces or JSF equivalent.

Table 14.3 For most Struts HTML tags and some Struts Bean tags, there is an equivalent tag in either the Struts-Faces tag library or the standard JSF tag library.

Struts Tag	Struts-Faces Replacement	JSF Standard Tag	Notes
<html:base>	<s:base>		
<html:button>		<h:commandButton>	
<html:cancel>		<h:commandButton id="cancel">	The `id` attribute must be "cancel" in order for it to be treated like the Struts tag. Also, the `immediate` property must be `false` (the default). If it's `true`, then the request will be processed as a normal JSF request instead of a Struts request.
<html:checkbox>		<h:selectBoolean>	
<html:errors>	<s:errors>		
<html:file>			No replacement at this time.
<html:form>	<s:form>		
<html:frame>			No replacement at this time.
<html:hidden>		<h:inputHidden>	
<html:html>	<s:html>		
<html:image>		<h:commandButton image="[url]"/>	
<html:img>		<h:graphicImage>	
<html:javascript>	<s:javascript>		
<html:link>	<s:link>		
<bean:message>	<s:message>		
<html:multibox>		<h:selectBoolean-Checkbox>	
<html:option>		<f:selectItem>	

continued on next page

Table 14.3 For most Struts HTML tags and some Struts Bean tags, there is an equivalent tag in either the Struts-Faces tag library or the standard JSF tag library. *(continued)*

Struts Tag	Struts-Faces Replacement	JSF Standard Tag	Notes
`<html:options>`		`<f:selectItems>`	You must modify your code to return `SelectItem` instances or a `Map` of name/value pairs instead of arbitrary JavaBeans.
`<html:options-Collection>`		`<f:selectItems>`	You must modify your code to return `SelectItem` instances or a `Map` of name/value pairs instead of arbitrary JavaBeans.
`<html:password>`		`<h:inputSecret>`	
`<html:radio>`		`<h:selectItem>` inside `<h:selectOneRadio>`	
`<html:reset>`		`<h:commandButton type="reset">`	
`<html:rewrite>`			No replacement at this time.
`<html:select>`		`<h:selectOneRadio>`, `<h:selectOneListbox>`, `<h:selectOneMenu>`, `<h:selectMany-Checkbox>`, `<h:selectMany-Listbox>`, or `<h:selectManyMenu>`	Choose the proper JSF tag based on the parameters you were using for the Struts `<html:select>` tag. (For example if `multiple` was `false`, use a `SelectOne` component; otherwise use a `SelectMany` component.)
`<html:submit>`		`<h:commandButton>`	
`<html:text>`		`<h:inputText>`	
`<html:textarea>`		`<h:inputTextarea>`	
	`<s:subview>`	`<f:subview>`	
`<bean:write>`	`<s:write>`		
`<html:xhtml>`			No replacement at this time.

Table 14.3 is by no means an exhaustive list of tags that you can use. You're free to mix and match JSTL tags, your own custom tags, and JSF component tags.

NOTE Struts-Faces provides automatic support for DynaBeans and DynaActionForms in JSF value-binding expressions. (DynaBeans are special JavaBeans that store values in a `Map` but expose them as normal properties; DynaActionForms use this feature to allow form properties to be declared in a configuration file instead of code.)

So, if you have a DynaBean available called `myBean` that has a `myProperty` property, you can reference it like a normal JavaBean with the following value-binding expression: `"#{myBean.myProperty}"`. For DynaActionForms, the map property is still supported for backward compatibility. So, if you have a DynaForm called `myForm` with a property called `myProperty`, you can reference the property with either `"#{myForm.myProperty}"` or `"#{myForm.map.myProperty}"`. For more information about DynaForms and DynaBeans, see the Struts site [ASF, Struts] or *Struts in Action* [Husted].

Struts-Faces also supports a special implicit variable, called `struts`, which provides access to Struts-specific objects in value-binding expressions. Table 14.4 lists the properties that it exposes.

Table 14.4 Using the `struts` implicit variable, you can access Struts-specific variables in value-binding expressions. This variable is an instance of the `org.apache.struts.faces.util.StrutsContext` class.

Property	Type	Description
`actionEvent`	`javax.faces.event.ActionEvent`	Current action event for this request (if any).
`actionMapping`	`org.apache.struts.action.ActionMapping`	Action mapping for the current request.
`actionServlet`	`org.apache.struts.action.ActionServlet`	The Struts `ActionServlet` instance.
`dataSource`	`javax.sql.DataSource`	Default application data source (if any).
`exception`	`java.lang.Throwable`	Exception thrown by a Struts tag (if any).
`externalContext`	`javax.faces.context.ExternalContext`	JSF external context.
`facesContext`	`javax.faces.context.FacesContext`	JSF context.

continued on next page

Table 14.4 Using the `struts` implicit variable, you can access Struts-specific variables in value-binding expressions. This variable is an instance of the `org.apache.struts.faces.util.StrutsContext` class. *(continued)*

Property	Type	Description
`locale`	`java.util.Locale`	Locale stored in the user's session for Struts-based localization.
`messageResources`	`org.apache.struts.util.MessageResources`	Default Struts message resources instance.
`moduleConfig`	`org.apache.struts.config.ModuleConfig`	Module configuration for the current module.
`cancelled`	`boolean`	Returns `true` if current request has been cancelled (indicated by a request attribute).

Now that you know which tags are available and how they map to the Struts HTML tags, let's move forward with some concrete examples.

BY THE WAY Some of our analysis is based on the Struts-Faces version of the Struts example application. The plain vanilla version is included in the standard Struts 1.1 distribution [ASF, Struts]. The Struts-Faces library includes two different versions that have been converted to use JSF tags: one that does not use Tiles, and one that does. The examples here may not match the examples in the Struts-Faces distribution exactly.

Converting a simple page

To give you an idea of how simple conversion can be, we'll start by modifying the Main Menu page from the Struts example application. This isn't a very complicated page, but it is fully internationalized and uses Struts Bean and HTML tags. The page in a browser is shown in figure 14.4. The original JSP source for the page appears in listing 14.1.

Listing 14.1 The original mainMenu.jsp from the Struts example application

```
<%@ page contentType="text/html;charset=UTF-8" language="java" %>
<%@ taglib uri="/WEB-INF/struts-bean.tld" prefix="bean" %>
<%@ taglib uri="/WEB-INF/struts-html.tld" prefix="html" %>
<jsp:useBean id="user" scope="session"
             type="org.apache.struts.webapp.example.User"/>
<html:html>
<head>
```

```
  <title><bean:message key="mainMenu.title"/></title>
  <html:base/>
</head>
<body bgcolor="white">
<h3><bean:message key="mainMenu.heading"/>
    <jsp:getProperty name="user" property="username"/>
</h3>
<ul>
  <li><html:link page="/editRegistration.do?action=Edit">
      <bean:message key="mainMenu.registration"/></html:link>
  </li>
  <li><html:link forward="logoff">
      <bean:message key="mainMenu.logoff"/></html:link>
  </li>
</ul>

</body>
</html:html>
```

To convert this page, we'll follow these steps:

1. Remove the Struts tag libraries.
2. Remove the `<jsp:useBean>` tag. This is no longer necessary, because value-binding expressions will find the `User` object in any scope.
3. Add the JSF standard tag libraries with the following directives:

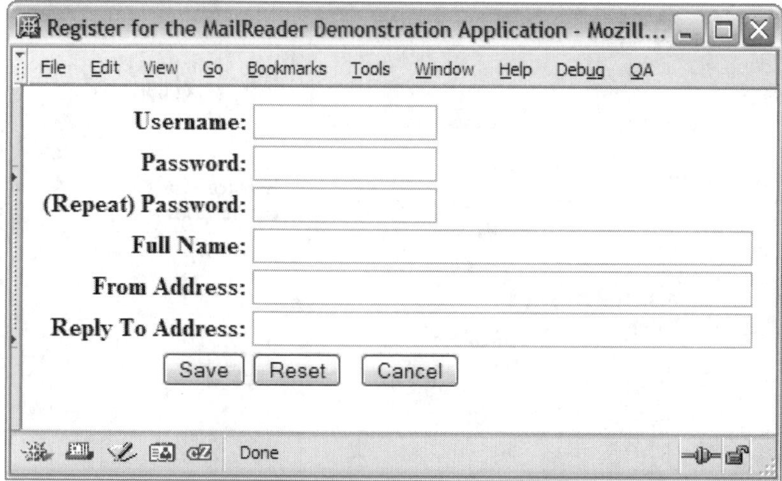

Figure 14.4 We'll start the conversion process with the Main Menu for the Struts example application.

```
<%@ taglib prefix="f"
          uri="http://java.sun.com/jsf/core" %>
<%@ taglib prefix="h"
          uri="http://java.sun.com/jsf/html" %>
```

4. Add the Struts-Faces tag library to the page with the following directive:

   ```
   <%@ taglib prefix="s"
             uri="http://jakarta.apache.org/struts/tags-faces" %>
   ```

5. Enclose all component tags in an `<f:view>` tag.
6. Convert all tags to equivalent Struts-Faces or standard JSF component tags (using tables 14.2 and 14.3).
7. Use `HtmlPanelGrid` or `HtmlDataTable` for layout (this is optional).
8. Change any ActionForwards that point to this page in struts-config.xml to use the `FaceServlet` prefix (/faces/). So, for example, the line

   ```
   <forward  name="success" path="/mainMenu.jsp"/>
   ```

   would be changed to

   ```
   <forward  name="success" path="/faces/mainMenu.jsp"/>
   ```

The converted page is shown in listing 14.2. What's great about this process is that the converted page has identical behavior to the previous page.

Listing 14.2 mainMenu.jsp converted to use JSF tags

```
<%@ page contentType="text/html;charset=UTF-8" language="java" %>
<%@ taglib prefix="f"
          uri="http://java.sun.com/jsf/core" %>       Import JSF
<%@ taglib prefix="h"                                  tag libraries
          uri="http://java.sun.com/jsf/html" %>

<%@ taglib prefix="s"                                  Replace Struts
          uri="http://jakarta.apache.org/              tag libraries
               struts/tags-faces" %>

<f:view>    Add view tag
<s:html locale="true">    Replace
<head>                    Struts tags
  <title>
    <s:message key="mainMenu.title"/>
  </title>
  <s:base/>
  <s:stylesheet path="/stylesheet.css"/>
</head>
<body>
```

```
<h:panelGrid columns="1"
             headerClass="list header"
             rowClasses="list row even,
                         list row odd"
             styleClass="list">
  <f:facet name="header">
    <h:panelGroup>
      <s:message key="mainMenu.heading"/>
      <h:outputText value="#{user.username}"/>
    </h:panelGroup>
  </f:facet>

  <h:outputLink value="editRegistration.do"
                styleClass="link">
    <f:param name="action" value="Edit"/>
    <s:message key="mainMenu.registration"/>
  </h:outputLink>

  <h:outputLink value="logoff.do" styleClass="link">
    <s:message key="mainMenu.logoff"/>
  </h:outputLink>

</h:panelGrid>

</body>
</s:html>
</f:view>
```

Use HtmlPanelGrid for layout

As listing 4.2 shows, updating the page is a combination of simply changing the tag library prefix and replacing or adding new tags. It's also important to note that we're building direct links to the appropriate Struts Actions (editRegistration.do and logoff.do). This means that when a user clicks on one of those links, the request will be processed directly by the Struts `ActionServlet`, not JSF's `FaceServlet`. These are what we called Struts requests in section 14.3.

Now that we've examined a simple example, let's look at something a bit more complicated.

Converting a more complicated page with client-side validation

Our second example is the Edit Registration page of the Struts sample application. It's shown in figure 14.5. The standard Struts JSP source for this page is shown in listing 14.3.

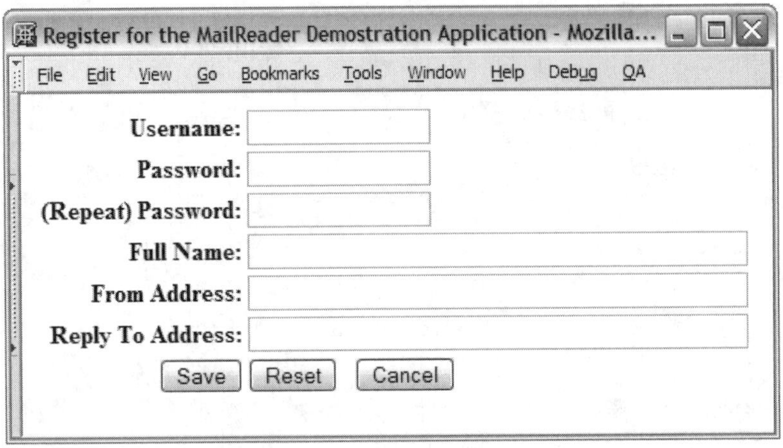

Figure 14.5 Our second example is the registration page of the Struts example application.

Listing 14.3 The original registration.jsp page from the Struts sample application

```
<%@ page contentType="text/html;charset=UTF-8" language="java" %>
<%@ taglib uri="/WEB-INF/struts-bean.tld" prefix="bean" %>
<%@ taglib uri="/WEB-INF/struts-html.tld" prefix="html" %>
<%@ taglib uri="/WEB-INF/struts-logic.tld" prefix="logic" %>

<html:html>
<head>
<logic:equal name="registrationForm"        <-(1) Logic tags used
             property="action"                    for conditionals
             scope="request" value="Create">
  <title><bean:message key="registration.title.create"/></title>
</logic:equal>
<logic:equal name="registrationForm" property="action"
            scope="request" value="Edit">
  <title><bean:message key="registration.title.edit"/></title>
</logic:equal>
<html:base/>
</head>
<body bgcolor="white">

<html:errors/>

<html:form action="/saveRegistration"
         onsubmit="return validateRegistrationForm(this);">
<html:hidden property="action"/>
<table border="0" width="100%">    <-(2) HTML table
                                         used for layout
  <tr>
```

```
  <th align="right">
    <bean:message key="prompt.username"/>:
  </th>
  <td align="left">
    <logic:equal name="registrationForm" property="action"
                 scope="request" value="Create">
      <html:text property="username" size="16" maxlength="16"/>
    </logic:equal>
    <logic:equal name="registrationForm" property="action"
                 scope="request" value="Edit">
    <html:hidden property="username" write="true"/>
    </logic:equal>
  </td>
</tr>

<tr>
  <th align="right">
    <bean:message key="prompt.password"/>:
  </th>
  <td align="left">
    <html:password property="password" size="16" maxlength="16"/>
  </td>
</tr>

<tr>
  <th align="right">
    <bean:message key="prompt.password2"/>:
  </th>
  <td align="left">
    <html:password property="password2" size="16" maxlength="16"/>
  </td>
</tr>

<tr>
  <th align="right">
    <bean:message key="prompt.fullName"/>:
  </th>
  <td align="left">
    <html:text property="fullName" size="50"/>
  </td>
</tr>

<tr>
  <th align="right">
    <bean:message key="prompt.fromAddress"/>:
  </th>
  <td align="left">
    <html:text property="fromAddress" size="50"/>
  </td>
</tr>
```

```
<tr>
  <th align="right">
    <bean:message key="prompt.replyToAddress"/>:
  </th>
  <td align="left">
    <html:text property="replyToAddress" size="50"/>
  </td>
</tr>

<tr>
  <td align="right">
    <html:submit>
      <bean:message key="button.save"/>
    </html:submit>
  </td>
  <td align="left">
    <html:reset>
      <bean:message key="button.reset"/>
    </html:reset>
     
    <html:cancel>
      <bean:message key="button.cancel"/>
    </html:cancel>
  </td>
</tr>
</table>
</html:form>

<html:javascript formName="registrationForm"
        dynamicJavascript="true"
        staticJavascript="false"/>
<script language="Javascript1.1"
        src="staticJavascript.jsp"></script>

</body>
</html:html>
```

❸ **JavaScript from Struts Validator**

Note that in addition to Struts HTML and Bean tags, this page uses Logic tags (❶) and HTML tables (❷) for layout. Consequently, the conversion process requires a little more effort. The integration with the Struts Validator (❸) doesn't require any extra conversion work, but we wanted to show how easy it is to integrate Struts validation. The declaration assumes that the `ValidatorPlugin` is configured in struts-config.xml, and that a rule for `registrationForm` has been declared in the plug-in's configuration file, validator.xml.

Here's the conversion process for this page:

1. Remove the Struts tag libraries.
2. Add the JSF standard tag libraries with the following directives:

```
<%@ taglib prefix="f"
           uri="http://java.sun.com/jsf/core"%>
<%@ taglib prefix="h"
           uri="http://java.sun.com/jsf/html"%>
```

3. Add the Struts-Faces tag library to the page with the following directive:

```
<%@ taglib prefix="s"
           uri="http://jakarta.apache.org/struts/tags-faces"%>
```

4. To replace the Struts Logic tags with the equivalent JSTL tags, add the JSTL tag library to the page: `<%@ taglib prefix="c" uri="http://java.sun.com/jstl/core" %>`
5. Enclose all component tags in an `<f:view>` tag.
6. Convert all Struts HTML or Bean tags to the equivalent Struts-Faces or standard JSF component tags (see tables 14.2 and 14.3).
7. Convert all Struts Logic tags to the equivalent JSTL tags. This is optional but recommended by the Struts team.
8. Change any ActionForwards that point to this page in struts-config.xml to use the `FaceServlet` prefix (/faces/). So, for example, the line

```
<forward name="success" path="/mainMenu.jsp"/>
```

would be changed to

```
<forward name="success" path="/faces/mainMenu.jsp"/>.
```

The converted page is shown in listing 14.4.

Listing 14.4 registration.jsp after conversion to JSF

```
<%@ page contentType="text/html;charset=UTF-8" language="java" %>
<%@ taglib prefix="c"
         uri="http://java.sun.com/jstl/core" %>       Add JSTL tag library
<%@ taglib prefix="f" uri="http://java.sun.com/jsf/core" %>   Import JSF
<%@ taglib prefix="h" uri="http://java.sun.com/jsf/html" %>   tag libraries
<%@ taglib prefix="s"
         uri="http://jakarta.apache.org/struts/tags-faces" %>   Replace Struts tag libraries

<f:view>   <-- Add view tag

<s:loadMessages var="messages"/>   <-- (1) Load MessageResources
<s:html locale="true">   <-- Replace Struts tags
<head>
```

```
  <title>                    Replace Struts Logic tags
  <c:choose>   <--           with equivalent JSTL tags
    <c:when test="${registrationForm.action == 'Create'}">
      <s:message key="registration.title.create"/>
    </c:when>
    <c:when test="${registrationForm.action == 'Edit'}">
      <s:message key="registration.title.edit"/>
    </c:when>
    <c:otherwise>
      UNKNOWN ACTION
    </c:otherwise>
  </c:choose></title>
  <s:base/>
  <s:stylesheet path="/stylesheet.css"/>
</head>
<body>

<s:errors/>

<s:form id="registration"
        action="/saveRegistration"
        focus="username"
        onsubmit="return validateRegistrationForm(this);"
        styleClass="center form">

  <h:inputHidden id="action"
                 value="#{registrationForm.action}"/>

  <h:panelGrid columns="2"
               styleClass="grid"                  (2) Replace HTML table
               headerClass="grid.header"              with HtmlPanelGrid
               columnClasses="grid.column0,
                              grid.column1">

    <%-- Grid header element --%>

    <f:facet name="header">
      <h:panelGroup>
        <c:choose>
          <c:when test="${registrationForm.action == 'Create'}">
           <s:message key="registration.header.create"/>
          </c:when>
          <c:when test="${registrationForm.action == 'Edit'}">
           <s:message key="registration.header.edit"/>
          </c:when>
          <c:otherwise>
           <h:outputText id="unknownActionTitle"
                         value="UNKNOWN ACTION"/>
          </c:otherwise>
        </c:choose>
```

```
  </h:panelGroup>
</f:facet>

<%-- Grid data elements --%>

<h:outputLabel for="username"
               styleClass="label">
  <s:message key="prompt.username"/>
</h:outputLabel>

<h:panelGroup>
  <c:choose>
    <c:when test="${registrationForm.action == 'Create'}">
      <h:inputText id="username"
                   size="16"
                   styleClass="field"
                   value="#{registrationForm.username}"/>
    </c:when>
    <c:when test="${registrationForm.action == 'Edit'}">
      <h:panelGroup id="usernameGroup">
        <s:write filter="true"
                 styleClass="value"
                 value="#{registrationForm.username}"/>
        <h:inputHidden id="username"
                 value="#{registrationForm.username}"/>
      </h:panelGroup>
    </c:when>
    <c:otherwise>
      <h:outputText id="unknownActionMessage"
                    styleClass="value"
                    value="UNKNOWN ACTION"/>
    </c:otherwise>
  </c:choose>
</h:panelGroup>

<h:outputLabel for="password"
               styleClass="label">
  <s:message key="prompt.password"/>
</h:outputLabel>

<h:inputText id="password"
             size="16"
             styleClass="field"
             value="#{registrationForm.password}"/>

<h:outputLabel for="password2"
               styleClass="label">
  <s:message key="prompt.password2"/>
</h:outputLabel>

<h:inputText id="password2"
```

```
                size="16"
                styleClass="field"
                value="#{registrationForm.password2}"/>

    <h:outputLabel for="fullName"
                   styleClass="label">
      <s:message key="prompt.fullName"/>
    </h:outputLabel>

    <h:inputText id="fullName"
                 size="50"
                 styleClass="field"
                 value="#{registrationForm.fullName}"/>

    <h:outputLabel for="fromAddress"
                   styleClass="label">
      <s:message key="prompt.fromAddress"/>
    </h:outputLabel>

    <h:inputText id="fromAddress"
                 size="50"
                 styleClass="field"
                 value="#{registrationForm.fromAddress}"/>

    <h:outputLabel for="replyToAddress"
                   styleClass="label">
      <s:message key="prompt.replyToAddress"/>
    </h:outputLabel>

    <h:inputText id="replyToAddress"
                 size="50"
                 styleClass="field"
                 value="#{registrationForm.replyToAddress}"/>

    <h:commandButton id="submit"
                     type="SUBMIT"
                     styleClass="submit"
                     value="#{messages['button.save']}"/>

    <h:panelGroup>
      <h:commandButton id="reset"
         type="RESET"
         styleClass="reset"
         value="#{messages['button.reset']}"/>
      <h:commandButton id="cancel"
         type="SUBMIT"
         styleClass="cancel"
         value="#{messages['button.cancel']}"/>
    </h:panelGroup>

  </h:panelGrid>
```

3 **Don't reference Struts Action**

```
</s:form>

<s:javascript formName="registrationForm"
              dynamicJavascript="true"
              staticJavascript="false"/>
<script language="Javascript1.1" src="staticJavascript.jsp"></script>

</body>
</s:html>
</f:view>
```

Replace Struts validation tag ❹

The biggest task with this page was converting the HTML table into an `<h:panelGrid>` component tag with a facet for the header, and child components (❷). Doing so, however, gives you some powerful possibilities for layout, and allows you to access `UIComponent` properties for the entire panel (like `rendered`, which lets you control whether or not a component is visible).

NOTE When you use the `<s:form>` tag, you can also register normal JSF event listeners (such as action listener or value-changed listener methods). Struts Actions are used as a replacement for JSF action methods—they don't interfere with the rest of the JSF event-processing model.

Curiously, when tags are converted to `<h:commandButton>`, no `action` attribute is specified (❸). This is because when the button is clicked, the Struts Action associated with the `<s:form>` element will be executed.

Also, note that we used the `<s:loadMessage>` tag to store the default `MessageResources` bundle under the key `bundle` (❶), and that the `UICommand` components (❸) use this bundle to localize their text.

It's also important to note that integrating Struts validation was as simple as converting any other tag (❹)—we just changed the `<html:javascript>` tag to `<s:javascript>`). So, if you're used to the way the Struts Validator works and you want to take advantage of its support of client-side JavaScript, you can do so in conjunction with JSF (as long as your form still subclasses Struts' `ValidatorForm`).

This is all that's required for converting most of your Struts JSP pages to use JSF. However, things are slightly more complicated in the world of Tiles, which we cover next.

Converting Tiles pages

Tiles is a powerful JSP templating system that's tightly integrated with Struts, but can also be used separately. If your JSP pages have Tiles tags, integrating them with JSF requires an extra two steps (assuming you've already configured the `FacesTilesRequestProcessor` as described in section 14.4.1):

1. For any JSPs that use Tiles tags, surround each `<t:insert>` tag with a Struts-Faces `<s:subview>` tag.
2. Add the /faces prefix to all references to that page (either in a Tiles XML file or a JSP).

So, let's assume you had a base layout JSP like the one shown in listing 14.5.

Listing 14.5 The original Struts version of layout.jsp

```
<%@ page contentType="text/html;charset=UTF-8" language="java" %>
<%@ taglib uri="/WEB-INF/struts-bean.tld" prefix="bean" %>
<%@ taglib uri="/WEB-INF/struts-html.tld" prefix="html" %>
<%@ taglib uri="/WEB-INF/struts-logic.tld" prefix="logic" %>
<%@ taglib prefix="t" uri="/WEB-INF/struts-tiles.tld" %>

  <html:html locale="true">
    <head>
      <title>
        <bean:message key="layout.title"/>
      </title>
    </head>
    <body>
      <table border="1" width="100%" cellspacing="5">
        <tr>
          <th colspan="2" align="center">
              <t:insert attribute="header" flush="false"/>
          </th>
        </tr>
        <tr>
          <td width="140" valign="top">
              <t:insert attribute="menu" flush="false"/>
          </td>
          <td align="left" valign="top">
              <t:insert attribute="body" flush="false"/>
          </td>
        </tr>
        <tr>
          <td colspan="2" align="center">
              <t:insert attribute="footer" flush="false"/>
          </td>
        </tr>
      </table>
    </body>
  </html:html>
```

All we need to do replace the Struts tag libraries with Struts-Faces and JSF tag libraries, and then surround each of the `<t:insert>` tags with an `<s:subview>` tag. The result is shown in listing 14.6.

Listing 14.6 Layout.jsp converted to use Struts-JSF tags

```
<%@ page contentType="text/html;charset=UTF-8" language="java" %>
<%@ taglib prefix="f" uri="http://java.sun.com/jsf/core" %>
<%@ taglib prefix="h" uri="http://java.sun.com/jsf/html" %>
<%@ taglib prefix="s"
           uri="http://jakarta.apache.org/struts/tags-faces" %>
<%@ taglib prefix="t" uri="/WEB-INF/struts-tiles.tld" %>

<f:view>
  <s:loadMessages var="messages"/>      <-(1) Load MessageResources
  <s:html locale="true">
    <head>
      <title><s:message key="layout.title"/></title>
      <s:stylesheet path="/stylesheet.css"/>
    </head>
    <body>
      <table border="1" width="100%" cellspacing="5">
        <tr>
          <th colspan="2" align="center">
            <f:subview id="header">
              <t:insert attribute="header"          (2) Surround with <f:subview> tags
                        flush="false"/>
            </f:subview>
          </th>
        </tr>
        <tr>
          <td width="140" valign="top">
            <f:subview id="menu">
              <t:insert attribute="menu" flush="false"/>
            </f:subview>
          </td>
          <td align="left" valign="top">
            <f:subview id="body">
              <t:insert attribute="body" flush="false"/>
            </f:subview>
          </td>
        </tr>
        <tr>
          <td colspan="2" align="center">
            <f:subview id="footer">
              <t:insert attribute="footer" flush="false"/>
            </f:subview>
          </td>
        </tr>
      </table>
```

```
    </body>
  </s:html>
</f:view>
```

Note that we added the Struts-Faces `<s:loadMessages>` tag (❶) so that we can expose the `MessageResources` to all pages that use this template.

You may have noticed that each `<f:subview>` tag (❷) has an identifier that happens to match the name of the Tiles attribute it surrounds. The names don't have to match, but the `<f:subview>` tag does require an identifier.

Since the layout now uses Faces components, its definition must be updated to use the /faces/ prefix so that the JSF servlet will process the page. So, if this layout is defined in a Tiles configuration file, the updated entry would look like this:

```
<definition name=".base" page="/faces/layout.jsp">
  <put name="header" value="/header.jsp"/>
  <put name="footer" value="/footer.jsp"/>
  <put name="menu" value="/blank.jsp"/>
  <put name="body" value="/blank.jsp"/>
</definition>
```

The only change here is the addition of the prefix before the filename of the definition. If this definition were in a JSP as opposed to in a Tiles configuration file, the change would have been made there instead. The bottom line is that anytime you use Struts-Faces or Faces tags on a page, the path must be updated with the /faces/ prefix, unless the file is inserted as part of a Tiles template. The inserted files header.jsp, footer.jsp, and blank.jsp don't require the prefix because they're included in a definition for a page that already has the prefix.

NOTE A side effect of converting a Tiles definition is that all JSPs inserted in the base template will also be processed by JSF. So if you add JSF components to the inserted pages, there's no need to update their Tiles definitions to have the /faces/ prefix (or the .faces suffix); only the file with the Tiles `<t:insert>` tags needs to have the prefix.

As you can see, Struts-Faces was designed to make integration with JSF easy. In most cases, all you have to do is replace Struts tags with Struts-Faces and JSF tags, and change paths that reference the JSP to include the proper prefix.

Just updating the JSPs gives you access to JSF's rich component model and its standard components. It also opens the door for developing custom components as well as using third-party ones. In many cases, this may be the extent of integration you want between Struts and JSF. You can continue to use the Struts Action classes and take full advantage of its controller functionality. However, if you want to take more advantage of JSF's functionality, that's entirely possible too. We take a look at some possibilities in the next sections.

14.4.3 Using JSF action methods and managed beans

So far, we've focused on updating JSPs to use JSF components. All of the procedures we've discussed integrate smoothly with Struts Actions; as a matter of fact, the process should allow you to avoid changing your Struts Actions at all.

One of the limitations of Struts, however, is that Actions and ActionForms are separate. JSF has no such limitation—backing beans can contain both properties and methods. Another nice JSF feature is the Managed Bean Creation facility. The ability to declare objects and have them created automatically can be quite useful.

Fortunately, Struts-Faces allows you to use these features in Struts applications, too. You can use ordinary action methods and managed beans just as you would in a pure JSF application. In order to access JSF event listeners, all you have to remember is not to use the Struts-Faces variant of the `<form>` tag. You can, however, mix both Struts-enabled forms and regular JSF forms:

```
<f:view>
...
   <s:form action="/hitMe">
    ...
    <h:commandButton value="Hit me with those digits!"/>
   </s:form>

   <h:form>
   ...
    <h:commandButton value="Hit me with those digits!"
                     action="#{myBean.hitMe}"/>
   </h:form>
</f:view>
```

In this snippet, the top form submits to the Struts Action `/hitMe`, while the bottom form submits to the JSF action method `myBean.hitme`. `myBean` could have been configured and created by the Managed Bean Creation facility as usual.

Of course, you don't have to mix the two types of forms on the same page. You can always use one or the other. And remember, you can still use normal JSF event handlers (value-changed listeners, action listeners, and any custom listeners) on any page that has been converted to use JSF components.

You may be wondering what happens if you use a JSF action method with a converted Struts application. The answer depends on what you want to happen. One option is to forward control to a Struts action; we discuss this next.

Invoking Struts Actions from JSF event handlers

Struts has no notion of server-side event handlers (other than Struts Actions themselves) for UI components. So, let's say you had an enhanced `UISelectOne` component that generated a `ValueChangedEvent` every time the user selected a new value. (We assume that the control generates client-side JavaScript to automatically submit the form.) If you wanted to forward control to a different Struts Action based on the value of the `UISelectOne` component, you could do so in a `ValueChangedListener`.

Also, if you've decided to migrate from Struts Actions to JSF action methods, you can start by simply wrapping existing Struts actions. Later, you can incrementally move the functionality from Struts Actions to JSF actions (presumably migrating the navigation rules as well).

Fortunately, it's easy to invoke Struts Actions from JSF event handlers. All that's necessary is to forward the request to the Struts Action using the `ExternalContext`. For example, let's say you wanted to forward control to a Struts Action called `hitMe` with a request parameter called `digits` that had the value "23". You could do so like this:

```
public String hitMe()
{
  FacesContext context = FacesContext.getCurrentInstance();
  String url = "/hitMe.do?digits=23";
  try
  {
    context.getExternalContext().dispatch(url);
  }
  catch (IOException e)
  {
    throw new FacesException(e);
  }
  finally
  {
    context.responseComplete();
  }
 return null;
}
```

All we're doing here is creating a URL to call the Struts Action directly, and then calling the `dispatch` method of the `ExternalContext` to actually forward the URL. In servlet environments, this just calls `RequestDispatcher.forward`, which internally forwards the request to the named resource. Since the Struts `ActionServlet` will process the forwarded request, we've given control back to the world of Struts, directing it to a specific Struts Action.

This example is an action method, but the same block of code (minus the return statement) could be used inside a `ValueChangedListener` or any other JSF event handler. This is a handy way to integrate JSF event handling with the normal Struts controller architecture.

If you're more interested in sharing business logic between the two controller architectures, then you're better off having the two different types of Actions call the same business logic directly. (If your business logic resides inside of a Struts Action, this is a good time to refactor it into separate classes.) We discuss the idea of using both controller architectures in the next section.

14.4.4 Who's controlling whom?

When you convert Struts JSPs to use JSF components, you're integrating with JSF's component model, but the back-end still uses Struts controller architecture, complete with its Action classes, ActionForwards, and so on. In the previous section, we showed how to call Struts Actions from JSF event handlers, but in that scenario, Struts is still controlling the final outcome.

With the Struts-Faces library, you can actually use the Struts controller architecture, JSF's controller architecture, or both at the same time. The general rule is that if you use the normal JSF `<h:form>` tag on a JSP page, the request will be handled like a normal JSF request. If you use the Struts-Faces `<s:form>` tag, the request will be handled as a JSF request, and then as a Struts request (instead of invoking action methods). When the request is handled as an ordinary JSF request, your JSP can either integrate with Struts (as shown in the previous section) or use standard JSF navigation features.

The primary reason for supporting both architectures is ease of migration. If you wanted to migrate your entire application to JSF, for example, you could start with the JSPs, and then slowly migrate the Actions and ActionForwards one by one. At some point, half your application would be using the Struts controller and the other half would use the JSF controller architecture. When you finished, your entire application's Action logic and navigation would be based on JSF.

In general, you should stick with one controller architecture or the other. If you begin to mix the two, your application could become messy and hard to decipher. Just imagine joining a project with a bunch of Struts Actions and ActionForwards intermixed with JSF action methods and navigation rules—it would be quite hard to figure out the application's logical flow. Restricting the core functionality—Actions and navigation—to one of the two architectures will make your applications easier to maintain.

14.5 Integrating JSF with non-Struts applications

All of our discussions about integrating Struts is fine and dandy, but what if you're not using Struts? What if you're using another foundation framework or no framework at all? We can make some observations from the way Struts-Faces is written.

Recall from section 14.4 that Struts-Faces works by allowing an application to use either JSF's `FacesServlet` or Struts' `ActionServlet` to process requests. This underscores a key fact about web applications—they can have multiple, cooperating servlets. If you think of JSF as "just another servlet," then things become a little clearer. As long as you've exposed your application objects in the proper web application scope, a JSF event handler can access it. Conversely, any objects your JSF code (or the Managed Bean Creation facility) create can be accessed by your non-JSF application logic, as long as it's all packaged in the same web application. Figure 14.6 shows an example of this.

Figure 14.6 shows that both your existing application and new JSF code can access the same application beans and business logic. Of course, if all of your business logic isn't packaged into easily accessible objects, this scenario won't work. (So, if you have all of your business logic in one big servlet, now might be the time to do some refactoring.)

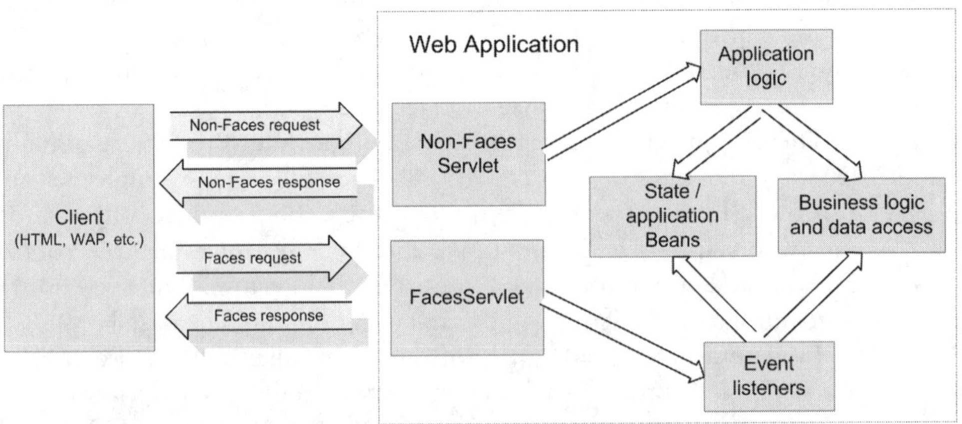

Figure 14.6 The key to integrating with JSF is understanding that you can have multiple servlets, and that application logic in a JSF environment and a non-JSF environment can access the same objects, as long as they're in the same web application.

The most important thing to keep track of is when a Faces request is being created, and when a Non-Faces request is being created. The rules are simple; see section 14.3 for details.

As is the case with Struts integration, we highly recommend that you use JSF's controller architecture *or* your existing one. Only use both while performing a complete migration. It is, however, acceptable to mix and match on a module basis.

So, if you have a new Order Tracking application that was built with JSF, it's perfectly logical to integrate it with a User Management module that was written using plain old servlets and WebMacro [WebMacro] for templating a few years ago and is widely deployed throughout your organization. This level of flexibility is one of the core design goals of JSF—it plays well with the existing servlet world, while simultaneously making that world more powerful.

Also, remember that JSF is an extensible architecture—just about every feature, from managed bean creation to displaying views—can be easily customized. Struts-Faces takes advantage of this extensibility to integrate the two frameworks seamlessly. See online extension appendix C for more information on extending JSF.

14.6 Summary

In this chapter, we took a look at integrating JSF with existing applications and frameworks. There are two different levels to JSF integration: using UI components (and associated event handlers, validation, converters, and so on), and using action methods and navigation (the controller functionality). Your level of integration will depend on the services your application currently provides and how they supplement the services JSF provides.

A concrete integration example is the Struts-Faces library [ASF, Struts-Faces], which allows you to use JSF within existing Struts applications. It provides a JSP tag library that replaces many Struts tags, and allows you to use UI components on pages that ultimately execute Struts Actions. It's also possible to use JSF actions and navigation in the same application.

Struts-Faces integrates with Struts by enhancing JSF's functionality, allowing both the Struts servlet and the JSF servlet to coexist. This is the approach you can use to integrate JSF with applications that don't use Struts. The important thing to remember is that since your application logic and business logic objects reside in normal web application scopes, they can be accessed by code that's executed by JSF actions or your existing application.

Part 4

Writing custom components, renderers, validators, and converters

In part 4, we show you how to create your own components, renderers, validators and converters. We explain the JSF APIs from a component developer's perspective, and also examine issues such as JSP integration and component packaging. Part 5 expands upon this foundation with several concrete examples. You will find part 5 in the online extension available for download at www.manning.com/mann.

15 The JSF environment: a component developer's perspective

This chapter covers

- How to write custom components, renderers, validators, and converters
- When to write a component or a renderer
- Internationalizing components
- Packaging components

As we've shown throughout this book, JavaServer Faces has several services that enable you to build web applications quickly. The real power of JSF, however, isn't the fact that it has some standard components available out of the box, or that IDE vendors provide additional components. The power lies in its component model and an extensible architecture that allows you and third parties to create your own user interface (UI) extensions—components, renderers, validators, and converters.

In this chapter, we'll introduce you to the classes and interfaces that you'll encounter when you build UI extensions, and give you advice for typical use cases. This chapter builds on the application environment details we discussed in chapter 11, so we highly recommend you read that chapter first. We also cover the more mundane side of the picture—configuration, and integration with a display technology like JSP.

NOTE This chapter provides an overview of how to create UI extensions and refers to detailed examples that are part of the online extension (http://www.manning.com/mann).

15.1 Three steps to UI extension nirvana

Implementing a custom JSF UI extension requires three key steps:

1. **Subclassing the appropriate classes and/or implementing the necessary interfaces:** Usually there is a specific class or interface you have to subclass. You may also need to implement additional interfaces or use other helper classes for additional functionality.
2. **Adding the proper configuration entries to a JSF configuration file:** Like most things in the world of JavaServer Faces, you can configure UI extensions in a JSF XML configuration file. As a matter of fact, this is how all of the default UI extensions are defined in the reference implementation [Sun, JSF RI]. For every extension you develop, you must have a corresponding configuration entry.[1]

   The configuration entries are used to initialize the `Application` instance, and also by tools for useful things like displaying an icon and a descriptive name on a component palette. In this chapter, we describe the basic entries required to register UI extensions; online extension appendix D covers every element in detail.

[1] You can also configure them in code, but this is rarely done by anyone other than those writing the code to parse the configuration files.

3 **Integrating your new class with a display technology such as JSP:** The last step is integrating your class with the display technology. Usually this means relating some set of XML tags, or special tokens, to a specific UI component, `UIComponent/Renderer` pair, `Validator`, or `Converter` instance. In the world of JSP, this means implementing custom tags. The tags map their attributes to user extension properties and attributes, and create new UI extension instances if necessary.

Because JSP is required by the JSF specification, we'll examine JSP integration in detail. This involves writing a tag handler class and updating a tag library descriptor (TLD). (We won't cover the ins and outs of developing tag handlers—only enough for you to begin developing JSF-specific tags; see *Web Development with JavaServer Pages, 2nd Edition* [Fields] for a deep discussion of the topic.) Even though we focus on JSP, integrating a UI class with another display technology is as simple as implementing the equivalent of a custom tag for that technology.

NOTE JSF was designed to work with JSP 1.2. In order to ensure that this code works with the multitude of environments that still use JSP 1.2, all of the JSP integration code presented in this book is based on JSP 1.2. You can develop JSF applications with JSP 2.0, but you cannot integrate UI extensions using JSP 2.0 tag files unless you duplicate the functionality of the JSP 1.2 base classes included with JSF.

In the rest of this chapter, we cover classes, interfaces, and configuration elements you'll need to perform these three steps for UI components, renderers, validators, and converters.

15.2 Developing UI components

The standard JSF components serve a larger purpose than just providing basic UI controls; they give you a base from which you can develop your own components. If you're as anxious as I am to avoid reinventing the wheel, then understanding how to leverage the work that Sun and its partners have done with JSF will save you a lot of time.

Before we begin, it's worthwhile to note that the skill set for UI component development is somewhat different than the skill set required for developing UIs or writing application code. Component development requires more detailed knowledge of HTTP, the Servlet API, and most important, the underlying markup language (in this case, HTML, and CSS). Remember, the purpose of developing a component is to hide the complexity of a particular piece of UI functionality. In other words, you, as a component writer, must deal with that complexity so that a front-end developer can happily drag the component from a tool palette and drop it onto a form.

The development process itself is relatively straightforward: write your UI component, register it in a JSF configuration file, and then integrate it with a display technology. Your UI component will usually subclass one of the existing components, such as `UIInput`, `UIOutput`, or `UIData`. These classes will typically subclass `UIComponentBase` (at some level) and implement one or more additional interfaces. (See chapter 11, figure 11.2 for a class diagram of the core UI component classes and interfaces.) If you want to provide strongly typed properties for renderer-dependent attributes, you can also write a renderer-specific component, like the standard HTML components. If you're using JSP, integrating a new component involves writing the tag handler and registering it in a TLD. All of the different pieces are pictured in figure 15.1.

So, now it should be clear what expertise you need, and what possible classes and files you need to work with. But when should you write a new component?

15.2.1 Deciding when to write a UI component

If you think you need to write a UI component, the first question you should ask yourself is "What, exactly do I need to do?" Writing a new UI components is a good solution for the following:

- Supporting standard HTML features, like frames or file uploads, that are not supported by the standard components.
- Providing nonvisual added functionality to an existing UI component, such as making the columns in `UIData` sortable automatically. (The MyFaces JSF implementation [MyFaces] has such a component.) If your changes are purely cosmetic, consider using a renderer instead. Our `RolloverButton-Renderer` (online extension chapter 17) is in this category—the only change it makes to `UICommand` is augmenting its output with JavaScript for rollovers.
- Creating a new type of component, like an RSS headline viewer (online extension chapter 18), a date input field with three drop-down listboxes (online extension chapter 16), a toolbar (online extension chapter 19), menus, tabbed panes, tree views, and so on.
- Supporting component functionality for another markup language that isn't supported in the standard component set. For example, some wireless

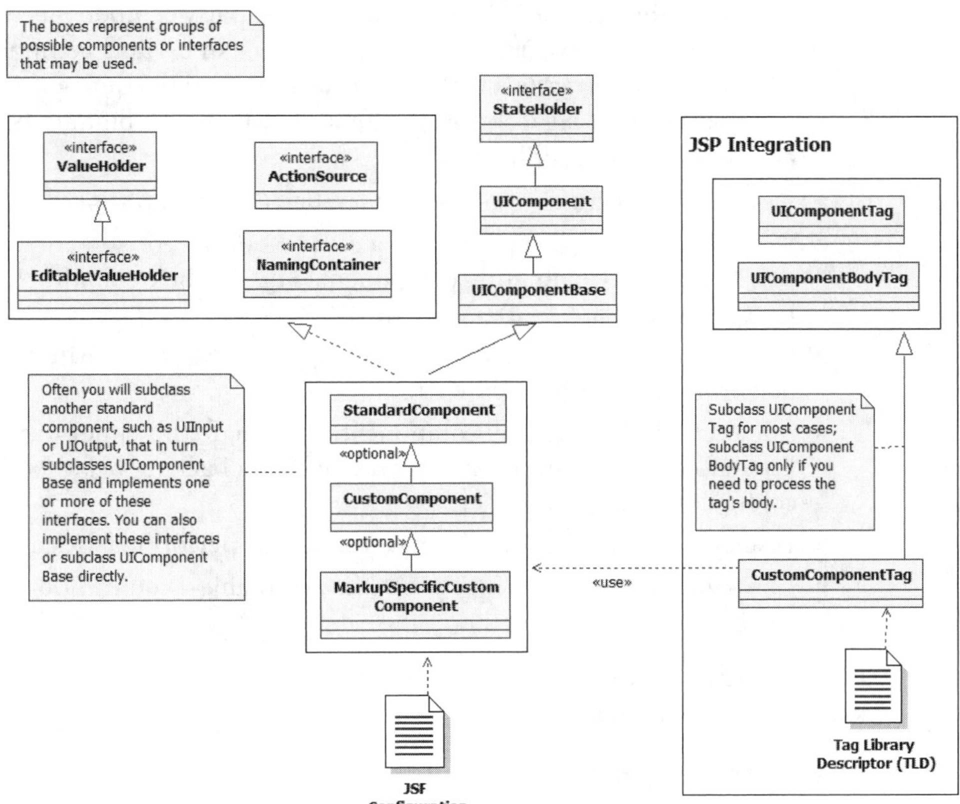

Figure 15.1 Class diagram of UI component development elements. Your UI component class will usually subclass one of the standard components, such as `UIInput` or `UIOutput`, which will subclass `UIComponentBase` and implement interfaces such as `ValueHolder`. You can optionally create a markup-specific subclass, like the standard HTML components (`HtmlOutputText`, `HtmlDataTable`, and so on). The component also must be registered in a JSF configuration file. If you're integrating with JSP, you need to write a custom component tag handler, which can subclass either `UIComponentTag` or `UIComponentBodyTag`, and must be configured in a tag library descriptor (TLD).

devices can visualize tickers and progress bars, which aren't supported by the standard components. You would typically develop a new renderer in this scenario as well. However, if you need to support a standard UI control (like a text field) for another device, then you're better off just writing a renderer and using an existing component (like `UIInput`).

You also should answer this question: "Can I do this any other way?" Remember, you can do all of these things *without* writing a new component:

- Use any of the standard components, or third-party components from your IDE vendor or elsewhere. Make sure there isn't an existing component you can use before you write a new one. To keep track of the third-party component market, visit JSF Central [JSF Central], which is a community site with an extensive product directory.
- Format an existing component. Remember, CSS can do a lot.
- Display an existing component on a different device, or add additional display behavior to an existing component. This can be done with a renderer instead (see section 15.3).
- Perform special business logic for a component. See if you can do this with one or more event listeners first.
- Add event listeners to a UI component. You can do this either with an event listener class or an event listener method in a backing bean; both can be configured through JSP.
- Display an object in a specific way—this can be performed with a converter.
- Check to make sure the user's input is acceptable—you can do this with a validator or validator method.

If you are still anxious to develop your own component (or at least interested in knowing how), read on.

15.2.2 Classes and interfaces

In chapter 11, we covered a good amount of the UI component world. There are some additional bits and pieces we omitted, however, that are helpful for component development—some `UIComponent` methods, and details on interfaces like `StateHolder` and `NamingContainer`, and so on. In the following sections, we provide additional information about the UI component classes and interfaces that will aid you on your component development journey.

UIComponent and UIComponentBase

All UI components descend from the `javax.faces.component.UIComponent` abstract base class. We covered the basic `UIComponent` methods in chapter 11, so we won't repeat them here; instead, we'll concentrate on the ones that pertain to component development.

Before we continue, however, it is important to repeat the distinction between attributes and properties. Recall that UI components can have renderer-independent properties (like `layout`) and renderer-specific attributes like `cellpadding`.

Both attributes and properties can be retrieved through the `attributes` property of `UIComponent`. The HTML component subclasses provide strongly typed properties for renderer-specific attributes, but doing so is not required.

Even though `UIComponent` isn't an interface, subclassing it directly isn't trivial—it has quite a few methods and has no default method implementations. Unless you have a lot of time on your hands, you're better off subclassing `UIComponentBase`, which provides default implementations of every method (except one). This means it already has support for managing event listeners, events, value-binding expressions, and so on. You can also subclass an existing component that has most of the functionality you desire; all of the standard components subclass `UIComponentBase` either directly or indirectly.

The remainder of this section refers to `UIComponentBase`, as opposed to `UIComponent`. Let's start with the `clientId` property:

```
public String getClientId(FacesContext context);
```

The `getClientId` method returns the component's client identifier. Recall that the client identifier is derived from the component identifier (the `id` property), and is the name used on the client. You should use this method any time you're outputting a client-side identifier, like the `name` or `id` attribute of an HTML element. (See chapter 2 for a thorough discussion of client identifiers.)

As we discussed in chapter 11, every component has a *type*, which is a standard name by which it can be referenced. For example, `UIOutput`'s type is `javax.faces.Output`, and `HtmlDataTable`'s type is `javax.faces.HtmlDataTable`. This type is configured in a JSF configuration file (see section 15.2.4). So that developers don't have to memorize each component's type, it is normally available as a constant:

```
public static final String COMPONENT_TYPE = "myNamespace.myComponentType";
```

This allows developers to use the constant to create new instances of your component through the `Application` class. You should declare this constant even if you subclass a concrete UI component class, since your new class is a new *type* of component (assuming that you're not trying to *replace* an existing component with your own implementation, which is what happens if you use an existing type). There is no property that exposes the type.

Throughout this book, we've grouped UI components into different families. The family is exposed as a read-only property:

```
public abstract String getFamily();
```

This is the only method that `UIComponentBase` doesn't implement. Usually you just return the `COMPONENT_FAMILY` constant:

```
public static final String COMPONENT_FAMILY = "myNamespace.myComponentFamily";
```

Families are used to help renderers decide if they know how to handle a particular component. They often map to the superclass—in other words, a UI component and all of its subclasses are usually in the same family because they have similar characteristics. Consequently, if you subclass a concrete UI component, there's no need to change the family unless you know that existing renderers won't be able to display your component.

NOTE For both `family` and type, the prefix "javax.faces." is reserved for standard JSF components. When you develop your own components, you can use the standard families if your component has similar behavior. This will allow JSF to select the proper renderer based on family and component type. You should not, however, create new families with the "javax.faces." prefix.

Once you've defined the type and `family`, it's time to implement the methods to perform the actual work. In simpler cases, this simply requires overriding one or more of the following methods:

```
public void encodeBegin(FacesContext context) throws IOException;
public void encodeChildren(FacesContext context) throws IOException;
public void encodeEnd(FacesContext context) throws IOException;
public void decode(FacesContext context);
```

The first three methods are for displaying (encoding) the component, and the latter is for interpreting browser input and updating the component accordingly (decoding). The encoding process starts with a call to `encodeBegin`. After `encodeBegin` completes, `encodeChildren` is called *if* the `getRendersChildren` method returns `true`. (It returns `false` by default, so you should override it and return `true` if your component wants to displays its own children. Otherwise, the child components will display themselves normally through calls to their own encoding methods.) Next, `encodeEnd` is called. If your component does not have children, you can put all of your encoding logic in `encodeBegin`.

TIP You should only begin encoding if the `rendered` property is `true`.

So, what is encoding logic? Basically just outputting markup directly to a `ResponseWriter` instance. Here's an example that outputs an `<input>` element:

```
public void encodeBegin(FacesContext context) throws IOException
{
  if (!isRendered())
  {
    return;
  }

  String clientId = getClientId(context);
  ResponseWriter writer = context.getResponseWriter();

  writer.startElement("input", this);
  writer.writeAttribute("name", clientId, "id");
  String value = (String)getValue();
  ...
  writer.writeAttribute("value", value, "value");
  ...
  writer.writeAttribute("type", "submit", "type");
  ...
  writer.endElement("input");
}
```

This code checks to make sure that the component should be rendered, and then writes an HTML input element with the component's current value. Note that the client identifier is output as the value of the `name` attribute. The output would look something like `"<input name='id01' value='Click me!' type='submit'>"`. As you can see, this code retrieves a `ResponseWriter` instance from the `FacesContext`, which it uses to output data. The `ResponseWriter` is suitable for all text output, and has useful methods for generating markup. Its `startElement` method's last parameter is the UI component itself; this is used by tools to associate output with your component. (Use `ResponseStream`, also available from the `FacesContext`, for binary output.)

BY THE WAY If you're thinking you should be able to declare the component's output in a template (like a JSP page or an XML file), you're not alone. This currently isn't supported in JSF 1.1, but will most likely be added in a future version of the specification.

All interpretation of client input is handled through the solitary `decode` method. If your component doesn't accept user input, this method will do nothing. Otherwise, you might use it to grab one or more response parameters and then apply them to your component's local value, performing conversions if necessary. You also might translate a request value into an event. Here's a sample decode method:

```
public void decode(FacesContext context)
{
  if (!disabled())
  {
    String type = (String)getAttributes().get("type");
    String clientId = getClientId(context);
    Map requestParameterMap =
         context.getExternalContext().getRequestParameterMap();

    /* If the type is not "reset", and there's a request
       parameter equal to the client id. The "x" and "y" are sent
       by the browser if an image was clicked for the button. We
       don't care what the values are, since no value is actually
       changed. We just want to make sure the request  parameter
       is there, which means that the button was clicked. */
    if (type == null || !type.equalsIgnoreCase("reset")) &&
          ((requestParameterMap.get(clientId) != null) ||
           (requestParameterMap.get(clientId + ".x") != null) ||
           (requestParameterMap.get(clientId + ".y") != null)))

      {
        queueEvent(new ActionEvent(this));
      }
}
```

This code first checks to make sure that the component is disabled. If not, the method looks for a request parameter that starts with the component's client identifier, and then creates and enqueues a new `ActionEvent` if it finds the right parameter (we cover `queueEvent` later in this section). Note that we use the client identifier in both the encoding and decoding methods. That's the whole point—to allow us to relate the client's representation of the component to the server instance.

TIP Do not decode a component if it has been disabled. A component is considered disabled if the `rendered` property is `false`. With HTML components, a component is also considered disabled if its `disabled` or `readonly` attribute is `true`. Non-HTML components may have different renderer-specific attributes that indicate whether they are disabled.

These four methods are the primary ones you'll use to encode or decode your component. You can, however, delegate rendering to a separate `Renderer` class instead of implementing it directly. As a matter of fact, this is what `UIComponentBase` does by default, so there's no need to override them if that is the behavior you desire. The renderer is determined by its type (like UI components):

```
public String getRendererType();
public void setRendererType(String rendererType);
```

UI components usually set their default renderers in their constructors. For example, here's the constructor for `UIInput`:

```
public UIInput()
{
  super();
  setRendererType("javax.faces.Text");
}
```

Note that unlike UI components, renderers usually don't declare constants, simply because you never know exactly what their concrete class is.

You can retrieve an instance of the current renderer (if one is available) from the current `RenderKit` based on the component's type and family. `UIComponentBase` has a convenience method that does this for you:

```
protected Renderer getRenderer(FacesContext context);
```

Renderers are quite powerful, but they're not really necessary for simpler components that you don't intend to use with other markup languages or redistribute. In these cases, you can just override the previous methods. (We discuss renderers in section 15.3.)

The following methods are used for event handling:

```
protected void addFacesListener(FacesListener listener);
protected FacesListener[] getFacesListeners(Class clazz);
protected void removeFacesListener(FacesListener listener);
public void queueEvent(FacesEvent event);
public boolean broadcast(FacesEvent event, PhaseId phaseId)
        throws AbortProcessingException;
```

`addFacesListener`, `getFacesListeners`, and `removeFacesListeners` are convenience methods for adding event listeners to your component. `UIComponentBase` manages the list of listeners for you, so you can support new types of listeners by just delegating to these methods. For example, here's how `UINavigator` (covered in online extension chapter 19) uses these methods:

```
public void addActionListener(ActionListener listener)
{
  addFacesListener(listener);
}

public void removeActionListener(ActionListener listener)
{
  removeFacesListener(listener);
}
```

```
public ActionListener[] getActionListeners()
{
  return (ActionListener[])getFacesListeners(ActionListener.class);
}
```

As you can see, these are just type-safe wrappers for the `UIComponent` methods, but they're required for `ActionSource` components like `UINavigator`. You will have to write these three for every type of event you need to support.

`UIComponentBase` also manages a list of all of the events currently enqueued on the component; the `queueEvent` method can be used to add a new event to this list. This is typically done during decoding, as shown earlier. The `broadcast` method dispatches an event to all interested listeners with a specific `PhaseId` value. Usually there's no need to override any of these methods, but you'll often use them.

BY THE WAY `UIComponentBase` also has several methods that are called for each phase in the Request Processing Lifecycle. They provide all component-based processing for each phase, recursively walking through the entire component tree. Usually, there is no need to override or call these methods directly, so we won't cover them here. For more information, see the JavaDocs included with your JSF implementation.

In addition to overriding these methods, your custom component will usually expose its own set of new properties such as `layout` or `pattern`. These are normal JavaBean properties that affect the component's behavior. You can enable value-binding expressions by using the `getValueBinding` and method of `UIComponent`, which we covered in chapter 11. As an example, here's the `required` property of the `UIInput` in the JSF reference implementation [Sun, JSF RI]:

```
private boolean required = false;
private boolean requiredSet = false;

public boolean isRequired()
{
  if (this.requiredSet)
  {
    return (this.required);
  }
  ValueBinding vb = getValueBinding("required");
  if (vb != null)
  {
    return (Boolean.TRUE.equals(vb.getValue(getFacesContext())));
  }
  else
```

```
    {
      return (this.required);
    }
  }

  public void setRequired(boolean required)
  {
    this.required = required;
    this.requiredSet = true;
  }
```

For retrieving the property, the basic algorithm is simple: if the value has been set, return it; otherwise, attempt to retreive its value-binding expression, evaluate it, and return that value instead. (The value-binding expression is set with the `setValueBinding` method, which is usually called in the JSP component tag handler.) Setting the property is basically the same as setting a normal property, except you must be able to determine whether or not it has been set. With primitives you can use a flag such as `requiredSet` in this example; with objects, you can check for `null`. (To avoid using a flag, you can also use the object wrappers for the primitive types.)

> **TIP** It's generally best to support value-binding expressions for any property you expect to be used by a front-end or application developer; this ensures that your UI component is as flexible as possible. (If you don't want to type this code repeatedly, it can easily be moved into a static utility method.)

In order to ensure that all UI components can manage saving their properties and any other state (either on the server or the client), this class also implements the `StateHolder` interface, which we cover next.

StateHolder

As we've discussed throughout this book, JavaServer Faces manages a tree of components for each view the user sees. It wouldn't be a good idea if it kept all of these trees hanging out in memory all the time—a single user could generate dozens of component trees, and with a lot of users, JSF would have to manage hundreds of trees simultaneously. That wouldn't be terribly performant.

To avoid this ghastly scenario, JSF has facilities for storing and retrieving a component's state. An implementation may remove views altogether or implement some sort of pooling mechanism and restore a component's state only when the original user needs to see the view again. Usually, the state is either stored on the server in the session or serialized and stored in the client (perhaps through a hidden field, as is the case with the standard render kit).

Regardless of how the JSF implementation handles this process, you usually only have to worry about the `javax.faces.component.StateHolder` interface, which has methods for saving and restoring state. `UIComponentBase` implements `StateHolder` (and provides default implementations of its methods). Any converters or validators that need to save their state should implement this interface as well.

A component's state is not saved if its `transient` property is set to `true`:

```
public boolean isTransient();
public void setTransient(boolean newTransientValue);
```

`UIComponentBase`'s default value for this property is `false`.

There are two additional methods that do the actual work of saving and restoring a component's state:

```
public Object saveState(FacesContext context);
public void restoreState(FacesContext context, Object state);
```

The `saveState` method should return a `Serializable` object that represents the current object's state. The `restoreState` method should use the `Serializable` object returned by `saveState` to restore the current object's state. As an example, let's look at how our example `UIHeadlineViewer` component (covered in online extension chapter 18) implements `saveState`:

```
public Object saveSate(FacesContext context)
{
  Object[] values = new Object[8];
  values[0] = super.saveState(context);
  values[1] = url;
  values[2] = showChannelTitle;
  values[3] = showItemTitle;
  values[4] = showItemCreator;
  values[5] = showItemPublishedDate;
  values[6] = showItemReceivedDate;
  values[7] = showItemDescription;

  return values;
}
```

There are a few things to point out here. First, we are returning an array of `Object` instances. We said before that we should be returning a `Serializable` object—fortunately, arrays are serializable. The first element of the array is set to equal the value of the superclass's `saveState` method.

`UIHeadlineViewer` subclasses `UIData`, so calling `super.saveState` returns all of the state associated with `UIData`'s functionality, as well as its superclass's (all the way up to `UIComponentBase`). When we say *state*, we mean the value of all properties and attached objects. For `UIData`, this means properties like `first` and `rows`, as well as any attached validators, value-change method bindings, and so on; for `UIComponentBase` this means the `clientId`, `id`, `rendered`, and `rendererType` properties, as well as any associated event listeners. The general rule of thumb is that each component should save the state of any properties or attached objects that it has added to its superclass.

All of the instance variables refenced in this method are exposed as properties of the `UIHeadlineViewer` component. The code simply returns an array of objects that contain the values of each variable that is exposed as a property.

If you need to save the state of a more complicated object, you can use `UIComponentBase`'s `saveAttachedState` helper method:

```
public static Object saveAttachedState(FacesContext context,
                                        Object attachedObject);
```

This method can be used to save any associated `Object`, `List`, or `null` value. These objects should either implement the `StateHolder` interface themselves or be serializable. For example, `UIComponentBase` in the JSF reference implementation [Sun, JSF RI] uses this method to save all associated event listeners:

```
values[7] = saveAttachedState(context, listeners);
```

Here, the result of `saveAttachedState` is stored in the array created by the `saveState` method (the `listeners` instance variable is a `List` of `FacesListener` instances).

The most important thing to remember when writing `restoreState` is that you're unwrapping the same data stored during the `saveState` method. Here's the corresponding `restoreState` method:

```
public void restoreState(FacesContext context, Object state)
            throws java.io.IOException
{
  Object[] values = (Object[])state;
  super.restoreState(context, values[0]);
  showDay = ((Boolean) values[1]).booleanValue();
  showMonth = ((Boolean)values[2]).booleanValue();
  showYear = ((Boolean)values[3]).booleanValue();
  showTime = ((Boolean)values[4]).booleanValue();
  startYear = ((Integer)values[5]).intValue();
  endYear = ((Integer)values[6]).intValue();
}
```

As you can see, `restoreState` is the opposite of `saveState`. We know that `saveState` returned an array of `Object` instances, so we can cast appropriately. We then call `super.restoreState` to ensure that the state of all of the superclass's properties and attached objects is restored. Finally, we retrieve each instance variable value directly from the array index in which it was originally stored.

If you saved an object with `saveAttachedState`, you can retrieve it with its opposite, `restoreAttachedState`, which is also a static method of `UIComponentBase`:

```
public static Object restoreAttachedState(FacesContext context,
                                          Object stateObj)
                     throws IllegalStateException;
```

Like `saveAttachedState`, `restoreAttachedState` works with `Objects`, `Lists`, and `null` values. Here's another example from the reference implementation's `UIComponentBase`:

```
List restoredListeners =
      (List)restoreAttachedState(context, values[7]);
if (restoredListeners != null)
{
  if (listeners != null)
  {
    listeners.addAll(restoredListeners);
  }
  else
  {
    listeners = restoredListeners;
  }
}
```

In this snippet, we retrieve a `List` of listeners using `restoreAttachedState`. If it isn't `null`, we either add its values to the existing `listeners` instance variable, or set `listeners` to equal the restored value if it was `null`.

TIP Because `saveState` and `restoreState` are called often, it pays to make sure they're efficient. Avoid using getters or setters if possible. Also, during development, you may end up with `ClassCastExceptions` if you change the type of an object and JSF attempts to reconstitute a saved object of the old type. This can happen if your implementation is saving state in the client. To avoid this, just make sure you reload the page (as opposed to posting to it).

So, the bottom line is that if your component, converter, validator, or listener has state—even something like a simple flag—you should implement the `StateHolder` interface. Renderers don't need to use this interface because they are stateless. If you're subclassing an existing Faces class, that class may already implement the interface (this is the case for *all* standard components because they all inherit from `UIComponentBase`). If so, you must call the superclass's `saveState` and `restoreState` methods and store their return values in the `Serializable` object you return from `saveState`. Conversely, you must also call the superclass's `restoreState` method to retrieve the superclass's state from the `Object` you returned from `saveState`. Usually, it's best just to use arrays, because they're fast and easy to use.

NOTE Usually `saveState` and `restoreState` are called when the `FacesServlet` is configured to store state on the client. When state is stored on the server, your UI objects might just be stored in the session. Because your object's behavior may change depending on whether these methods are called, it's important to test it with both state saving options (client and server).

That's all there is to say about `StateHolder`. Let's move on to the next interface, `EditableValueHolder`.

EditableValueHolder

All input controls should implement the `javax.faces.component.EditableValueHolder` interface (as does `UIInput`). We covered this interface in chapter 11, but there are a few additional methods that are important for writing components.

These methods center around handling component values. Recall that input controls actually have two types of values: a submitted value and a local value. The *submitted value* is the value entered by the user, before any conversions or validations have occurred. The *local value* is the real value of the component, after successful conversion and validation, before any associated model object is updated through a value-binding expression.

The user's input is stored directly in the `submittedValue` property:

```
public Object getSubmittedValue();
public void setSubmittedValue(submittedValue);
```

This is typically the value retrieved from the incoming request, and is usually set by the component or renderer in its `decode` method:

```
Map requestMap = context.getExternalContext().
                 getRequestParameterMap();
if (requestMap.containsKey(clientId))
{
    setSubmittedValue((String) requestMap.get(clientId);
}
```

Here, we simply retrieve a `Map` of the request parameters, grab the user's input (which is the request parameter for the component's client identifier), and set the `submittedValue` property. As you can see, no conversion takes place whatsoever.

We have already discussed the `value` property, but let's take another look at it:

```
public Object getValue();
public void setValue(Object object);
```

This is a bit of a strange property. Whenever you call `setValue`, you are setting the local value directly. However, when you call `getValue`, you will receive the local value if it is non-`null`. Otherwise, you'll receive the value of any associated value-binding expression.

In order to determine if the local value has been set, you can use the `localValueSet` property:

```
public boolean isLocalValueSet();
public void setLocalValueSet(boolean localValueSet);
```

UI components usually update the local value during the Process Validations phase of the Request Processing Lifecycle, or the Apply Request Values phase (if the `immediate` property is set to `true`). When the local value is set (via `setValue`), this flag is set to `true`. If a model object is updated during the Update Model Values phase, the local value is set to `null`, and `localValueSet` is set to `false`.

Keeping track of this value-chain can be somewhat confusing, so this is the basic pattern:

- The `submittedValue` property is set during decoding.
- The `value` property (the local value) is set after successful validation, and the `submittedValue` property is cleared.
- If there is a value-binding for the `value` property, the `value` property is cleared after successfully updating the model.
- During encoding, the `submittedValue` is displayed if it is non-`null`, and the `value` property is displayed otherwise. This ensures that users see the last value they entered.

`UIInput`, which is the superclass of all standard input controls, handles all of this processing, so you won't need to implement it yourself as long as you subclass a standard input control. You will, however, need to know what is going on.

NOTE You should only access `submittedValue` when decoding and validating the component.

Now that you know all there is to know about UI component values, let's look at something simpler: the `NamingContainer` interface.

NamingContainer

A naming container ensures that all of its child components have a unique client identifier. In practice, this usually means that the client identifiers of the children are prefixed by the client identifier of the parent. So, if the parent's client identifier is "foo," its children's might be "foo.id01," "foo.id02," and "foo.id03." (For more on identifiers and naming containers, see chapter 3.)

Normally your component won't be a naming container unless it processes child components. For example, `UIData` and `UIForm` are standard components that are naming containers. Often your component will subclass one of the standard components that already implements this interface. For example, the `UIHeadlineViewer` component (covered in online extension chapter 18) subclasses `UIData`, so it's automatically a naming container.

If your component doesn't subclass an existing naming container, it must implement the `javax.faces.component.NamingContainer` interface, which is a marker interface [Grand] (and consequently has no properties or methods) located in the `javax.faces.component` package. `UIComponentBase` recognizes parent naming containers by default, so usually implementing this interface is enough. Alternatively, you can subclass the `javax.faces.component.UINamingContainer` class, which adds a default type and family (which you would normally override anyway).

`NamingContainer` is not only the simplest component interface we're covering—it's also the last. There is, however, one other code-related issue we should cover.

15.2.3 Event handling with method bindings

There are two interfaces that fire events: `ActionSource` (for action events) and `EditableValueHolder` (for value-change events). Recall from chapter 11 that these interfaces maintain a list of event listeners, but also allow you to specify an additional event listener via a method-binding expression.

For `ActionSource`, the additional listener is specified with the `actionListener` property:

```
public MethodBinding getActionListener();
public boid setActionListener(MethodBinding actionListenerMethod);
```

For `EditableValueHolder`, it is the `valueChangeListener` property:

```
public MethodBinding getValueChangeListener();
public void setValueChangeListener(MethodBinding valueChangeMethod);
```

The normal event listeners are handled automatically by `UIComponentBase`, but these method bindings must be handled separately, unless you're subclassing a concrete class like `UICommand` or `UIInput` that has already performed this work for you.

Because these are `MethodBinding` instances, they can't be added to the event listener list. Instead, they must be executed by your component's `broadcast` method for integration with the normal event-handling process. Here's an example for an `ActionSource`:

```
public void broadcast(FacesEvent event)
            throws AbortProcessingException
{
  super.broadcast(event);
  MethodBinding binding = getActionListener();
  if (binding != null &&
      (isImmediate() &&
          event.getPhaseId().equals(PhaseId.APPLY_REQUEST_VALUES) ||
      (!isImmediate() &&
          event.getPhaseId().equals(PhaseId.INVOKE_APPLICATION))))
  {
    FacesContext context = FacesContext.getCurrentInstance();
    binding.invoke(context, new Object[] { event });
  }
}
```

First, note that we call the superclass's `broadcast` method. This calls all of the ordinary event listener instances. Next, we check to see if the `actionListener` property is non-`null`. If so, we check to see if the `immediate` property is `true`. If it is, we execute the method after the Apply Request Values phase; otherwise, we execute it during the Invoke Application phase. Executing the method-binding expression simply involves calling its `invoke` method with the event as the parameter in a single-element array. (See chapter 11 for coverage of the `MethodBinding` class.)

With this simple bit of code, we support listener methods in addition to listener classes. That's it for the world of UI component base classes and interfaces. Now, let's move on to the exciting world of component configuraton.

15.2.4 Registration

Inside an application configuration file, you declare a component with the `<component>` element:

```
<component>
  <component-type>UIInputDate</component-type>
  <component-class>org.jia.components.UIInputDate</component-class>
</component>
```

The `<component-type>` element specifies the component's type, and `<component-class>` specifies the concrete implementation class. With this definition, we can retrieve a new `UIInputDate` instance with a simple call to the `Application` class:

```
UIInputDate myInputDate = (UIInputDate)application.
            createComponent(UIInputDate.COMPONENT_TYPE);
```

Usually, this type will match the component's `COMPONENT_TYPE` constant, which is `"jia.InputDate"` in this case. So the following code would have the same effect:

```
UIInputDate myInputDate = (UIInputDate)application.
            createComponent("jia.InputDate");
```

Those two elements are all the `Application` instance needs to create your component. However, you can fully describe a component, including icons, attributes, and properties. The more information you provide, the better your component will function with tools. Listing 15.1 shows most of the possible `<component>` child elements.

Listing 15.1 A more complete example of registering a component with JSF

```
<component>
    <description>A simple date entry component.</description>
    <display-name>Input Date</display-name>
    <component-type>jia.InputDate</component-type>
    <component-class>
      org.jia.components.UIInputDate
    </component-class>
    <property>
        <description>CSS Style</description>
        <display-name>styleClass</display-name>
        <icon>
            <small-icon>icons/styleClass.jpg</small-icon>
        </icon>
        <property-name>styleClass</property-name>
        <property-class>String</property-class>
    </property>
    <property>
        <description>
          True if the year is to be displayed.
        </description>
        <display-name>showYear</display-name>
        <icon>
            <small-icon>icons/showYear.jpg</small-icon>
        </icon>
        <property-name>showYear</property-name>
        <property-class>Boolean</property-class>
        <default-value>false</default-value>
    </property>
    <property>
        <description>
          True if the day of the week should be displayed.
        </description>
```

```
            <display-name>showDay</display-name>
            <icon>
                <small-icon>icons/showDay.jpg</small-icon>
            </icon>
            <property-name>showDay</property-name>
            <property-class>Boolean</property-class>
            <default-value>true</default-value>
            <suggested-value>true</suggested-value>
        </property>
        <property>
            <description>
              True if the month should be displayed
            </description>
            <display-name>showMonth</display-name>
            <icon>
                <small-icon>icons/showMonth.jpg</small-icon>
            </icon>
            <property-name>showMonth</property-name>
            <property-class>Boolean</property-class>
            <default-value>true</default-value>
            <suggested-value>true</suggested-value>
        </property>
        <property>
            <description>
              True if the time should be displayed.
            </description>
            <display-name>showTime</display-name>
            <icon>
                <small-icon>icons/showTime.jpg</small-icon>
            </icon>
            <property-name>showTime</property-name>
            <property-class>Boolean</property-class>
            <default-value>false</default-value>
        </property>
    </component>
```

In addition to the component's type and class, this entry provides a display name, description, and small and large icons. It also tells the tools that the component accepts a single attribute called `styleClass` of type `String`, and that it has four properties of type `Boolean`: `showYear`, `showDay`, `showMonth`, and `showTime`. You can see that both the `<attribute>` and `<property>` elements also accept a display name, description, icon, name, class, default value, and required value. Only the name and class are required.

If you're not particularly interested in creating such a complete component definition, remember that many of the elements are optional, and that tools like the Faces Console [Holmes] simplify the process greatly.

NOTE JSF IDEs often require additional metadata in order to import custom components. Unfortunately, the details vary between vendors. This will be standardized in a future version of the specification.

Now that you know how to register components with JSF, let's take a look at how to integrate them with JavaServer Pages.

15.2.5 JSP integration

JavaServer Faces provides two abstract base classes you can use for writing JSP component tags: `UIComponentTag` and `UIComponentBodyTag`. Most of the time, you can subclass `UIComponentTag` directly. If you need to process the body of the tag, you must subclass `UIComponentBodyTag` instead. The only standard component tags that do this are the `<f:view>` and `<f:verbatim>` tags (in the JSF in the reference implementation [Sun, JSF RI]). The `<f:view>` tag processes the body to save its state properly, and `<f:verbatim>` outputs its body (almost) literally. Most of the time, subclassing `UIComponentTag` will be sufficient.

In addition to subclassing the appropriate base class, you'll need to declare the tag inside a tag library definition (TLD), which is an XML file that defines a set of tags.

UIComponentTag

In the simplest cases, you can create a new component tag by just subclassing `javax.faces.webapp.UIComponentTag` and associating it with a component/renderer pair. This association is performed by overriding two read-only properties: `componentType` and `rendererType`. Here's how `UIComponentTag` defines the `componentType` property:

```
public abstract String getComponentType();
```

All you have to do is return a `String` representing the component's type. For example, the `HeadlineViewer_TableTag` class, which integrates our custom `UIHeadlineViewer` component with JSP, defines this read-only property as follows:

```
public String getComponentType()
{
  return UIHeadlineViewer.COMPONENT_TYPE;
}
```

This associates the `HeadlineViewer_TableTag` class with a `UIHeadlineViewer`'s component type.

NOTE The fact that the componentType property is a single String means that a JSF component tag is usually associated with a single component. A component, however, can be associated with many different tags.

In addition to specifying the component type, you must specify the renderer type by overriding the rendererType property:

```
public abstract String getRendererType();
```

This property is a String that maps to a specific renderer type. If the component renderers itself, this method should return null. However, if rendering should be delegated to a renderer, you'll need to specify a value. For example, our UIHeadlineViewer component uses the standard Table renderer, so here's how the Navigator_ToolbarTag class implements this method:

```
public String getRendererType()
{
  return "javax.faces.Table";
}
```

TIP Note that the name of the tag handler class, HeadlineViewer_TableTag, includes the component type and renderer types that the tag supports. This is a convenient way to name tag handler classes, since they are usually associated with a single component/renderer pair.

If no renderer type is associated with the tag class, you can just use the component type itself in the name of the tag handler. For example, the tag handler class for UIInputDate is named InputDateTag.

Tag handlers can have properties, which are exposed as element attributes when used in JSP. For example, here's an example of using the component tag for our UIInputDate component:

```
<jia:inputDate showDay="false"/>
```

The attribute showDay maps to a Boolean property of the InputDateTag class. InputDateTag must map the showDay property to an attribute or property of UIInputDate. UIComponentTag supports a few basic component properties by default: id, rendererType, and rendered. If your custom component doesn't add any properties and the associated renderer (if any) doesn't require any special attributes, then there's no need to override any other methods.

However, if your component has its own properties (as is usually the case), you also need to override the setProperties method:

```
protected void setProperties(UIComponent component);
```

This is where you map properties of your tag class to properties or attributes of your component. The first thing to remember when implementing this method is to call the superclass's implementation, or else the basic properties like `rendererType` and `renderer` won't be updated properly. (This will also be true if you create tag handler class hierarchies; you always want to ensure that the superclass's properties are properly transferred to the component instance.)

Other than that, for each property or attribute you'd like to expose via your custom tag, you need to

- Add the property to the tag handler class
- Associate the tag handler property with the appropriate component property or attribute in the `setProperties` method

For example, our `UINavigator` component has a `headerLabel` property, and its renderer also uses a `headerClass` attribute. Both of these are exposed as properties of the `Navigator_ToolbarTag` class:

```
public String getHeaderLabel()
{
  return headerLabel;
}
public void setHeaderLabel(String headerLabel)
{
  this.headerLabel = headerLabel;
}

public String getHeaderClass()
{
  return headerClass;
}

public void setHeaderClass(String headerClass)
{
  this.headerClass = headerClass;
}
```

Here's how `setProperties` uses these two properties:

```
protected void setProperties(UIComponent component)
{
  super.setProperties(component);
  UINavigator navigator = (UINavigator)component;

  ...
  if (headerLabel != null) { navigator.setHeaderLabel(headerLabel); }
  ...
  Map attributes = navigator.getAttributes();
```

```
    if (headerClass != null)
    {
      attributes.put("headerClass", headerClass);
    }
    ...
  }
```

We've left out additional details for the sake of clarity, but you can see that this snippet does a few things. First, it calls the superclass's `setProperties` method, which is a requirement in most cases. Then, if the tag handler's `headerLabel` property isn't `null`, we set the component's `headerLabel` property to be equal to the tag handler's `headerLabel` property. Because `headerClass` is actually a renderer-specific attribute, we set the component's `headerClass` attribute to be equal to the tag handler's `headerClass` property (if the tag handler's property isn't `null`). This can be done by retrieving the component's `attributes` property, which is a `Map`, and simply adding a new name/value pair for the `headerClass` property.

In most cases, this is basically what you'll do with `setProperties`—set component properties or attributes based on the properties of the tag handler class itself. Think of this method as an initialization method—it's only called when the associated component is first created.

If you add properties to your tag handler, you'll need to override the `release` method as well:

```
public void release();
```

This is a standard method of the `javax.servlet.jsp.tagext.Tag` interface (which `UIComponentTag` implements) that is guaranteed to be called before the tag is garbage collected. In it, you should release any resources you've acquired.

So, to continue with the `Navigator_ToolbarTag` example, here's an abbreviated version of its `release` method:

```
public void release()
{
  headerClass = null;
  ...
  headerLabel = null;
  ...
}
```

All we're doing here is setting the instance variables for the tag's properties to `null`.

These are all of the methods you generally have to override when developing a new component tag. If, however, your tag is for a facet, you must also override `getFacetName`:

```
protected String getFacetName();
```

All you have to do is return a `String` that represents the facet's name, like "header".

`UIComponentTag` also has some useful utility methods:

```
public UIComponent getComponentInstance();
public static UIComponentTag
                getParentUIComponentTag(PageContext context);
protected boolean isSuppressed();
protected boolean isValueReference(String value);
```

As its name suggests, `getComponentInstance` returns the `UIComponent` instance that is related to this tag (the results are valid only while the tag, or its children, are being executed). The static method `getParentUIComponentTag` retrieves the parent `UIComponentTag` instance, whose associated `UIComponent` is often the parent of the `UIComponent` associated with the current tag.

The `boolean suppressed` property returns `true` if the component should not be displayed. A component shouldn't be displayed if its rendered property is `false`, it's the child of a component whose `rendersChildren` property is `false`, it is a facet (facets are displayed by their parents), or its parent component's `suppressed` property is `true`.

If you need to determine whether or not a tag's property is a value- or method-binding expression, call `isValueReference`. This method is essential if you'd like to support value-binding expressions in your tag properties, like the standard component tags. You'll often find yourself using `isValueReference` like this:

```
if (immediate != null)
{
  if (isValueReference(immediate))
  {
    navigator.setValueBinding("immediate",
                              app.createValueBinding(immediate));
  }
  else
  {
    navigator.setImmediate(Boolean.getBoolean(immediate));
  }
}
```

Here, we check to see if `immediate` is a value-binding expression. If so, we retrieve a `ValueBinding` instance from the `Application` and set the value-binding for that property; otherwise, we just set the property directly. This is code you'll typically write inside `setProperties`.

NOTE Any tag property you want to support value-binding expressions must be of type `String`.

You may remember that `UIComponent` (and also `Renderer`) both have three key methods for displaying a component—`encodeBegin`, `encodeChildren`, and `encodeEnd`. `UIComponentTag` has these methods as well:

```
protected void encodeBegin() throws IOException;
protected void encodeChildren() throws IOException;
protected void encodeEnd() throws IOException;
```

These methods perform the same functions as their counterparts in the other classes; as a matter of fact, by default, they simply call `UIComponent`'s method of the same name. These methods are called internally by `UIComponentTag`; you only need to override them if you'd like to augment or replace the default functionality. (If you do override them, be sure to check the `suppressed` first.)

WARNING Avoid the temptation to put rendering logic in these methods; such work should be handled by the UI component or renderer.

If you've developed JSP custom tags before, you know that output starts with the `doStartTag` method and completes with the `doEndTag` method of the `Tag` interface. In `UIComponentTag`, the associated `UIComponent` instance is created and initialized in `doStartTag` and `encodeBegin` is also called if the component doesn't render its own children. In `doEndTag`, the list of child components or facets is updated, both `encodeBegin` and `encodeChildren` are called if the component renders its children, and then `encodeEnd` is called.

Because a significant amount of default processing takes place in these methods, you usually won't need to override them. You can, however, modify their return values with the following two methods:

```
protected int getDoStartValue() throws JspException;
protected int getDoEndValue() throws JspException;
```

`UIComponentTag`'s implementation of `doStartTag` returns the value of `getDoStartValue` upon successful completion. By default, `getDoStartValue` returns `Tag.EVAL_BODY_INCLUDE`, which tells the JSP implementation to evaluate the body of the tag, processing any custom tags it may have and outputting any other text. If you don't want the body to be processed, override `getDoStartValue` to return `Tag.SKIP_BODY`.

The default implementation of `doEndTag` returns the value of `getDoEndValue` if there are no errors. `getDoStartValue` returns `Tag.EVAL_PAGE` by default, which tells the JSP implementation to continue processing the rest of the page normally. If you want to skip processing the rest of the page, override `getDoEndValue` to return `Tag.SKIP_PAGE` instead.

For most cases, this is all you need to know about `UIComponentTag`; just add the appropriate properties, override a few methods, and you're ready to go. Now, let's look at `UIComponentBodyTag`, a subclass of `UIComponentTag` that processes its body.

UIComponentBodyTag

`UIComponentBodyTag`, in the package `javax.faces.webapp`, is an abstract class that subclasses `UIComponentTag` that also implements the `javax.servlet.jsp.tagext.BodyTag` interface. There's no need to subclass it unless you need to process the body content of the tag. For example, the `<f:verbatim>` JSF core tag processes its body; it simply sets the value of the associated `UIOutput` instance to equal the `String` value of the body.

Instead of evaluating the body of a tag and including it in the page's primary output stream, `BodyTags` buffer the results and store them in a separate `javax.servlet.jsp.tagext.BodyContent` instance. In order to accomplish this, `UIComponentBodyTag` overrides the `getDoStartValue` method of `UIComponentTag` and returns `BodyTag.EVAL_BODY_BUFFERED` instead of `Tag.EVAL_INCLUDE_BODY`.

The `BodyContent` instance can be retrieved via the `getBodyContent` method:

```
public BodyContent getBodyContent();
```

The `BodyContent` class has some methods for accessing the evaluated content of the tag's body, including methods for retrieving the associated `Writer`, and the body as a `String`.

The `BodyTag` lifecycle involves two additional methods in addition to the `doStartTag` and `doEndTag` defined in the `Tag` interface:

```
public void doInitBody() throws JspException;
public int doAfterBody() throws JspException;
```

The `doInitBody` method is called before the body is evaluated, and `doAfterBody` is called after it is evaluated. These methods won't be called unless the tag's body is nonempty. The default implementation of `doInitBody` does nothing, and `doAfterBody` simply returns the value of this method:

```
protected int getDoAfterBodyValue() throws JspException;
```

As with `getDoStartValue` and `getDoEndValue`, you can override this method to change the return value of `doAfterBody`. By default, this method returns `BodyTag.SKIP_BODY`, which tells the JSP implementation to end processing of the body and move on to the `doEndTag` method. If you want your tag to process the body multiple times, override this method to return `IterationTag.EVAL_BODY_AGAIN`.

Most of the time, you'll override the `doAfterBody` method to process the tag's body, and modify the component's value accordingly. There are at least two things you can do with the tag's body. First, you can set the value of the associated component based on its contents. This is what the `<f:verbatim>` tag does. You can also output new content based on the body; this is what the `<f:view>` tag does. If the state saving method is `client`, it will output the state of the page (which is sent in the form of hidden fields for the HTML render kit). This state is, of course, based on the body of the page.

Tag library integration

JSP custom tags are grouped into tag libraries through a TLD, which is an XML file that's usually located in the WEB-INF/lib directory in a web application, or the META-INF directory of a JAR file. A TLD simply maps a custom tag handler class to a JSP tag and declares which properties should be exposed as JSP tag attributes.

For example, all of the custom component tag handlers from this book are declared in the jia.tld file. Here's a snippet:

```
<!DOCTYPE taglib PUBLIC
  "-//Sun Microsystems, Inc.//DTD JSP Tag Library 1.2//EN"
  "http://java.sun.com/dtd/web-jsptaglibrary_1_2.dtd">
<taglib>
  <tlib-version>1.0</tlib-version>
  <jsp-version>1.2</jsp-version>
  <short-name>
    JSF in Action Custom Tags
  </short-name>
  <uri>jsf-in-action-components</uri>
  <description>
    Sample custom components, renderers,
    validators, and converters from
    JSF in Action.
  </description>
...
  <tag>
    <name>headlineViewerTable</name>
    <tag-class>
      org.jia.components.taglib.HeadlineViewer_TableTag
    </tag-class>
    <body-content>JSP</body-content>
    <attribute>
      <name>url</name>
      <required>false</required>
      <rtexprvalue>false</rtexprvalue>
    </attribute>
...
    <attribute>
```

❶ Tag library description

❷ Tag description

❸ New properties or attributes

```
        <name>showItemTitle</name>
        <required>false</required>
        <rtexprvalue>false</rtexprvalue>
      </attribute>
  ...
      <attribute>
        <name>id</name>
        <required>false</required>
        <rtexprvalue>false</rtexprvalue>
      </attribute>
  ...
      <attribute>
        <name>binding</name>
        <required>false</required>
        <rtexprvalue>false</rtexprvalue>
      </attribute>
  ...
      <attribute>
        <name>onclick</name>
        <required>false</required>
        <rtexprvalue>false</rtexprvalue>
      </attribute>
  ...
      <attribute>
        <name>width</name>
        <required>false</required>
        <rtexprvalue>false</rtexprvalue>
      </attribute>
    </tag>
  ...
  </taglib>
```

❸ New properties or attributes

❹ Inherited properties or attributes

❺ HTML attributes

As the listing shows, all TLDs start with the library's description (❶). Pay attention to the <uri> node; this is what must be included in any JSPs that use these components, like so:

```
<%@ taglib uri="jsf-in-action-components" prefix="jia" %>
```

After the tag library description (which is, essentially, that library's header), each TLD has one or more tag descriptions (❷). The description maps a tag name to a tag handler class, and also describes each valid attribute. Here, there are a set of attributes specific to this custom component (❸), as well as attributes inherited from the parent component (❹). In either case, some of these may also be HTML pass-through attributes (❺). The key is that you must declare *every* single attribute your tag will support, regardless of its purpose or origin. If you expect someone to type it into a JSP, it must be declared. Also note that all declared attributes must have <rtexprvalue> set to false.

Once you have registered your tag handler with a tag library and included it as shown, you can access it in JSP, like so:

```
<jia:headlineViewerTable url="http://www.jsfcentral.com/jsfcentral.rss"
                         styleClass="hviewer"
                         channelTitleClass="hviewer-channel-title"
                         itemTitleClass="hviewer-item-title"
                         itemClasses="hviewer-item-even, hviewer-item-odd"
                         rows="5"/>
```

(We left out some of the declarations for these attributes, but you get the idea.)

We've now fully covered the JSF component environment. However, the world of UI components isn't complete without their siblings, renderers.

NOTE Integrating UI components with JSP can be tedious if the extension has several properties. Most of the standard components fall into this category, because there are so many HTML attributes for each element. (Each attribute must be exposed as a property of your JSP component tag.) To deal with this issue, both the reference implementation [Sun, JSF RI] and MyFaces [MyFaces] include tools that automatically generate tag handlers based on component and renderer definitions in a JSF configuration file. These tools aren't quite user-friendly or polished (for instance, the RI's tool is available only if you download the source), but they do exist, and will likely be officially released in the future.

15.3 Developing renderers

When we covered `UIComponentBase` in section 15.2.2, we discussed four methods for encoding and decoding. When a component encodes and decodes itself, it's said to use the *direct implementation* rendering model. In many cases, this model works well. Another technique is the *delegated implementation* model, which offloads rendering duties to an associated `Renderer` instance.

All of the standard components use delegated implementation, and `UIComponentBase` does this by default. The chosen `Renderer` instance is defined by the component's `rendererType` property. That property is used by a `RenderKit` instance to look up the proper `Renderer` instance. (A `RenderKit` manages a set of `Renderer` instances; JSF ships with one for HTML 4.01 by default.)

The indirect association between components and renderers is important; it allows the same component to be displayed by the proper `Renderer` instance as long as the current `RenderKit` knows about the specified renderer type. For example, `UIGraphic`'s `rendererType` property is set to "javax.faces.Image" by default. If an HTML render kit is currently in use, it will return a `Renderer` instance of type

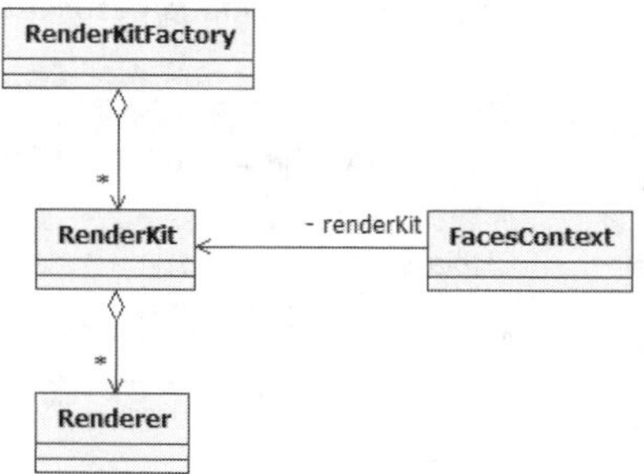

Figure 15.2
`Renderer` instances are managed by a `RenderKit`, which in turn is managed by a `RenderKitFactory`. You can retrieve the current `RenderKit` instance from the `FacesContext`.

`javax.faces.Image`, which will display an HTML `<img>` tag. If another render kit, such as one that outputs normalized XML, is selected, a different `Renderer` instance with the same type will be selected, and may display a `<graphic_image>` tag instead.

All of the renderer-related classes are shown in figure 15.2. As you can see, a `RenderKitFactory` is responsible for managing `RenderKit` instances. Each `RenderKit` can contain one or more `Renderers`, and the current `RenderKit` can be retrieved from the `FacesContext`.

You may have noticed that there are no concrete classes in this figure—only abstract ones. The JSF specification has no requirements in this area—it defines only the renderer types and behavior for the standard HTML `RenderKit`; nothing more. This means that you can't portably subclass an existing `Renderer` class, because there are no standard class names or methods.

Renderers are associated with a UI component type and family; table 15.1 lists all of the renderer types in the standard HTML render kit, and their corresponding UI components and families.

Table 15.1 Renderer types for the standard render kit. Each renderer type is associated directly with an HTML-specific component.

Family[a]	Component	Renderer Type[b]	HTML Rendering Behavior
Command	`UICommand`, `HtmlCommandButton`	`Button`	A form button that is an action source and can execute an action method.
	`HtmlCommandLink`	`Link`	A hyperlink that is an action source and can execute an action method.
Data	`UIData`, `HtmlDataTable`	`Table`	A table with customizable headers, footers, and other properties.
Form	`UIForm`, `HtmlForm`	`Form`	An input form; must enclose all input components.

continued on next page

Table 15.1 Renderer types for the standard render kit. Each renderer type is associated directly with an HTML-specific component. *(continued)*

Family[a]	Component	Renderer Type[b]	HTML Rendering Behavior
Image	`HtmlGraphicImage`	`Image`	Displays an image based on its URL.
Input	`HtmlInputHidden`	`Hidden`	An input field of type "hidden".
	`HtmlInputSecret`	`Secret`	An input field of type "password".
	`UIInput`, `HtmlInputText`	`Text`	An input field of type "text".
	`HtmlInputTextarea`	`Texte-area`	A text area (multiline input field).
Message	`UIMessage`, `HtmlMessage`	`Message`	Displays messages for a specific component.
Messages	`UIMessages`, `HtmlMessages`	`Messages`	Displays all messages (component-related and/or application-related).
Output	`HtmlOutputFormat`	`Format`	Outputs parameterized text.
	`HtmlOutputLabel`	`Label`	A text label for an input field.
	`HtmlOutputLink`	`Link`	A hyperlink that's not associated with a user command.
	`UIOutput`, `HtmlOutputText`	`Text`	Plain text, with optional CSS formatting.
Panel	`HtmlPanelGrid`	`Grid`	A table with customizable headers, footers, and other properties.
	`HtmlPanelGroup`	`Group`	Groups components together for use inside of other components, and to apply common styles or hide/display a group of components.
Checkbox	`HtmlSelectBoolean-Checkbox`	`Checkbox`	A single checkbox.
SelectMany	`HtmlSelectMany-Checkbox`	`Checkbox`	A table with a list of checkboxes, grouped together.
	`UISelectMany`, `HtmlSelectMany-Listbox`	`Listbox`	A listbox that allows you to select multiple items.
	`HtmlSelectManyMenu`	`Menu`	A listbox of size one.

continued on next page

Table 15.1 Renderer types for the standard render kit. Each renderer type is associated directly with an HTML-specific component. *(continued)*

Family[a]	Component	Renderer Type[b]	HTML Rendering Behavior
SelectOne	`HtmlSelectOneRadio`	`Radio`	A table of radio buttons, grouped together.
	`HtmlSelectOne-Listbox`	`Listbox`	A listbox that allows you to select a single item.
	`UISelectOne`, `HtmlSelectOneMenu`	`Menu`	A drop-down listbox that allows you to select a single item.

[a] *Standard families have the prefix "javax.faces".*
[b] *Standard renderer types have the prefix "javax.faces".*

You may have noticed that there are similar tables in chapters 4 and 11. There are a few key differences, however. This table only lists components with visual representations, since these are the ones that use renderers. Also, we've listed base UI component classes, since each one has a default renderer type. There's one other important point: the description we've been using for the HTML components is basically the renderer behavior. That doesn't mean the renderer performs all of the work—it just means that people normally think in terms of a visual representation, so it's easier to explain what the component *looks* like—and that *is* the job of the renderer.

TIP It's actually possible to replace a default renderer, so if you created and registered a new renderer with the type `javax.faces.Listbox`, it would be used instead of the standard renderer.

Writing a new renderer requires that you subclass the `Renderer` class and register your new class with JSF through an application configuration file. If you write your own renderer from scratch, it can require a reasonable amount of work to support features like pass-through HTML attributes. Sometimes it's possible to delegate to an existing `Renderer` instance in order to take advantage of the work that JSF implementations already perform (we show this technique in online extension chapter 17). JSP integration for renderers is the same as it is for UI components because the JSP component tags represent a component/renderer pair. Figure 15.3 shows the different elements required for developing a new renderer.

One important point figure 15.3 makes clear is that renderers require UI components to function. A given renderer can (and often does) work with one or more types of components, but they have an intimate relationship with each one

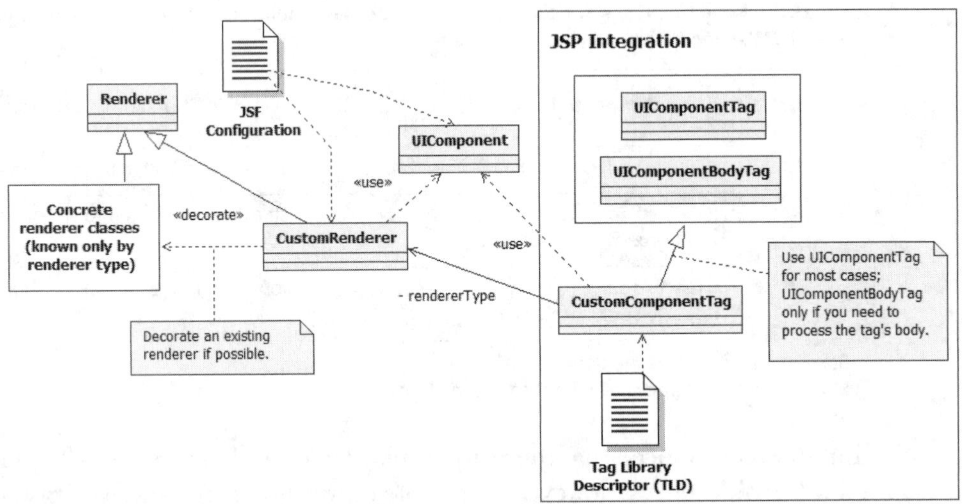

Figure 15.3 A diagram representing the different classes and elements required for developing a custom renderer. You start by subclassing the `Renderer` class, and optionally delegating to an existing `Renderer`. `Renderers` work directly with specific UI components, and are integrated with JSP via custom tags that work with a component/renderer pair.

(or at least with a particular superclass). UI components, on the other hand, usually don't know much at all about their renderers; this makes it easy to swap in new renderers.

Now that we've discussed exactly what renderers are, let's talk about when it's necessary to write one.

15.3.1 Deciding when to write a renderer

To determine when it's necessary to develop a new renderer, ask yourself the quintessential question once again: "What, exactly, do I need to do?" Writing a renderer is a good solution if you want to do the following:

- Augment or enhance the display of an existing component. Our `RolloverButton` renderer is a good example of this—all it does is add a little bit of JavaScript to the standard `Button` renderer behavior. This is best achieved by decorating [GoF] an existing renderer.
- Display the same component in different ways (perhaps to different client devices). Suppose you wanted to display a `UIData` component via scalable vector graphics (SVG). The solution is to write a new renderer just for that

device. (You would probably write a set of Renderer classes for that device and group them into a RenderKit.)

- Consolidate rendering duties for different types of components (usually with the same superclass). For example, you may write three different types of components that can be displayed as a list of bulleted items. You would only need one bulleted list renderer.

If you're still not sure, take a look at section 15.2.1, which discusses when to write a UI component. Often, it's not clear at first which one you should be developing; in some cases, you need both. Also, remember that you can always use the standard renderers with your own custom components, provided that the renderer understands your component's superclass (see online extension chapter 18 for an example).

We discuss the rendering classes in the next sections; all of these classes are located in the javax.faces.render package.

15.3.2 Renderer

Renderer is an abstract class in the javax.faces.render package that knows how to display one or more components to a specific client type. It can also translate responses from the client into component values.

WARNING There's only a single instance of each Renderer type available throughout the life of an application, so they must be thread-safe.

Four of Renderer's methods are also found in UIComponent:

```
public void decode(FacesContext context, UIComponent component)
public void encodeBegin(FacesContext context, UIComponent component)
public void encodeChildren(FacesContext context,
          UIComponent component)
public void encodeEnd(FacesContext context, UIComponent component)
```

The only difference between these signatures and the ones in UIComponent is that they take the actual UIComponent as a parameter in addition to the context. This is because a single Renderer instance is used to render all components that have its renderer-Type. These methods serve the same function as those in UIComponent; as a matter of fact, UIComponentBase just passes the call directly to the appropriate Renderer, if there is one. (See section 15.2.2 for an overview of these methods.) Renderer has default implementations of these methods that do not perform any processing, except for encodeChildren, which iterates through any child components and calls their encoding methods.

The `Renderer` class also duplicates `UIComponent`'s `rendersChildren` property:

```
public boolean getRendersChildren()
```

The default implementation returns `false`. Override this method to return `true` if your `Renderer` will display its children.

Every `UIComponent` has a `clientId` property, which represents their name in the client's world. Sometimes these simple strings may not make sense to the client. For those cases, `Renderer` has a `convertClientId` method:

```
public String convertClientId(FacesContext context, String clientId);
```

This method gives the renderer a chance to translate the component's `clientId` property into something that makes sense for the particular requirements of the client. By default, this method just returns the `clientId` unmodified.

This class also exposes a method that performs the conversion process during the Process Validations phase:

```
public Object getConvertedValue(FacesContext context,
                                UIComponent component,
                                Object submittedValue);
```

If you override this method, it should convert `submittedValue` to a form suitable for the component (using any converter retrieved from the `component` parameter, if necessary) and return the converted value. The default implementation performs no conversion; it simply returns `submittedValue`.

If you override `decode`, you should call this method (and implement it if necessary). This way, subclasses of your `Renderer` can simply override `getConvertedValue` to change that part of the decoding process.

NOTE If you're wondering where to put properties your renderer can use to display a component, remember that `UIComponent` has an `attributes` property where you can store renderer-dependent name/value pairs. These attributes are usually set by the tag handler (or its equivalent if you're not using JSP) or in code. `Renderers` access information through `UIComponent` attributes because there's only one `Renderer` instance available and there could be dozens of `UIComponent` instances using that single `Renderer` instance. (The strongly typed renderer-dependent properties of the standard HTML components are really aliases for renderer-dependent attributes.)

That's all there is to the `Renderer` class. In simpler cases, you only need to override the `encodeBegin` method.

You may have noticed that a `Renderer`'s type isn't a property of the class. It's actually a key that's usually configured in a JSF configuration file and passed into its `RenderKit`, which we describe in the next section.

15.3.3 RenderKit

A `RenderKit` represents a collection of `Renderer` instances, keyed by their type. All of the `Renderers` within a particular `RenderKit` instance are usually related in some way. For example, the default `RenderKit` has `Renderer` instances that only know how to output HTML. Other render kits may display different dialects of HTML (perhaps DHTML with lots of JavaScript), or some other type of markup altogether, like SVG. Render kits can also be used to provide different "skins" that use the same type of markup with a different look and feel. As a matter of fact, there's an open source skinning toolkit, called Xkins, that makes use of this concept [Xkins].[2]

The pattern-conscious will note that this is more or less an Abstract Factory [GoF], and is also conceptually similar to the `java.awt.Toolkit` class, which creates different instances of components tailored for specific platforms. `RenderKits` don't actually *create* `Renderer` instances, though; they merely store a single instance of each type. (The instances are usually created when a JSF implementation parses its configuration files and registers them with the appropriate `RenderKit`.)

There is rarely a need to subclass `RenderKit`, since you can add new `Renderer` instances to it through a configuration file, so we'll focus on how to use it in your code. The class, located in the `javax.faces.render` package, is an abstract base class; you must retrieve a concrete implementation from a `RenderKitFactory` (described next). It has one method for adding a `Renderer` instance, and one for removing it:

```
public void addRenderer(String rendererType, Renderer renderer);
public Renderer getRenderer(String rendererType);
```

Usually you won't be calling `addRenderer` directly; `Renderer` instances can be added to a `RenderKit` declaratively in a JSF configuration file. As a matter of fact, you can create new `RenderKit` instances via configuration as well; we cover configuration in section 15.3.4.

`getRenderer` is useful in cases where you need to retrieve a `Renderer` instance but you only have the type. (If you're working inside a `UIComponentBase` subclass,

---

[2] Using more than one `RenderKit` at a time isn't currently supported by the reference implementation [Sun, JSF RI]. That doesn't mean other implementations won't support this feature, however.

you can use its getRenderer method instead.) All of the literal renderer type values are listed in table 15.1. If no Renderer instance can be found, the method returns null.

When you're developing custom components and renderers, you need to worry about only two RenderKit methods. Usually you'll be adding your own renderers to an existing RenderKit via a configuration file.

Just like Renderers, each RenderKit is associated with an identifier. The identifier isn't a property of the RenderKit itself; it's a key used to retrieve an instance from a RenderKitFactory. The key for the standard RenderKit is defined in the RenderKitFactory class itself. You can retrieve a RenderKitFactory instance from the FactoryFinder class. Here's how you retrieve the default RenderKit:

```
RenderKitFactory rkFactory =(RenderKitFactory)FactoryFinder.
                    getFactory(FactoryFinder.RENDER_KIT_FACTORY);
RenderKit defaultRenderKit =
   rkFactory.getRenderKit(RenderKitFactory.DEFAULT_RENDER_KIT,
                facesContext);
```

This code retrieves a RenderKitFactory instance from the FactoryFinder, and then gets the default RenderKit from the RenderkitFactory. This is a useful technique if you want to access a specific RenderKit. If you're interested in the current RenderKit instance, you can get from FacesContext:

```
RenderKit currentRenderKit = facesContext.getRenderKit();
```

This code retrieves the current RenderKit instance by using the renderKitId property of the UIViewRoot instance retrieved form the current FacesContext. Remember, an application developer can change the current RenderKit at any time, as long as the JSF implementation supports that capability.

That's all you need to know in order to write your own renderers. Now, let's examine how you can register them with JSF.

15.3.4 Registration

Configuring renderers is quite similar to configuring components; it's just a matter of declaring the renderer in an application configuration file. Instead of a <component> element, you use a <renderer> element, but you can specify the display name, icon, description, and so on as well. The main difference is that you must nest a <renderer> element inside a <render-kit> element. So, if you wanted to add a custom renderer to the default render kit, you could do it like so:

```
<render-kit>
  <renderer>
    <renderer-type>jia.Toolbar</renderer-type>
```

```
    <renderer-class>
      org.jia.components.ToolbarRenderer
    </renderer-class>
  </renderer>
</render-kit>
```

This specifies a renderer of type `jia.Toolbar` whose Java class is `org.jia.components.ToolbarRenderer`. We could get a handle to this `Renderer` via the default `RenderKit` like so:

```
Renderer toolbarRenderer = (ToolbarRenderer)
       defaultRenderKit.getRenderer("jia.Toolbar");
```

You can also associate a `Renderer` with a specific `RenderKit`:

```
<render-kit>
  <render-kit-id>org.foobar.WML</render-kit-it>
  <renderer>
    <renderer-type>jia.Toolbar</renderer-type>
    <renderer-class>
      org.jia.components.ToolbarRenderer
    </renderer-class>
  </renderer>
</render-kit>
```

This associates the `Toolbar` renderer with a `RenderKit` that has the identifier `org.foobar.WML`. You can also associate renderers with a render kit by its class name:

```
<render-kit>
  <render-kit-class>org.foobar.WMLRenderKit</render-kit-class>
  <renderer>
    <renderer-type>jia.Toolbar</renderer-type>
    <renderer-class>
      org.jia.components.ToolbarRenderer
    </renderer-class>
  </renderer>
</render-kit>
```

This associates the renderer with an instance of the `org.foobar.WMLRenderKit` class.

So far, we've been showing the simplest definition of a `Renderer`. Like custom components, tools will work better with your custom renderer if you provide additional information. Listing 15.2 shows a more complicated example that includes most of the possible elements.

Listing 15.2 A more complete example of registering a renderer with JSF

```
<renderer>
  <description>
    A Toolbar renderer.
  </description>
```

```
<display-name>Toolbar</display-name>
<icon>
  <small-icon>icons/toolbar_small.gif</small-icon>
  <large-icon>icons/toolbar_large.gif</large-icon>
</icon>
<component-family>jia.Navigator</component-family>
<renderer-type>jia.Toolbar</renderer-type>
<renderer-class>
  org.jia.components.ToolbarRenderer
</renderer-class>
<attribute>
  <description>The CSS style for the header.</description>
  <display-name>headerClass</display-name>
  <icon>
    <small-icon>icons/toolbar_css.gif</small-icon>
  </icon>
  <attribute-name>headerClass</attribute-name>
  <attribute-class>String</attribute-class>
</attribute>
<attribute>
  <description>The CSS style for each item.</description>
  <display-name>itemClass</display-name>
  <icon>
     <small-icon>icons/toolbar_css.gif</small-icon>
  </icon>
  <attribute-name>itemClass</attribute-name>
  <attribute-class>String</attribute-class>
</attribute>
<attribute>
  <description>
    The CSS style for the selected item.
  </description>
  <display-name>selectedItemClass</display-name>
  <icon>
     <small-icon>icons/toolbar_css.gif</small-icon>
  </icon>
  <attribute-name>selectedItemClass</attribute-name>
  <attribute-class>String</attribute-class>
</attribute>
<attribute>
  <description>
    The CSS style for the each item's icon.
  </description>
  <display-name>iconClass</display-name>
  <icon>
     <small-icon>icons/toolbar_css.gif</small-icon>
  </icon>
  <attribute-name>iconClass</attribute-name>
  <attribute-class>String</attribute-class>
</attribute>
<attribute>
```

```
    <description>
      Direction - either HORIZONTAL or VERTICAL
    </description>
    <display-name>layout</display-name>
    <icon>
       <small-icon>icons/toolbar_layout.gif</small-icon>
    </icon>
    <attribute-name>layout</attribute-name>
    <attribute-class>String</attribute-class>
    <default-value>VERTICAL</default-value>
    <suggested-value>VERTICAL</suggested-value>
  </attribute>
</renderer>
```

This example adds a display name, description, and icon. It also specifies the component family that the renderer supports. In addition, the entry defines five attributes of type `String`: `headerClass`, `itemClass`, `selectedItemClass`, `iconClass`, and `layout`. Each `<attribute>` element can have a description, display name, and icon, a name, a class, a default value, and a suggested value. Only the name and class are required. Note that there are no `<property>` elements as there are with components.

That's all there is to configuring renderers. Generally, it's best to start out with the simple case (only specify the type and class name) and then add more information as necessary. If you're going to be redistributing your components or renderers for use by people you don't know, we highly suggest you provide as much metadata as possible, and even include icons if possible. This will make your components appear more professional.

NOTE Just as with components, JSF IDEs often require additional metadata in order to import custom renderers. Unfortunately, the details vary between vendors. This will be standardized in a future version of the specification.

Now, let's see how JSP fits into the picture.

15.3.5 JSP integration

Integrating a renderer with JSP is part of the same process as integrating a component with JSP. This is because the base JSP tag classes, `UIComponentTag` and `UIComponentBodyTag`, are both designed to work with a component/renderer pair. Consequently, you'll need to write a new tag handler for every unique component/renderer combination. See section 15.2.5 for details on subclassing `UIComponentTag` and `UIComponentBodyTag`.

This completes our discussion of the rendering environment. Next we examine validation.

15.4 Developing validators

We've discussed validation—the act of verifying a component's local value—throughout this book. JSF includes a few standard validators—`LengthValidator`, `DoubleRangeValidator`, and `LongRangeValidator`, and so on. Each input control can have one or more validators associated with it. You can also handle validation directly in backing beans with a single validator method. (For more information on validation, see chapter 6.)

Validation in backing beans (which make use of `EditableValueHolder`'s `validator` property) is useful for application-specific logic that's tied to the backing bean itself. (See chapters 11 and 13 for more information.) However, if you'd like to write reusable validation logic that isn't specific to a backing bean, or you'd like to associate multiple validation routines with a single input control, you'll need to create a custom validator.

The process is simple enough: it requires implementing the `Validator` interface, registering the validator's class with JSF, and optionally creating a custom tag handler. This is depicted in the class diagram shown in figure 15.4. If your

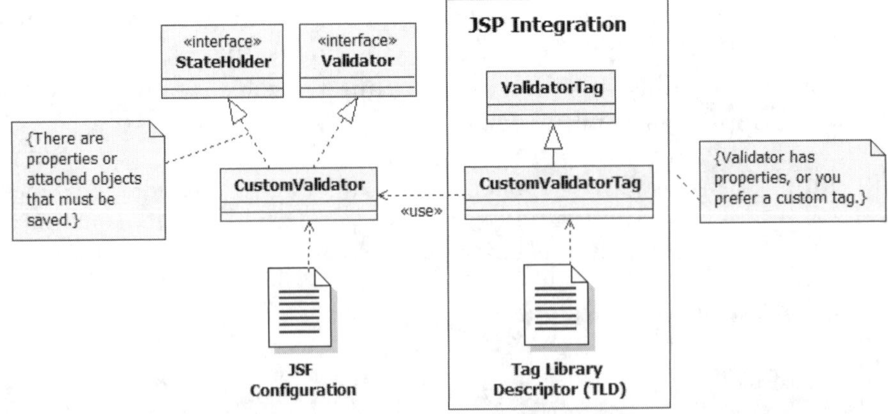

Figure 15.4 To create a new validator, you must implement the `Validator` interface and register the new class in a JSF configuration file. If your validator maintains any state, it can also implement the `StateHolder` interface. To integrate with JSP, you must also write a tag handler class and register it in a tag library descriptor; this is only necessary if you have developer-configurable properties or you prefer that developers use a custom tag as opposed to the generic `<f:validator>` tag.

Validator has properties that it would like to save between requests, it must also implement the StateHolder interface.

Now, let's examine the Validator interface.

15.4.1 Validator

Creating a custom validator requires implementing a single interface: javax.faces.validator.Validator. Every EditableValueHolder maintains a collection of Validator instances. New instances can be added to the collection either in code or declaratively (in JSP or another display technology). During the Request Processing Lifecycle, JSF will call the input control's validate method, which executes each associated Validator instance.

Every Validator has an identifier that is configured in a JSF configuration file (and isn't exposed as a property). However, it is customary to store the default identifier in a constant, as it is with custom components:

```
public final String VALIDATOR_ID =
                    "jia.RegularExpressionValidator";
```

This specifies a default validator identifier of jia.RegularExpressionValidator.

The Validator interface has a single method:

```
public void validate(FacesContext context, UIComponent component,
                     Object value)
              throws ValidatorException;
```

When you implement this method, first check to see if the component's value is correct. If it's not, throw a new ValidatorException instance. ValidatorException has two constructors: one that simply accepts a FacesMessage instance, and one that excepts a FacesMessage instance and the original Throwable that caused the problem.

For example, here's the validate method for our RegularExpressionValidator (online extension chapter 20). It checks to see if an input control's value matches a regular expression:

```
public void validate(FacesContext  context,
                     UIComponent component, Object value)
              throws ValidatorException
{
  ...
  if (!isValid(value))
  {
    ...
    throw new ValidatorException(new FacesMessage(messageText, null));
  }
}
```

You can see how simple the main algorithm is—check to see if the component's value is valid, and if not throw a `ValidatorException`. If an exception is thrown, JSF will automatically add the `FacesMessage` instance to the message queue. Otherwise, the component's `valid` property will be set to `true`. The actual validation happens in the `isValid` method, which is a simple helper method:

```
protected boolean isValid(String value)
{
  ...
  return pattern.matcher(value).matches();
}
```

This method simply returns `true` if the value matches the validator's `pattern`, which is a precompiled regular expression.

> **TIP** Placing your primary validation-checking algorithm in another method makes unit testing easier, because the method won't require JSF-specific objects like `FacesContext`.

Your validator may have additional properties that affect how it performs its work. `RegularExpressionValidator` has an `expression` property that contains the actual regular expression the `isValid` method uses. Validators can also store and retrieve attributes on the UI component instance. If your validator does have properties, you'll need to implement the `StateHolder` interface (covered in section 15.2.2). Otherwise, you can't guarantee that the value of the properties will be remembered between requests. (Validators themselves are automatically saved by `UIInput`.) A validator should also have a no-argument constructor so that it can be created by the `Application` object's `createValidator` method.

That's all there is to writing a validator. Now, let's look at how to register one with JSF.

15.4.2 Registration

Registering a validator is similar to registering a component or a renderer. It just requires a little bit of XML in a JSF configuration file. In the simplest case, all you need to specify is the identifier and class:

```
<validator>
  <validator-id>jia.RegularExpressionValidator</validator-id>
  <validator-class>
    org.jia.validators.RegularExpressionValidator
  </validator-class>
</validator>
```

This registers a validator called with the identifier `jia.RegularExpressionValidator`, whose class is `org.jia.validators.RegularExpressionValidator`.

Now that the class has been registered, we can create a new instance in code like so:

```
Validator validator =
  application.createValidator("jia.RegularExpressionValidator");
```

If the validator has a constant for its identifier, you would normally use that instead:

```
Validator validator = application.createValidator(
                        RegularExpressionValidator.VALIDATOR_ID);
```

It's also possible to provide additional elements in the validator declaration, such as a description, and supported properties and attributes. These are usually used by tools, although adding a description is certainly not a bad thing. An example is shown in listing 15.3.

Listing 15.3 A more complete example of registering a validator with JSF

```
<validator>
    <description>
      Validates an input control based on a regular expression.
      </description>
    <display-name>RegularExpressionValidator</display-name>
    <icon>
      <large-icon>images/regex_large.gif</large-icon>
      <small-icon>images/regex_small.gif</small-icon>
    </icon>
    <validator-id>jia.RegularExpressionValidator</validator-id>
    <validator-class>
      org.jia.validators.RegularExpressionValidator
    </validator-class>
    <property>
        <description>Regular expression.
        </description>
        <icon>
          <small-icon>images/regex.gif</small-icon>
        </icon>
        <property-name>expression</property-name>
        <property-class>java.lang.String</property-class>
    </property>
    <property>
        <description>
           Error message to be dispayed (optional).
        </description>
        <property-name>errorMessage</property-name>
        <property-class>java.lang.String</property-class>
```

```
    </property>
  </validator>
```

As you can see, the listing includes additional elements like a description, and an icon, and also describes each of its properties. The <property> elements for validators are the same as the <property> element for UI components and renderers; they have several possible elements, including an icon, a default value, and a suggested value.

That's all the work required for registering a validator with JSF. Now, let's examine JSP integration.

15.4.3 JSP integration

If your validator doesn't have any properties, you can use the JSF core <f:validator> tag instead of writing your own custom tag handler. This tag just takes a validator identifier as a parameter. So, if our RegularExpressionValidator didn't have any properties, we could use it like this:

```
<h:inputText>
  <f:validator validatorId="jia.RegularExpressionValidator"/>
</h:inputText>
```

This works fine for simple cases. However, if your validator has properties, or you'd rather have front-end developers use a specific tag instead of remembering a validator identifier, you can create your own validator custom tag. All such tags must subclass the ValidatorTag class, which happens to be the same class used by the JSF core tag library.

In addition to subclassing the ValidatorTag, you'll need to declare the tag inside a tag library definition (TLD).

ValidatorTag

ValidatorTag is a class in the javax.faces.webapp package that implements most of the core functionality you'll need. The first thing you'll do when you subclass ValidatorTag is decide which of your validator's properties your tag should support. All of these properties should be exposed as attributes in the tag library definition.

Once you've created getters and setters for the tag's properties, there are three methods you need to worry about. The first is setValidatorId:

```
public void setValidatorId(String validatorId);
```

This method associates your tag handler with a specific validator. You usually call it in your constructor like this:

```
public RegExpValidatorTag()
{
  super();
  setValidatorId(RegularExpressionValidator.VALIDATOR_ID);
}
```

This associates a tag handler called `RegExpValidatorTag` with `RegularExpression-Validator`. This is the same identifier defined during the registration process (see section 15.4.2.)

All of the work happens in the `createValidator` method:

```
protected Validator createValidator() throws JspException;
```

This is where the `Validator` instance is actually created and configured based on the tag handler's properties, so you'll need to override it if you're setting any of the validator's properties. The most important thing to remember is to call the superclass's `createValidator` method first:

```
protected Validator createValidator() throws JspException
{
  RegularExpressionValidator validator =
          (RegularExpressionValidator)super.createValidator();
  ...
  validator.setExpression(expression);
  ...
  validator.setErrorMessage(errorMessage);
  ...
  return validator;
}
```

In this example, we retrieve the `Validator` instance from the superclass and then proceed to set its properties (based on properties of the tag handler).

Finally, as with any tag handler, you must override the `release` method:

```
public void release();
```

All that's necessary here is to reset any instance variables to the default value, which is typically `null`:

```
public void release()
{
  super.release();
  expression = null;
  errorMessage = null;
}
```

Note that we call the superclass's `release` method as well.

Once you've written the custom tag handler, you'll need to integrate it with a tag library, as shown in section 15.2.5.

That's all there is to creating custom validators. For a detailed example, see online extension chapter 20. Now, let's examine the world of custom converters.

15.5 Developing converters

Type conversion is a critical, but often overlooked, feature of any good web framework. In JSF, type conversion is handled by a converter, which is a simple class that converts a Java object to and from a string for display. A UI component can be associated with a single converter, and converters can be registered by type or by identifier.

JSF ships with converters for all of the basic data types (`boolean`, `Short`, `int`, and so on) that are registered by type. It also includes two other converters—`Number` and `DateTime`—that are registered by identifier. When a component or renderer displays its value, it looks for a registered converter, and if it can't find one, it will use the converter for the value's type. (For more on type conversion, see chapter 6.)

You can easily write your own converters, and just like the standard ones, they can be registered by type or identifier. All you need to do is implement the `Converter` interface, register the converter with JSF, and optionally create a JSP custom tag handler. (If your converters have properties that must maintain their state, you must also implement the `StateHolder` interface.) These elements are depicted in figure 15.5. Writing a new converter is similar to writing a new validator—just compare figures 15.4 and 15.5.

Let's begin our type conversion tour with the `Converter` interface.

15.5.1 Converter

A `ValueHolder` can be associated with a single converter (either in code or declaratively). All converters must implement the `Converter` interface, found in the `javax.faces.convert` package. Like validators, converters have identifiers that are registered in a JSF configuration file, and often exposed through a constant:

```
public final static String CONVERTER_ID = "jia.User";
```

This constant can be used to create new instances of your converter through the `Application.createConverter` method.

The `Converter` interface only has two methods:

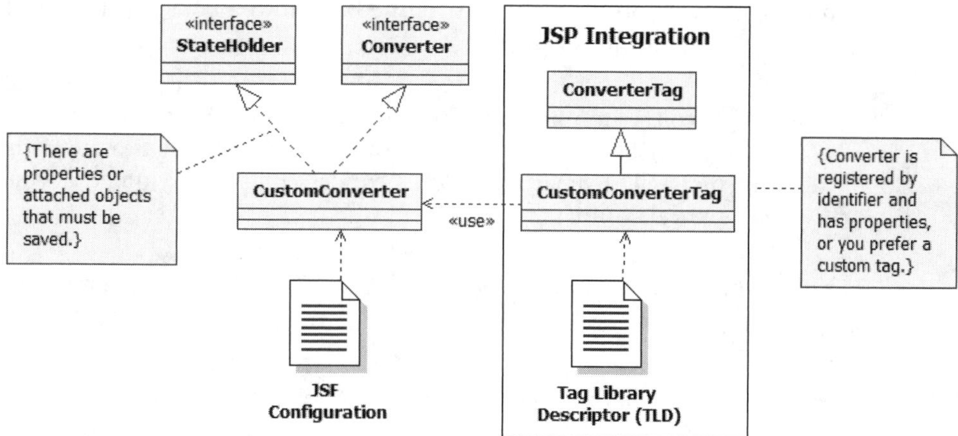

Figure 15.5 To write a converter, you implement the `Converter` interface, and then register the converter in an application configuration file. If your converter has properties that must be remembered in between requests, it must implement the `StateHolder` interface. If your converter is registered by identifier and has configurable properties, or you want to make life easier for end users, you can also create a JSP custom tag, which must be registered with a TLD.

```
public Object getAsObject(FacesContext facesContext,
                UIComponent uIComponent, String string)
              throws ConverterException;
public String getAsString(FacesContext facesContext,
                UIComponent uIComponent, Object object)
              throws ConverterException;
```

The `getAsObject` method should convert an `Object` into a `String`, and is executed during the Process Validations phase, or the Apply Request Values phase if the component implements `EditableValueHolder` and the `immediate` property is `true`.

The `getAsString` method is the opposite of `getAsObject`: it translates an `Object` into a `String`. It is executed during the Render Response phase, when the component is displayed.

If possible, these methods should be symmetrical, so the following code should return `true`:

```
Foo foo = new Foo(...);
String string = fooConverter.getAsString(context, component, foo);
Foo convertedFoo = (Foo)converter.getAsObject(context,
                                  component, string);
return foo.equals(convertedFoo);
```

This may not always be possible, however. For example, our example `UserConverter` (covered in online extension chapter 20) may convert a `User` object into a `String` that includes only the first name. So if any `User` property other than `firstName` was non-`null`, conversion from the first name back into a `User` object would lose the value of the remaining properties.

TIP If you write unit tests for your converter (which, as always, we recommend), be sure to write a test that ensures that the two methods are symmetrical. Even if you don't expect complete symmetry, you can test partial symmetry.

In either method, you throw a new `ConverterException` if conversion is not possible. Here's how `UserConverter` implements the `getAsObject` method:

```
public Object getAsObject(FacesContext context,
                UIComponent component, String displayString)
{
  User user = new User();
  FacesMessage message = getStringAsUser(user, displayString);
  if (message != null)
  {
    throw new ConverterException(message);
  }
  return user;
}
```

The algorithm is simple: convert the value, throw an exception if there is an error, and return the converted value otherwise. As you can see, one of `ConverterException`'s constructors (it has many) takes a `FacesMessage` as a parameter. This `FacesMessage` instance will be added to the message queue and possibly displayed to the user. The actual conversion process has been delegated to the `getStringAsUser` method.

TIP Placing the core conversion logic in a separate method that doesn't use JSF classes makes unit testing easier.

Converters can also have additional properties that affect the conversion process. For example, `UserConverter` has a `style` property that helps it decide whether or not to display the first name, the last name, or both. If your converter has properties whose state you would like to save between requests, it should implement the `StateHolder` interface. Converters can also make use of attributes stored on the UI component instance. They should also have a no-argument constructor so that they can be created by the `Application` object's `createConverter` method.

This concludes our tour of the `Converter` interface; once you've implemented and tested it properly, you'll need to register your new converter with JSF.

15.5.2 Registration

Registering a new converter requires a `<converter>` entry in a JSF configuration file. You can register a converter by identifier and/or by type. Here's an example of registering it by identifier:

```
<converter>
  <converter-id>jia.User</converter-id>
  <converter-class>
    org.jia.converters.UserConverter
  </converter-class>
</converter>
```

This relates a converter called `jia.User` with the class `org.jia.converters.UserConverter`.

Here's an example of registering the converter by type:

```
<converter>
  <converter-for-class>java.lang.Boolean</converter-for-class>
  <converter-class>
    javax.faces.convert.BooleanConverter
  </converter-class>
</converter>
```

This is the way the reference implementation [Sun, JSF RI] registers the `BooleanConverter` for `Boolean` objects. Anytime JSF encounters a component value of type `Boolean` and there is no specific converter registered, it will use the `BooleanConverter`.

As is the case with all custom components and component helpers, there are additional elements you can define that make it easier for tools to work with your converters. A more complete example is shown in listing 15.4.

Listing 15.4 A more complete example of registering a converter with JSF

```
<converter>
  <description>
    Converts a User object to and from a String.
  </description>
  <display-name>UserConverter</display-name>
  <icon>
    <small-icon>images/user_small.gif</small-icon>
    <large-icon>images/user_large.gif</large-icon>
  </icon>
  <converter-id>jia.User</converter-id>
  <converter-class>
    org.jia.converters.UserConverter
  </converter-class>
  <property>
    <description>
```

```
        The display style for the user's name.
      </description>
      <property-name>style</property-name>
      <property-class>java.lang.String</property-class>
    </property>
    <property>
      <description>
        Determines whether or not the user's role should be shown.
      </description>
      <property-name>showRole</property-name>
      <property-class>java.lang.String</property-class>
      <default-value>false</default-value>
    </property>
  </converter>
```

Listing 15.4 shows additional elements like the description, a display name, an icon, and details about specific properties. For the complete range of possibilities, see online extension appendix D.

Now that you have seen how to register a new converter with JSF, let's look at integrating it with JavaServer Pages.

15.5.3 JSP integration

If you registered your converter by type *only*, then there's no need to worry about JSP integration at all. JSF will automatically use your converter when it tries to convert the registered type and the associated component doesn't have another converter registered. If, however, your converter is registered by identifier, front-end developers will want to associate it with a component using JSP.

Like validators, there is a tag in the JSF core tag library that you can use for associating a converter with a component. This tag works fine when your converter has no properties, so we could use it with our `User` converter like so:

```
<h:inputText>
  <f:converter converterId="jia.User"/>
</h:inputText>
```

Of course, in cases where your converters have properties, or you prefer that front-end developers use a specific tag as opposed to a generic tag and an identifier, you'll need to develop your own custom tag handler. You can do this by subclassing the `ConverterTag` class.

ConverterTag

`ConverterTag` is a concrete class in the `javax.faces.webapp` package; it's the same class used to implement the `<f:converter>` tag. When you subclass it, in addition to overriding its methods, you'll want to provide properties that map to the set of properties and/or attributes that your converter supports. Its interface is similar to that of `ValidatorTag`; there are three methods of importance. The first is `setConverterId`:

```
public void setConverterId(String converterId);
```

Use this method to specify the identifier of the converter that's associated with this tag. Usually, you'll call this method in the constructor, and the `converterId` should match the identifier registered for the converter in an application configuration file. Here's an example from the tag handler for `UserConverter`:

```
public UserConverterTag()
{
  super();
  setConverterId(UserConverter.CONVERTER_ID);
}
```

This associates the tag handler with a converter registered under the identifier `jia.User` (which is the same identifier we chose in section 15.5.2).

The method where all of the magic occurs is `createConverter`:

```
protected Converter createConverter() throws JspException;
```

This is where a new `Converter` instance is created (based on the identifier set by `setConverterId`). It's also where any properties of the converter instance should be configured. So, if your converter has additional properties, you'll need to override it. Here's an example:

```
protected Converter createConverter() throws JspException
{
  UserConverter converter = (UserConverter)super.createConverter();
  ...
  converter.setStyle(styleType);
  ...
  converter.setShowRole(Boolean.valueOf(showRole).booleanValue());
  ...
  return converter;
}
```

First, we retrieve a new `UserConverter` instance from the superclass's `createConverter` method. Then, we simply set the appropriate properties of the `UserConverter` based on properties of the tag handler. Finally, we return the newly created object.

ConverterTag also has a release method, like all JSP tag handlers:

```
public void release();
```

You should override this method to reset any instance variables to their default values:

```
public void release()
{
  super.release();
  style = null;
  showRole = null;
}
```

Once you've created a new ConverterTag, you'll need to add it to a JSP custom tag library, as shown in section 15.2.5.

Converters, along with the other UI extensions—validators, renderers, and UI components—form JSF's powerful component model. But what about internationalization and localization?

15.6 Handling internationalization

UI extensions have two primary sources of text that a user may see: strings declared as properties or attributes of UI components, and messages. Internationalization of properties and attributes is usually performed by the application or front-end developer, often with value-binding expressions (see chapter 6), so this is not a concern for the component developer. Messages, however, should be fully internationalized.

Fortunately, we examined the process of internationalizing messages in chapter 13. Messages for UI extensions have the same requirements: load a resource bundle (checking the default application's bundle first), grab the proper localized string based on the view's current locale, and then create a new FacesMessage instance with the localized string. This is best implemented using a factory method, as we did in chapter 13.

15.7 Packaging UI extensions

We've walked through all of the different UI extensions: components, renderers, validators, and converters. When you write extensions, you can either include all of their configuration information and classes with your application code, or package one or more extensions in a separate JAR file. The first choice makes sense if you don't intend to redistribute the extensions separately. Otherwise, you should create a separate JAR file with all of the required classes, an application

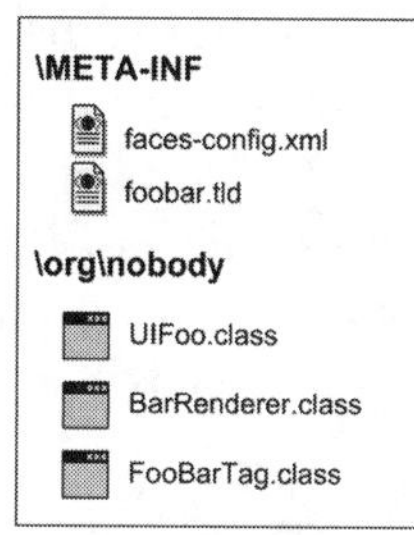

Figure 15.6
A directory structure for UI extensions packaged together inside a JAR. The only requirement is that faces-config.xml and any TLDs be in the META-INF directory. All class files should be placed in their usual directories.

configuration file, and any TLDs. This way, anyone can drop this JAR in any application's library path (such as WEB-INF/lib) and the application has immediate access to your components.

The structure of the JAR file is simple: place your class and resource bundles in their normal directories, and place your configuration file (which must be called faces-config. xml), and any tag libraries, in the META-INF directory. Figure 15.6 shows the directory structure for a fictional `UIFoo` component with a `Bar` renderer and a JSP tag handler.:

As you can see, the only real issue is making sure that there's a faces-config.xml file in the META-INF directory. This should contain all registration information for the UI components in the JAR file *only*—no need to worry about any application-level information. When a JSF application initializes, it will load that application's configuration file, and also search for faces-config.xml in all of the JARs in the web application's resource path.

15.8 Summary

In this chapter, we surveyed the component developer's landscape. A component developer deals with UI components, renderers, validators, and converters. Collectively, these are known as user interface extensions.

No matter which type of object you're developing, there are three specific developmental steps: write the class, register the class with JSF via a configuration file, and integrate it with a display technology. For JSP, integration usually includes developing a custom tag handler and registering the tag handler with a JSP tab library.

JSF provides base classes and interfaces for all UI components and helpers, as well as base JSP custom tag implementations. Internationalization is only necessary for messages that an extension may generate, and is similar to internationalizing messages in applications. You can also package any number of UI extensions in a JAR file, which can be dropped into any JSF application's library path.

Congratulations! You have reached the end of the print edition of *JavaServer Faces in Action*. If you're thirsty for more, don't worry—there are five additional chapters and four appendices available online. The additional material isn't just fluff either—it's chock-full of information that includes:

- Several in-depth examples of writing custom UI components and renderers: a date input control, a rollover button, an RSS viewer, and a toolbar
- Examples of developing a validator and a converter
- More than 80 pages showing how to build part of the case study using RAD-style, drag-and-drop support for JSF inside Oracle JDeveloper [Oracle, JDeveloper], IBM WebSphere Studio [IBM, WSAD], and Sun Java Studio Creator [Sun, Creator]
- Details on extending JSF by decorating or replacing pluggable classes for evaluating expressions, displaying views, and more
- Extensive listing of time zones, country codes, and language codes

If any of these topics sound appealing, check out the *JSF in Action* online extension (available exclusively to those who have purchased this book) at http://www.manning.com/mann.

Now that we've finished the plug, here are a few key points about JSF you should remember:

- JSF is a standard, best-of-breed, user interface framework for building web applications in Java (developed through the Java Community Process [JCP]).
- With JSF, you program in terms of UI components and events, rather than HTTP requests and responses.
- JSF can integrate with Struts [ASF, Struts], Spring [Spring], and other frameworks.
- All JSF applications are standard Java web applications built on top of the Servlet API, and can integrate with other servlet-based applications.
- You can build JSF applications without JSP, but JSP is the default display technology (see appendix A for examples of alternatives).
- You can use JSTL and other custom tags with JSF (with some restrictions).

- Integrated development environments (IDEs) have powerful support for JSF, allowing rapid application development (RAD) via a familiar, drag-and-drop environment (see online extension appendix B for full-fledged examples.)
- JSF has a powerful and extensible architecture (see online extension appendix C for more information).

Thanks for reading *JavaServer Faces in Action*.

A Using JSF without JSP

Throughout this book, we've made a point of saying that JSF can be used without JSP. Given the fact that all of our examples were based on JSP, it may be hard to see how another display technology would fit into the picture. Supporting different display technologies is possible because of JSF's core feature: the component model. UI components are pure objects, and a view is just a tree of UI components. So, as long as the tree is created, it doesn't matter how.

There is also another, subtler aspect: terminology. For example, the canonical term for a page is *view*, and each view has a *view identifier*, not a page name or URL. By default, a view identifier is just the filename, but it could be something else, like "TradeCaptureScreen." The identifier could map to a template (like JSP), or it could map to something else entirely, like a Java class.

In this appendix, we'll examine how JSF can be used without JSP, and then survey examples of building views with pure Java and the XML User Interface Language (XUL) [XUL]. We'll then discuss some other possibilities for using JSF without JSP.

A.1 How JSF handles display technologies

One of the most powerful features of JSF is its pluggable architecture. Nearly every feature—from action handling to resolving EL variables—can be replaced or extended. The view handler is responsible for creating and displaying a view as well as restoring it when the user requests the same view again. The default view handler displays views simply: it forwards the request to the web container, ensuring that it has a proper JSP filename. (Of course, it's not quite *that* simple, but you get the idea.) When the JSP container processes the page, the JSP tags perform the real work of creating the view.

Other display technologies can be supported just by replacing the view handler, which is configured in an application configuration file. The view handler has a simple interface, and as long as you implement it properly, it doesn't matter how you do it. A view handler can parse an entirely different type of template, or it can load a Java class, as long as it subclasses the `ViewHandler` abstract base class. (For an example `ViewHandler` implementation, see online extension appendix C.)

Fair enough—it's possible. But what does JSF look like without JSP?

A.2 Creating views with class-based pages

If you've done any Swing programming, you should be familiar with creating and configuring UI components in code. We showed some examples of manipulating

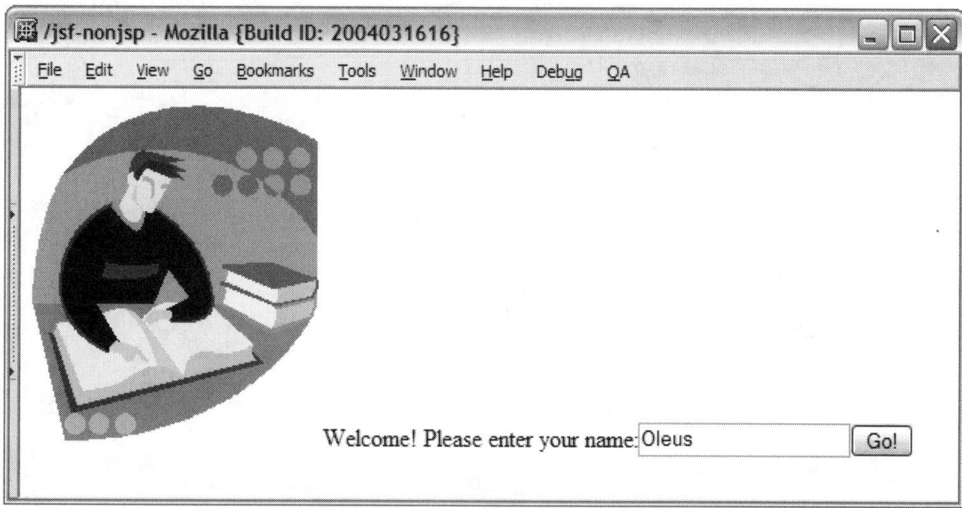

Figure A.1 Sample view: a form that displays an image and collects a username. This view can be created by the Smile code in listing A.1 or the XUL definition in listing A.2.

JSF UI components in code, but it's always been in conjunction with a JSP template. As it turns out, you can use the same techniques to create the entire view in Java code.

Exploiting this possibility is the goal of the Smile open-source JSF implementation [Smile]. Smile's goal isn't to implement every feature of the JSF specification; it's intended to provide support for class-based pages (CBP) to other implementations. CBPs are views that are created entirely in Java; as a matter of fact, a view identifier maps directly to a specific Java class, and no JSP is involved.

NOTE This section is based on Smile [Smile] 0.32, which is based on JSF 1.0 beta. This version does not implement many core features of the specification. The project goal is, however, to provide support for CBP on top of any JSF implementation, with MyFaces [MyFaces] as the default. (As of this writing, the Smile site states that they will be merging with MyFaces, which, according to mailing list discussions, is no longer true.)

Let's examine a simple login view, as shown in figure A.1. To create this view in Smile, all that's necessary is to implement an interface and write a single method, as shown in listing A.1.

Listing A.1 The Smile code for the view in figure A.1

```
package org.jia.smile;

import javax.faces.component.*;
import javax.faces.component.html.*;
import javax.faces.context.*;

import net.sourceforge.smile.component.Screen;
import net.sourceforge.smile.context.Page;
import net.sourceforge.smile.context.PageUtils;

public class Login implements Page      <-(1) Implement Page interface
{
  public Login()
  {
  }

  public void init(FacesContext ctx,      (2) Implement init method
                   UIComponent root)
  {
    Screen screen = new Screen();      <-(3) Instantiate Smile form

    PageUtils.addChild(root, screen);      <-(4) Add to root of view

    screen.setId("getName");

    HtmlGraphicImage graphic = new HtmlGraphicImage();
    graphic.setId("logoGraphic");
    graphic.setURL("/images/logo.gif");
    PageUtils.addChild(screen, graphic);

    HtmlOutputText outputText = new HtmlOutputText();
    outputText.setId("userNameLabel");
    outputText.setValue("Welcome! Please enter your name:");
    PageUtils.addChild(screen, outputText);

    HtmlInputText inputText = new HtmlInputText();
    inputText.setId("userNameInput");
    inputText.setValue("Oleus");
    PageUtils.addChild(screen, inputText);

    HtmlCommandButton commandButton = new HtmlCommandButton();
    commandButton.setId("userNameButton");
    commandButton.setValue("Go!");
    PageUtils.addChild(screen, commandButton);
  }
}
```

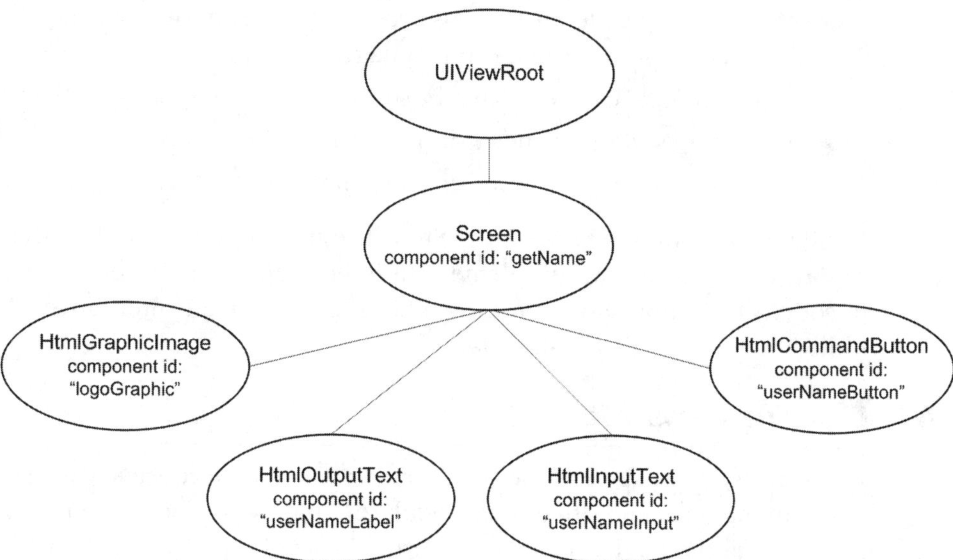

Figure A.2 The JSF component tree generated by the code in listing A.1. The `UIViewRoot` contains a `Screen` instance (which is a subclass of `UIForm`), which has child `HtmlGraphicImage`, `HtmlOutputText`, `HtmlInputText`, and `HtmlCommandButton` components.

Smile views are defined in page descriptors, which implement the `Page` interface (❶). All that's necessary is to implement the `init` method (❷) and build the component tree. The root component for Smile views is the `Screen` class (❸), which subclasses `UIForm`. Creating the view is simply a matter of creating the proper components and adding them to the view, starting with the `Screen` (❹). Smile also has a useful class to assist in the process of building the tree, called `PageUtils`.

In this example, we create the concrete HTML components, but this certainly isn't a requirement. The concrete components are, however, simpler to manipulate in code. This code generates the component tree shown in figure A.2.

BY THE WAY This code is based on JSF 1.0 beta because that is the latest version supported by Smile. Code written for an updated version of Smile would most likely use the `Application` class's factory methods.

As the figure shows, this is an ordinary JSF component tree that can be created with JSP as well (although `Screen` is a Smile-specific component).

Creating views in code has some specific consequences:

- Manipulating code with Java is accessible to developers who aren't familiar with HTML or other markup languages.
- View templates can be created by subclassing or composing different objects.
- There are no dependencies on JSP or any other template engine.
- Views are pure JSF and pure Java (no template text, HTML, or JSP custom tags).

It will be interesting to see how the Smile project progresses, and if other organizations or companies will implement different approaches to building JSF views in code. The bottom line, however, is that this is a viable alternative to JSP, and while immature, Smile exists today.

A.3 Creating views with XUL

Users of the Netscape web browser, or its open-source cousins Mozilla, Firefox, and Camino, may know that underneath the snappy browser lies a powerful platform for building web applications. At the heart of it is XUL [XUL], which allows you to define views using plain XML files. XUL is quite powerful in its own right, but the key is the fact that it defines a standard language for describing user interfaces.

Because XUL defines an XML dialect, it's entirely possible to integrate it with JSF. All that's necessary is to write a new view hander that can map JSF components to XUL elements. The JSF reference implementation [Sun, JSF RI] has an example that provides support for a few XUL elements.

NOTE This example uses XUL as a replacement for JSP, but still uses the standard HTML render kit to output HTML to a web browser. It's also possible to output XUL directly to a Mozilla-based browser, which can be done by writing a new render kit.

As an example, let's create the simple view shown in figure A.1 with XUL instead of JSP. The XUL behind this view is shown in listing A.2.

Listing A.2 Sample XUL view for page shown in figure A.1

```
<?xml version="1.0"?>

<page>
  <window id="getName">
    <image id="logoGraphic" url="/images/logo.gif" />
    <label id="userNameLabel"
           value="Welcome! Please enter your name:" />
```

```
    <textbox id="userNameInput" value="" />
    <button id="userNameButton" action="next" value="Go!"/>
  </window>
</page>
```

You can see from the listing that XUL has an entirely different set of XML elements than JSP component tags. However, the XUL view handler knows how to translate these elements into JSF components. Table A.1 shows how these tags map to JSF components.

Table A.1 Each JSF component maps to an XUL tag.

JSF Component	XUL Tag
UIViewRoot	<page>
UIForm	<screen>
UIGraphic	<graphic>
UIOutput	<label>
UIInput	<textbox>

The sample XUL view handler only creates the base objects, but it certainly *could* create concrete HTML components such as `HtmlForm` and `HtmlOutputText`. Once it has parsed the XML view definition, the view handler creates the ordinary JSF component tree shown in figure A.3. This could have been created with JSP (or Java code) as well.

The XUL example included with the JSF RI [Sun, JSF RI] is rudimentary—it is intended to be an example, and has only partial XUL support. However, it provides a concrete example of how JSF can be used with other template formats.

XUL is quite powerful—it is, after all, the basis of Mozilla's cross-platform user interface. We hope to see more complete integration between JSF and XUL in the future.

A.4 Other options

Class-based pages and XUL are only a couple possibilities for alternate display technologies. The possibilities are pretty endless, and include:

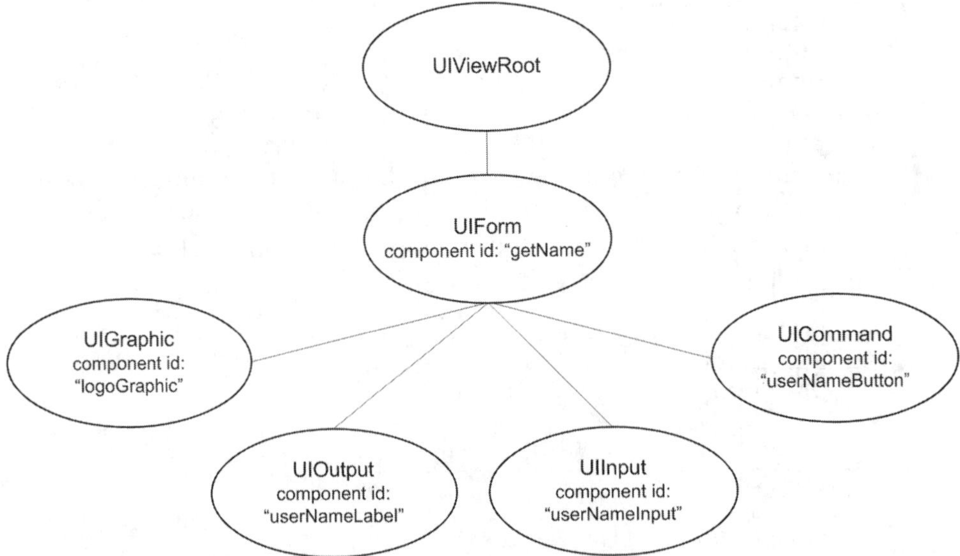

Figure A.3 JSF component tree generated by markup in listing A.2.

- Other template languages such as Velocity [ASF, Velocity]
- XML scripting engines like Jelly [ASF, Jelly]
- XML processing frameworks like Cocoon [ASF, Cocoon]
- Custom XML dialects
- Scripting languages like Jython [Jython] or Groovy [Groovy]
- Custom HTML templates (similar to Tapestry [Tapestry])

One of these options—namely, Cocoon integration—is already under way through the Keel meta-framework [Keel], which is lead by Michael Nash, a JSF Expert Group member. He's even written an article on the topic [Nash].

For an example of custom HTML templates, see Hans Bergsten's article on using JSF without JSP [Bergsten].

Also, if you're concerned about how well JSP works with JSF, keep in mind that the community is working toward tighter integration between the two technologies. This is the goal of the next major releases of JSP and JSF, which will work to align the expression languages and improve interoperability with custom tags, among other things. As of this writing, both of these releases are currently scheduled to be included in the next release of J2EE (5.0), which is due out in late 2005.

NOTE If you require tools support, you may not have many alternatives to JSP. Check with your vendor to make sure it supports your desired alternative before committing.

As the JSF landscape evolves, more options will become available; you can find all of the latest developments at the JSF Central community site [JSF Central].

references

[Alur, Crupi, Malks] Alur, Deepak, John Crupi, and Dan Malks. 2003. *Core J2EE Patterns*. Upper Saddle River, NJ: Prentice Hall.

[ASF, Cocoon] Apache Software Foundation. "Cocoon XML web application framework." http://cocoon.apache.org.

[ASF, Digester] Apache Software Foundation. "Jakarta Commons Digester (reads XML files into Java objects)." http://jakarta.apache.org/commons/digester.

[ASF, Jelly] Apache Software Foundation. "Jakarta Commons Jelly Java and XML-based scripting and processing engine." http://jakarta.apache.org/commons/jelly.

[ASF, Struts] Apache Software Foundation. "Struts web application framework." http://struts.apache.org.

[ASF, Struts-Faces] Apache Software Foundation. "Struts-Faces integration library." http://cvs.apache.org/builds/jakarta-struts/nightly/struts-faces.

[ASF, Tapestry] Apache Software Foundation. "Tapestry web application framework." http://jakarta.apache.org/tapestry/index.html.

[ASF, Tiles] Apache Software Foundation. "Tiles JSP templating framework." http://jakarta.apache.org/struts/userGuide/dev_tiles.html.

[ASF, Tomcat] Apache Software Foundation. "Tomcat web container." http://jakarta.apache.org/tomcat/index.html.

[ASF, Velocity] Apache Software Foundation. "Velocity template engine." http://jakarta.apache.org/velocity/index.html.

[Barcia Series 2004] Barcia, Roland. 2004. "Developing JSF Applications Using WebSphere Studio V5.1.1 (5-part series)." http://www-106.ibm.com/developerworks/websphere/techjournal/0401_barcia/barcia.html.

[Bayern] Bayern, Shawn. 2002. *JSTL in Action*. Greenwich, CT: Manning.

[BEA, WebLogic] BEA. "WebLogic J2EE application server." http://www.bea.com/framework.jsp?CNT=index.htm&FP=/content/products/server.

[Bergsten] Bergsten, Hans. 2004. "Improving JSF by Dumping JSP." http://www.onjava.com/pub/a/onjava/2004/06/09/jsf.html.

[Friedl] Friedl, Jeffrey E. F. 2002. *Mastering Regular Expressions*. Sebastopol, CA: O'Reilly & Associates, Inc.

[Fowler, Dependency Injection] Fowler, Martin. 2004. "Inversion of Control Containers and the Dependency Injection Pattern." http://www.martinfowler.com/articles/injection.html.

[Fowler, Enterprise] Fowler, Martin. 2003. *Patterns of Enterprise Application Architecture*. Boston: Addison-Wesley.

[GoF] Gamma, Erich, Richard Helm, Ralph Johnson, and John Vlissides. 1995. *Design Patterns: Elements of Reusable Object-Oriented Software*. Reading, MA: Addison-Wesley.

[Grand] Grand, Mark. 1998. *Patterns in Java, Vol. 1*. New York: John Wiley & Sons.

[Groovy] "Groovy Java scripting language." http://groovy.codehaus.org.

[Hunter] Hunter, Jason. 2001. *Java Servlet Programming*. Sebastopol, CA: O'Reilly & Associates.

[Husted] Husted, Ted. 2003. *Struts in Action*. Greenwich, CT: Manning.

[Holmes] Holmes, James. "Faces Console JSF configuration editor." http://www.jamesholmes.com/JavaServerFaces/console.

[IBM, WAS] IBM. "WebSphere Application Server." http://www-306.ibm.com/software/info1/websphere/index.jsp?tab=products/appserv.

[IBM, WSAD] IBM. "WebSphere Studio Application Developer J2EE IDE." http://www.306.ibm.com/software/awdtools/studioappdev.

[Informa] "Informa Java RSS library." http://informa.sourceforge.net.

[JBoss, Hibernate] JBoss. "Hibernate object/relational persistence and query engine." http://www.hibernate.org.

[Jython] "Jython Java-based Python implementation." http://www.jython.org.

[JSF Central] "JSF Central JavaServer Faces community and FAQ." http://www.jsfcentral.com.

[JSR 227] "Java Specification Request 227: A Standard Data Binding & Data Access Facility for J2EE." http://www.jcp.org/en/jsr/detail?id=227.

[Keel] "Keel meta-framework for server-side applications." http://www.keelframework.org.

[Kobrix] "Kobrix Software. Tag Interface Component Library." http://www.kobrix.com.

[Microsoft, ASP.NET] Microsoft. "ASP.NET web application framework." http://www.asp.net.

[MyFaces] "MyFaces open source JSF implementation." http://www.myfaces.org.

[Nash] Nash, Michael. 2004. "Spinning Your Code with XSLT and JSF in Cocoon." http://www.developer.com/lang/article.php/10924_3348311_1.

[New Atlanta, ServletExec] New Atlanta Communications. "ServletExec web container." http://www.newatlanta.com/products/servletexec/index.jsp.

[OpenSymphony, SiteMesh] OpenSymphony. "SiteMesh web-page layout and decorating framework." http://www.opensymphony.com/sitemesh.

[OpenSymphony, WebWork] "WebWork web application framework." http://www.opensymphony.com/webwork.

[Oracle, ADF] Oracle. "Application Development Framework." http://otn.oracle.com/products/jdev/index.html.

[Oracle, ADF UIX] Oracle. "ADF UIX components." http://otn.oracle.com/products/jdev/collateral/papers/9.0.5.0/adfuix_roadmap/adfuix_roadmap.html.

[Oracle, AS] Oracle. "Oracle Application Server." http://otn.oracle.com/products/ias/index.html.

[Oracle, JDeveloper] Oracle. "JDeveloper J2EE IDE." http://otn.oracle.com/products/jdev/index.html.

[Salmon, SOFIA] Salmon. "Salmon Open Framework for Internet Applications." http://www.salmonllc.com/website/Jsp/vanity/Sofia.jsp.

[Schalk] Schalk, Chris. 2004. "How to Use JSF with JDeveloper 10g." http://otn.oracle.com/products/jdev/howtos/10g/jsf_howto/jsf.html.

[Smile] "Smile open source JSF implementation (with Java views)." http://smile.sourceforge.net.

[Spring-Faces] "JSF integration code for Spring (open source)." http://jsf-spring.sourceforge.net.

[Sun, Creator] Sun Microsystems. "Java Studio Creator JSF IDE." http://wwws.sun.com/software/products/jscreator/index.html.

[Sun, i18n] Sun Microsystems. "Java Tutorial, Internationalization Trail." http://java.sun.com/docs/books/tutorial/i18n/index.html.

[Sun, JDO] Sun Microsystems. "Java Data Objects specification." http://java.sun.com/products/jdo/index.jsp.

[Sun, JRL] Sun Microsystems. "Java Research License." http://www.java.net/jrl.html.

[Sun, JSF Spec] Sun Microsystems. "JavaServer Faces specification." http://java.sun.com/j2ee/javaserverfaces.

[Sun, JSF RI] Sun Microsystems. "JSF reference implementation." http://java.sun.com/j2ee/javaserverfaces.

[Sun, JSP] Sun Microsystems. "JavaServer Pages specification." http://java.sun.com/products/jsp/index.jsp.

[Sun, JSAS] Sun Microsystems. "Java System Application Server." http://wwws.sun.com/software/products/appsrvr/home_appsrvr.html.

[Sun, JSTL] Sun Microsystems. "JavaServer Pages Template Library." http://java.sun.com/products/jsp/jstl/index.jsp.

[Sun, Portlet] Sun Microsystems. "Portlet specification." http://www.jcp.org/en/jsr/detail? id=162.

[Sun, Servlet] Sun Microsystems. "Servlet specification." http://java.sun.com/products/servlet/index.jsp.

[Syndi8] "Syndic8 RSS and Atom news feed aggregator." http://www.syndic8.com.

[Szyperski] Szyperski, Clemens. 2002. *Component Software, Beyond Object-Oriented Programming*. New York: Addison-Wesley.

[TheServerSide] The Middleware Company. "TheServerSide.com enterprise Java community." http://www.theserverside.com.

[W3Schools] Refsnes Data. "W3Schools web technology tutorial site." http://www.w3schools.com.

[WebMacro] Semiotek. "WebMacro open source template language." http://www.webmacro.org.

[XUL] The Mozilla Organization. "XML User Interface Language." http://www.mozilla.org/projects/xul/.

index

Symbols

A

Index entries with page numbers 703 and higher refer to the online extension.

Index entries with page numbers 703 and higher refer to the online extension.

B

Index entries with page numbers 703 and higher refer to the online extension.

Index entries with page numbers 703 and higher refer to the online extension.

Index entries with page numbers 703 and higher refer to the online extension.

Index entries with page numbers 703 and higher refer to the online extension.

Index entries with page numbers 703 and higher refer to the online extension.

Index entries with page numbers 703 and higher refer to the online extension.

I

Index entries with page numbers 703 and higher refer to the online extension.

J

Index entries with page numbers 703 and higher refer to the online extension.

Index entries with page numbers 703 and higher refer to the online extension.

Index entries with page numbers 703 and higher refer to the online extension.

M

Index entries with page numbers 703 and higher refer to the online extension.

N

O

Index entries with page numbers 703 and higher refer to the online extension.

R

Index entries with page numbers 703 and higher refer to the online extension.

S

Index entries with page numbers 703 and higher refer to the online extension.

Index entries with page numbers 703 and higher refer to the online extension.

T

U

Index entries with page numbers 703 and higher refer to the online extension.

Index entries with page numbers 703 and higher refer to the online extension.

Index entries with page numbers 703 and higher refer to the online extension.

V

Index entries with page numbers 703 and higher refer to the online extension.

W

Index entries with page numbers 703 and higher refer to the online extension.

X

Index entries with page numbers 703 and higher refer to the online extension.